W9-AHC-750

Woman's Day Encyclopedia of Cookery

VOLUME 12

in 12 volumes—over 2,000 pages—
with more than 1,500 illustrations in color,
1,000 entries and 8,500 recipes
1,200 menus, 50 specialty cook books
and a host of delightful features by distinguished food writers.

Prepared and edited by the Editors of Woman's Day
Editor: EILEEN TIGHE
Managing Editor: EVELYN GRANT *Food Editor:* GLENNA MCGINNIS
Art Consultant: HAROLD SITTERLE *Photographic Editor:* BEN CALVO
Associates: OLIVIA RISBERG, CHARLOTTE SCRIPTURE,
CAROLYN STORM, JOHANNA BAFARO

SPECIAL PROJECT STAFF
Editor: NIKA STANDEN HAZELTON *Art Director:* LEONARD A. ROMAGNA
Associates: L. GERALDINE MARSTELLER, HELEN FEINGOLD,
SUSAN J. KNOX, INEZ M. KRECH

FAWCETT PUBLICATIONS, INC. NEW YORK

Copyright © 1966 by Fawcett Publications, Inc.,
publishers of Woman's Day

All rights reserved.

FIRST EDITION

No part of this book may be reproduced in any form without permission in writing from the publisher, except by a reviewer who wishes to quote brief passages in connection with a review written for inclusion in a magazine, newspaper or broadcast.

PRINTED AND BOUND BY
FAWCETT-HAYNES PRINTING CORPORATION
ROCKVILLE, MARYLAND

Table of Contents

VOLUME 12

TOPPING TO ZWIEBACK
plus
150 WAYS TO BE A BETTER COOK

Definitions and 440 Recipes
How to buy, store, prepare, cook, and serve •
Nutritive Food Values • Caloric Values

TORTE 1853
TORTILLA 1856
TRIPE 1858
TROUT 1859
TRUFFLE 1861
TUNA COOK BOOK 1862
TURKEY COOK BOOK 1870
TURNIPS 1878
TURNOVERS 1879
UPSIDE-DOWN CAKE 1881
VACHERIN 1884
VANILLA 1884
VARIETY MEAT 1885
VEAL COOK BOOK 1888
VEGETABLE COOKERY 1898
VENISON 1908
VICHYSSOISE 1910
VITAMINS 1912
VOL-AU-VENT 1913
WAFFLES 1914
WALNUTS 1915
WATER CHESTNUTS 1919
WATERMELON 1920
WEDDING CAKE 1922
WELSH RABBIT 1923
WESTERN COOKERY 1924
WEST COAST SALADS 1934
WHITEFISH 1938
WHITE SAUCE 1939
WILD RICE 1940
WINE 1941
YAMS 1950
YEAST 1951
HOW TO COOK SUPERBLY:
Yeast Rolls and Buns 1952
YOGURT 1957
YORKSHIRE PUDDING 1958
ZABAGLIONE 1960
ZUCCHINI 1960
150 WAYS TO BE A BETTER COOK 1964
100 MENUS 1972

To help you plan more varied meals with the recipes in this volume

GENERAL INFORMATION 1976
COMPLETE RECIPE INDEX
FOR THE 12-VOLUME WOMAN'S DAY
ENCYCLOPEDIA OF COOKERY 1977

Foreword

To the best of our knowledge, no work of this magnitude ever has been undertaken by any author, editor, or publisher in America. The editors of Woman's Day, with a special staff of experts, present to you this Encyclopedia of Cookery, a comprehensive and colorful library on all culinary matters. The twelve-volume encyclopedia contains in its 2,000 pages over 8,500 recipes from all over the world, 1,500 food illustrations in color, 1,200 menus, 50 special cook books and over 1,000 food definitions. In addition, there are full details about all foods, their nutritive and caloric values, how to buy, serve, prepare, and cook them. There is a history of food and cooking, articles on nutrition, diet, entertaining, menu planning, herbs and spices. Every topic of culinary interest is covered. Five years of intensive work have gone into its preparation, backed by twenty-five years of food and cookery experience in the publication of Woman's Day.

We think you will find this Encyclopedia of Cookery the most complete and authoritative work ever published on the subject. It is a library for everyone who cares about good food and the fine art of preparing it.

The Editors

TOPPING—A covering or garnish for foods. Toppings are also used to add to the flavor of many dishes. Some toppings are thin and glazy while others are puffy and light. Whipped cream, fudge sauce, sugar glazes, hard sauce, honey caramel toppings, buttered crumbs, mashed potatoes, cheese, and melted chocolate are all used for toppings.

WHIPPED-CREAM TOPPING

Whip 1 cup heavy cream with 2 tablespoons cocoa and 2 teaspoons sugar until almost stiff. Serve on plain cake. Makes about 2 cups.

TORTE—A rich cake or pastry, made with eggs, sugar, jam, liqueur, and little or no flour, with nuts or dry bread crumbs often used instead of flour. Tortes can be baked in layers put together with luscious fillings, such as buttercream. They may be frosted in an elegant manner with rich icings and/or whipped cream or meringues. Tortes can also be decorated to the nth degree with glacé fruits, nuts, or candied flowers; in short, anything that will dress up a cake.

ALMOND BRANDY TORTE

3 eggs
1 cup sugar
1 teaspoon ground mace
Grated rind of 2 lemons
1 cup fine dry bread crumbs
1 cup good-quality brandy
1¾ cups finely ground blanched almonds (about ½ pound)
Simple Lemon Icing
Toasted almonds, cut into halves

Beat eggs and sugar until light. Add mace and lemon rind. Stir in bread crumbs and brandy alternately. Blend in almonds. Pour into greased and floured deep 8-inch cake pan. Bake in preheated moderate oven (350°F.) for 30 to 35 minutes, or until cake tests done. Cool. Ice with Simple Lemon Icing. Decorate top with toasted almond halves. Makes 12 servings.

Simple Lemon Icing

Sift 2 cups confectioners' sugar into bowl. Gradually beat in 2 tablespoons fresh lemon juice. Beat to spreading consistency. If necessary, add a little more sifted confectioners' sugar or lemon juice.

VIENNESE TORTE

1½ cups sugar (use fine granulated)
⅔ cup sifted all-purpose flour
1 tablespoon Dutch-type cocoa
1 cup finely ground hazelnuts
9 egg whites
1 cup heavy cream, whipped and sweetened to taste
1 tablespoon rum
12 marrons glacés
Candied violets

Sift together sugar, flour, and cocoa; add hazelnuts. Beat egg whites until very stiff. Fold into sugar mixture. Grease and flour 3 cookie sheets. Pipe mixture from pastry bag or spread in 9-inch layers on cookie sheets. There should be 3 layers. Bake in preheated slow oven (300°F.) for 30 minutes, or until layers are barely golden. Cool. Combine whipped cream and rum. Fill layers with whipped cream and put together. Spread a thin layer of whipped cream on top. Arrange *marrons glacés* in a circle on the top, 1 inch from edge. Fill spaces between them with candied violets. Pipe a decorative whipped-cream border around top.

FRENCH CHOCOLATE TORTE

4 ounces (4 squares) unsweetened chocolate
¼ cup water
½ cup sweet butter, cut into pieces
½ cup sugar
3 large or 4 small eggs, separated
½ cup ground unblanched almonds
2 teaspoons rum or brandy
⅓ cup all-purpose flour
Sour-cherry jam
Chocolate Icing

Melt chocolate in water over low heat, stirring constantly. Remove from heat. Stir in butter and stir until completely melted. Blend in sugar. Cool. Beat in egg yolks, one at a time. Blend in nuts and flavoring. Stir in flour and blend well. Fold in stiffly beaten egg whites. Grease and flour two 8-inch layer-cake pans. Divide batter between pans. Bake in preheated moderate oven (350°F.) for about 25 minutes, or until cakes test done. Cool. Put sour-cherry jam between the layers and spread a thin layer of jam over top. Frost top and sides of cake thickly with Chocolate Icing. Makes 12 to 16 servings.

Chocolate Icing

1½ cups sugar
1½ cups hot water
2 ounces (2 squares) unsweetened chocolate
⅓ cup cornstarch
¼ cup cold water
1 tablespoon rum or brandy extract

Combine sugar, hot water, and chocolate in heavy saucepan. Over medium heat, bring to a boil. Lower heat and cook for

5 minutes, stirring constantly. Mix cornstarch and cold water to a smooth paste. Stir mixture into chocolate syrup. Cook for 3 or 4 minutes, stirring constantly to avoid lumping. Remove from heat. Blend in extract. Beat until cool enough to spread. Makes enough for top and sides of two 8-inch layers, about 2 cups.

Note: This icing should be flavored in the same manner as the French Chocolate Torte, to match flavors.

JAEGERTORTE
(Hunter's Torte)

1 cup fine dry bread crumbs
3 tablespoons sherry
2 tablespoons fresh lemon juice
5 eggs, separated
1¼ cups sugar
1 cup almonds, blanched and shredded
1 teaspoon baking powder
½ teaspoon salt
⅔ cup apricot jam or currant jelly
4 egg whites

Soak bread crumbs in sherry and lemon juice. Beat egg yolks until light. Gradually beat in 1 cup sugar; beat until mixture is thick and lemon-colored. Beat in bread crumbs, ¾ cup of the almonds, and the baking powder. Beat the 5 egg whites with salt until stiff. Fold lightly into batter. Put batter into greased and floured 9-inch shallow baking dish suitable for serving. Bake in preheated moderate oven (350°F.) for 20 to 25 minutes, or until cake tests done. Reduce oven heat to slow (300°F.). Remove torte from oven. Cool slightly in dish. Spread with apricot jam. Beat the 4 egg whites until frothy. Add ¼ cup sugar, 1 tablespoon at a time, beating well after each addition. Meringue should be stiff and glossy. Spread meringue evenly over torte. Sprinkle with remaining almonds. Bake for 10 to 15 minutes, or until top is honey-colored. Cool, and serve from baking dish. Makes 10 to 12 servings.

MOCHA TORTE

8 eggs, separated
1 cup sugar
1½ cups cake flour
½ cup butter, melted and cooled
5 cups Mocha Buttercream
1 cup slivered toasted almonds
Whole coffee beans

Beat egg yolks and sugar until light and fluffy. Gradually beat in flour, 2 tablespoons at a time. Beat egg whites until stiff. Gently fold into mixture. Stir in butter, stirring just sufficiently to blend. Grease and flour four 8-inch layer-cake pans. Divide batter among pans. Bake in preheated moderate oven (350°F.) for about 15 minutes, or until layers test done. Remove from pans and let cool. Reserve 1 cup Mocha Buttercream. Spread remaining Mocha Buttercream between layers, over sides, and on top. Stick almonds on sides of torte. Put remaining cup of Mocha Buttercream into pastry bag with fluted tube. Pipe a row of large rosettes around edge of torte. Pipe more rows of rosettes on top of torte until it is completely covered. Top each rosette with a coffee bean. Chill before serving. Makes 16 servings.

Mocha Buttercream

1 cup sugar
⅔ cup strong or espresso-type coffee, cold
12 egg yolks, well beaten
2½ cups sweet butter, softened
¼ cup triple-strength coffee, cold

In heavy saucepan cook sugar and ⅔ cup coffee to thread stage (234°F. on a candy thermometer). Pour syrup slowly over egg yolks, stirring constantly. Beat mixture until cold and foamy. Gradually beat in butter, a little at a time, alternately with ¼ cup coffee. Beat only until mixture is smooth. If cream separates, keep beating until smooth. Chill to spreading consistency before using. Makes about 5 cups.

SWEDISH VARMLANDSTÅRTA

3 egg whites
½ cup granulated sugar
¼ cup finely chopped hazelnuts
2 tablespoons cocoa
Buttercream
Slivered toasted almonds

Beat egg whites until very stiff. Gradually beat in sugar. Beat until stiff and glossy. Beat in nuts and cocoa. Grease 2 cookie sheets and mark 8-inch circles on each sheet. Spread the meringue mixture out into 8-inch circles and bake in preheated slow oven (300°F.) for 30 to 35 minutes. Lower heat to very slow (275°F.) for the last 5 to 10 minutes. Loosen the layers while they are still warm and let them cool before the Buttercream is spread on them. Spread Buttercream on the tops of layers. Put layers together and sprinkle cake with slivered toasted almonds. Makes 8 to 10 servings.

Buttercream

3 egg yolks
2 tablespoons sugar
⅓ cup light cream
⅓ cup butter

Put egg yolks, sugar, and cream in a saucepan and let simmer while whipping firmly until the cream thickens. Let cool. Cream butter until light and fluffy. Gradually beat in the cooled cream mixture, 1 teaspoon at a time. Beat until well blended and fluffy.

CHERRY TORTE WITH CREAM

1½ cups sifted all-purpose flour
2 egg yolks
9 tablespoons sugar
Grated rind of 1 lemon
½ cup butter, softened and cut into small pieces
¼ cup finely grated hazelnuts or filberts
6 cups pitted fresh bing cherries (about)
½ teaspoon ground nutmeg
½ cup heavy cream
½ cup slivered blanched almonds

Put flour in a bowl. Make a well in the center. Add 1 egg yolk, 1 tablespoon of the sugar, the grated lemon rind, and butter. Stir with a fork until mixture blends and forms a dough. Knead with the hands on a lightly floured board until dough is smooth. Pat dough with the fingers into the bottom and sides of a 9-inch pie pan, pressing the dough into a high edge on the side of the pan. Sprinkle dough with grated hazelnuts. Chill for 2 hours. Put pitted cherries on top of dough in overlapping circles, making 2 layers. Sprinkle with remaining sugar and nutmeg. Bake in preheated moderate oven (350°F.) for 15 minutes. Beat remaining egg yolk with cream and pour mixture over cherries. Sprinkle top with slivered almonds. Continue baking in moderate oven (350°F.) for 30 minutes, or until dough is golden brown and cherries are tender. Serve warm. Makes 6 to 8 servings.

APRICOT TORTE

4 eggs
1 cup sugar
½ teaspoon salt
⅔ cup sifted all-purpose flour
⅔ cup cornstarch
1 package (11 ounces) dried apricots
¾ cup dark corn syrup
¼ cup cold water
½ cup chopped almonds or walnuts

Beat eggs in large mixing bowl until fluffy. Gradually add ⅔ cup sugar and salt, beating until mixture doubles in bulk and mounds slightly when dropped from spoon. Sift flour and ½ cup cornstarch over egg mixture; fold in. Pour into 2 greased and floured 9-inch layer-cake pans. Bake in preheated moderate oven (350°F.) for about 25 minutes, until top springs back when lightly touched. Cool slightly. Remove from pan. Cool completely on a rack; then cut each cake into 2 layers with a sharp thin knife.

Put apricots in saucepan, cover with water, and bring to a boil. Simmer, uncovered, for 30 minutes, stirring occasionally. Add ½ cup corn syrup and remaining ⅓ cup sugar; stir until sugar is melted. Purée mixture, using an electric blender or a strainer. Reserve ¾ cup. Stack cake layers, using all but ¾ cup purée as filling; use about ½ cup between each layer.

Blend remaining 2 tablespoons cornstarch and water in saucepan. Stir in reserved ¾ cup purée and remaining corn syrup. Stirring constantly, bring to boil, and simmer for 1 minute. Cool slightly. Pour over cake. Spread evenly over top and sides with spatula. Cover sides with chopped nuts. Serve with whipped cream, if desired. Makes 8 servings.

Viennese Torte

SWEDISH SANS RIVAL TORTE

5 egg whites, at room temperature
½ teaspoon cream of tartar
2 cups sifted confectioners' sugar
1½ cups blanched almonds
1 cup sweet butter
¼ cup water
1 cup granulated sugar
3 egg yolks
1 teaspoon vanilla extract
24 slightly toasted blanched almonds, halved

Beat egg whites with cream of tartar until foamy throughout. Using an egg beater or electric mixer, beat in confectioners' sugar, 2 tablespoons at a time, beating after each addition until sugar is thoroughly blended. (Do not beat in sugar any faster or meringue will not stand up.) Grind 1 cup of the almonds. Carefully fold almonds into meringue. Cut out three 8-inch squares from wax paper or plain brown paper such as packing paper. Place on greased cookie sheets. With spatula, spread meringue on squares. Bake in preheated very slow oven (275° F.) for about 20 minutes or until light golden and firm to the touch. Remove from cookie sheet. When cooled, carefully peel off paper from meringue squares.

■ Meanwhile make buttercream. Beat butter until light and fluffy. Boil water and ⅓ cup of the sugar until syrup spins a 2-inch thread when dropped from spoon (232°F. on candy thermometer). Beat egg yolks until well blended. Pour sugar syrup over egg yolks, a little at a time, beating constantly. Beat until cooled. Add butter very carefully, a little at a time, to prevent curdling. Stir in vanilla. (If cream curdles, place over hot water and beat until smooth.)

■ To make praline powder, melt remaining ⅔ cup sugar over lowest possible heat. Add remaining ½ cup whole blanched almonds and stir until almonds are coated with sugar. Pour mixture onto buttered cookie sheet. Cool thoroughly until hard. Break praline into very small pieces with rolling pin or grind coarsely in meat grinder.

■ To assemble torte, stir half of ground praline into buttercream. Spread ⅔ of this mixture on the 3 meringue layers and sandwich them together. Spread remaining ⅓ on sides. Sprinkle sides with remaining praline. Decorate top with toasted almond halves in a decorative pattern. Makes 10 to 12 servings.

OPERA TORTE

Cake:

2 cups sifted confectioners' sugar
1⅓ cups sifted cornstarch
6 eggs, separated
¼ teaspoon cream of tartar
¼ cup water
1 teaspoon vanilla extract

Filling:

1 tablespoon unflavored gelatin
¼ cup cold water
4 egg yolks
6 tablespoons sugar
3 tablespoons cornstarch
2 cups milk
1 tablespoon vanilla extract
1 cup heavy cream, whipped
3 tablespoons brandy (optional)

Almond Paste:

1 cup blanched almonds
2 cups confectioners' sugar
1 teaspoon almond extract
2 egg whites, slightly beaten
Green food coloring

Topping:

½ cup sifted confectioners' sugar

Grease four 8-inch layer-cake pans and line the bottoms with wax paper.

■ To make the cake, sift together 3 times 1 cup confectioners' sugar and the cornstarch. Beat the egg whites, cream of tartar, and water in a large bowl until the mixture forms soft peaks. Gradually beat in remaining 1 cup confectioners' sugar, a little at a time. Continue beating until stiff peaks form when beater is raised. Add egg yolks and vanilla; beat in just until well blended. Fold in sugar-cornstarch mixture, a little at a time, and blend thoroughly. Divide batter among pans and bake in a preheated moderate oven (350°F.) for 30 minutes, or until top of cake springs back when touched lightly with finger. Cool before removing from pans.

■ Meanwhile, make the filling. Soften gelatin in cold water. Combine egg yolks, sugar, cornstarch, and milk in top part of double boiler. Cook over simmering, not boiling, water until mixture is smooth and thick. Stir constantly. Remove from heat and beat in gelatin and vanilla. Cool, beating occasionally to keep smooth. Fold in whipped cream and brandy. Chill before using.

■ While filling chills, make almond paste. Put almonds through nut grinder twice, or grind fine in electric blender. Combine with sugar, almond extract, and egg whites. Work with spoon until smooth. Stir in a few drops of green food coloring to color the paste light green. Knead almond paste with hands until it is very smooth and the sugar has been completely absorbed. This may take from 5 to 10 minutes. Roll out on wax paper into an 8-inch circle.

■ To assemble the Torte, neatly spread filling on cake layers; the top layer should also be spread with filling. Put layers together. Place almond paste over filling on top layer. Sift confectioners' sugar through a paper lace doily onto almond paste to form decorative pattern. Remove doily carefully. Makes 10 to 12 servings.

Note: This handsome delicate cake is at its best if served very cold, almost frozen.

TORTILLA—The daily bread of Mexico, made since time immemorial by the Indians and later by the Mexicans, in the shape of a round, flat, thin cake resembling a pancake. Tortillas are cooked on a griddle until done, but not browned. They are eaten as is, or stuffed and rolled with meat, cheese, etc., in which case they are called *tacos*.

The word tortilla means "little cake." True tortillas are made with a lime-treated cornmeal dough called *masa*, but they are also made with wheat flour. The *masa* needed for them can be bought fresh in the Mexican-American border districts, and dried in all stores catering to people of Mexican and Central American origin. Tortillas are also sold canned.

Tortillas should be served hot. The Mexicans put them in a hot dish and cover them with a napkin to keep them hot. If cooled, they can be reheated in preheated moderate oven (350°F.). Before putting in the oven, brush them with water, or rub with dampened hands to moisten them.

WHITE CORN TORTILLAS

Boiling water
2 cups masa
1 teaspoon salt

Stir boiling water into *masa* to make a stiff dough. Add salt. Let stand for 1 hour. With damp hands, pat dough into 5-inch round cakes. They should be as thin as possible. Bake on greased griddle, turning frequently to cook through thoroughly. Makes about 12.

Note: The dough may also be rolled out between 2 sheets of clear plastic or wax paper, and trimmed to size.

TORTILLA DE HARINA DE TRIGO (Wheat Tortillas)

2 cups all-purpose flour
1 teaspoon baking powder
1 teaspoon salt
½ cup lard
¾ cup water (about)

Sift dry ingredients together into mixing bowl. Cut in lard as when making pie dough. Add enough water to make a soft dough. Roll out thinly on floured board. Cut into 5-inch rounds. Bake on lightly greased griddle, turning frequently to cook through. Makes about 16.

CHILI-FILLED TORTILLAS

Fry tortillas in small amount of cooking oil until crisp. Spread heated canned chili con carne on each tortilla. Cover with shredded lettuce. Sprinkle with a little French dressing and some grated Parmesan cheese. Fold over; garnish with black olives, green onions, and tomato wedges.

Tortilla de Harinha de Trigo *Chili-Filled Tortillas*

CHICKEN-FILLED TORTILLAS WITH TOMATO SAUCE

- 12 tortillas
- 2 tablespoons cooking oil
- 1 green onion, minced
- 1 cup (one 8¼-ounce can) tomatoes, drained and chopped
- 2 cups chopped cooked chicken
- Salt
- 1 cup (8-ounce can) tomato sauce
- 1 hot dried red pepper
- Dash of oregano

Fry tortillas in 1 tablespoon of the oil until crisp. Cook onion in remaining oil for 2 minutes. Add tomatoes; cook for 5 minutes. Add chicken, heat, and add salt to taste. Spread on tortillas and fold over. Top with remaining ingredients, heated together. Makes 12.

TOSTADAS

Cut canned tortillas into 6 or 8 wedge-shape pieces. Fry in deep fat (375°F. on a frying thermometer) for 2 to 3 minutes, until golden brown. Drain on absorbent paper and sprinkle with salt. These will stay crisp for several weeks if kept in an airtight container, or they may be frozen for longer storage.

TORTONI—An Italian dessert in which whipped cream is flavored with sherry, rum, or other liquor, combined with macaroon crumbs, put into little paper cups, sprinkled with more crumbs or with almonds, and frozen. The classic is Biscuit Tortoni.

BISCUIT TORTONI

- ½ cup coarsely ground dried almond macaroons
- 1 cup light cream
- ⅓ cup sugar
- ¼ cup sherry
- 1 cup heavy cream, whipped
- ½ cup blanched almonds, minced and toasted

Soak the ground macaroons in the light cream for 30 minutes. Add sugar and sherry; freeze until mushy. Fold in whipped cream and pack into eight ¼-cup paper or foil cups. Sprinkle with the almonds and freeze until firm. Makes 8 servings.

COFFEE TORTONI

- 1 egg white
- 1 tablespoon instant coffee powder
- ⅛ teaspoon salt
- 6 tablespoons sugar
- 1 cup heavy cream
- 1 teaspoon vanilla extract
- ⅛ teaspoon almond extract
- ¼ cup toasted blanched almonds, finely chopped

Turn refrigerator control to coldest setting. In small bowl mix egg white, coffee, and salt. Beat with rotary beater until almost stiff. Gradually beat in 2 tablespoons of the sugar and beat until stiff. Whip cream and fold in remaining sugar and the flavorings. Fold in meringue and nuts. Spoon into ¼-cup paper or foil cups and freeze in freezing compartment of refrigerator until firm. Makes 8 servings.

SHERRY TORTONI

Melt ½ pound marshmallows in ⅔ cup sherry in top part of double boiler; cool to room temperature. Whip 2 cups heavy cream; fold into marshmallow mixture. Spoon into 8 individual soufflé cups or double thickness of paper baking cups which have been set in muffin pans. Sprinkle with very finely chopped almonds or cake or cookie crumbs. Freeze; wrap individually in foil or plastic wrap and return to freezer. Makes 8 servings.

TOSS, TO—In culinary usage the phrase means to mix a food lightly, usually with a fork and spoon. Tossing is done in order to allow all parts of the food to come into contact with other ingredients; a salad, for instance, is tossed so that the ingredients will be well coated with the dressing.

TOURNEDOS—A meat cut, consisting of small filets of beef taken from the tip of the tenderloin. They are also known as filet steaks. Since the meat of the filet is very lean, the tournedos are circled with a strip of pork fat secured with string; the string, and usually the fat, is removed before serving. Tournedos are sautéed in butter or broiled. They are served, usually on bread rounds so that the delicious meat juices will not be wasted, with different accompaniments and sauces, such as mushrooms, artichokes, etc.

TRIFLE—A dessert of English origin made from jam-covered, spirit-soaked spongecake, over which a rich custard is poured. The trifle is then covered with whipped cream and handsomely decorated with glacé fruit and almonds. Another name for it is tipsy cake. But trifle need not be so elaborate. It may be simple spongecake soaked with fruit juice, covered with fresh or canned fruit, and decorated with whipped cream.

Trifles can also be varied in other ways. Instead of using spongecake, macaroons may be the base. Cake crumbs too have been used to advantage. Instead of covering the cake with whipped cream, it may be covered with a sugared meringue and quickly baked in the oven, as in a meringue pie.

The name trifle is also given to fruit desserts served with custard and whipped cream.

A TRUE ENGLISH TRIFLE

2 layers of plain spongecake
1 dozen ladyfingers, split
1 cup apricot, strawberry, raspberry, or any other jam
1 cup good-quality sherry or Madeira
½ cup brandy
8 egg yolks
½ cup sugar
4 cups light cream, scalded
1 teaspoon vanilla extract
½ teaspoon almond extract
1 cup heavy cream, whipped
Angelica strips and candied cherries
Blanched almonds and tiny macaroons

Line silver or crystal dish with one of the spongecake layers. Make a border with the ladyfingers, allowing them to protrude ½ inch over edge of the dish. Spread spongecake layer with jam and sprinkle with half of sherry. Top with second cake layer. Combine remaining sherry and the brandy and pour over cakes. Let stand until cake has absorbed the liquid. In top part of a double boiler beat egg yolks with sugar until thick. Slowly stir in scalded cream. Cook over simmering, not boiling, water, stirring constantly, until thickened. Remove from heat and stir in vanilla and almond extracts. Cool. Pour custard over cake layers. Chill. Spread top of trifle with whipped cream or pipe ornamental swirls of whipped cream through pastry tube. Cut angelica into strips and cut candied cherries into halves and quarters. Decorate trifle with glacé fruit in any fancy pattern. Arrange almonds and tiny macaroons around border. Chill before serving. Makes 16 servings.

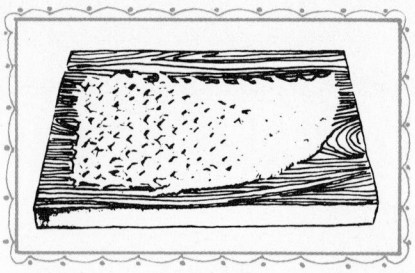

TRIPE—The inner lining of the stomach of beef. There are three kinds: honeycomb, pocket, and plain or smooth. Honeycomb tripe is considered the most desirable.

Availability and Purchasing Guide—Honeycomb, pocket, and plain tripe are all available fresh, pickled, and canned. The fresh and canned tripe are widely available; pickled tripe is not often found outside the New England area.

Tripes à la mode de Caen, the most famous of French tripe dishes, is available canned.

Storage—Refrigerate fresh and pickled tripe.

☐ Fresh, refrigerator shelf: 1 day
☐ Pickled, refrigerator shelf: 2 to 3 days
☐ Canned, kitchen shelf: 1 year

Nutritive Food Values—A good source of protein.

☐ Fresh, 3½ ounces = 100 calories
☐ Pickled, 3½ ounces = 62 calories

Basic Preparation—Fresh tripe, although it has been cooked before it is sold, requires additional cooking. Pickled tripe is usually sold thoroughly cooked, but should be parboiled before using. Canned tripe is ready to heat and serve.

☐ **To Cook Fresh Tripe**—Put in kettle and cover with water. Add 1 tablespoon salt. Simmer, covered, for 1½ hours, or until tender. Drain and dry between paper towels. Cut into serving pieces and serve with hot tomato sauce, or use in recipes.

☐ **To Sauté Fresh Tripe**—Dip serving pieces of cooked fresh tripe into 1 beaten egg mixed with 2 tablespoons water; then into fine dry bread crumbs. Sauté tripe in small amount of hot fat in skillet until golden-brown on both sides. Serve with hot tomato sauce or lemon wedges.

☐ **To Broil Fresh Tripe**—Brush serving pieces of cooked fresh tripe with melted butter or margarine. Broil about 3 inches from heat for 5 minutes. Turn and brush with butter. Broil for 5 minutes longer, or until golden brown. Brush again with butter and season with salt, pepper, and paprika.

☐ **To Parboil Pickled Tripe**—Put tripe in saucepan and cover with cold water. Bring to boil, cover, and simmer for about 15 minutes. Drain, and dry between paper towels. Cut into serving pieces.

☐ **To Panfry Pickled Tripe**—Roll pieces of parboiled pickled tripe in a mixture of half flour and half cornmeal. Fry in ⅛ inch of hot bacon fat or lard until well browned on both sides and crisp. Put on a hot platter and put a small pat of butter or margarine on each piece.

BATTER-FRIED TRIPE

1 pound fresh tripe, cooked
1 cup all-purpose flour
¼ teaspoon salt
1 teaspoon baking powder
1 egg, beaten
½ cup milk
1 teaspoon cooking oil
Bacon fat or lard
Chili sauce or ketchup

Cut tripe into 1½-inch squares. Mix dry ingredients. Add next 3 ingredients and beat until smooth. Dip pieces of tripe in the batter and fry in hot bacon fat in skillet until browned on both sides. Serve with chili sauce. Makes 4 servings.

TRIPES À LA MODE DE CAEN

The most famous tripe recipe in French cookery

2 pounds fresh tripe
3 carrots, scraped and cut into rounds

6 whole cloves
3 garlic cloves, chopped
3 ounces salt pork, diced
8 peppercorns
1 calf's foot, cut into 3 pieces, or 1 veal knuckle, cracked
Large bouquet garni (1 celery stalk with tops, ¼ leek, 1 bay leaf, 3 parsley sprigs, ¼ teaspoon ground thyme
6 slices of bacon
¾ cup water
1½ cups dry white wine

Wipe tripe and cut into cubes. Put in a large earthenware pot a layer of carrots and half of cloves, garlic, salt pork, and peppercorns. Add a layer of tripe. Repeat the process. Put calf's foot and *bouquet garni* in the center of the pot. Cover the last layer of tripe with slices of bacon. Fill casserole three-fourths full with water mixed with white wine. Cover tightly and bake in preheated moderate oven (350° F.) for 5 hours, or until tripe is tender. Add boiling water if needed. Remove calf's foot and *bouquet garni.* Thicken sauce with cornstarch before serving if desired. Makes 6 to 8 servings.

TRIPES À LA LYONNAISE

2 pounds fresh tripe, cooked
¼ cup butter or cooking oil
4 large onions, thinly sliced
Salt and pepper to taste
¼ teaspoon ground nutmeg

Cut tripe into squares. Heat 2 tablespoons of the butter, add onion slices and sauté until pale yellow. Remove onions. Add tripe and remaining butter. Brown tripe on both sides. Add sautéed onions. Cook over medium heat, stirring, for 8 minutes. Season with salt and pepper and stir in nutmeg. Serve very hot. Makes 6 large servings.

CRISP BREADED TRIPE

1 pound fresh tripe
1 egg
⅓ cup undiluted evaporated milk
1 teaspoon salt
⅛ teaspoon pepper
½ teaspoon crumbled dried sage
1 small onion, grated
1¼ cups fine dry bread crumbs

Wash tripe; cover with seasoned water and simmer for about 1½ hours, or until tender. Drain, and cool. Cut into 16 pieces. Combine beaten egg, evaporated milk, salt, pepper, sage, and onion. Dip tripe into mixture, then coat with crumbs. Arrange pieces 1 inch apart on greased cookie sheet. Let stand for 30 minutes. Bake in preheated hot oven (400°F.) for 20 minutes, or until browned. Makes 4 servings.

STEWED TRIPE WITH VEGETABLES

1 pound fresh tripe
2 cups water
2 cups (one 1-pound can) tomatoes
1 bay leaf
2 whole cloves
4 peppercorns
½ green pepper, chopped
1 onion, chopped
1½ teaspoons salt
⅛ teaspoon pepper
½ teaspoon Worcestershire
4 medium potatoes
All-purpose flour
About 2 cups (one 1-pound can) whole green beans, drained

Cut tripe into 1-inch squares. Add water and all ingredients except last 3. Simmer, covered, for 2 hours. Add potatoes and simmer for 1 hour longer. Thicken with flour mixed with a little cold water. Add beans, and heat. Makes 4 servings.

TRIPE CREOLE

Cut 1 pound cooked fresh tripe into strips. Simmer for 30 minutes with 1 tablespoon cooking oil, 1 sliced onion, 2⅓ cups (one 1-pound, 3-ounce can) tomatoes, 1 minced garlic clove, and salt, pepper, ground nutmeg, and herbs to taste. Makes 4 servings.

TROUT—The name given to a large group of fishes of the family *Salmonidae.* Although most varieties are fresh-water fish and favor clear cool waters, a few, such as the sea trout and some of the rainbow trout, live in the sea and ascend rivers to breed. Trout vary greatly in size and coloration according to their environment, but they all have one thing in common: they are a fine sporting fish. They are also one of the most delicious fish to eat; their flesh is lean and delicate.

Among the most widely known are the rainbow trout, *Salmo gairdnerii,* native to the streams of California, but now found in other parts of the United States and throughout the world; the brook, or speckled, trout, *Salvelinus fontenalis,* of the eastern United States; the steelhead, or salmon-trout, which is a variety of the rainbow trout; the cutthroat trout, *Salmo clarkii,* and the Dolly Varden, *Salvelinus malma,* both found in cold waters from California to Alaska.

Trout can be broiled, baked, poached, or panfried, usually whole.

Availability—Trout are available whole, fresh and frozen. Trout are also available canned. Smoked or kippered trout are available.

Storage

☐ Fresh, refrigerator shelf, raw: 1 to 2 days
☐ Fresh, refrigerator shelf, cooked: 4 to 5 days
☐ Frozen, refrigerator frozen-food compartment, prepared for freezing: 2 months
☐ Frozen, freezer, prepared for freezing: 4 to 6 months

Caloric Values

☐ Brook trout, 3½ ounces, raw = 101 calories
☐ Rainbow trout, 3½ ounces, raw = 195 calories

Basic Preparation

☐ **To Poach**—Put cleaned trout in a flat pan and barely cover with hot Court Bouillon. Cover and simmer for 4 to 6 minutes, or until fish flakes easily with a fork. Serve with béarnaise or other sauce.

Court Bouillon

Combine 1 quart water, 3 tablespoons fresh lemon juice or 1 tablespoon vinegar, and 1½ teaspoons salt. Bring to a boil and cook for 3 minutes before using for poaching fish.

☐ **To Panfry**—Dip cleaned trout into milk and roll in flour. Fry in hot butter or margarine in skillet until well browned on both sides and fish flakes easily with a fork. Season with salt and pepper.

☐ **To Bake**—Put cleaned trout in a well-greased shallow baking pan. Sprinkle with salt and pepper and brush with melted butter or margarine. Bake in preheated hot oven (400°F.) for 15 to 20 minutes, or until fish flakes easily with a fork. Season with salt and pepper.

☐ **To Broil**—Put cleaned trout on broiler rack and brush with melted butter or margarine. Broil about 3 inches from the heat for 3 to 5 minutes, depending on the thickness of the fish. Turn and brush again with butter. Broil for 5 to 8 minutes longer, brushing once or twice with butter. Season with salt and pepper.

☐ **To Fry Brook Trout**—Clean and wash fish, allowing 2 or 3 per person. Dry thoroughly. Dip each fish into undiluted evaporated milk, then into seasoned cornmeal. Fry in shallow fat until golden-brown on both sides.

☐ **To Freeze**—Eviscerate fish and leave whole or remove head. Wash thoroughly and drain. Wrap in moisture- vapor-proof wrapping, excluding as much air as possible. Seal.

TROUT EN PAPILLOTE

1 steelhead trout (4 to 5 pounds)
Salt and pepper
½ cup butter or margarine
1 tablespoon chopped fresh mint

Have trout cleaned but do not remove head. Sprinkle lightly inside and out with salt and pepper. Arrange a large sheet of foil in bottom of shallow baking dish.

Truite au Bleu

Spread butter on foil. Put fish on foil and sprinkle with mint. Roll up and twist ends of foil. Bake fish in preheated hot oven (400°F.) for about 50 minutes. Put, still wrapped, on hot platter. Cut portions through bones and all. Serve with cream sauce or other preferred sauce. Makes 4 to 6 servings.

RAINBOW TROUT, ROCKY MOUNTAIN STYLE

4 rainbow trout, about 1 pound each
1½ teaspoons salt
¼ teaspoon pepper
Yellow cornmeal
Butter or margarine

Sprinkle cleaned trout inside and out with salt and pepper, mixed together. Roll in cornmeal and panfry in hot butter for 5 minutes on each side, or until golden-brown and fish flakes easily with a fork. Makes 4 servings.

BROOK TROUT MEUNIÈRE

4 brook trout
All-purpose flour seasoned with salt and pepper
½ cup clarified butter
⅓ cup chopped parsley
Lemon wedges

Wash trout and drain, leaving head and tail on. Dip fish into flour. Melt ¼ cup butter and sauté trout until firm and brown. Put trout on a serving platter and cover with chopped parsley. Add remaining butter to pan drippings. Cook over medium heat until butter becomes golden-brown. Spoon butter over fish. Serve with lemon wedges. Makes 4 servings.

TRUITE AU BLEU

3 cups water
1 cup vinegar
6 peppercorns
1 small bay leaf
1 teaspoon salt
4 trout, freshly dressed
Melted butter
Hot boiled potatoes

Bring first 5 ingredients to a boil. Drop in trout and simmer just long enough to cook fish through, about 4 minutes for the average fish. Serve hot with melted butter and boiled potatoes, and asparagus, if desired. Makes 4 servings.

TROUT, ENGLISH STYLE

6 trout
3 tablespoons butter or margarine
2 tablespoons olive oil
All-purpose flour
Salt and pepper
1 egg, slightly beaten
1 cup fine dry bread crumbs

Wash and dry trout. Heat butter and olive oil in a large skillet. Dredge fish with flour, and sprinkle with salt and pepper. Dip in egg, then in the crumbs, and sauté quickly in the hot fat. Serve with tartare sauce. Makes 6 servings.

COMMANDER'S PALACE TROUT ALEXANDER

3 pounds speckled trout
Milk and water
Salt and pepper
3 bay leaves
½ cup butter
¾ pound mushrooms, sliced
1 garlic clove, minced
4 scallions with green tops, minced
¼ pound each of cooked shrimps and lobster
2 tablespoons all-purpose flour
1 cup heavy cream

Skin and bone trout. Place pieces side by side in a buttered shallow saucepan. Add milk to cover fish halfway and add about half as much water as milk. Sprinkle lightly with salt, add bay leaves, and cover the pan. Bring liquid to a boil. Reduce heat and simmer slowly for about 15 minutes, or until the fish flakes readily at the touch of a fork. Reduce the broth in which the fish was poached to ½ cup and reserve it for use in the sauce. Melt butter, add mushrooms and garlic, and sauté for 5 minutes, stirring occasionally. Add scallions and simmer for 5 minutes longer. Add shrimps and lobster. Heat thoroughly. Sprinkle with flour and cook, stirring, for 2 more minutes. Gradually stir in 1 cup milk, the cream, and reserved fish broth. Simmer the sauce for 10 minutes, stirring, over low heat until smooth and thickened. Season to taste with salt and pepper. Pour sauce around the fish on the platter and serve at once. Makes 4 servings.

TRUFFLE ***by Lucy Kavaler***—"Sensual men of fashion consume them to whet their appetite for lovemaking." With these words an Italian writer of the 1470's expresses the age-old belief about the aphrodisiac qualities of truffles.

Modern science does not back up this legend, but the popularity of the truffle, which is a fungus growing beneath the ground, does not depend upon lovers alone. Adding its incomparable flavor to the best *pâté de foie gras,* the truffle is appreciated by the true gourmet. Anthelme Brillat-Savarin, 19th-century French expert on the art of dining, recommended stuffing turkeys with truffles, and lyrically declared this "a luxury only for the tables of the great or . . . homes of kept women." Some cooks cut truffles into fancy shapes and use them to decorate platters of cold chicken or meats, while others stretch the expensive delicacy by chopping it very fine and adding it to a cream sauce flavored with Madeira. One inspired chef some years back created truffled ice cream. Ward McAllister, social arbiter of the extravagant gilded age of the 1890's, beseeched such friends as *the* Mrs. Astor to serve *filet de boeuf* with truffles rather than mushrooms.

But neither McAllister nor the modern gourmet would be likely to recognize the truffle in its natural state. Unlike the appealing mushroom, the truffle is an extremely ugly fungus. Belonging to the *Ascomycetes* class of fungi, the truffle is a roundish dark-brown ball with a thick, warty, rindlike surface. Within lies a series of elaborate folds, which contain the spores or seeds. In the Middle Ages its appearance gave rise to the legend that truffles were formed from witches' spit, which was believed to be dark in color, rather than the white of normal humans. Although the average truffle weighs but a few ounces, every so often a king-size specimen tipping the scales at two-and-a-half pounds is found.

Finding the truffle at all is quite a feat, as no part of it ever appears above ground. The fungus grows in the woods on the roots of oaks or beeches, taking nourishment from the trees and giving them back water and minerals from the soil in a perfect example of the harmony of nature. The only giveaway of the whereabouts of a truffle is its odor, and the human sense of smell is not keen enough to detect that. Animals love truffles just as much as people do, which has turned out to be very fortunate for those of us who appreciate good food. The Russians tried to use bear cubs and the Sardinians employed goats, but dogs and pigs have proved to be the best hunters.

It takes several years to teach a pig to hunt, and a trained animal is worth its weight in truffles. Tenderly treated by its master, it is trundled to the forest in a wheelbarrow. The pig snuffles along the ground until attracted by the delectable smell. It digs up the truffle, and then comes the critical moment: the owner must prevent the animal from eating the fungus without discouraging it to the point where it will not go on to find more truffles. An acorn or other tidbit is, therefore, substituted, while the truffle is whisked away.

Many different kinds of truffle lie hidden beneath the soil, but not all of them are edible. Unfortunately, none of the forty varieties growing in the United States is good, so gourmets must rely on imports, primarily from southern France and northern Italy. Of the Italian truffles, the Piedmont is the most renowned. But the reputation for best flavor belongs to the *Tuber melanosporum,* which grows in the oak forests of Périgord in France.

It is possible, but by no means easy, to increase truffle production by planting groves of oaks or beeches, putting bits of truffle in the soil nearby, and waiting. The first harvest appears from six to ten years later. It is easy to see why truffles remain such a luxury.

In the desert, however, truffles can be a lifesaving, rather than a luxury food. The desert truffle, known scientifically as *Terfezia,* is different from the species eaten in America or Europe and does not require a tree partner. Hungry nomads traveling over the burning wastes of the Sahara watch for the telltale sign that reveals the hidden fungus. A truffle pushes the sand up an infinitesimal amount, just enough to cast a shadow at sunset or sunrise. The Arabs roast the truffles in the hot ashes of the fire and then dip them into salt. Any leftover truffles are dried and taken along to provide sustenance on the weary journey to the oasis.

Availability and Purchasing Guide—Fresh truffles are not available in the United States.

Canned truffles are available in most gourmet food stores. They are put up in several sizes of cans or jars, some being very small, and all being very expensive: a seven-ounce can costs about $20.

Storage—If only a part of a can is used, it should be tightly covered and refrigerated since the full flavor and aroma are quickly lost after a can is opened. If the opened can must be kept for some time, pour bacon or poultry drippings over the remaining truffles, cover, and store in the refrigerator.

Nutritive Food Values—Truffles, like mushrooms, are low in calories and have very little nutritive value. They are served for the delicate flavor and aroma they give to foods.

Basic Preparation—Canned truffles have already been cooked so they are added to the food they are to accompany just long enough to heat them through.

☐ **To Use in Salads**—Truffles are mixed with diced boiled potatoes or artichoke hearts and the salad seasoned with a dressing made of salad oil, lemon juice, salt, and pepper. Never use other herbs as they will mask the delicate flavor of the truffles.

Truffles are diced and inserted into pieces of meat. They are sometimes minced and added to dressing for fowl or game.

TRUSS, TO—To tie a bird with string, holding the wings and legs tightly to the body. This is done before cooking so that the bird will not loose its shape.

To truss a bird, fold wing tips back under. With a long piece of clean string, tie the leg tips together tightly and make a taut loop around the tail. Have the two ends of the string of reasonably even length. Cross the string over the back of the bird. Take it across the wings to hold them closely to the body. Finally, tie the string securely to what is left of the bird's neck. Remove string after bird is cooked.

All types of poultry and game bird may be trussed, but it is not absolutely necessary to truss a duck since its legs are short and close to the body. In barbecueing, a bird is trussed to keep the bird well balanced on the roasting rod so that the bird will cook evenly. Let roasted or barbecued birds stand for twenty minutes before removing cord, and then carve.

TRY OUT, TO—To render, that is, to heat fat or fat meat, such as salt pork or bacon or kidney fat, until the fat melts and can be separated from the remaining tissue. The tried-out fat is then used for cooking, or stored in solid form for future use.

TUNA—This salt-water game fish belongs to the mackerel family. It is also called tunny fish or horse mackerel. Tuna is found in almost all the seas of the temperate and warm zones of Asia, Africa, and America. In some parts of the world tuna can be enormous, reaching weights of 1500 pounds.

There are several varieties, including the albacore, bluefin, skipjack, and yellowfin.

Tuna is one of the best sporting fish and a fine food fish, fresh or canned.

Availability and Purchasing Guide—Because of its size fresh tuna is usually sold in steaks. Bluefin steaks are available from July to October; albacore from May to September. Frozen tuna steaks are available year round.

Canned tuna is sold packed in water or oil or seasoned oil, chunk style or solid pack. The all-white meat tuna comes from the albacore. A tuna-and-noodles dish is available canned.

Storage

- ☐ Fresh, refrigerator shelf, raw: 1 to 2 days
- ☐ Fresh, cooked; and canned, opened, refrigerator shelf: 3 to 4 days
- ☐ Fresh, prepared for freezing; or frozen, refrigerator frozen-food compartment: 2 to 3 weeks
- ☐ Fresh, prepared for freezing; or frozen, freezer: 3 to 4 months
- ☐ Canned, kitchen shelf: 1 year

Nutritive Food Values—A good source of protein.

- ☐ Fresh, 3½ ounces, raw = 145 calories
- ☐ Canned in oil, 3½ ounces, solids and liquid = 288 calories
- ☐ Canned in water, 3½ ounces, solids and liquid = 127 calories

Basic Preparation—Fresh tuna can be broiled, panfried, and baked. Canned tuna can be used in an endless variety of dishes. However, remember to drain and wash the oil or brine from canned tuna before using in cooked dishes.

☐ **To Broil Fresh Tuna**—Put steaks, cut into serving pieces, on broiler rack and brush with melted butter or margarine. Broil for 3 to 4 minutes on each side, depending on thickness of steak. Brush again with butter and season with salt and pepper. Serve with lemon wedges.

☐ **To Panfry Fresh Tuna**—Put steaks, cut into serving pieces, in hot butter or margarine in skillet and panfry for 3 to 5 minutes on each side, or until golden-brown. Serve with lemon wedges.

☐ **To Bake Fresh Tuna**—Put steaks, cut into serving pieces, in buttered shallow baking pan. Brush with melted butter or margarine. Bake in preheated hot oven (400°F.) for 8 to 10 minutes per pound, or until fish flakes easily with a fork. Time will depend on thickness of steak. Serve with lemon wedges.

TUNA COOK BOOK

FRESH TUNA

TUNA EN BROCHETTE

2 pounds fresh tuna steaks
1 slender loaf French bread
½ cup butter, melted
¼ cup olive oil
3 tablespoons fresh lemon juice
1 teaspoon salt
Bay leaves

Slice tuna ¾ inch thick, remove skin and dark meat, and cut into pieces slightly smaller than the diameter of the bread. Slice bread thin. Mix remaining ingredients except bay leaves and marinate fish in mixture for 1 hour. Impale a slice of bread on a skewer and add a slice of fish and a bay leaf; repeat until skewers contain 3 slices of fish and 4 of bread. Do not push too close together. Broil, basting with remaining marinade and turning until browned on all sides, for about 15 minutes. Makes 6 servings.

FRESH TUNA TARRAGON

2 pounds tuna steaks
White wine (about 1½ cups)
1 tablespoon crumbled dried tarragon
All-purpose flour
Salt
¼ cup butter or cooking oil

Marinate tuna steaks in white wine to cover for 2 hours. Drain. To the marinade add tarragon and let soak. Dry steaks, dust lightly with flour, sprinkle with salt, and sauté in butter on both sides until brown. Add the wine and tarragon mixture and cook at high heat until the wine is reduced to half. Remove fish to a hot platter, pour sauce over, and serve at once. Makes 4 to 6 servings.

CANNED TUNA: APPETIZERS AND SOUP

TUNA AND HORSERADISH CANAPÉS

1 can (about 7 ounces) tuna, drained and flaked
1 tablespoon minced celery
3 tablespoons mayonnaise
½ cup soft butter or margarine
3 tablespoons well-drained prepared horseradish
8 slices of toast, each cut into 4 triangles
Chopped parsley

Mix tuna, celery, and mayonnaise to a paste. Add butter and horseradish and mix well. Spread on toast and sprinkle with parsley. Makes 32 triangles.

TUNA DIP, FINES HERBES

1 can (about 7 ounces) tuna
1 package (3 ounces) cream cheese
¼ cup sherry
2 tablespoons minced parsley
2 tablespoons minced chives or 1 teaspoon dried chives
1 teaspoon minced tarragon or ¼ teaspoon dried tarragon
Dairy sour cream
Salt to taste

Combine all ingredients, adding enough sour cream to make of spreading or dunking consistency. Season with salt to taste and, if you wish, 1 or 2 tablespoons chopped capers or nuts. Makes about 1 cup.

TUNA APPETIZER

Here is a good first course, or a main dish for a light luncheon. It is very simple. Arrange large flakes of tuna (white preferred) on lettuce leaves on 4 individual plates. Whip ¼ cup heavy cream; fold in ½ cup mayonnaise, 2 teaspoons fresh lemon juice, and 1 teaspoon crushed dillseed (use a mortar and pestle, or a heavy bowl and wooden spoon). Spread sauce over tuna and top with a bit of pimiento or sliced stuffed olive. Makes 4 servings.

CABBAGE AND TUNA PIROG

1 package hot-roll mix
4 cups finely chopped cabbage

1 onion, chopped
¼ cup butter or margarine
1 or 2 cans (about 7 ounces each) tuna
2 tablespoons dillweed
Salt and pepper
1 egg
1 tablespoon water

Make hot-roll mix according to directions on the box. Cook cabbage and onion in butter until wilted. Add tuna, flaked, and dillweed. Season to taste with salt and pepper. After dough has risen, divide into halves and roll each half into a rectangle about 9 x 11 inches. Put one rectangle in a shallow baking pan and spread with tuna-cabbage mixture. Moisten edges, top with second rectangle, and seal. Brush the top with egg beaten with water. Bake in preheated hot oven (400° F.) for 15 to 20 minutes, or until nicely browned. Cut into squares. Makes 12 servings.

TUNA TREAT

2 medium tomatoes, peeled and seeded
2 hard-cooked eggs, chopped
1 green pepper, chopped
¼ cup drained tuna fish
2 flat anchovy fillets, chopped
Salt and pepper to taste
4 slices of white bread
Butter
½ cup Russian dressing (about)
Worcestershire

Chop tomatoes and drain well. Mix with next 4 ingredients. Season. Remove crusts from bread and toast slices. Cut toast into quarters and butter each piece. Spread with tuna mixture and cover with dressing. Sprinkle a drop of Worcestershire on each. Makes 16.

TUNA COCKTAIL

Combine 1 can tuna (white preferred) and ½ cup minced celery. Mix ½ cup mayonnaise, 2 teaspoons each of grated horseradish and grated onion, and 2 tablespoons fresh lemon juice. Combine tuna with sauce. Serve in cocktail glasses and garnish with slivered almonds, pimiento, or olives. Makes 4 servings.

TUNA FISH MOUND

2 cans (8 ounces each) tuna fish, drained
¼ cup minced chives
2 large sweet pickles, minced
2 teaspoons A-1 sauce
3 tablespoons ketchup
3 tablespoons grated Parmesan cheese
2 tablespoons mayonnaise

Combine the ingredients and mix well. Spoon into a round 3-cup mold or bowl. Refrigerate. When ready to use, turn out on a plate. Decorate with sliced stuffed olives. Surround with crackers. Makes 4 to 6 servings.

TUNA CHOWDER

¼ cup diced salt pork or bacon
1 onion, chopped
2 cans (about 7 ounces each) tuna in oil
2 cups hot water
1 cup diced potatoes
2 cups milk
Salt and pepper
1 tablespoon minced parsley

Cook salt pork until crisp. Remove and reserve. To fat in pan add onion and oil drained from tuna. Cook until onion is wilted; then add the water and potatoes. When potatoes are almost tender, add tuna, milk, and salt and pepper to taste. Simmer until potatoes are done. Add salt pork. Top with parsley. Makes 4 servings.

CANNED TUNA: MAIN DISHES

TUNA-NOODLE CASSEROLE

½ pound noodles
1 garlic clove, minced
½ cup minced green onions
3 tablespoons butter or margarine
¼ cup all-purpose flour
2 cups milk
2 cans (about 7 ounces each) tuna
2 tablespoons sherry (optional)
Salt and pepper
3 tablespoons bread crumbs
2 tablespoons minced parsley
2 tablespoons melted butter

Cook noodles in salted water, and drain. In the meantime, sauté garlic and onions in butter until wilted; add flour, blend over heat, and add milk. Cook, stirring constantly, until thickened and smooth; add tuna, sherry, and salt and pepper to taste. Other ingredients of your choice may be added with the tuna. Put in a 1½-quart casserole. Mix crumbs, parsley, and butter, and sprinkle on top. Reheat in preheated moderate oven (350°F.) for about 15 minutes. Makes 6 to 8 servings. Some suggestions for other ingredients: sliced cooked mushrooms, pimientos, sliced olives, nuts, tiny shrimps, hard-cooked eggs, some halved or quartered artichoke hearts, cooked peas, green beans, or Limas.

The seasonings may be varied, too: curry, chili powder, mustard, dill, tarragon, chives, basil, and thyme all blend happily with tuna; so does tomato, so a little tomato paste could be added.

TUNA FLORENTINE

1 pound spinach, cooked, chopped, and seasoned
2 tablespoons butter or margarine
3 tablespoons all-purpose flour
2 cups milk
¼ cup grated Swiss cheese
⅓ cup grated Parmesan cheese or ½ cup grated Cheddar
2 cans (about 7 ounces each) tuna

Put spinach in a large shallow baking dish and keep hot. Make a *roux* with the butter and flour; add milk, Swiss cheese, 2 tablespoons of the Parmesan, and the oil and juice from the tuna. Cook over hot water for 20 minutes. Add tuna, flaked, and pour over spinach. Sprinkle top with remaining Parmesan and broil until brown and bubbly. Makes 6 servings.

CURRIED TUNA

2 cups chopped onions
1 cup chopped apples
½ cup butter or margarine
2 tablespoons curry powder
2 cups canned tomatoes
Salt
2 cans (about 7 ounces each) tuna
Hot cooked rice
Chutney

Sauté onions and apples in butter until wilted. Add curry powder and tomatoes; cover and simmer for 30 minutes. Season with salt to taste. Separate tuna into flakes; add, and heat. Serve with rice, chutney, and any other desired condiments. Makes 4 servings.

SWEET-AND-SOUR TUNA

1 cup (one 7-ounce can) pineapple tidbits
½ cup vinegar
¼ cup sugar
1 tablespoon soy sauce
2 tablespoons cornstarch
4 green onions, sliced diagonally
1 green pepper, sliced thin
2 tomatoes, peeled, seeded, and cut into eighths
2 cans (about 7 ounces each) tuna

Drain syrup from pineapple and combine it with vinegar and sugar. Mix soy sauce with cornstarch, and add. Cook, stirring constantly, until clear and thickened. Add onions, green pepper, pineapple, and tomatoes, and simmer for 4 minutes. Add tuna, broken into large flakes, and cook just long enough to heat. Serve with chow-mein noodles if desired; or ¼ cup split almonds can be added to this dish. Makes 4 to 6 servings.

TUNA AND RICE

¼ cup butter or margarine
1 small onion, minced
1 cup uncooked rice
Pinch of ground saffron
2¾ cups hot fish or chicken bouillon
½ cup grated Parmesan cheese
1 can (about 7 ounces) tuna, drained

Melt butter, add onion, and cook until lightly colored. Add rice and stir for 3 minutes. Put saffron in ½ cup of the bouillon; add remaining bouillon to the rice. Cook over low heat, stirring occasionally. When the liquid is absorbed, add saffron-flavored bouillon and cook until the rice is tender. Remove from heat and stir in cheese and tuna. Mix lightly. Makes 6 servings.

TUNA MARKA

2 cans (about 7 ounces each) tuna, white preferred
½ cup chopped green onions
1 tablespoon butter
½ cup sliced water chestnuts
2 teaspoons slivered fresh or candied gingerroot

2 cups dairy sour cream
Salt and pepper
Hot cooked rice

Drain tuna oil into pan, add onions and butter, and cook until wilted. Add tuna, broken into large flakes, water chestnuts, gingerroot, sour cream, and salt and pepper to taste. Heat gently. Serve with rice. Makes 6 servings.

TUNA AND POTATO TART

1 tablespoon chopped onion
1 tablespoon butter
1 can (about 7 ounces) tuna
2 cups seasoned mashed potatoes
2 tablespoons minced parsley
Salt and pepper if necessary
Pastry for 1-crust 10-inch pie, baked
6 eggs
1 tablespoon melted butter

Cook onion in butter until wilted. Add tuna, potatoes, parsley, and salt and pepper if needed. Spread in the pie shell; make 6 depressions in the potato mixture, drop a raw egg into each, and drizzle a little melted butter over each. Bake in preheated moderate oven (375°F.) until eggs are set. Makes 6 servings.

TUNA AND CHILI FONDUE

1 can (about 7 ounces) tuna
½ cup minced celery
2 tablespoons minced onion
¼ cup minced canned green chilies
¼ cup mayonnaise or salad dressing
1 teaspoon chili powder
¼ teaspoon salt
12 slices of bread
2 cups grated sharp Cheddar cheese
3 eggs, beaten
1 cup milk
¼ cup cream
¼ teaspoon salt
Dash of hot pepper sauce

Combine first 7 ingredients. Spread on half of the bread and make sandwiches. Cut each sandwich into quarters and arrange in a square baking dish, putting cheese between layers and on top. Combine remaining ingredients and pour over all. Bake in preheated slow oven (300° F.) for 50 minutes, or until set and nicely browned. Makes 6 servings.

TUNA PIZZA

1 package hot-roll mix
2 cans (about 7 ounces each) tuna chunks
¼ cup olive oil
1 garlic clove, crushed
Pitted ripe olives
2 cans tomato sauce
1 teaspoon crumbled dried oregano
Salt and pepper
½ pound Mozzarella cheese, sliced

Prepare hot-roll mix according to directions on package. Divide into two parts. Roll each portion into a large round about ¼ inch thick. Put on greased cookie sheet or two 12-inch pizza pans. Drain tuna, reserving liquid. Combine 3 tablespoons olive oil and the garlic, and paint surface of dough liberally. Separate tuna chunks, and divide between the two pizzas, arranging so that the surfaces are fairly well covered. Arrange olives in spaces left. Combine oil drained from tuna, any garlic oil remaining, tomato sauce, oregano, and salt and pepper to taste, and spread over tuna. Divide Mozzarella cheese between the two, paint tops with remaining 1 tablespoon olive oil, and bake in preheated hot oven (425° F.) for 20 minutes, or until nicely browned around the edges. Makes 6 to 12 servings.

TUNA MORNAY IN RICE RING

5 cups hot cooked rice
½ cup slivered almonds
6 tablespoons melted butter
2 cans (about 7 ounces each) tuna, drained and washed
Mornay Sauce

Mix well rice, almonds, and butter. Pack in 8- or 9-inch ring mold and keep warm. Heat tuna in top part of a double boiler. Make Mornay Sauce and add 1 cup to hot tuna. Keep it and remaining sauce hot while you unmold rice. Fill center with tuna; top with remaining sauce. Makes 6 servings.

Mornay Sauce

¼ cup butter
¼ cup all-purpose flour
2 cups milk
2 tablespoons grated Parmesan cheese
¼ cup grated Swiss cheese
½ teaspoon powdered mustard
Salt and pepper

Cook butter and flour together for a minute; add milk and stir until thickened. Add cheeses, mustard, and salt and pepper to taste; then cook, stirring constantly, for 10 minutes. Makes about 2 cups.

BRANDADE DE THON

1 cup dried white beans, washed
4 garlic cloves
2 tablespoons heavy cream or olive oil
1 can (7 ounces) tuna, drained and washed
Salt
¼ cup each of grated Swiss and Parmesan cheese
2 tablespoons butter or margarine
½ cup soft stale-bread crumbs

Cook white beans and garlic in water until tender, usually about 2 hours. Drain and purée, or whirl in a blender until smooth, with cream, tuna, and a little of the bean liquid. When smooth, season to taste with salt, and add grated Swiss and grated Parmesan cheese. Put in a shallow baking dish, dot with butter, and sprinkle with bread crumbs. Bake in preheated moderate oven (375°F.) for about 20 minutes. Makes 6 servings.

TONNO CON PISELLI
(Tuna with Peas)

This is a very easy, very simple dish. Combine 1 can (about 7 ounces) of tuna, 1 tablespoon olive oil, 2 cups cooked peas, and salt and pepper to taste. Heat. Makes 4 servings.

TUNA GREEN-BEAN CASSEROLE

2 tablespoons minced onion
2 tablespoons butter or margarine
2 tablespoons all-purpose flour
1 cup milk
¼ cup chicken bouillon
1 tablespoon or more prepared mustard
½ pound green beans, cooked
2 hard-cooked eggs, chopped
1 can (about 7 ounces) tuna, flaked
1 tablespoon minced parsley
½ teaspoon crumbled dried tarragon (optional)
Salt and pepper
¼ cup fine dry bread crumbs
2 tablespoons melted butter or margarine

Cook onion in butter until wilted. Add flour, milk, and bouillon, and cook, stirring constantly, until thickened. Add mustard, beans, eggs, tuna, parsley, and tarragon. Taste, and add salt and pepper if necessary. Put in a 1-quart casserole and sprinkle with crumbs and melted butter, mixed. Bake in preheated hot oven (400° F.) for about 20 minutes. Makes 4 servings.

TUNA-MACARONI BAKE

8 ounces macaroni
1 can (10½ ounces) cream-of-mushroom or chicken soup
¾ cup milk
1 can (7 ounces) tuna, flaked
Grated rind of ½ lemon
¼ teaspoon pepper
¼ teaspoon seasoned salt
3 cups shredded sharp Cheddar cheese
1½ cups crushed potato chips

Cook macaroni in boiling salted water until tender; drain and add soup, milk, tuna, lemon rind, pepper, seasoned salt, and 2 cups cheese. Mix well. Put in shallow baking dish; cover with potato chips mixed with remaining cheese. Bake in preheated moderate oven (350°F.) for about 40 minutes. Makes 6 to 8 servings. Can be frozen.

TUNA MUSHROOM MACARONI

2 cups (8 ounces) elbow macaroni
1 medium onion, chopped
2 tablespoons butter or margarine
¼ cup all-purpose flour
1 teaspoon seasoned salt
1½ teaspoons paprika
½ teaspoon garlic salt
¼ teaspoon crumbled dried oregano
¼ teaspoon pepper
2½ cups milk
½ cup dairy sour cream
2 cans (6½ to 7 ounces each) tuna, drained
¼ pound mushrooms, sliced
2 tablespoons grated Parmesan cheese

Cook macaroni according to package directions. Drain and reserve. Cook onion in butter until tender. Stir in flour and seasonings. Gradually add milk and cook over low heat, stirring, until thickened. Mix in sour cream, tuna, and mushrooms; heat. Stir in cooked macaroni and turn into 2-quart casserole. Sprinkle with additional paprika and Parmesan cheese. Bake in preheated moderate oven (375° F.) for 30 minutes. Makes 6 servings.

West Coast Salad
Tuna Mornay in Rice Ring
Fresh Tuna Tarragon
Sweet = and = Sour Tuna

INDIVIDUAL TUNA PIES

Pastry

1 cup all-purpose flour
½ teaspoon salt
⅓ cup shortening
Cold water

Sift flour with salt. Cut in shortening until mixture resembles coarse cornmeal. Add cold water and stir until dough cleans the bowl. Knead on lightly floured board until smooth. Roll dough into 12-inch square; cut into four 6-inch squares.

Tuna Filling

1 can (7 ounces) tuna fish, drained
2 tablespoons chopped onion
1½ teaspoons Worcestershire
¼ cup mayonnaise
¼ teaspoon salt
Dash of pepper

Combine tuna fish with remaining ingredients. Spread some of mixture over lower half of each pastry square; fold top half over mixture. Moisten edges with water. Seal with tines of fork. Put on oiled cookie sheet. Makes 4 pies.

TUNA VÉRONIQUE

¼ cup sliced onion
¼ cup butter or margarine
¼ cup all-purpose flour
¼ teaspoon each of salt, crumbled dried marjoram, and monosodium glutamate
Dash of pepper
1 cup vegetable bouillon
2 cups milk
1 egg, slightly beaten
3 cans (6½ to 7 ounces each) tuna, drained and flaked
1½ cups seedless grapes or 2 cans (8¾ ounces each), drained
Toast points

Cook onion in butter until crisp-tender, about 3 minutes. Quickly stir in flour and seasonings. Gradually stir in bouillon and milk. Bring to boil, stirring constantly; boil for 1 minute. Beat some of hot sauce into egg; return to heat; cook and stir for 1 minute. Add tuna and grapes. Reheat until piping hot. Serve on toast points; garnish with paprika and parsley, if desired. Makes 6 servings.

DOUBLE-BOILER TUNA SOUFFLÉ

2 tablespoons butter or margarine
1 small onion, minced
3 tablespoons all-purpose flour
¾ teaspoon salt
½ teaspoon celery salt
⅛ teaspoon pepper
¾ cup milk
2 eggs, separated
1 can (about 7 ounces) tuna, drained and flaked
Juice of ½ small lemon

Melt butter in top part of double boiler. Add onion and cook over direct heat until golden. Blend in flour and seasonings. Put over boiling water and gradually add milk, stirring. Cook until thickened, stirring. Beat egg whites until stiff; set aside. Beat yolks until thick and lemon-colored. Add tuna and lemon juice to yolks. Gradually beat in hot sauce. Return to top part of double boiler. Fold in egg whites. Cover and cook over simmering water for 45 minutes, or until firm. Makes 4 servings.

TUNA FRITTERS

2 cups biscuit mix
¼ cup wheat germ
1 egg, well beaten
1 cup milk
2 cans (7 ounces each) flaked tuna, drained

Mix biscuit mix with wheat germ. Add egg beaten with milk. Fold in tuna. Drop by tablespoonfuls into hot shallow fat (360°F. on frying thermometer) and fry until golden-brown, turning once. Serve with chili sauce if desired. Makes 12.

TUNA PASTRIES

Moisten flaked drained tuna fish with melted butter and dairy sour cream. Season to taste with salt, cayenne, and mustard. Fill bought 1-inch patty shells with mixture. Top with a little piece of pimiento.

TUNA TETRAZZINI

1 can (4 ounces) sliced mushrooms
Water
1 cup evaporated milk, undiluted
¼ cup butter or margarine
2 tablespoons all-purpose flour
½ teaspoon salt
⅛ teaspoon white pepper
1 can (7 ounces) tuna, drained and flaked
1½ cups, about (half of 8-ounce package) fine noodles, cooked
1 cup soft bread cubes

Drain mushrooms; reserve liquid; add water to liquid to make 1 cup. Add to milk. Melt 2 tablespoons butter in a saucepan; blend in flour, salt, and pepper. Gradually stir in milk mixture and cook over low heat, stirring, until thickened. Add tuna, mushrooms, and noodles. Put in 1½-quart casserole. Melt remaining butter, mix in bread cubes, and toss. Arrange around edge of casserole. Bake, uncovered, in preheated moderate oven (375°F.) for about 20 minutes. Makes 4 servings.

TUNA CORNISH PIES

1 package (10 ounces) piecrust mix
2 tablespoons toasted sesame seeds (optional)
½ cup chopped celery
¼ cup chopped green pepper
2 tablespoons chopped onion
1 tablespoon butter or margarine
1 can (10½ ounces) condensed cream-of-mushroom soup, undiluted
2 tablespoons chopped pecans
1 tablespoon fresh lemon juice
1 teaspoon curry powder
2 cans (6½ to 7 ounces each) tuna fish, drained and finely flaked
Mushroom Cream Sauce

Combine dry piecrust mix and sesame seeds. Prepare according to package directions. Roll into six 7-inch pastry circles. Cook celery, green pepper, and onion in butter until crisp-tender, about 3 minutes. Combine cooked vegetables, ½ cup soup (reserve remaining soup for sauce), pecans, lemon juice, and curry powder; blend. Stir in tuna. Place about ⅓ cup tuna mixture on each pastry circle; fold over and seal. Slash tops to allow steam to escape. Bake in preheated hot oven (425°F.) for 20 to 25 minutes, or until lightly browned. Serve with Mushroom Cream Sauce. Garnish with parsley and radish roses, as desired. Makes 6 servings.

Mushroom Cream Sauce

Cook 1 tablespoon chopped onion in 1 teaspoon butter. Stir in reserved undiluted soup, an additional 1 can (10½ ounces) undiluted condensed cream-of-mushroom soup, 1 can (6 ounces) sliced mushrooms, and ⅓ cup of the mushroom liquid. Heat to serving temperature. Makes about 2 cups.

CASHEW TUNA CASSEROLE

2 cans (7 ounces each) tuna, flaked
1½ cups chopped cashew nuts
½ pound fresh mushrooms
⅓ cup diced onion
6 tablespoons butter or margarine
3 tablespoons flour
2½ cups milk
Salt and pepper
½ cup crushed potato chips

Drain tuna and flake. Mix tuna with cashew nuts. Sauté mushrooms and onion in 3 tablespoons butter until onion is golden. Add to tuna mixture. Spoon mixture into shallow 1½-quart casserole. Melt 3 tablespoons butter. Stir in flour. Gradually stir in milk. Cook over low heat, stirring constantly, until smooth and thickened. Season with salt and pepper to taste. Pour sauce over tuna mixture. Sprinkle potato chips over top. Bake in preheated moderate oven (350°F.) for about 25 minutes. Makes 6 servings.

ITALIAN TUNA FRITTATA

2 tablespoons olive oil
1 green pepper, chopped
1 onion, chopped
8 eggs
1 cup (6- or 7-ounce can) tuna, flaked
½ teaspoon salt
⅛ teaspoon white pepper

Heat olive oil. Sauté green pepper and onion for 5 minutes. Beat eggs; add tuna and seasonings. Mix well and pour into skillet with vegetables. Cook, lifting edges with spatula and tilting skillet to allow uncooked egg to run under. Divide into 4 portions and turn each to brown. Serve on toast spread with mayonnaise. Makes 4 servings.

CANNED TUNA: SALADS

TUNA-VEGETABLE MOLD

1 box (3 ounces) lemon-flavored gelatin

1 cup hot water
1 cup cold water
2 tablespoons vinegar
2 tablespoons minced onion
½ teaspoon salt
1 can (about 7 ounces) tuna, drained and flaked
¾ cup diced celery
¾ cup diced raw carrots
¼ cup diced sweet pickles
Salad greens
Mayonnaise

Dissolve gelatin in hot water. Add cold water, vinegar, onion, and salt. Chill until thickened but not firm. Fold in tuna, celery, carrots, and pickles. Pour into 1½-quart mold and chill until firm. Unmold on salad greens and serve with mayonnaise. Makes 4 to 6 servings.

MARINATED TUNA

2 cans (about 7 ounces each) tuna, drained
2 tablespoons fresh lemon juice
2 teaspoons chopped chives
1 teaspoon instant minced onion
¼ teaspoon ground rosemary
¼ teaspoon cracked pepper
Dash of ground cloves
½ teaspoon salt
1 cup dairy sour cream

Separate tuna into bite-size chunks. Mix remaining ingredients, pour over tuna, and toss lightly with fork. Chill for at least 1 hour. Makes 4 servings.

HOT TUNA-POTATO SALAD

6 slices of bacon
¼ cup sugar
6 tablespoons vinegar
2 tablespoons water
1 teaspoon celery seeds
1 egg, beaten
4 medium potatoes, cooked and cut into chunks
¾ cup diced celery
1 medium onion, chopped
1 can (about 7 ounces) tuna, drained
Seasoned salt
Salt and pepper

Cook bacon until crisp. Remove bacon and reserve ¼ cup fat. Add sugar, vinegar, water, and celery seeds to fat in skillet; bring to boil and simmer for 5 minutes. Stir small amount of mixture into egg. Put back in skillet, mix well, and remove from heat. Pour mixture over potatoes, celery, onion, and tuna and mix well; season to taste. Put in 1½-quart casserole and crumble bacon on top. Bake in preheated moderate oven (350° F.) for about 30 minutes. Makes 4 to 6 servings.

WEST COAST SALAD

1 large or 2 medium heads romaine
2 hard-cooked eggs, chopped
3 green onions, finely minced
1 can (about 7 ounces) tuna
6 slices of bacon
2 tablespoons or more wine vinegar
Pepper and salt

Wash romaine, dry, and chill; break into pieces and put in a large bowl. Add eggs, onions, and tuna broken into pieces. Cook bacon until crisp; drain and crumble into bowl, reserving fat. Add vinegar to bacon fat in same pan, also a few grindings of pepper. Heat and pour over salad, mixing gently. Add salt if necessary. Makes 6 servings.

TUNA, POTATO, AND BEAN SALAD, GENOA STYLE

1 can (about 7 ounces) tuna
1 cup cooked sliced potatoes
1 cup cooked cut green beans
1 tablespoon minced onion
½ cup minced celery
2 tablespoons each of olive oil and vinegar
½ teaspoon salt
Pepper
½ cup mayonnaise

Drain tuna, reserving oil and liquid. Combine tuna, broken into large pieces, potatoes, beans, onion, and celery. Add tuna oil to olive oil, vinegar, salt, and a little pepper. Combine with mayonnaise, and mix carefully with salad. Chill. Makes 6 servings.

TUNA COLESLAW WITH GRAPES

2 cups finely sliced cabbage
1 cup seedless grapes or Tokays, Black Ribiers, or Muscats, cut into halves and seeded
2 tablespoons minced onion
¼ cup mayonnaise
⅓ cup dairy sour cream
1 teaspoon fresh lemon juice
Salt and pepper to taste
1 can (about 7 ounces) tuna

Combine all ingredients except tuna and mix thoroughly. Separate tuna chunks and fold in lightly but well. Makes 6 servings.

TUNA RADICCIO

1 quart curly endive, escarole, or dandelion leaves
1 can (about 7 ounces) tuna
8 fillets of anchovies, chopped
¼ cup each of minced green olives, parsley, and green onions
1 hard-cooked egg, chopped
½ cup sliced radishes
¼ cup each of sliced green pepper and shredded salami
½ cup olive oil
1 garlic clove, pressed
2 to 3 tablespoons vinegar
Salt and pepper to taste

Wash greens very well, and shred. Combine with other ingredients; mix well. Makes 6 servings.

SALUBRIOUS TUNA SALAD

1 can (about 7 ounces) tuna, drained and flaked
1 cup cottage cheese
2 tablespoons each of chopped celery, green pepper, onion, and ripe olives
Salt and pepper
Dillweed, chili powder, or curry powder
Lettuce leaves

Combine tuna with cottage cheese, celery, green pepper, onion, and ripe olives. Add salt and pepper to taste, and a little dillweed. Serve on lettuce leaves and accompany with crisp crackers. Makes 4 to 6 servings.

Note: If dietetic tuna is used, this is a good low-calorie, high-protein dish.

APPLE-TUNA SALAD

1 large red apple, cored and cut into wedges
2 tablespoons fresh lemon juice
1 orange, peeled and sliced
½ cup red grapes, split and seeded
1 can (7 ounces) tuna, drained and flaked
Salad greens
¼ cup mayonnaise
2 tablespoons orange juice

Mix apple wedges and lemon juice. Arrange fruits and tuna on greens. Mix mayonnaise and orange juice and pour over top. Makes 2 servings.

CANNED TUNA: SANDWICHES

TUNA-CAPER OPEN-FACE SANDWICHES

Mash 1 can (about 7 ounces) tuna with 2 tablespoons butter and 2 teaspoons capers. Spread on rounds of bread and decorate each with a thin slice of hard-cooked egg and a whole caper. Makes about ¾ cup.

WALNUT TUNA SPREAD

Flake 1 can (about 7 ounces) tuna well. Combine with 1 cup finely chopped or ground walnuts, 1 teaspoon fresh lemon juice, and enough mayonnaise to moisten (about ¼ cup if the tuna is drained, less if it isn't). Makes about 2 cups.

SAVORY TUNA SANDWICH SPREAD

1 can (about 7 ounces) tuna, drained
3 tablespoons mayonnaise
2 tablespoons minced celery
Dash of Worcestershire
1 tablespoon chili sauce or ketchup
1 or 2 tablespoons fresh lemon juice
1 cucumber
White toast or bread

Mix all ingredients except last 2. Peel and thinly slice cucumber. Cover half of toast slices with cucumber and spread with mixture; top with remaining toast to make sandwiches. Makes about 1¼ cups.

Note: Above mixture can be used for hot canapés if desired. Put each cucumber slice on a toast round of the same size, spread with mixture, and broil until hot.

TURBOT—A large European salt-water flatfish that belongs to the flounder family. The turbot, which is brown and speckled in color and weighs an average of ten pounds, is a highly prized food fish, since its flesh is most delicate and delicious. Its closest American relative is the halibut.

TURKEY—A native American game bird which is related to the pheasant. There are a number of varieties. Wild turkeys were once unbelievably numerous throughout the United States and Central America, living in the forests in small flocks and coming out to the clearings only to feed. They are fast on their feet and when pursued they run rather than fly, although when they must fly, they fly high and fast, at speeds estimated at fifty miles per hour or more.

The Indians domesticated turkeys long before the arrival of the early settlers. The Spanish *conquistadores* took birds domesticated by the Aztec Indians of southern Mexico back with them to Spain as early as 1519. Interestingly, some of these European turkeys were brought back to the New World later and crossed with the native wild varieties.

The turkey is a bird not only native to America, but, because of its associations with Thanksgiving, it is the most American of all food birds. So much so that Benjamin Franklin, in a letter to his daughter Sara Bache, wrote: "I wish the Bald Eagle had not been chosen as the Representation of our Country; he is a Bird of bad moral Character, like those among men who live by sharpening and robbing . . . The turkey is a much more respectable bird, and withal a true original Native of America."

Availability and Purchasing Guide—Turkeys are sold in two styles: oven-ready (sometimes called "ready-to-cook" or "eviscerated") and dressed. Oven-ready turkeys are drawn and cleaned, ready for roasting. This style comes fresh or frozen-fresh and is often individually packaged. The neck and cleaned giblets are wrapped and put into the cavity of the bird. If you buy this style, you'll need about 1 pound per person.

Dressed turkeys have the head and feet on; the feathers are removed, but the birds are not drawn. The butcher will draw the bird for you. Have him pull the leg tendons and cut the neck off close to the body. Buy about 1¼ pounds per person, as you lose about ⅕ of the weight in drawing. To be sure of the final weight in order to time the roasting, ask the butcher to weigh the drawn bird. If bird is frozen, allow ample thawing time, 24 hours for each 6 pounds of turkey in the refrigerator. At room temperature, allow 1 hour per pound.

Frozen stuffed turkeys are available. Contrary to most unstuffed frozen turkeys, these are roasted without thawing. A roast-meat thermometer is necessary in cooking these birds.

Fresh or frozen turkey parts such as whole breasts and drumsticks are available, packaged separately. Frozen turkey dinners and frozen turkey slices in giblet gravy are available, as is turkey pie and frozen, boned rolled turkey roasts.

Smoked turkey, some of which is ready to eat, some requiring further cooking, is available.

Canned boned turkey, turkey à la king, turkey and noodles, and turkey soups, are available. Turkey dinners prepared as baby and junior foods are also available.

Storage

- ☐ Fresh, refrigerator shelf, raw: 6 to 8 days
- ☐ Fresh, refrigerator shelf, cooked, 4 to 5 days
- ☐ Fresh, prepared for freezing; or frozen, refrigerator frozen-food compartment, raw: 2 to 3 weeks
- ☐ Fresh, prepared for freezing; or frozen, freezer, raw: 6 months
- ☐ Fresh, refrigerator frozen-food compartment, prepared for freezing, cooked: 2 to 3 weeks
- ☐ Fresh, freezer, prepared for freezing, cooked: 3 months

To store leftover turkey, remove stuffing from bird and put stuffing in a separate container. When cold, cover, and store in refrigerator. If there is a lot of meat left, cool the entire carcass, wrap in foil or wax paper, and store in the refrigerator. Otherwise, remove the meat from the bones and refrigerate meat. Or wrap and freeze it. If you plan to make soup, crack the bones, wrap, and refrigerate. If you have time, make, cool, and refrigerate the broth, so the bones can be discarded.

Nutritive Food Values—A good source of protein.

- ☐ 3½ ounces, raw = 218 calories
- ☐ 3½ ounces, roasted = 263 calories

Basic Preparation—If turkey is frozen, thaw in refrigerator in original wrapping. Put in shallow pan and allow 1 to 3 days for thawing. A thawed, fresh ready-to-cook turkey can be kept on the refrigerator shelf at 38°F. for 1 to 2 days. After thawing, it is important to remove the original wrapping and to rewrap very loosely. Do not refreeze.

☐ **To Roast**—When ready to prepare turkey, rinse bird inside and out with cold water, drain and pat dry. Rub skin and cavity lightly with salt. Insert stuffing and stuff neck cavity; fasten skin to back with a skewer. Stuff body cavity loosely and close with skewers or stitching. Fold wings and bring wing tips onto the back. (If bird is too big for this, let wings stay close to body of bird.) Push drumsticks under band of skin at tail or tie them to tail with string. Line a shallow roasting pan with foil to avoid messy clean-up. Place bird on a rack in the foil-lined pan. Brush all over with vegetable oil. Roast according to directions on foil package or in preheated slow oven (325°F.), according to the Timetable at left, basting several times with drippings in pan. When turkey breast is brown, cover with a loose tent of foil. To make tent, tear off a sheet of heavy foil 5 to 10 inches longer than turkey. Crease lengthwise through center. Place over the bird and press the foil gently at drumsticks and breast to anchor it. Differences in the shape and tenderness of individual birds may necessitate increasing or decreasing the cooking time slightly. Cut band of skin or string at drumstick 1 hour before bird is done. Remove from oven 30 minutes before serving.

A roast meat thermometer placed in the center of the inside thigh muscle or in the thickest part of the breast muscle should register approximately 185°F. when turkey is done. Turkey is done when thickest part of drumstick feels very soft when pressed between fingers.

When dinner is set for a definite hour, start the bird 20 to 30 minutes ahead of

TIMETABLE FOR ROASTING TURKEY

PURCHASED READY-TO-COOK WEIGHT	OVEN TEMPERATURE	INTERIOR TEMPERATURE	GUIDE TO TOTAL ROASTING TIME
6 to 8 lbs.	325°F.	185°F.	2 to 2½ hours
8 to 12 lbs.	325°F.	185°F.	2½ to 3 hours
12 to 16 lbs.	325°F.	185°F.	3 to 3¾ hours
16 to 20 lbs.	325°F.	185°F.	3¾ to 4½ hours
20 to 24 lbs.	325°F.	185°F.	4½ to 5½ hours

schedule to avoid delay should the turkey take longer to cook than was estimated.

☐ **To Stuff**—Stuff the bird just before you're ready to roast it. If desired, stuffing can be prepared ahead and refrigerated. Do not add liquid or eggs until ready to use. For Basic Bread Stuffing recipe plus variations see chart below. Extra stuffing can be put in a baking pan and baked in preheated hot oven (425°F.) until well browned after the turkey is removed from the oven. Spoon some of the drippings over the top before baking. If you have your own favorite recipe, allow about 1 cup of stuffing per pound of drawn bird.

☐ **To Prepare Giblets**—Wash giblets; cook neck, heart, and gizzard for about 2 hours in boiling salted water with a bay leaf, an onion, and a few celery leaves. Add liver during last 20 minutes. Drain, reserving broth for gravy. Remove meat from neck; grind or chop with the heart, gizzard, and liver. Giblets can be prepared a day ahead and refrigerated. Add to stuffing or gravy.

☐ **To Make Gravy**—For 6 cups gravy: pour drippings from roasting pan into bowl, skim off fat, and put ½ cup fat into saucepan. Blend in ½ cup flour. Measure skimmed drippings, and add water to make 6 cups. Cook fat and flour until bubbly. Add liquid all at once and cook until thickened, stirring constantly. Season to taste. Ground or chopped cooked giblets can be added.

☐ **To Bone Turkey**—Wash poultry and pat dry. Remove wings. With a sharp knife with a sharp point cut the bird down the center back downward to the tail. Remove the tail section. Using the point of the knife against the bones of the bird cut away the skin and flesh from the back and ribs. When the legs are reached cut the joint at the hip to remove the leg, bone and all. The bones will be removed from the legs later. Do the same with the wings, leaving the wing bone for later removal. Continue cutting the meat away from the bones until the breastbone is reached. Carefully cut the skin away from the top of the breastbone so that the skin remains in one piece. Now with the sharp knife cut and scrape away the meat from the leg and wing bones. In doing this the wing and leg will be turned inside out when the bone is removed. Turn legs and wings right side out. Now the bird is ready for stuffing or rolling. When preparing a turkey, if it is not to be stuffed and will only be rolled into a boneless roast, it may be cut into halves through the breastbone skin and then rolled and tied. This is done when a turkey is quite large.

☐ **To Freeze**—Clean and eviscerate turkey. Wash well and drain. Wrap giblets separately in moisture- vapor-proof material. Seal, and freeze. Tie turkey so that wings and legs lie close to body. Wrap in moisture- vapor-proof material, excluding as much air as possible. Seal, and freeze.

To freeze cooked turkey, remove meat from bones. If desired, use bones for making broth or soup which can be frozen in freezer jars or containers. Leftover gravy can also be frozen. Separate large slices from scraps, and package types and amounts of meat for the particular recipes in which you plan to use it. Tear off generous strips of heavy-duty foil, put meat in the center, and fold ends over tightly, making several double folds. Fold sides in the same way. Secure with string or freezer tape, and mark the contents with a freezer pencil (white-meat slices for pie; chopped light and dark for salads, mixed light and dark strips for turkey ragout). It's also a good idea to date packages. Frozen cooked turkey will retain its good quality for up to 3 months.

BASIC BREAD STUFFING, WITH SOME VARIATIONS

	(DRAWN WEIGHT)				
	8 to 11 lbs.	11 to 15 lbs.	15 to 19 lbs.	19 to 25 lbs.	Directions
Basic Bread Stuffing					
Butter or margarine, cups	½	⅔	1	1⅓	Cook all ingredients except crumbs in skillet for 5 minutes. Toss with crumbs.
Medium onions, minced	2	3	4	5	
*Poultry seasoning, tablespoons	1	1½	2	2½	
Salt, teaspoons	1½	2	3	4	
Pepper, teaspoons	¾	1	1½	2	
Chopped parsley, cups	⅓	½	¾	1	
Chopped celery leaves, cups	¾	1	1½	2	
Soft stale-bread crumbs, quarts	2½	3½	4½	6	
Egg Stuffing					
Same as Basic Stuffing **plus** eggs	2	3	4	5	Beat slightly, and add with crumbs.
Oyster Stuffing					
Same as Basic Stuffing **plus** oysters, pints	1	1½	2	2½	Drain oysters, and chop. Cook with onion mixture.
Chestnut Stuffing					
Same as Basic Stuffing bread crumbs, quarts	½	¾	1	1½	Cook chestnuts in boiling water for 15 minutes. Remove shells and brown skins, and chop. Add with crumbs.
plus chestnuts, pounds	1	1½	2¼	3	
Nut Stuffing					
Same as Basic Stuffing **plus** chopped nuts, cups	1	1½	2	2½	Add with crumbs.
Corn-Bread Stuffing	Same as Basic Stuffing; but substitute crumbled unsweetened cornbread, made with eggs, for half of bread crumbs				
Rice Stuffing					
Same as Basic Stuffing, but **omit** crumbs; **add** raw rice, cups	2¼	3¼	4½	5½	Cook rice in boiling salted water until nearly tender. Drain.

**Or use thyme and sage, or other herbs, to taste.*

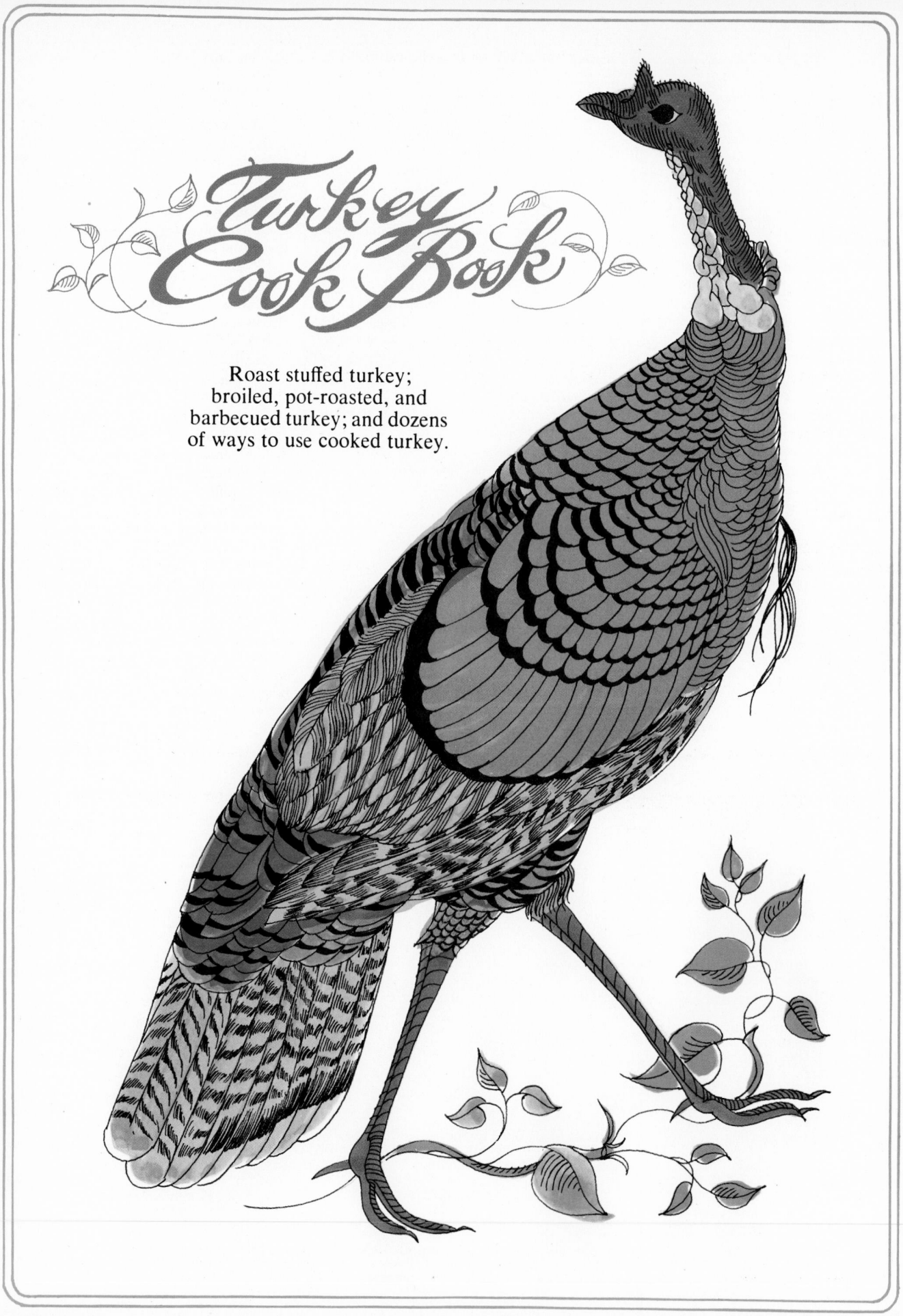
Turkey Cook Book
Roast stuffed turkey;
broiled, pot-roasted, and
barbecued turkey; and dozens
of ways to use cooked turkey.

BROILED TURKEY

Have a 4- to 6-pound turkey split into halves lengthwise. Fold wing tips into back. Put, skin side down, in broiler pan without rack. Brush with cooking oil and season to taste with salt and pepper and a little sugar. Put pan about 9 inches from heat. Turkey should just begin to brown after 20 minutes of cooking. Broil slowly until well browned, about 40 minutes. Turn and baste with pan drippings. Broil until brown and done, for 40 to 50 minutes. Baste with pan drippings several times during broiling.

PANFRIED TURKEY

Dredge pieces of cut-up turkey with seasoned flour. Put turkey, meatiest pieces first, in about ½ inch of hot fat or cooking oil in a heavy skillet and fry until golden-brown. Reduce heat, add 2 tablespoons water; cover, and cook slowly for 45 to 60 minutes, or until tender. Turn pieces several times to assure even cooking. Uncover pan for the last 10 minutes to recrisp skin.

POT-ROASTED TURKEY, JAMAICA STYLE

1 ready-to-cook turkey, about 6 pounds
¼ cup butter or margarine
1½ cups chicken broth
¾ cup sliced celery
1 medium onion, chopped
½ teaspoon garlic salt
2 dried red peppers, crushed
1 tablespoon vinegar
¼ teaspoon ground allspice
½ cup sliced green olives
1 medium green pepper, sliced
2 tablespoons cornstarch
Salt and pepper

Brown turkey on all sides in the butter in Dutch oven. This should take 20 to 30 minutes. Put turkey on rack. Add next 7 ingredients. Cover and simmer for 2 to 2½ hours, or until tender. Add olives and green pepper and cook for 10 minutes longer. Remove turkey to a hot platter and thicken liquid in Dutch oven with cornstarch blended with a little cold water. Season to taste with salt and pepper and pour over turkey. Makes 8 servings.

ROAST BONELESS TURKEY ROLL

Thaw frozen roll in the refrigerator, allowing 1 to 2 days. When thawed, remove wrapper, leaving string on. Rinse roll in cold water. Drain and pat dry. If not preseasoned, sprinkle with salt and pepper. Put on rack in shallow roasting pan. Brush with melted butter or margarine. Insert roast-meat thermometer in center of roll. Roast as directed on package label. Or roast in preheated moderate oven (350°F.) for 2 to 2½ hours for a 3- to 5-pound roll. Meat thermometer should register 170°F. to 175°F. when roll is done. Brush occasionally with pan drippings or melted butter during the roasting. If roll is becoming too brown, cover loosely with a tent of foil.

BARBECUED TURKEY ROLL

One 5- to 7-pound turkey roll, thawed
1 cup bottled barbecue sauce

Place turkey roll in roasting pan. Add about ¼ inch water to pan and cover. Roast, covered, in preheated moderate oven (350°F.) to an internal temperature of 170°F. to 175°F. on meat thermometer. This will take 2½ to 3¼ hours. Half an hour before the roast is done, pour barbecue sauce over turkey. Baste several times with liquid in pan. Makes 10 to 12 servings.

BARBECUED TURKEY STEAKS

Have butcher cut 1-inch-thick steaks from a large frozen tom turkey. Some steaks will be all white meat, some part dark meat, and some all dark meat. Marinate for several hours in 1 part oil and 1 part white wine, herbed if desired. Broil for 10 minutes, basting with marinade.

BOILED TURKEY, VEGETABLE, AND DUMPLING DINNER

1 ready-to-cook turkey, about 6 pounds
5 cups water
1 onion, cut up
2 celery stalks, cut up
1 tablespoon salt
½ teaspoon pepper
¼ cup all-purpose flour
2 packages (10 ounces each) frozen mixed vegetables
Savory Dumpling Batter

Wash turkey. Simmer with water and next 4 ingredients for 2½ hours, or until very tender. Lift out turkey, and remove meat from bones; keep hot. Strain broth; thicken with flour mixed with a little cold water. Add mixed vegetables, and bring to boil. Drop in Savory Dumpling Batter by tablespoonfuls. Simmer, covered, for 15 minutes. Put turkey on platter; lift out dumplings and vegetables and arrange around turkey. Pour some of gravy over turkey, and serve remainder in bowl. Lefover small pieces of turkey can be used for salad. Makes 4 to 6 servings.

Savory Dumpling Batter

2 cups sifted all-purpose flour
2 teaspoons baking powder
1½ teaspoons salt
4 egg yolks
⅔ cup milk
½ cup chopped parsley
2 tablespoons chopped green-onion tops

Sift dry ingredients. Beat egg yolks with milk; add to dry ingredients together with the parsley and onion tops. Mix lightly until blended.

PUERTO RICAN TURKEY SAUSAGE

1 turkey (about 10 pounds)
½ pound boiled ham
9 eggs
1 can (2 ounces) truffles, sliced (optional)
1 can (4 ounces) sliced mushrooms, drained
2 teaspoons salt
1 teaspoon ground nutmeg
1½ teaspoons pepper
Cracker crumbs, about ½ cup
Chicken broth

Remove skin and meat from turkey bones. Grind turkey skin, meat, and ham twice through the finest blade of a meat grinder. Beat in 7 eggs, one at a time. Stir in truffles, mushrooms, salt, nutmeg, and pepper. Blend well. It may be necessary to add some cracker crumbs. Shape mixture into 5 rolls 2 to 3 inches in diameter and 6 to 8 inches long. Roll in 2 beaten eggs. Roll in cracker crumbs. Wrap roll in cheesecloth and tie ends to seal tightly. Put roll into a deep kettle. Add enough hot chicken broth just to cover. Cover kettle and simmer for 1 hour. Remove roll from broth and chill. Remove cheesecloth; cut roll into thin slices. Makes 15 to 20 servings.

Note: This is a large recipe; after cooking it can be cooled and refrigerated until needed.

SPIT-ROASTED TURKEY

Select a turkey weighing 10 to 12 pounds. Wash turkey and dry. Sprinkle cavity with salt and a little thyme or marjoram. Add a stalk of celery and a few slices of onion. Truss turkey securely, having both wings and legs close to body and neck skin skewered on at back. Drive spit from a point just in front of the tail, having it go through back and come out at about the top of the wishbone. Rub skin with cooking oil. Insert a meat thermometer in the thickest part of the thigh. Connect spit to the motor and roast over medium fire until meat thermometer registers 175°F., or until leg moves easily in joint. Allow about 15 minutes cooking time for each pound of bird. Baste frequently as it turns with melted margarine. Makes 6 to 8 servings.

COOKED TURKEY

TURKEY SOUP

1 roast-turkey carcass
2 quarts water
2 teaspoons salt
¼ teaspoon pepper
2 celery stalks, including leaves, diced
1 medium onion, peeled and sliced
Few parsley sprigs
1 bay leaf

Scrape any stuffing from turkey bones. Put carcass in kettle and add remaining ingredients. Bring to boil, cover, and simmer for 2 hours. Strain. Pick off any meat from bones and add to soup. Makes about 1½ quarts.

Note: If desired, add ¼ cup rice or ⅓ cup elbow macaroni or noodles to strained soup. Simmer, covered, for about 15 minutes.

TURKEY AND COCKTAIL SAUCE

Mix 1 cup chili sauce, 2 tablespoons each of prepared horseradish and fresh lemon juice, 1 teaspoon salt, and ¼ teaspoon pepper. Chill. Put in bowl in center of platter, and arrange diced cooked turkey around bowl. Serve with toothpicks for dipping turkey pieces into sauce. Good for buffet with deviled eggs, cheese, celery, green and ripe olives, hot garlic bread, marble cake, and grapes. Makes 1¼ cups sauce.

TURKEY PÂTÉ

2 cups lightly packed ground turkey meat and skin
1 onion, minced
2 hard-cooked eggs, minced
½ cup ground almonds
Salt and pepper to taste
A generous dash of hot pepper sauce
2 tablespoons brandy
Enough mayonnaise to bind

Combine all ingredients except mayonnaise. Then bind with mayonnaise until a just-stiff paste is formed. Place in a bowl or container. Decorate with aspic, truffles, or sliced olives, if desired. Chill. Serve as an hors-d'oeuvre or as a snack. Makes about 3 cups.

TURKEY PIE, BREADSTICK TOPPING

½ cup all-purpose flour
1 cup cold turkey or chicken broth
3 cups hot broth
1 package (10 ounces) frozen peas
2 cups (one 1-pound can) onions, drained
2 cups carrot chunks, cooked
2 cups diced cooked turkey
Salt and pepper
1 can ready-to-bake breadsticks
1 egg yolk
1 tablespoon water

Blend flour and cold broth; stir into hot broth and cook, stirring constantly, until thickened. Add peas and simmer for a few minutes. Add onions, carrots, and turkey; season to taste with salt and pepper and pour into 2-quart baking dish. Put in preheated very hot oven (450°F.). Separate breadsticks, and weave on a greased cookie sheet to fit top of baking dish, stretching slightly if necessary. Trim ends to fit. Brush with egg yolk mixed with water. Bake with casserole for about 10 minutes. Press topping down slightly on pie. Good with parsley potatoes, mixed green salad, and honeydew with berries. Makes 6 servings.

TURKEY HAWAIIAN

2 eggs, beaten
½ cup all-purpose flour
½ teaspoon salt
Water
2 cups cubed cooked turkey
Fat for frying
1 can (13½ ounces) pineapple chunks
2 tablespoons cornstarch
1 tablespoon butter
1 tablespoon chicken-stock base
1 each of green and red peppers, cut into eighths
1 tablespoon soy sauce
1 can (8 ounces) onions, drained

Combine first 3 ingredients and 3 tablespoons water; beat until smooth. Add turkey, and stir until all pieces are coated. Drop into hot shallow fat, and brown on all sides; keep warm. Drain pineapple juice into saucepan. Blend in cornstarch. Add butter, pineapple, and remaining ingredients. Simmer for 5 minutes, stirring frequently. Add turkey, and serve at once. Makes 4 servings.

TURKEY PAPRIKA

2 large onions, sliced
1 garlic clove, minced
¼ cup butter or margarine
1 can (10½ ounces) tomato purée
¼ cup paprika
Salt and pepper to taste
2 cups turkey broth or 2 chicken bouillon cubes dissolved in 2 cups water
3 cups cut-up leftover turkey
1 cup dairy sour cream

Brown onions and garlic slightly in butter. Add remaining ingredients except sour cream. Simmer for about 20 minutes. Just before serving, top with sour cream. Serve with noodles or rice. Makes 6 servings.

PRESSED TURKEY

Mix 1 cup turkey broth and 3 cups minced cooked turkey in saucepan. Simmer until broth is nearly evaporated. Season to taste with salt and pepper. Let stand until cold. Pour into a 3-cup bowl; weight with a plate. Chill overnight. Then unmold, and cut into slices. Garnish with parsley and serve with mayonnaise. Makes 4 to 6 servings.

Note: Prepare this a day ahead.

TURKEY AND BROCCOLI AMANDINE

4 ounces (about 2 cups) medium noodles
1 package (10 ounces) frozen broccoli, cooked
2 tablespoons butter or margarine
2 tablespoons all-purpose flour
1 cup each of undiluted evaporated milk and turkey or chicken broth
1 cup diced Cheddar cheese
½ teaspoon monosodium glutamate
1 teaspoon Worcestershire
¼ teaspoon pepper
2 cups diced cooked turkey
Salt
¼ cup toasted slivered blanched almonds

Cook and drain noodles; put in shallow baking dish. Cut broccoli into 1-inch pieces, and reserve blossoms. Arrange stems on noodles. Make a sauce with butter, flour, and liquids. Add cheese, monosodium glutamate, Worcestershire, and pepper; stir until cheese is melted. Add turkey and salt to taste; pour over ingredients in dish. Arrange broccoli blossoms on top, and sprinkle with almonds. Bake in preheated moderate oven (350°F.) for about 30 minutes. Good with tomato juice, peas, and fudge cake. Makes 4 servings.

TURKEY RAGOUT

To 2 cups leftover turkey gravy add ¼ cup sherry, 1 teaspoon Worcestershire, ½ teaspoon monosodium glutamate, 1 tablespoon currant jelly, and salt and pepper to taste. Heat, stirring to blend jelly. Add 2 cups cooked turkey cut into strips. Heat. Good with mashed potatoes, snap beans and mushrooms, radishes, green onions, and cheesecake. Makes 4 servings.

TURKEY CURRY

1 onion, minced
1 tart apple, peeled and chopped
¼ cup butter or margarine
⅓ cup all-purpose flour
1 to 2 tablespoons curry powder
1½ teaspoons salt
⅛ teaspoon pepper
¼ teaspoon ground ginger
1 cup turkey broth
1 cup milk
½ cup heavy cream
Juice of ½ lemon
3 cups diced cooked turkey

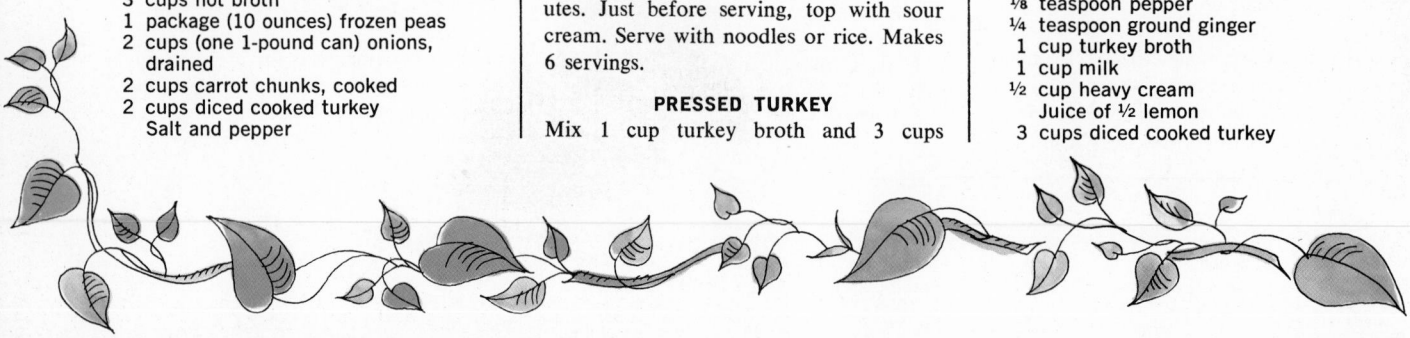

Spit-Roasted Turkey

Cook onion and apple in butter in top part of a double boiler over direct heat until onion is golden. Blend in flour and seasonings. Add broth, milk, and cream; cook over boiling water, stirring constantly, until thickened. Cook, covered, for 10 minutes longer. Add lemon juice and turkey. Heat thoroughly. Good with fluffy rice, sautéed bananas, cashews, chutney, raisins, and lemon bread pudding. Makes 4 servings.

TURKEY CHOW MEIN

1 large onion, sliced
2 cups sliced celery
2 tablespoons cooking oil
2⅓ cups (one 1-pound, 3-ounce can) bean sprouts, drained
1½ cups chopped cooked turkey
2 chicken bouillon cubes
1½ cups hot water
2 tablespoons soy sauce
2 tablespoons cornstarch
¼ cup cold water
Salt and pepper
Chow-mein noodles

Cook onion and celery in oil for 10 minutes. Add bean sprouts, turkey, and bouillon cubes dissolved in hot water. Bring to boil and simmer for 5 minutes. Add soy sauce. Stir in cornstarch blended with cold water. Cook, stirring constantly, until thickened. Season to taste with salt and pepper. Serve over noodles, with additional soy sauce if desired. Makes 4 servings. Good with broccoli, jellied tomato salad, and apple cobbler.

Turkey Chop Suey

Use recipe above. Omit noodles; serve on hot cooked rice.

BAKED TURKEY AND RICE

1 cup uncooked rice
¼ cup butter or margarine
¼ cup all-purpose flour
1¼ cups turkey or chicken broth
½ cup sauterne or other dry white wine
1 can (3 ounces) sliced mushrooms, undrained
Few parsley sprigs, chopped
1 teaspoon instant minced onion
⅛ teaspoon ground sage
1 cup grated sharp Cheddar cheese
2 cups diced cooked turkey
Salt and pepper
Paprika to taste

Cook and drain rice. Make a sauce with next 4 ingredients. Add mushrooms, parsley, onion, sage, and half of cheese. Stir until cheese is melted. Stir in rice and turkey; season to taste with salt and pepper. Put in shallow baking dish, and sprinkle with remaining cheese and the paprika. Bake in preheated moderate oven (375°F.) for about 30 minutes. Good with zucchini, sliced tomatoes, and apple crunch (made from mix). Makes 6 servings.

TURKEY CREOLE IN RICE RING

1 onion, chopped
½ medium green pepper, chopped
1 can (3 ounces) sliced mushrooms, undrained
2 celery stalks, diced
2 tablespoons butter or margarine
2⅓ cups (one 1-pound, 3-ounce can) tomatoes
1 bay leaf
1 teaspoon seasoned salt
¼ teaspoon pepper
½ teaspoon monosodium glutamate
1 teaspoon Worcestershire
1 teaspoon sugar
1½ cups diced cooked turkey
1 tablespoon cornstarch
1 tablespoon water
2 cups uncooked long-grain rice
½ cup chopped parsley

Cook first 4 ingredients in butter for 5 minutes. Add tomatoes, seasonings, and sugar. Simmer, uncovered, for 10 minutes. Remove bay leaf; add turkey, and heat. Blend cornstarch and water. Stir into hot mixture and cook, stirring constantly, until slightly thickened. Cook and drain rice. Add parsley, and mix lightly. Pack into oiled 2-quart ring mold. Unmold on hot platter; fill with Turkey Creole. Good with frozen asparagus, cottage-cheese salad, and pineapple upside-down cake. Makes 6 servings.

SHERRIED TURKEY WITH POTATOES

¼ cup butter or margarine
¼ cup all-purpose flour
2 tablespoons chicken-stock base
1¼ cups water
½ cup heavy cream
¼ cup sherry
Salt and pepper to taste
1 can (3 ounces) mushrooms, undrained
2 envelopes instant mashed potatoes
6 large slices of cooked turkey or 2 cup pieces of turkey
3 tablespoons grated Parmesan cheese
Paprika

Make a sauce with first 6 ingredients. Add seasonings and mushrooms. Prepare potatoes as directed on label, and put in shallow baking dish. Arrange turkey on potatoes. Cover with the sauce. Sprinkle with cheese and paprika. Bake in preheated hot oven (425°F.) for about 20 minutes; or put under broiler until golden-brown and bubbly. Good with Brussels sprouts with almonds, fresh-pear and orange salad, and poundcake. Makes 6 servings.

TURKEY WITH WELSH-RABBIT SAUCE

3 tablespoons butter or margarine
3 tablespoons all-purpose flour
1 teaspoon salt
Dash of cayenne
⅛ teaspoon pepper
1 teaspoon prepared mustard
1 teaspoon Worcestershire
2 cups milk
2 cups (½ pound) sharp Cheddar cheese, shredded
4 to 6 large slices cooked turkey
Hot toast

Melt butter; blend in flour and seasonings. Add milk and cook, stirring constantly, until thickened. Add cheese and cook until cheese is melted. Arrange turkey on broilerproof platter or baking dish; cover with the sauce. Put under broiler until bubbly. Serve on toast. Good with frozen mixed vegetables, sliced cucumbers with French dressing, and fresh plums. Makes 4 to 6 servings.

SAVORY TURKEY SQUARES WITH MUSHROOM SAUCE

3 cups coarsely chopped or ground cooked turkey
2 cups soft bread crumbs
1 cup turkey broth or 1 chicken bouillon cube and 1 cup water
⅔ cup minced celery
2 tablespoons minced parsley
1 teaspoon monosodium glutamate
3 eggs, slightly beaten
1 tablespoon fresh lemon juice
2 tablespoons instant minced onion
1 pimiento, chopped
⅔ cup light cream
Salt and pepper
Mushroom Sauce

Mix all ingredients except last three. Season to taste with salt and pepper. Pour into baking dish (12 x 7 x 2 inches) and put in pan of hot water. Bake in preheated moderate oven (350°F.) for 50 to 60 minutes. Cut into squares and serve with Mushroom Sauce. Makes 6 to 8 servings.

Mushroom Sauce

In saucepan blend ¼ cup soft turkey fat or butter and ¼ cup flour; heat until bubbly, stirring. Gradually stir in 2 cups turkey broth and cook, stirring, until thickened. Drain 1 can (3 ounces) chopped mushrooms and add to sauce. Season to taste with salt, pepper, and poultry seasoning.

CUCKOO'S EGGS

1 cup each of minced turkey and smoked ham
¾ cup Béchamel sauce
Salt and pepper to taste
Dash of ground nutmeg
Fine dry bread crumbs
6 tablespoons cooking oil
Chopped spinach, mashed turnip, or mashed potato

Mix turkey, ham, Béchamel sauce (medium white sauce made with half milk, half chicken broth), salt, pepper, nutmeg, and ½ cup fine dry bread crumbs. Shape into 8 balls; roll in bread crumbs and fry in very hot oil. Serve each egg in a nest of spinach. Makes 4 servings.

TURKEY PUDDING

¼ pound bacon, diced
1 cup minced cooked turkey
1½ cups cooked spaghetti or noodles
3 tablespoons grated cheese
3 to 4 tablespoons turkey gravy
Salt and pepper
1 cup soft white bread crumbs
Parsley
1 hard-cooked egg, chopped

Cook bacon. Drain fat, leaving 2 tablespoons in pan. Add turkey, spaghetti, cheese, gravy, and salt and pepper to taste. Heat well. Heavily grease a loaf pan (9 x 5 x 3 inches) and sprinkle soft bread crumbs over bottom and sides. Fill with turkey mixture, pressing with spoon to pack tightly. Bake in preheated very hot oven (450°F.) for 15 to 20 minutes. Garnish with parsley and chopped hard-cooked egg. Serve with additional hot turkey gravy. Makes 4 servings.

TURKEY PIE WITH CORN-BREAD TOPPING

1 can (10½ ounces) cream-of-mushroom soup
1 cup milk
1 cup cooked peas
1 pimiento, sliced
1½ cups cubed leftover turkey
¾ cup sifted all-purpose flour
¾ cup yellow cornmeal
2 teaspoons baking powder
¾ teaspoon salt
¼ cup shortening
1 egg, slightly beaten
¾ cup milk

In saucepan heat soup, milk, peas, pimiento, and turkey. Put in shallow 2-quart baking dish. Mix flour, cornmeal, baking powder, and salt. Cut in shortening. Mix egg and milk; add to dry ingredients; mix well. Pour over turkey mixture. Bake in preheated hot oven (425°F.) for about 25 minutes. Makes 4 servings.

PINWHEEL TURKEY PIE

4 carrots, cut up
2 potatoes, cut up
½ cup chopped parsley
3 cups cut-up leftover turkey
2 cups turkey gravy or chicken bouillon, thickened
Salt and pepper to taste
Parsley Pinwheels

Partially cook carrots and potatoes in boiling salted water. Drain; add remaining ingredients except Parsley Pinwheels and simmer until vegetables are tender, adding more water if necessary. Serve topped with Parsley Pinwheels. Makes 6 servings.

Parsley Pinwheels

Cut ½ cup butter or margarine and ½ pound cream cheese into 2 cups sifted all-purpose flour and ¼ teaspoon salt. Roll out ¼ inch thick on floured board to form a rectangle about 12 x 8 inches. Sprinkle with parsley. Beginning at end, roll up jelly-roll fashion. Cut into ½-inch slices, and bake on cookie sheet in preheated hot oven (400°F.) for about 20 minutes.

LAYERED TURKEY LOAF

3 envelopes unflavored gelatin
3 cups cold turkey or chicken broth
2 cups diced cooked turkey
Celery salt
Salt
2 tablespoons chopped parsley
1½ cups bottled cranberry-juice cocktail
1 cup diced celery
½ cup chopped walnuts
Salad greens
Mayonnaise

Soften 2 envelopes gelatin in ½ cup of the broth; stir over very low heat until gelatin is dissolved. Add to remaining broth. Chill until slightly thickened. Add turkey, seasonings to taste, and parsley. Put half in a loaf pan (9 x 5 x 3 inches) and chill until firm. Soften 1 envelope gelatin in ¼ cup cranberry cocktail. Dissolve over very low heat; add to remaining cocktail with ¼ teaspoon salt, the celery, and nuts; chill until slightly thickened. Spoon over firm layer; chill until firm. Pour remaining turkey mixture over cranberry layer; chill until firm. Unmold on greens; serve with mayonnaise. Good with mushroom soup, baked potatoes, chocolate meringue pie. Makes 6 to 8 servings.

CALIFORNIA TURKEY BAKE

4 slices of bread
Prepared garlic spread
4 eggs, separated
2 cups milk
2 teaspoons seasoned salt
⅛ teaspoon pepper
¼ cup sliced ripe olives
2 pimientos, chopped
2 cups diced cooked turkey

Trim crusts, and spread each slice of bread with small amount of garlic spread. Cut into 1-inch squares. Beat egg whites until stiff; set aside. Beat egg yolks and next 3 ingredients until foamy. Add bread, olives, pimientos, and turkey. Fold in egg whites. Pour into shallow baking dish; bake in preheated slow oven (325°F.) for 50 minutes, or until firm. Good with frozen peas, grapefruit and avocado salad, and raisin pie. Makes 6 servings.

TURKEY-SAUSAGE SQUARES

1 pound sausage meat
1 onion, minced
2 cups soft stale-bread crumbs
1 cup diced celery and leaves
2 eggs, beaten
2 cups diced cooked turkey
1 cup milk
1 teaspoon poultry seasoning
Turkey gravy
Seasoned salt and pepper to taste

Cook sausage meat until done but not browned, breaking up with fork. Remove meat, and pour off all but 2 tablespoons of the fat. Cook onion in the fat for 5 minutes. Mix meat and onion with all ingredients except gravy and salt and pepper. Stir in 1 cup leftover gravy and salt and pepper. Pour into shallow baking dish, and bake in preheated moderate oven (350°F.) for about 45 minutes. Cut into squares, and serve with additional heated gravy. Good with baked acorn squash, mixed green salad, and Tokay grapes. Makes 6 to 8 servings.

TURKEY SALAD

2 cups diced leftover turkey
1 cup sliced celery
¼ cup French dressing
2 cups halved seeded Malaga or Tokay grapes
Salt and pepper
Salad greens
½ cup cooked salad dressing
⅓ cup dairy sour cream
¼ cup toasted slivered almonds

Marinate turkey and celery in French dressing for 1 hour. Add grapes, and season to taste with salt and pepper. Arrange on salad greens. Combine boiled

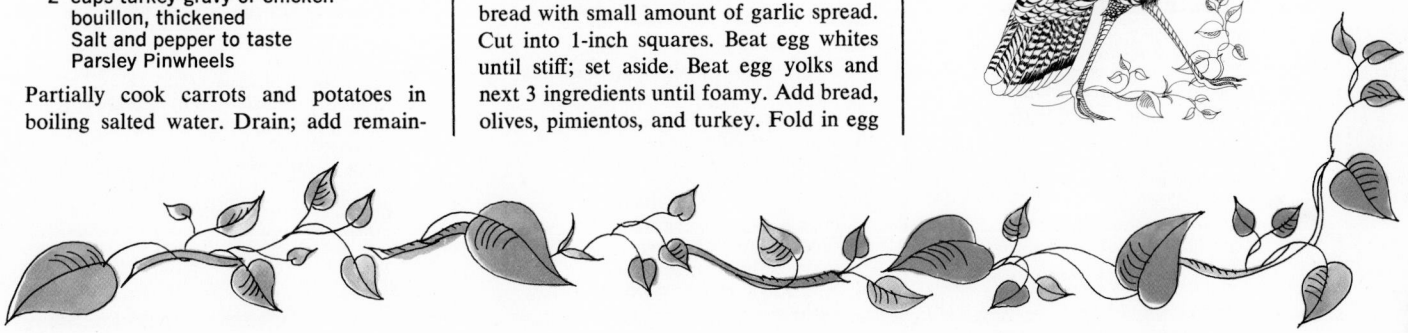

Turkey Hawaiian ***Turkey Creole in Rice Ring***

dressing and sour cream. Top salad with this mixture, and garnish with slivered almonds. (Mayonnaise or bought salad dressing can be substituted for the cooked dressing and sour cream.)

BROILED TURKEY SALAD

1 teaspoon instant minced onion
1 tablespoon fresh lemon juice
2 cups diced cooked turkey
¾ teaspoon salt
⅛ teaspoon pepper
½ cup mayonnaise
1½ cups finely diced celery
¼ cup canned buttered chopped almonds
2 cups finely crushed potato chips
1 cup grated Cheddar cheese

Mix onion and lemon juice. Add remaining ingredients except last 2. Mix well; chill. Divide among 4 individual baking dishes, or put in 9-inch pie pan. Mix chips and cheese and completely cover top of salad. Put under broiler just until top is golden, but salad is still cold. Good with marinated tomatoes, cucumbers, watercress, French bread, and fruit cup. Makes 4 servings.

FRESH TANGERINE AND TURKEY SALAD

2 cups diced cooked turkey
1 cup diced celery
1 teaspoon finely chopped onion
1¼ teaspoons salt
¼ teaspoon ground white pepper
2 cups diced tangerine sections, well drained (about 5 tangerines)
3 tablespoons mayonnaise
1 tablespoon fresh lemon juice
Lettuce
Tangerine sections for garnish

Mix together first 6 ingredients. Blend mayonnaise with lemon juice; add and mix lightly. Serve on lettuce. Garnish with tangerine sections. Makes 4 servings.

OPEN TURKEY SANDWICHES WITH CHEESE SAUCE

4 slices of toast
4 large slices of cooked turkey
3 tablespoons butter or margarine
3 tablespoons all-purpose flour
¼ teaspoon salt
⅛ teaspoon pepper
1 cup milk
¼ pound process American cheese, cut up (1 cup)

Arrange toast in shallow baking dish. Cover with turkey. Melt butter in saucepan; blend in flour, salt, and pepper. Add

Turkey and Broccoli Amandine ***Turkey Pie, with Breadstick Topping***

milk gradually and cook until thickened, stirring constantly. Add cheese and cook until cheese is melted. Pour sauce over turkey. Then brown under broiler. Makes 4 servings.

BAKED TURKEY-CHEDDAR SANDWICHES

12 slices of firm bread
3 eggs, beaten
¾ cup milk
½ teaspoon seasoned salt
Butter or margarine
1 can (10½ ounces) cream-of-mushroom soup
½ cup each of undiluted evaporated milk and turkey or chicken broth
½ teaspoon bottled thick condiment sauce
¼ teaspoon pepper
2 cups diced cooked turkey
½ cup grated Cheddar cheese

Dip bread into mixture of eggs, milk, and seasoned salt. Brown on both sides in hot butter. Put 6 slices in shallow baking dish. Mix soup, evaporated milk, broth, condiment sauce, pepper, and turkey. Spoon on toast slices. Top with remaining slices, and sprinkle with cheese. Bake in preheated hot oven (400°F.) for 15 to 20 minutes. Good with succotash, sliced-tomato and watercress salad, and baked fresh pears. Makes 6 servings.

TURKEY COMBINATION SANDWICHES

2 packages (3 ounces each) cream cheese, softened
1½ ounces (¼ cup) blue cheese, crumbled
⅓ cup minced pimiento-stuffed olives
1 teaspoon grated onion
6 slices of whole-wheat bread
Mayonnaise
6 slices of cooked turkey
Sliced leftover poultry stuffing
2 cups (one 1-pound can) whole-berry cranberry sauce, chilled and sliced
Lettuce leaves
6 slices of white bread

Mix first 4 ingredients. Spread whole-wheat bread with mayonnaise. Cover with turkey and poultry stuffing. Top with cranberry sauce, then with lettuce. Spread cheese mixture on white bread and invert on lettuce. Secure with picks and cut diagonally into halves. Makes 6 sandwiches.

Note: If not available, stuffing can be omitted. Or prepare stuffing and bake in a small loaf pan. Cool; chill.

TURMERIC—The irregularly shaped root of a tropical plant which is related to ginger. It is one of the essential spices in Indian cooking. When washed, cooked, and then dried, the turmeric root has a mild aroma and a mustardlike bitter taste. One of its characteristics is the brilliant gold color it adds to the dishes in which it is used. Turmeric is the "secret ingredient" of many prepared mustards with a bright yellow color, and it is always present in curry powder.

Turmeric flavors and colors curried meat, poultry, fish, and shellfish; deviled and creamed eggs; sauces for eggs, chicken, fish, or shellfish; egg, potato, or chicken salads; and rice dishes. It may be cooked in butter and the butter added to potatoes, corn, snap beans, and cabbages, or it may be used plain in all sorts of relishes and pickles.

Ground turmeric is widely available and the whole root may be purchased in herb specialty shops.

SAFFRON PILAU

¼ cup butter
1 small onion, minced
1 garlic clove, minced
2 whole cloves
½ teaspoon ground turmeric
⅛ teaspoon ground cuminseed
1½ cups uncooked rice
Salt
Few shreds of saffron

In the butter gently cook onion and garlic until they are transparent but not brown. Add cloves, turmeric, and cuminseed, and cook for 2 or 3 minutes. Then add rice, salt, the saffron which has been softened in a bit of warm water, and boiling water to cover rice by 1 inch. Proceed with favorite method for boiling or steaming rice until done. Makes 4 servings.

Note: If unaccompanied by other eastern dishes, serve with a sprinkling of tiny onion rings, fried crisp and brown; slivers of almonds, fried or toasted; or seedless raisins, puffed in water, then fried a bit.

PEAR CHUTNEY

2 pounds onions, chopped
10 pounds hard cooking pears, peeled and quartered
2 tablespoons salt, or more to taste
½ cup preserved gingerroot, cut into chunks
2 hot dried peppers or ½ teaspoon cayenne
8 sweet green peppers, chopped
4 cups sugar
3 tablespoons flour
2 tablespoons ground turmeric
¼ cup powdered mustard
2 quarts cider vinegar

Grind onions and pears in grinder, using coarse blade. Mix with salt and let stand overnight. In morning drain off liquid. Cover pulp with cold water and drain again. Mix remaining ingredients and stir until smooth. Boil for 5 minutes. Add to pear mixture and boil for about 40 minutes, or until thick, stirring constantly to prevent sticking. Pour while hot into sterilized jars. Seal and cool. Makes about 8 pints.

TURNIP—A root vegetable that is a member of the *Brassica* genus; there are several varieties. The flesh varies in texture; the finer-fleshed turnips are eaten as a vegetable and the coarser ones are fed to livestock. Turnips are white-fleshed. Some varieties have purple tops. (The so-called yellow turnip or Swedish turnip is actually the closely related rutabaga.) Turnip tops are eaten as greens and are used for forage.

Turnips originated in the temperate zone of Europe and have been grown for some 4,000 years. They are a cool-weather vegetable and are popular in northern Europe and Great Britain. They came to the New World via Mexico, arriving in Virginia in 1610 and New England in 1628. Since they are not much trouble to grow and are useful to man and beast, the early and later settlers raised them for both. Turnips and turnip greens are particularly appreciated in our Southern states.

Availability—Fresh turnips are available year round with peak season from October to March.

Turnip greens are also available canned and frozen.

Purchasing Guide—Turnips are sold either bunched, with the tops left on or with tops removed. The tops should be fresh and green and the roots smooth, firm, and a good weight for their size.

Storage—Turnips keep best in a very cool, well-ventilated storage place at about 55° F., the old root cellar, in fact. If such storage is unavailable, refrigerate.

☐ Fresh, refrigerator shelf, raw: 1 month
☐ Fresh, refrigerator shelf, cooked: 2 to 3 days
☐ Fresh, prepared for freezing; or frozen, refrigerator frozen-food compartment: 2 to 3 months
☐ Fresh, prepared for freezing; or frozen, freezer: 1 year

Nutritive Food Values—A fair source of vitamin C. The greens are an excellent source of vitamins A and C, and a good source of calcium, iron, and riboflavin.

☐ Turnip, 3½ ounces, cooked = 23 calories
☐ Fresh turnip greens, 3½ ounces, solids and liquid = 20 calories
☐ Canned turnip greens, 3½ ounces, solids and liquid = 18 calories
☐ Frozen turnip greens, 3½ ounces, cooked and drained = 23 calories

Basic Preparation—Wash, pare, and slice or dice. Small turnips may be left whole.

☐ **To Cook**—Cook, covered, in 1 inch of boiling salted water until tender, for 12 to 15 minutes. Drain; season, and serve with melted butter or margarine. Sliced turnips may be seasoned and baked in a covered casserole in preheated moderate oven (375°F.) for about 45 minutes.

☐ **To Freeze**—Wash, peel, and cut into 1-inch cubes. Blanch in boiling water for 2 to 2½ minutes. Chill in cold water for 3 to 4 minutes. Drain. Pack into freezer container, leaving ½-inch headspace. Seal.

TURNIPS IN SOUR CREAM

2 pounds fresh turnips
1¼ teaspoons salt
½ teaspoon celery salt
1 cup dairy sour cream
¼ teaspoon ground ginger
⅛ teaspoon white pepper

Peel turnips and dice into medium cubes. Cook in boiling salted water until soft.

Drain. Mash, and season with remaining ingredients. Serve hot. Makes 6 servings.

FLUFFY TURNIPS

2 pounds fresh turnips
1 can (10½ ounces) beef consommé
½ teaspoon sugar
2 teaspoons finely chopped onion
2 tablespoons chopped parsley

Pare and cube turnips. Cook with consommé over medium heat for 12 to 15 minutes, or until tender. Mash in same liquid until fluffy. Add remaining ingredients. Reheat and serve with meat dish. Makes 6 servings.

FINNISH STUFFED TURNIPS

12 small to medium-size turnips
Boiling water
1 tablespoon salt
¼ cup butter or margarine
⅔ cup soft bread crumbs
¼ cup chopped almonds

Scrub turnips, rinse, drain, and peel. Cook, covered with salted boiling water, for 12 to 15 minutes, or until soft. Drain, and cool. Spoon out a little of the center. Chop removed centers and mix with 2 tablespoons butter and all but 2 tablespoons of the bread crumbs. Stuff hollowed turnips with crumb mixture and sprinkle with about half of almonds. Brown remaining butter. Put stuffed turnips in a casserole, pour browned butter over, and sprinkle well with remaining crumbs and almonds. Bake in preheated moderate oven (350°F.) for 20 minutes, or until lightly browned. Baste frequently with any butter in casserole or extra melted butter. Makes 6 servings.

TURNIP SALAD

Mix together 4 cups finely grated young raw turnips, 1 cup thick dairy sour cream, 1 tablespoon sugar, 1 tablespoon vinegar, and 1 teaspoon salt. Serve on crisp shredded lettuce. Makes 6 to 8 servings.

TURNOVER—A filled pastry in a triangular or semicircular shape. The pastry used may be a standard pastry, puff paste, or egg pastry, rolled out into a circle or a square. The filling, which may be savory or sweet, is placed on half the pastry, which is then folded over to enclose the filling and either baked or deep fried. Turnovers can be served hot or cold.

Commercially made apple, blueberry, and cherry turnovers are sold frozen; other turnovers are sold in the bakery department of food stores; refrigerated bake-and-serve turnovers are sold in the dairy department.

CHICKEN-LIVER TURNOVERS

Cook 2 slices of bacon until crisp, and crumble. In the bacon fat cook ½ pound chicken livers. Chop livers fine; mix with bacon and a little mayonnaise; season. Roll Flaky French Crust about ⅛ inch thick. Cut into 2-inch rounds. Put a dab of filling on one side of each round, and fold over, pinching together. Prick with fork and crimp around edge. Brush with egg yolk beaten with 1 tablespoon milk. Bake in preheated very hot oven (450° F.) for 10 minutes. Makes about 3 dozen.

Flaky French Crust

2 cups plus 2 tablespoons sifted all-purpose flour
¾ teaspoon salt
1 cup soft butter
2 egg yolks
¼ cup light cream
2 tablespoons dry white wine

Sift flour and salt into bowl. Cut in butter. Add combined egg yolks, cream, and wine; mix with fork until blended and smooth. Knead lightly in bowl until bubbles begin to appear on the surface of dough. Cover and chill for 1 hour. Roll to ⅛-inch thickness on floured board. Fold twice lengthwise and then twice crosswise. Chill for 15 minutes. Roll and fold twice more. Store, wrapped in moisture-proof paper, in refrigerator until needed.

CORNED-BEEF TURNOVERS, MUSHROOM SAUCE

Mince half of 12-ounce can corned beef; add ¼ cup undiluted cream-of-mushroom soup from 10½-ounce can, 1 grated small onion, and 2 chopped parsley sprigs. Add seasoning to taste. Roll pastry (made with 1½ cups all-purpose flour) into a rectangle (16 x 8 inches) on floured board. Cut into eight 4-inch squares. Spoon meat mixture on one corner of each square; moisten edges with water; fold over in triangles; crimp edges with fork; brush with undiluted evaporated milk. Put on cookie sheet; bake in preheated hot oven (425°F.) for about 20 minutes. Dilute remaining soup with ⅓ cup milk; heat; add ½ teaspoon Worcestershire. Serve as sauce for turnovers.

SAMOSAS
(Curried Meat Turnovers)

2 tablespoons instant minced onion
2 tablespoons water
2 tablespoons butter or margarine
¼ teaspoon each of garlic powder, ground cinnamon, ground ginger, and cayenne
2 teaspoons ground coriander
¼ cup chopped fresh tomato
1½ cups finely ground lamb or beef
1¼ teaspoons salt
¼ cup water
2 teaspoons fresh lemon juice
Pastry for Samosas
Egg white, beaten slightly

Soften onion in 2 tablespoons water. Sauté in butter. Add spices and stir and cook for 1 minute. Add tomato, lamb, and salt. Stir and cook for 2 to 3 minutes. Add water and lemon juice, and cook until all the liquid is absorbed. Turn out onto a plate to cool. Roll Pastry very thin on a lightly floured board. Cut into circles with a 2½-inch cookie cutter. Brush edges lightly with beaten egg white. Place rounded ½ teaspoon of mixture in center of each. Fold over dough and crimp edges with a fork, being sure they are well sealed. Fry in hot deep fat (360°F. to 375°F. on a frying thermometer) until golden-brown. Drain on absorbent paper. If desired, use your own pastry recipe and bake the puffs in preheated hot oven (400°F.) for 12 to 15 minutes. Serve as an accompaniment to cocktails or tomato juice. Makes about 60 turnovers.

Pastry for Samosas

2 cups sifted all-purpose flour
1 teaspoon salt
¼ cup butter or margarine
7 tablespoons yogurt

Sift flour with salt. Melt butter and add to flour. Mix well. Stir in yogurt gradually, working it with hands for about 5 minutes. Knead until satiny and smooth. Makes pastry for 60 turnovers.

BLUEBERRY TURNOVERS

In saucepan mix ¼ cup sugar, ⅛ teaspoon salt, and ⅓ cup all-purpose flour. Add 2 tablespoons fresh orange juice and about 1⅔ cups (one 14-ounce can) blueberries with syrup. Cook, stirring constantly until very thick; cool. Roll 1 recipe of pastry (2¼ cups all-purpose flour) and cut into twelve 4½-inch rounds. Put 2 tablespoons blueberry mixture on half of each round, moisten edges, and fold over. Seal edges with a fork. Fry in small amount of fat until golden-brown on both sides.

RAISIN-ORANGE TURNOVERS

1¾ cups seedless raisins
1¾ cups water
¼ cup orange juice
⅓ cup brown sugar, firmly packed
1 tablespoon quick-cooking tapioca
½ teaspoon ground cinnamon
¼ teaspoon salt
1 tablespoon vinegar
1 tablespoon butter or margarine
2 teaspoons grated orange rind
Standard pastry made with 2 cups flour
Light cream (optional)

Combine raisins, water, and orange juice in saucepan. Bring to a boil and boil for 5 minutes. Then add sugar, tapioca, cinnamon, and salt. Cook, stirring constantly, until mixture comes to a boil. Remove from heat; add vinegar, butter, and orange rind. Cool. Roll pastry very thin (less than ⅛ inch) and cut into 6-inch circles or 5-inch squares. Put about 3 tablespoonfuls of filling on one side of each circle or square, moisten edges, fold over, and seal edges with floured fork.

Brush lightly with cream, if desired. Bake in preheated hot oven (425°F.) for about 20 minutes. Makes 8 to 10.

MARMALADE TURNOVERS

Roll standard pastry ⅛ inch thick and cut into 4-inch circles. Put 1 tablespoon marmalade on one side of circle. Dot with butter and sprinkle lightly with cinnamon. Moisten edges, fold over, and press edges together. Seal with floured fork. Bake in preheated hot oven (425° F.) for about 15 minutes.

TURTLE and TORTOISE—These are members of the reptilian order Chelonia. They live in salt and fresh waters as well as on land, and are distinguished by their shells. Most of them have hard shells or carapaces, but there are soft-shell varieties. They come in many sizes and colors. In general usage the word turtle is used to describe aquatic types, while the word tortoise is reserved for the forms living on land.

Some turtles are enormous, growing to more than seven feet and weighing as much as 1,000 pounds. For eating purposes, the most famous one is the green turtle, which lives in warm ocean waters and sports a smooth greenish or olive shell. This turtle is made into a thick gelatinous soup which is considered an extraordinary treat by many people. Turtle soup is always served with the addition of sherry or Madeira, with a thin slice of lemon floating on it.

The people of Philadelphia prize the snapping turtle, a large fresh-water turtle of North America. It is traditionally made into snapper stew, and the meat is dished up in a rich cream sauce.

Turtle steak, another delicacy, is highly regarded in the South, especially on the Florida Keys, where commercial turtle fishing is concentrated. At its best it tastes like fine veal, but it can also be very tough. It is seldom available except locally.

There are many varieties of tortoise, known by such local names as the gophers of Florida. These are eaten in stews and soups.

Turtles and tortoises lay eggs which in many cases are also eaten as a delicacy. The eggs most widely eaten are those of the green sea turtle. Usually, turtles' eggs are boiled in heavily salted water. The white does not get hard, as with hens' eggs, but the yolk does and it is rich.

Generally speaking, turtles and tortoises are far more popular in America, with its tradition of living off the land, than in Europe. The exception is turtle soup, which was and is greatly fancied by English gourmets.

Availability—The fresh-water common snapping turtle or snapper is occasionally sold live in food stores, generally in the eastern half of the United States. Market sizes range from 4 to 25 pounds. The alligator snapping turtle is found in southern areas and is usually marketed in New Orleans and St. Louis. It often attains a weight of 200 pounds. Several species of soft-shell turtles are available in the southern areas of the United States where they are caught. Other fresh-water turtles are the Mississippi turtle, the Pacific pond turtle, the Mobile and Suwanee turtle, and the chicken turtle. These are available in local areas only. Green turtles, the most famous of the sea turtles, are available only in local areas. Fishing for them is centered around Key West, Florida.

Frozen turtle meat from the snapping turtle is available in some markets.

Canned turtle meat, green-turtle meat, turtle soup, green-turtle soup, and snapper soup are available.

Storage—Live turtle must be cooked immediately.

- ☐ Fresh, cooked; and canned, opened, refrigerator shelf: 1 to 2 days
- ☐ Canned, kitchen shelf: 1 year
- ☐ Frozen, refrigerator frozen-food compartment: 2 months
- ☐ Frozen, freezer: 1 year

Nutritive Food Values—High in protein.

- ☐ Green turtle, 3½ ounces, raw = 89 calories
- ☐ Canned green turtle, 3½ ounces = 106 calories

Basic Preparation

☐ **To Dress a Live Turtle**—The head must be removed first. Cause snapping turtle to grasp a stick. The head can then easily be pulled forward and cut off. Heads of other species can be forced to protrude by pressing the upper shell. Run a sharp knife along the edges of the skin where it joins the shell; then pull the skin back over the legs to the feet and disjoint the feet. Remove the lower part of the shell by cutting through the bridges which join the upper and lower shell. In both the snappers and soft-shells the bridges are soft. When the bridges are cut, the lower shell is readily removed by inserting a sharp knife under it and lifting the shell up and off. Remove entrails; then remove four quarters from the upper shell.

TURTLE SOUP

3 pounds turtle meat
Water
¼ cup butter or margarine
2 medium onions, minced
¼ cup all-purpose flour
1 cup canned tomatoes
½ garlic clove, minced
2 bay leaves
Few parsley sprigs
6 whole cloves
¼ teaspoon ground mace
1 teaspoon sugar
Juice of 1 lemon
½ cup sherry
2 hard-cooked eggs, minced

Have turtle meat cut into 1-inch cubes. Put meat with 3 quarts water in kettle and bring to boil; simmer for 10 minutes. Strain, reserving broth. Melt 3 tablespoons of the butter in kettle. Add turtle meat and brown on all sides. Remove meat and add remaining butter to kettle. Add onions and brown lightly. Add flour and stir until browned. Add turtle meat and next 8 ingredients. Add enough water to broth to make 4 quarts and add to mixture in kettle. Bring to boil, cover, and simmer for 3 hours. Strain, add sherry, and reheat, if necessary. Serve with a garnish of minced egg. Makes about 3 quarts.

TURTLE STEAK WITH SOUR-CREAM SAUCE

1½ pounds of turtle steaks, cut paper-thin
All-purpose flour
6 tablespoons butter or margarine
Salt and pepper
Paprika
½ cup dry white wine
1 cup dairy sour cream
Chopped parsley

Pound turtle steak with the edge of a plate. Dip steaks in flour. Melt butter in skillet with cover, add turtle steaks, and brown quickly on both sides. Season with salt and pepper to taste and add 1 tablespoon paprika. Add wine, cover, and simmer for 1 hour. Remove turtle to a hot platter. Stir sour cream into drippings in skillet and heat, stirring constantly. Pour over turtle and sprinkle with paprika and parsley. Makes 4 to 6 servings.

UPSIDE-DOWN CAKE—A cake baked in a different manner from other cakes, and one that does not necessarily require an oven. Brown or white sugar and butter are spread in the bottom of a pan and covered with a design of fruit and occasionally nuts which are then topped with a cake batter of some kind. After baking, the cake is turned out of the pan upside down. The sugar and butter mixture forms a glaze with the fruit juices and the cake remains moist. The cake batter may be a spongecake, a muffin batter, a yellow cake made from scratch or from a mix, a spice cake, or perhaps, for an old-fashioned version, gingerbread. Smaller versions may be made in custard cups or muffin pans. Upside-down cakes are also called skillet cakes because they can be baked on top of the stove, using a covered skillet over either gas or electric thermostatically controlled surface units. They can also be baked in covered electric skillets.

Usually an upside-down cake is served warm, either plain or with whipped cream or a dessert sauce. On some occasions main-dish upside-down cakes may be made, using ground meat and perhaps corn bread as a topping.

Upside-down cakes are typically American and are not found in European cooking. They date back to the days of the early settlers who did not always have a bake oven in their homes. Thanks to the ingenuity of these early homemakers, their families did not have to forego the pleasure of eating cake.

APRICOT-PRUNE UPSIDE-DOWN CAKE

- ¼ cup water
- ½ cup brown sugar, firmly packed
- ½ cup butter or margarine
- 1 cup sweetened cooked dried-apricot halves
- 1 cup cooked pitted prunes
- 2 cups sifted cake flour
- 2 teaspoons baking powder
- ¼ teaspoon salt
- 1 cup granulated sugar
- 1 egg
- ¾ cup milk
- 1 teaspoon vanilla extract
- Whipped cream (optional)

Mix water, brown sugar, and ¼ cup of the butter, melted. Pour into wax-paper lined pan (9 x 9 x 2 inches). Arrange fruits in mixture, alternating apricots and prunes. Sift flour, baking powder, and salt together. Cream the remaining butter; gradually add granulated sugar and beat well. Add egg and beat until light. Add sifted dry ingredients alternately with milk, beating until smooth after each addition. Stir in vanilla. Pour into pan over fruit. Bake in preheated moderate oven (350°F.) for 45 to 50 minutes. Then invert pan on serving plate and peel off paper. Serve warm, with whipped cream, if desired. Makes 6 large or 9 small servings.

Pineapple Upside-Down Cake

Combine ¼ cup melted butter and ⅔ cup firmly packed brown sugar. Mix well and spread in pan (9 x 9 x 2 inches). Drain 1 can (8½ ounces) sliced pineapple and sprinkle 2 tablespoons of the syrup over sugar mixture in pan. Cut pineapple slices into quarters and arrange on sugar mixture. Sprinkle with ½ cup chopped nuts. Prepare cake batter as directed in recipe above. Pour into pan over pineapple and proceed as directed. Makes 6 large servings.

Blueberry Upside-Down Cake

Combine ¼ cup melted butter and ½ cup firmly packed brown sugar. Mix well and spread in pan (9 x 9 x 2 inches). Mix 2 cups washed fresh blueberries and

Ambrosia Upside-Down Cake

2 teaspoons grated lemon rind. Put in pan, distributing evenly. Prepare cake batter as directed in recipe for Apricot-Prune Upside-Down Cake. Pour into pan over berries and proceed as directed. Makes 6 large servings.

Cherry Upside-Down Cake

Combine ¼ cup melted butter and ½ cup firmly packed brown sugar. Mix well and spread in pan (9 x 9 x 2 inches). Mix 2 cups (one 1-pound can) water-packed pitted red sour cherries, drained (reserve liquid), and 2 teaspoons grated lemon rind. Put in pan, distributing evenly. Prepare cake batter as directed in recipe for Apricot-Prune Upside Down Cake. Pour into pan over cherries and proceed as directed. Serve baked cake with Cherry Sauce. Makes 6 large servings.

Cherry Sauce

Blend 2 tablespoons sugar and 2 teaspoons cornstarch. Add reserved cherry juice and cook until thickened.

AMBROSIA UPSIDE-DOWN CAKE

⅓ cup butter or margarine
¾ cup firmly packed light brown sugar
6 slices of canned pineapple
1 package cake mix: yellow, orange, or orange-coconut
1 can (11 ounces) mandarin oranges
Coconut
6 maraschino cherries

Melt butter in pan (13 x 9 x 2 inches). Sprinkle with brown sugar. Arrange slices of pineapple on sugar. Prepare cake mix as directed on label. Pour over pineapple slices and bake as directed for pan size. Turn out on rack, and cut into 6 serving pieces. Drain mandarin oranges. Arrange sections around each cake serving; sprinkle with coconut; put a maraschino cherry in each pineapple ring. Makes 6 large servings.

GINGER-MINCE UPSIDE-DOWN CAKE

1 package dry mincemeat
½ cup boiling water
3 tablespoons butter
2 tablespoons brown sugar

1½ cups canned sliced apples
1 package gingerbread mix

Break mincemeat into saucepan. Add boiling water, and cook for 3 minutes, stirring occasionally. Cool. Melt the butter in a baking pan (8 x 8 x 2 inches). Sprinkle brown sugar on butter. Arrange apple slices in pan, and pour mincemeat over apples. Prepare gingerbread mix as directed on the package. Pour over the mincemeat. Bake in preheated moderate oven (350°F.) for about 35 minutes. When done, turn upside down on serving plate. Makes 8 servings.

UTENSIL—An instrument, vessel, tool, or implement. When the word is applied to kitchen equipment, it refers to the utensils used in the preparation, cooking, serving, or storing of food. Following is a check list of utensils needed in a well-equipped kitchen. Those preceded by an asterisk are probably most essential to the largest number of families.

Baking pans: corn-stick pan; custard cups; loaf pan (9 x 5 x 3 inches) for bread, loaf cakes, meat loaf; muffin pans

*Beaters and mixers, 2 or more of following: whisk for beating and mixing; rotary beater with heavy-duty gear construction; portable electric mixer; stationary electric mixer

Blender, electric, for puréeing, chopping, mixing batters, sauces, beverages

*Boards for cutting and rolling: small one for cheese, vegetables; medium for carving meats; largest for piecrust and breadmaking

*Bowls, graduated (from 1 pint to 4 quarts), for mixing and storing

*Broiling pan, if there isn't one in the range

Cake pans: *8- or 9-inch round or square layer pans (2 or 3); 8- or 9-inch square loaf pan; *13 x 9-inch loaf pan; angel-food pan; springform pan

*Can, bottle, jar openers; alone or in combination:
- Beer-type can opener
- Bottle opener
- Corkscrew
- Electric can opener, a real convenience item
- Hand can opener, either mounted on wall or to keep in a drawer (an emergency one needed for odd cans and odd times even if an electric opener is available)
- Jar opener

*Casseroles with covers: graduated sizes, starting with 2-quart

*Coffeemaker, electric or non-electric percolator, drip, vacuum, or espresso

*Cookie sheets, cutter, press; decorating tubes and tips; cake racks

*Collander, sieve, strainers—need at least 1 large and 1 tea-strainer size

*Covered pan, at least 6 to 10-quart with trivet. May be a Dutch oven, kettle, or saucepan to be used for meats, soups, quantity cooking, canning, and blanching.

*Cutlery (paring knives, chef or butcher knife, carving knife, slicer, utility) and other small tools (rubber and metal spatulas, spoons—including slotted and wooden, forks, apple corer, baster, pastry fork or blender, vegetable peeler, nutcracker, skewers, ladle, shears, potato masher, tongs, pastry brush).

Deep fryer, electric or non-electric

*Double boiler, 2- or 3-quart. Use bottom as an extra saucepan; some upper pans can be used as casseroles.

Egg poacher, electric or non-electric

*Flour sifter, 1-cup and 5-cup sizes most frequently used

*Graters, grinder, shredders, juicer, ice crusher, electric or non-electric. Frequently available in combination or as attachments to mixer. Singly they are more frequently non-electric.

*Griddle, grill, waffle iron; electric or non-electric. One appliance often serves two purposes, and some of the grills serve as heated serving trays.

Ice-cream freezer, electric or non-electric

*Knife sharpener, electric, available alone or in combination with another appliance. Non-electric usually serves this one purpose only.

*Measuring cups graduated from ¼ cup to 1 cup for dry measure; 1 cup, 2 cups, and 4 cups for liquid measure.

*Measuring spoons

Molds for salads, desserts, breads, cakes, puddings

*Pantryware: canisters, salt and pepper shakers, scoops

*Pie pans, one or two each 8-inch and 9-inch

Pressure cooker, electric or non-electric. Useful for certain stews, soups, pot roasts, canning

*Protective mats, tiles, trivets

*Roasting pan, with a rack. Useful size is 10 x 12 inches; 12 x 15 inches, or in between.

Rolling pin, cover, pastry cloth

*Saucepans, for a small family, start with a 1-quart and a 2-quart.

Scales, especially for families on special diets

*Skillets: 7-inch and 10-inch are good starting sizes. Other sizes and omelet pan can come later.

Steamer for steaming rice, puddings, vegetables; for blanching

*Storage accessories: vegetable bins, dinnerware racks, utensil trays, and drawer dividers for use in drawers

*Storage containers with covers for pantry shelves, refrigerator, and freezer storage

*Teakettle, 2- or 3-quart size

Teapot, 1 or 2 depending on tea service

*Thermometers: candy, frying, freezer, meat, and oven

*Toaster, electric or non-electric

Warmers: electric hot trays, casseroles, etc., and their non-electric cousins, the chafing dishes, casseroles, etc., which use canned heat or candles to keep foods warm

VACHERIN—A delicious creamy white dessert cheese made in France and Switzerland from whole milk mixed with cream. It has a firm leathery crust over a very soft paste, similar to ripe Brie.

Vacherin is also the name of a French or Swiss meringue cake made usually in the shape of rings which are stacked on each other and filled with fruit, ice cream, whipped cream, mousse, etc. It is a very festive dessert.

VACHERIN À LA SUISSE
(Meringue Shell)

Beat 5 egg whites, a pinch of salt, and ¼ teaspoon cream of tartar until the whites are stiff and form soft peaks. Gradually add 1¼ cups sugar, 1 tablespoon at a time, beating after each addition. When the meringue becomes very stiff, after about ⅔ of the sugar has been added, fold in remaining sugar at one time and add 1 teaspoon vanilla extract. Grease and flour 2 cookie sheets or cover them with baking paper. Trace 5 circles, 7 inches in diameter, on the sheets. Spread one of the circles with a layer of meringue ¼ inch thick. Put rest of meringue in a large pastry bag with a plain tube and pipe rings of the mixture around the rims of the other 4 circles. Make about 12 small rosettes of meringue in addition, but reserve some of the mixture. Bake the meringue in preheated very slow oven (250°F.) for about 45 minutes. Meringue should be crisp and dry with no tears adhering to it. Remove from oven and loosen meringues carefully. Around the edge of the flat circle spread a thin ridge of unbaked meringue. Put one of the baked rings on this. Brush the top of the ring lightly with more unbaked meringue and top with another ring. Repeat this process until all the rings are piled up and you have a large meringue shell. Coat the outside with the remaining unbaked meringue and return to the oven until the shell is thoroughly dried out. Turn off the heat and let the *vacherin* remain in the oven for several hours to cool and dry slowly. To serve, fill the shell with fresh fruit, sweetened whipped cream, sherbet, frozen mousse, or scoops of variflavored ice creams. Decorate with the meringue rosettes and chopped pistachio nuts. Cut into wedges at the table. Makes 6 to 8 servings.

VANILLA ***by Lucy Kavaler***—One of the loveliest of orchids with lemon-yellow waxy outthrust petals; it has no odor, yet it is the source of the most aromatic of flavors. The tropical plant *Vanilla planifolia* bears its fruit in the form of a bean pod, which also has virtually no scent or flavor. When dried and cured, however, the bean develops the taste and smell that is generally associated with vanilla, a delicate sweetness ideal for flavoring baked goods, ice cream, and candies.

Vanilla is a part of our earliest memories; its haunting fragrance carries us back to childhood, to cakes baking in the oven, to little bottles of dark-brown extract sniffed and surreptitiously applied as perfume. Even as grown-ups, we find that the scent, like that of cinnamon, cloves, and other spices, brings an aura of far-off places into our everyday kitchens.

It is indeed only fitting that vanilla's history takes in the romantic Spanish conquistadors. More than four centuries have passed since the day when bold dashing Hernán Cortés drank his first cup of *xocoatl* at the court of Montezuma, ruler of the Aztecs. To make this beverage, he learned, the Indians powdered the beans of the cacao tree together with bean pods, renamed *vainilla,* meaning "little scabbard," by the Spaniards.

The combination of vanilla and chocolate has been a particularly happy one from Aztec times to the present. A rich creamy flavor results, and so the best chocolate candy, cakes, and frostings are enhanced with vanilla. Hot chocolate can leave the nursery and become a drink for grown-ups when a few drops of vanilla extract are added.

With the invention of ice cream in the 17th century, vanilla began to outrank other flavors. "Make mine vanilla," cry the vast majority of ice-cream eaters today. It is three times as popular as any other flavor and accounts for half of the staggering three-quarters of a billion gallons of ice cream consumed here in a year. The ice-cream industry thus seizes the lion's share of vanilla bean imports, but enough is left to add mellow sweetness to cakes, cookies, candies, and other desserts. Leaf through any cook book and observe how many such recipes call for vanilla.

This widespread use is particularly surprising, because few natural products have been as difficult to obtain in cultivation as vanilla. It remained a luxury flavor for three centuries, as no one, outside of the Mexican Indians, could manage to obtain a crop of beans. The problem was that the transplanted orchid would bear no fruit. Superstitious plantation owners were convinced that the curse of Montezuma lay upon them. At last in 1836 a French botanist discovered that the curse lay in the sexual structure of the plant; it could be pollinated by a single species of bee, native only to Mexico. A freed slave then worked out a way of pollinating the plants by hand. This slow and painstaking method, used to this day, made it possible to raise vanilla in many areas of the world. Madagascar, in particular, became a center for the French "Bourbon" beans, so called because the crop was also produced on the island of Bourbon, now Réunion, in the Indian Ocean. But artificial pollination and the appearance of the fruit are merely the preamble to a long and tedious curing and drying process. Fully six months are devoted to transforming the thick green pods into the long thin dark-brown green-bean-shape sticks we know. Even then the job is not done, as most cooks and food processors find it easier to use extracts, made by dissolving the chopped beans in alcohol and water, filtering the resulting liquid, and aging it in glass-lined tanks.

In this form the flavor, as the skilled cook knows, is highly concentrated, and the tiniest quantity carries its sweetness through an entire cake or batch of cookies. A number of chefs, especially in Europe, still like to work with the vanilla bean, both for baking and for making ice cream. In one family of French origin a recipe handed down for generations advises splitting the pod, separating the pulp from it, scalding both pulp and pod with heavy cream, then removing the pod and retaining the flavored cream as a base for old-fashioned ice cream. Many ice-cream lovers will buy only those commercial brands that contain black seed specks, proof that natural vanilla was utilized. The absence of these specks, however, does not necessarily imply the presence of artificial flavor. When manufacturers use extracts, the seeds have been filtered out.

The suspicious gourmet, though, has good reason for his doubt. All too often there is no more than a drop of pure vanilla extract in mass-produced vanilla ice cream, cakes, cookies, and candies. Instead the taste comes from such unromantic origins as waste wood-pulp liquor. Unpalatable though this sounds, the flavor created is a brother, albeit not a twin, of the natural product. Where the planters had trouble in making the orchid reproduce, chemists have been baffled in their efforts to determine the chemical composition of the bean. They have succeeded in duplicating only vanillin, the chief but not the sole source of the taste. The synthetic is stronger and cheaper than the natural extract, which accounts for its wide commercial use. One artificial-flavor producer insists doggedly that despite its centuries-long popularity in ice cream, natural vanilla endures cold poorly and should be reinforced by at least a little of the stable synthetic.

However it is made, we all eat and serve vanilla ice cream. As Ralph Waldo Emerson, American essayist, pointed out more than a century ago: "We dare not trust our wit for making our house pleasant to our friend and so we buy ice cream."

Availability—Pure vanilla extract is widely available. Vanilla beans are available in specialty food stores.

VANILLA SUGAR

Cut a 1-inch piece of vanilla bean into small pieces. Place in covered jar with 1 cup sifted confectioners' sugar. Let stand at least overnight before using. Used for sprinkling on cookies and cakes.

VANILLA FRESH-FRUIT CUP

1 large unpeeled pear, diced
2 cups fresh orange sections
½ cup seeded grapes
2 tablespoons sugar
1 tablespoon fresh lemon juice
1 teaspoon vanilla extract
Fresh mint leaves

Combine all ingredients except mint leaves. Chill for 2 to 3 hours. Garnish with mint and serve as appetizer or dessert. Makes 6 servings.

Note: Vanilla brings out the sweetness in fruits so less sugar is necessary.

SUGGESTED USES FOR VANILLA

- Add 6 to 8 drops of vanilla extract to a cup of hot tea. The vanilla flavor won't be discernible but it will bring out the flavor of the tea.
- Add vanilla extract to taste to the egg-and-milk mixture when making French toast.
- For fruit-salad dressing, mix ¼ teaspoon vanilla extract, ¼ cup mayonnaise, and ¼ cup heavy cream, whipped.
- Add vanilla extract to taste to the cream or milk to be used for morning cereal. Less sugar will be needed.

VARIETY MEAT—The name given to those edible parts of an animal other than the skeletal muscle which is usually known as "meat."

Variety meats include liver, sweetbreads, kidneys, brains, heart, tongue, tripe, and oxtails. Partially prepared meats, such as sausages, are also sometimes looked upon as variety meats. For additional information see entries for individual variety meats.

RAGOUT OF VARIETY MEATS

½ pound each of beef liver, beef kidney, beef heart, fresh tongue, and oxtail
1 cup cider vinegar
1 cup red wine
2 garlic cloves, minced
1 bay leaf
6 whole cloves
1 teaspoon pepper
3 tablespoons bacon fat
1 teaspoon dried hot pepper
3 tablespoons chopped chives
1 tablespoon salt
1 large onion, sliced
2 medium green peppers, seeded and chopped

3 tablespoons chopped parsley
½ pound Italian sweet sausages, sliced
2 tablespoons tomato paste
½ cup pitted green olives
Cornmeal Sauce

Pour boiling water over the variety meats. Drain and chop meat, removing bone from oxtail, into small cubes. Cover with vinegar and wine, 1 garlic clove, the bay leaf, cloves, and pepper. Marinate for several hours. Melt bacon fat and add remaining garlic, hot pepper, and chives. Add meat and cook until brown. Add water to cover, and salt. Allow mixture to come to a boil and add onion, green peppers, parsley, sausages, and tomato paste. Cover and cook until meats are tender. Add olives. Serve with Cornmeal Sauce. Makes 6 to 8 servings.

Cornmeal Sauce

1 tablespoon bacon fat
1 small onion, chopped
3 cups water
1 teaspoon salt
Yellow cornmeal

Melt bacon fat and sauté onion until golden. Add water and salt and bring to a boil. Stir in enough cornmeal to give mixture the consistency of a very thick cream sauce.

VEAL—Young beef four to fourteen weeks of age is known as veal. It is most abundant in late winter and spring. During the rest of the year most of the meat sold as veal is actually calf, from animals fourteen weeks to one year of age.

Availability—All year round. Most plentiful in late winter and spring. For information on the cuts of veal available, see Retail Cuts of Veal—Where They Come From, page 1887.

The veal variety meats available are liver, kidney, heart, brains, sweetbread, and tongue.

Boneless veal rolls weighing from 4 to 8 pounds, boneless veal leg roasts weighing from 4 to 6 pounds, and small veal steaks are all available frozen.

Strained and chopped veal and veal with vegetables and cereal are available in baby and junior foods.

Purchasing Guide—The color of lean veal meat varies with the age of the animal, becoming redder with increasing age. Young, milk-fed veal will have grayish-pink lean. The texture should be fine and velvety. Veal has very little exterior fat and what it has should be firm and creamy white. It has no marbling.

Storage—Remove from market paper or loosen wrapper; store unwrapped or loosely wrapped in coldest part of refrigerator.

☐ Ground veal, stew meat, and variety meats, refrigerator shelf, raw: 1 to 2 days
☐ Chops, steaks, roasts, and cutlets, refrigerator shelf, raw: 2 to 3 days
☐ Veal and gravy, refrigerator shelf, cooked and covered: 4 to 5 days
☐ All types, refrigerator frozen-food compartment, raw, prepared for freezing: 1 to 2 weeks
☐ All types except ground, freezer, raw, prepared for freezing: 6 to 7 months
☐ Ground veal, freezer, raw, prepared for freezing: 2 to 3 months
☐ Veal and gravy, freezer, cooked, prepared for freezing: 2 to 3 months

Veal, once thawed, should not be refrozen.

Nutritive Food Values—An excellent source of protein, iron, and niacin; a fair source of riboflavin.

☐ Arm steak, 3½ ounces, cooked = 298 calories
☐ Blade steak, 3½ ounces, cooked = 276 calories
☐ Breast, 3½ ounces, stewed with gravy = 346 calories
☐ Cutlet, 3½ ounces, cooked = 277 calories
☐ Loin chop, 3½ ounces, cooked = 421 calories
☐ Rib chop, 3½ ounces, cooked = 318 calories
☐ Rump chop, 3½ ounces, cooked = 232 calories
☐ Rump, 3½ ounces, roasted = 174 calories
☐ Sirloin, 3½ ounces, roasted = 175 calories

Basic Preparation—The cuts of veal generally used for roasting come from the shoulder, rib, loin, or leg sections. The cuts used for stuffing and braising are the breast, birds, and chops. The neck, flank, and shanks are used for cooking in liquid. See Retail Cuts of Veal—Where They Come From, page 1887. Since veal is a very lean meat, broiling, except for kidneys and sweetbreads, is not recommended.

☐ **To Roast**—Wipe meat with a damp cloth and put on a rack in shallow roasting pan. Sprinkle with salt and pepper. If desired, rub with a cut garlic clove. Or sprinkle with herbs such as marjoram, thyme, or crumbled bay leaf. If roast has little fat covering, lay several strips of fat bacon or salt pork on top. Do not cover or add water. Insert a meat thermometer into center of thickest part of meat. Roast in preheated slow oven (300°F. to 325°F.) until meat thermometer registers 170°F. See Timetable for Roasting, below, for length of time required. Plan to have roast done 15 to 20 minutes before serving to allow for making gravy.

☐ **To Make Gravy**—For each cup of gravy desired, use 2 tablespoons drippings, 2 tablespoons all-purpose flour, and 1 cup liquid. Lift roast from pan and pour off all fat except the amount needed. Leave any brown bits in the pan. Blend in flour completely. Put pan over moderately low heat and cook and stir until mixture bubbles and begins to brown. Remove from heat and gradually stir in water or other liquid; combine thoroughly. Return pan to heat. Continue cooking and stirring over low heat until gravy thickens and is cooked, for 3 to 5 minutes. Season, and strain, if desired. **Note:** If pan drippings are not brown, a liquid gravy coloring may be added to attain proper color.

☐ **To Panfry Chops, Patties, and Steak**—Brown meat on both sides in a small amount of fat in heavy skillet. Enough fat should be used to cover the surface of the skillet. After meat is browned on both sides, season to taste with salt and pepper. Continue cooking over medium

TIMETABLE FOR ROASTING VEAL

CUT	APPROX. WEIGHT (POUNDS)	OVEN TEMPERATURE	INTERIOR TEMPERATURE WHEN REMOVED FROM OVEN	APPROX. COOKING TIME (MINUTES PER POUND)
Leg	5 to 8	300 to 325°F.	170°F.	20 to 35
Loin	4 to 6	300 to 325°F.	170°F.	30 to 35
Rib (rack)	3 to 5	300 to 325°F.	170°F.	35 to 40
Rolled Boned Shoulder	4 to 6	300 to 325°F.	170°F.	40 to 45

heat, turning occasionally, until meat is done. Do not cover during cooking.

☐ **To Braise**—Meat is browned slowly, seasoned, and a little liquid such as water, broth, or vegetable juice is added; the heat is lowered to the point where the meat barely simmers, the pan is covered tightly, and cooking continues until meat is completely tender. The meat cooks by steam. For cooking time, see Timetable for Braising Veal, below.

☐ **To Cook in Liquid**—The procedure is almost exactly as above, but a larger quantity of liquid is added, usually enough to cover the meat. Recipes, however, are generally required because of the differences in flavors, other foods to be added, the size, shape, and thickness of the meat, and a few changes in procedure, such as flouring the meat. The cut of meat is also usually specified, although this may be interchangeable within a group according to size and taste.

☐ **To Prepare Brains**—Veal brains weigh about ½ pound. Soak in cold salted water for 15 minutes. Wash in cold running water. Drain, cool, and remove outer membrane. Simmer for 10 minutes in boiling salted water. Drain, cut into slices, and dredge with seasoned flour. Or dip in fine dry bread crumbs seasoned with salt and pepper. Sauté in butter or margarine until lightly browned, sprinkle with parsley, and serve with lemon wedges.

☐ **To Prepare Hearts**—Veal hearts weigh about ¾ pound. They are tender and delicate in flavor and are usually cooked by moist heat, as in braising. To braise hearts, wash well under cold running water. Remove veins and arteries. Put in a bowl and cover with cold water, add 2 tablespoons vinegar, and let stand overnight in the refrigerator. Then drain and wipe dry. Brown on all sides in hot butter or margarine. Sprinkle with all-purpose flour and brown slightly. Add 2 cups beef bouillon. Bring to boil, cover, and simmer for 2½ to 3 hours, or until tender. Serve sliced, with the pan liquid.

☐ **To Prepare Kidneys**—Veal kidneys weigh 8 to 12 ounces each and are so tender that they need very little cooking. They are usually broiled or panfried. To broil kidneys, remove the capsule and white core, rinse well, and cut crosswise into ½-inch slices. Saturate with melted butter and season with salt and pepper. Broil 3 inches from heat for about 5 minutes on each side. To panfry kidneys, prepare and slice as above. Season with salt and pepper and brown in hot butter for about 2 or 3 minutes on each side.

☐ **To Prepare Liver**—Veal liver weighs 2 to 3 pounds and comes from milk-fed animals. It is mild in flavor, light in color, and tender. Calf's liver is also mild in flavor and tender but is slightly darker in color. Liver is often panfried. To panfry, try to get slices that are of the same thickness, about ¼ inch. Remove capsule and thin outer membrane to prevent curling. Dredge with all-purpose flour, if desired, and panfry in hot butter for 1 to 3 minutes on each side.

☐ **To Prepare Tongue**—Veal tongue weighs ½ to 2 pounds. It is cooked in liquid. To cook tongue, put in kettle. Add ½ teaspoon salt per pound of tongue and water to cover. Add a few peppercorns, 1 large onion stuck with 2 or 3 whole cloves, 1 bay leaf, 1 sliced carrot, 1 celery stalk, and a few parsley sprigs. Bring to boil, cover, and simmer for 2 to 3 hours, or until tender. Cool in the liquid, pull off skin, and cut off roots. Serve sliced with mustard or horseradish.

☐ **To Prepare Sweetbreads**—Veal sweetbreads are white and tender. A pair weighs about 1 pound. They should be precooked before using them in recipes. Put in saucepan and cover with boiling water. Season with salt. Simmer, covered, for 25 minutes. Drain. Hold under cold running water and slip off membrane with fingers. With knife, cut out dark veins and thick connective tissue. Split very thick sweetbreads into halves lengthwise. Use at once or refrigerate.

TIMETABLE FOR BRAISING VEAL

CUT	AVERAGE WEIGHT OR THICKNESS	APPROX. TOTAL COOKING TIME
Breast, stuffed	3 to 4 pounds	1½ to 2½ hours
Breast, rolled	2 to 3 pounds	1½ to 2½ hours
Veal birds	½ x 2 x 4 inches	45 to 60 minutes
Chops (all except shoulder)	½ to ¾ inch	45 to 60 minutes
Steaks or cutlets	½ to ¾ inch	45 to 60 minutes
Shoulder chops	½ to ¾ inch	45 to 60 minutes
Shoulder cubes	1 to 2 inches	45 to 60 minutes

RETAIL CUTS OF VEAL—WHERE THEY COME FROM

TENDER

1. Shoulder Section
   - Arm roast
   - Blade roast
   - Arm steak
   - Blade steak
   - Rolled shoulder
2. Rib Section
   - Rib roast
   - Crown roast
   - Rib chops
   - Frenched rib chops
3. Loin Section
   - Loin roast
   - Rolled stuffed loin
   - Loin chops
   - Kidney chops
   - Sirloin roast
   - Sirloin steak
   - Rolled double sirloin
   - Cube steak
4. Leg Section
   - Standing rump
   - Shank half of leg
   - Rolled leg
   - Center leg
   - Boneless cutlets
   - Round steak
   - Escallops
   - Rolled cutlets (birds)
   - Heel of the round
5. Breast Section
   - Breast
   - Stuffed breast
   - Stuffed chops

LESS TENDER

- Neck slices
- Riblets
- Fore shanks
- Brisket pieces (front of breast section)
- Brisket rolls

GROUND VEAL (may come from any section, but generally from neck, breast, shanks, and flank)

- Ground veal
- Patties
- Mock chicken legs (ground veal on skewers)

CUBE STEAKS

- Cube steaks
- Rolled cube steaks (birds)

DICED VEAL

- City chicken (diced veal on skewers)
- Veal for stew (generally from forequarter cuts)

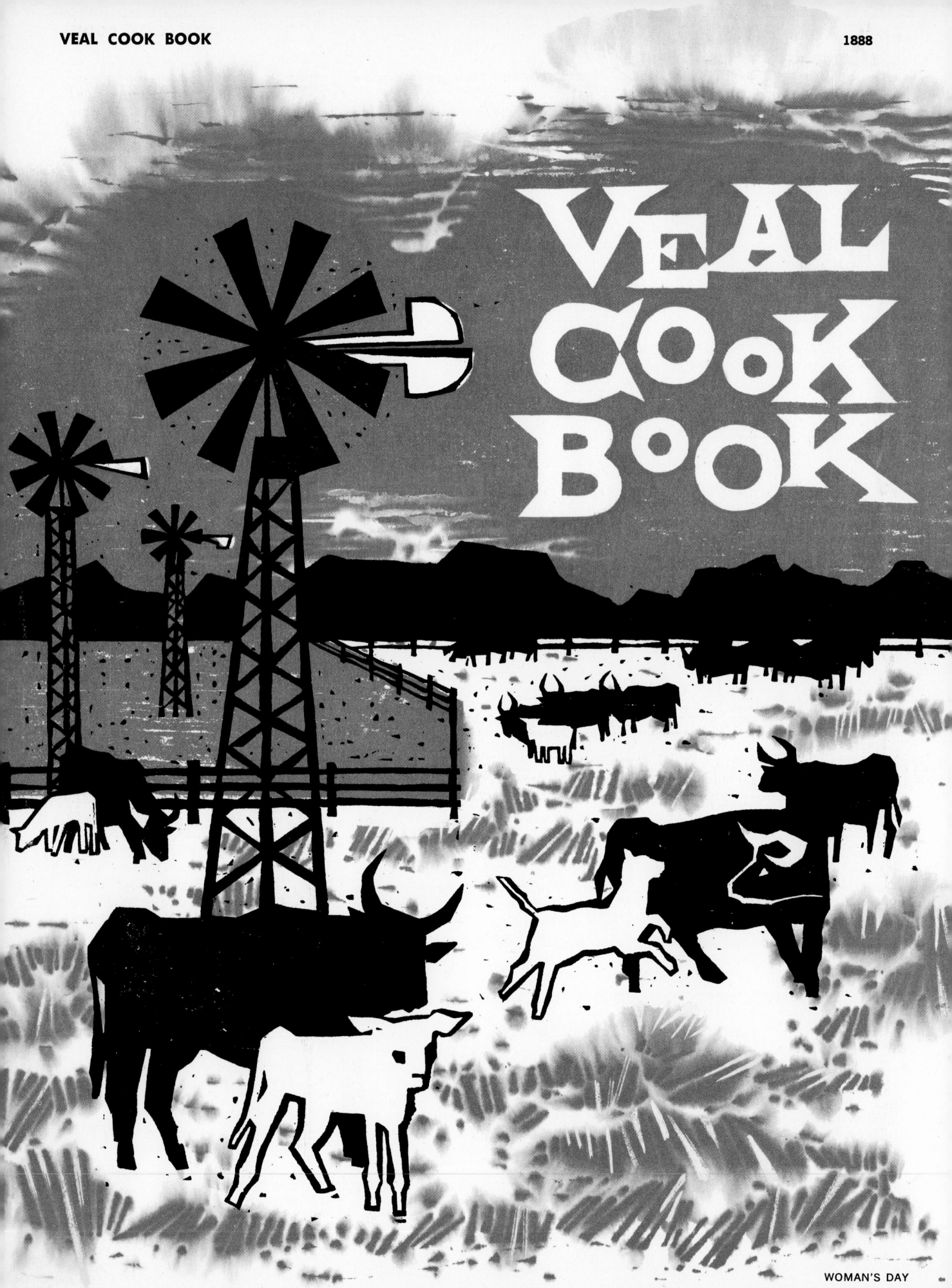
VEAL
COOK
BOOK

LEG AND SHOULDER OF VEAL IN LARGE PIECES

ROAST LEG OF VEAL

3 pounds boneless leg of veal
¼ pound lean salt pork
3 to 4 slices of prosciutto or cooked ham
3 garlic cloves, cut into small pieces
1 teaspoon each of salt and pepper
½ teaspoon each of ground ginger and nutmeg
Crumbled dried basil
Olive or corn oil
½ cup each of tomato juice and sherry or Madeira

Buy a leg of veal and have the butcher bone, roll, and tie it. Have the butcher lard the meat with strips of the pork and small rolls of the ham. If you own a larding needle, you can do it yourself. Jab the meat in several places with a sharp knife and insert the pieces of garlic. Combine salt, pepper, ginger, and nutmeg and rub this mixture on the leg. Arrange it in a baking dish and sprinkle with a little dried basil and plenty of olive oil. Mix tomato juice with sherry and add to the pan. Insert a meat thermometer in the flesh and roast in preheated moderate oven (350°F.) for 30 minutes. Baste with the pan juices and continue roasting for another 30 minutes. Baste again, adding more wine and tomato juice if needed. Lower heat to slow (300°F.) and continue cooking for another 30 minutes, or until the thermometer registers an internal temperature of 165°F. Serve with roasted potatoes, a good green salad, and hot French bread. Use the pan juices as a sauce. Makes 6 servings.

BRAISED LEG OF VEAL

½ cup plus 2 tablespoons butter
1 garlic clove, minced
1 teaspoon salt
¼ teaspoon ground rosemary
Pinch of thyme
Pepper to taste
1 small leg of veal, boned and tied
2 cups thinly sliced onions
2 celery stalks, trimmed and cut into 2-inch lengths
1 carrot, scraped and cut into 1-inch lengths
1 bay leaf
Chicken bouillon or water
1 tablespoon cornstarch
¼ cup dry sherry

Cream 2 tablespoons butter with garlic, salt, rosemary, thyme, and pepper. Rub this over the meat. Put remaining butter, onions, celery, carrot, and bay leaf in heavy casserole or Dutch oven. Put meat on the bed of vegetables and cover. Bake in preheated moderate oven (375°F.) for about 2 hours, or until veal is very tender. Turn the meat several times as it cooks and, if necessary, add a little bouillon to keep it from becoming dry. Remove meat and strain broth. Measure it and add enough bouillon to make 2 cups. Boil the liquid rapidly. Blend cornstarch with wine and stir it into the gravy. Cook, stirring constantly, until smooth. Serve the meat with the sauce. Makes about 8 servings.

VITELLO TONNATO
(Veal with Tuna)

3½ pounds veal cut from the leg
Celery (about 8 stalks)
Olive oil (1⅓ cups)
3 carrots
10 anchovy fillets
½ sour pickle
2 cans (7 ounces each) tuna fish
1 cup dry white wine
2 garlic cloves
Salt, pepper, and ground thyme to taste
2 egg yolks
1½ cups uncooked rice
6 green onions, sliced
1 red onion, chopped
½ green pepper, chopped
12 each ripe and green olives, chopped
¼ cup minced parsley
Tarragon vinegar

Simmer veal, 4 celery stalks, ½ cup olive oil, 1 carrot, next 5 ingredients, and seasonings for about 3 hours. When tender, cool in pot. Purée ingredients except meat in an electric blender or force through a food mill. Beat egg yolks and stir in ½ cup oil, a few drops at a time. When thickened, beat in puréed mixture. Cook, and cool rice. Add 2 chopped carrots, 1 cup diced celery, green and red onion, green pepper, olives, parsley, remaining oil, vinegar, and salt and pepper to taste. Add a little purée. Serve veal sliced very thin with the purée as a sauce and with the rice salad. Garnish with artichokes and pimientos, if desired. Makes 8 servings.

JELLIED VEAL SLICES

4 to 5 pounds veal shoulder
2 garlic cloves
3 to 4 tablespoons butter
1 teaspoon each of salt and pepper
1 cup white wine
1½ cups bouillon or water
Bones from the meat
1 pound veal neck
1 teaspoon chopped fresh tarragon
1 onion, stuck with 2 cloves
½ bay leaf

Have the shoulder boned, rolled, and tied. Make small incisions in the meat with a sharp knife and insert slivers of garlic. Melt the butter in a deep Dutch oven or a heavy kettle and brown meat on all sides. Sprinkle with salt and pepper. Add white wine and bouillon. Add bones, veal neck, tarragon, onion, and bay leaf; cover with a tight lid. Bring to boil, remove to preheated slow oven (325°F.), and bake for 2½ hours, or until the meat is fork-tender. Cool the meat. Remove strings, cut into serving slices, and arrange on a deep platter. Strain the broth through a linen towel or several thicknesses of cheesecloth and cool very quickly over ice. Remove every trace of fat. Cook down by one third and spoon over veal slices. Chill. Serve with a garniture of chopped parsley, sliced stuffed olives, and hard-cooked eggs, and pass a tarragon-flavored mayonnaise or anchovy vinaigrette sauce. Makes 8 servings.

ARROSTO DI VITELLO
(Veal Roast)

3- pound boneless veal roast
Salt and pepper
½ cup butter or margarine
½ cup minced onion
½ cup white wine
1 tablespoon all-purpose flour
1 cup sliced fresh mushrooms
1 tablespoon crumbled rosemary leaves

Season meat with salt and pepper to taste. In a skillet, sear meat on both sides in butter until golden-brown. Remove from skillet. Brown onion; add wine and flour and stir well; add mushrooms and rosemary. Put meat on a rack in a roasting pan. Pour contents of skillet over meat. Roast in preheated moderate oven (350°F.) for 1¾ hours. Serve sauce with mashed potatoes or polenta. Makes 6 to 8 servings.

VEAU SAUMONÉ
(Veal with Salmon)

3 to 4 pounds leg of veal
1 cup white wine
3 parsley sprigs
2 fresh dill sprigs or 1 teaspoon dillweed
2 cans (7 ounces each) salmon
1 teaspoon salt
1 teaspoon pepper
2 egg yolks
½ cup cooking oil (about)

Have the butcher bone, roll, and tie veal. Place meat in a deep casserole or baking dish with a tight cover and add white wine, parsley, dill, salmon, salt, and pepper. Cover tightly and bake in preheated moderate oven (350°F.) for 2½ to 3 hours, or until the meat is tender. Let it cool in the juices and then remove it to the refrigerator to chill. Put the salmon and juices through a food mill or fine sieve, or purée them in an electric blender. Beat egg yolks until light and lemon-colored and gradually add oil. Slowly beat in the puréed salmon mixture. Taste for seasoning and add more chopped parsley or dill if necessary. You can do this whole process in an electric blender if you have one. When ready to serve, cut the veal into thin slices and arrange them on a platter. Pour the sauce over and serve with a rice salad. Makes 6 to 8 servings.

Veau Saumoné with Tarragon

Substitute fresh or crumbled dried tarragon for the dill in recipe for *Veau Saumoné*.

VEAL SHOULDER WITH CHEESE SAUCE

3 to 4 pounds boneless shoulder of veal, rolled and tied
Melted butter and white wine
Slices of baked ham
¼ cup butter or margarine
¼ cup all-purpose flour
1½ cups scalded milk
2 egg yolks
¼ cup lukewarm cream
Salt
Grated Swiss cheese
Grated Parmesan cheese
Chopped parsley

Place veal in a roasting pan and insert a meat thermometer. Roast in preheated slow oven (325°F.), basting often with a mixture of melted butter and white wine. When the veal has reached an internal temperature of 160°F. (in about 2 hours), remove it and cut into even slices. Arrange these slices, alternating them with slices of baked ham, in a baking dish. Pour the pan juices over the meat. In a skillet melt butter and blend in flour. Cook for a few minutes and slowly add scalded milk. Cook and stir until smooth and thickened. Continue cooking for a few minutes, stirring constantly. Beat egg yolks lightly and beat in cream. Slowly add this mixture to the sauce, blend it in thoroughly, and heat well but do not let it boil or the sauce will curdle. Season to taste with salt. Sprinkle the meat liberally with grated Swiss cheese, pour the sauce over it, and sprinkle the top with grated Parmesan cheese. Run under the broiler, sprinkle with chopped parsley, and serve from the baking dish. Makes 6 to 8 servings.

SHOULDER OF VEAL WITH RAVIOLI STUFFING

1 veal shoulder (4 to 5 pounds) with pocket for stuffing
Salt and pepper
3 cups finely ground or minced cooked chicken meat
4 cooked chicken livers, finely ground or minced
½ cup each of sliced green onions with tops and chopped fresh parsley
¼ cup grated Parmesan cheese
¼ cup heavy cream
1 teaspoon salt
½ teaspoon each of ground black pepper and crumbled dried tarragon
⅛ teaspoon ground nutmeg
Olive oil
About ¾ cup chicken broth or bouillon
½ cup dry white wine

Sprinkle veal, inside and outside pocket, generously with salt and pepper. To make stuffing, thoroughly mix together the remaining ingredients except olive oil, chicken broth, and ¼ cup of the white wine. Taste stuffing and correct seasoning with salt and pepper. Spoon stuffing lightly into veal pocket; close with small skewers or sew. Tuck under and skewer tight any thin edges of meat to make a compact shape. Then with string tie into a roll. Rub roast surface with olive oil.

Shoulder of Veal with Ravioli Stuffing

NUTMEG

Place on rack in roasting pan. Bake in preheated slow oven (300°F.) for 3 to 3½ hours. Baste frequently with chicken broth. During last 30 minutes, baste with reserved wine. Allow to stand for 30 minutes before carving. Makes 10 10 servings.

Note: To make a sauce to serve over veal slices, loosen pan drippings. Add dry white wine (about 2 cups). Heat, stirring, until wine is slightly reduced. Garnish with whole cherry tomatoes or, if desired, hollow out tomatoes and fill with whipped cream, seasoned with grated Parmesan cheese and chopped parsley.

VEAL STEAK, CHOPS, CUTLETS, AND ESCALLOPS

MARINATED VEAL STEAK

Have a 1-inch-thick steak cut from the leg; remove the outside skin. In a shallow dish put ½ cup olive oil and 2 crushed garlic cloves and let the steak marinate in this for several hours, turning occasionally. Broil over a low fire for 7 to 9 minutes on each side. No further basting should be necessary, as the meat will have absorbed enough of the oil to moisten it. Serve with fettuccine and a zucchini and tomato casserole.

VEAL CHOPS PAPRIKA

- 6 loin veal chops
- 1 egg, beaten
- 2 tablespoons milk
- ¼ cup cracker meal
- ¼ cup cooking oil
- Salt and pepper
- 1 medium onion, chopped
- ¼ pound mushrooms, sliced
- 1 tablespoon paprika
- 1 bay leaf
- 1 can (10½ ounces) condensed tomato soup
- ⅓ cup water
- ½ cup dairy sour cream

Dip chops into combined egg and milk, then into cracker meal. Brown on both sides in 3 tablespoons oil in skillet. Remove chops to shallow casserole and sprinkle with salt and pepper. Put 1 tablespoon oil in skillet. Add onion and mushrooms; brown lightly and place on chops. Mix remaining ingredients and pour over top. Bake in preheated moderate oven (350°F.) for about 45 minutes. Makes 6 servings.

VEAL CHOPS SOUBISE

- 6 large veal chops
- Milk
- 4 large onions, minced
- Butter or margarine (about ⅔ cup)
- All-purpose flour
- 2 tablespoons cooking oil
- 1 teaspoon salt
- ½ teaspoon pepper
- ½ cup grated Parmesan cheese
- Grated Swiss cheese

Soak veal in enough milk to cover for 1 hour. Sauté onions in ¼ cup butter in a heavy skillet, then steam the onions in the butter over a very low heat. They should be transparent and just tender, not browned. Remove the chops from the milk and dry them on absorbent paper. Dust them lightly with flour and, in a separate pan, brown on both sides in ¼ cup butter heated with the oil. Lower heat and season the chops with salt and pepper. Continue to cook, turning once, until they are tender. Arrange the chops in a flat baking dish. Blend the liquid

Veal Chops Soubise

from the onion with the milk in which the chops were soaked. You will need about 1½ cups liquid. To the pan in which the chops were cooked, add enough butter to make 3 tablespoons fat. Blend in ¼ cup flour and simmer gently for 3 or 4 minutes. Slowly add the milk-onion liquid, stirring constantly. Cook and stir until the sauce is smooth and thickened. Season to taste with salt and pepper and add grated Parmesan cheese. Continue cooking until the cheese is thoroughly blended into the sauce. Spread each chop with some of the drained steamed onion. Pour the sauce over all and sprinkle liberally with grated Swiss cheese. Run under the broiler or heat in preheated hot oven (475°F.) until the cheese melts and browns lightly. Serve with duchesse potatoes, green peas, and seeded breadsticks. Makes 6 servings.

BREADED VEAL CUTLET
(Wiener Schnitzel)

This is the classic veal dish of Vienna. For 4 persons, buy 4 cutlets, or 1½ pounds veal cutlet. Beat 2 eggs lightly; set out a bowl of all-purpose flour seasoned with salt and pepper and another bowl of fine dry bread crumbs. Heat cooking oil and butter mixed in a large skillet. You will need at least ½ inch of fat in the pan. Dip each cutlet into flour, then into beaten egg, and finally into bread crumbs. Sauté the cutlets in the hot oil and butter until they are well browned on both sides and tender. Arrange the cutlets on a hot platter and on each one place a slice of lemon topped with a rolled anchovy. Surround with mounds of chopped hard-cooked egg and tiny mounds of capers. Sprinkle the whole lightly with chopped parsley.

VEAL CUTLETS, SICILIAN STYLE

3 slices of leg of veal, about ¼ inch thick
½ pound salami, sliced
½ pound mortadella or bologna, sliced
½ pound sliced prosciutto or cooked ham
¼ cup fine dry bread crumbs
5 garlic cloves, minced
2 tablespoons chopped parsley
1 teaspoon crumbled dried basil
5 or 6 hard-cooked eggs
¼ cup olive oil
Salt and pepper to taste
5 or 6 slices of bacon
2 cups tomato sauce

Have the bone removed from the veal slices, but leave each slice in one whole piece. Ask the butcher to pound these large cutlets very thin. On a large sheet of heavy wax paper, arrange the slices side by side the long way, so that they overlap slightly. Pound the overlapping areas thoroughly to press them together. On the veal arrange rows of overlapping slices of salami. Top these with rows of mortadella and finally with prosciutto or cooked ham. Sprinkle the surface with bread crumbs, 3 garlic cloves, the parsley, and basil. Down the center place a row of shelled hard-cooked eggs. Sprinkle with olive oil and salt and pepper. Roll up very carefully in the paper as for a jelly roll, making certain that the eggs stay in place in the center. Remove paper, and tie the rolled meat firmly in several places. Place the roll in a baking dish and stripe the top with bacon slices.

Veal Cutlets, Sicilian Style

Pour tomato sauce over all and add remaining garlic. Bake in preheated moderate oven (350°F.) for 1 hour, basting from time to time with the tomato sauce. Remove to a hot platter, or serve from the baking dish. Serve with green noodles, good green salad, and hot crisp Italian bread. Makes 8 servings.

Note: This is exceptionally good sliced and served cold the next day.

STUFFED VEAL ROLLS

6 pieces of veal cutlet (about 1¼ pounds)
Salt and white pepper to taste
¾ cup fine dry bread crumbs
Few parsley sprigs, chopped
Grated rind of 1 lemon
¼ teaspoon ground thyme
¼ teaspoon crumbled dried basil
5 tablespoons butter or margarine
3 tablespoons milk
1 tablespoon all-purpose flour
1 teaspoon seasoned salt
1 cup chicken bouillon
1 tablespoon fresh lemon juice

Season veal with salt and pepper. Mix next 5 ingredients, 2 tablespoons melted butter, milk, and salt and pepper to taste. Spread on veal pieces and roll up. Secure with toothpicks or string. Brown on all sides in remaining butter. Remove meat rolls to shallow 1½-quart casserole. Blend flour and seasoned salt into butter remaining in pan. Add bouillon, lemon juice, and pepper to taste. Bring to boil, stirring; pour over meat rolls. Cover and bake in preheated moderate oven (350° F.) for about 45 minutes. Makes 6 servings.

VEAL ESCALLOPS
(Scallopine, Escalopes, Scallops, or Collops)

Veal escallops are small slices of veal cut very thin and then flattened even more with a meat pounder. They can be cut from the tenderloin, the sirloin, or the leg; the best come from the tenderloin. Be sure they are paper-thin. If your butcher doesn't pound them enough, do it yourself. Place each escallop between 2 pieces of wax paper, and pound with a meat pounder; or, if you don't have one, use the flat side of a cleaver or any heavy flat object. You might even use the bottom of a heavy skillet.

VEAL ESCALLOPS, MARSALA

1½ pounds thin veal escallops
All-purpose flour
3 tablespoons butter or margarine
3 tablespoons cooking oil
Salt and pepper
Ground ginger
Marsala
¼ cup chopped parsley

Dust veal with flour and brown quickly on both sides in butter mixed with oil. Season to taste with salt and pepper and add a dash of ground ginger. Cover with Marsala and continue cooking until the wine is reduced to half. Turn the escallops once during this process. When the wine is reduced and the meat is tender, remove the escallops to a hot platter and add another ¼ cup Marsala to the pan. Bring the juices to a boil, add parsley, and pour over the meat. Serve with rice. Makes 4 servings.

Note: This is the classic *scallopine* dish of southern Italy.

VEAL ESCALLOPS WITH LEMON

Place 8 (1½ pounds) very thin veal escallops on large shallow plate and cover with fresh lemon juice. Place another plate on top and let meat stand for 30 minutes. Remove from lemon juice, dust lightly with flour, and sauté for 3 or 4 minutes on each side. Season; add ¼ cup finely chopped parsley. Toss escallops in parsley. Makes 4 servings.

VEAL AND BACON TERRINE

12 bacon slices
2 pounds veal escallops
¾ cup chopped green onions
¾ cup chopped parsley
Pepper
Crumbled dried thyme
½ bay leaf, crumbled
1½ pounds Canadian bacon, thinly sliced
½ cup dry white wine or dry vermouth

Line a bread pan or mold, both bottom and sides, with slices of bacon. In the bottom put a layer of veal escallops and sprinkle them slightly with green onions and parsley, a little pepper, thyme, and bay leaf. Place a layer of sliced Canadian bacon on this and add another layer of veal scallops. Repeat the seasonings. Continue these layers until all the veal and Canadian bacon are used. Stripe the top with more slices of regular bacon and add wine. Place a lid on the mold or cover with several layers of heavy foil. Bake in preheated slow oven (300°F.) for 2 hours. Remove the mold from the oven and take off the lid. Add several layers of heavy foil and place a plate on top. Put weights on the plate. You can use canned goods, a heavy electric iron, or any weighty object. Let the terrine stand until thoroughly cool. Place in the refrigerator to chill. When ready to serve, turn the meat with the jellied broth that formed around it onto a decorative platter. Serve cut into very thin slices. Makes 8 servings.

Note: Excellent for cocktails or for a picnic or buffet.

ROLLATINE WITH HAM

Rollatine are escallops of veal spread with stuffing and then rolled and tied or fastened with toothpicks.

8 very thin veal escallops
8 thin slices of ham
8 sage leaves
¼ cup butter or margarine
¼ cup cooking oil
All-purpose flour
Salt and pepper to taste
⅓ cup white wine

On each escallop place a piece of ham and pound thoroughly to press the two together. Top the ham with a leaf of sage and roll the escallop up firmly. Tie it with string or fasten with toothpicks. In a large skillet heat butter and oil. Dust the rolls with flour and brown them in the hot butter and oil, rolling them around to be sure they are evenly colored. Season with a little salt (the amount depends on the saltiness of the ham) and pepper, and add white wine. Cover the skillet and cook gently for 8 to 10 minutes, turning the rolls once or twice during the cooking. In the center of a hot platter, place a mound of cooked noodles dressed with butter and cheese, and arrange the rolls around the noodles. Makes 4 servings.

BREAST OF VEAL

BREAST OF VEAL WITH SAUSAGE STUFFING

1 breast of veal, about 3 pounds
1½ pounds sausage meat
3 cups soft bread crumbs
½ cup sliced green onions
¼ cup chopped parsley
6 anchovy fillets, chopped
1 egg, slightly beaten
1 teaspoon salt
½ teaspoon pepper
1 teaspoon crumbled dried thyme
4 large onions, sliced
4 carrots, scraped and cut into strips
4 or 5 parsley sprigs, chopped
Butter (about ⅓ cup)
1 cup chicken bouillon or white wine

Have the butcher cut a pocket in veal breast. Combine the sausage with bread crumbs, green onions, parsley, anchovy fillets, egg, salt, pepper, and thyme. Stuff the pocket of the veal breast with this mixture and sew it up or fasten it with skewers. Mix onions, carrots, and parsley together and spread them on the bottom of a baking pan. Dot the bed of vegetables with butter and place the veal on top. Add bouillon and sprinkle the meat with salt and pepper. If you use a seasoned bouillon for liquid, you may not need additional seasoning. Rub the veal breast with butter and roast in preheated hot oven (450°F.) for 30 minutes, basting from time to time. After 30 minutes, or as soon as the veal begins to brown nicely, cover the pan and lower the heat to slow (325°F.). Continue roasting for 1¾ to 2 hours. About 15 minutes before the meat is done, remove the cover to finish browning the top. Makes 6 servings.

Note: To serve cold, slice, and serve with a well-seasoned mayonnaise and a green salad.

SIMMERED BREAST OF VEAL

3- pound breast of veal

½ pound lean bacon
1 tablespoon salt
Water
4 onions, peeled
6 carrots, scraped
1 celery stalk
2 or 3 parsley sprigs
1 pound garlic sausage or Kielbasa
3 turnips, peeled and halved
6 medium potatoes, peeled
1 small head green cabbage, quartered
About 2 cups (one 1-pound can) tiny French-style peas, drained

Place veal and bacon in a large kettle and add salt and water to cover. Place a lid on the kettle and bring to a boil. Lower the heat and simmer gently for 1¼ hours. Add onions, carrots, celery, and parsley; continue cooking for 30 minutes. Add sausage, turnips, potatoes, and cabbage. Cook for a final 15 minutes, adding peas during the last few minutes. Remove the veal breast to a hot platter and arrange the sausage, bacon, and vegetables around it. Serve with a good hot mustard and a tomato and cucumber salad. Makes 6 servings.

BELGIAN VEAL BLANQUETTE

2 pounds breast of veal, cut for stew
5 tablespoons butter or margarine
2½ cups beef consommé
⅛ teaspoon crumbled dried thyme
1 bay leaf
12 shallots or 12 scallions, bulb end only
⅛ teaspoon ground nutmeg
Salt and pepper
½ pound ground veal
½ pound ground pork
½ cup fresh bread crumbs
¼ cup milk
1 egg
12 fresh mushroom caps
2 tablespoons all-purpose flour
2 egg yolks
Juice of ½ lemon

In a flameproof casserole lightly brown pieces of veal in 3 tablespoons butter. Add 1 cup consommé and herbs, shallots, and nutmeg. Season to taste with salt and pepper. Add water to cover. Bring to a boil. Lower heat, cover, and simmer over low heat until meat is just tender, about 1 hour. In a bowl mix ground veal, pork, bread crumbs, milk, and egg. Roll mixture into tiny meatballs the size of a nut. Sauté balls in remaining butter. Add mushroom caps and sauté until lightly browned. Add to stew. Cover and simmer for 10 minutes. To the pan drippings, add flour. Gradually stir in remaining consommé. Cook, stirring constantly, over low heat until smooth and thickened. Gradually stir hot sauce into egg yolks and lemon juice. Simmer sauce for 5 minutes. Add to stew. Blend well and reheat slightly. Serve with rice or mashed potatoes. Makes 6 servings.

BARBECUED VEAL BREAST AND VEGETABLES

2 to 2½ pounds veal breast
2 tablespoons shortening
4 large potatoes, halved
4 carrots, halved lengthwise
1 onion, chopped
1 garlic clove, minced
1 can (8 ounces) tomato sauce
¼ cup vinegar
1 tablespoon sugar
1½ teaspoons salt
⅛ teaspoon pepper
Dash of cayenne
1 teaspoon Worcestershire
1 teaspoon powdered mustard

Cut meat into serving pieces. In Dutch oven or top-stove casserole, brown meat slowly on all sides in shortening. Remove from heat and add potatoes and carrots. Mix remaining ingredients and pour over meat and vegetables. Bake, covered, in preheated moderate oven (350°F.) for 2 hours, or until meat and vegetables are tender. Makes 4 servings.

VEAL BREAST IN MUSHROOM SAUCE

2 pounds veal breast
2 tablespoons shortening
1 can (10½ ounces) cream-of-mushroom soup
¼ soup-can water

Brown veal in shortening. Add soup and water. Simmer, covered, for about 2 hours, or until tender. Makes 4 servings.

VEAL SHANKS, NECK, AND SHIN

VEAL WITH BULGUR AND DILL

¼ cup all-purpose flour
2 teaspoons salt
Few grindings of pepper
3 pounds veal-neck slices
2 tablespoons shortening
1 cup chopped onions
2 cups undiluted canned consommé
½ cup white wine
2 garlic cloves, crushed
1 cup bulgur (cracked wheat)
Salted water
1 package (9 ounces) frozen artichoke hearts
1 cup dairy sour cream
1 tablespoon dillweed
Salt and pepper

Combine flour, salt, and pepper; rub into veal slices. Brown veal in shortening slowly, using a large flameproof casserole or a skillet. Add onions, consommé, wine, and garlic. Cover and simmer for 1½ hours, or until tender. In the meantime cook bulgur in 2 cups salted water for 15 minutes; also cook artichoke hearts. Strain meat juice and vegetable juices, and purée in blender. Add sour cream, dill, and salt and pepper to taste. Combine half of this sauce with the bulgur and mound in the center of a platter or chop plate. Surround with veal slices and garnish with artichoke hearts. Serve remaining sauce separately. Makes 6 servings.

Note: If you wish, sprinkle with minced parsley or dill, or paprika for more color.

VEAL IN ASPIC

2 pounds carrots
2 pounds onions
2 pounds shank of veal
1 celery stalk
1 teaspoon Worcestershire
¼ teaspoon hot pepper sauce
2 bay leaves
Salt and pepper to taste
2½ quarts water
2 envelopes unflavored gelatin
Watercress
Radish roses

Scrape carrots and peel onions; put in kettle with meat, celery, and seasonings. Add water and bring to a boil over a gentle heat. Cook very slowly until the meat falls from the bones. The broth should then be strained through a dampened linen napkin into a clean pan, placed back over heat, and reduced to half its quantity. Remove all bones from the meat and cut meat into small even dice. When the broth has reduced sufficiently, remove from heat, stir in gelatin softened in ½ cup cold water, and pour over the diced meat. Pour all into a 2-quart mold and chill until set; stir occasionally while still liquid to prevent meat from sinking to the bottom of the mold. Unmold on platter and garnish with watercress and radish roses. Makes 6 to 8 servings.

JELLIED HERB VEAL LOAF

4 pounds neck of veal
2 pounds shin of veal
1 veal knuckle
1 onion stuck with 2 whole cloves
1 bay leaf
1 teaspoon crumbled dried thyme
2 or 3 carrots
Celery stalks and leaves
Water
1½ tablespoons salt
Pepper
Sliced hard-cooked eggs
Worcestershire

Place meat and bones in a deep kettle and add onion stuck with cloves, bay leaf, thyme, carrots, and some celery. Cover with cold water and bring to a boil. Boil rapidly for 5 minutes and then skim off any scum that has formed. Add salt and a few grinds of pepper. Lower the heat, cover the kettle, and simmer for 2½ hours, or until the meat is very tender. Remove the meat and set the broth aside to cool. When the meat is cool enough to handle, separate all the lean and discard bone, fat, and gristle. Chop the meat rather coarsely. Oil a mold and place a layer of the chopped veal in the bottom. Add a layer of sliced hard-cooked eggs and more chopped meat. Continue until the meat is used. Skim the fat from the broth. Strain it and return it to the heat to cook down. Season with Worcestershire. Cool the reduced broth and pour over the meat in the mold. The broth should just barely reach the top of the chopped veal. Place in the refrigerator to chill and gel. Serve sliced, with a vegetable salad and thin bread-and-butter sandwiches, or thin slices of bread spread with chive and parsley butter. Makes 12 servings.

INDIVIDUAL JELLIED HERB VEAL LOAVES
Arrange the layers of meat and egg in recipe for Jellied Herb Veal Loaf in individual molds. Top with broth, chill, and gel. Turn out onto individual salad plates garnished with lettuce. Add a dollop of herbed mayonnaise (mayonnaise blended with chopped chives and parsley) and serve as a main course for a summer luncheon. Makes 10 to 12 servings.

SMALL PIECES OF VEAL

VEAL STEW

1 pound dried marrow beans
6 cups water
½ pound salt pork, thinly sliced
2 pounds boneless veal stew meat
1 large onion, sliced
2 garlic cloves, minced
1 tablespoon paprika
¼ teaspoon crumbled dried thyme
½ teaspoon crumbled dried marjoram
¼ teaspoon pepper
4 large carrots, sliced
1 green pepper, cut into eighths
4 outer celery stalks, sliced
Chopped parsley

Wash beans, add the water, and bring to boil; boil for 2 minutes. Let stand for 1 hour. Fry salt pork for about 5 minutes; add veal, onion, and garlic; brown lightly. Stir in paprika, thyme, marjoram, and pepper. Add to beans and water. Simmer, covered, for 1½ hours, or until beans and meat are almost tender, adding more water if necessary. Add carrots, green pepper, and celery; simmer for 25 minutes longer, or until vegetables are tender. Add salt if desired. Sprinkle chopped parsley over stew. Makes 8 servings.
Note: Stew can be made a day or two before. Cool, refrigerate, and reheat at serving time. (Or serve 4 for 2 meals.) Green pepper can be omitted or pimiento can be substituted for it.

VEAL WITH DANDELION GREENS

1 pound boneless veal, diced
2 tablespoons butter or margarine
2 onions, sliced
3 small carrots, quartered
½ cup diced celery
2 large mushrooms, quartered
½ cup water
1 pound dandelion greens, cooked
Pinch of basil or ½ bay leaf, crushed
Salt and pepper

Brown veal in butter in heavy kettle; add vegetables and water. Cover and simmer until tender, about 1 hour. Add greens; season with basil and salt and pepper to taste and heat for 5 minutes. Makes 4 servings.

HAWAIIAN VEAL STEW

1½ pounds stewing veal, cut into 2-inch pieces
3 tablespoons butter or margarine
2½ cups (one 1-pound, 4-ounce can) pineapple cubes, drained
1½ teaspoons seasoned salt
1 tablespoon paprika
1 bay leaf
¼ teaspoon pepper
1 onion, sliced
2 tablespoons all-purpose flour

Brown veal on all sides in butter in kettle. Add next 6 ingredients and 4 cups water. Bring to boil, cover, and simmer for 1½ hours. Thicken with flour blended with ¼ cup water. Serve plain, on toast, or on hot cooked rice. Makes 6 servings.

VEAL AND PEPPERS, ITALIAN STYLE

1½ pounds boneless lean veal
3 tablespoons olive oil
2 green peppers, cut into eighths
1 can (3 ounces) sliced mushrooms
Pinch of crushed red pepper
2 cans (8 ounces each) tomato sauce
Salt and pepper

Cut meat into bite-size pieces. Heat oil in skillet and brown meat on all sides. Add green pepper, cover, reduce heat, and cook for 10 minutes, stirring occasionally. Add mushrooms and liquid, red pepper, and sauce. Simmer, covered, for 30 minutes longer, or until tender. Season to taste. Makes 4 servings.

VEAL MEXICAN

2½ pounds shoulder of veal, cubed
Butter or lard
3 garlic cloves
1 tablespoon chili powder
1 teaspoon crumbled dried oregano
1 teaspoon salt
Dash of hot pepper sauce
2 cups tomato sauce
1 can (6 ounces) peeled green chilies, chopped

Brown veal cubes on all sides in butter (the Mexicans use lard). When the cubes are all nicely browned, add garlic, chili powder, oregano, salt, hot pepper sauce, and tomato sauce. Cover and simmer very gently for about 2 hours, or until veal cubes are thoroughly tender. Add chilies to veal and heat through. Taste for seasoning; you may want to add more chili powder and hot pepper sauce. Serve on hot rice with refried beans or black beans. Makes 6 servings.

VEAL WITH GARLIC SAUCE

This is a French version of Veal Mexican. Prepare the dish as above, but omit the chili powder and chilies and add 4 garlic cloves. Makes 6 servings.

GROUND VEAL AND LEFTOVER COOKED VEAL

OLD-FASHIONED VEAL LOAF

2 pounds veal, ground
1 pound pork, ground
1 cup fine dry bread crumbs
2 garlic cloves, chopped
¼ cup grated onion
½ cup chopped parsley
2 eggs, slightly beaten
1 teaspoon crumbled dried thyme
1 teaspoon salt
1 teaspoon pepper
Bacon slices

Place the ground meats in a deep bowl and mix thoroughly with bread crumbs, garlic, onion, parsley, eggs, thyme, salt, and pepper. Form the meat mixture into a firm loaf shape. Place a layer of bacon slices on the bottom of a shallow roasting pan or baking dish and arrange the loaf on top. Stripe the top of the meat with more bacon slices. Roast in preheated moderate oven (350°F.) for 1½ hours, basting occasionally with the pan juices. Serve hot with creamy mashed potatoes and green beans. Makes 8 servings.

VEAL LOAF WITH ITALIAN SAUSAGES

This is an elegant buffet dish to be served hot or cold. Make veal-and-pork mixture in recipe above. Buy 6 to 8 Italian sausages and boil them for 10 minutes. Cool and remove the skins. Arrange half of the veal-pork mixture on bacon slices in the bottom of a baking dish. Put the skinned sausages on the meat and add the rest of the mixture. Press down firmly. Top with more bacon and bake as above. Makes 8 to 10 servings.

WHITE DOME

½ cup sliced mushrooms
Lemon juice
Butter or margarine
2 cups ground cooked veal
¾ cup condensed cream-of-chicken soup
2 cups mashed potatoes
Grated cheese
¼ cup fine dry bread crumbs

Sprinkle mushrooms with lemon juice. Sauté mushrooms in butter. Add meat and soup to mushrooms. Heat until thick. Grease baking dish; fill with heated pudding mixture, piling it up in the shape of a pyramid. Cover with a thick layer of mashed potatoes which have been mixed with 2 tablespoons grated cheese. Pour over a little melted butter; top with ¼ cup bread crumbs mixed with 2 tablespoons grated cheese. Bake in preheated hot oven (425°F.) for 20 minutes. Makes 6 servings.

AVOCADOS STUFFED WITH VEAL

2 large ripe avocados
1 teaspoon onion juice
Salt and pepper to taste
2 cups cold cooked veal
Dash of hot pepper sauce
1 tablespoon melted butter or gravy
½ teaspoon poultry seasoning

Cut avocados lengthwise into halves and remove seeds. Mix other ingredients and pile into the halved shells. Bake in preheated hot oven (400°F.) for 20 minutes. Makes 4 servings.

VEAL SALAD

2 cups diced cooked veal
¼ cup chopped onion
¼ cup chopped celery
½ cup toasted blanched almonds
1 cup mayonnaise
1 teaspoon crumbled dried tarragon
1 tablespoon fresh lemon juice
Salad greens

Mix veal with onion, celery, and almonds. Blend mayonnaise with tarragon and lemon juice. Add enough of the mayonnaise to the veal mixture to bind it. Heap on greens; garnish with the rest of the mayonnaise, and with tomatoes, ripe olives, and toasted almonds, if desired. Serve with herbed French bread. Makes 4 servings.

VEAL AND CHEESE STEAKS

Juice of 1 lemon
Salt and pepper
½ cup bouillon or white wine
4 slices of cooked veal
1 egg, beaten
½ cup fine dry bread crumbs
4 slices of Swiss cheese
Slivered blanched almonds
Paprika

Mix lemon juice with salt, pepper, and bouillon. Pour mixture over veal. Let stand for 1 hour. Drain. Dip veal into egg and then into crumbs. Brown in hot fat on one side only. Cover unbrowned side with cheese, almonds, and paprika. Bake in a shallow pan in preheated hot oven (400°F.) until cheese sizzles, about 10 minutes. Makes 4 servings.

VEAL VARIETY MEATS

VEAL BRAINS IN MUSHROOM SAUCE

1 pound veal brains
1 teaspoon salt
1 tablespoon vinegar
1 can (10½ ounces) cream-of-mushroom soup
¾ cup milk
2 tablespoons grated cheese
2 tablespoons dry bread crumbs
1 tablespoon margarine

Wash brains in cold water; remove membrane. Cover with water, add salt and vinegar, and simmer for 15 minutes. Drain; drop into cold water and drain again. Heat mushroom soup with milk. Add coarsely cut brains. Pour into shallow 1-quart casserole or pie plate. Sprinkle with cheese and crumbs; dot with margarine. Brown in preheated hot oven (400°F.) for 10 minutes. Makes 4 servings.

ROAST VEAL KIDNEYS

Have the butcher leave all the fat on veal kidneys. Put the whole kidneys on the spit, and roast them over the charcoal for about 40 minutes, or until a small incision shows that they are done to your liking. Slice through fat and all, and serve with *Maître d'Hôtel* Butter made by creaming together ½ cup butter, 1 teaspoon minced parsley, 1 tablespoon fresh lemon juice, and a little freshly ground black pepper.

VEAL KIDNEYS IN VERMOUTH

4 veal kidneys
Milk
6 tablespoons butter or margarine
1 medium onion, chopped
¼ cup parsley, chopped
Salt and pepper
Boiled rice
¼ cup dry vermouth
¼ cup beef bouillon

Remove the fat and cut the kidneys into thin slices. Soak in milk for 1 hour. Melt butter in a skillet and sauté onion and parsley gently. Drain sliced kidneys and dry them on absorbent paper. Add them to the pan and cook quickly, turning slices to brown on both sides. Season to taste with salt and pepper and arrange on a bed of rice. To the pan add vermouth and bouillon. Heat and blend with the onion and parsley. Pour over the kidneys and rice. Makes 4 servings.

MOTTRAM KIDNEY IN CREAM

Mince 1 veal kidney into pea-size pieces. Sauté 2 tablespoons chopped onion in 2 tablespoons butter until transparent. Add another tablespoon butter and the kidney, and cook quickly for 2 to 3 minutes. Sprinkle with 1 teaspoon flour, pour in ¼ cup heavy cream, and season with salt and pepper. Cook for a few seconds so that the cream will heat, and serve on toast. This is enough for 4 persons, 6 if each serving is topped with a poached egg.

VEAL LIVER STEAK, BÉARNAISE

You will need about 8 ounces of veal or calf's liver per serving. Ask the butcher to cut it rather thick, 1 to 1½ inches. Broil over charcoal or in a broiler until crusty brown on the outside and still pink and rare in the center. Brush with a mixture of melted butter and oil several times during the broiling. Season to taste. If you are broiling over charcoal, move the coals close to the meat for the last minute to char the outside a bit. Sprinkle with parsley; serve Quick Béarnaise Sauce separately. Good with onion slices baked in beef broth and sprinkled with grated cheese, and fried or sautéed potatoes.

Quick Béarnaise Sauce

1 teaspoon crumbled dried tarragon
2 teaspoons chopped green onion
2 teaspoons chopped parsley
3 tablespoons wine vinegar
1 tablespoon water
3 egg yolks
2 teaspoons fresh lemon juice
½ teaspoon salt
Few grains of cayenne
½ cup butter

In a small pan cook tarragon, green onion, parsley, wine vinegar, and water. Cook gently until almost a glaze. Put egg yolks in an electric blender with lemon juice, salt, and cayenne. Flick the blender on and off rapidly just long enough to blend the eggs. Melt butter and bring just to boiling. With the blender on high, add the butter until sauce is blended and thickened. Add the tarragon mixture and beat until well mixed.

SWEETBREAD AND CUCUMBER SALAD

Prepare 2 or 3 pairs of veal sweetbreads as directed on page 1887. Chill, and cut into ¼-inch slices. Peel 2 medium or 1 large cucumber. Split, remove seeds, and cut into very thin slices. Arrange sliced cucumbers in a bowl and sprinkle with salt. Let stand for 30 minutes. Wash off salt and drain well. Mix cucumbers with 6 thinly sliced green onions and the sliced sweetbreads. Add enough well-seasoned homemade mayonnaise to bind, and heap in a salad bowl. Garnish with more mayonnaise, tomato wedges, sliced hard-cooked eggs, and ripe olives. Makes 6 servings.

VEGETABLE—Although the word can properly be used as an adjective to describe any kind of plant life, as distinguished from animal life, in common usage vegetables are those plants or parts of plants eaten by man. They include the leafy vegetables such as spinach, lettuce, and cabbage; the stem vegetables, such as celery and asparagus; the roots and tubers of which beets, turnips, carrots, and potatoes are examples; flower vegetables such as broccoli and cauliflower; seeds and seed pods, which include beans and peas; edible fungi, such as mushrooms and truffles; and those fruits classed as vegetables because of the way they are cooked and served: tomatoes and squash, for example.

Modern methods of transportation, refrigeration, and storage have made most vegetables available year round. Canned and frozen vegetables are universally available. Some vegetables are available dried; a few are available pickled. Puréed and chopped vegetables are sold as baby and junior foods.

Nutritive Food Values—Vegetables are a source of vitamins and minerals. They are good sources of vitamin A and C. Vegetables supply varying amounts of thiamine, riboflavin, and niacin. The minerals present are calcium, phosphorus, and iron. Vegetables are necessary in maintaining the neutrality of the blood and the regularity of the digestive system. For specific food values see the individual vegetable entries.

VEGETABLE COOKERY

by James A. Beard

A colorful display of fresh vegetables is a magnificent sight to behold. Deep-purple eggplant, plump green peppers, bright tomatoes, slender young scallions, miniature beans and carrots make as beautiful a centerpiece as any bouquet of flowers. But often it is dismaying to encounter them after they have been cooked—overdone, waterlogged, colorless, and tasteless. It is amazing to me that most people mistreat these crisp delicacies.

Indeed, the art of vegetable cookery has been tragically neglected in most of the world's cuisines. The English are noted for overcooking vegetables until they are mushy; most Europeans do little better; we Americans use scant imagination and less variety; Latins tend to ignore them. The French and Italians do some vegetable dishes well, but it is only the Chinese who approach vegetables with true appreciation and artistry.

I recall some of my vegetable-eating experiences with horror. I was once served beans cooked for hours with hog jowl, and spinach drowned in water and cooked with salt pork. Then I have tried to gulp down Brussels sprouts cooked to a gray mass. This was in England, of course.

On the other hand, I have enjoyed beans cooked just until barely tender and still crisp and then sautéed in good sweet butter, a dish so delicious I could have made a meal of it. I have eaten perfect spinach, barely wilted in the skillet with oil and garlic and soy sauce—one of my favorites; and Brussels sprouts steamed in butter until crisply done, each one a buttery nugget of flavor.

Vegetable cookery, then, need not be dull. With our bountiful supply in this country, there is no excuse for not giving vegetables a chance to shine at the table. Using choice tender young vegetables, good butter or oil, fine seasonings, and some care, anyone can turn out tasty dishes. Vegetables need not always be boiled. They can go into the skillet to be braised; they can be cooked in interesting combinations; they can go into delicate soufflés; they can be dressed with a variety of sauces. If you do boil them, and some are most delicious this way, do not drown them in a large pot full of water. Spread them out in skillet and use just enough water to cover them barely. Cook until they are crisply done, not mushy, and drain them well. A watery vegetable is most unappetizing. This method retains the garden-fresh flavor and texture that is the vegetable's most appealing quality.

For example, here is asparagus:

ASPARAGUS

True asparagus lovers can eat a pound per serving; for others, perhaps ½ to ¾ pound will do. Break or cut off the tough stalk ends and peel them up a ways if you wish. Remove scales and wash off sand which may collect under them. Arrange the stalks in a skillet and add just enough salted water to cover. Bring to a boil and cook for 4 to 6 minutes, testing frequently with a fork. The asparagus stalks should be just pierceable and still crisp. Drain thoroughly. Good fresh asparagus really needs nothing but freshly ground pepper and salt. But here are a variety of ways to dress it: melted butter and freshly ground pepper, hollandaise sauce or maltaise sauce, freshly grated Parmesan cheese.

- As a main luncheon dish: for each portion top several stalks of asparagus with a fried egg and spoon 2 tablespoons of melted butter and some freshly grated Parmesan cheese over all. Top with freshly grated black pepper.
- Another luncheon dish: for each portion, top several stalks of buttered asparagus with a thin piece of frizzled ham. Or place the asparagus on top of a slice of ham. Add melted butter and grated cheese.
- Combine 3 tablespoons of Dijon mustard with 1 tablespoon of fresh lemon juice and about 6 tablespoons of softened butter. Beat with a fork until it is a creamy paste. Serve with hot asparagus.
- Serve cold asparagus with a good vinaigrette sauce: 6 tablespoons of olive oil to 2½ tablespoons of wine vinegar, and salt and pepper to taste. Or you may add a tablespoon of Dijon mustard to the vinaigrette and beat it in well.
- Serve cold asparagus with a well-flavored homemade mayonnaise.
- Serve either cold or hot asparagus as follows: for each portion, add a hard-cooked egg to the plate. Pass lemon quarters, olive oil, and mustard. Each person crushes the egg with a fork and blends in olive oil, mustard, and lemon juice to taste, making a rather thick sauce. This is seasoned to taste with salt and pepper and eaten with the asparagus.

CORN

Good fresh corn is another vegetable that is at its best when cooked quickly and served simply. The sooner corn is cooked after picking the sweeter it is.

Put the ears in a skillet with cold water to cover. Omit salt; it tends to toughen the corn. Bring just to a boil and then let the ears stand in the boiling water for 1 minute. Eat at once with coarse salt, freshly ground pepper, and plenty of sweet butter.

- Corn steamed in butter: Just before cooking, cut the kernels from 6 ears of corn. Melt ½ cup butter in a skillet, and when it is just bubbling, add the corn. Cook until the kernels are just heated through, 3 or 4 minutes. Shake the pan well and add salt and freshly ground pepper to taste. Spoon onto hot plates or onto rounds of toast fried crisp in butter or oil.
- Variations: Add 3 tablespoons of finely chopped green pepper and a hint of finely chopped garlic to the pan 3 minutes before you put in the corn. Blend well.
- Add ½ cup of crisp bacon cracklings.
- Add 2 tablespoons of finely chopped pimiento and 2 dashes of hot pepper sauce.
- Cook the corn in ¼ cup butter, season to taste, and just before serving stir in 4 to 6 tablespoons of heavy cream.
- Cook corn in ¼ cup butter and stir in 3 tablespoons of *Duxelles* (see below).

DUXELLES

This is a delicious addition to many vegetable dishes as well as a fine seasoning for sauces and eggs. It will keep in the refrigerator for a fortnight and is also good when frozen.

½ cup butter, approximately
2 pounds mushrooms, chopped very fine (stems and all)
1 garlic clove, finely chopped
2 shallots or 1 small onion, finely chopped
Additional butter, if needed
Salt

Melt the butter in a heavy skillet and add the mushrooms, garlic, and shallots. Cook very slowly, stirring occasionally, until the liquid is cooked out and the mushrooms are fairly black in color. Add more butter if needed and season with salt to taste when the mixture begins to cook down. Store in a jar or crock.

MADAME FRAIZE'S TOMATOES PROVENÇAL

This is another simple but perfect vegetable dish that takes advantage of the fresh ripe flavor. Madame Fraize has a small restaurant in Maillane, France, near Avignon. She treats vegetables with real respect. She not only cooks them beautifully, but even serves a "vegetable course."

Use ripe but firm tomatoes. Split them into halves and sauté, cut side down, in olive oil until the cut side is delicately caramelized in the oil. Season to taste.

VEGETABLES À LA GRECQUE

Any number of vegetables may be cooked in this sauce and served cold. They are thoroughly delicious as a first course, or

Vegetables à la Grecque ■ ***Gratin of Greens***

with cold meats or fish as a main luncheon dish. Or you may serve several vegetables *à la grecque* on a combination hors-d'oeuvre luncheon tray with any or all of the following: stuffed eggs, sliced salami, sliced tomatoes, sardines, anchovies, thinly sliced ham. Such a tray, plus good French bread, makes a fine buffet luncheon for summer.

Most vegetables cooked in this manner may be kept in the refrigerator for several days.

Sauce à la Grecque

1½ cups water
¼ cup olive or peanut oil
Juice of 2 lemons
1 teaspoon salt
2 or 3 garlic cloves
1 bay leaf
1 parsley sprig
1 celery top
1 teaspoon crumbled dried thyme
Fennel sprig or fennel seeds (optional)
½ teaspoon white pepper
Dash of hot pepper sauce

Combine all ingredients and bring to a boil. Boil for 5 minutes. Add the vegetables and simmer until just tender. Do not overcook. Let them cool in the sauce and serve chilled with some sauce spooned over. Or drain and serve with vinaigrette sauce.

Or the vegetables can be removed when they are done, the sauce cooked down until somewhat reduced, then cooled and poured over the vegetables. Top with chopped parsley, chives, and fresh tarragon. Variations on the Sauce: Substitute white wine for half of the water. Use wine vinegar instead of lemon juice. Add 1 to 2 tablespoons tomato paste.

Vegetables to be cooked à la grecque:

12 small artichokes (about 2 inches) or 12 hearts
2 pounds large-stalked asparagus
About 20 scallions
12 to 14 leeks (about 2 inches) (trim and soak in acidulated water)
12 tiny whole eggplants (about 2 inches) or 1 large eggplant, sliced
12 to 16 small whole zucchini (about 2 inches) or 8 larger zucchini, halved
12 to 16 young whole carrots (about 2 inches)
About 1 pound mushrooms, small ones preferred
4 to 6 celery hearts, halved
3 fennel heads, quartered
28 to 30 small white onions

■ **Variation** for Onions *à la Grecque*—Use 1 cup oil and 1 cup water. When the onions are just beginning to be tender, add 1 tablespoon tomato paste, a pinch of ground saffron, and ½ cup raisins. Cook for several minutes, or until the raisins are puffed and the sauce is thick and rich.

Makes approximately 8 servings for a first course.

BRAISED VEGETABLES

There are several ways to braise vegetables. The old French method was to cook them in boiling water for an hour or more and then bake them for another hour. The result is absolutely tasteless.

I prefer to poach vegetables in broth, or water plus bouillon cubes or beef extract, until they are just barely tender, and then finish them off in butter or oil. You may save the broth for sauces and gravies. Or sometimes I use half broth and half white wine for the poaching. This gives added flavor.

Poached vegetables may be drained and then tossed in hot butter or oil and seasonings; or they may be arranged in a flat baking dish, dotted with butter, and covered loosely with a piece of foil or parchment paper to be finished off in a preheated moderate oven (350°F.). This takes 12 to 15 minutes.

When serving braised vegetables, remember most of them are properly knife and fork foods.

Braised Celery

Choose 1 good heart of celery for each person. Trim them neatly and cut off the tops. Tops can be saved for seasoning other dishes. Split the hearts into halves and wash well. Place them in a skillet large enough for all to lie flat. You may need 2 skillets. Barely cover the celery with broth, water, and bouillon cubes, or broth and white wine. Season with salt to taste and add a dash of hot pepper sauce. Bring to a boil and reduce the heat at once to a simmer. Cook the celery, turning once or twice, until it is just tender. The time will vary according to the thickness of the hearts and your taste for tenderness. Drain the broth from the skillet and turn the celery cut side down. For 6 celery hearts, add 4 to 5 tablespoons butter and 2 or 3 twists of the pepper grinder. Heat for 5 minutes over a medium heat. Turn the celery over and heat for another 3 or 4 minutes.

If you wish, you may add a few spoonfuls of the broth during the last minute or two.

To braise in the oven, remove the cooked celery hearts from the broth and place them cut side up in a baking dish. Add a few spoonfuls of broth. Dot heavily with butter and place a piece of foil or parchment very loosely over the top. Heat in a preheated moderate oven (350° F.) for 12 to 15 minutes. Variations: 1. Sprinkle with freshly grated Parmesan cheese just before serving.

2. To serve cold, let the poached celery cool in the broth and serve with a vinaigrette sauce or French dressing. When topped with anchovy fillets and a bit of pimiento, this dish is called Celery Victor.

Braised Fennel

Prepare in the same way given for celery hearts (see above). I find that sometimes, if the fennel heads are very large, it is better to quarter them or cut them into slices. This is an excellent accompaniment for fish or game.

Braised Endive

Choose uniform-size heads of Belgian endive. Follow the recipe for braised celery, but add 1 or 2 thin slices of lemon to the broth.

Braised Lettuces

Tiny heads of limestone (Bibb) lettuce or Boston (butter) lettuce are best for braising. Romaine braises well. Iceberg lettuce is not good. Proceed as for braised celery, but watch the poaching closely for there is a great difference in cooking time, since some lettuces are more tender than others. If you are poaching rather loose-leafed heads, it is wise to tie them together lightly so they will hold their shape. Remove the strings before serving, of course.

Braised Chinese Cabbage

Cut this vegetable into quarters trimmed to fit your skillet and leave the root on. Proceed as for celery.

Braised Leeks

Clean the leeks well and poach as for celery. Reheat in butter and serve.

■ **Variations**—1. Poach leeks until just tender, remove from the broth, and wrap with strips of partially cooked bacon. Place on a rack and bake in preheated slow oven (250°F.) until the bacon is crisp.

2. Chill the cooked leeks in the broth. Drain and arrange in a serving dish. Add a good vinaigrette sauce or French dressing, and top with strips of anchovy if you wish.

BRAISED LEEKS, NICOISE

Another method of braising calls for steaming or simmering the vegetables in butter or oil plus seasonings. This gives a richer dish.

12 uniform-size leeks
⅓ cup olive or peanut oil
2 garlic cloves, finely chopped
2 tomatoes, peeled and cut into sixths
Finely grated rind of 1 lemon, or thinly sliced and chopped rind
1 tablespoon fresh lemon juice
Salt and pepper to taste
½ cup soft black olives, pitted
Chopped parsley

Wash the leeks well and cut into 1- to 1½-inch rounds. Heat the oil in a heavy skillet and add the leeks. Cover and cook for exactly 9 minutes over a medium heat. Add the remaining ingredients except the parsley and cook, uncovered, for another 6 to 8 minutes. Do not let the mixture become mushy. Top with chopped parsley. This is excellent with veal or lamb. Makes about 8 servings.

BRAISED ONION SLICES

2 tablespoons butter or margarine
2 tablespoons olive oil
4 large onions, peeled and cut into 1-inch slices
1 teaspoon salt
¼ cup broth
½ teaspoon pepper
¼ cup whiskey (optional)

Melt the butter in a heavy saucepan. Add olive oil. Add the onions and sear over high heat for 2 minutes. Add salt, broth, and pepper and reduce the heat. Cover and simmer for 10 minutes. Add the whiskey, if desired, and let the sauce cook down slightly. Makes 4 to 6 servings.

■ **Variation**—Add 2 tablespoons of raisins that have been soaked in the whiskey.

CLASSIC RATATOUILLE

Interesting combinations of vegetables and seasonings can make rich, flavorful dishes. These are often cooked in butter or oil in the skillet. This is a classic example.

⅓ cup olive oil
2 large onions, sliced
3 garlic cloves (or more, to taste), chopped
2 small eggplants, cubed
4 small zucchini, sliced
2 green peppers, cut into strips
1 head of fennel, sliced
2⅓ cups (one 1-pound, 3-ounce can) Italian plum tomatoes
1 teaspoon crumbled dried basil
1½ teaspoons salt
½ teaspoon chopped parsley
Pepper to taste

Heat the olive oil in a heavy skillet and add the onions and garlic. Heat and toss until wilted. Add the eggplants, zucchini, peppers, and fennel, and mix well over a brisk heat. Add the tomatoes, seasonings, and parsley; cover, and simmer for about 1 hour, stirring occasionally. Remove the cover and cook down until most of the liquid has evaporated and the mixture is thick. Serve hot or serve cold with additional oil and a little vinegar. Makes 6 servings.

■ **Variations**—1. Add 2 celery hearts cut into thin slices.

2. Thirty minutes before the ratatouille is done, add 1 pound of small whole mushrooms or 1 pound of large mushrooms, sliced.

3. Substitute 1 or 2 sliced cucumbers for the zucchini.

CAPONATA

This is the Italian *ratatouille* and it is almost always served cold. There are many versions but this is the one I have enjoyed most.

1 large or 2 small onions, thinly sliced
1 celery stalk, thinly sliced
½ cup olive or peanut oil
2 medium or 3 small eggplants, unpeeled and cut into strips
1½ cups Italian plum tomatoes
Salt and pepper
1 teaspoon crumbled dried basil
2 garlic cloves, chopped
2 tablespoons tomato paste
⅓ cup capers
½ cup soft black Italian or Greek olives, pitted
1 lemon, thinly sliced
Tomato quarters
Chopped parsley

Sauté the onions and celery in oil until just golden. Add the eggplant strips and sauté lightly, tossing them well with the onions and celery. Add the tomatoes and cook down, uncovered. Do not let the vegetables overcook. Season with salt and pepper to taste and add the basil and garlic. Cook for 10 minutes. Stir in the tomato paste, capers, olives, and lemon slices and cook for another 10 minutes.

Chill the *caponata* for a day or so before serving. Serve garnished with tomato quarters and chopped parsley. Add oil and vinegar if you wish. Makes 4 servings.

CAULIFLOWER SAUTÉ WITH LEMON

1 medium-size cauliflower
Olive oil
Salt and pepper
Fresh lemon juice

Wash the cauliflower and soak it in salted cold water for 1 hour. Drain, and cut into flowerets. Cover with fresh cold salted water and cook slightly. The flowerets should be quite firm.

Heat olive oil in a large skillet and add the drained flowerets. Sauté them quickly, turning to brown on all sides. Remove to a hot serving dish and season to taste with salt and pepper; add lemon juice. Makes 4 servings.

■ **Variation**—serve cold, dressed with lemon juice, sesame-seed oil, salt and pepper.

OKRA AND TOMATOES WITH LEMON

1 pound small fresh okra
½ cup olive oil
3 or 4 onions, peeled and coarsely chopped
2 garlic cloves, peeled and chopped
About 3½ cups (one 1-pound, 13-ounce can) tomatoes
Salt and pepper
1 teaspoon coriander, tied in a cheesecloth bag
Lemon wedges

Trim the cone-shape tops from the okra, wash them, and dry them thoroughly with paper towels.

Heat the oil in a large skillet and add the onions and garlic. Cook gently until tender. Add the okra and cook, tossing lightly, until they are slightly browned. Add the tomatoes, salt and pepper to taste, and the bag of coriander. Cover the skillet and simmer gently until the okra is tender; this depends on its size and age. Remove the cheesecloth bag. Serve with lemon wedges. Steamed rice is a good accompaniment. Makes 4 servings.

Note: This dish is equally good served cold with lemon wedges. If fresh okra is not available, substitute the frozen.

ZUCCHINI IN TOMATO SAUCE

3 tablespoons olive oil
1 garlic clove, finely chopped
7 cups (two 1-pound, 13-ounce cans) Italian plum tomatoes
1 teaspoon salt
1 teaspoon sugar
½ teaspoon pepper
3 tablespoons tomato paste
12 small zucchini, peeled
2 tablespoons chopped fresh basil

Heat the olive oil, add the garlic, and cook for 3 minutes. Add the tomatoes and bring to a boil. Lower the heat and simmer slowly for 20 to 25 minutes, stirring occasionally. Add next 3 seasonings and tomato paste, and simmer for 10 more minutes. Add the zucchini and cook until just pierceable with a fork, about 15 minutes. Stir in the basil, and cool. Serve cold. Makes 8 to 10 servings.

MADAME FRAIZE'S CABBAGE AND ZUCCHINI SKILLET

5 tablespoons olive oil, goose fat, or bacon fat
1 head cabbage (about 1½ pounds), coarsely chopped
1 large onion, thinly sliced
3 or 4 zucchini, peeled and cut into ½-inch slices
1 garlic clove, finely minced
Salt and pepper

Heat the oil in a skillet and add the cabbage. Toss it about well, and cover. Cook quickly for 5 minutes, stirring twice. Add the onion and re-cover. Reduce the heat and cook slowly for 45 minutes. Add the zucchini and garlic, re-cover, and cook slowly for another 30 to 45 minutes. Add more oil if needed. Season to taste and cook for another 15 minutes. Serve very hot with braised meats or boiled beef. It is good with sausage also. Makes 6 servings.

■ **Variations**—1. Add another garlic clove and ¼ cup tomato paste with the zucchini. 2. Add pitted black olives and crisp bits of bacon for the last 10 minutes.

HARICOTS VERTS MAILLANOISE
(Green Beans, Maillane Style)

Vegetables simply boiled until tender but still crisp often gain added interest when tossed with imaginative seasonings.

2 pounds tiny green beans
Salted water
3 tablespoons olive oil
1 garlic clove, finely chopped
Chopped parsley
Salt (optional)

Cook the beans in salted water until just crisply tender. Drain well. In a skillet heat the olive oil and garlic. Add the beans and toss as you would a salad. Add parsley, and additional salt if needed. Makes 6 to 8 servings.

CARROTS WITH DILL

Boil 12 whole carrots until just crisply tender. Drain. Melt ½ cup of butter in a skillet and roll the carrots around in the butter until they are well saturated. Add salt, chopped fresh dill to taste, and freshly ground pepper.

Serve in a divided dish with fresh or frozen peas in butter.

Makes 4 servings.

BROCCOLI ALLA PIEMONTESE

Cook 1 or 2 bunches of broccoli according to your favorite recipe until it is just barely tender, not mushy. Drain. Sauté 2 finely chopped garlic cloves in enough olive oil to cover the bottom of a large skillet. When the garlic is lightly browned, add the broccoli and spoon the hot oil over it. Season with salt and pepper to taste, toss in ½ cup dry white wine, and let it cook down very quickly. Serve the broccoli with the pan juices poured over it. Makes 4 to 8 servings.

GRATIN OF GREENS

Sometimes vegetable combinations are finished off in the oven with a topping of cheese or crumbs. This makes a hearty dish.

2 pounds spinach, washed and chopped rather fine
Olive oil
Salt and pepper
2 pounds Swiss chard, washed and chopped fine
2 pounds zucchini, diced
1 cup cooked rice
3 garlic cloves, chopped
6 eggs
Crumbs

Cook spinach in skillet with olive oil until just wilted. Season with salt and pepper. Drain. Prepare the chard in the same manner. Cook the zucchini in oil until just tender. Combine the vegetables with the rice and garlic and mix thoroughly. Put in a well-oiled baking dish, add 3 to 4 tablespoons olive oil, and heat in preheated slow oven (300°F.) for 20 minutes.

Beat the eggs well and pour them over the vegetables. Sprinkle with crumbs and return to the oven to cook until the eggs are just set. Serve warm or cold. Makes 6 to 8 servings.

■ **Variations**—1. Add a bit of flaked codfish as well as the rice and omit the eggs.

2. Use some finely chopped celery tops as well as the spinach and chard, and blend ½ cup grated Parmesan cheese with the eggs.

3. Substitute mustard greens for the chard.

4. Substitute finely chopped beet greens or turnip greens for one of the other greens.

5. Add pitted black olives to the dish.

GRATIN OF EGGPLANT

1 large onion, coarsely chopped
½ cup olive oil
4 tomatoes, peeled, seeded, and chopped, or about 2 cups plum tomatoes
1 large eggplant, sliced
Salt and pepper to taste
½ teaspoon crumbled dried thyme
½ tablespoon all-purpose flour
Grated Swiss cheese

Sauté the onion in the oil and add the tomatoes. Let them cook for 5 to 8 minutes. Add the eggplant and seasonings and cook very slowly, covering the pan for part of the cooking time. When the eggplant is tender but not mushy, sprinkle with the flour and blend it into the juices. Add the grated cheese and run under the broiler to melt. Makes 4 servings.

STUFFED BAKED EGGPLANT

Many people think of stuffed vegetables as a way of using up leftovers, but the stuffed vegetable dish can be an important taste combination and elegant party fare.

2 small eggplants
Olive oil
2 garlic cloves
2 cups croutons
16 to 20 anchovy fillets
Salt and pepper
Grated rind of 1 lemon
2 tablespoons fresh lemon juice

Halve the eggplants and scoop out the flesh. Chop rather coarsely and sauté in ⅓ cup of olive oil with finely chopped garlic. Sauté the croutons separately in garlic-flavored oil. Chop the anchovies rather fine and combine with the eggplant and croutons. Toss well. Season to taste and add the lemon rind and lemon juice.

Stuff the eggplant halves with this mixture and dribble with olive oil. Place in a baking dish with a little warm water. Bake in preheated moderate oven (375° F.) for 35 minutes, or until done and well browned. Makes 4 servings.

STUFFED ZUCCHINI

12 to 14 small zucchini, halved
Olive oil
⅔ cup bread crumbs or croutons
3 garlic cloves, finely chopped
12 black olives, chopped
2 tablespoons capers
12 to 14 anchovy fillets, coarsely chopped
2 tablespoons chopped parsley

Scoop out the zucchini and discard the seeds and a small amount of the flesh. Sauté the halves quickly in olive oil. Then parboil them for 5 to 10 minutes. Cool. Heat 6 tablespoons of olive oil and sauté the crumbs and garlic for 2 minutes. Add the chopped black olives, the capers, and part of the chopped anchovies. Stuff the zucchini with this mixture; sprinkle with additional crumbs and brush with oil. Arrange in a baking dish and bake in preheated moderate oven (375° F.) for 20 minutes, brushing once with more oil. Serve cold, garnished with chopped parsley and the rest of the anchovies. Makes 6 or 7 servings.

ZUCCHINI WITH WALNUTS

¼ pound walnuts
6 medium zucchini
2 tablespoons butter or margarine
Salt and pepper

Reserve a few walnut halves for garnish and chop the remainder. Slice unpeeled zucchini about ⅛ inch thick. Sauté in butter, stirring constantly. When zucchini is almost tender, add the chopped walnuts and salt and pepper to taste. Continue cooking until tender. Garnish with walnut halves. Makes 6 servings.

VEGETABLE SOUFFLÉS

Onion or Shallot Soufflé

This is a spring favorite at the Four Seasons Restaurant in New York.

For the vegetables:

6 shallots, peeled and chopped, or 1 medium onion, chopped
3 tablespoons butter

For the basic soufflé mixture:

3 tablespoons all-purpose flour
3 tablespoons butter or margarine
¼ cup milk
½ teaspoon salt
Dash of hot pepper sauce
¾ cup sharp Cheddar or Gruyère cheese, grated
4 egg yolks
6 egg whites

Sauté the shallots in butter until nicely colored and cooked through.

Prepare the soufflé mixture: combine the flour and butter in a skillet and cook for a few minutes. Gradually stir in the milk, salt, and hot pepper sauce, and continue stirring until thickened. Add the shallots, the cheese, and the egg yolks, lightly beaten. Cook, stirring constantly, over very low heat for 5 minutes, or until the cheese is melted and the mixture blended. Cool. Beat the egg whites until stiff but not dry. They should still have a fine gloss. Fold half of the whites in quite thoroughly. Add the rest of the whites and fold in lightly. Pour into a buttered 1½-quart soufflé dish and bake in preheated moderate oven (375°F.) for 25 to 30 minutes, or at 400°F. for a little less time. The soufflé is done when it is high and brown. Makes 6 servings.

Broccoli Soufflé

Prepare the basic soufflé mixture as above. Add 1 cup of puréed cooked broccoli and ½ garlic clove, finely minced. Frozen broccoli may be used.

Caponata* ■ *Celery Victor

Spinach Soufflé

1 garlic clove, chopped
2 tablespoons olive oil
¾ cup chopped fresh or frozen spinach
2 teaspoons fresh lemon juice
Pinch of ground nutmeg

Sauté the garlic in oil for a minute. Add the spinach, lemon juice, and nutmeg and heat through for 4 or 5 minutes. Add to the basic soufflé mixture (page 1904). Cool slightly and fold in the egg whites. Pour into a buttered 1½-quart soufflé dish and bake in preheated moderate oven (375°F.) for 30 to 35 minutes. Makes 6 servings.

Green-Bean Soufflé

To the basic soufflé mixture (page 1904) add:

1 cup finely chopped or puréed cooked green beans
¼ cup crisp bacon pieces

Add the beaten egg whites, pour into a buttered 1½-quart soufflé dish, and bake in preheated moderate oven (375°F.) for 30 to 35 minutes.

TANGERINE SWEETS

6 cooked sweet potatoes
48 tangerine sections
1 jar (8 ounces) honey
Parsley

Peel and slice each potato lengthwise into 4 slices. Put in shallow ovenproof serving dish. Arrange 2 tangerine sections on each potato slice. Cover with honey and bake in preheated moderate oven (350° F.) for 30 minutes, or until heated through. Garnish with parsley. Makes 6 servings.

ONIONS IN ONIONS

3 Spanish onions, 3 inches in diameter
Salt
18 pearl onions (use canned, if preferred)
¼ cup butter or margarine
¼ cup all-purpose flour
2 cups milk
Pepper

Cook Spanish onions in boiling salted water to cover until barely tender. Cook pearl onions in the same manner until done (if using canned ones, heat through). Melt butter, and blend in flour. Gradually add milk, and cook, stirring constantly, until thickened. Season to taste with salt and pepper. Drain the pearl onions, and combine with the sauce. Remove outer skins from Spanish onions, and cut each into halves crosswise. Remove center rings to leave a hole about 1 inch in diameter. Put 3 pearl onions in each hole and pour the cream sauce over all. Put under broiler until golden brown. Makes 6 servings.

Onions in Onions

Tangerine Sweets

Zucchini with Walnuts

VENISON—The edible flesh of a wild animal taken by hunting. The word is most often used in reference to deer meat. It comes from the Latin term for hunt and quarry.

For practically all cooking purposes, recipes for deer, moose, and elk are interchangeable. What should be remembered is that the flavor of venison depends on the animal's food and the tenderness of the meat depends on the animal's age. Venison is apt to be tough; it should, therefore, be treated like any such meat, and be either marinated or pot-roasted.

PIT-COOKED VENISON

This is a favorite way of cooking freshly killed meat in camp. Dig a pit about 18 inches square and line with rocks. Build a fire in the pit and let it burn down until you have about 6 inches of red coals. Place a 5- or 6-pound boned roast on 2 thicknesses of heavy-duty foil large enough to cover roast. Season with salt and pepper and any other seasonings you desire. Fold foil over the roast, sealing edges well. Place in the pit and bank coals around it. Fill the pit with dirt and cover with a dampened piece of canvas weighted down with rocks. Leave for 5 to 6 hours. Carefully remove roast from pit and open foil. Use the juices to serve over the sliced roast. Makes 8 servings.

VENISON STEAKS OR CHOPS

8 venison steaks or chops, 1½ inches thick
Burgundy
Freshly ground pepper
Seasoned all-purpose flour
Butter (about ⅓ cup)
½ pound fresh mushrooms, sliced
6 slices of bacon, cut into julienne strips
¼ cup minced onion
½ cup diced celery

Place steaks in a shallow pan and pour wine over just barely to cover; sprinkle liberally with pepper. Marinate overnight. Remove meat from marinade; dry on paper towels. Turn in seasoned flour and sauté in butter until nicely browned and tender. In another skillet simmer in 2 tablespoons butter the mushrooms, bacon, onion, and celery. When lightly browned, add wine marinade and bring to the boiling point. Serve steaks on a heated platter; pour sauce with vegetables over the meat. Makes 8 servings.

SPICY BARBECUED ROAST VENISON

4-pound venison roast (leg, rump, or shoulder)
2 tablespoons olive oil
1 cup chili sauce
1 cup water
2 tablespoons vinegar
1 tablespoon Worcestershire
1 teaspoon salt
¼ teaspoon pepper
⅛ teaspoon each of celery salt, ground cinnamon, and ground cloves
1 small onion, finely chopped
½ lemon, thinly sliced
½ cup currant jelly

Brown roast on all sides in olive oil, then place in a roasting pan. Add all the remaining ingredients except jelly to the pan juices and heat to boiling, scraping bottom of pan to loosen all particles. Pour sauce over meat and roast in preheated moderate oven (350°F.) until meat reaches the desired degree of doneness, about 1½ hours for rare, 2 to 2½ hours for medium or well done, basting occasionally with sauce. Add more water if necessary. Remove meat to serving platter and strain basting sauce. Measure and add water if needed to make ½ cup of sauce. Add jelly and cook over moderate heat, stirring constantly, until jelly is melted and sauce is smooth. Serve hot in a sauceboat to spoon over sliced meat. Makes 8 to 10 servings.

VENISON POT ROAST

1 cup dry red wine
1 cup water
1½ teaspoons salt
2 bay leaves
10 whole cloves
5 whole allspice
2 chili peppers
1 large onion, sliced
One 5- to 6-pound venison roast (any cut) or chuck or rump beef
2 tablespoons bacon fat

Combine all ingredients except meat and bacon fat to make a marinade. Put meat in deep container; do not use aluminum. Pour marinade over meat. Cover and marinate in refrigerator for 2 days. Drain and reserve marinade. Dry meat. Strain marinade. In Dutch oven brown meat on all sides in hot bacon fat. Add ½ cup reserved marinade. Simmer, covered, over low heat for 2 to 3 hours, or until meat is tender. (Cooking time depends on cut and age of the venison.) Check occasionally, add more marinade to prevent sticking. Remove pot roast to hot serving dish and slice thickly. Keep hot. Make gravy in the usual manner. Pour gravy over meat. Serve with wild rice or buttered noodles. Makes 6 to 8 servings.

MEAT-ON-A-STICK

2 pounds venison round steak
¼ cup olive oil
¼ cup dry red wine
2 tablespoons Worcestershire
1 teaspoon garlic salt
½ teaspoon crumbled dried oregano
½ teaspoon salt
¼ teaspoon pepper

Remove fat and bone from meat and cut meat into 1-inch cubes. Mix remaining ingredients and pour over meat in a mixing bowl. Marinate for 2 hours, stirring occasionally. Thread meat on individual skewers or sticks and broil, either over charcoal or in the oven, until meat reaches the desired degree of doneness, turning to brown each side. About 3 minutes on each side will result in a crusty outside and pink juicy inside if sticks of meat are placed about 5 inches from heat.

When hunters cook meat-on-a-stick in camp, they cut green willow branches and peel them to use for sticks.

Makes enough for ten 8-inch sticks.

VENISON RAGOUT

2 tablespoons butter or margarine
2 tablespoons all-purpose flour
1 cup chicken bouillon or 1 chicken bouillon cube dissolved in 1 cup water
1 tablespoon Worcestershire
1 tablespoon currant jelly
2 cups 1-inch cubes of cooked venison
Salt and pepper to taste

Brown butter in skillet. Add flour and continue to cook until flour browns. Add bouillon, stirring constantly until thickened. Add Worcestershire and jelly and cook over low heat, stirring constantly, until jelly is melted. Add meat and seasonings and heat until meat is heated through. Makes 4 servings.

VENISON STROGANOFF

2 pounds venison round steak, cut ¾ inch thick
2 tablespoons shortening
1 large onion, peeled and chopped
½ teaspoon salt
⅛ teaspoon pepper
1 can (10½ ounces) beef bouillon
¼ pound fresh mushrooms
2 tablespoons butter or margarine
2 tablespoons all-purpose flour
1 teaspoon prepared mustard
1 cup dairy sour cream

Remove bone and fat from meat and cut into strips about ¼ inch wide and 1½ inches long. Brown meat in shortening in a heavy skillet. Transfer meat to a 2-quart casserole and add onion, salt, and pepper. Heat bouillon in skillet, scraping bottom of pan to loosen all particles. Pour over meat and bake, covered, in preheated moderate oven (350°F.) for 1½ hours, stirring occasionally if meat on top becomes dry.

Wash and slice mushrooms and sauté

in butter until golden. Stir in flour. Drain the liquid from the meat and add gradually while stirring. Cook over low heat, stirring constantly, until smooth and thickened. Add mustard and sour cream and blend well. Pour over meat. Serve over cooked rice. Makes 4 to 6 servings.

BRINE-CURED VENISON ROLL

8 to 10 pounds venison flank and scraps
1 medium onion, peeled and chopped
2 quarts water
1½ cups rock salt
¾ teaspoon saltpeter

Spread out flank, sewing together if you have several small ones. Sprinkle with onion and any scraps or meat trimmings. Roll tightly and tie securely. Boil water with salt until salt is dissolved. Add saltpeter (this is to preserve the color of the meat). Cool the brine, add the meat roll, and store in a stone crock or glass or pottery bowl. Put a plate on top with a weight to keep the meat immersed in the brine. The meat may be left in the brine from 2 weeks to 2 months. When ready to use, remove the meat, rinse with fresh water, and boil in water to cover for 2 hours. Then remove from the liquid and place in a loaf pan. Put a weight on top to press it into a firm roll. Cut into thin slices for sandwiches or dice it and serve it cold with a pickle relish or in a salad. Makes 12 to 14 servings.

VENISON SAUSAGE

4 pounds venison scrap meat
½ pound beef suet
¼ cup smoked salt
2 teaspoons salt
1½ teaspoons ground sage
½ teaspoon ground allspice
¼ teaspoon cayenne

Grind the venison and the suet through the coarse blade of a meat grinder. The suet will be easier to grind if it is cold. Mix in the seasonings thoroughly and grind again through the medium blade. Mix again thoroughly, using your hands. Stuff into casings and tie into convenient lengths. Drop into boiling water and cook until the sausage floats, 20 to 30 minutes. After cooking, the sausage may be wrapped in foil and frozen. Makes 8 to 10 servings.

VENISON CHOPS PARMESAN

8 venison chops
1 tablespoon butter
2 medium onions, peeled, quartered, and sliced
1 tablespoon shortening
Salt and pepper
1 cup beef bouillon or 1 bouillon cube dissolved in 1 cup hot water
8 slices of French bread, toasted
1 cup dairy sour cream
1 tablespoon Worcestershire
3 tablespoons grated Parmesan cheese

Trim fat from chops. Melt butter and sauté onions until they are limp and straw-colored. Remove onions and add shortening. Brown chops on both sides and sprinkle with salt and pepper. Top with onions and bouillon. Simmer, covered, until meat has reached the desired degree of doneness, 15 to 30 minutes. Arrange toast on serving dish or individual plates, top each slice with a chop, and keep warm. Add sour cream and Worcestershire to pan drippings and stir until mixed and heated. Pour over chops and sprinkle with Parmesan cheese. Makes 8 servings.

HUNTER'S CHILI

1 pound small red chili or kidney beans
½ teaspoon baking soda
1 tablespoon salt
1 pound each of venison and moose scraps, trimmed from neck, shoulder, shanks, or ribs, (or all venison or all moose may be used)
¼ cup shortening
1 large onion, peeled and chopped
4 to 6 tablespoons chili powder
2 tablespoons all-purpose flour
3 garlic cloves, peeled and minced, or put through garlic press
4 teaspoons crumbled dried oregano
2 teaspoons ground cuminseed
1½ teaspoons crumbled dried sage or ¾ teaspoon ground sage

Soak beans overnight in water. In the morning add baking soda and bring to a boil. Boil for 10 minutes. Drain and rinse. Cover beans with water, add salt, and bring to a boil. Meanwhile, trim all fat and tendons from meat and cut into small cubes. Brown in shortening, then add to the beans. Cook onion in remaining shortening until golden brown, stirring occasionally. Add chili powder and flour, and mix. Then add to beans and meat. Rinse the pan with a little water, stirring to remove all particles, and add to chili. Add remaining ingredients and cover. Simmer for 4 hours, stirring occasionally, adding more water if necessary. Makes 6 to 8 servings.

VENISON SHANKS WITH ROSEMARY

6 slices of venison from upper shank, cut 1 inch thick
Olive oil
6 medium potatoes, peeled and halved
Salt and pepper
Basting Sauce

Rub meat with olive oil and place in a large flat roasting pan. Brown in preheated extremely hot oven (500°F.), turning once to brown both sides. Place potatoes around meat and sprinkle both with salt and pepper to taste. Reduce heat to slow (325°F.) and roast for 1 hour more, basting frequently with Basting Sauce. Makes 6 servings.

Basting Sauce for Venison

1 cup chicken bouillon
½ cup dry red wine
½ cup tomato sauce
2 tablespoons olive oil
2 tablespoons grated onion
1 garlic clove, peeled and minced, or put through garlic press
1 teaspoon salt
½ teaspoon crumbled dried rosemary or 1 teaspoon chopped fresh rosemary
⅛ teaspoon pepper
Pinch of cayenne

Combine all ingredients in a small saucepan and heat to boiling. Keep warm over very low heat while using to baste venison shanks.

VENISON MEATBALLS

2 pounds venison, ground
1 medium onion, peeled and chopped
1 garlic clove, peeled and minced, or put through a garlic press
1 cup tomato juice
1 cup dry bread crumbs
1 teaspoon Worcestershire
1½ teaspoons salt
½ teaspoon pepper
Water
All-purpose flour

Mix together thoroughly all ingredients except water and flour, and form into balls the size of a golf ball. Brown them in shortening and transfer to a 2-quart kettle. Pour a small amount of water into the skillet and heat, scraping the bottom to remove all particles. Pour over meatballs and add enough water to cover them. Simmer, covered, for about 45 minutes. Pour off the liquid and measure. Mix a smooth paste of flour and water, measuring 2 tablespoons water and 1½ tablespoons flour for each cup of liquid. Gradually add the hot liquid, stirring constantly, and cook until thickened. Correct seasoning. Serve with Herbed Wild Rice (page 1940). Makes 6 to 8 servings.

VERBENA, LEMON (*Lippia citriodora*) —This perennial shrub, originally from Argentina and Chile, is now found in many mild climates. Its size varies greatly according to the conditions under which it is grown: outdoors in warm climates it reaches over ten feet; inside in pots it grows to a height of less than ten inches. The long, narrow, pointed leaves are yellow-green. Dried or fresh, these leaves have a delicate lemony flavor and smell. They may be used to garnish fruit cups or fruit salads, or put into jellies. A crushed leaf in the bottom of a cup or glass gives a delicious flavor to a sweet drink. Lemon verbena tea is one of the most popular of the herb teas. Its lemony fragrance makes it a natural for cologne and sachets, too.

VERMICELLI—A variety of pasta consisting of long thin strands, thinner than spaghetti. The name is Italian and means "little worms."

Vermicelli is cooked like any other pasta in plenty of boiling salted water, and served either with a sauce or with butter and grated Parmesan cheese. It may be served also as a soup, in bouillon.

VERMOUTH—A fortified white wine, flavored with various herbs, barks, seeds, spices, etc. The principal aromatic agent in vermouth consists of flowers of the shrub *Artemisia absinthium,* also known as wormwood; (the far more toxic leaves of the same plant are used in the making of absinthe). The name is derived from the German *wermut,* meaning "wormwood."

Vermouth is used principally as an apéritif and as a cocktail ingredient. There are two main types: French and Italian. The French is pale in color and quite dry. The Italian is darker and usually has a base of muscat wine. It is quite sweet. French-type wines are, however, made in Italy and Italian-type ones made in France. Both are produced in many other countries, including Spain, England, Argentina, and the United States. They are based on similar aromatics, including artemisia flowers, bitter-orange peel, camomile, aloes, cardamom, and anise. American vermouths are excellent and compare favorably with the imported ones.

VICHYSSOISE—A very elegant cold leek and potato cream soup invented by Louis Diat, the great chef of the Ritz-Carlton Hotel in New York.

Chef Diat often told of the origin of Cream Vichyssoise Glacée, as the soup is properly called. When he lived as a child on the family farm in a small village in central France, not far from Vichy, one of Europe's most famous watering places, his mother used to make the hot leek and potato soup that is standard French fare. In the summer, the children cooled their hot soup with milk.

When Chef Diat took over the kitchens of the Ritz-Carlton, he was interested in cool dishes to serve during the hot summer season. The time was shortly before World War I when cold jellied dishes were just beginning to be introduced. As Chef Diat remembered the cooled soup of his childhood, he began to add refinements to it and made it into the perfect summer soup.

As for naming the soup, he first thought of his little native village, but he realized that no one would know the place, and decided that since Vichy was a nearby town, and one that his rich customers would know very well from having taken the cure there, the name "Vichyssoise," "From Vichy," would be the right one.

THE ORIGINAL CREAM VICHYSSOISE GLACÉE

From *Cooking à la Ritz* by Louis Diat (Lippincott, 1941)

4 leeks, white part only
1 medium onion
2 tablespoons sweet butter
5 medium potatoes
4 cups water or chicken broth
1 tablespoon salt
2 cups milk
2 cups medium cream
1 cup heavy cream

Finely slice the white part of the leeks and the onion, and brown very lightly in the sweet butter; then add the potatoes, also sliced finely. Add water and salt. Boil gently for 35 to 40 minutes. Crush and rub through a fine strainer, or whirl in a blender. Return to heat and add milk and the medium cream. Season to taste and bring to a boil. Cool, and then rub through a very fine strainer. When soup is cold, add the heavy cream. Chill thoroughly before serving. Finely chopped chives may be added when serving. Makes 8 servings.

VINAIGRETTE—A sauce which is a mixture of oil, vinegar, salt, and pepper, sometimes with the addition of herbs. The sauce is one of the simplest and best of salad dressings, and there are countless variations of it. It takes its name from *vinaigre,* the French word for vinegar.

VINEGAR ***by Lucy Kavaler***—Vinegar, a mixture of acetic acid and water, is a kitchen workhorse, needed for pickling, preserving, tenderizing tough meat and fowl, and adding sour pungency to dishes ranging from vinegar pie to tomato ketchup and salad dressing.

No one can say when vinegar first came into use. It was old when Ruth in the Bible dipped her morsel of bread into vinegar, when Caesar's legions mixed it with drinking water. Vinegar was probably discovered by ancient peoples accidentally, along with wine. Yeasts and bacteria are ever present in the air, too small to be seen by the naked eye. In the days before recorded history, yeasts must have fallen by chance into uncovered earthenware jugs of fruit juice and caused the juice to ferment and become wine. And in time the bacteria *Acetobacter* dropped into the wine and soured and transformed it into acetic acid and water. The name, derived from the French words *vin aigre,* "sour wine," is an apt description of the way vinegar is made. Despite the winy origin, no alcohol remains; the action of the *Acetobacter* sees to that.

Although it started with wine, vinegar making did not stop there, and imaginative cooks throughout the world have invented such variants as banana vinegar, or date, pear, orange, pineapple, peach, raspberry, honey, molasses, rice, or brandy. In America the cider vinegar made out of fermented apple juice is the most popular, and a white distilled vinegar based on dilute alcohol is also widely used. The English years ago began to employ malt in an economical effort to dispose of sour ale and beer, and still like malt vinegar best. Subtleties of flavor are achieved with herbs and leaves. The chef of a luxury restaurant makes an incomparable marinade for beef by using a vinegar he has flavored himself. He first crushes basil and a garlic clove, then pours boiling vinegar over them, places the mixture in a jar, shakes it once a day for ten days, and at last strains it through a thin cloth.

The strangest of all formulations was devised by a gang of thieves looting Marseille during the Black Plague of the Middle Ages. They choked down a mixture of cloves, sage, rosemary, rue, pimiento, calamus (a root), caraway, nutmeg, and vinegar, in the belief that this hair-raising brew would protect them from the disease. But even they seem unimaginative when compared to Cleopatra who made vinegar history on the night when she dissolved a perfect pearl and drank it down with a flourish to show Mark Antony that she could consume a fortune in one meal. Nobody has ever found out what she thought of the flavor.

Anyone aware that the difference between good and superlative cuisine lies in just such basic ingredients as vinegar, must consider strength as well as flavor. Vinegar's bite and sourness is in direct proportion to the amount of acetic acid in it, and a four per cent vinegar will be far less pungent than one with five per cent or higher. The term "forty- or fifty-grain strength" is used by some manufacturers instead, "grain" standing for ten times the acetic-acid content. The strength

The Original Cream Vichyssoise Glacée

has no effect on the calorie count, which is nil, making vinegar the dieter's delight the world over.

One of the most universal of all foods, vinegar is an essential of characteristic dishes of nations separated by thousands of miles and totally different customs and cooking practices. Consider the German *sauerbraten* and potato salad, the Japanese rice *sushi,* the American barbecued chicken, the Chinese sweet-and-sour pork, the kosher herring. Eating an old artichoke, say the French with a smile, will make you old quickly, but a young one with *sauce vinaigrette* will add years to your life. Although the pickle is definitely not a part of gourmet cookery, few gourmets anywhere in the world would pass up the pleasure of biting into a sharp sour salty one, be it dill, tomato, watermelon, beet, pumpkin, or cauliflower. The natural affinity of vinegar for salads has also won international recognition.

King Richard II of England was so fond of "salat," as it was then known, that his cook wrote down the directions: "Take parsel, sawge (sage), garlec, chibollas (small onions), leeks, myntes, fenel, ton tressis (watercress) . . . waishe hem clene . . . myng (mix) hem wel with rawe oile. Lay one vinegar and salt and serve it forth." In 14th-century England or 20th-century America, the classic salad dressing called "French" is regularly served forth.

Salad dressings, pickles, and seasoning do not exhaust the uses for vinegar; some are completely independent of the palate. Louis XIII of France, for example, ordered his generals to cool their cannons with vinegar. Less royal personages find that it removes the smell of onions from their fingers, helps to hard-cook cracked eggs without mess, controls the pervasive odor of cooking cabbage, and best of all, leaves shampooed hair soft and silky.

Availability and Purchasing Guide—The most common types of vinegar, such as red-wine, cider, and distilled vinegar, come in pint or quart bottles. Many others are available and they vary in size with the manufacturer and the kind of vinegar. Some of the special vinegars are imported: rosé wine vinegar, tarragon, chianti vinegar. Others are made in the United States and include basil white-wine vinegar, eschalot red wine, garlic red wine, red wine, rosé wine, tarragon red wine, white wine, white wine and vinegar with tarragon sprigs.

Table vinegars should be bought in small quantities. Vinegars for canning or preserving can be bought in larger bottles.

Storage—Store in a dark, cool place and keep airtight. Avoid using sediment that may form in bottom of bottle if stored a long time. Mold indicates spoilage; do not use. Cider or distilled vinegar will keep for about 6 months on the pantry shelf once opened, or almost indefinitely if not opened. Other vinegars will keep for 2 to 3 months.

Vinegar which has developed "mother," a jellylike membrane, can still be used. The vinegar should be strained through a fine strainer.

HERB VINEGAR
(from fresh herbs)

Put 2 cups minced fresh herb leaves in 1 quart cider vinegar and let jar stand in a warm place for 2 weeks, shaking mixture every day. Then strain, bottle, and seal. Makes 1 quart.

HERB VINEGAR
(from dried herbs)

Scald 1 quart of cider vinegar. Add 1½ tablespoons dried herbs. Let stand in jar in a warm place for 2 weeks, shaking mixture every day. Strain, bottle, and seal. Makes 1 quart.

SPICED RAISIN RELISH

1½ cups seeded raisins
⅓ cup sugar
⅓ cup cider vinegar
¼ teaspoon ground cinnamon
Dash of ground cloves

Simmer all ingredients, covered, for 15 to 20 minutes. Cool, and serve as a relish with ham or other meat. Makes about 1½ cups.

VITAMIN—A powerful organic compound indispensable to nutrition which is found in small quantities in foods. Absence of vitamins can cause serious health disorders, or even death. The fat-soluble vitamins (vitamins A, D, E, K) found in natural foods are more easily absorbed than vitamins in pill form, but with other vitamins, there is no significant difference. Each vitamin has its own function in the closely interwoven body processes. Vitamin values of commercial preparations, based on feeding tests on animals and on the latest chemical or microbiological methods of assay, are expressed in weights of pure vitamins in milligrams (mg.) or micrograms (mcg.). Vitamins A and D are also expressed in International Units. Research in vitamins has made this subject more complex as additional vitamins are found and their specific functions in the body are determined.

The fat-soluble vitamins are not lost easily in cooking, because they do not dissolve in water. However, water-soluble vitamins (vitamins B complex and C) may be partially lost in cooking water, but in normal practice enough is retained to afford complete protection. The risk is usually greatest in vitamin C loss, but in acid foods this loss is relatively slow. Losses in vitamins occur when fresh produce is stored too long or cooked too long in too much water. Cooking water should be used to prevent the loss of valuable vitamins. Dietary allowances specifying the amounts of vitamins needed are only approximations. These figures vary with age, sex, and activity. A well-varied diet will provide the necessary vitamins. Long-range good eating is important since vitamin deficiencies at their beginning are hard to detect. Once discovered, they may have progressed to a severe and chronic stage which will take months or even years to remedy.

FAT-SOLUBLE VITAMINS

Vitamin A is necessary for good eyesight and eyes that adapt readily to changes from light to dark. It is especially important for skeletal growth and normal tooth structure. Vitamin A is also necessary for the health of the mucous membranes lining the nose, throat, and other air passages, the alimentary canal, and the genitourinary tracts. It also regulates the permeability of membranes inside nearly *all* body cells, and functions in the entire body. Vitamin A can be stored in the body in the liver. The recommended daily allowance is 5,000 International Units per day. The food sources are fish-liver oils, animal livers, yellow-colored vegetables and fruits, green-colored vegetables and fruits, all milk products that include milk fat.

Vitamin D is necessary to prevent rickets and promote normal bone growth. Huge overdoses have been known to have specific toxicity. Daily requirement for children is 400 International Units. Vitamin D can be stored in the body in the liver. Vitamin D is formed from fatty material in the skin by ultraviolet light as in sunlight and is found in limited amounts in food. Fish-liver oils and other vitamin-D-fortified foods, chiefly milk products, are the usual sources of vitamin D. Vitamin D is stable to heating, aging, and storage.

Vitamin E is essential in muscle functions and serves as an anti-oxidant in body cells. The daily requirement is not stated. Food sources include wheat and corn germ and most seed oils, and it is found in moderate amounts in cereals, egg yolk, legumes, nuts, leafy vegetables, and vegetable oils.

Vitamin K is necessary in the formation of prothrombin which is vital to the proper clotting of blood. Large doses have been given to surgical patients and premature babies to prevent hemorrhaging. The adult daily requirement is unknown. Food sources are cabbage, cauliflower, spinach, and other leafy vegetables; pork liver, soybean oil, and other vegetable oils. It is moderately stable to heat, light, and exposure to air.

WATER-SOLUBLE VITAMINS

Vitamin C or ascorbic acid is necessary in the prevention of scurvy leading to sore mouth, swollen gums, hemorrhages, bone fragility, weakened capillary walls, and muscle weakness. It is unstable when heated and exposed to air, and may be destroyed by drying and storage. It is found naturally in citrus fruits, strawberries, cantaloupes, tomatoes, sweet peppers, cabbage, potatoes, kale, broccoli, and turnip greens. The adult human daily requirement is 70 mg. for women and 75 mg. for men.

Thiamine (B-1) is necessary to maintain the appetite; in preventing beriberi (a disease affecting the nerves and digestive system), fatigue, and constipation; and in preserving the health of the nerves. It is unstable to heat and air in alkaline foods. In acid foods, such as cereals, meats, breads, peanuts, and walnuts, it is somewhat more stable to heat and air. The adult human daily requirement is 0.8 to 1.2 mg. for women and 0.9 to 1.2 mg. for men. It is found naturally in wheat and nearly all seed germ, pork, liver, organ meats, whole grains, enriched products, nuts, legumes, yeast, and potatoes.

Riboflavin (B-2) is necessary for the proper use in the body of carbohydrates and amino acids, preventing eye sensitivity and cataract. It is stable to heat in cooking, to acids and exposure to air, but unstable in the presence of light. It is found in liver, milk, meat, eggs, legumes, enriched products, yeast, and green leafy vegetables. The adult human daily requirement is 1.2 to 1.8 mg. for women and 1.3 to 1.7 mg. for men.

Niacin or niacinamide (a related compound) is necessary in the prevention of pellagra (a disease involving the nerves and skin), and is an essential part of carbohydrate and amino-acid metabolism. It is stable to heat, light, and exposure to air, acid, and alkali. The adult human daily requirement is 13 to 20 mg. for women and 15 to 19 mg. for men. It is found in liver, poultry, meat, fish, whole grains, enriched products, legumes, yeast, and mushrooms.

Pantothenic acid is necessary to growth and health and serves as a catalyst in the utilization of fats, sugars, and amino acids. It is moderately unstable to acid, alkali, heat, and certain salts, but it is extremely widely distributed. The adult human requirement has not been established. It is found in liver, organ meats, eggs, peanuts, legumes, mushrooms, salmon, yeast, wheat germ, and whole grains.

Vitamin B-6 (pyridoxine, pyridoxal, pyridoxamine) is necessary in nerve functions and to the proper metabolism of fats and amino acids. It is only moderately stable to heat, light, and air. The adult human daily requirement is about 1.5 to 2.0 mg. It is found in liver, pork, organ meats, legumes, seeds, grains, leafy foods, and potatoes.

Biotin is necessary for cell respiration. A deficiency in biotin causes fatigue, loss of appetite, nausea, and anemia. It is found in organ meats, egg yolks, milk, fruits, and leafy vegetables. Deficiencies are extremely rare.

Folacin and B-12 are necessary for blood cell formation and prevention of anemia. B-12 is closely related to nerve function. They are found in organ meats, milk, eggs, fish, and most leafy vegetables.

VODKA—A potent colorless spirit, distilled from a grain or potato mash. Vodka does not have a definite aroma or taste.

Russians, Poles, and other Slavic people toss their vodka down in thimble-size glasses, accompanied by *zakuski* or appetizers. In recent years vodka has become a popular drink in the United States.

VOL-AU-VENT—A delicate light pastry made from puff paste in the shape of a wide tower which looks like an enormous patty shell. Its cavity is filled with a sauced or creamed food. Like a patty shell, a *vol-au-vent* has a lid or top, which is removed before filling and put back afterward, like a hat.

The term is French, and it means "flying in the wind." Supposedly the great French chef Carême was experimenting with puff paste shapes one day. When he baked the first *vol-au-vent,* he noticed that the puff-paste dough had baked into its airy towerlike shape. Joyfully, he cried that it was "flying in the wind," and the name stuck.

CHICKEN-MUSHROOM VOL-AU-VENT

1 pound sweet butter
4 cups all-purpose flour
1 teaspoon salt
1 tablespoon fresh lemon juice
1¼ cups cold water (about)
1 egg, slightly beaten
Chicken-Mushroom Filling

Shape the butter into a brick about 3 x 5 x ¾ inches. Roll butter in 3 tablespoons of the flour, coating all sides. Wrap in wax paper, and chill. Put remaining flour in a large bowl. Make a well in the center. Add salt and lemon juice. Gradually begin to add water, only enough to make a rather firm, slightly sticky dough. Knead dough thoroughly on floured board for 20 minutes. Pound it on the table at intervals to achieve the right consistency. It should be very elastic and smooth. Form it into a ball; place on well-floured cloth. With a rolling pin, make the ball of dough into the shape of a four-leaf clover. Roll ends out, leaving the center thick. Well rolled, the dough will have a thick cushion in the center and four thinner "petals." Put brick of butter in the center of the four-leaf clover. Fold "petals" over dough by stretching them over butter and sealing all the edges so that the butter is completely enclosed. Wrap in wax paper, and chill for 20 minutes. On a well-floured cloth, gently roll out the block of dough as evenly as possible into a rectangle slightly less than ⅓ inch thick, and about 3 times as long as it is wide. Do not roll over the ends but flatten them gently to same thickness as the rest of the dough. Fold dough into thirds, making three layers, and chill for 20 minutes. Turn folded sides toward you, and roll out dough, and fold again into thirds. (Rolling, folding, and turning is called a "turn.") It is necessary to make a total of 6 turns, after which the dough is ready for use. The dough should be chilled between each turn. Roll chilled dough to ½-inch thickness. Cut out two 7-inch circles. Brush one with water and put the other on top. Roll remaining dough ¼ inch thick and cut out 2 more 7-inch circles. Cut out centers to leave two rings 1½ inches wide. Reserve one of the centers. Brush outer edge of double circle with water and lay 1 ring on top. Moisten this ring and top with remaining ring. Prick the bottom inside with a fork and let stand for 10 minutes. Scallop bottom edges with fingers and dull edge of a knife. Cut crisscross lines on reserved center and put on top. Brush whole shell except the edges with egg. (Egg on edges might prevent rising.) Bake in preheated extremely hot oven (500°F.) for 5 minutes. Reduce heat to moderate (350°F.) and bake for 30 minutes longer. Remove the center cover and scoop out soft center. Fill shell with Chicken-Mushroom Filling. Replace cover in center. Makes 6 servings.

Chicken-Mushroom Filling

½ pound mushrooms, sliced
¼ cup butter or margarine
¼ cup all-purpose flour
1 teaspoon salt
¼ teaspoon pepper
2½ cups light cream
3 cups diced cooked chicken
2 egg yolks
2 tablespoons sherry

Cook mushrooms in the butter until lightly browned. Blend in flour and seasonings. Gradually add cream and cook, stirring constantly, until thickened. Add chicken, and heat. Beat egg yolks with the sherry and add to mixture. Cook, stirring, for 2 or 3 minutes longer.

WAFFLE—A crisp, light quick bread made from a pour batter which always contains eggs. Waffles are made in a waffle iron, a utensil with two metal parts hinged together. Each section of the iron has an embossed surface, the crisscross design of which is imprinted on the waffle as it bakes.

Waffles are a very old form of cake or bread, and in Europe there are century-old, elaborately patterned waffle irons, often in the shape of hearts. The word itself is ancient, and traces its origins back to old German words meaning weave and honeycomb. Looking at the pattern of a waffle, we can see both images in it.

Waffles should be uniformly brown, crisp, and tender. Crispness results from baking the waffle for a sufficient length of time.

Serve waffles with butter and syrup, creamed mixtures, sauces, or ice cream.

Commercially prepared waffle mixes are available, as are frozen precooked waffles which can be heated in a toaster.

BASIC WAFFLES

1½ cups all-purpose flour
2 teaspoons baking powder
½ teaspoon baking soda
¼ teaspoon salt
1 tablespoon sugar
3 eggs, separated
¾ cup dairy sour cream
¾ cup sweet milk or buttermilk
¼ cup lard or vegetable shortening, melted
¼ cup butter, melted

Sift dry ingredients together. Beat egg yolks, sour cream, and milk. Add to dry ingredients, alternating with fats cooled to room temperature. Stir until batter is smooth and free from lumps. Fold in egg whites, beaten stiff. Cook waffles according to directions for your particular waffle iron. Serve with syrup, honey, preserves, etc. Makes 4 waffles.

Note: These are fluffy crisp waffles with enough body to hold up when topped with creamed chicken or meat. They freeze well, too.

■ **To Freeze**—Cool; wrap each leftover waffle in foil and freeze. Or freeze flat and wrap. To reheat, it is not necessary to thaw. Place each unwrapped section in toaster set at light and toast until section is heated through. These waffle sections become crisp when cool. If you prefer, place unwrapped sections side by side on a flat cookie sheet and put under grill until heated and sufficiently browned. Do not keep over 2 weeks in the freezer.

■ **To Use Leftover Batter**—Store leftover waffle batter in refrigerator in covered jar. Before cooking add 1 teaspoon baking powder dissolved in 1 tablespoon milk for each cup batter. If batter is still too stiff, add an extra tablespoon or 2 of milk. Cook as directed.

Bacon Waffles

Cut thin strips of breakfast bacon into halves. Place one of these pieces over the top of each waffle section before closing iron. Cook according to directions for your iron, and serve. The bacon should be crisp and brown.

Ham Waffles

Add ½ cup ground baked ham to Basic Waffle batter before cooking.

Blueberry, Currant, Raisin, Nut, or Date Waffles

Add ½ cup blueberries, currants, raisins, chopped nuts, or pitted dates (cut into thirds) to Basic Waffle batter before cooking.

Cheese Waffles

Add ½ cup grated Parmesan or shredded Cheddar cheese to Basic Waffle batter before cooking.

Spice Waffles

Add to Basic Waffle batter before cooking: ½ teaspoon ground cinnamon plus ½ teaspoon coriander seeds (pounded or ground) and ¼ teaspoon ground nutmeg. Or use 1 teaspoon cinnamon alone, or vary it by adding a little nutmeg, clove, or ginger; ½ teaspoon caraway seed is a distinctive addition if you like the flavor.

Rice Waffles

Add ⅔ cup fluffy cooked rice to Basic Waffle batter.

CORN WAFFLES

2 eggs, separated
1½ cups milk
⅓ cup melted shortening
1 cup cream-style corn
2 cups sifted all-purpose flour
2 teaspoons baking powder
½ teaspoon salt

Beat egg yolks with rotary beater until thick. Add milk, shortening, and corn. Add to sifted dry ingredients; mix until smooth. Then fold in stiffly beaten egg whites. Bake in hot waffle iron. Serve hot with butter and syrup. Or serve with creamed chicken or ham, as a main dish. Makes 6 waffles.

BROWNIE WAFFLES

½ cup butter, melted (or ¼ cup each butter and margarine)
2 ounces (2 squares) unsweetened chocolate, or 2 envelopes no-melt chocolate
1 cup sugar
½ teaspoon vanilla extract
2 eggs
1½ cups all-purpose flour
1 teaspoon baking powder
⅛ teaspoon ground cinnamon (optional)
½ cup milk
1 cup finely chopped pecans, almonds, or walnuts

Melt butter and chocolate in heavy saucepan; add sugar and beat well. Add vanilla, and cool. Add eggs one at a time, beating well. Sift flour, baking powder, and cinnamon. Add alternately with milk to first mixture. Add nuts. Bake according to directions for your particular waffle iron. When first taken from the iron, the waffle will be soft, but it gets crisp as it cools.

If any batter is left over, refrigerate. Before cooking add ½ teaspoon baking powder mixed with 1 teaspoon of water, for each cup of batter. This batter keeps several days, covered, in the refrigerator. Freezing is not advised. Makes 4 waffles.

■ **Variation**—You can use half dairy sour cream, half milk, plus ½ teaspoon baking soda and 1 teaspoon cream of tartar, instead of milk and baking powder.

Note: Serve a waffle section to each person and top each with a scoop of vanilla ice cream and hot fudge sauce. It makes a marvelous dessert and is fun to cook at the table. Cut recipe in half for a small group.

CHERRY WAFFLES

Waffles for 4 servings
Grated orange rind
1 can (1 pound) water-packed pitted red sour cherries
¼ cup sugar
1 tablespoon cornstarch
⅛ teaspoon salt
1 tablespoon fresh lemon juice
Red food coloring
Buttered chopped blanched almonds

Prepare waffles using mix or your favorite recipe, adding a little grated orange rind to batter. Drain cherries and measure juice. Mix sugar with cornstarch and salt. Add enough water to the juice to make 1 cup. Add mixture gradually to cornstarch mixture. Cook over low heat, stirring constantly, until smooth and thickened. Stir in cherries, lemon juice, and food coloring. Serve hot on waffles with a sprinkling of buttered chopped almonds.

OLD COLONY GINGERBREAD WAFFLES

1 cup plus 2 tablespoons all-purpose flour
1¼ teaspoons baking powder
¼ teaspoon baking soda
1 teaspoon ground ginger
¼ teaspoon ground clove
¼ teaspoon ground nutmeg
¾ teaspoon ground cinnamon
⅓ cup butter and lard, mixed (or use vegetable shortening in place of lard)
½ cup boiling water or coffee
⅓ cup firmly packed dark-brown sugar
½ cup dark molasses
1 egg, well beaten

Sift dry ingredients. Add shortenings to boiling water and stir until dissolved. Then add sugar and molasses. Cool to room temperature. Add to dry ingredients; add egg and beat until batter is smooth. Pour into waffle iron. Use about ¾ cup batter for each waffle. Serve one section to a person. These waffles become crisp as they cool. Extra batter can be refrigerated for several days in a covered container. Cooked sections can be frozen. See Basic Waffles, page 1914, for freezing. Makes 2 large waffles.

Note: These waffles are delicious for dessert topped with cinnamon-flavored whipped cream; Mock Devonshire Cream, soft custard or vanilla pudding; with caramel, chocolate, or butterscotch sauces. Other favorite toppings, especially during the Christmas holidays, are: hard sauce, Orange Hard Sauce, brandy sauce, or heated mincemeat, well laced with spirits.

SAUCES FOR OLD COLONY GINGERBREAD WAFFLES

Mock Devonshire Cream

Those who have tasted rich, golden Devonshire Cream know there is no substitute, but here's a recipe which approaches it somewhat and is delicious in its own right. Blend a 3-ounce package of cream cheese, at room temperature, with 2 to 3 tablespoons heavy cream or dairy sour cream. When smooth, fold in 2 tablespoons confectioners' sugar and ½ teaspoon vanilla extract. Makes ½ cup.

Orange Hard Sauce

Blend ¼ cup butter, at room temperature, with 1 cup confectioners' sugar, 1 teaspoon grated orange rind, and 2 to 4 tablespoons fresh orange juice. The mixture should not be stiff or runny. Taste, adding more orange juice if the sauce will take it without separating. If desired, substitute 1 or 2 tablespoons Grand Marnier, Curacao, or Triple Sec for some of the orange juice. Cover and chill until firm. Pass with the waffles. If any sauce is left over, use on puddings, as a filling for cakes, or a frosting for sweet muffins. Makes about ⅞ cup.

HONEY BUTTER

1 cup honey
½ cup butter

Be sure both ingredients are at room temperature. Add honey slowly to softened butter and beat with a fork. When well blended, heat gently. Serve hot. Makes 1½ cups.

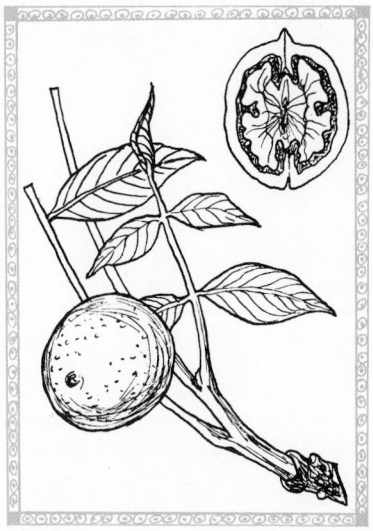

WALNUT—The edible nut of the fruit of the walnut tree. The most commonly

Waffles

known walnut is the English, or Persian, walnut, *Juglans regia.* This hard-shelled nut has a wrinkled white kernel with two very irregularly shaped halves covered with a light brown skin. The shell is thin and light tan; it is made up of two distinct halves. In the United States this species of walnut is generally called a California walnut. The black walnut, *J. nigra,* a native American nut, has a dark brown, deeply ridged shell covering a strongly flavored kernel. Butternuts, or white walnuts, *J. cinerea,* are also native to America.

The English walnut was known in Old English as *wealhhnutu,* which meant "Welsh" or "foreign nut." It had been cultivated for centuries in the Mediterranean region, from which it spread to temperate zones everywhere. Pliny the Elder reported in the 1st century A.D. that the tree had been introduced from Persia; it was known in Italy in the 1st century B.C. according to an earlier writer. Many varieties now exist. One in France is called the Titmouse walnut because the shell is so thin that birds, and especially the titmouse, can crack it open and eat the kernel. Walnut oil, expressed from the kernel, is used in France like olive oil.

The Indians of North America relied heavily on butternuts and black walnuts for their food. Butternut oil was used as a seasoning; the kernel thickened and flavored their meat and vegetable dishes. Both black walnuts and butternuts, as the Indians knew, are better when used in combination with other foods than when eaten plain. The black walnut meat is extremely oily, which adds to its food value but does not make it too tasty if eaten fresh. After being stored for a while it dries out and the flavor improves. These nuts are widely used in cakes, cookies, confections, and ice cream.

English walnuts are one of the most popular of all nuts for eating out-of-hand. Walnut meats also make a delicious addition to all sorts of cakes and cookies.

Today, the United States leads the world in walnut production; other countries which grow them include France, Italy, Turkey, Iran, Yugoslavia, Rumania, China, and India.

Availability and Purchasing Guide—Nuts and nutmeats are available year round in bulk, in film bags, and in vacuum cans. They are graded according to variety, size, and grade. Variety is determined by shape, hardness of shell, and flavor. Sizes in the shell and shelled are indicated by the number in an ounce or by the diameter of smallest and largest nuts or nutmeats. There are three sizes of walnuts: large, medium, and babies. Grade is based on color and condition of nuts and nutmeats. When choosing walnuts in the shell, look for those which are clean and free from scars, cracks, or holes, and well filled, so the kernel does not rattle.

For full flavor and freshness, when choosing shelled walnuts, look for those which are plump and meaty, and crisp and brittle; limp shriveled nutmeats indicate staleness.

☐ 2 pounds in-shell walnuts = 1 pound shelled = 4 cups

Storage—Store in-shell walnuts in a cool dry place; store shelled walnuts, tightly covered, in the refrigerator or freezer. Walnuts remain fresh longer in the shell, in larger pieces, and uncooked.

☐ In shell, kitchen shelf: 2 to 3 months
☐ Shelled; or vacuum-packed, opened, refrigerator shelf: 6 months
☐ Shelled, refrigerator frozen-food compartment or freezer: 1 year
☐ Vacuum-packed, kitchen shelf: 1 year

Nutritive Food Values—Some protein, iron, and B vitamins. Walnuts are high in fat.

☐ English, 3½ ounces, shelled = 651 calories
☐ Black, 3½ ounces, shelled = 628 calories

Basic Preparation

☐ **To Shell**—Use nutcracker; the shell of California walnuts is thin and nutmeat removes easily. Black walnuts must be cracked with a hammer, and the meats picked out with a nut pick.

☐ **To Chop**—Use a long straight knife and wooden board, or a chopping bowl and chopper.

☐ **To Grind**—Use a special nut grinder, except for butters and paste, for which you should use a meat grinder or blender.

☐ **To Roast**—Spread walnuts in shallow baking pan; dot with butter (1 tablespoon for 2 cups walnuts). Bake in preheated moderate oven (350°F.) for about 20 minutes, or until golden, stirring occasionally. Spread on paper towels to cool.

HO T'AO CHI JING
(Walnut Chicken)

2 pounds chicken breasts
2 tablespoons cornstarch
2 egg whites, unbeaten
1 cup California walnut meats
¼ cup cooking oil
1 cup diced celery
1 can (5 ounces) water chestnuts, quartered
⅓ cup chicken bouillon
3 tablespoons soy sauce
1 tablespoon sherry
1 teaspoon sugar
3 slices of fresh gingerroot, minced

Remove chicken meat from bones and cut into ½-inch cubes. Mix 1 tablespoon cornstarch with 1 tablespoon water and beat into egg whites with a fork. Add chicken and mix until each piece is coated. Boil walnuts in water to cover for 3 minutes. Drain and dry between paper towels. Deep fry in hot oil (375°F. on a frying thermometer) until golden-brown. Remove and keep warm. In another pan, heat oil. Add chicken, celery, and water chestnuts. Fry for 3 to 4 minutes. Mix bouillon, soy sauce, sherry, sugar, gingerroot, and 1 tablespoon cornstarch. Add to chicken mixture; cook, stirring, until thickened. Serve garnished with walnuts. Makes 4 to 6 servings.

WALNUT SHORTBREAD

1 cup soft butter
1 cup confectioners' sugar
1 teaspoon vanilla extract
2⅓ cups sifted all-purpose flour
Walnut halves

Cream butter. Gradually beat in sugar. Add vanilla extract. With hands work in flour and knead until bowl is clean. Chill thoroughly. Roll out on lightly floured board to ½-inch thickness. Cut with 2-inch scalloped or other fancy cutter. Decorate with nuts. Bake on ungreased cookie sheets in preheated moderate oven (350°F.) for 20 to 25 minutes. Store airtight. Makes 24.

BLACK-WALNUT BRITTLE

In saucepan mix ½ cup light corn syrup, 2 cups sugar, ⅓ cup water, ¼ teaspoon salt, and 3 tablespoons butter. Bring to boil, stirring until sugar is dissolved. Add 1 cup coarsely broken black walnuts and cook, stirring almost constantly, until a small amount of mixture separates into hard brittle threads when dropped into very cold water (300°F. on a candy thermometer). Add 1 teaspoon vanilla extract and pour onto buttered cookie sheet to cool. When cold, break into pieces. Makes about 1¼ pounds.

WALNUT BONBONS

⅓ cup soft butter
⅓ cup light corn syrup
½ teaspoon salt
1 teaspoon vanilla extract
4½ cups (1 pound) sifted confectioners' sugar
Red and green food coloring
California walnut halves

Blend first 4 ingredients; mix in sugar and knead until blended. Divide mixture into halves and color one half red and the other green. Shape mixtures into 1-inch balls and press a walnut half on each side of each ball. Store airtight. Makes 4 dozen.

BLACK-WALNUT WAFERS

2 eggs
1 cup firmly packed light brown sugar
⅔ cup sifted all-purpose flour
¼ teaspoon each of salt and baking powder
1 cup finely chopped black walnuts

Beat eggs until light. Add sugar and beat

until thick. Add sifted dry ingredients and nuts; mix well. Drop by scant teaspoonfuls onto greased cookie sheets. Bake in preheated hot oven (400°F.) for 5 minutes. Let stand for ½ minute before removing. Makes about 5 dozen.

CHOCOLATE BUTTERSCOTCH BARS

- ⅔ cup shortening, melted
- 2¼ cups firmly packed light brown sugar
- 3 eggs
- 2¾ cups sifted all-purpose flour
- ½ teaspoon salt
- 2½ teaspoons baking powder
- 1 cup chopped California walnuts
- 1 cup (6 ounces) semisweet chocolate pieces
- 1 teaspoon vanilla extract

Add shortening to sugar and mix well. Add eggs, one at a time, beating well after each addition. Add sifted dry ingredients, nuts, chocolate, and vanilla. Spread in greased pan (15 x 10 x 1 inch). Bake in preheated moderate oven (350° F.) for about 25 minutes. While warm, cut into 50 bars.

HUNGARIAN WALNUT BARS

- 2¼ cups sifted all-purpose flour
- ¼ teaspoon salt
- 1 cup granulated sugar
- 1 cup soft butter
- 2 egg yolks
- 1 tablespoon brandy
- 4 cups finely chopped California walnuts
- ½ cup firmly packed light brown sugar
- 1½ teaspoons ground cinnamon
- 4 unbeaten egg whites
- Confectioners' sugar (optional)

Sift flour, salt, and ½ cup of the granulated sugar. Blend in butter; add egg yolks and brandy. Pat evenly into greased and floured pan (15 x 10 x 1 inch). Bake 15 minutes. In heavy saucepan put remaining granulated sugar, the walnuts, brown sugar, cinnamon, and egg whites. Cook, stirring, over low heat until sugars dissolve. Increase heat and cook until mixture no longer clings to sides of pan. Spread on baked mixture. Return to oven for 15 minutes longer. Cool slightly. Cut into bars 1 x 3 inches. Dust cookies with confectioners' sugar, if desired. Store in airtight container. Makes 50.

SERBIAN WALNUT STRIPS

- 4½ cups (1 pound) walnuts, ground
- 1 cup granulated sugar
- 1 teaspoon fresh lemon juice
- 4 egg whites, unbeaten
- ¾ cup confectioners' sugar

Mix walnuts and granulated sugar. Add lemon juice and 3 egg whites. Knead until mixture sticks together. Pat out on sugared board to rectangle 3 inches wide and ½ inch thick. Beat remaining egg white stiff and gradually beat in confectioners' sugar. Spread over walnut mixture. Cut into strips 1½ x ¾ inch. Arrange cookies in rows on well-greased cookie sheets. Bake in preheated very slow oven (200°F.) for 20 minutes. Makes 6 dozen.

WALNUT CRESCENTS

- 1 cup soft butter or margarine
- Confectioners' sugar
- 1½ teaspoons water
- 2 teaspoons vanilla extract
- 2 cups unsifted all-purpose flour
- 1 cup chopped California walnuts

Cream butter and ¼ cup confectioners' sugar. Add remaining ingredients and mix well. Shape into rolls about ½ inch in diameter and cut into 1-inch pieces. Put on ungreased cookie sheets and pull ends down slightly to form crescent shapes. Bake in preheated moderate oven (375°F.) for about 15 minutes. While warm, roll in confectioners' sugar; roll again when cool. Makes about 6 dozen walnut crescents.

BAKED BONBONS

- 2½ cups (1 pound) pitted dates
- 2 cups (½ pound) shelled California walnuts
- 3 egg whites
- ¾ cup sugar
- 1 teaspoon vanilla extract
- Food coloring

Grind dates and nuts together twice and shape into 72 small balls. Beat egg whites until they begin to hold their shape. Gradually add sugar and continue beating until mixture is stiff but not dry. Add vanilla and divide into halves. Tint half pink and half green. With a teaspoon roll date balls in meringue and put on greased cookie sheets. Swirl top of each. Bake in preheated very slow oven (250°F.) for 30 minutes. Makes 6 dozen.

WASSAIL—A drink once popular in England for special occasions such as Christmas and Twelfth Night. It consisted of ale or wine flavored with spices. Other ingredients such as toast, sugar, and especially roasted apples were added.

A wassail was originally a toast made to someone's health or good luck as you gave him a cup of wine. The word came from the Old Norse *ves heill,* or "Be in good health." Wassail bowls and wassailing were Old English festive customs. The wassail bowl was surrounded with merriment. Often at Christmas, groups of Christmas carolers would go a-wassailing, traveling from house to house caroling their hosts in return for a cup of the delicious wassail. In those days the custom of singing was so connected with the drink itself that a wassail meant a carol. It is hard to tell whether more drinking or singing went on.

OLD-TIME WASSAIL BOWL

- 6 baking apples
- ½ cup sugar
- Whole cloves
- ½ teaspoon each of ground cinnamon and nutmeg
- 1 tablespoon grated lemon rind
- 2 quarts muscatel
- 4 eggs, separated

Core apples and peel down to about 1 inch from the stem end. Fill cavities with the sugar and bake in preheated moderate oven (350°F.) for 30 minutes to 1 hour, or until tender but still firm. Time will depend on kind of apples. When done, stud apples with whole cloves. Add ground spices and lemon rind to the wine and heat in top part of a double boiler over hot water. Beat egg whites until stiff. Then beat egg yolks until thick and lemon-colored. Fold egg yolks into whites. Put apples in bottom of wassail (punch) bowl. Add egg whites to wine and pour over apples. Serve in warm mugs. Makes 2 quarts, plus the apples.

WASSAIL BOWL

- 4 quarts apple cider
- 1 cup firmly packed brown sugar
- 1 can (6 ounces) frozen lemon-juice concentrate
- 1 can (6 ounces) frozen orange-juice concentrate
- 6 each of whole cloves and allspice
- 1 tablespoon ground nutmeg
- 24 cinnamon sticks

Put cider, sugar, and fruit juices (undiluted) in kettle. Tie cloves and allspice in a small cheesecloth bag. Add to cider with nutmeg. Cover and simmer for 20 minutes. Remove spice bag. Serve beverage hot in mugs with a cinnamon stick in each mug. Makes twenty-four 6-ounce mugs.

WATER—Water is one of the most essential substances on the face of the earth, if not the most important. Technically it is a chemical compound, H_2O, which consists of two atoms of hydrogen united with one atom of oxygen in every water molecule. Water is present in a solid state as ice or snow; as a liquid it is the water we know; in a gaseous state it is steam or water vapor. All vegetables and animals, certainly not excluding man, contain water. Man can live longer without food than he can without water.

Chemically pure water of two parts hydrogen and one part oxygen is obtainable only by filtration and distillation. It does not exist naturally. The purest water obtainable in natural form is rain water in places remote from human habitation, taken after the rain has been falling long enough to have cleared the atmosphere, or water obtained from melting snow that has fallen in the polar regions. Water in some mountain lakes resulting from melting snow and resting on impermeable rocks is also relatively pure.

Such water is known as "soft," in contrast to "hard" water which implies a mineral content of eight or more grains to the gallon. Minerals vary greatly.

Those most often found in hard water are lime and magnesia salts. These minerals are not harmful in any way and a small amount actually improves the flavor of the water. Soft water is often flat by contrast.

So called "pure water" provided by communities for drinking water is not pure in the chemical sense, but is uncontaminated by sewage. In large cities, chlorine is sometimes added to insure further protection.

Spring water is frequently regarded as the highest type of pure water because of its bright and sparkling appearance. This is due primarily, however, to the presence of minerals. When minerals are present in sufficient amount to be of alleged medicinal value, the water is classed as mineral water.

Distilled water is ordinary water filtered, boiled in vacuum boilers to remove volatile organic matter, converted into steam in stills, and finally condensed and aerated. Aeration removes the flat taste of the distilled product. This water is free of salts and organic matter. It should be stored in siphons or corked bottles to insure its continued purity.

Water can be sterilized at home by boiling, thus killing all organic matter. It, too, should be carefully stored.

Spring water and mineral water are widely available; bottled and distilled water can be bought in small quantities in drugstores. Electric water distillers are available for homes. They remove taste and odor-producing minerals and salts, and eliminate fluorides and detergents. Water-tap filters which remove objectionable taste, odor, discoloration, and cloudiness are also available. Activated charcoal within the filter removes chlorine, sulphur, rust, scale, and algae.

Electric water coolers of half-gallon size are available for home use, as well as water containers with spigots for refrigerators. These are helpful in conserving water since they eliminate the prolonged running of tap water to obtain a cool drink.

WATER CHESTNUT—The fruit of a water plant of the genus *Trapa* with floating leaves and small white flowers. The nutlike fruit kernel resembles a true chestnut in shape and color, but is crunchy in texture. Native to Asia, it is widely used in Oriental cookery. Water chestnuts can be used in poultry, meat, seafood, and egg dishes, and add a pleasant crispness when combined with soft foods.

Canned water chestnuts are widely available in the United States and can be bought in most food stores. Pickled water chestnuts are also available.

Caloric Value

☐ 3½ ounces, raw = 79 calories

DUCK HASH

¼ cup butter or margarine
1 small onion, chopped
2 cups diced cooked potatoes
2 cups chopped cooked duckling
½ cup chopped water chestnuts
½ cup diced green pepper
½ cup consommé
1 teaspoon salt
¼ teaspoon pepper
½ teaspoon grated lemon rind
¼ cup heavy cream
Buttered soft bread crumbs

Melt butter, add onion, and cook until golden. Add potatoes and brown lightly. Add next 8 ingredients and cook for several minutes. Put in shallow baking dish and sprinkle with crumbs. Bake in preheated moderate oven (350°F.) for about 30 minutes. Makes 4 servings.

ROAST PORK WITH CHINESE VEGETABLES

¼ teaspoon salt
½ cup diced mushrooms
½ pound Chinese cabbage, diced
¾ cup diced water chestnuts
¼ cup diced bamboo shoots
12 snow-pea pods (frozen can be used)
¼ cup diced celery
¼ cup water
2 cups diced roast pork
1 teaspoon cornstarch
Dash of pepper
¼ teaspoon sugar
½ teaspoon monosodium glutamate
¼ cup blanched almonds, toasted

Put salt in hot, well-greased skillet. Add mushrooms, cabbage, water chestnuts, bamboo shoots, snow-pea pods, and celery. Stir-fry for 30 seconds. Add the water, cover, and cook for 2 minutes. Add the roast pork and stir. Blend cornstarch with a little water and add to first mixture with pepper, sugar, and monosodium glutamate. Cook, stirring, for 30 seconds. Put in serving dish and garnish with almonds. Makes 4 servings.

WATER-CHESTNUT AND RICE STUFFING

1 medium onion, minced
1½ cups diced celery
⅓ cup butter or margarine
1⅓ cups cooked rice
1 cup chopped water chestnuts
2 teaspoons grated fresh gingerroot or other spice or herb to taste
Salt and pepper to taste

Cook onion and celery in the butter for 5 minutes. Add remaining ingredients and mix lightly. Use as stuffing for duck. Makes about 4 cups.

WATERCRESS—This is the most popular and widely eaten of the cresses, plants of the mustard family which includes peppergrass or garden cress, winter cress or rocket, and spring or Belle Isle cress. All have crisp green leaves and a pungent, rather bitter taste, each variety with its own characteristics. Peppergrass is sometimes sprinkled over such dishes as beet soup; the more bitter winter and spring cresses should be cooked with another herb like spinach to cut their strong flavor. All the cresses may be boiled as potherbs; and all of them are delicious in salads, usually with other greens. Minced cresses are sprinkled on cream soups, or used minced to garnish vegetables. Watercress, the most widely available of the cresses, is used as garnish for canapés and seafood appetizers; as garnish for meats, poultry, and fish; minced and blended into cottage- or cream-cheese spreads or omelets and egg dishes; minced and added to biscuit dough or piecrust; used like sorrel; sprinkled over carrots, cauliflower, potatoes, green beans, and sweet vegetables.

Watercress gets its name because it grows in cold running water. It is a native of temperate Europe, and is naturalized in the brooks and ponds of North America. The word "cress" alone has a long history; it is perhaps related to the Latin word for grass, and even further back to the Sanskrit verb meaning "to eat," especially gnawing or nibbling. It would then be a distantly removed linguistic cousin to the word "grass." Humans, having only one stomach, cannot digest grass, but cress has long been eaten by man.

The Greeks and Romans both esteemed watercress. The old Greek proverb, "Eat cress and learn more wit," was taken seriously by the Romans who ate it with vinegar as a remedy for deranged minds. Later, cress's reputation for curing madness diminished, but it was thought to have other miraculous qualities. One Renaissance Englishman wrote: "The eating of water cress doth restore the wanted bloom to the cheeks of old-young ladies." John Evelyn, the 17th-century Englishman of letters who wrote a book about salads, decided that watercress was "best for raw and cold Stomachs, but nourish little." Evelyn was right about many things but wrong about watercress. Modern nutritionists recommend its use for its high vitamin content, as well as its goodly amounts of iron.

Availability—Watercress is available all year round with peak supplies in May,

June, and July.

Purchasing Guide—It is sold in small bunches. Look for fresh deep greens and crisp stems with no yellowing or wilting.

Storage—Store away from light and heat. To keep, wash well, shake water from the leaves, and refrigerate in a tightly covered jar.

☐ Refrigerator shelf: 7 days

Nutritive Food Values—A good source of vitamins A and C and supplies a variety of minerals including iron if eaten in large amounts.

Basic Preparation—Wash thoroughly in several changes of water to remove all traces of sand. Remove all tough stems and wilted portions. When cooked, it should be cooked for a very short time.

CREAM-OF-CORN-AND-CRESS SOUP

1 small onion, chopped
¼ cup butter or margarine
1½ cups cut fresh corn
1½ teaspoons suet
½ teaspoon sugar
1 cup water
1½ cups milk
⅛ teaspoon white pepper
1 cup chopped watercress
2 egg yolks, beaten
½ cup light cream
Paprika

Sauté onion in butter in saucepan for 2 or 3 minutes. Add corn, suet, sugar, and water. Bring to boil and simmer, covered, for about 10 minutes. Add milk, pepper, and cress; cook for 2 or 3 minutes longer. Force mixture through a food mill or purée in a blender. Add egg yolks and cream; heat gently. Serve with a sprinkling of paprika. Makes about 1 quart or 4 servings.

CHICKEN AND WATERCRESS SOUP

Heat together 1 can (10½ ounces) chicken soup, 1 can water, and 1 vegetable bouillon cube. Stir until cube dissolves. Add ½ cup chopped watercress. Serve immediately. Makes 2 or 3 servings.

WATERCRESS SALAD

To a bowlful of freshly washed and crisped watercress in bite-size pieces, add 2 or 3 hard-cooked eggs, peeled and sliced. Add 2 or 3 chopped fresh green onions and salt and pepper to taste. Top with 1 or 2 tablespoons olive oil to taste. Toss with a dash or so of wine vinegar. Makes 4 servings.

WATERCRESS SANDWICH

Mix potted meat with chopped watercress and celery. Moisten with mayonnaise or salad dressing.

SOUR-CREAM WATERCRESS SAUCE

½ cup salad dressing
½ cup dairy sour cream
½ teaspoon salt
¼ teaspoon pepper
Few drops of hot pepper sauce
½ cup chopped watercress

Mix together all ingredients. Makes about 1½ cups sauce.

WATERMELON—A member of the gourd family, native to Africa, and most commonly a spherical fruit with pink or red flesh and many seeds. There are many varieties among which are yellow and white watermelons as well as the red. Seeds may be white, red, brown, black, green, or speckled. The rind is usually dark green. Watermelons average twenty-four to forty pounds, although there are some small two- to ten-pound varieties, and even some monstrously large ones. The flesh is sweet with a high water content.

In the United States watermelons are a universally popular summer dessert, but in the dry countries of Africa and in Near Eastern countries such as Iraq, watermelons are not confined to the dessert course. There they are an important staple food and an animal feed. They are especially valuable in countries where water is scarce, because they are such a thirst-quenching delight. In some parts of Asia the seeds are roasted and eaten as snacks. Americans prize their watermelon-rind pickles; the Orientals preserve entire halves of watermelon in salt or brine.

Watermelons were cultivated by the ancient Egyptians. The warmer parts of Russia and the Near East have long been able to grow these melons. Eventually, with many other foods, their culture spread to Europe. The botanists of the 16th and 17th centuries described all the varieties of watermelon we know today.

Watermelons were grown in this country quite early in its history. They were found in Massachusetts gardens as early as 1629, and in Florida not too long afterward. Watermelons are most successfully raised in a warm climate, and they flourish throughout the South of this country.

Availability—Watermelons are sold whole, halved, quartered, or by the slice. They are available in May, June, July, and August.

Pickled watermelon rind and dried watermelon seeds are also available.

Frozen melon-ball mixtures which include watermelon are available.

Purchasing Guide—Watermelons should be symmetrical in shape and firm to the touch. The shape varies from long oval to small cannonball. The skin is smooth with a deep green to gray color with a yellowish underside. The flesh is red with black seeds dispersed throughout.

Storage—Wrap cut surfaces in wax paper. Use within 1 or 2 days.

☐ Refrigerator shelf: 1 to 2 days

Nutritive Food Values—A good source of vitamin A and a fair source of vitamin C.

☐ 3½ ounces = 26 calories

Basic Preparation—Chill before serving. Cut into wedges or cubes, removing seeds. Serve with fresh lime or lemon juice, if desired.

FROSTY WATERMELON SOUP

1 envelope unflavored gelatin
¼ cup cold water
6 cups diced fresh watermelon
¼ cup sugar
⅓ cup fresh lime juice
¼ teaspoon salt
Fresh mint sprigs

Soften gelatin in cold water. Place over hot water to melt until ready to use. Press watermelon through a sieve. Add sugar, lime juice, and salt. Stir in melted gelatin. Chill until mixture has thickened slightly, 3 to 4 hours. Serve in chilled bouillon cups. Garnish with sprigs of fresh mint. Makes 1 quart, or 5 servings.

MOLDED WATERMELON SALAD

1 box (3 ounces) watermelon-flavored gelatin
1 cup hot water
3 tablespoons fresh lemon juice
¼ cup fresh orange juice
½ cup muscatel
2 cups diced watermelon
Salad greens
Dairy sour cream

Dissolve gelatin in hot water. Add next 3 ingredients. Chill until slightly thickened. Fold in melon and pour into 1½-quart mold. Chill until firm. Unmold on greens: serve with sour cream. Makes 6 servings.

RIPE WATERMELON PICKLE

4 quarts diced red watermelon, seeded
5 cups sugar
¼ teaspoon salt
½ cup cider vinegar
2 slices of lemon
1 tablespoon cracked whole cinnamon
1 teaspoon whole cloves

Put diced melon in colander and with the hands squeeze out as much juice as possible. Let drain for 1 hour. Put melon, sugar, salt, vinegar, and lemon in large heavy kettle. Add spices tied in cheesecloth bag. Cook slowly for 50 to 60 minutes. Stir occasionally to prevent sticking. Pack at once into hot sterilized jars and seal. Makes about 2 pints.

WATERMELON-LIME COOLER

Take one-fourth of a good-size watermelon, and remove all seeds. Pound flesh or press through a food mill to remove juice. There should be about 3 cups. Add the juice of 1 large lime, and sugar to taste. Put a cube of watermelon and a slice of lime in each of 4 tall glasses. Add ice cubes, and pour watermelon-juice mixture over ice. Makes 4 servings.

Watermelon-Lime Cooler

SPICED WATERMELON HONEY

3 pounds watermelon rind
1 cup water
6 cups sugar
3 lemon slices
3 pieces of whole dried gingerroot
½ teaspoon whole cloves
2 cinnamon sticks
¼ teaspoon salt

Remove all green outer rind and red meat from watermelon rind; discard. Force remaining rind through food chopper, using coarse blade. Measure; there should be 6 cups. Put in kettle with water. Cook slowly, uncovered, for 25 minutes, or until melon is translucent. Add sugar and lemon. Tie spices in a cheesecloth bag and add with salt to first mixture. Cook slowly, stirring frequently, for 1 hour, or until thickened. Remove spice bag; ladle mixture into hot sterilized jars; seal. Makes 2½ pints.

WATERMELON-MARASCHINO PICKLE

2 pounds (about 2½ quarts) prepared watermelon rind
1 tablespoon powdered slaked lime (buy in drugstore)
Water
Cider vinegar
1 teaspoon salt
2½ pounds (5 cups) sugar
1 tablespoon each of whole allspice and cloves
6 small pieces of cinnamon stick
1 jar (4 to 6 ounces) maraschino cherries, drained

To prepare rind, pare and remove all green and pink portions from watermelon rind. Cut into 1-inch pieces and soak for 3 hours in lime dissolved in 1 quart water. Drain rind; cover with fresh cold water and cook, covered, for 1 hour, or until tender. Drain and cover with a weak vinegar (1 cup to 2 cups water) and let stand overnight. Drain. In preserving kettle bring to boil 3 cups vinegar, the salt, ½ cup water, the sugar, and the spices tied in a piece of cheesecloth. Cover and let stand for 1 hour. Add watermelon and simmer, covered, for 2 hours. Add cherries about 20 minutes before pickle is done. Discard spice bag and spoon pickle at once into hot sterilized jars; cover with boiling syrup. Seal jars. Makes 4 pints.

WATERMELON SHERBET

3 cups watermelon juice
½ cup sugar
⅛ teaspoon salt
1 envelope unflavored gelatin
Juice of 1 lemon

Mix first 3 ingredients. Remove about ¼ cup to small saucepan. Soften gelatin in juice in saucepan. Dissolve over hot water or very low heat. Add with lemon juice to first mixture. Freeze in crank-type freezer. Makes about 1 quart.

Note: To make juice, force watermelon pulp through a food mill or sieve. To get 3 cups juice, you will need about one-fourth of a good-size watermelon.

WATERMELON ALMOND SHERBET

1 watermelon
2 tablespoons cornstarch
1 teaspoon almond extract
⅓ cup sugar
½ teaspoon salt
1 teaspoon grated lemon peel

Remove the rind and 1 inch of white from melon and put red meat through food chopper, accumulating 4 cups pulp and juice. In saucepan over low heat cook the other ingredients. When well blended, stir in melon and restore to cooking temperature. Beat thoroughly and freeze. Makes 8 servings.

WEDDING CAKE—A white cake, often with spices and candied peel added, and flavored with almond extract, traditionally baked in tiered layers, covered with white frosting, and decorated. The first piece is supposed to be cut by the bride and groom together. This cake was formerly called the bride's cake. The groom's cake was a cake made with a dark batter, having molasses, raisins, candied fruits, nuts, and spices in it. Nowadays, the kind of cake served is a matter of choice. Formerly both bride's and groom's cakes were offered.

WEDDING CAKE
(Bride's Cake)

5¼ cups sifted cake flour
6 teaspoons baking powder
2 teaspoons salt
3 cups sugar
8 egg whites
1 cup shortening at room temperature
2 cups milk
1 teaspoon almond extract
1½ teaspoons orange extract
Ornamental Frosting

Mix flour, baking powder, salt, and 2 cups sugar. Beat egg whites in a large bowl until foamy. Gradually add remaining sugar, beating only until meringue will hold up in soft peaks. Stir shortening in mixing bowl just to soften. Sift in dry ingredients. Add 1½ cups of the milk and the flavorings. Mix until all flour is dampened. Then beat for 2 minutes at low speed in electric mixer. Add remaining milk and meringue and beat for 1 minute longer in mixer. Line bottoms of 1 square pan (10 x 10 x 2 inches) and 2 square pans (8 x 8 x 2 inches each) with paper. Pour batter into pans to equal depths. Bake in preheated slow oven (325°F.) for 45 minutes, or until done. Cool on racks. When cold, brush cakes to remove any loose crumbs. Trim one of the 8-inch cakes to make a 5-inch square. Put 10-inch cake on a large flat tray or plate. Spread top and sides with a thin layer of Ornamental Frosting. Cover top of cake smoothly with more Frosting. Center 8-inch cake on top of 10-inch cake and frost. Center 5-inch cake on 8-inch cake. Frost. Then spread Frosting over entire cake to give a flat, even base for decorating. Force remaining Frosting through a pastry tube to make flowers, garlands, etc. Makes 50 servings.

Ornamental Frosting

½ cup soft butter or margarine
½ teaspoon salt
12 cups (3 pounds) sifted confectioners' sugar
5 egg whites, unbeaten
¼ cup light cream (about)
2 teaspoons vanilla extract

Cream butter. Add salt and part of the sugar gradually, blending after each addition. Add remaining sugar, alternately with the egg whites first, then with the cream, until of the right consistency for spreading. Beat after each addition until smooth. Add vanilla, and blend. (While frosting cake, keep bowl of frosting covered with a damp cloth to prevent excessive evaporation.) Makes 5 cups, or enough to frost one 10 x 10 x 2-inch cake and two 8 x 8 x 2-inch cakes and to decorate.

Note: Favors are occasionally put into the bride's cake: a thimble, tiny horseshoe, ring, button, or other favorite silver charms should first be wrapped in wax paper. Make small cuts at random in cake and insert charms before frosting cake.

WEDDING CAKE
(Groom's Cake)

4 cups sifted all-purpose flour
1 teaspoon baking powder
½ teaspoon each of ground cloves, cinnamon, and mace
2 cups butter or margarine
2¼ cups (1 pound) firmly packed brown sugar
10 eggs, well beaten
½ pound each of candied cherries and pineapple
1 pound dates, seeded and sliced
1 pound each of seedless raisins and currants
½ pound citron, thinly sliced
¼ pound each of candied orange and lemon peel.
2 cups chopped nuts
1 cup each of honey and molasses
½ cup cider

Sift flour, baking powder, and spices together 3 times. Cream butter. Gradually add sugar; cream until light and fluffy. Add eggs, fruits, peels, nuts, honey, molasses, and cider. Gradually add sifted dry ingredients, beating after each addition until blended. Spoon into 3 loaf pans (10 x 5 x 3 inches each), greased, lined with heavy paper, and greased again. Bake in preheated very slow oven (250°F.) for 3½ to 4 hours. Makes 80 servings.

Note: Half of cake is often served at the wedding reception and the remainder put in gift boxes for the guests to take home.

WEIGH—In cookery to weigh means to calculate accurate amounts of required ingredients by the use of scales. The recipes in this Encyclopedia are based upon measurements rather than weights, and while household scales can be helpful in cookery, they are not absolutely essential. However, one of the areas in which they are almost a necessity is in canning, where amounts of ingredients in recipes are often given in weights. Scales are also helpful in the preparation of food for special diets.

EQUIPMENT

A number of different models of household scales are available. They are of two types generally: those which use weights, and the spring type. The first are the more accurate; and for this reason, weight scales are the ones used commercially. Both types of scales come in various sizes. Gram scales are a type of weight scale and are helpful for special diets. Weight scales which weigh both ounces and grams are now available.

AVOIRDUPOIS WEIGHT

Unit	Weight	Metric Equivalent
Pound	16 ounces or 7000 grains	0.453 kilograms
Ounce	16 drams or 437.5 grains	28.349 grams
Dram	0.0625 ounces or 27.343 grains	1.771 grams
Grain	0.0023 ounces or 0.036 drams	0.0648 grams

Weights and Equivalent Measures of Common Foods

Beans, dried navy: 1 pound=2⅓ cups uncooked=6 cups cooked
Beans, dried kidney: 1 pound=2½ cups uncooked=6¾ cups cooked
Beans, dried Lima: 1 pound=2½ cups uncooked=6 cups cooked
Butter, unwhipped: 1 pound or 4 sticks=2 cups
Butter, whipped: ¼ pound or 1 stick=½ cup
Cheese, cottage: ½ pound=1 cup
Cheese, cream: 3 ounces=6 tablespoons
Cheese, grated: 4 ounces=1 cup
Chestnuts: 1½ pounds in-the-shell=1 pound shelled
Chicken: 3½ pounds drawn chicken=2 cups cooked, diced
Chocolate: 1 ounce=1 square
Cocoa: 1 pound=4 cups
Coconut, finely grated: 3½ ounces=1 cup
Coffee: 1 pound=5 cups
Cornmeal: 1 pound=3 cups
Dates: 1 pound=2½ cups pitted, cut
Flour, all-purpose: 4 ounces=1 cup sifted
Flour, cake: 4 ounces=1 cup plus 2 tablespoons, sifted
Flour, whole-wheat: 7 ounces=1 cup
Macaroni: 8 ounces=2 cups uncooked=4 to 5 cups cooked
Meat, beef: 1 pound=3 cups cooked minced
Meat, beef: 1 pound uncooked=2 cups ground
Mushrooms: ½ pound sliced raw=2½ cups
Noodles: 2⅔ ounces=1 cup uncooked=1 cup cooked
Oats, rolled, quick-cooking: 1 pound=5⅔ cups uncooked
Oil: 2 cups=1 pound
Peanuts: 1 pound in-the-shell=⅔ pound of nutmeats
Peanuts: 1 pound shelled=3¼ cups
Peas, dry: 1 pound, cooked=2½ cups
Peas, split: 1 pound=5½ cups cooked
Peas, split: 1 pound, uncooked=2 cups uncooked=5 cups cooked
Pecans: 1 pound in-the-shell=½ pound nutmeats
Pecans: 1 pound shelled=4¼ cups
Potatoes: 1 pound=3 medium
Potatoes: 1 pound raw, unpeeled=2 cups cooked, mashed
Raisins, seedless whole: 1 pound=2¾ cups
Rice: 1 pound=2½ cups uncooked=8 cups cooked
Spaghetti: 8 ounces=2½ cups uncooked=4 to 5 cups cooked
Sugar, granulated: 1 pound=2¼ cups
Sugar, brown, firmly packed: 1 pound=2¼ cups
Sugar, confectioners': 1 pound=3½ cups
Walnuts: 1 pound in-the-shell=½ pound of nutmeats
Walnuts: 1 pound shelled=4½ cups
Yeast: 1 package active dry yeast=¼ ounce or 2 teaspoons

Can Sizes

Industry Term	Approximate Net Weight	Approximate Cups
6 ounce	6 ounces	¾
8 ounce	8 ounces	1
Picnic	10½ to 12 ounces	1¼
12 ounce	12 ounces	1½
No. 300	14 to 16 ounces	1¾
No. 303	16 to 17 ounces	2
No. 2	1 pound, 4 ounces or 1 pint, 2 fluid ounces	2½
No. 2½	1 pound, 13 ounces	3½
No. 3 cylinder	3 pounds, 3 ounces or 1 quart, 14 fluid ounces	5¾
No. 10	6½ pounds to 7 pounds, 5 ounces	12 to 13

Frozen Food Packages

Vegetables	9 to 16 ounces
Fruits	10 to 16 ounces
Canned Frozen Fruits	13½ to 16 ounces
Frozen Juice Concentrates	6 and 12 ounces
Soups	10 ounces

WELSH RABBIT or RAREBIT—A popular dish of melted cheese poured over toast. Beer, ale, wine, or even milk may be added to the rabbit. When topped with a poached egg it is called a Buck or Golden Buck.

WELSH RABBIT

½ pound sharp Cheddar cheese, diced or crumbled
⅓ cup milk
¼ teaspoon powdered mustard
1 teaspoon Worcestershire
Dash of cayenne
1 egg, well beaten
Toast or crackers

Put cheese in a heavy skillet and melt over very, very low heat, stirring constantly. As cheese melts, gradually add milk, stirring to blend. Add seasonings. Then add egg and cook, stirring, over very, very low heat until smooth and thickened. Serve on toast. Makes 4 to 6 servings.

WELSH RABBIT WITH BEER

2 tablespoons butter or margarine
1 pound sharp Cheddar cheese, shredded
½ teaspoon powdered mustard
Dash of cayenne
½ teaspoon salt
1 teaspoon Worcestershire
½ cup beer, ale, or milk
2 eggs, slightly beaten
8 slices of toast
Parsley

Melt butter in top part of double boiler or chafing dish over direct heat. Add cheese, and heat, stirring occasionally, until cheese is melted. Put over boiling water, add seasonings, and pour in the liquid mixed with eggs. Cook until thick, stirring frequently. Serve on toast with garnish of parsley. Makes 4 servings.

GOLDEN BUCK

½ pound sharp process American Cheddar cheese
¾ cup light cream or evaporated milk
1 teaspoon Worcestershire
½ teaspoon prepared mustard
Toast
4 eggs, poached

Melt cheese in top part of double boiler over hot water. Gradually add cream, stirring constantly. Add seasonings. Pour over toast and top each slice with a poached egg. Makes 4 servings.

WESTERN
COOKERY
by Idwal Jones

The Pacific Coast, like ancient Gaul, has been divided into three parts: California, Oregon, and Washington. California's sea frontage runs upward for 780 miles, or roughly the distance from the toe of Italy to the heart of Sweden. Its lower zone, from the Mexican border up to Santa Barbara, is arid, but irrigation has long made it a copious producer of edibles of almost every variety. It yields oranges, lemons, grapefruit, olives, almonds, dates, avocados, and other subtropical fruits and vegetables.

The zone has had its own traditional cuisine that began with the settlement of the Spaniards in the late 1700's, and the planting of grapevines by friars in their mission gardens at San Diego.

The Spanish and Mexican influence on tastes in food are perceptible on every hand. The ubiquitous *frijoles,* and the beans' accompaniment, the hot chili peppers, red, green, or black, are grown in vast amounts. Also the inevitable tomato, which was widely eaten here when elsewhere in the country it was shunned as the "poisonous" love apple.

Southern Californians have a deep-rooted fondness for barbecues, with meat grilled outdoors, served with thin fried disks of cornmeal paste known as tortillas, and as enchiladas when rolled up with cheese and a fiery stuffing. These are the customary dishes for social gatherings of every kind even at fashionable Santa Barbara, where the *Visitadores* go a-riding in Spanish garb to meet at their annual fiesta. Barbecues, a reminder of the old pastoral days, are clung to with a persistence that gives rise to some wonderment, for they are held at night, and their survival does seem curious, for in southern California dusk is followed by a drop in temperature, and the steaks must be whisked from the grill on sizzling-hot plates.

But the barbecue is as enduring as folklore, and nowadays has been improved by the serving of lettuce dressed with lemon juice, olive oil, and a topping of grated cheese.

A singularity of California is that in its great central valley, a flat corridor running between two ranges of mountains and seldom more than an hour and a half from the ocean, the climate is uniform throughout. Around Sacramento oranges may even be picked a fortnight earlier than at Los Angeles, 500 miles to the south. A warm dry plain this, where a succession of grain, sugar-beet and red-bean fields, also fruit orchards, and vineyards, their lines wheeling as they open and close like the ribs of a fan, stretch onward to infinity. At intervals occur pasturages where cattle graze in the blue shadow of scrub oaks, a touch faintly reminiscent of deer parks in England. Beyond this irrigated domain with its sparse settlements lies the delta area, another country. Here the San Joaquin and Sacramento Rivers and a plenitude of lesser streams pour their waters into a chain of warm inland seas. And when the Pacific sends in its chill, punctual tides, the area is cloaked with a dense gray mist that here, as in San Francisco, is known as the tule fog.

In the Delta area food problems are unknown. Its repertory of foodstuffs is extravagant. In its 200 square miles exist folk of several backgrounds, each with their own type of cookery. Sikhs in turbans work the asparagus, rice, and artichoke fields. Chinese work the oyster beds, catch shrimps, and raise hogs, poultry, and fat white ducks for San Francisco's large Chinatown. Their eating houses are to be found at nearly every waterside wharf. The Italian and Portuguese fishermen are also hunters of feathered game that swarm in for the winter. Basques keep the area supplied with dairy stuffs, beef, and also marsh-bred lambs that forage in the bulrush tracts.

Ark dwellers, many of whom own a parcel of land on which they raise pigs and vegetables, especially the tomato, often pull up anchor to follow the "run" of some particular fish: shad, striped bass, salmon-trout, or a score of other varieties. Sturgeon, protected by law for many years, may again be caught, although angling for it is no gentle pastime.

Sturgeon has gone into the folklore of this area where the big fish was harried out of existence by the crews of rival fishing syndicates. At the city markets sturgeon could be bought for eight cents the pound, and its roe sold at fifty cents the bucketful. In the Delta it was salted down in barrels, and the ranch cooks braised cuts of it in red wine, or salted it down as if it were pork. Those were the lush days, still recounted by the older fishermen when they huddle around the stove in some waterside tavern until the fog has lifted.

The Delta is fortunate in having so close to it a market such as San Francisco. It is uniquely cosmopolitan. From its earliest days it has known every type of foreign cookery and adopted them all.

To procure seafood, its fishing fleet ranges the coast from Mexico where it catches abalone and tuna, visits Monterey Bay where fish of a hundred and fifty kinds abound, goes up to Alaska for the salmon, halibut, and so forth, and returns with this bounty to its base at Fisherman's Wharf. This is a congeries of fish bazaars and eating places, simple or elaborate, and a popular haunt of the citizens. They like shellfish, the Pacific crab, clams, and oysters, which are found nearer home. The native oysters, coppery and the size of a nickel, are sold not by the dozen but by the hundred. But above all reigns the favorite, the mammoth Pacific crab. On the wharf it is boiled outside in large iron pots that steam like so many geysers.

Dominant here are the crab fishermen, Italians of the third generation, who belong to an ancient guild hardly less devoted to the opera than to the netting and the cooking of crab. The local fish stew, the aromatic *cioppino,* and a much-fancied crab salad, are but two of their specialties. One story has it that *cioppino* was first made here by a Genoese captain who, deserted by his crew in the frenzy of the gold rush, turned his ship into a restaurant.

The Italians also introduced the artichoke, using it in dishes like the *frittata di carciofini* and also as a salad. They prefer their artichokes, which are of the globe kind, in young and tender bud. For eighty years San Francisco has been getting them from Colma, a village founded by Italians, a brief run southward on the "artichoke coast."

Colma came into renown when the champion athletes of the early 1900's, finding that the sandy rim made an agreeable run, chose the village as their training quarters. At its weather-beaten hotel they consumed artichokes in a variety of dishes, with a grating of hard cheese.

In cookery of this order, as in France where the soundest cookery is basically peasant, wine is indispensable. The culinary use of it is widespread, for the state has twenty-four districts where wine making is a hereditary craft. Three among them are Sonoma, a drowsy Spanish pueblo, and St. Helena, early settled by Germans, whose wineries seem like ancient châteaux. The winery of the classic vineyard at Livermore, however, has a plain workaday look, with a roof of galvanized iron.

Oregon is half forest, and for the rest valleys, small in the mountains and large in the central part, drained by wide rushing streams like the Willamette, the Rogue, and the Hood. Most Oregonians are country-bred, of New England descent, and their market towns have an old-fashioned air. In the Cascade Range, with its innumerable lakes and rivers, the coaching days endured longer than elsewhere, for the railroads came in late.

A typical farm in the Cascade uplands is a ten-acre forest clearing, fenced in to keep out the wild broom and rhododendrons, various deer, and the black bear. The cows amble wherever they choose, as do the goats, all of the silky Angora strain. Berries of every description, cultivated or wild, and the gooseberry which is extremely rare in California, grow wantonly, their branches sagging to earth. Oregon raspberries, peculiarly fragrant and of giant size, are prized above all. Raspberry jelly is made in almost every rural kitchen, and large amounts of it somehow turn up at luxury shops in the East.

Come winter, the cranberry, grown in the extensive bogs along the coast, makes its fitting appearance, for the game season has opened. Hunters bring in quail, wild pigeons, bobtailed deer, rabbits, and strings of pheasants, both of Chinese and Mongolian origin. These birds are prolific breeders, and myriads of them are turned loose from the state hatcheries.

To ward off any dearth in the flow of apple pies, the family orchard is customarily planted to apples of various kinds, like the Gravenstein, Gascoyne's Scarlet, American Mother, the quince-flavored Grieve, Egremont Russet, and other favorites, each with its own time for ripening. The daughter of the household is usually the guardian. She may have cut her teeth on apples, taken a course in pomology, and learned pastry making in her mother's kitchen.

One young lady, thus trained, entered a pie competition at a fair in the Rogue Valley. Apple culture is almost a religion and judges of apple pie regard as anarchic any departure from the fixed and ancient ways of making it. This modern young lady waited nervously for the verdict, one novice among the contestants, thirty-five in all. She won the blue ribbon, the judges lauding her pie for its old-fashionedness.

To achieve that was her intention. And she had used a recipe used by an ancestress who had cooked pies for President John Adams.

For all the popularity of the apple, it must yield to that of the pear, of which Oregon grows five times as many. Cherries also, especially the plump Ox-heart and Kentish cherries, which go into ambrosial tarts, are much grown. Bees thrive on their blooms and in the mountains, covered for months with wild sage, oregano, and the various thymes, beekeeping is much practiced. You look for bee farms in small nooks, shielded from rough winds, where rosemary grows magnificently and often makes a hedge. Country people prize rosemary honey and chunks of it in the comb, dark, glistening, and flavorsome, make part of their breakfast.

In the Northwest are secluded tracts of intensely green meadowland watered by innumerable brooks splashing down from the Cascade Mountains. Cows wade deep through fields of sorrel, cloves, and sown alfalfa. A dairy region is this, settled by German and Swiss farmers, whose homesteads are thriftily kept. They send their cream by truck to Astoria, on the Columbia River, and to the cheese factories in Tillamook.

Although their farms may be modern, womenfolk cling as tenaciously to old customs as do the Pennsylvania Dutch. Butter for their own use they make in the home dairy, a shed open to the breeze from the meadows. They form it into pats, stamped with a design of bees, a cow's head, or a maid in a sunbonnet.

In autumn the farmer presses apples to make cider, in which meat and ocean fish are generally braised. His garden supplies the white cabbage for the sauerkraut barrel; massive beets and turnips, always baked with cuminseed, and considerable red chard and fence-climbing spinach, destined for soup. What would the farm do without the plum tree? Its favorite dessert is raised dumplings, first boiled, then baked with plums in a heavily buttered sauce.

This cuisine has not spread much beyond the farms. The little pigs that live out with the cows are better known, especially at the innumerable villages on the Oregon coast. Smacks from California on their way to procure huge oysters at Tokeland on Willapa Bay in Washington pause at them to buy a hogshead cheese, an agreeable change in a diet that is largely fish. This hogshead cheese, prepared with old cider and herbs, is of a texture so firm that they often must hack it with jackknives.

Much fancied hereabouts is salmon, which comes largely from the estuary of the Columbia, the river that separates the state from Washington.

So abounding in large forests is Washington, and so thinly is it settled, that it is likely to retain its frontier character for decades to come. Its dwellers on the western side, almost wholly Nordic, have a strong awareness of the Pacific. The profusion of bays, sounds, estuaries, and gulfs, all packed with islands, has made this region a salt-water province. Here stand all its large ports and cities, growing with tomorrow in mind.

Deeper inland the axes ring, timbers fall, and in the wake of the loggers rise villages where life goes rustically forward. The early newcomers, except for the woodsmen who trekked in from Michigan and Wisconsin, were followed by settlers of the Down East strain, who arrived with their heirlooms, plows, and young trees from their home orchards.

The cookery here is still basically plain American, although modified by that of the later migrants and a food supply that lacked nothing in the way of fresh-water fish, deer and elk meat, greenstuffs, wild herbs, and salmon from the river and sea. Canadians have made popular their *Salmon tindish,* jugged hare, marinated deer and bear steaks, larded beef tongues, curried rabbit, and dishes involving the pigeon, pheasant, and partridge. Sausage, a viand that Canadians have never permitted to suffer in quality, are now found everywhere. Mostly they are of the highly spiced Oxford type.

In no roster of Washington foods should split-pea soup be omitted. Since the early days of the fur trade when it was introduced here by the French-Canadian voyageurs and trappers, it has been a country mainstay. Caldrons of this soup, laced with scraps of smoked pork, simmer at campfires in sixteen Indian reservations.

Along the western shore, where British people chose to settle, although not because of its moister air and fogs, one finds steak-and-kidney pudding and of course, plum pudding. Solidly planted here are the Germans, who brought with them their incomparable pancakes.

Latterly have come Finns, much devoted to cranberry-growing. But none have influenced Washington cookery more than the people from Sweden, who must be thanked for their ways of coping with lobsters and crabs, which they barbecue. To supply Seattle, the town on Puget Sound, which must consume nearly a million crabs each week, boats bring in loads of them from northern waters. The Alaskan crab, like its Japanese cousin, measures a foot and a half across the disc, and has legs three feet long.

Of all the customs in Washington none is of older usage than that of feasting at barbecues. The cook, in mackinaw and coonskin hat with tail, tends a grid on which succulent young pigs are roasting over a low fire of hardwood. With a bunch of twigs dipped into oil, he anoints the piglets until they are done and of a hue as golden as a sunset. When done, he sluices them with water from the brook, the skin instantly crackles, and the piglets are carved with the edge of a dinner plate. Applesauce, and plum tartlets are passed round, with mugs of chilled cider.

Merry occasions are these barbecues, evocative of the pioneer days, served in traditional style, and with foods eaten on the land from which they sprang.

APPETIZERS AND SOUPS

WINE PICNIC PÂTÉ

A wine picnic is a California institution. A glorious day planned for visitors from the East is often a trip to the Napa Valley vineyards (or the Livermore Valley or Santa Clara Valley) for a day of wine tasting and a picnic. A favorite bottle of wine purchased at the winery, a good cheese, and a loaf of French bread make a simple picnic.

- ¾ cup butter or margarine
- 1 pound chicken livers
- ½ pound fresh mushrooms
- 1 teaspoon salt
- ⅓ cup finely chopped green onions
- ½ cup of white wine
- 1 garlic clove, mashed
- Pinch of dillweed
- 4 drops of hot pepper sauce

Melt ¼ cup of the butter in frying pan. Add chicken livers, mushrooms, salt, and green onions; simmer for 5 minutes. Add wine, garlic, dillweed, and hot pepper sauce. Cover and cook slowly for 10 minutes more, or until chicken livers and mushrooms are very tender. Cool slightly and whirl in a blender until smooth, or press through a sieve. Blend in remaining butter. Taste and add additional salt if necessary. Pack into a crock; chill overnight. Makes about 3 cups.

SPLIT-PEA SOUP

- ½ pound salt pork, diced
- 1 cup chopped onion
- 2 garlic cloves, finely minced
- 1 pound green split peas
- 2 quarts water or broth
- 1 bay leaf
- Few celery leaves
- Freshly ground pepper to taste

Cook salt pork in kettle until browned. Remove pork and reserve. In fat remaining in kettle, cook onions and garlic for 2 or 3 minutes. Add peas and remaining ingredients except pork. Bring to a boil, cover, and simmer for 2 hours, or until peas are mushy. Purée through sieve, food mill, or in blender. Add pork and reheat. Makes about 2 quarts.

CHERRY SOUP SCANDINAVIAN

Use either sweet or tart cherries for this soup and sweeten accordingly.

- 1 cup water
- About ¾ cup sugar
- 2 lemon slices
- ⅛ teaspoon each of ground cinnamon and cloves
- 4 cups pitted fresh or frozen bing cherries
- 1½ tablespoons cornstarch
- 2 tablespoons water
- Red food coloring (optional)
- Heavy cream

Combine in a saucepan the water, sugar, lemon, cinnamon, and cloves. Bring to a boil and add cherries. Bring to a boil again and cook gently for about 2 minutes. Blend cornstarch and water and stir into cherries. Stirring gently, bring to a boil again. Cook until sauce thickens slightly and clears. Remove lemon slices. Add a few drops of food coloring if you wish. Chill. Serve as first course, or as dessert with cream. Makes 4 servings.

FISH AND SHELLFISH

There are innumerable "authentic" versions of this famous California dish, each with its adherents. This recipe is for a combination of fish, but it's basic enough to be used with lobster alone, or with crab, or just about any other denizen of the sea.

CIOPPINO

- 1½ pounds fish*
- ½ pound raw shrimps
- 1 large Dungeness crab
- 12 clams
- ½ cup olive oil
- 1 teaspoon minced garlic
- 1 cup chopped onion
- 1 cup chopped green onions
- ½ cup minced green pepper
- 1 can (8 ounces) tomato sauce
- 3½ cups (one 1-pound, 13-ounce can) tomatoes
- 2 cups red table wine
- 1 teaspoon salt
- ¼ teaspoon coarsely ground pepper
- ¼ teaspoon dried oregano
- ¼ teaspoon dried basil
- Parsley
- Hot garlic bread

*This fish should be a firm-fleshed one, like sea bass, rockfish, or even shark. Have it cut into good-size pieces. Have shrimps shelled and cleaned, the crab cleaned and cracked, the clams scrubbed. If there are no clams, use mussels, cockles, or oysters. To make the sauce, heat olive oil, next 11 ingredients, and ½ cup parsley together; then simmer for 5 minutes. Now arrange the fish, shrimps, and crabs in layers in a 3-quart kettle or casserole. Pour on the sauce, cover, and simmer over low heat or bake in preheated slow oven (300°F.) for 30 minutes, or until the fish is done. Add the clams and as soon as they open up, sprinkle with more chopped parsley and serve with lots of hot garlic bread. Bibs are almost a necessity when eating Cioppino. Makes 6 to 8 servings.

SHRIMPS

Most of the shrimps eaten in the West these days come from somewhere else: the Gulf of California, the Gulf of Mexico, or even more remote places. We do eat lots of them: as appetizers, main dishes, first courses, and salads. Here is a popular way to serve them.

SHRIMPS VICTORIA

- 1 pound raw shrimps
- 2 tablespoons minced shallots
- ¼ cup butter or margarine, or more
- ½ pound mushrooms
- 1 tablespoon all-purpose flour
- ½ teaspoon salt
- Pepper
- 3 tablespoons sherry
- 1½ cups dairy sour cream
- Hot cooked wild rice (optional)

Shell and clean the shrimps, and sauté them, along with the minced shallots, in the butter until shrimps are pink. Add the mushrooms and cook for 5 minutes, adding another tablespoon butter if needed. Sprinkle with the flour, salt, and some freshly ground pepper. Add sherry and sour cream and correct seasonings. Cook gently until hot and serve with wild rice if desired. Makes 6 servings.

PRAWNS IN CREAM

Generally speaking, there is no difference between a shrimp and a prawn, but Westerners title their largest shrimps (of several species) prawns.

- 2 pounds raw prawns or large shrimps
- Boiling salted water
- ¼ cup butter
- ½ cup heavy cream
- ¼ cup dry sherry
- 2 tablespoons finely chopped parsley
- Salt and pepper

Drop prawns into boiling water to cover and cook gently for 5 minutes. Drain, shell, and devein. Melt butter in large frying pan or chafing dish. Add prawns and cook them, turning gently, until lightly browned. Add cream, sherry, parsley, and salt and pepper to taste. Heat thoroughly. Spoon into crisp pastry cups or onto small toast points. Makes 6 servings.

CRABS

Westerners are unanimous in acknowledging that the Dungeness crab is the best

in the world, and many non-Westerners agree. It is sweet and meaty, and considerably larger than its Eastern cousins. Then there is the enormous King Crab from Alaska, which sometimes measures ten feet from claw to claw. When cooked and frozen, they are inclined to be a little stringy, but when frozen raw (they're *all* frozen, alas), they have a fine delicate flavor. Cracked Crab is a great favorite from San Diego to the Olympic Peninsula.

CRACKED CRAB

Dungeness crabs are cleaned, the legs and claws cracked open, the body cut into 4 sections. The pieces are heaped onto a bed of ice, and the participants shell out the meat and consume it simply with homemade mayonnaise, crusty French bread, and plenty of dry white wine. A good-size Dungeness crab will serve 2 not-too-hungry people.

HOT CRAB SALAD

On the West Coast the sweet Dungeness crab is used.

- 1 pound flaked crabmeat (about 2 cups)
- 1 cup sliced celery
- ½ cup finely chopped green pepper
- 2 hard-cooked eggs, chopped
- 1 cup mayonnaise
- 1 tablespoon each of fresh lemon juice and Worcestershire
- ¾ cup fine soft bread crumbs
- 2 tablespoons melted butter

Combine crabmeat, celery, green pepper, eggs, mayonnaise, lemon juice, and Worcestershire. Turn into buttered baking dish (about 1½ quarts). Sprinkle top with bread crumbs. Dot with butter. Bake in preheated slow oven (325°F.) for 30 minutes. Makes 4 servings.

BROILED KING-CRAB LEGS

If you can get uncooked King crabs, they're better. Use the large middle sections of the legs, one for each serving. Split the shells with a heavy pointed knife, the length of the leg (the shell is tough, not brittle, rather like heavy plastic), and make a cross cut in the middle. Lay back the shell just enough to allow the insertion of the sauce, which is a simple one: equal parts of melted butter and fresh lemon juice. Broil the crab legs over charcoal, cut side up, and baste several times with the sauce during the cooking. If crabs are precooked, this will take only long enough to allow the bottom side to become brown; if raw, the whole thing will turn red first. Serve in the shell.

OYSTERS

The West Coast abounds in oysters of all sizes, from the tiny Olympias, no larger than a shirt button, to the gigantic Willapas, which must be cut into two or four pieces to eat. Bluepoints from Eastern waters have been planted too, and flourish in some places. The little San Francisco Bay oysters, with their slightly greenish color and coppery taste, have all but disappeared because of overfishing and the pollution of the Bay, but once in a great while they are available. Since the days of the Gold Rush, Westerners have consumed oysters in large quantities and in every conceivable way, including this one.

PEPPER PAN ROAST

- ¼ cup minced onion
- ¼ cup minced green pepper
- 1 garlic clove, crushed
- 1 cup butter or margarine
- 1 pint oysters

Cook onion, green pepper, and garlic in the butter for 2 or 3 minutes. Remove garlic, add drained oysters, and cook until plump, a very few minutes. Serve with toast. Makes 2 generous servings.

SALMON

Salmon is the king of fish in the Pacific Northwest, and the chinook is the king of salmon. Rich, moist, and delicious, it is good in all sorts of ways, but best simply broiled and served with lemon, butter, and parsley. The earliest settlers in the Northwest found the Indians roasting split salmon over open fires, and that is still a favorite method of cooking these magnificent fish.

BARBECUED SALMON STEAKS

When an event occurs that calls for feeding a crowd, a whole salmon outdoor barbecue is traditional. On the beach, the whole salmon is often butterflied and cooked on a plank. Any barbecue treatment of salmon should be simple; salmon and wood-fire flavors are full and almost sufficient.

- 4 salmon steaks, about ¾ inch thick
- ⅓ cup fresh lemon juice
- 3 tablespoons melted butter
- 1 tablespoon each of brown sugar and grated onion
- ½ teaspoon powdered mustard
- 1 teaspoon salt
- Pepper to taste

Wash salmon and pat dry. Combine lemon juice, butter, brown sugar, onion, mustard, salt, and pepper. Brush over surfaces of salmon. Allow to stand for 15 minutes. Place fish in a well-greased hinged wire grill or on a greased barbecue grill. Cook over moderately hot coals, turning once and basting with remaining marinating sauce, for about 4 minutes on each side, or until fish flakes easily when tested with a fork. Can be broiled, for 5 to 8 minutes on each side. Makes 4 servings.

SALMON MAYONNAISE

- 5-pound piece of salmon
- Court Bouillon
- 1 envelope unflavored gelatin
- ¼ cup water
- Mayonnaise
- Ripe olives, pimiento, almonds, and deviled eggs

Wrap the salmon in cheesecloth, leaving enough extra at the ends to make handling easy. Cook it in the Court Bouillon until it reaches an internal temperature of 160°F., about 10 minutes to the pound. Remove, unwrap, and allow to cool. Dissolve the gelatin in the water. Mix with 3 cups mayonnaise and cover the fish completely with the mixture. Garnish with rings of ripe olives, pieces of pimiento, and halves of blanched almonds. Surround with deviled eggs. Pass extra mayonnaise, made with lemon juice instead of vinegar. Makes 10 servings.

Court Bouillon

- 3 quarts water
- 1 quart white wine
- 1 cup wine vinegar
- 3 onions
- 9 whole cloves
- 4 carrots, finely diced
- 2 celery stalks
- 1 bay leaf
- 1 teaspoon crumbled dried thyme
- Few parsley sprigs
- 1 tablespoon salt

Put liquids in kettle. Stud onions with the cloves. Add with remaining ingredients to liquids. Cover and simmer for 1 hour. Strain.

MEAT, POULTRY, AND GAME

LAMB SHANKS BAKED IN FRUITED WINE

Westerners, generally, use a lot of fruits with meats.

- 4 lamb shanks
- Salt and pepper to taste
- All-purpose flour
- 1 cup dry red wine
- 1 cup each of dried apricots and pitted prunes, each cooked until just tender
- ½ cup each of golden raisins and sugar
- 2 tablespoons each of vinegar, fresh lemon juice, and honey

Green Goddess Salad Dressing
on Romaine and Shrimp
Strawberries de Luxe
California Omelet
Lamb Shanks Baked in Fruited Wine

½ teaspoon each of ground cinnamon and allspice

Season lamb shanks with salt and pepper; dust with flour. Place in a baking pan. Cover and bake in preheated moderate oven (350°F.) for about 1½ hours, or until meat is tender. Meantime, combine remaining ingredients in a saucepan. Bring to a boil, then simmer for 5 minutes. Drain excess fat from lamb; pour fruit sauce over. Cover and bake in hot oven (400°F.) for 30 minutes more. Serve lamb with fruit sauce spooned over. Makes 4 servings.

Out of the Pyrenees, great numbers of Basques came to the West to be sheepherders here. Now almost every Basque settlement stages a grand early-summer festival—a Basque barbecue picnic. Tender spring lamb is grilled over great outdoor wood fires to be the *pièce de résistance.*

BASQUE BARBECUED LAMB

Ask your butcher to bone a leg of lamb, leaving seam open ("butterfly" it). During barbecuing, apply the baste with a brush of fresh parsley. Thin portions of the meat will be well done, thick portions slightly pink.

Butterflied leg of lamb (5 to 6 pounds before boning)
¾ cup dry red or white wine
¼ cup each of olive oil and wine vinegar
¼ cup chopped parsley
2 garlic cloves, minced or mashed
1 teaspoon mixed dried herbs
1 teaspoon salt
¼ teaspoon pepper

Brush meat all over with baste made by combining remaining ingredients. Place meat on grill, fat side up, over medium coals. Cook for 50 to 60 minutes, basting frequently and turning occasionally. To carve, start at one end and cut across the grain into thin slices. Makes 6 to 8 servings.

CALIFORNIA OMELET

1 tablespoon minced green onion
1 small garlic clove, minced or mashed
2 tablespoons butter or margarine
1 large tomato, peeled, seeded, and diced
12 pitted ripe olives, halved
1 ripe but firm avocado, peeled and diced
6-egg French omelet

Cook onions and garlic in butter until just soft. Add tomato and olives and heat through. Add avocado, remove from heat, and keep warm. Meantime, make omelet. Spread avocado filling down center of omelet, fold, and turn onto a warm platter. Makes 4 servings.

CHICKEN-AVOCADO TOSTADA

The Western *tostada,* borrowed from Mexico, has come to mean not just the tortilla fried crisp (as is the immediate Mexican translation), but a great hot and cold sandwich-salad, built upon a crisp fried tortilla and the West Coast's plentiful avocados.

4 corn tortillas
Cooking oil for frying
1 can (15 ounces) chili with beans, heated
6 cups shredded iceberg lettuce
1 can (7 ounces) green chili sauce, chilled
1 cup shredded or grated Parmesan cheese
12 thin slices of chilled cooked chicken
2 avocados, peeled and sliced lengthwise
Radishes, tomato wedges, green onions, olives to garnish

Fry tortillas, one at a time, in hot deep or shallow fat until crisp and brown. Drain; place one on each serving plate. Spoon hot chili over top of tortillas. Toss shredded lettuce with about half of the green chili sauce; pile part of the lettuce in a stack over hot chili; arrange part in a bed around tortillas. Sprinkle about 2 tablespoons of the cheese over each serving. Arrange chicken and avocado slices on top of the center stacks of lettuce. Sprinkle with remaining chili sauce, then with remaining cheese. Garnish each serving with radishes, tomato wedges, green onions, and olives. Makes 4 servings.

SHERRIED ARTICHOKE CHICKEN

1 frying chicken (about 3 pounds), cut into serving pieces
Salt, pepper, paprika
6 tablespoons butter or margarine
2 cups (one 1-pound can) artichoke hearts, drained
¼ pound fresh mushrooms, sliced
3 tablespoons finely minced onion
2 tablespoons all-purpose flour
⅔ cup chicken bouillon
¼ cup sherry
½ teaspoon crumbled dried rosemary

Sprinkle chicken generously with salt, pepper, and paprika to taste. In a frying pan brown chicken pieces on all sides in 4 tablespoons of the butter; transfer to a casserole. Arrange artichoke hearts between chicken pieces. Add remaining butter to the drippings in frying pan; add mushrooms and onion and sauté until just tender. Sprinkle flour over mushrooms and stir in chicken bouillon, sherry, and rosemary. Cook, stirring, for a few minutes; pour over chicken. Cover and bake in preheated moderate oven (375° F.) for 40 minutes, or until chicken is tender. Makes 4 servings.

CURRIED RABBIT

1 frying rabbit (about 4 pounds)
Seasoned all-purpose flour
⅓ cup shortening
2 cups chopped onions
2 garlic cloves
1 large apple, peeled and chopped
Juice of ½ lemon
1 tablespoon curry powder, or more
Salt and pepper to taste
Water

Have rabbit disjointed and cut into serving pieces. Dust generously with seasoned flour, and brown on all sides in hot shortening. Remove to a kettle. In drippings left in skillet cook onions, garlic, and apple for 2 or 3 minutes. When the mixture is wilted, add it to the meat, along with the lemon juice and curry powder. (Curry powders vary a good deal in strength, so use your own judgment.) Add salt, pepper, and water to cover (or part water and part canned tomatoes); cover and simmer for 2½ hours, or until done. Correct seasoning, and if necessary, thicken the sauce with a little flour-and-water paste. Serve with curry condiments. Makes 6 to 8 servings.

VEGETABLES

POTATOES IN PARSLEY SAUCE

This way with potatoes comes from the French side of the Basque population.

3 tablespoons olive oil
½ cup each of finely chopped onion and parsley
1 large garlic clove, minced or mashed
4 medium-large boiling potatoes, peeled and cut into ¼-inch slices
1½ cups chicken or beef bouillon
Salt and pepper to taste

In olive oil in a large kettle slowly sauté onion, parsley, and garlic until soft, about 15 minutes. Add potatoes and cook, gently stirring, for a few minutes. Add bouillon and salt and pepper. Bring to a boil; reduce heat, cover, and simmer until potatoes are tender. Taste and correct seasoning. Makes 4 to 6 servings.

ARTICHOKE FRITTERS

Here only the bottoms *(fonds)* of the artichokes are used. The frozen or canned ones will do, but they won't be as good as

freshly cooked artichoke bottoms.

1 cup all-purpose flour
½ teaspoon salt
1 teaspoon baking powder
⅔ cup milk
2 teaspoons melted butter
1 egg, well beaten
12 large artichoke bottoms
Fat for deep frying

Mix flour, salt, and baking powder in a bowl. Add milk and beat until smooth. Add butter and egg. If the batter seems too thick, add a little more milk. Cut the cooked artichoke bottoms into quarters, dip into the batter, and fry in deep hot fat (370°F. on a frying thermometer) until browned. Drain on paper towels and serve piping hot. Makes 6 servings.

CHILLED ARTICHOKES WITH GARLIC MAYONNAISE

6 large artichokes
Fresh lemon juice
Boiling salted water or salted water and dry white wine
1 cup mayonnaise
1 garlic clove, mashed
Paprika
Lettuce

Wash artichokes thoroughly in cold water; drain. Turn each artichoke on its side and cut straight across top, about one third of the way down, to slice off thorny tip. Cut off stem, making a flat base. Remove small leaves around base. With scissors, cut thorns from tips of outer leaves. Rub cut edges with lemon juice. Turn artichoke on cut end and press firmly to separate leaves slightly. With a small spoon or melon-ball cutter, carefully and thoroughly scoop out the center fibrous leaves and fuzzy core. Stand artichokes in 1 inch of boiling salted water, or 2 parts salted water, 1 part dry white wine, in large kettle. Cover and simmer for 40 minutes, or until tender. Drain; cover with clear plastic wrap; chill for 1 hour or more. Combine mayonnaise and garlic. Spoon into cored artichokes. Sprinkle with paprika. Serve on lettuce-lined salad plate. Makes 6 servings.

FRIED BEANS

Garlic, onions, or chili powder may be added for extra seasoning, but this is the basic way to fry *frijoles*. A small dish of beans is served at every meal in most Mexican cafés.

1 pound dried Mexican pink or pinto beans
6 cups water
1 tablespoon salt
½ cup lard, bacon fat, or ham fat

Wash the beans and put in kettle. Add the water. (Unless beans are very old and hard, soaking is not necessary.) Cook until tender but not mushy, for 2 hours or more; add the salt. Melt the lard in a heavy pot (the Mexicans use a *cazuela,* a large earthenware pot with sloping sides and rounded bottom). Then add the beans, a few at a time, mashing them with a spoon and adding a little of the bean liquid. Continue until all the beans and liquid are used; then cook and stir until the mixture becomes thick. Makes 6 servings.

■ **Variation**—Refried beans *(frijoles refritos)* are even better. The fried beans are reheated with more lard until hot and a little crispy around the edges; stir the crisp bits into the center.

SALADS

AVOCADO SALAD

Avocados are a welcome addition to many salads. They are often diced and added to a mixed green salad, sliced and served with sliced oranges, or used as edible containers for chicken salad. They are best, perhaps, simply served on the half shell, their centers filled with a dressing made with ½ cup each of wine vinegar and olive oil, and 2 tablespoons each of minced parsley, green pepper, and green onions, with salt and pepper to taste.

MEXICAN SALAD

Mexicans are partial to all sorts of salads, and as with us, the mixed green salad rates high. Sliced radishes, green peppers, and cucumbers are frequently added, and the dressing is apt to be a rather tart one: 2 parts oil to 1 part vinegar, with perhaps a little chili powder added for extra tang.

On Christmas Eve, however, there is a very special salad, the *Ensalada de Noche Buena,* which resembles somewhat the ambrosia of our Southern states.

ENSALADA DE NOCHE BUENA (Christmas Eve Salad)

6 beets, cooked
4 oranges, peeled
4 bananas, peeled
4 apples, peeled and cored
¼ cup sugar
3 limes
1 cup peanuts
1 head of lettuce
Seeds of 2 pomegranates
1 cup tart French dressing

Dice the beets, oranges, bananas, and apples. Combine them and sprinkle with the sugar. Let stand for 30 minutes. Slice the limes very thin and chop the peanuts coarsely. Shred lettuce and line a bowl with it. Put diced fruits on top, spread over them the slices of lime, sprinkle with peanuts and pomegranate seeds, and pour French dressing over all. Bring to the table in all its glory, and mix well before serving. Makes 12 servings.

CAESAR SALAD

Numerous chefs and restaurateurs have claimed to be the originators of this popular salad, but the best guess is that it started in Tia Juana, during prohibition, at a restaurant called Caesar's. It's very good and filling, which is really all that matters.

1 garlic clove
¾ cup olive oil
2 cups croutons (made from stale Sourdough Bread, page 1932)
2 large or 3 small heads of romaine
Pepper to taste
½ teaspoon salt
2 eggs
Juice of 1 large lemon
6 or 8 anchovy fillets (optional), snipped into bits
½ cup grated Parmesan cheese

Crush garlic, add to olive oil, and let stand overnight. Brown croutons in ¼ cup of this garlic oil, stirring so that they will brown on all sides. Drain on paper towels. Break romaine into a large bowl. Add a generous grinding of fresh black pepper and the salt. Then dress with remaining garlic oil, turning so that every leaf is glossy with oil. Soft-cook the eggs for just 1 minute (do this ahead), and break them into the middle of the salad. Squeeze the lemon juice directly over the eggs, and mix so that there is a thick creamy look to the lettuce. Add anchovy if desired. Taste for seasoning, and add more salt, pepper, or lemon if it's needed. Add the cheese, and toss. Add the croutons last. Serve at once, so croutons remain crisp. Makes 10 to 12 servings.

GREEN GODDESS SALAD DRESSING ON ROMAINE AND SHRIMP

8 to 10 anchovy fillets
1 green onion
¼ cup each of minced chives and parsley
1 tablespoon crumbled dried tarragon soaked in vinegar, then strained, or 2 tablespoons minced fresh tarragon
3 cups mayonnaise
¼ cup tarragon vinegar

Chop anchovies and onion together until finely minced. Mix lightly but thoroughly

with chives, parsley, tarragon, mayonnaise, and vinegar. Makes about 1 quart dressing. Store unused dressing in a covered container in refrigerator for a week or more.

Note: This dressing goes on a salad of broken romaine in a salad bowl rubbed with a cut clove of garlic, often generously embellished with chilled cooked tiny sweet San Francisco Bay shrimps, prawns, Dungeness (Pacific Coast) crabmeat, lobster, or chicken. Eastern counterparts or frozen or canned seafood can substitute for the western seafood. Prawns here are the very large shrimps.

BREAD AND PANCAKES

SOURDOUGH BREAD

There are dried sourdough starters on the market these days which take a good deal of work out of making this wonderful bread. However, it's fun to start from scratch, and if all goes well you'll have some of the best bread in the world.

- 2 cups Sourdough Starter
- 3 cups all-purpose flour
- 1½ tablespoons butter or margarine, melted
- 2 tablespoons sugar
- 1 teaspoon salt
- ½ teaspoon baking soda
- Milk

Start mixing dough about 8 hours before bread is to be baked. Put Sourdough Starter in bowl. Add 2 cups of the flour and the remaining ingredients except soda and milk; mix well. Add enough more flour to make a dough that is fairly stiff. Shape into a ball and put in a greased bowl. Grease top of dough. Cover and let stand in a warm place for 4 to 6 hours. Dissolve soda in a little water and knead into dough, mixing thoroughly. Put in well-greased loaf pan (9 x 5 x 3 inches). Brush with milk, cover, and let rise until doubled in bulk. Bake in preheated hot oven (400°F.) for about 45 minutes.

Sourdough Starter

- 1 teaspoon active dry yeast
- ¼ cup warm water
- 2 tablespoons sugar
- 1 tablespoon vinegar
- 1 teaspoon salt
- 2 cups all-purpose flour
- Potato water (or warm water)

Dissolve yeast in the warm water. Add next 4 ingredients. Then add enough potato water to make a creamy batter (about 2 cups). Put in a stone crock or bowl, cover and let stand in a warm place for 2 to 3 days to ferment. It will become bubbly and have a sour odor. Makes about 2½ cups.

ORANGE RYE BREAD

Many Scandinavians settled in the Northwest. Their descendants there still maintain the delicious renown of Scandinavian home-baking.

- 1 package active dry yeast or 1 cake compressed yeast
- ¼ cup water*
- 1½ cups lukewarm water
- ⅓ cup sugar
- ¼ cup molasses
- 2 tablespoons shortening
- Grated peel from 2 oranges
- 1⅛ teaspoons salt
- About 2½ cups each of sifted rye flour and all-purpose flour

Sprinkle dry yeast or crumble cake yeast into warm water. *Use very warm water (105°F. to 115°F.) for dry yeast; use lukewarm water (80°F. to 90°F.) for compressed. Let stand for a few minutes, then stir until dissolved. In a large mixing bowl combine lukewarm water, sugar, molasses, shortening, orange peel, salt, and dissolved yeast. Gradually add flours, beating until smooth. On a lightly floured board knead dough lightly; turn into a greased bowl. Cover and allow to rise in a warm place until almost doubled in bulk. Punch down and shape into 2 loaves. Place each in a greased loaf pan (9 x 5 x 3 inches). Allow to rise again in a warm place until almost doubled in bulk. Bake in preheated moderate oven (375°F.) for 40 minutes. Makes 2 loaves.

SEATTLE DUTCH BABIES

These popoverlike eggy pancakes are still a Seattle specialty.

- 3 eggs
- ½ cup each of all-purpose flour and milk
- 2 tablespoons melted butter
- ½ teaspoon salt
- Melted butter
- Lemon wedges
- Confectioners' sugar

In a mixing bowl beat eggs with a French whip or fork until blended. Add flour to eggs in 4 additions, beating after each addition until just smooth. Add milk in 2 additions, beating slightly after each. Lightly beat in 2 tablespoons melted butter and the salt. Thickly butter two 9-inch pie pans. Pour half of the batter into each. Bake in preheated hot oven (400°F.) for 10 minutes. Reduce heat to moderate (350°F.) and bake for 5 minutes longer. Serve immediately. Offer melted butter, lemon wedges, and confectioners' sugar for toppings. Makes 4 dessert servings, or 2 main-dish servings.

DESSERTS

WASHINGTON PLUM DUMPLINGS

There are two kinds of fruit dumplings. The old-fashioned variety was made by dropping spoonfuls of sweet dumpling batter into boiling stewed fruit, cooking until done, then serving with the sweetened fruit as a sauce. These, I think, are better.

- 4 fresh plums
- Sugar
- ¼ teaspoon ground cinnamon or nutmeg
- 2 cups sifted all-purpose flour
- 2¼ teaspoons baking powder
- ½ teaspoon salt
- ⅓ cup butter or margarine
- ⅔ cup milk (about)
- 1 egg white, slightly beaten

Cut plums into halves and remove stones. Mix 2 tablespoons sugar and the cinnamon. Sprinkle on cut sides of plums and put halves back together. Sift flour, baking powder, salt, and 2 tablespoons sugar. Cut in butter until mixture looks like coarse meal. Add milk, mixing until soft dough is formed. Knead on lightly floured board for 30 seconds. Roll dough out to ¼-inch thickness. Cut into four 4-inch squares. Put a plum on each square. Moisten edges of dough and bring corners up over the plums, pressing edges together. Put in a greased shallow baking pan. Prick with a fork. Brush with egg white and sprinkle with sugar. Bake in preheated moderate oven (350°F.) for about 30 minutes. Serve plain, or with cream. Makes 4 servings.

RASPBERRY JAM SCONES

Oven-fresh scones, dripping with raspberry jam made from the local crop of spicy raspberries, have long been a food treat at the West Washington State Fair near Seattle. The tradition extended to the Seattle World's Fair. In this home recipe, you bake the jam right into the scones. You could use any tart berry jam.

- 2 cups sifted all-purpose flour
- 1 tablespoon each of baking powder and sugar
- ¾ teaspoon salt
- ¾ cup butter or margarine
- 2 eggs
- ¼ cup milk
- ½ cup thick jam
- Sugar

Sift together flour, baking powder, sugar,

and salt into mixing bowl. Cut in ½ cup of the butter until particles are fine. Beat eggs slightly with milk, add to dry ingredients, and toss with a fork to mix and form a soft dough. Divide dough into halves. On a lightly floured board, roll out each half into a 10-inch circle. Place one dough circle in a 10-inch layer-cake pan or on a cookie sheet. Spread with half of the remaining soft butter, then with the jam. Top with second circle. Spread it with remaining butter and sprinkle lightly with sugar. Bake in preheated hot oven (425°F.) for 20 minutes. Cut into wedges and serve warm. Makes 8 servings.

LIME-FROSTED PAPAYA

Usually Westerners serve papaya for a first course, a salad, or a dessert, simply chilled, halved (with the seeds scooped out), and with a slice of lime. Occasionally, for dessert, it is filled with a scoop of coconut or ginger ice cream or fresh lime sherbet.

- 3 chilled ripe papayas, halved and seeded
- Washed fresh grape or fig leaves (optional)
- 6 scoops of fresh lime sherbet
- 6 thin slices of lime
- Light rum (optional)

Place each papaya half on a large grape leaf on a dessert plate. Put a scoop of sherbet in each half. Garnish each with a lime slice. Sprinkle lightly with rum if you wish. Makes 6 servings.

RED-WINE-BAKED PEARS

Washington, Oregon, and California account for about 80 per cent of the nation's commercial pear production, and the pear tree is a favorite in home orchards. Winter Bosc is considered the best variety for baking, but the summer Bartlett and other varieties work well in this recipe, too.

- 6 medium-size pears, with stems
- 6 whole cloves
- 1½ cups dry red wine
- ¾ cup each of sugar and water

Pierce blossom end of each unpeeled pear with a clove. Place pears in a deep casserole, on sides or standing on end. Combine wine, sugar, and water, and pour over pears. Cover and bake in preheated hot oven (400°F.) for 30 minutes, basting occasionally. Uncover and continue baking, basting, for 15 minutes more, or until pears are tender. Serve hot or cold with remaining wine sauce. Makes 6 servings.

NORTHWEST HUCKLEBERRY (OR BLUEBERRY) BUCKLE

- ¼ cup butter or margarine
- ½ cup sugar
- 1 egg
- 1 teaspoon vanilla extract
- 1 cup sifted all-purpose flour
- 1 teaspoon baking powder
- ¼ teaspoon salt
- ⅓ cup milk
- 2 cups fresh huckleberries or blueberries or 1 package (10 ounces) frozen blueberries, thawed and drained
- Spice-Crumb Topping

In a mixing bowl cream together butter and sugar. Beat in egg and vanilla. Sift together flour, baking powder, and salt. Add to creamed mixture alternately with milk. Turn into buttered 8- or 9-inch square baking pan. Sprinkle evenly with huckleberries, then with Spice-Crumb Topping. Bake in preheated moderate oven (375°F.) for 40 minutes, or until toothpick inserted in center comes out clean. Makes 8 servings.

Spice-Crumb Topping

Combine ½ cup sugar, ⅓ cup all-purpose flour, ½ teaspoon ground cinnamon, and ¼ teaspoon ground nutmeg. Cut in ¼ cup butter or margarine to make a crumbly mixture.

Serve these cakelike squares warm with butter as a coffeecake, or with heavy cream, a thin hot lemon sauce, or lemon or vanilla ice cream for dessert. Use frozen blueberries when fresh berries are out of season.

STRAWBERRIES DE LUXE

By drawing on the strawberries locally grown up and down the West Coast, strawberries are "in season" almost the whole year round.

- Large strawberries with stems
- Dairy sour cream
- Sifted light brown sugar

Arrange strawberries in a large crystal bowl (imbedded in ice, if you wish) in center of table. Provide each guest with a sectioned dessert plate or 2 small cups on a dessert plate, one section filled with sour cream, the other with brown sugar. Holding each strawberry by the stem, dip first into sour cream, then into brown sugar.

You could arrange this dessert so each person can reach to a central serving: Use a three-tiered stand with one item filled with sour cream, one with brown sugar, one with strawberries.

ALMOND DEEP-DISH APPLE PIE

- 1½ cups all-purpose flour
- ½ teaspoon salt
- ½ cup butter or margarine
- ¼ cup lard
- ¼ cup finely grated almonds
- Water as needed
- 6 to 8 medium apples, peeled and sliced
- ¾ cup sugar
- Juice and grated rind of 1 small orange
- 3 tablespoons rum or brandy
- Heavy cream

Mix flour and salt. Cut in ¼ cup butter and the lard. Add nuts, and enough water to hold ingredients together. Refrigerate while you make the filling.

Put the apples in a shallow baking dish (about 2 inches deep). Combine ¼ cup melted butter, the sugar, orange juice and rind, and mix lightly with the apples. Now roll out the chilled pastry, not too thin, cut 2 or 3 tiny holes in it, and cover the apples, pressing the pastry against the edges of the dish; trim. Bake in preheated very hot oven (450°F.) for 15 minutes. Then reduce heat to slow (325°F.) and bake until the apples are tender. When done, pour rum into the holes, using a small funnel. Serve warm with heavy cream. Makes 6 to 8 servings.

SOUR-CREAM APPLE TORTE

- 6 large firm apples, peeled and thinly sliced
- 1 cup sugar
- 6 eggs
- 2 cups dairy sour cream
- 2½ teaspoons vanilla extract
- Pinch of salt
- 1 package (6 ounces) zwieback, crushed into fine crumbs (about 2 cups crumbs)
- ¼ cup sugar
- ½ teaspoon ground cinnamon
- About 1½ tablespoons soft butter

Place apples in a heavy pan, sprinkle with sugar (no water), and cook over very low heat until apples are tender. Beat eggs slightly; blend in sour cream, vanilla, and salt. Carefully stir egg mixture into apples, and continue cooking slowly, stirring gently, until mixture thickens slightly. Remove from heat. Mix zwieback crumbs with sugar and cinnamon. Coat bottom and sides of a 9-inch springform pan with soft butter. Press two thirds of the crumb mixture onto sides and bottom of pan. Carefully spoon in apple custard. Sprinkle remaining crumbs over top. Bake in preheated slow oven (325°F.) for 1 hour. Allow to cool. Chill if you wish. Makes 10 to 12 servings.

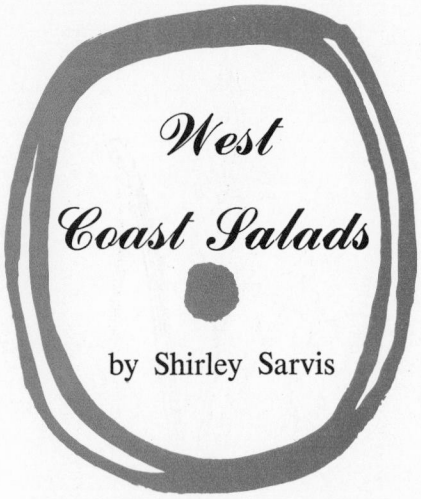

There is a mystifying phenomenon in the order of courses in the West. The salad comes first. No one seems to know quite how this tradition got started, but for over a century now, Westerners have deviated from the continental example set by their eastern cousins and put the salad course before the meat course instead of after. Maybe the custom began in Spanish California where southwest barbecues and festival feasts offered an abundance of food, but in no particular order. Maybe it's a carry-over from Gold Rush days when a hotel or mining-camp cook could make a salad quickly to appease the appetites of hungry workingmen until the main part of the meal could be prepared. Perhaps it was the warm California climate that prompted people to want to eat something cool and refreshing first. It could have been the invention of early Westerners: a way to show off their wonderful variety of fresh fruits and vegetables to visitors from the East.

While we've been searching and sleuthing with food historians to try to find the reason for the first-course Western salad, we've come up with some theories of our own: the delicacy of a Western salad makes it deserving of a place at the forefront of a meal. The nuances of a wonderfully subtle salad can best be appreciated before tastes are dulled by spicier, richer foods. The goodness of a fine Western salad justifies its lead position; it deserves the total attention guests can give only to the first item served. There is opportunity for much more play and display in the serving of a salad early in the meal. Guests are concentrating on the food. The table is clear of other dishes and distractions.

Certainly commercial produce growers have promoted the emphasis the big salad gets by being first course; lettuce and other salad ingredients are important crops in the Western economy; but the foremost theory put forth by food historians and popular conjecturers alike is that, in the early days of the West, the first-course salad simplified dinner and suited the necessarily casual style of living. We think that is a strong argument in favor of serving salad first today, and not just in the West. It is a simplification that meets the needs of today's casual living: it eliminates both a first course and a later salad course; it eases the task of the homemaker-hostess who has no help; yet it offers all the elegance of an introductory course at dinner.

A careful Western hostess takes great pride in the finesse of her salad, honoring the fine points of salad making. She capitalizes on her good fortune at having a profusion of fruits and vegetables to choose from. She arranges her greens and other ingredients to make the most of them.

Following are six salads, in themselves six reasons why a Western salad comes first. They are typical of the favorite first courses of Western hostesses. Different although they are, they all have in common certain essential qualities: delicacy, simplicity, some traditional first-course ingredients such as seafood, fruit, cheese, artichokes, and colorful attractive display.

BROWNED-BUTTER WILTED LETTUCE

Less familiar than wilting lettuce with hot bacon drippings and vinegar is wilting it with bubbling browned butter. More delicate is the result, and more suited to the role of a first-course salad. Select just the tender, light-colored leaves from the heart of butter (sometimes called Boston or butterhead) lettuce. Tear them into pieces slightly smaller than you would for most green salads to carry out the theme of delicacy. Prepare butter and dress the salad at the table so your audience can see the butter brown and then tenderly wilt the lettuce leaves. Over a candle warmer, heat the butter slowly, just until it turns a deep-golden color. Pour it, foaming, over torn lettuce and snipped chives. Toss, and serve at once.

About 2 quarts torn and loosely measured hearts of butter or Boston lettuce
2 tablespoons snipped chives
¼ cup butter

Place lettuce in salad bowl. Sprinkle with chives. Heat butter until it melts and foams and browns; watch carefully, do not let it burn. Pour hot butter over lettuce and chives. Toss lightly. Serve at once. Makes 4 servings.

CRAB AND GRAPEFRUIT SALAD WITH AVOCADO MAYONNAISE

In the West this salad no doubt derived from the local fondness for Pacific Coast crab. Inlanders and Easterners can substitute King crab, canned or frozen. Arrange crab and grapefruit individually, building each on a base of finely shredded iceberg lettuce.

1 ripe avocado
⅓ cup mayonnaise
4 teaspoons fresh lemon juice
¼ teaspoon garlic salt
Finely shredded iceberg lettuce
1 large chilled grapefruit, peeled and cut into sections, removing all membrane
½ pound chilled Pacific crab legs

Peel avocado and mash with a fork. Mix in mayonnaise, lemon juice, and garlic salt. Line chilled salad plates with the shredded lettuce. Arrange grapefruit sections and crab legs over lettuce. Spoon some of the dressing on top of each salad; pass remaining dressing. Makes 4 servings.

CALIFORNIA PARMESAN-WALNUT SALAD

Grate Parmesan cheese yourself and toast the walnuts slightly to taste this salad at its best. Your blender can speed the grating of hard cheese; to toast walnuts, place in preheated hot oven (400°F.) for just a few minutes. Use a combination of several of your favorite salad greens.

¼ cup salad oil
3 tablespoons tomato juice
1 tablespoon fresh lemon juice
1 teaspoon grated or scraped onion
¼ teaspoon each of salt, pepper, and sugar
¼ teaspoon crumbled dried sweet basil
1 quart coarsely torn and loosely measured salad greens
⅓ cup coarsely broken California walnuts, lightly toasted
¼ cup grated Parmesan cheese

Beat or shake together first 8 ingredients to make dressing. Place greens in chilled salad bowl and sprinkle with walnuts and cheese. Pour over salad just enough dressing to coat ingredients lightly. Toss; serve at once. Makes 4 servings.

SPECIAL MIXED GREEN SALAD

Its total simplicity is the beauty of this salad: the playing of one green against another in contrast. There is the bite of dark-green watercress brushing the icy crunch of romaine smoothed by suedelike petals of butter lettuce. Crumbles of blue cheese echo the peppery spice of watercress. Oil and vinegar dress it. Although loyal Westerners would choose a blue from an Oregon cheesery, you may use as well your favorite piquant blue-veined cheese or perhaps a Danish Bleu or Roquefort.

Make a simple oil and vinegar dressing seasoned with just salt and pepper—about ¾ cup salad oil to ¼ cup wine vinegar—

but taste! Proportions depend on the strength of the vinegar you use.

- 3 cups each of butter lettuce hearts and romaine leaves, coarsely torn and loosely measured
- 3 cups watercress leaves
- 2 ounces blue cheese
- Oil and vinegar dressing

Place salad greens in chilled salad bowl. Crumble blue cheese over top. Pour on just enough dressing to coat each leaf lightly. Toss gently. Serve at once. Makes 6 servings.

GINGER CHEESE SALAD BOWL

This is a salad to begin in the kitchen and finish at the table. First, line a large salad bowl with torn mixed salad greens and top with some seedless green grapes, toasted almonds, and cheese cubes. Placing the arranged salad bowl before your guests, dress, toss, and serve.

- ½ cup salad oil
- 4 teaspoons fresh lemon juice
- 4 teaspoons dry sherry
- 1½ teaspoons ground ginger
- 1½ teaspoons wine vinegar
- ¼ teaspoon salt
- ⅛ teaspoon each of sugar and pepper
- 4 cups coarsely torn and loosely measured salad greens
- 1 small package (3 ounces) cream cheese
- 4 teaspoons grated orange peel
- ¾ cup seedless green grapes or other seeded fresh grapes
- ⅓ cup diced almonds, lightly toasted
- 1 tablespoon finely sliced green onions with tops (optional)

Shake together or beat with a fork the first 8 ingredients to make a dressing. Place salad greens in salad bowl. Press all sides of cream cheese block into grated orange peel until peel adheres; cut block into about ⅜-inch cubes; place together on salad greens. Arrange grapes and almonds in separate sections on top of greens. If you like, sprinkle all over with onions. At table, pour on just enough dressing to moisten ingredients; toss salad lightly. Makes 4 servings.

WESTERN ANTIPASTO SALAD

The Western Italian population influenced the eating of the marinated appetizer, or antipasto salad. Heating the marinade brings out the flavors of the vegetables it dresses.

- ½ cup salad oil
- ¼ cup red-wine vinegar
- ¼ teaspoon salt
- ⅛ teaspoon freshly ground pepper
- 1 large garlic clove, minced or mashed
- 1 package (9 ounces) frozen artichoke hearts, cooked just until tender, then drained
- ¼ pound fresh mushrooms, sliced
- ½ cup pitted black olives
- 2 tablespoons each of chopped pimiento and freshly chopped parsley
- Romaine

Shake or beat together salad oil, vinegar, salt, pepper, and garlic. Pour into saucepan and just heat through. Beat again to mix thoroughly and pour over artichoke hearts, mushrooms, olives, pimiento, and parsley. Cool, then cover and chill thoroughly for at least 2 hours; gently stir occasionally. At serving time, line individual salad plates with romaine leaves. Arrange marinated vegetables on top, spooning some of the marinade over romaine. Makes 4 to 6 servings.

WHALE—A mammal belonging to the order Cetacea. It lives in the deep sea and is valued commercially for its flesh and for its oil, which nowadays is used mainly in the manufacture of cosmetics, lubricants, and textiles.

Whales have been caught since the Middle Ages, but the emphasis on their products has shifted as civilization progresses. In the Middle Ages they provided food for Europe, and in the 17th, 18th, and 19th centuries they were caught chiefly for their oil, used for lighting and in the manufacture of soap. Whale meat today is a staple food item in Norway and other Scandinavian countries, where whale fishing and processing are important industries. During World War II, when food was extremely scarce in these countries, whale meat helped the people to survive. It is an inexpensive meat, of a rather brilliant, dark-red color. Since whale meat is tough, it has to be cooked like any tough meat, that is, marinated, pot-roasted, or otherwise tenderized.

Availability—Frozen whale steaks are available in specialty food stores.

Nutritive Food Values—Very high in vitamin A with traces of thiamine and riboflavin.

☐ Whale meat, 3½ ounces, raw = 156 calories

WHEAT—The grain of a grass of the genus *Triticum*. It is the most widely grown and prized of all the cereal grains, and the most important in all but the Asiatic countries. The little wheat kernels grow in beads at the top of stalks or straw. The harsh straw and chaff are winnowed off to leave only the tiny grains to which man owes so much. The flour made by grinding wheat grain is the best of all flours for breadmaking because of the presence of gluten, a form of protein which makes a soft and spongy dough.

A grain of wheat has three main parts. The outer covering is the bran, the inner part the endosperm, and the tiny nucleus within the endosperm is the germ. If the entire kernel is ground, the result is whole-wheat flour, graham flour, or entire-wheat flour. If just the endosperm is used, the result is flour—wheat flour—and plain flour.

There are hard and soft wheats used for making various kinds of flour. Hard wheats are made into bread and all-purpose flours; soft wheats are made into pastry, cake, and all-purpose flours. A special kind of hard wheat, durum, is ground to make the semolina used for making pasta. Besides flours, wheat is made into various ground products: semolina; farina, ground wheat with the bran and most of the germ removed; cracked wheat, cleaned wheat cracked into fragments; wheat cereals, made from the whole wheat or part of the wheat kernel.

Wheat is thought to be the oldest of man's grains and it has been cultivated for so many thousands of years that it is difficult to say exactly when the first wheat harvest was made. It was probably grown originally in the fertile plains of the Euphrates Valley. From there it spread east and west until now it covers the globe. We do know that it is largely to grains that we owe the initial transition from nomadic to settled life. When man stops long enough in one place to harvest his crops, a whole new way of life begins, differing from the wandering life of the earliest hunters and gatherers of wild foods. Grains are the chief of those "fruits of the fields" that sustain life. They need not be consumed immediately, they can be stored against need, and in themselves they bear the seed of their renewal.

Civilizations everywhere have long honored bread and wheat. In classical times, Demeter, goddess of the fields and fertility (the Romans knew her as Ceres, hence the word "cereal"), was at the heart of the Eleusinian mysteries, the secret cult that has been called the fountainhead of Greek culture. In ancient friezes she is pictured holding shafts of wheat. It was said that she gave the first grain to the hero Triptolemus, telling him to diffuse its blessing throughout the world. Triptolemus quite evidently followed her instructions; wheat is now, except in oriental rice-growing countries, the most widely eaten grain in the world.

In this country, the colonists of Virginia and Massachusetts brought the grain to our shores quite early. However, the climate of the eastern seaboard proved not so satisfactory for wheat as for the native corn, and the crop never became an important one. When the frontier expanded to what is now the middle and far west, the pioneers found the perfect home for their crop. The original wheat fields were considerably smaller than the vast expanses we know today. Old-fashioned methods of plowing, reaping, and winnowing made large production difficult. As mechanical progress made possible quick and efficient farming and harvesting processes, the wheat farmers expanded their crops. Such inventions as the reaper and efficient winnower have changed the food habits of Americans.

Availability and Purchasing Guide—Wheat flour is available in the following forms:

Whole-Wheat, Graham, or *Wheat Flour*—These terms are synonymous for flour made from any cleaned, unrefined, unbleached wheat other than durum or red durum wheat.

Gluten Flour is a high-protein whole-wheat flour from which the starch has been removed.

Flour, White, Plain, All-Purpose, or *General-Purpose Flour*—These terms are synonymous for refined wheat flour. It is available bleached or unbleached.

Cake Flour—This is a highly refined bleached flour.

Self-Rising Flour—Refined bleached flour to which leavening ingredients and salt have been added.

Enriched Flour—This is refined bleached flour to which vitamins and minerals have been added.

Instant-Type Flour—This flour is in granular form, making it easier to pour and pack than other flours.

Other wheat products available are cereals, including hot cooked, quick-cooking, and ready-to-eat; bulgur or wheat pilaf (parboiled wheat); wheat germ, the rich embryo of the wheat grain; and a variety of crackers such as graham and shredded wheat crackers.

Since cereal products are not visible when purchased, select a brand in which you have confidence. Individually wrapped servings cost more than the large economy-size boxes. Cereals requiring long cooking are usually less expensive than the quick-cooking or ready-to-eat varieties. Select the cereal that is most convenient and economical for your use.

Storage—Flour should be stored at room temperature in tight containers. In hot weather, only small amounts should be kept on hand.

Cereals should be stored tightly covered in a cool dry place. Ready-to-eat cereals are packaged with an inner wrapping. Open carefully to keep this lining intact. The lining should be kept tightly folded to preserve the freshness of the cereal. Whole-grain cereals, even though unopened, should be refrigerated because of their fat content.

- ☐ Kitchen shelf, dry or uncooked cereal: 2 to 3 months
- ☐ Refrigerator shelf, cooked cereal: 2 to 4 days
- ☐ Whole-grain cereals, dry or uncooked, refrigerator shelf: 5 to 6 months

Nutritive Food Values—In white flour, starch is present in greater proportion and is more digestible than it is in whole-wheat flour. Therefore, it is higher in caloric value. If enriched, white flour contains added thiamine, riboflavin, niacin, and iron. Calcium and vitamin D may also be added. Whole-wheat flour, which contains all the nutrients available in the whole grain, is high in phosphorus, potassium, and has moderate amounts of protein, niacin, thiamine, and riboflavin. The caloric values of 3½ ounces of the most commonly available wheat flours are:

- ☐ Whole-wheat flour = 333 calories
- ☐ Flour, enriched or unenriched = 364 calories
- ☐ Self-rising, enriched = 352 calories

Wheat cereals are moderately high in calcium, phosphorus, and sodium and contain good amounts of thiamine, riboflavin, and niacin. The amounts vary with the enrichment of the cereal. The caloric values of 3½ ounces of the most commonly available wheat products are:

- ☐ Bulgur, dry = 357 calories
- ☐ Bulgur, canned, unseasoned = 168 calories
- ☐ Bulgur, canned, seasoned = 182 calories
- ☐ Wheat germ = 363 calories
- ☐ Whole-wheat crackers = 403 calories
- ☐ Graham crackers, plain = 384 calories
- ☐ Graham crackers, chocolate-coated = 475 calories
- ☐ Graham crackers, sugar-honey-coated = 411 calories
- ☐ Cereal, rolled wheat, cooked = 75 calories
- ☐ Cereal, wheat, whole-meal, cooked = 45 calories
- ☐ Cereal, wheat and malted barley, quick-cooking = 65 calories
- ☐ Cereal, wheat and malted barley, instant = 80 calories
- ☐ Cereal, wheat-flakes, ready-to-eat = 354 calories
- ☐ Cereal, wheat germ, ready-to-eat = 391 calories
- ☐ Cereal, puffed wheat, ready-to-eat = 363 calories
- ☐ Cereal, puffed wheat with sugar and honey, ready-to-eat = 376 calories
- ☐ Cereal, shredded wheat, ready-to-eat = 354 calories
- ☐ Cereal, shredded wheat with malt, salt, and sugar, ready-to-eat = 366 calories
- ☐ Cereal, bran with sugar and malt, ready-to-eat = 240 calories
- ☐ Cereal, bran with sugar and wheat germ, ready-to-eat =238 calories
- ☐ Cereal, bran flakes, ready-to-eat = 303 calories
- ☐ Cereal, bran flakes with raisins, ready-to-eat = 287 calories

WHEY—The liquid part of milk which remains after the thicker part, or curd, is removed. The curd is used in making cheese. Whey contains sugar, minerals, and lactalbumin. Although some whey cheese is also made, most whey is further separated, with the fattier parts used in making butter and the remainder fed to livestock.

WHIP, TO—To beat an ingredient with an egg beater, a whisk, an electric beater, or a fork until it is light and puffy due to the air incorporated into it by the beating.

The secret of successful whipping is to do it quickly and thoroughly. Anything whipped should be used quickly, or the air incorporated in it will escape and the food will become limp.

WHISKEY or WHISKY—A spirit distilled from such grains as barley, rye, and corn, and subsequently refined, colored, and flavored by various processes. Each country produces a distinctive type of whiskey. There are differences in the method of production, the grains used, and of great importance, the character of the water. The water in Scotland, for example, rises through red granite, contributing to the flavor of Scotch whisky. Whiskey, by the way, is "whisky" in Scotland and Canada; in Ireland and the United States it is spelled with the "e."

The Latin term used to describe distilled spirits was *aquavitae*, "water of life." The Scotch and the Irish translated it to *usquebaugh* in Gaelic. The name was later contracted to *uisge* and still later anglicized to whiskey.

The four steps of whiskey production are malting, fermenting, distilling, and aging. First the grain is cleaned and then it is prepared for fermentation by a process called malting. During malting the grain is ground and then cooked with water to form a mash. Malt is added. Malt enzymes change the starch in the grain to sugar.

The next step is fermentation by yeast. In this process the grain sugars are converted to alcohol.

Distilling separates the alcohol from the waters. The vapors are caught, condensed, and drawn off as new whiskey which is colorless and harsh. Aging in wooden barrels is the final process, the one which provides the mellow beverage that is eventually bottled.

Whiskey, strictly defined by the United States Federal standards, is a grain spirit, distilled at less than 190 proof and one day old. Thirty-three whiskey variations are listed among the United States Standards, but general usage divides whiskey into two major sub-divisions, straight whiskey and blended whiskey. *Straight* whiskey is whiskey which is unmixed with other liquors or substances (except distilled water used for reduction of proof), such as straight bourbon whiskey and straight rye whiskey. Federal law requires that straight whiskey be aged in new charred oak barrels for at least two years. A *blended* whiskey is a balanced blending of straight whiskeys and neutral grain spirits (a high distillate, at least 190 proof, of any fermented mash), containing at least twenty per cent straight whiskeys and bottled at not less than eighty proof. The blend may combine several, or sometimes many, straight whiskeys with extremely light-bodied, almost flavorless, spirits (neutral grain spirits), and sometimes a blending agent such as sherry in very small amounts, resulting in a blended whiskey that is light in body.

The word *proof* applied to distilled spirits indicates the amount of alcohol in a liquor. Proof is twice the percentage of alcohol. Example: a 100-proof whiskey contains fifty percent alcohol. All whiskeys have a bottling proof between eighty and 110. Proof indicates potency, not necessarily quality.

A *bonded* whiskey is straight whiskey, produced and bottled in accordance with the Federal Bottling-in-Bond Act. It must be at least four years old, must be bottled at 100 proof, must have been produced in a single distillery, by the same distiller, and be the product of a single season and year. It must have been bottled at an internal revenue bonded warehouse under United States Government supervision.

Imported whiskeys come to the United States from Ireland, Canada, and Scotland. *Irish whiskey* (the Irish spell it with an "e" as do Americans) varies in the processing as well as in flavor depending on whether it is made in Northern Ireland or in the Republic of Ireland to the south. Both use barley malt and small cereal grains, and in the south these include oats and wheat with the unmalted barley and rye.

All *Scotch whisky* is a blend of malt whisky, made from malted barley, and grain whisky, made from malted and unmalted grains. These two types of whisky are distilled differently before they are blended. In addition there are four varieties of malt whisky, each coming from a different part of Scotland: Highland Malts come from the north of Scotland; Lowland Malts from the South; and Islay Malts and Cambeltown Malts from the Island of Islay and from Campbeltown on the Firth of Clyde respectively, both in western Scotland. Barley is the principal grain used, and the smoky flavor of Scotch is acquired in the process of drying the malted barley over peat fires, a process distinctive to Scotland.

Most *Canadian whisky* on the American market is a blend of heavy and light-bodied grain mashes and is similar to American whiskeys.

Caloric Values

- ☐ Bourbon, 1½ ounces, 86 proof = about 125 calories
- ☐ Irish, 1½ ounces, 86 proof = about 125 calories
- ☐ Rye, 1½ ounces, 86 proof = about 125 calories
- ☐ Scotch, 1½ ounces, 86 proof = about 110 calories

WHITEBAIT—A small salt-water fish, one and a half to four inches in length, which is the fry of the common herring or sprat. Whitebait are generally found in the Thames estuary in England and along the coast of the North Sea. The name is also given to various other small fish which are similar to the European whitebait, such as the smelts found off the California coast, to many silversides, and to some of the anchovies found in salt and fresh waters in the United States.

These little fish are generally fried in deep fat but they can be sautéed or broiled. They are available fresh in large eastern markets in November, December, and part of January. They should be stored in the refrigerator and eaten as soon as possible.

If whitebait is frozen, it should be frozen whole. Since they are so small, it is best to cover the fish with water in a small pan and freeze until ice is formed. Wrap the entire block of ice in moisture-vapor-proof material, excluding as much air as possible. Seal.

PANFRIED WHITEBAIT

Soak whitebait in ice water for 1 to 2 hours. Drain on a towel and roll in cornmeal. Panfry quickly in hot olive oil, shaking the pan often to move the fish about. Turn them carefully with a wooden spoon. Season with salt and pepper to taste and serve plain or with tartare sauce.

Chili Whitefish

WHITEFISH—A fatty fresh-water fish caught all year round in the Great Lakes in other North American lakes and streams, and in Alaska. Whitefish belongs to the salmon family. Some Arctic varieties live in salt water.

Whitefish can be prepared in almost any of the ways that fish is prepared: broiled, panfried, baked, baked stuffed, or poached.

Recipes occasionally call for white fish, two words. This does not mean the species of fish known as whitefish, but refers to any white-meated fish such as cod, flounder, sole, etc.

Availability—Whitefish weighs 2 to 6 pounds and is available year round fresh, whole or filleted. It is also sold frozen, in fillets, and smoked whole drawn.

Purchasing Guide—Fresh fish should have bright, clear bulging eyes; gills that look and smell clean; scales that are shiny and lie close to the skin; and firm flesh with some spring to it when pressed with a finger.

Storage—Fresh fish is very perishable. Wrap in moisture-proof paper or place in tightly covered container in coldest part of refrigerator.

Keep frozen fish solidly frozen until ready to use. Once thawed, use immediately. Do not refreeze.

- ☐ Fresh, refrigerator shelf, raw: 1 to 2 days
- ☐ Fresh, prepared for freezing; or frozen, refrigerator frozen-food compartment: 2 to 3 weeks
- ☐ Fresh, prepared for freezing; or frozen, freezer: 3 to 4 months
- ☐ Fresh, refrigerator shelf, cooked: 3 to 4 days
- ☐ Smoked, refrigerator shelf: 1 week

Nutritive Food Values—Very high in protein and vitamin A, phosphorus and potassium; has some thiamine, riboflavin, and niacin.

- ☐ Fresh, 3½ ounces, raw = 155 calories
- ☐ Fresh, 3½ ounces, baked and stuffed = 215 calories
- ☐ Smoked, 3½ ounces = 155 calories

Basic Preparation

☐ **To Broil**—Put split fish, skin side down, on oiled broiler rack. Dot with butter or brush with oil. Broil 4 to 5 inches from unit, basting occasionally with butter or oil, for 6 to 10 minutes, or until fish flakes easily with a fork. Do not turn. Season with salt and pepper.

☐ **To Panfry**—Cut fish fillets into serving-size portions. Sprinkle both sides with salt and pepper. Dip in a mixture of beaten egg and milk, using 1 egg to 1 tablespoon milk. Roll in fine dry bread crumbs, cracker crumbs, cornmeal, or flour. Put in ⅛-inch hot fat in heavy skillet and panfry over medium heat until browned on one side. Turn and brown on other side. Allow about 5 minutes for each side.

☐ **To Bake**—Cut fish fillets into serving-size portions. Sprinkle both sides with salt and pepper. For each 2 pounds of fish, mix 2 tablespoons fresh lemon juice with ¼ cup melted butter or margarine. Dip fish into this mixture and put in shallow baking dish. Pour any remaining butter mixture over fish. Bake in preheated moderate oven (350°F.) for 25 to 30 minutes. Sprinkle with paprika.

☐ **To Poach**—Cut fillets into serving-size portions. Put in a wire basket or on a plate. If plate is used, tie in a piece of cheesecloth. Lower the fish into salted boiling water or Court Bouillon (at right). Simmer for 10 minutes, or until fish flakes easily when tested with a fork.

☐ **To Freeze**—Clean and eviscerate fish. Remove head and wash thoroughly. Dip pieces of fish in a solution of 1½ teaspoons ascorbic acid and 4 cups water for 20 seconds. Drain, and wrap pieces in moisture- vapor-proof wrapping, excluding as much air as possible. Seal.

BAKED WHITEFISH WITH BREAD STUFFING

1 large onion, chopped
Butter or margarine
1 cup soft stale-bread crumbs
¼ cup minced parsley
½ teaspoon crumbled thyme leaves
Salt
Dash of pepper
1 egg, well beaten
1 whole whitefish, about 4 pounds
Lemon wedges

Sauté the onion in ¼ cup butter until golden. Add next 3 ingredients, ½ teaspoon salt, the pepper, and egg; mix well. Fill cavity of fish with the stuffing, and sew up. Put in a well-oiled baking dish, sprinkle with salt, and dot with butter. Bake in preheated hot oven (400°F.) for 25 to 35 minutes. Serve with lemon wedges. Makes 4 to 6 servings.

CHILI WHITEFISH

1 pound whitefish fillets
1 tablespoon each of cooking oil and vinegar
2 tablespoons minced onion
1 teaspoon salt
2 teaspoons steak sauce
⅓ cup chili sauce
¼ cup water
1 tablespoon capers
1 cup cooked green peas

Cut fish into serving pieces. Bring oil, vinegar, onion, salt, steak sauce, chili sauce, and water to boil in top part of a double boiler. Add capers and fish. Cover and cook over boiling water for 25 minutes, stirring several times. Add peas; heat. Makes 4 servings.

COLD WHITEFISH

Poach a whole whitefish in Court Bouillon. Remove it from the broth, cool, and chill. Remove the skin but leave head and tail intact. Mask with a mixture of ½ cup each of mayonnaise and dairy sour cream to which you add 1 teaspoon prepared mustard, 2 tablespoons finely chopped onion, 2 tablespoons capers, 1 tablespoon finely chopped anchovy fillets, and 2 tablespoons tomato purée or strained chili sauce. Serve with vinegar, salt, and pepper to taste.

Court Bouillon

8 to 10 shallots, chopped finely, or 12 green onions
1 garlic clove, chopped
1 leek, chopped
2 or 3 carrots, scraped and sliced
¼ cup chopped parsley
1 teaspoon each of salt and pepper
1 bay leaf
Pinch of dried thyme
1 cup dry white wine
4 cups water

Mix shallots with garlic, leek, carrots, and parsley; add salt, pepper, bay leaf, and thyme. Cover with white wine and water. Put Court Bouillon on the range, bring to boil, and simmer for about 20 minutes. Strain through a fine sieve and use as directed in recipe.

SMOKED WHITEFISH AND RICE

½ pound smoked whitefish
¼ cup butter or margarine
½ cup light cream
4 hard-cooked eggs, diced
2 cups hot cooked rice
½ teaspoon curry powder
⅛ teaspoon pepper

Split whitefish and remove bones and skin. Flake fish with fork. Melt butter and stir in remaining ingredients. Add fish and mix lightly with fork. Heat gently. Makes 4 servings.

SMOKED WHITEFISH PLATTER

Remove the skin and arrange a whole smoked whitefish, with head and tail intact, on a bed of watercress. Garnish with lemon wedges and serve with strips of buttered pumpernickel for a smörgåsbord or with cocktails.

WHITE SAUCE—This term is applied to sauces which are light or blond in color, as opposed to the brown sauces which are made with brown stock. Some of the white-sauce group, such as Sauce Velouté, are made with white stock; that is, stock made with veal and/or chicken as opposed to beef stock, a brown stock. The term also applies specifically to a simple sauce made with cream or milk and with a white *roux:* that is, a combination of butter and flour which isn't browned. This sauce is also known as béchamel. Béchamel sauce is available in jars.

First Aid for White Sauce

■ **Lumpy Sauce**—If the *roux* is hot and the liquid near the boiling point, the sauce should not be lumpy. However, if it is, strain it through a fine sieve or whirl it in a blender. Simmer over low heat for 5 minutes.

■ **Too-Thin Sauce**—Boil it down over moderate heat, stirring constantly, until it is of the desired consistency. Or thicken it with *beurre manié,* a paste of butter and flour which has been kneaded together. Blend ½ tablespoon butter with ½ tablespoon flour to a smooth paste. Remove sauce from heat and beat in *beurre manié.* Return to heat and boil for 1 minute, stirring constantly.

■ **To Store**—Scrape the sides of the pan with a spatula and add to sauce in pan. To prevent a skin from forming on the top, float a little milk or light cream or melted butter on top. Keep hot over hot water, but do not cover sauce. Or cool and refrigerate, or freeze.

To Make White Sauce

Melt the butter, stir in the flour, and cook it for two minutes without coloring. Then add hot milk and/or cream gradually or all at once. Cook sauce over moderate heat, stirring constantly, until thickened and smooth. It should be cooked for at least five minutes, or the raw taste of the flour will come through. Remove sauce from the heat and season with salt and white pepper. (Black pepper would mar its whiteness.) It is now ready for the addition of cheese and other ingredients, or to be served as is over fish, meats, and vegetables, or used as the basis for soups, soufflés, and creamed dishes.

White sauce comes in varying degrees of thickness, depending on the use. The table that follows gives the proportions of ingredients for different consistencies:

To Make White Sauce

Consistency	Fat	Flour	Liquid	Use In
Thin	1 tablespoon	1 tablespoon	1 cup, hot	Soups
Medium	2 tablespoons	2 tablespoons	1 cup, hot	Sauces
Thick	3 to 4 tablespoons	3 to 4 tablespoons	1 cup, hot	Croquettes, souffles, pie fillings

WHITING—A small gray and white saltwater fish sometimes called kingfish or silver hake. One variety is found along the Middle Atlantic coast, another variety off the New England coast. Whiting grow to an average length of twelve inches and weigh from one to four pounds. The fish has tender white flesh, fine in texture, flaky, with a delicate flavor. It can be broiled, panfried, baked, or poached.

Availability—Sold whole fresh or frozen, filleted, salted, or smoked.

Purchasing Guide—See Whitefish, page 1938.

Storage—See Whitefish, page 1938.

Nutritive Food Values—A good source of protein.

☐ Fresh, 3½ ounces, raw = 105 calories

Basic Preparation—See Whitefish, page 1938.

WHITING CREOLE

1 small onion, chopped
2 tablespoons butter or margarine
½ cup diced celery
½ cup chopped green pepper
2 canned pimientos, chopped
3½ cups (one 29-ounce can) tomatoes
1 tablespoon cornstarch
2 tablespoons water
Salt and pepper
2 tablespoons chopped parsley
6 small whiting

Cook onion in the butter for 2 or 3 minutes. Add celery, green pepper, and pimiento and cook for 2 or 3 minutes longer. Add tomatoes, bring to a boil and simmer, covered, for 1 hour. Mix cornstarch and water and stir into mixture. Season to taste and add parsley. Put fish in the mixture and simmer for 7 minutes, or until fish flakes easily with a fork. Makes 6 servings.

MARINATED WHITING

1½ pounds whiting fillets
½ cup highly seasoned French dressing
Paprika

Cut 1½ pounds whiting fillets into serving pieces. Refrigerate fish in ½ cup highly seasoned French dressing for several hours. Arrange fish on broiler rack; broil under medium heat for 5 minutes on each side, brushing with dressing used for marinating. To serve, pour drippings over fish; sprinkle with paprika. Makes 4 servings.

CREAMED SMOKED WHITING

1½ pounds boneless smoked whiting
2 cups milk
1 bay leaf
Pinch of ground thyme
10 peppercorns
1 slice of onion
¼ cup butter
¼ cup all-purpose flour
¼ cup light cream
Dash of cayenne
1 tablespoon chopped pimiento
2 hard-cooked eggs, chopped

Soak fish in milk with bay leaf, thyme, peppercorns, and onion for 1 hour. Then put over very low heat, and simmer gently for 10 minutes. Flake fish. Melt butter and blend in flour. Add strained milk and cream slowly. Add fish and remaining ingredients. Makes 4 servings.

WILD RICE—A native American grass, *Zizania aquatica,* that bears a grain used for food. It is a tall plant that grows in water in the western Great Lakes area and has never been domesticated. The Indians have used it as a cereal for many centuries and today it is still gathered by local Indian tribes and marketed for consumption as a luxury food.

Wild rice should not be overcooked. It is more delicate than other rice, with a truly delicious flavor. It can be used like regular rice, but it is especially good with poultry and game birds.

Availability—Widely available packaged, uncooked, instant, or precooked, and in combination with white rice.

Storage—Store in covered container in a cool dry place. Will keep almost indefinitely.

Nutritive Food Values—High in protein, phosphorus, and potassium, with some riboflavin, thiamine, and niacin.

☐ 3½ ounces, uncooked = 353 calories

Basic Preparation—Wash ¾ cup uncooked wild rice in 3 or 4 changes of cold water, removing any foreign particles. Add 1 teaspoon salt to 3 cups boiling water. Add rice gradually so that water continues to boil. Cover and simmer, stirring occasionally with a fork, for 30 to 45 minutes, or until rice is tender and all of water is absorbed. Add butter to taste. Makes 2¼ cups.

HERBED WILD RICE

1 cup uncooked wild rice
1 teaspoon salt
¼ cup butter, melted
1 teaspoon grated onion
¼ teaspoon each of pepper and ground sage
⅛ teaspoon ground thyme

Rinse wild rice thoroughly in running water. Cover with water and bring to a boil. Drain and rinse. Cover with water again, add salt, and simmer until tender, about 30 minutes. Drain and rinse in hot water. Add remaining ingredients and mix thoroughly. Makes 6 to 8 servings.

SHRIMPS WITH WILD RICE

2 packages (10 ounces each) frozen shelled deveined shrimps
1 cup uncooked wild rice
1 garlic clove, minced
¼ cup olive oil
2 cans (8 ounces each) tomato sauce
1 sauce-can water
½ teaspoon ground oregano
½ teaspoon crumbled dried basil
1 large green pepper, seeded and cut into chunks
Salt and pepper

Thaw shrimps. Cook rice according to package directions and put in 2-quart casserole. Sauté garlic in olive oil in a skillet for 5 minutes. Add all ingredients except shrimps and salt and pepper. Bring to boil and simmer for 10 minutes. Add shrimps; season to taste. Pour shrimp mixture over rice. Cover and bake in preheated moderate oven (350°F.) for about 30 minutes. Makes 6 servings.

WILD RICE STUFFING

1 cup wild rice
4 cups chicken broth
1 cup diced celery
¼ cup instant minced onion
½ cup butter or margarine, melted
1 can (4 ounces) mushroom crowns
½ teaspoon marjoram leaves
¼ teaspoon oregano leaves
¼ teaspoon pepper
1 teaspoon seasoned salt
¼ teaspoon thyme leaves
Salt to taste

Wash wild rice well. Add to boiling chicken broth, bring to boil again, cover and simmer for 30 to 45 minutes, or until rice is tender, stirring occasionally with fork. All of broth should be absorbed. Sauté celery and onion in the butter for 2 or 3 minutes. Drain mushrooms, reserving 2 tablespoons liquid. Add mushrooms and liquid to rice with remaining ingredients, including celery mixture. Makes 6 cups, or enough to stuff a 10-pound turkey.

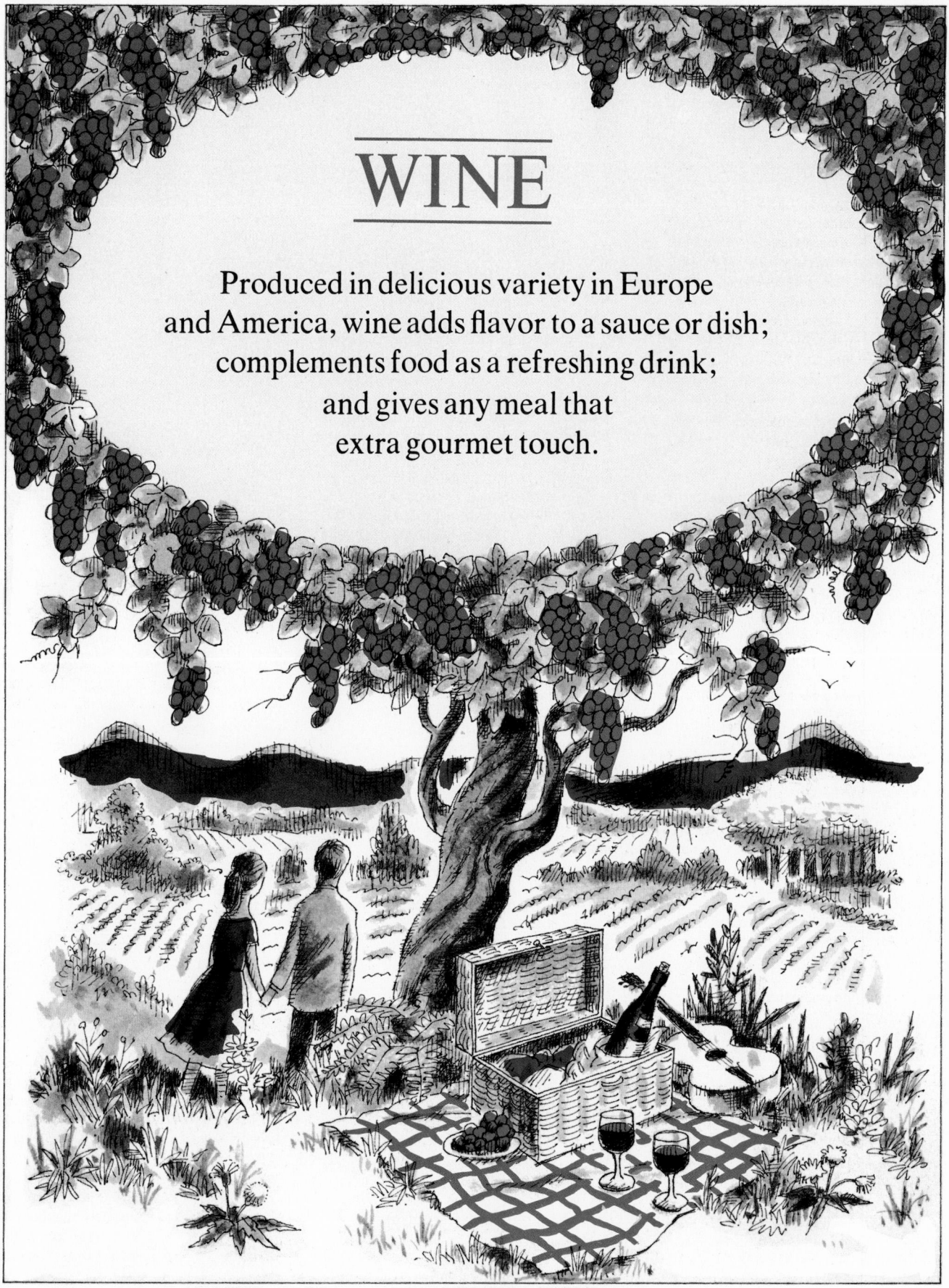
WINE
Produced in delicious variety in Europe
and America, wine adds flavor to a sauce or dish;
complements food as a refreshing drink;
and gives any meal that
extra gourmet touch.

Wine is the product of the natural fermentation of the juice of the grape. The term is also used to describe beverages made from other fruit juices or vegetable juices by adding sugar and yeast and fermenting the mixture. Examples are dandelion wine and elderberry wine. But strictly speaking wine is the product of the vine, for grapes contain naturally all the ingredients needed for a normal fermentation of the juice. No sugar nor yeast need be added.

The origin of wine goes back so far into the dim mists of the past that we have no records of when or where the first wine was made. There are evidences in archaeological discoveries that it was known in the Near East as long as 10,000 to 12,000 years ago. Ancient Egyptian frescoes depict scenes of grape harvesting and wine making. Excavators found winepresses in the Minoan ruins of Crete, and the palace of the Assyrian kings contained a huge wine cellar with a detailed record of its contents.

The Bible has many references to wine and to its ceremonial use, and no doubt from earliest times the fermented juice of the grape had been connected with religious rites. Primitive man must have thought that the natural phenomenon of the fermentation was magical, and certainly the joyous feeling that comes from drinking the beverage must have seemed magical too. This was indeed a divine gift.

Some of the complicated ways of treating wines were developed in ancient times. The Greeks of the classic age used pitch to seal their wine jars and this gave the wine a taste of resin. Today the modern Greeks still like the flavor and add resin to many of their wines to give them a distinctive taste. The Romans at their lavish banquets sipped wines that were strongly perfumed and spiced. The vermouths of today are versions of these aromatic drinks.

Early Phoenician merchants who ranged far afield, even into the Atlantic Ocean, spread the vine throughout the Mediterranean area. Wherever Roman legions went they took the vine and the knowledge of wine making with them—into France, Spain, Portugal, up the Rhine and Moselle valleys of Germany and even into southern England.

In more recent times, European colonizers have transported the custom around the earth—to Canada, Australia, New Zealand, South Africa, and South America. In our own country Spanish friars planted vineyards at their missions in what is now California, and later the settlers of the English colonies along our east coast experimented with the native wild grapes and also imported French vines. In the early years of the Republic, Thomas Jefferson was a noted wine enthusiast and brought many clippings from Europe for planting in Virginia.

To our ancestors wine was both a pleasure and a necessity. It was a pleasure, of course, because the fermented juice of the grape was—and is—a refreshing drink that enhanced food and cheered the soul; it was a necessity because the water supply was often tainted. Even milk sometimes brought serious illness or death. Wine was always safe.

The Characteristics of Wine

The characteristic qualities of a wine—its color, aroma, taste, body—are results of the soil, climate, grape variety, and finally of the vintner's art. In each wine region, through generations of experiment, growers have tended to concentrate on certain grape varieties that seem to do best in the soil and climate of the area. The vines are so sensitive to their environment that vineyards only a few yards apart will produce wines of entirely different qualities even when planted with the same grape variety. A slight change in the chemical content of the soil or the slant of the sun's rays can affect the wine's distinctive characteristics.

Strangely enough, the greatest wines come from soil that would seem most useless—sandy, chalky, or rocky—and from climates that are somewhat severe. France's great Burgundies come from the northern part of the region; Champagne is a northern district in France. In Germany, the farther north you go in the Rhine and Moselle valleys, the better the wine. It has often been said that vines that struggle for survival produce the best grapes.

Certainly the art of the vintner is important. He must decide just the right time for the harvest; he must supervise the fermentation; he must see that the new wine is properly stored in the right sort of container and at the right temperature to insure maturing.

With all these influences at work, it is not surprising that wine can vary from poor to great. The truly great wines—the big velvety Burgundies, the delicate Bordeaux, the rich whites of Germany—are, of course, limited in quantity because only small areas can produce such perfection. But there are many other fine wines that are not so important yet make delicious drinking, and there is a large supply of good honest *vin ordinaire* for everyday drinking.

People of wine countries, such as France and Italy, and wine lovers the world over enjoy the simple *vin du pays,* or regional wine, with their daily meals. Such wines are often called "gulping" wines, for their refreshing, thirst-quenching qualities hold no subtleties, no rich aroma to beguile the senses. They are good healthy accompaniments for family dinners or casual parties. The truly great wines are reserved for those very special occasions when time can be taken to savor each drop.

Types of Wine

Generally speaking, wines may be divided into four categories: *natural still wines*—red, white, and rosé (pink)—sometimes called "table" wines; *sparkling wines,* such as champagne; *fortified wines,* such as sherry and port; and *aromatic wines,* such as vermouth. Red table wines are dry and rosés are nearly always dry to dryish. White table wines and wines in the other categories vary from dry to very sweet.

The color of the wine does not necessarily reflect the color of the grape. Red wines, of course, are made from red grapes. The fruit is pressed, and the skins and pips are allowed to stay in the must to color it. Then the new wine is drawn off. White wines may be made in the same manner from white grapes, or they may be made from red grapes. In this case, the grape skins and pips are removed from the juice as the fruit is pressed. Some champagne is made by this method. Red grapes are used to make rosés, and the skins and pips are left in the must just long enough to turn it pink. Rosés are also made by mixing red and white wines, but the result is less satisfactory.

New wine is put in casks in the "caves" or cellar of the winery and left to age. Some wines stay in the cask only a few weeks or months before bottling; others are not bottled for years. Wine is a living, breathing thing even in the bottle, and the maturing process continues until the bottle is uncorked, or until it passes its prime, becomes old and flat and finally "dead."

In general white wines are drunk when they are young and fresh—within two to three years. The great whites of Germany and the sweet whites of Bordeaux last longer. Reds, with the exception of Beaujolais, which is drunk young, take longer to mature. Great reds, such as very fine Bordeaux and Burgundies, may take as long as ten to twenty years to reach their peak, and some Bordeaux have been known to live for sixty years.

In making champagne, the fermentation is halted by means of temperature control before all the sugar has turned to alcohol. The wine is bottled and the following spring, when the temperature rises, the remaining sugar ferments in the bottles, creating the bubbly effervescence. Some other sparkling wines are made by adding sugar to force a second fermentation or by adding carbon dioxide. The "manufactured" sparkling wines are not as fine.

Fortified wines are made by adding a dose of brandy to the wine to give it more strength. The brandy is usually distilled from the same wine. Aromatic wines, often also fortified, are flavored with various infusions – herbs, seeds, spices.

Storage of Wines

Remember, wine in the bottle is alive, and like all living things it is sensitive and should be handled with some care. It does not like being tossed about, does not like vibration, light, or temperature extremes. Store it in a dark, fairly cool spot away from heating units and drafts. A cool corner in the basement or an unheated closet are likely spots. The ideal temperature is 50 to 60 degrees or even a touch higher. The important points are that there should be no sudden fluctuations in "climate" and that the wine should rest undisturbed.

If you do not have such a spot, buy wine in small quantities and keep it in a dimly lit corner. Use it up within a few weeks.

Store wine bottles on their sides so that the corks are kept in touch with the liquid. If they dry out, they will shrink and let the air in to spoil the wine.

Older wines, like older people, dislike disturbances much more than young wines. If you are fortunate enough to find a bottle of fine aged Bordeaux or Burgundy, do not jiggle it home from the wine shop and serve it immediately. Give it a chance to rest quietly for several days or even weeks after you carry it home.

Once a living wine is opened it can not be recorked and returned to storage. Some table wines can be recorked and used again for one or two days, but older wines tend to die quickly and champagne loses its effervescence. If you have wine left over, it is wise to use it in cooking the next day. Fortified wines, with the exception of very dry (fino) sherry and a fine vintage port, will keep for a few weeks, although there is some deterioration. Fino sherries lose their brilliance within a week and a fine old port shows marked changes within a day or two. Opened bottles of aromatic wines will keep for a few weeks.

Wine with Food

Over the years much has been written about when to serve certain types of wine and which wines to serve with which foods. There are no strict rules. Even connoisseurs disagree and have indulged in many spirited arguments on the subject. Certainly customs vary from country to country. You may find that in a red-wine region you will be served red wine with fish, and you may dine in Spain and find sherry served throughout the meal.

Still some foods and wines do seem to complement each other, just as cheese goes with bread and bacon with eggs. Here are the most widely accepted rules:

Apéritifs: Dry sherry, dry champagne, a light dry white wine such as an Alsatian or a California Riesling, dry vermouth.

With fish: Dry white wine, dry champagne.

With beef, lamb, and mutton: Red wine, dry champagne.

With veal: Dry white wine, dry champagne.

With pork: Dry champagne, a light flowery white such as an Alsatian, a dry Moselle, or a California Riesling.

With chicken and turkey: Dry champagne, red wine, or dry white wine. There is disagreement among wine drinkers on whether to drink white or red with poultry. Your best guide is the method of cooking. A young chicken gently roasted on the spit goes well with a dry white wine. But a red goes with *coq au vin*. Some people like a light red with the Thanksgiving turkey, and others prefer a white.

With duck: Red wine, dry champagne.

With game: A good red wine, dry champagne.

With cheese: A good red wine.

With dessert and fruit: A sweet white wine, such as a rich German wine, a sauterne, or a slightly sweet champagne.

At the end of the meal: Port or other sweet fortified wine such as a sweetish sherry or Madeira.

Wine, with the exception of dry champagne, does not seem to go well with eggs, salads, or highly spiced dishes such as curries and chilies. Champagne is the one all-purpose wine that can be served with almost any food and throughout the meal. Rosés are at their best with picnic foods or informal buffets combining a variety of foods.

Serving Wines

Red table wines: With one or two exceptions, these should be served at room temperature. The exceptions—Beaujolais from France and (sometimes) the Italian Valpolicella—gain by being lightly chilled. For all other reds, place the bottle in the room in which it is to be served a few hours in advance. An hour or so before serving, remove the cork to give the wine a chance to breathe. This will bring out the flavor and aroma.

Very old red wines, such as great Burgundies and Bordeaux, often develop sediment and must be handled with care. Remove them from their resting place to the dining room a day in advance and stand them upright to let the sediment slip to the bottom. Take out the cork several hours before serving and decant the wine. To do this, hold the bottle up to the light so that you can watch the liquid. Tip it slowly and let the wine slip gently into a decanter and keep your eye on the wine in the bottle. The minute you see cloudy sediment moving into the neck of the bottle, stop pouring. Let the decanter stand, upstoppered, until ready to serve.

Dry white table wines, champagnes, rosés: These should be lightly chilled. Do not let them get too cold. Between 50 and 55 degrees is right. The best method is to nestle the bottle in a bucket filled with ice for 15 to 20 minutes before serving. Or place it in the refrigerator for 2 to 3 hours. Open the bottle just before serving.

Dry sherries, dry Madeiras, and vermouths: Chill lightly. Vermouths may be served over ice.

Dessert wines: Sweet white wines, port, sweet sherries, and other dessert wines should be served at room temperature.

If you are serving more than one wine at dinner, serve the lesser before the greater and white before red. Of course you may follow a red wine at dinner with a sweet white or champagne at dessert.

One word of caution: do not serve your best wines after a prolonged cocktail party, but reserve them for true wine lovers and an occasion when they will be the sole stars. The other times, a pleasant table wine will serve the purpose.

Very tart salad dressings and sauces do not go very well with wine since they tend to kill the wine's delicate flavor. Decide which one you will feature, and match the other to it. Curry kills the taste of all wine, and beer, preferably imported, should be drunk with curries.

Also, do not have any highly scented flowers on your dinner table. Their sweet smell will overpower the wine's bouquet —and much of the pleasure of wine drinking is connected with the wine's own delightful aroma.

A question that is frequently brought up is how much money you should spend for a bottle of wine. The answer is: it depends on the occasion. Great wines are expensive, and unless you are an expert on recognizing them and their just price at the wine merchant's, have an idea of how much a specific kind or vintage is worth. You can do this by asking for the wine by name at different reputable stores and comparing the prices. But bear in mind that for a good bottle of table wine you should pay no more than $3.00 top price. Most likely, it will cost between $1.50 and $2.50 a bottle. Very often, you can pick up a pleasant wine for less, depending on where it comes from and its supply.

Wineglasses

Two or three generations ago, elegant families and fine restaurants and hotels had great arrays of different wineglasses. There was a special shape for each kind of wine: one for sherry, one for white wine, one for the great German whites, one for claret (red Bordeaux), one for red Burgundies, and so on. One needed the vast mansions of that era with the cupboard space and servants that went with them to care for such a collection.

Today's apartments and modern servantless homes do not permit such extravagance. Nor do we serve the elaborate seven-course meals with five different wines that were once fashionable. We have solved the problem with the all-purpose wineglass with a medium-size tulip-shape bowl. It serves equally well for whites and reds, for sherries, ports, champagnes, and vermouth on the rocks. It is nice to have a slightly larger-bowled glass for champagne if possible, for the larger bowl holds the bubbles better. But it is not necessary.

Wineglasses should be filled not more than two thirds full. This gives the bouquet (or aroma) a chance to fill the rest of the glass, and gives the drinker a chance to inhale the perfume as he sips the wine. Traditionally, the host pours a small amount of the wine into his own glass first and tastes it to be sure it is all right before he serves his guests.

A fifth bottle of wine or champagne should give you six to seven glasses, and a bottle of dessert wine eight to ten glasses. These are rough figures, of course, and depend on the size of the glasses. If you serve champagne throughout the meal, count on a half bottle for each guest.

Major Wine Regions and Their Products

FRANCE

Bordeaux – This area in southwestern France produces red wines, often called "clarets," that are famous for their clear jewellike color and for their delicate flavor and bouquet. The great Bordeaux wines are all château-bottled. That is, each is the product of an individual vineyard, bottled by the proprietor, and carrying the name of the château on its label. Among the famous names are Lafite, Latour, Haut-Brion, Margaux, Cheval Blanc, and Pétrus. These wines are scarce and expensive.

There are many less well-known châteaux in Bordeaux producing wines that range from excellent down to average or ordinary. The price generally reflects the quality. Other vineyards sell their grapes or bulk wine to shippers who bottle it under the label of the region or district, such as Médoc or St. Julien.

The principal grape variety used in red Bordeaux wines is Cabernet Sauvignon.

White Bordeaux wines are seldom dry. They vary from sweetish to very sweet. The Graves district produces the driest,

Champagne with canapés, olives, and chicken pastries

Red Burgundy with broiled steak and tomato half

although even these seem better with fruit than with a main course. Good vineyards in Graves are Olivier and Domaine de Chevalier.

From Sauternes in Bordeaux comes France's greatest dessert wine, Château d'Yquem. It is rich, perfumed, and round, and owes its special qualities to the fact that the grapes are gathered when overripe, even shriveled, and covered with mold called "noble rot." Other sauternes are less rich but still sweet. Rich white wines also come from the nearby district of Barsac. All go best with fruit or dessert.

Burgundy—This region of France also produces world-famed red wines. The big Burgundies come from the northern section, Côte de Nuits. They are noted for their full-bodied velvety texture, rich aroma, and deep-red color. The wines are bottled by the proprietors and carry the name of the vineyard or commune. Outstanding names in red Burgundies include Romanée-Conti, Le Chambertin, Le Corton, Le Richebourg, La Tâche, Musigny.

Among the less important vineyards, many produce fine red Burgundies that make delightful drinking, although they may not have the deep velvety quality of the bigger wines.

The grape variety used in red Burgundies is Point Noir.

The best white Burgundies rank near the top as white dinner wines and they come from the section known as the Côte de Beaune. They are dry to dryish, full-bodied with fine bouquets. Among these are Le Montrachet, Meursault, and Corton-Charlemagne.

From the southernmost part of Burgundy come two very pleasant light wines, the red Beaujolais and the white Pouilly-Fuissé. These wines are often served *en carafe* in French restaurants.

A little to the northwest of Burgundy is the tiny Chablis district, home of the wine of the same name. Chablis is very dry, with a flinty taste and a faintly greenish tinge. It is the traditional drink with oysters, particularly on the half-shell.

Champagne—The world's most glamorous wine derives its name from this region in northern France where it is produced. Champagne is a blended wine made usually from red and white grapes. A small amount made solely from white grapes is known as *blanc de blancs*.

Champagne producers buy grapes from various vineyards, and each company blends the resulting wines according to its own recipe. Nonvintage champagnes are blends of wines of various years—and a nonvintage from a fine house can be a good buy.

Champagnes range from dry to sweet and the labeling can be confusing. The dryest is labeled *brut; extra-sec* is dryish; *sec* is actually sweetish; *demi-sec* is sweet; and *doux* is very sweet.

Rhône Valley—This southern region of France makes both white and red wines, often unusually good. The sun is hot in the Rhône Valley and the red wines in particular often have a slightly scorched or earthy taste, making them rougher than the sophisticated reds of Burgundy and Bordeaux. But they have a hearty quality that goes well with hearty meats. The Hermitage and Côte Rôtie are robust; the reds from Châteauneuf-du-Pape are lighter.

hite Bordeaux with broiled chicken and green beans

Port with dessert, a strawberry sponge roll

Rhone white wines are light, dry, and slightly flinty in taste. White Hermitage and Chante-Alouette are the best known. The most outstanding rosé also comes from the Rhône valley—Tavel. It is drier than most pink wines and has a clear rosy color.

Loire Valley—Tourists flock to this picturesque valley to see the beautiful châteaux and while there they enjoy the delicious local wines. Reds, whites, and rosés are all produced but it is the whites that are the favorites. They are mostly light, delicate, and dry. Leading names are Pouilly-Fumé, Sancerre, and Muscadet. Vouvray is a white wine that ranges from dryish to sweet.

Alsace—This northeast corner of France borders on Germany and has many historical connections with that country. The same grape varieties are used here as in the German vineyards, and the wines resemble the lightest of the German whites. They are dry with a slightly flowery quality and go well with Alsatian foods, such as pork or sausage dishes. The wines are labeled with the grape names, the two best known being Riesling and Gewürztraminer.

French Vermouth—This is a dry vermouth with a flavor of herbs and seeds. In France it is drunk as an apéritif either plain or in a vermouth cassis: vermouth over ice with a touch of crème de cassis and a dash of soda. Crème de cassis is a syrup made from black currants.

GERMANY

Among the greatest and most costly wines in the world are the white wines of the Rhine and Moselle districts in Germany. The important Rhine wines are big and serious, full-bodied with deep perfumes. Moselles are lighter, more lively, and with flowery bouquets.

German wines range from dry to very sweet and even one vineyard may produce wines of varying sweetness. This is done by harvesting the grapes at intervals. Some are picked at the normal time to make a dry wine. Others are left to become overripe in order to make a sweeter wine. The final harvesting is of grapes that have shriveled and developed "noble rot." Bottle labels designate the ripeness of the grapes and amount of sweetness: *Spätlese* means dry to dryish; *Auslese* means sweetish; *Beerenauslese* means sweet; *Trockenbeerenauslese* means very sweet and rich.

Regional wines are labeled with the name of the village; wines bottled by the proprietor are labeled with the village name followed by the name of the vineyard. For example, Bernkasteler Doktor is wine from the Doktor vineyard in the village of Bernkastel. Three or four of the greatest vineyards omit the name of the village and use the vineyard name only. Among these are Schloss Vollrads, Schloss Johannisberg, and Steinberg. Some villages with outstanding vineyards are:

Rhine Valley—Bodenheim, Oppenheim, Nierstein, Hochheim, Winkel, Erbach, Oestrich, Geisenheim.

Moselle Valley—Bernkastel, Piesport, Wehlen, Trittenheim, Wiltingen, Ockfen.

These are but a few of the many German towns and villages where fine vineyards are located.

ITALY

Italian wines do not include any "greats" but many of them are good, sound, agreeable wines. The reds are often earthy, even a little rough, and they go well with hearty Italian food and with barbecued meats. The best known is chianti, and the finest chianti comes in regular claret bottles, not the straw-covered round bottles. Other good reds are Valpolicella, Barolo, Bardolino.

Italian white wines are light and pleasing, and they can be dry, sweetish, or sweet. Soave is a soft dry white; Orvieto and Est! Est! Est! come either dry or sweet.

Italy also produces a sweet sparkling wine, Asti Spumante, and a well-known rich dessert wine, Marsala. Italian vermouths are dryish to sweet. The sweet vermouth is often served as an apéritif with a dash of Campari (Italian bitters) and a twist of lemon peel.

SPAIN

Spanish table wines are exported in very small amounts. It is the fortified sherries for which the country is famed. Sherry is not a vintage wine, but a blend of wines of various ages. By the *solera* system, as the method is called, young sherries are gradually, over a period of years, mixed with increasingly older sherries to give body, maturity, and flavor.

Sherries range from very dry to very sweet, depending on the grape varieties used. They are labeled as follows: *manzanilla,* light and dry; *fino,* pale and dry; *amontillado,* nutty and dryish; *golden,* medium sweet; *oloroso,* rich and sweet; *cream,* heavy and very sweet. Each firm puts out a variety of sherries.

PORTUGAL

Port is a fortified wine blended from many grape varieties and is always sweet. The finest ports, well aged, are very rich. *Vintage port,* a blend of great wines of an outstanding year, is matured in the bottle for 20 years or longer. These rare wines have a deep-red color and a deep aroma. They must be decanted. *Crusted port,* a little less fine than vintage, is aged in the bottle for about 10 years. It, too, must be decanted.

Ruby port is a young wine matured in the cask. It is light, with an agreeable fruity flavor. *Tawny port* is an older ruby port that has faded to a tawny color and become mellower. There is some white port made from white grapes.

As with sherry, the firms in Portugal each ship several wines and indicate the type on the labels.

UNITED STATES

California—Wine making in California dates back almost two hundred years, when the first vines were planted by Franciscan friars. For the past hundred years, California vintners have experimented with many different grapes and today most California wine is made from European grape varieties. The finest vineyards are located to the north, around the San Francisco Bay region, and most are planted with several kinds of grapes to produce a number of wines, both white and red.

The best wines are labeled with the name of the grape variety, although a few have specific names devised by the vintner or company producing them. Leading red table wines are labeled Cabernet Sauvignon, Pinot Noir, and Zinfandel. The Riesling is a good white table wine and Grenache a good rosé. Two sound wines for everyday drinking are labeled Mountain White and Mountain Red.

California vineyards also produce good champagnes and good fortified wines, such as sherries and ports.

New York—The New York Finger Lakes district has several outstanding wine companies producing wines from native grapes. These grapes, having been developed from the wild varieties found in this country, have flavors that are often called "foxy." The wines, as a result, are very different from those made from European grapes.

As with California wines, the best are labeled with the name of the grape, such as Elvira, Diana, Delaware. The whites are more successful than the reds.

Some European grape varieties are planted in New York but they are used mainly in blends.

Good champagne is made in this region and also some pleasant sherries.

Ohio—A small vineyard area in northern Ohio produces some interesting wines from native American grapes. These wines are labeled with the name of the grape variety.

Cooking with Wine

Cooking with wine is like cooking with any other flavoring, from onions through thyme or vanilla extract. The wine should be used to round out the flavor of a dish, and in some cases, as with meats, to tenderize it before cooking, in a marinade, or during cooking. Wine should always be used sparingly in cookery.

When wine is not part of a recipe, but you feel you would like to add some to the dish you're cooking, add a very little at a time, and taste as you go along.

The alcohol in wine and all spirits evaporates in cooking above the boiling point so that only the flavor remains. Preferably use a dry wine of good quality (a wine that you would like to drink) in your cooking since you will be tasting the wine's flavor.

Don't be hidebound about such rules as "white wines for white meats" and "red wines with red meats." Such dishes as chicken, veal, or beef are excellent with either wine. Fish is an exception. It is better cooked with white wine.

When cooking a sauce or other dish with wine, bring it to the boiling point to let the alcohol evaporate and do not cover the pan.

When cooking with fortified wines or spirits such as brandy, it is best to flambé the dish to let the alcohol evaporate completely. Pour the spirits into a heated spoon and then over the hot food, such as a meat. Set a match to it and let the flame burn down by itself. The alcohol will then have evaporated and only the flavor of the spirits remains.

Meats that have been marinated or soaked in wine to tenderize them must be well dried before cooking.

All meat to be cooked in wine must be well browned before the wine is added.

All dishes cooked with wine can be reheated successfully. A few slices of carrots mitigate the raw tartness of some red wines.

When sherry is used in cooking, especially in seafood dishes, it should be a dry sherry and used most sparingly.

SOLE IN WHITE WINE

- ¼ cup butter
- 2 shallots or 4 green onions, finely chopped
- 6 fillets of lemon sole or flounder
- 1½ cups dry white wine (about)
- Salt and pepper to taste
- 1 teaspoon crumbled dried tarragon
- 1 tablespoon chopped parsley
- ¼ cup all-purpose flour
- 1 cup heavy cream
- Buttered crumbs or grated cheese

Use 1 tablespoon of the butter to butter an oval or oblong baking dish (about 11 x 14 inches) or a fish poacher, which usually measures 12 x 16 inches, and a piece of paper cut to fit. Place shallots on bottom and arrange fillets on top. Barely cover with dry white wine. Season with salt and pepper. Add tarragon and parsley. Cover with the buttered paper and put in preheated moderate oven (350°F.) for about 15 minutes, or until fish is just cooked through.

Remove paper; if you are to serve fish in the baking dish, pour off the liquid, but keep fish warm with the buttered paper over it. Measure liquid from the fish and reduce to 1 cup, if need be, over high heat. Prepare cream sauce by heating remaining 3 tablespoons butter and the flour together over low heat. Stir in fish liquid and the heavy cream. Correct seasoning. When sauce is thickened, simmer for 4 or 5 minutes. Pour sauce over fillets. Sprinkle with a few buttered crumbs. Put under preheated broiler for 3 or 4 minutes to glaze. Makes 4 to 6 servings.

DAUBE PROVENCALE

- 4 to 5 pounds chuck or rump of beef, rolled and tied
- 3 garlic cloves
- 1 onion stuck with 2 cloves
- 1 teaspoon crumbled dried thyme
- ½ teaspoon crumbled dried rosemary
- 1 teaspoon pepper
- 1 pig's foot, split
- 2 carrots
- 2 teaspoons salt (about)
- Coarse dry red wine
- 2 tablespoons tomato paste
- 1 cup stoned black olives
- 1 pound macaroni

Put all ingredients in a bowl except wine, tomato paste, olives, and macaroni. Add enough wine to cover. Let stand in refrigerator for 12 to 24 hours. Remove to casserole or Dutch oven. Cover tightly and either simmer on top of stove, or bake in preheated very slow oven (200° F.) for 4 to 6 hours, or until meat is tender. Add tomato paste and black olives (Italian or Greek type) and cook for another 30 minutes. Skim off excess fat.

Put meat and pig's foot on a platter and slice meat. Reserve sauce. Garnish platter with additional boiled onions and carrots if you wish. Cook macaroni in boiling salted water until done to your taste, and drain. Mix with thick luscious sauce and serve with the *daube*. This is called *macaronnade*. A *daube* is much better made one day and allowed to rest for 24 hours, when all fat can be removed. Then it can be eaten either cold in its own jelly or heated and served with *macaronnade,* as above. Makes 6 to 8 servings.

FILET OF BEEF WITH SHERRY

- 4 tomatoes, peeled, seeded, and chopped
- 5 tablespoons butter
- Salt and pepper
- 1 teaspoon sugar, if needed
- 12 mushroom caps
- ¼ cup water mixed with ¼ cup sherry
- 6 tournedos cut from the filet, about 1½ inches thick, each wrapped and tied with a piece of salt pork or bacon
- ¼ cup finely chopped beef fat or ¼ cup butter and 2 tablespoons cooking oil
- 1 teaspoon meat extract
- 6 pieces of fried toast, about the size of the tournedos
- ½ cup sherry

Cook tomatoes in butter until most of liquid has evaporated. Season with salt and pepper. Add sugar if needed. Set aside. Poach mushrooms in water and sherry mixture. Set aside. Using heavy skillet, sauté tournedos in hot beef fat until meat reaches desired state of rareness. Season tournedos with salt and pepper. Add meat extract to pan. Turn tournedos and cook for a few seconds longer to brown nicely. Remove to hot platter and put on fried toast. Top with a spoonful of tomato mixture and a mushroom cap. Add sherry to skillet and let it cook down very quickly with the pan juices. Pour over tournedos. Makes 6 servings.

CHICKEN BRAISED WITH WINE

- 7 tablespoons butter
- 3 tablespoons cooking oil
- 1 roasting chicken (3½ to 4 pounds)
- Salt and pepper to taste
- 1 teaspoon crumbled dried thyme
- 1 onion stuck with 2 cloves
- 1 small carrot
- Dry red wine
- 16 small white onions
- 1 teaspoon sugar
- 12 to 16 mushroom caps
- Beurre manié (butter and flour kneaded together)
- Chopped parsley

Melt 3 tablespoons of the butter and the cooking oil in a heavy skillet. Brown chicken over fairly high heat until nicely colored on all sides. Season with salt and pepper. Transfer to a casserole or baking dish which can be covered. Add thyme, onion with cloves, carrot, and enough full-bodied red wine to cover the chicken. Simmer, covered, in preheated slow oven (300°F.) for 1 to 1½ hours, or until chicken is just tender. Do not overcook. It may be that you will have to reduce temperature to slow (250°F.) if it seems to be cooking too quickly.

While casserole is cooking, sauté white onions in remaining butter. Cover pan or skillet and steam onions until tender. Add sugar at the last minute, to caramelize and give onions color. Sauté mushroom caps until lightly browned in the skillet in which you browned the chicken, adding more butter if needed. Season them with salt and pepper.

Remove chicken when it is tender, cut into serving pieces, and arrange on a hot platter. Reduce wine sauce over a high heat. Correct seasoning and thicken sauce with small balls of *beurre manié*. Pour sauce over chicken and top with chopped parsley. Garnish with glazed onions and mushroom caps and serve with boiled potatoes. Drink the same type wine used for Coq au Vin. Makes 4 to 6 servings.

Duckling Rosé

DUCKLING ROSÉ

1 duckling, about 5 pounds, cut in quarters
Salt
Paprika
Powdered ginger
1 tablespoon grated onion
1 cup rosé
⅓ cup brown sugar, firmly packed
⅓ cup granulated sugar
1 tablespoon cornstarch
1 teaspoon grated orange rind

Remove any excess fat from duckling and put bird quarters in shallow baking pan. Roast, uncovered, in preheated hot oven (400°F.) for 30 minutes. Remove from oven and drain off fat. Sprinkle duckling pieces with salt, paprika, ginger, and the onion. Pour ¼ cup of the wine into pan. Cover tightly with foil and roast for 45 minutes longer, or until duckling is tender. Mix ¼ teaspoon salt, remaining wine, and other ingredients in saucepan. Cook, stirring constantly, until thickened. Pour over duckling and roast, uncovered, for about 10 minutes longer, or until glazed, basting frequently. Makes 4 servings.

CABBAGE IN WHITE WINE

6 tablespoons goose fat, bacon fat, or olive oil
1 large head cabbage, coarsely shredded
Salt and pepper to taste
1 small onion, sliced
1 cup very dry white wine or vermouth

Heat fat in large heavy skillet or deep pan over medium heat. Put cabbage in it and cook, turning several times, until it is lightly browned. Season with salt and pepper. Add onion and white wine. Turn down heat and simmer, covered, until cabbage is soft and well blended, stirring occasionally. Makes 4 servings.

PRUNES IN WINE

36 prunes
Port
1 cup sugar
Heavy cream, whipped

Soak prunes in enough good port to cover them. Let stand for 24 hours. Heat sugar with 1 cup port and stir until sugar is dissolved. Add port from prunes and cook for 3 minutes. Then add prunes and cook until they reach the boiling point. Cool prunes in the wine and put in refrigerator for 24 hours. Serve with port-flavored whipped cream. Makes 6 servings.

WINTERGREEN—A trailing evergreen plant, native to eastern North America, which takes its name from the fact that it keeps its foliage during the winter. Also known as teaberry and checkerberry, it is a low hardy shrub with white flowers and small bright red berries.

The whole plant may be eaten, and probably often was by the Indians of our northeast coast. Wintergreen oil, an important flavoring material, used in medicine and in candy, soft drinks, chewing gum, and dentifrices, was once obtained exclusively from the leaves of the plant, but nowadays the twigs and bark of the sweet birch are more used to give wintergreen flavor than the plant itself.

WOODCOCK—The name is used to describe two related birds, the European woodcock, *Scolopex rusticola,* and a similar but smaller American bird, *Philohela minor*. Both are migratory birds and are considered the best of winged game.

The American woodcock is ten to twelve inches long and weighs about ten ounces, the female being the larger. It has a rounded body, short legs, brownish-gray feathers, and a bill that is extremely sensitive at the tip.

Woodcock can be prepared or cooked in the same way as other game birds. When young, it can be roasted or broiled; if of unknown age, it is best pot-roasted and finished with a sour-cream gravy. Frozen dressed woodcock is available in specialty food stores and stores specializing in game.

BAKED WOODCOCK

Cut cleaned and drawn bird into serving pieces. Dip into milk and flour seasoned with salt and pepper. Brown on all sides in hot butter. Place meat in casserole and add enough sweet or sour cream to cover. Add 7 or 8 crushed juniper berries for flavor (optional). Bake, covered, in preheated moderate oven (350°F.) until tender. Baking time depends on the age and size of the bird, but it is tender when easily pierced with a fork.

Note: If the bird is baked in sour cream, the appearance of the sauce will be curdled, but this is as it should be. If this is objectionable, thicken the sauce with a little flour mixed with water into a smooth paste. Strain sauce before serving to remove juniper berries.

WOODRUFF, SWEET (**Asperula odorata**)—A spreading plant with small white flowers whose slim yellow leaves are used to flavor beverages. The sweet woodruff plant is a clumpy little one, growing only about eight inches tall; it provides a good ground cover. The characteristic odor of its leaves is released when they are somewhat dried; they then smell like new-mown hay. The leaves may be used to flavor cold fruit drinks and wine cups. Fruit cups, too, may be garnished with a sprig. And the traditional May wine or *Maibowle* is made by steeping woodruff in Rhine wine.

MAIBOWLE

2 bunches woodruff
½ cup super fine sugar, or sugar to taste
½ cup brandy
3 bottles Moselle or Rhine wine
Ice
1 bottle champagne
½ cup fresh strawberries (optional)

Wash woodruff and shake dry. Place in deep bowl with sugar, brandy, and 1 bottle of the wine. Cover bowl; let stand overnight at room temperature. Before serving, strain mixture and pour over ice in punch bowl. Add remaining still wine and the champagne. Float strawberries in punch bowl, for decorative appearance. Makes 8 to 10 servings.

WORCESTERSHIRE SAUCE—A thin, dark, pungent seasoning sauce, containing garlic, soy, vinegar, anchovies, tamarinds, onions, shallots, molasses, sugar, salt, and spices. The sauce was originally made in Worcester, England, and is used with meats. It can also be used as a seasoning ingredient in gravies, soups, tomato juice, meat loaves, cheese rabbits, etc. Worcestershire is made in the United States but is also available imported from England.

WORMWOOD (**Artemisia absinthium**)—This spreading, shrubby perennial grows to a height of four feet. It has lobed gray-looking leaves covered with silky hair. These leaves have some culinary use, for they may be put on top of roast goose to cut grease. A mixture of the leaves and flowers is sometimes drunk for colds, digestion, and even rheumatism. Wormwood is best known, however, as a flavoring ingredient in absinthe, a powerful spirit now illegal in this country. Absinthe-type cordials made without wormwood are available.

YAM—One of the various plants of the genus *Dioscorea,* a tropical group with twining or creeping stems and broad leaves. The yam is a thick tuber which develops at the base of the stem. There are more than 150 species of this widely used root growing in Central and South America, the West Indies, and tropical Asia. Some varieties grow up to 100 pounds; some are no larger than a small potato. The consistency varies from coarse and mealy to tender and mushy, with some crisp varieties.

There are as many ways of preparing yams as there are varieties of the tuber. They may be used in soup, like mashed potatoes, mashed and then fried or baked, boiled or baked in their jackets, cooked with meat in stews, or cut into slices and fried. Most yams have a bitter taste when raw, which disappears when they are cooked.

People often think that yams and sweet potatoes are the same thing, but although they resemble each other closely in taste, they belong to entirely different families of plants. For culinary purposes, yams and sweet potatoes are interchangeable and not even an expert with a refined palate would be sure to be able to tell the difference in a cooked dish.

Few true yams are cultivated in the United States, but certain moist-fleshed varieties of sweet potato are called "yams." The "air potato" or Asian species is grown to some extent for food and the cinnamon vine is cultivated as an ornamental plant for its cinnamon-scented white blossoms. But throughout the West Indies and most parts of Central and South America the yam is the principal food of the working class.

The name "yam" is a development from the Sengalese word *nyami,* to eat: African slaves named the strange sweet-potato-like tubers they saw for the first time in the West Indies. In the southern parts of this country sweet potatoes are often casually referred to as yams; although this is not accurate, in the kitchen it does not make any real difference.

Availability—Yams are available all year round in stores catering to people of Puerto Rican, South or Central American, or West Indian origin.

Purchasing Guide—Select firm yams with unwrinkled skins. Some yams have a white, yellow, or even purple flesh. Some are sold by the piece or by weight in pieces cut from the larger yams.

Storage—Uncut yams should be stored in a cool dark dry place. Cooked yams should be refrigerated.

- ☐ Kitchen shelf: 1 week
- ☐ Refrigerator shelf, cooked: 4 to 5 days
- ☐ Refrigerator frozen-food compartment, cooked: 3 months
- ☐ Freezer, cooked: 1 year

Caloric Value

- ☐ 3½ ounces, raw = 101 calories

Basic Preparation—Peel, wash, and slice

or cube. Can be cooked in any way potatoes are cooked.

ORANGE YAMS

4 medium yams
¼ cup firmly packed brown sugar
2 tablespoons butter or margarine
Grated rind of 1 orange
¼ cup fresh orange juice
½ teaspoon salt
⅛ teaspoon pepper

Cook yams in small amount of boiling water until tender. Drain and peel. Mash while hot. Add remaining ingredients and beat until light and fluffy. Put in broiler-proof dish and brown lightly in broiler. Good with duck or other poultry, or with ham. Makes 4 servings.

PUERTO RICAN YAM AND CHEESE CRULLERS

2 cups grated peeled yams
½ cup sifted all-purpose flour
2 tablespoons cooking oil
1 teaspoon salt
¼ cup grated Cheddar cheese
1 egg, well beaten
3 tablespoons milk
Fat or oil for deep frying

Combine all ingredients except fat. Beat until well blended. Drop mixture by teaspoonfuls into deep hot fat (375°F. on a frying thermometer) and fry until golden-brown on all sides. Drain on absorbent paper. Can be served with guava jelly if desired. Makes 4 dozen crullers.

YAM CUSTARD PIE

2 cups cold mashed cooked yams
3 eggs, separated
1 cup less 2 tablespoons sugar
2 tablespoons melted butter
½ teaspoon salt
1 cup milk
Pastry for 1-crust 9-inch pie, unbaked
½ teaspoon vanilla extract
¼ cup shredded coconut

Beat yams and egg yolks together until light and fluffy. Beat in ½ cup sugar, the butter, salt, and milk. Pour into pastry-lined pie pan. Bake in preheated moderate oven (350°F.) for 40 minutes, or until set. Beat egg whites until foamy. Gradually beat in remaining sugar and continue beating until stiff. Add vanilla; pile meringue lightly on pie. Sprinkle with coconut. Bake in hot oven (425°F.) for 5 minutes. Cool. Makes 6 to 8 servings.

YAM SPICECAKE

2 cups sifted cake flour
¾ teaspoon salt
2 teaspoons baking powder
¼ teaspoon baking soda
1 teaspoon each of ground cinnamon and nutmeg
⅛ teaspoon ground cloves
½ cup soft butter or margarine
¾ cup sugar
2 eggs
1¼ cups cold mashed cooked or canned yams
½ cup milk
Fluffy white frosting
¼ cup coarsely chopped nuts

Sift first 7 ingredients. Cream butter, add sugar, and cream until light and fluffy. Add eggs, one at a time, beating thoroughly after each addition. Beat in yams. Add sifted dry ingredients and milk, beating only until smooth. Line two 8-inch layer-cake pans with wax paper. Pour batter into pans. Bake in preheated moderate oven (350°F.) for about 35 minutes. Turn out on racks and peel off paper. Cool, and frost. Top with nuts.

Two thousand yeasts packed together would occupy barely the space required to write their name. Each of these tiny organisms has but one cell and reproduces in the most primitive way, by budding. Yeasts float unseen in the air around us, lie in the soil, fall onto plants and on our food. Although they could hardly be more different from mushrooms or truffles, they belong to the same group of living things, the fungi. Like all fungi, they require moisture and sugar or starch in order to grow, but unlike other fungi, the genus *Saccharomyces* changes the food it consumes into alcohol and carbon dioxide in a process known as fermentation.

A delicate goblet filled with champagne, a slice of soft white bread, a bottle of cold hearty beer are very different from one another, but all are linked by this single organism, the yeast. The carbon dioxide given off by the growing yeast pushes its way through flat heavy dough, lifting it into a light fluffy loaf. The alcohol imparts delightful and intoxicating qualities to grape juice and unappetizing grain mashes, transforming them into wines, whiskeys, and beer.

Mothers in ancient Egypt worried about their children's diet and sent jugs of beer to school. Their modern counterparts frown on alcohol for minors and so nowadays adults alone manage to down ninety-one million barrels of the foaming drink every year. Barley and corn malt provide the starch that nourishes the brewers' yeasts. Some beer makers add fresh yeasts to each brew, while others save a little of the fermented liquid from one time to the next. Long before the true nature of fungi was understood, a scientist, forgotten now, observed that the same yeasts which fermented beer could also make bread and cakes rise. And the brewers handed their leftovers to bakers and housewives.

When America was young, it was the custom for a bride to receive a bit of a yeast starter from her mother. Each time she baked, she would keep some of the yeast-filled dough. Prospectors and trappers in the Northwest carried a similar lump of sourdough in their packs to make the tasty bread that bears its name. Today sourdough bread is a San Francisco specialty and only a few women still use starters handed down in the family for hundreds of years, but both home baked and commercially baked bread and coffeecake are as dependent on yeast as ever they were.

The brewers' yeast was sent back to the beer makers long ago, replaced by bakers' yeast, which is composed of strains specially selected for both their flavor and their ability to produce a lot of carbon dioxide and rather little alcohol. The yeast is compressed, with 3,500 billion yeast organisms going into a one-pound cake. Even this treatment does not quiet the active fungi, and they must be refrigerated or they will start to grow before being put into the dough. Yeast-makers have discovered that the organisms can be kept under control by further drying to send them into a resting stage. This active dry yeast cannot function, even without refrigeration, until it is revived with warm water.

The same packages of compressed or active dry yeasts are used by those who make their own wines. This sounds delightfully wicked and reminiscent of bootleggers and Prohibition, but actually the law allows the fermentation of 200 gallons a year for home use. Until recently the great wines of France were fermented only by the wild yeasts that settled on the grapes. Each vineyard, a Frenchman explains, has slightly different yeasts and these account for some of the subtle differences in wine flavor. Unfortunately, yeasts are scarce in dry seasons. Scientists, recognizing the uncertainties of nature, isolated the chief wine-making yeast strains and produced pure cultures in the laboratory. These are used exclusively in America and by a growing number of European vintners as well.

The question, what makes one wine sweet and another dry, would trap many a quiz program contestant. The answer has nothing to do with sweet or sour grapes. A wine is dry when the yeasts have been allowed to complete the fermentation process and to transform all the sugar in the juice into alcohol; when fermentation is incomplete, some sugar is left and sweetens the wine. The bubbles in champagne that tickle the nose arise when additional yeasts and sugar are placed in white wine and a second fermentation occurs. In order to make the gin for a martini and the Scotch for a highball, the yeasts must do their familiar work in a grain mash which is then distilled.

Quite another species of yeast, *Torulopsis* or *Candida utilis,* cannot perform the miracle of fermentation, but may become a miracle food of the future. In the hour it takes to prepare dinner, the population of the world increases by 3,600. It has been estimated that more than six billion people will be on earth by the year 2,000, many of them hungry unless new sources of food, such as torula yeast, are utilized. Torula reproduces at such speed that half a ton yields 6,000 to 7,000 tons of protein in a mere twenty-four hours. And these yeasts will thrive in mashes made of rotten fruits, sugar wastes, or molasses. During World Wars I and II there were unnerving reports that "the Germans are making steaks out of sawdust." The truth was nearly as strange. They were growing torula yeasts on the liquid left over when logs are made into wood pulp. Even today in the food-rich United States several paper mills are using their wastes in this way. Torula adds protein and vitamins to a number of canned soups, baby foods, pet foods, and TV dinners.

Although torula is really more a hope for the future than a food of the present, knowledge about this yeast can sometimes mean the difference between life and death. In World War II when Dutch prisoners of war were starving in a Japanese prison camp in Java, a botanist among them suggested growing torula yeast on scraps of rotten potatoes, spoiled fish, and ammonia distilled from urine. The yeast flourished on these repellent nutrients and provided more than 130 pounds of food a week, just enough to keep the men alive until liberation.

Availability—Packaged active dry yeast is widely available. Cakes of compressed yeast are also available, but are less widely distributed. The ⅔-ounce cake of compressed yeast is the equivalent of one package of active dry yeast. Since the dry yeast keeps much better than the compressed and equally good results are obtained with it, this type is much more in demand.

Storage

- ☐ Compressed, refrigerator shelf: 2 weeks
- ☐ Dry, kitchen shelf: until time dated on package

Nutritive Food Values—A good source of B vitamins.

- ☐ Baker's compressed, 3½ ounces = 86 calories
- ☐ Baker's dry, active, 3½ ounces = 282 calories
- ☐ Brewer's dry, 3½ ounces = 283 calories
- ☐ Torula, 3½ ounces = 277 calories

USING YEAST

There is a difference in compressed and active dry yeasts in that different temperatures of water are required for dissolving them. Lukewarm water (80°F. to 90°F.) should be used for the compressed. A drop of liquid which feels cool when placed on the inside of the wrist is lukewarm, or the right temperature for the compressed. Active dry yeast can be dissolved in slightly warmer water (110° F. to 115°F.). Compressed yeast will dissolve in milk but dry yeast should always be dissolved in water. If no water is called for in a recipe, ¼ cup water should be substituted for an equal amount of milk.

Some of the following questions are often asked about yeast:

Q. Is it possible to get yeast dough too warm?

A. Yes. If the rising place is too warm, some of the yeast will be killed. A temperature of 145°F. will kill yeast.

Q. How can one tell if compressed yeast is still good?

A. Fresh compressed yeast will "break clean" when crumbled into the water. If compressed yeast is old, it will be mushy.

Q. What is the purpose of salt in bread?

A. Salt imparts a pleasant flavor to bread and a small quantity also helps to point up other flavors. The main purpose, however, is to control the yeast action so the rising is not too rapid.

Q. How can one tell when enough flour has been added to the dough when a range is given?

A. Add one-half the flour amount specified, beat until smooth, then add more flour until it begins to clean the sides of the bowl and can be handled.

Q. How can one tell when dough has risen enough?

A. Press a finger deep into side of dough. If the dent remains, the dough has doubled or, in other words, it has risen enough. Be sure to check at minimum time given, so dough does not get *too* light.

How to Cook Superbly: Yeast Rolls and Buns

By Helen Evans Brown

Probably no experience so delights a cook as the feeling of yeast dough under her hands as she kneads it for bread or rolls. It seems alive, and that's because it is. Yeast is a plant, a living plant, and watching and feeling it grow as the dough rises is truly exciting. And then there's that wonderful aroma while it's baking! But most gratifying of all are the delectable results, achieved with so little effort. What a joy to produce light hot rolls for a family dinner, even though you've only been home an hour or two, or to make your own hamburger buns for the children. But when your miniature Parker House rolls are in such demand at the church fair, why should you announce that anyone could make them as well? Receipts for yeast rolls vary, but forming them into different shapes is the same. Some doughs stay in the refrigerator for several days, some can be baked as soon as they have risen. Dough can also be frozen for a short time, but it's more satisfactory to bake the rolls first, then freeze them.

EQUIPMENT

You'll need only the regular kitchen equipment: a large mixing bowl, a pastry board, cookie cutters, a rolling pin, cookie sheets, and muffin pans, as well as the usual measures, saucepans, spoons, and knives. It's also nice to have a heavy-duty electric mixer with a dough hook, if you have neither the time nor strength for kneading.

MIXING, KNEADING, AND RAISING

There was a time when milk for yeast rolls or bread had to be scalded, then cooled to lukewarm. This was to avoid any bacteria that might be in the milk and affect the yeast. As almost all of today's milk is pasteurized, this is unnecessary. However, the milk should be warm so that the yeast will work faster. I have found that the quickest way to mix the ingredients is to heat the water or milk to about as hot as the finger can stand, add butter, sugar, and salt to it, and stir until the butter is melted and the mixture is lukewarm. This won't take long if the butter is cold. The yeast is crumbled or sprinkled into warm water, then stirred until dissolved. Now add the beaten eggs, then beat in part of the flour. Vigorous beating at this point gets best results. Use a spoon or electric or hand beater. Add flour gradually until the mixture is too stiff to beat, then continue adding flour and mix until the desired consistency is reached, usually soft but not sticky. I use my hands for this, but a wooden spoon may be used. As the moisture content of flour varies, it is impossible to give the exact amount of flour needed. When making most rolls, sufficient flour has been added when the mixture leaves the side of the bowl, and is soft but not sticky. Now turn it out on a floured board, sprinkle with a little flour, and cover with a cloth. Let stand for 10 minutes, then start kneading if the recipe calls for it. To do this, fold the dough toward you, then, using the heels of your lightly floured hands, push it away. Give it a half turn, and repeat and repeat until the dough is smooth and shiny. While kneading, you may have to sprinkle a little more flour on the board to keep the dough from sticking. Now butter a large bowl; put the dough in it. Turn the dough in the bowl so that the top is greased, and cover. Put in a warm place—80°F. is ideal—to rise. (Refrigerator rolls do not require this raising period.) If you have an oven with a pilot light, put it in there with the door slightly ajar. When the dough has doubled in bulk, it is ready. If you are unsure, stick your forefinger into the dough. It is right if the imprint remains. Now knock down; this means to punch it in the middle with your fist. It will fall immediately. Give it two or three turns to smooth the dough (some recipes call for a second kneading at this point); you are now ready to form and bake your rolls.

TO DISSOLVE YEAST

Use very warm water (105°F. to 115°F.) for dry yeast; use lukewarm (80°F. to 90°F.) for compressed.

EGG GLAZE

If you want your rolls beautifully shiny and browned, brush them, before baking, with a mixture of 1 slightly beaten egg and 1 tablespoon milk or water. The French call this gilding *dorure*.

SHAPING AND BAKING VARIOUS ROLLS

■ **Breadsticks**—Roll the dough about ½ inch thick, cut into ½-inch strips (use a ruler and pastry wheel), and cut each strip 8 inches long. Roll strips under the palms of your hands (really under the inside of your fingers) to make even sticks about 9 inches long. Arrange on a buttered cookie sheet (be careful not to stretch them when lifting), leaving space between them. Let rise until almost doubled, and bake in preheated hot oven (425°F.) for 5 minutes; reduce heat to slow (300°F.) and bake for 15 minutes longer, or until crisp.

■ **Butterfly Wings**—Roll dough ¼ inch thick and cut into strips 6 inches wide; roll like a jelly roll. Seal edge, cut into 2-inch pieces, and put on a buttered cookie sheet, sealed side down, and swirls at the sides. Using a round pencil, a wooden dowel, or the handle of a wooden spoon, press firmly across the center of each roll, parallel with cut sides. Cover and let rise until doubled in bulk. Bake in preheated hot oven (425°F.) for 10 to 15 minutes, or until nicely browned. In rising, the cut sides spread like wings, hence the name.

■ **Butter Rolls**—Roll dough very thin, about ⅛ inch. Brush with melted butter, then cut into 2-inch strips. Pile in stacks of six, and then cut each stack into 1-inch pieces. Put in buttered muffin tins, cut side up; cover and let rise until doubled in bulk. Bake in preheated hot oven (425°F.) for 10 to 15 minutes, or until nicely browned.

■ **Cloverleaf Rolls**—Form dough into smooth round balls of about ½ ounce each, and 1¼ inches in diameter. To form a smooth ball, work with fingers and thumbs, smoothing from top to bottom. Place 3 balls, smooth side up, in each buttered muffin tin; cover and let rise until almost doubled in bulk. Bake in preheated hot oven (425°F.) for about 15 minutes, or until brown. If you use small muffin pans, be sure to make the balls smaller, or they'll pop right out of the pans.

■ **Crescent Rolls**—Roll dough into a circle about 8 inches in diameter, and cut into 8 pie-shape pieces. Or roll dough and cut into 4-inch squares, then cut each square into halves from corner to corner. Starting at the long side of the triangle, roll toward the tip, stretching the dough a little as you roll. Bend tips in to form a crescent and put on a buttered cookie sheet. Cover and let rise until doubled in bulk. Bake in preheated hot oven (425°F.) for 10 to 15 minutes.

■ **Dinner Rolls**—Form dough into balls, then roll under fingers to make cylinders with pointed ends. Put on buttered baking sheets, glaze, then slit lengthwise with a very sharp knife or razor blade. Let rise until doubled in bulk and bake in preheated hot oven (425°F.) for 10 to 15 minutes.

■ **Figure-Eight Rolls**—Roll dough ¼ inch thick and cut into ½-inch strips. Cut strips about 8 inches long, dampen one end, and form into circles. Or cut dough with a 3-inch round cutter, and remove center with a 2-inch cutter. Give circles of dough a single twist, forming a figure 8. Put on buttered cookie sheets and let rise until doubled in bulk; then bake in preheated hot oven (425°F.) for 10 to 15 minutes, or until brown.

■ **Bowknot Rolls**—Roll dough ¼ inch thick and cut into strips as for Figure-Eight Rolls. Tie in a knot and tuck one end under, then up through the center; tuck other end under. Put on buttered cookie sheets and let rise until doubled in bulk. Bake in preheated hot oven (425°F.) for about 15 minutes.

■ **Finger Rolls**—Roll dough about ⅓ inch thick and cut with a finger-roll cutter especially made for the purpose. Let rise until doubled in bulk and bake in preheated hot oven (425°F.) for 10 to 15 minutes, or until brown.

■ **Hamburger Buns**—Roll dough ½ inch thick, allow to rest for a few minutes, then cut with a round 4-inch cutter. Put on buttered cookie sheets, let rise until doubled in bulk, then bake in preheated hot oven (425°F.) for 10 to 15 minutes, or until brown.

■ **Pan Rolls**—Form dough into 1½- or 2-ounce balls. To have them uniform,

form dough into a long roll about 1½ inches in diameter, and cut into 1½-inch pieces. Form into smooth rounds, working from the top with fingers and thumbs. Put smooth side up in a buttered deep-sided square or round cake pan, almost touching if you want soft-sided rolls, about 1½ inches apart if you want browner sides. Let rise until doubled in bulk. Bake in preheated hot oven (425° F.) for 12 to 15 minutes, or until brown.

■ **Parker House Rolls**—Roll dough ¼ inch thick and cut with a round cookie cutter in any size you prefer. Brush with melted butter, and crease each round through the center with a round pencil or handle of a wooden spoon. Fold over at the crease and press edges gently together. Place close together if you want them to have soft sides, farther apart if you prefer the all-brown variety. Cover and let rise until doubled in bulk, then bake in preheated hot oven (425°F.) for 12 to 15 minutes.

■ **Pepper and Salt Sticks**—Make like Breadsticks (page 1953), but before baking brush with Egg Glaze (page 1953), and sprinkle with cracked black pepper and coarse salt. Bake like Breadsticks.

■ **Ring of Rolls**—Roll dough ¼ inch thick and cut into rounds with a cookie cutter. Dip rolls into melted butter and arrange in a ring in 9-inch pie pan, having each round overlap half the one next to it; a 9- or 10-inch pie pan takes about 20 rolls. Let rise until doubled in bulk, and bake in preheated hot oven (400°F.) for 15 to 20 minutes. Serve whole; guests break off their own portion according to their appetites.

■ **Salt Sticks**—Make like Pepper and Salt Sticks, but use caraway seeds with the coarse salt instead of the cracked pepper.

CRUSTY ROLLS

If you want a crust on your rolls, form as described above, but bake in preheated moderate oven (350°F.) for about 25 minutes, or until brown.

YIELD

It is difficult to tell just how many rolls you can get from the following recipes, as it depends upon the size and type you are going to make. Miniature rolls use about ½ ounce of dough (a 1¼-inch ball), regular-size rolls from 1½ to 2 ounces of dough (1¾- to 2¼-inch balls). I have given the approximate total weight of these doughs so that you can figure them out for yourself.

Cloverleaf, crescent, bowknot, figure-eight, and pan rolls: freshly baked and golden brown from the oven.

BAKING
POWDER
SALT

PLAIN YEAST ROLLS

These are not rich, but a good plain roll, lower in calories than most.

- 1½ cups milk
- ¼ cup butter or margarine
- 2 tablespoons sugar
- 1 teaspoon salt
- 2 packages active dry yeast or 2 cakes compressed yeast
- ½ cup water*
- 5 cups (about) all-purpose flour

Heat milk as described under Mixing, Kneading, and Raising on page 1953, add butter cut into pieces, sugar, and salt. Stir until lukewarm. Sprinkle or crumble yeast into water. *Use very warm water (105°F. to 115°F.) for dry yeast; use lukewarm (80°F. to 90°F.) for compressed. Let stand for a few minutes, then stir until dissolved. Stir in dissolved yeast. Beat in 4 cups of the flour as on page 1953, adding more flour until the dough is soft but not sticky; proceed as on page 1953 (kneading, rising, etc.). Form into any type of roll, let rise, and bake in preheated hot oven (425°F.) as described on page 1953. Makes about 2½ pounds of dough.

REFRIGERATOR ROLLS

A good recipe if hot rolls are wanted several days running, or if you want to mix them ahead and bake a few days later. The dough, when refrigerated, keeps for about 6 days if made with water, but only 3 days if milk is used.

- 1½ cups milk or water
- ½ cup butter or margarine
- ⅓ cup sugar
- 2 teaspoons salt
- 2 packages active dry yeast or 2 cakes compressed yeast
- ½ cup water*
- 2 eggs, beaten
- 6 cups (about) all-purpose flour

Heat milk as hot as your finger can stand. Add butter cut into pieces, sugar, and salt. Stir until the butter is melted and the mixture is lukewarm. Sprinkle or crumble yeast into water. *Use very warm water (105°F. to 115°F.) for dry yeast; use lukewarm (80°F. to 90°F.) for compressed. Let stand for a few minutes, then stir until dissolved. Add eggs and dissolved yeast to butter mixture. Add 4 cups of the flour and beat well. Add as much additional flour as is needed to make a soft dough. Turn out on a lightly floured board and knead until satiny and elastic. Butter a large mixing bowl, put in dough, turn over to grease top, and cover tightly. Put the dough in the refrigerator and remove as much as is needed at a time. Form into rolls, let rise until doubled, and bake in preheated hot oven (425°F.) for 12 to 15 minutes, as on page 1953. Weight is 3 pounds, 6 ounces.

NO-KNEAD FEATHER ROLLS

- 1 cup water
- ¼ cup butter or margarine
- 2 tablespoons sugar
- 1 teaspoon salt
- 1 package active dry yeast or 1 cake compressed yeast
- ¼ cup water*
- 1 egg, beaten
- 3 cups all-purpose flour

Heat water as hot as your hand can stand; add butter cut into pieces, sugar, and salt. Stir until butter is melted and the mixture is lukewarm. Sprinkle or crumble yeast into water. *Use very warm water (105°F. to 115°F.) for dry yeast; use lukewarm (80°F. to 90°F.) for compressed. Let stand for a few minutes, then stir until dissolved. Add dissolved yeast and egg to first mixture. Beat in flour to make a very soft dough; it will be too soft to knead. Brush top with melted butter, cover, and let rise until doubled in bulk. Stir down and spoon into buttered 2-inch muffin tins and allow to rise in a warm place until the dough has almost reached the top of the pans. Bake in preheated hot oven (425°F.) for 12 to 15 minutes. Makes about 18 rolls.

CORNMEAL ROLLS

- 1 package active dry yeast or 1 cake compressed yeast
- ¼ cup water*
- 1 cup milk
- ¼ cup butter or margarine
- 1 cup cornmeal
- 2 tablespoons sugar
- 1 teaspoon salt
- 2 eggs, beaten
- 3 cups (about) all-purpose flour

Sprinkle or crumble yeast into water. *Use very warm water (105°F. to 115°F.) for dry yeast; use lukewarm (80°F. to 90°F.) for compressed. Let stand for a few minutes, then stir until dissolved. Heat milk, add butter cut into pieces, cornmeal, sugar, and salt. Stir until butter is melted and mixture is lukewarm. Add yeast mixture, eggs, and flour; mix well, adding more flour if needed to make a soft but not sticky dough. Turn out on a floured board and knead until satiny and elastic. Cover and let rise until doubled in bulk. Knock down, form, and let rise until doubled. Bake in preheated hot oven (425°F.) for 12 to 15 minutes. Dough weighs about 2¼ pounds.

WHOLE-WHEAT ROLLS

- 1 cup milk
- 2 tablespoons sugar
- ⅓ cup butter or margarine
- 1 teaspoon salt
- 2 packages active dry yeast or 2 cakes compressed yeast
- ½ cup water*
- 2 cups all-purpose flour
- 1½ cups (about) whole-wheat flour

Heat milk, add sugar, butter cut into pieces, and salt. Stir until lukewarm. Sprinkle or crumble yeast into water. *Use very warm water (105°F. to 115°F.) for dry yeast; use lukewarm (80°F. to 90°F.) for compressed. Let stand for a few minutes, then stir until dissolved. Add dissolved yeast and flours to first mixture. Beat well, turn out on a floured board, and knead until satiny and elastic. Cover and let rise until doubled in bulk. Knock down and knead lightly, then form into rolls; pan rolls, cloverleaf, parker house are good shapes for this dough. Bake in preheated hot oven (425°F.) for 12 to 15 minutes. Dough weighs about 2 pounds.

SQUASH ROLLS

- 1 cup water*
- ¾ cup sugar
- 1 package active dry yeast, or 1 cake compressed yeast
- Cooking oil
- 2 teaspoons salt
- 1 cup strained cooked winter squash
- ½ cup nonfat dry-milk solids
- 5 cups all-purpose flour (about)

*Use very warm water (105°F. to 115°F.) for dry yeast; use lukewarm (80°F. to 90°F.) for compressed. Put water and sugar into the large bowl of electric mixer. Sprinkle dry yeast or crumble cake into mixture. Let stand for 5 minutes; then stir until dissolved. Add 3 tablespoons oil, the salt, squash, and dry milk. Beat well at low speed. Gradually beat in 2 cups of the flour. (Or beat with rotary beater.) Scrape beaters, and add remaining flour by hand, mixing well. Let stand in a warm place until doubled in bulk, about 1 hour. Put on a floured board and knead gently. Roll to 1-inch thickness. Cut with floured 2½-inch cutter. Roll edges lightly in oil so that the baked rolls will separate readily. Put in greased baking pan (13 x 9 x 2 inches), and let rise until doubled, about 30 minutes. Bake in preheated hot oven (400°F.) for about 20 minutes. Makes about 15.

YOGURT—A semisolid milk product that has been made acid by the addition of bacterial cultures which have much greater acidifying power than natural ferments. Apart from being a refreshing and nourishing food, yogurt is said by many to have excellent medicinal qualities in keeping the intestinal system healthy, helping to clear up skin diseases, etc. Buttermilk, clabbered milk, kumiss, etc., are all dairy products related to yogurt.

Yogurt stems from the Balkans, and in the Balkans and the Near East it is consumed several times daily, either as is or used in cooking. It has been used there for so many centuries that no one knows how long, and the people of these regions claim that their unquestionable hardiness and longevity is due to the constant consumption of yogurt.

Yogurt can be made from any kind of milk, and although cows' milk is now most commonly used, it is still made from sheeps' and goats' milk wherever these animals are raised in the Balkans.

In America, yogurt is made commercially either plain or flavored with fruits and extracts. However, yogurt can also be made at home. Plain yogurt is an excellent ingredient in cooking, introducing an interesting flavor twist to familiar foods.

Availability—Yogurt made from whole milk or partially skimmed milk is widely available plain or flavored with vanilla or such fruits as prune, strawberry, pineapple, apricot, etc. The fruit-flavored yogurts are actually plain yogurt with the fruit in the bottom of the container.

Storage—Store in the coldest part of refrigerator.

☐ Refrigerator shelf: 2 to 3 days

Nutritive Food Values—A good source of vitamin B and calcium.

☐ Plain, 3½ ounces, made from whole milk = 62 calories

☐ Plain, 3½ ounces, made from partially skimmed milk = 50 calories

HOMEMADE YOGURT

¼ cup plain yogurt
1 quart non-fat milk (fresh or made from granules)

Let the yogurt stand at room temperature for 3 to 4 hours. Heat milk to 120°F. on a candy thermometer. Do not overheat. Cool to 90°F. Add the yogurt and mix thoroughly. Turn into a bowl or 4 individual containers. Do not stir or move containers. Cover and keep barely lukewarm until a curd has formed. Store in refrigerator. Makes 1 quart.

BULGARIAN COLD CUCUMBER SOUP

4 cups plain yogurt
½ cup chopped walnuts
2 cups diced cucumbers
Salt and white pepper to taste
2 garlic cloves, crushed

Beat yogurt until smooth. Combine walnuts, cucumbers, salt, pepper, and garlic. Add to yogurt and blend. Chill thoroughly. At serving time, you may add 1 ice cube to each serving. Makes 4 to 6 servings.

LAMB BARYANI

2 cups uncooked rice
Salt
4 onions
Butter or margarine
½ teaspoon ground coriander
½ teaspoon turmeric
1½ cups plain yogurt
1 pound boneless lamb, sliced
Seeds from 2 cardamom pods
¼ teaspoon ground cinnamon
3 whole cloves
¼ teaspoon chili powder
Water
2 hard-cooked eggs
Rosewater

Cook rice in boiling salted water. Drain. Slice 2 onions and cook until golden-brown in 2 tablespoons butter. Mix onion with coriander, turmeric, 1 teaspoon salt, and the yogurt. Rub mixture into lamb and let stand for 30 minutes. Pound remaining onions in a mortar with a pestle, or grind fine. Add lamb mixture and cook, uncovered, in skillet until some of the liquid has evaporated. Alternate layers of meat mixture and rice in a 3-quart casserole. Sprinkle top layer with cardamom seed, cinnamon, cloves, and chili powder. Pour 3 tablespoons butter, melted, over top. Add 2 or 3 tablespoons of water. Cover tightly and bake in preheated moderate oven (350°F.) for about 45 minutes. Garnish with eggs, cut into wedges. Sprinkle with a few drops of rosewater. Makes 6 to 8 servings.

STUFFED VEAL CUTLETS

2 pounds Italian-style veal cutlets
½ teaspoon crumbled dried rosemary
6 hard-cooked eggs, sieved
1 tablespoon minced onion
¼ cup minced fresh pineapple
¼ teaspoon ground cinnamon
¼ cup dry bread crumbs
¼ cup plain yogurt (about)
⅓ cup butter or margarine
1 cup rich beef bouillon
1 cup canned tomatoes

Pound meat until very thin. Sprinkle meat with rosemary and let stand for 2 hours. Mix eggs with onion, pineapple, cinnamon, crumbs, and enough yogurt to make a thick mixture. Put some of the filling on each cutlet. Roll up meat and skewer with toothpicks or fasten with a string. Brown veal in butter on all sides. Add bouillon and tomatoes. Cover and bake in preheated slow oven (300°F.) for 2 hours. Thicken liquid if desired. Makes 4 to 6 servings.

STEAK KABOBS

1½ pounds boneless tender steak, cut into 1½-inch cubes
½ cup plain yogurt
1 tablespoon minced shallot or green onion
Pepper and salt to taste

In refrigerator marinate meat in remaining ingredients, except salt, for 1 to 2 days, turning occasionally. Thread on large skewers, and broil over hot charcoal for about 15 minutes, turning frequently. Season with salt. Makes 3 or 4 servings.

EGG AND TONGUE WITH YOGURT SAUCE

¼ cup butter or margarine
6 eggs
Salt and pepper to taste
6 slices of cooked tongue
6 slices of hot thin toast
1 cup plain yogurt
2 tablespoons soft butter
1 teaspoon paprika
2 tablespoons chopped fresh dill

Melt butter; slip eggs into butter and fry until whites are firm and yolks are still soft. Sprinkle with salt and pepper. Put a slice of tongue on a piece of toast. Top with hot fried egg. Beat yogurt until smooth and spoon yogurt over egg. Beat butter with paprika and put a small amount of butter and chopped dill on top of yogurt. Makes 6 servings.

CHICKEN TANDOORI

2 broiler-fryers, about 2½ pounds each
1 whole cardamom pod
1½ pints plain yogurt
1½ tablespoons fresh lime juice
1½ tablespoons butter or margarine, melted
1 garlic clove, crushed
1 teaspoon chili powder
½ teaspoon ground coriander
⅛ teaspoon ground ginger

Split chickens into halves, and discard backbones. Remove skin except from the wings. Cut small slits in meat in several places. Put in large bowl. Remove seed from cardamom pod, and crush. Mix with remaining ingredients, and pour over chickens. Marinate for at least 6 hours, or overnight. Broil slowly, covered with the marinade, for 25 to 30 minutes on each side, or until chicken is tender. Makes 4 servings.

EGGPLANT WITH YOGURT

2 medium eggplants
1 teaspoon minced garlic
1 cup plain yogurt
Salt and pepper to taste

Bake eggplants in preheated hot oven (425°F.) for about 40 minutes, turning occasionally. Peel off skin, and discard. Chop the pulp; add garlic, yogurt, and salt and pepper. Makes 6 servings.

YOGURT ONIONS

½ cup milk
3 tablespoons butter or margarine
8 onions, sliced
3 egg yolks
1 cup plain yogurt
Salt to taste
½ cup grated cheese
¼ cup whole-wheat cracker crumbs or wheat germ

In a saucepan combine milk, butter, and onions. Simmer for 20 minutes. Drain and put onions in a shallow casserole. Mix egg yolks with yogurt and salt. Pour mixture over onions. Sprinkle top with cheese and crumbs. Bake in preheated moderate oven (350°F.) for about 20 minutes, or until onions are tender. Makes 4 to 6 servings.

CARROTS À LA SULTANA

6 carrots, scraped and cut into thin slices
2 teaspoons fresh lemon juice
½ cup all-purpose flour
½ teaspoon salt
¼ cup chicken bouillon
1½ cups olive oil
1 egg white, stiffly beaten
1 cup plain yogurt
1 garlic clove, mashed
Thinly sliced unpeeled cucumber

Sprinkle carrots with lemon juice. Mix flour with salt. Gradually beat in bouillon and 1 tablespoon of the oil. When smooth, fold in egg white. Heat remaining oil until very hot. Dip carrot slices into batter and fry until brown and crisp. Drain on absorbent paper. Mix yogurt with garlic. Pour mixture over carrots. Serve at once with thinly sliced cucumber. Makes 6 servings.

AVOCADO SALAD WITH YOGURT DRESSING

3 large avocados
Fresh lemon juice
Salt to taste
2 cups fresh grapefruit sections
24 stuffed green olives
1½ cups cubed melon
1 cup drained mandarin orange sections
Yogurt Dressing

Halve avocados, remove pits, and cut into cubes. Sprinkle with lemon juice and salt. Toss all fruits together and chill until ready to serve. Just before serving mix salad with Yogurt Dressing. Makes 6 servings.

Yogurt Dressing

1 cup plain yogurt
2 tablespoons honey
1 teaspoon fresh lemon juice
1 tablespoon pineapple juice
1 teaspoon grated lemon rind
⅛ teaspoon salt

Beat yogurt until smooth and beat in remaining ingredients. Chill until ready to serve.

CUCUMBER YOGURT SALAD

1 cucumber, peeled
½ teaspoon salt
1½ cups plain yogurt
Cayenne, paprika, black pepper

Shred cucumber on coarse shredder. Sprinkle with salt. Let stand at room temperature for 1 to 2 hours. Drain, and squeeze out water. Beat yogurt and season with cayenne, paprika, and black pepper to taste. Fold cucumbers into yogurt. Chill. Makes 4 to 6 servings.

CHEESE, CUCUMBER, AND GRAPEFRUIT SALAD

2 cups creamed cottage cheese
1 tablespoon fresh lemon juice
¼ cup plain yogurt
¾ teaspoon salt
2 cups chilled fresh-grapefruit sections
1 cup coarsely grated cucumber
1 tablespoon chopped parsley
Salad greens

Gently mix cottage cheese, lemon juice, yogurt, and salt. Drain grapefruit sections, and chop coarsely. Fold grapefruit, cucumber, and parsley into cottage cheese mixture. Serve at once on salad greens. Makes 6 servings.

SPINACH-COTTAGE CHEESE SALAD

2 to 3 cups raw spinach, washed and well drained
6 radishes, thinly sliced
1 tablespoon minced onion
2 tablespoons French dressing
¼ cup plain yogurt
⅛ teaspoon marjoram
2 cups creamed cottage cheese
Stuffed-olive slices

Tear spinach into bite-size pieces. Add radishes, onion, and French dressing; toss lightly. Add yogurt and marjoram to cheese; blend. Arrange 6 mounds of cheese mixture on spinach. Garnish each mound with olive slices. Makes 6 servings.

SHRIMP AND CUCUMBER SANDWICHES

⅓ cup shredded cucumber, drained
1 cup cooked shrimps, chopped
2 teaspoons minced green onion
1½ teaspoons fresh lemon juice
⅛ teaspoon dried dillweed
¼ cup plain yogurt
Salt to taste
8 slices of white bread
Butter or margarine

Mix all ingredients except last 2. Cut crusts from bread, if desired. Spread bread with butter, then with first mixture. Makes 4 sandwiches.

YOGURT, CUCUMBER, AND RADISH RELISH

1 pint plain yogurt
¾ cup minced cucumber with skin
½ cup radish slices
½ teaspoon paprika
Salt and pepper to taste
1 teaspoon chopped parsley

Mix all ingredients except parsley. Chill well, and stir before serving. Sprinkle with parsley. Makes 4 to 6 servings.

YOGURT HONEY CAKES

3 cups water
2½ cups sugar
1½ teaspoons fresh lemon juice
½ teaspoon vanilla extract
1 cup plain yogurt
¼ cup light cream
2 eggs
2 cups sifted all-purpose flour
1 teaspoon baking soda
1 cup butter or margarine
Honey
Sweetened whipped cream

Mix water with sugar and lemon juice. Bring to a boil, lower heat, and simmer for five minutes. Stir in vanilla. Keep warm.

Beat yogurt with cream and eggs. Sift flour with baking soda. Gradually stir flour into yogurt mixture. Heat butter and drop dough mixture by tablespoons into the hot butter. Brown on both sides. When cooked, drop dough into hot sugar syrup. Let stand in syrup for 5 minutes. Remove with a slotted spoon and arrange on a serving platter. When cool, split each cake into halves, spread with honey, and top with whipped cream. Makes about 20.

YOGURT FROTH AYRAN

2 cups plain yogurt
½ teaspoon salt
1 cup ice water
Mint leaves

Beat yogurt until frothy, about 5 minutes. Beat in salt and ice water and beat for another 2 minutes. Serve in tall glasses garnished with mint sprigs. Makes 4 servings.

YORKSHIRE PUDDING—A traditional British accompaniment for roast beef, consisting of a savory batter of eggs, milk, and flour baked in the beef drippings. Yorkshire pudding must be puffy, crisp, and golden-brown. It is sliced into squares and served at the same time as the meat, along with roast potatoes and a green vegetable, in the usual English way. The batter is usually baked in a shallow baking dish, but it can also be baked in muffin pans or other small baking pans of various shapes.

Yorkshire pudding takes its name from Yorkshire, a county in the north of England. The food in Yorkshire is excellent farm food, and anyone who has traipsed over the Yorkshire moors can never forget the bountiful farm meals served in this historic county.

YORKSHIRE PUDDING

2 eggs
1 cup milk
1 cup all-purpose flour
½ teaspoon salt
Beef drippings (about ¼ cup)

Beat together eggs and milk. Sift together flour and salt. Stir into the egg mixture. Beat batter until smooth and well blended. Pour about ¼ cup beef drippings into a baking pan (11 x 7 inches or 9 x 9 x 2 inches). If the beef was roasted in such a pan, remove meat and keep hot; discard all but ¼ cup drippings from the pan. Pour batter into pan. Bake in preheated hot oven (450°F.) for 10 minutes. Reduce heat to moderate (350°F.) and bake for 10 to 15 minutes longer, or until puffy and golden-brown. Makes 4 servings.

Bûche de Noël

YULE LOG—The Yule log is a huge piece of wood symbolically burned around Christmastime. It may be burned on Christmas Eve; some countries burn it a bit every day for the twelve days of the Christmas season. In some places it is kept until the next year to light the new Yule log. In parts of France a bit of the log is kept throughout the year to insure a good season of crops and help cattle bear their offspring easily.

In all Christmas celebrations, light plays an important part, as a symbol of hope and deliverance from spiritual and physical darkness. The candles on our Christmas trees and the burning Yule log are symbols of our desire for light. So is a cake in the shape of a Yule log, which is traditional in England and in France, where it is known under the name of *Bûche de Noël.* The cake is made like a jelly roll, filled with a creamy filling, and decorated to resemble the bark of a tree.

BÛCHE DE NOËL
(Yule Log)

5 eggs, separated
¼ teaspoon cream of tartar
1 cup granulated sugar
1 tablespoon grated orange rind
2 tablespoons sherry
1 cup sifted cake flour
¼ teaspoon salt
Confectioners' sugar
Coffee Cream Filling
Chocolate Frosting
Grated pistachio nuts
Marzipan (optional)

Beat egg whites until foamy. Add cream of tartar and beat until stiff. Gradually beat in ½ cup sugar, 1 tablespoon at a time. Beat egg yolks until thick and lemon-colored. Beat into egg yolks remaining ½ cup sugar, the orange rind, and sherry. Fold egg-yolk mixture into egg whites. Sift flour with salt. Fold gradually into egg mixture. Pour into foil-lined jelly-roll pan (1 x 15 x 10 inches). Bake in preheated moderate oven (375°F.) for about 20 minutes. When baked, turn out on towel sprinkled with confectioners' sugar. Carefully remove foil from cake. Roll up cake in the towel from the 10-inch end and let stand until cold. Unroll carefully and spread with Coffee Cream Filling.

Reroll and spread the entire roll with Chocolate Frosting. Run tines of fork the length of the cake to resemble bark. Cake can also be iced using a star tip on a pastry bag and running lengthwise lines of frosting over the sides and top of the entire cake. Sprinkle grated pistachio nuts along the "bark" of the cake and trim with marzipan leaves. Makes 8 to 10 servings.

Coffee Cream Filling

Chill 2 cups heavy cream with ¼ cup confectioners' sugar and 1 tablespoon instant coffee powder. When chilled for 2 or more hours, whip until thick enough to spread. Spread on cooled cake.

Chocolate Frosting

Melt 3 ounces (3 squares) unsweetened chocolate and 3 tablespoons butter or margarine. Mix 4 cups confectioners' sugar, ⅛ teaspoon salt, 7 tablespoons milk, and 1 teaspoon vanilla extract. Add chocolate mixture and blend well. Let stand, stirring occasionally, until of spreading consistency.

ZABAGLIONE or ZABAIONE—A dessert of Italian origin, made of eggs, sugar, and wine beaten until thick over boiling water and served either warm or cold in dessert or parfait glasses. It is also used as a sauce for fruit.

ZABAGLIONE

4 egg yolks
¾ cup sugar
¾ cup Marsala

Combine ingredients in top part of a double boiler. Cook over simmering, not boiling, water, beating constantly with a wire whip or an egg beater, for about 10 minutes, or until very thick. Serve immediately in glasses or small coffee cups. Makes 4 to 6 servings.

Cold Zabaglione

Proceed as above. Set pan in a basin filled with cracked ice. Beat zabaglione until thoroughly cold. Pour into glasses or cups and keep refrigerated. Unless the zabaglione is beaten until thoroughly cold, it will not remain frothy but will collapse and separate. Makes 4 to 6 servings.

ZEPPOLE—A doughnutlike pastry of Italian origin. It consists of pieces of dough which may be filled with bits of cooked cauliflower, anchovies, etc., before frying. The dough can also be fried plain and sprinkled with salt, or with sugar and cinnamon.

ZEPPOLE

1 teaspoon active dry yeast
¾ cup warm water
1 egg
2 cups all-purpose flour
½ teaspoon salt
Cooking oil

Sprinkle yeast into water. Let stand for a few minutes; then stir until dissolved. Beat in egg, flour, and salt. When smooth, cover and let stand in a warm place until doubled in bulk. Beat down and let rise again until doubled. Drop by tablespoonfuls into 1 inch of hot oil (375°F. on a frying thermometer). When browned on one side, turn and brown on the other. Drain on absorbent paper. Serve as a bread with butter or sprinkled with sugar and cinnamon as a dessert. These are also good dipped in honey or syrup. Makes about 20.

Note: For variety, flour hands and shape tablespoonfuls of dough around a small piece of cooked cauliflower or an anchovy before frying. Cubes of Mozzarella or a teaspoonful of Ricotta can be used in the same way.

ZUCCHINI—A variety of summer squash developed in Italy. It is also known as vegetable marrow or Italian marrow. Zucchini is cylindrical in shape but larger at its base than at its top. The skin has a lacy pattern of green and yellow that concentrates to give the appearance of stripes. It grows to be ten to twelve inches long and two to three inches thick, and has pale-green flesh and a delicate flavor.

Availability—Fresh zucchini is available in some food stores year round with the peak season from May to July. Frozen zucchini is available.

Purchasing Guide—Look for zucchini that have tender rinds, are glossy in appearance, and free from blemishes. They should be fairly heavy for their size. Choose zucchini that are small with a narrow diameter. They are best when 6 to 7 inches long and 1 to 1½ inches thick.

Storage—Buy in small amounts. Keep in the vegetable compartment of the refrigerator.

- ☐ Fresh, refrigerator shelf or vegetable compartment, uncooked: 3 to 4 days
- ☐ Refrigerator shelf, cooked: 4 to 5 days
- ☐ Fresh, prepared for freezing; or frozen, refrigerator frozen-food compartment: 2 to 3 weeks

☐ Fresh, prepared for freezing, or frozen, freezer: 6 to 12 months

Nutritive Food Values—Provides fair quantities of vitamin A and C, and small amounts of other vitamins.

☐ 3½ ounces, cooked and drained = 12 calories

Basic Preparation—Wash but do not peel. Remove stem and blossom ends. Cut into ½-inch slices or cubes.

☐ To Cook—Have about 1 inch of water boiling in a saucepan. Add zucchini and salt to taste. Cook, covered, for 10 to 15 minutes, or until tender. Drain, and season to taste.

Zucchini may also be baked, creamed, or used for fritters. Young zucchini can be sautéed in butter until tender. Season to taste with salt, pepper, and garlic.

☐ To Freeze—Use young zucchini. Wash and cut into ½-inch slices. Blanch in boiling water for 3½ minutes. Chill in cold water for 5 minutes. Drain. Pack into containers, allowing ½-inch headspace. Seal.

ZUCCHINI CHICKEN

1 broiling-frying chicken (about 2½ pounds), quartered
11 tablespoons olive oil
1 pound tomatoes, finely chopped
2 green peppers, finely chopped
2 medium zucchini, coarsely chopped
1 small onion, coarsely chopped
Bouquet garni (mixed herbs in cheesecloth bag)
Salt to taste
All-purpose flour to thicken

Brown chicken pieces in 3 tablespoons of the oil. Remove pieces from pan and add remaining oil and all other ingredients except *bouquet garni,* salt, and flour. Fry briefly, stirring constantly. Add chicken and *bouquet garni* and simmer, covered, until chicken is done, about 30 minutes. Remove *bouquet garni.* Season with salt. Thicken with a flour and water paste if desired. Makes 4 servings.

LAMB-STUFFED ZUCCHINI

Here's a fine way to use up leftover lamb. Select 6 small zucchini, 6 or 7 inches long and about 1½ inches in diameter, and remove pulp with an apple corer; or split lengthwise and scoop out some of the pulp. Mix 1 cup minced cooked lamb, 1 cup cooked rice, 2 tablespoons minced onion, 1 tablespoon minced parsley, ¼ teaspoon ground oregano, and enough gravy, mayonnaise, cream sauce, or sour cream to moisten. Add salt to taste and stuff zucchini. If any stuffing is left over, form it into small balls and put with zucchini in a baking dish. Pour over 3 cups of tomato sauce seasoned with oregano, basil, or dill. Bake in preheated moderate oven (350°F.) for 30 minutes, or until the zucchini are tender. Makes 3 servings.

Zabaglione

ZUCCHINI ZITI

½ cup minced onion
½ cup butter or margarine
½ cup minced green pepper
1½ to 2 pounds zucchini, sliced
3 cups peeled, seeded, and chopped tomatoes
1 teaspoon salt
½ teaspoon pepper
1 can (4 ounces) sliced mushrooms, undrained
1 pound ziti or other short pasta

Sauté onion in hot butter for 2 minutes. Add all other ingredients except ziti. Cover and cook over low heat for about 30 minutes, stirring frequently. Zucchini slices should be tender, but still preserve their shape. Serve on hot cooked ziti. Makes 6 servings.

BAKED ZUCCHINI AND CORN

3 ears of corn
1 pound unpeeled zucchini, thinly sliced
1 medium onion, thinly sliced
¼ cup butter or margarine, melted
1 teaspoon salt
¼ teaspoon pepper
1 teaspoon chili powder, or to taste
1 can (8 ounces) tomato sauce

Grate corn kernels from cobs. Mix corn and remaining ingredients except sauce. Put in shallow 1½-quart baking dish. Pour sauce over top. Bake, uncovered, in preheated moderate oven (350°F.) for about 45 minutes. Makes 6 servings.

ZUCCHINI AND PEPPER STEW

1 can (6 ounces) tomato paste
1 stalk celery, sliced
1 carrot, sliced
½ cup cooking oil
1 cup water
4 large green peppers, sliced
2 medium zucchini, diced
4 small potatoes, peeled and diced
1 large onion, chopped
1 garlic clove, minced
Salt and pepper
Grated Parmesan cheese

Put first 3 ingredients in saucepan, bring to boil and simmer, covered, for about 1 hour. Heat oil in skillet and add next 6 ingredients. Cook until slightly browned. Add to first mixture and simmer for 10 minutes, or until vegetables are tender. Season with salt and pepper to taste and serve with the cheese as a main dish. Makes 6 servings.

SAUTÉED ZUCCHINI ITALIAN STYLE

1½ pounds zucchini, each 5 to 6 inches long
3 tablespoons olive oil or butter or margarine
½ teaspoon salt
⅛ teaspoon pepper

Wash zucchini. Do not peel. Cut into crosswise slices ⅛ inch thick. Heat oil in a 9- to 10-inch skillet. Add zucchini. Cook until slices are translucent and the edges are lightly browned, turning with a spatula to cook uniformly. Add more oil if needed. Sprinkle with salt and pepper. Makes 6 servings.

ZUCCHINI OMELET

2 tablespoons olive oil
1 small zucchini, diced
1 celery stalk, diced
2 fresh tomatoes, peeled
½ teaspoon salt
Dash of pepper
4 eggs, beaten
2 tablespoons grated Parmesan cheese
½ teaspoon crumbled dried thyme

Heat oil in skillet and sauté zucchini and celery until celery is tender. Add tomatoes, salt, and pepper. Cook, covered, for 10 minutes, stirring frequently. Mix beaten eggs, cheese, and thyme and pour over vegetables. Cook over low heat for 8 to 10 minutes on each side. Makes 4 servings.

ZUCCHINI AND CUCUMBERS IN SOUR CREAM

2 zucchini, about 8 inches long
1 cucumber, 8 inches long
½ inch of boiling water
¾ teaspoon salt
½ cup chopped green onions
2 tablespoons butter or margarine
½ cup dairy sour cream
⅛ teaspoon pepper
Chopped parsley

Wash zucchini and cucumber. Cut into crosswise slices ¼ inch thick. Put zucchini slices in a saucepan with boiling water and salt. Cover, bring to boiling point, reduce heat, and cook for 15 minutes, or until almost tender. Add cucumber slices and cook only until crisp-tender, about 3 minutes. Drain if necessary. In the meantime sauté green onions in butter. Add to zucchini and cucumbers along with sour cream and pepper. Mix lightly. Heat, but do not boil. Sprinkle with chopped parsley. Makes 6 servings.

ZUCCHINI WITH CREAMY CHEESE TOPPING

12 zucchini, about 5 inches long
Salt
2 eggs
All-purpose flour
Margarine
2 cups dairy sour cream
1 cup shredded sharp Cheddar cheese

Wash and trim zucchini. Cook in small amount of boiling salted water until tender, about 10 minutes. Drain and cool. Beat eggs with ¼ teaspoon salt. Roll zucchini in flour, then dip into egg, and fry in hot margarine until browned on both sides. Put in shallow broiler-proof baking dish and pour sour cream over top. Sprinkle with cheese. Put under broiler until golden-brown. Makes 6 servings.

ZUCCHINI PICKLES

2 pounds zucchini
½ pound onions
¼ cup salt
2 cups sugar
2 cups cider vinegar
1 teaspoon celery seeds
1 teaspoon ground turmeric
½ teaspoon prepared mustard
2 teaspoons mustard seeds

Wash zucchini and cut into thin slices. Peel and quarter onions and cut into thin slices. Cover with water and add salt. Let stand for 2 hours, then drain. Bring to a boil the sugar, vinegar, and spices and pour over the vegetables. Let stand for 2 hours. Boil for 5 minutes and pack in 4 hot sterilized pint jars. Seal. Makes 4 pints.

ZWIEBACK—A sweet biscuit or rusk which is first baked and then sliced and toasted in the oven to make it into a kind of dry toast. The word comes from the German, and means "baked twice." Commercially made zwieback is available.

Caloric Value

☐ 3½ ounces = 423 calories

ZWIEBACK

1 package active dry yeast or 1 cake compressed yeast
¼ cup water*
1 cup milk
4 cups all-purpose flour
1 egg, beaten
½ cup granulated sugar
¼ cup melted butter
1 teaspoon vanilla extract
½ teaspoon salt
Confectioners' sugar
Fresh lemon juice

Sprinkle dry yeast or crumble cake into water. *Use very warm water (105°F. to 115°F.) for dry yeast; use lukewarm (80°F. to 90°F.) for compressed. Let stand for a few minutes, then stir until dissolved. Scald milk and cool to lukewarm. Add milk and 2 cups of the flour to yeast. Beat thoroughly. Stand in warm place for about 1 hour, or until light and bubbly. Beat in remaining ingredients except confectioners' sugar and lemon juice and remaining flour; if necessary, add a little more flour to make a medium-stiff dough. Stand in warm place and let rise until doubled in bulk. Punch down and turn out on lightly floured board. Knead for about 5 minutes. Shape dough into 2½-inch round buns. Place buns on greased cookie sheet, about 1 inch apart. Allow to rise again in warm place until doubled in bulk. Bake in preheated hot oven (400°F.) for 10 minutes. Lower heat to moderate (350°F.) and bake for 15 minutes longer. Cool buns. Slice into ¾-inch slices. Return to slow oven (300°F.) and bake for 40 minutes, or until the slices are lightly browned on both sides. Mix confectioners' sugar with lemon juice to prepare a thin icing. When zwieback are cold, frost with lemon icing. Makes about 2 dozen.

Zucchini Chicken

150 WAYS TO BE A BETTER COOK

by Frances Rosien

SEASONING

1. Pep up the same old mayonnaise (1 cup) with 1 teaspoon curry powder; 1 tablespoon chutney; 1 tablespoon prepared horseradish; 1½ tablespoons tart jelly; 2 tablespoons of the juice from sweet pickles (a delightful marinade for coleslaw, too); or 1 tablespoon dill-pickle juice for an interesting variation.

2. Make a *bouquet garni* to flavor boiled beef, fish, stews, hearty soups. Merely tie sprigs of celery, parsley, a bay leaf in a square of cheesecloth and throw into the pot; remove after cooking. Other herbs and vegetables, such as fennel, leek, marjoram, tarragon, can be added.

3. Experiment with the clean-cut flavor of dried dill: sprinkled on a green salad; dusted on top of creamed vegetables; as an interesting zip to delicate meats like veal and poultry; added to the butter sauce for Lima beans, green beans, fresh peas.

4. Be cautious with strong herbs and spices. Remember you can always add more. Start with pinches and build up to taste, particularly with bay leaf, sage, or garlic.

5. Try to cook on the day before you serve it anything with multiple spices, herbs, or onions. It's twice as good the second day if the flavors are allowed, as the French say, "to marry."

6. Toss a dash of vanilla extract into recipes containing chocolate.

7. Invest in a vanilla bean. Keep it in the sugar canister you reserve for baking.

8. Serve hot chocolate or cocoa with cinnamon stick as a stirrer. It looks and tastes wonderful.

SOUP SLEIGHT OF HAND

Two soups are better than one. Served hot or cold, they start the most mundane meal with a bang. These are interesting:

9. One can split pea with ⅓ can tomato and ½ can cream-of-asparagus; add water to make proper thickness.

10. One can cream-of-celery, ⅓ can tomato, 1 cup cooked celery, and 1 can crabmeat make a beautiful bisque; thin to desired consistency with water.

11. One can black-bean soup added to chili or stew shortens the cooking time and produces that desirable deep-brown, days'-long-cooking taste.

12. Rice with a difference: Mix about 3 cups consommé with 1 cup rice that has been browned for about 3 minutes in the skillet with 1 tablespoon butter or oil. Bake, covered, in preheated moderate oven (350°F.) for about 30 minutes.

HOT BREADS, BISCUITS, AND PANCAKES

Hot breads give an everyday family meal a company touch. Try these for rave reviews: For the average-size loaf of bread (French or Italian style or any with a crisp crust), use 1 cup butter or margarine and add:

13. The juice and grated rind of 1 lemon.

14. The heads from a package of frozen broccoli.

15. Two tablespoons of any of these: celery seed, dried dill, chopped fresh parsley, poppy seed.

16. Five tablespoons sugar, 1 teaspoon ground cinnamon, a shake or two of ground nutmeg or mace. Spread thickly on each slice (not cut completely through), wrap in foil, heat thoroughly in oven.

Saltine crackers, too, make delightful accompaniments for salad and soup meals. Try these:

17. Top about 2 dozen crackers with a mixture of 1 cup grated Cheddar cheese, the whites of 2 eggs, 1 tablespoon chili powder. Spread and brown in hot oven for about 3 minutes.

18. Spread crackers with peanut butter and dab of mayonnaise; put under broiler for quick toasting.

Canned biscuits are wonderful time-savers, special treats when used with imagination. Here are some ideas:

19. Split into halves, dip into melted butter, roll in sugar-and-cinnamon mixture. Bake.

20. Cut each biscuit into three portions, deep fry, and roll immediately in grated Cheddar or Parmesan cheese flavored with a little garlic salt. Great appetizers.

21. A delicious teatime or coffee-break goodie! Split biscuits and spread between the layers a mixture of chopped walnuts, dates, candied orange peel, enough honey to moisten; top with brown sugar and dots of butter or margarine. Bake.

22. Make quick snacks by splitting and filling unbaked canned biscuits with chopped peanuts, crisp bacon, and mayonnaise. Bake.

23. Serve piping-hot buttered biscuits on top of warm stewed fruit; cover with thick sweet cream, dash of ground cinnamon.

Use pancakes as a base for unusual main dishes. Here are some ways:

24. Spread with a cooked mixture of hamburger, onions, green pepper, and a spicy barbecue sauce.

25. Cover with chili, onions, and cheese; brown in oven.

26. Use as a base for creamed eggs, with slivers of ham, bacon, and mushrooms.

27. Serve with tuna or chicken à la king topped with Parmesan cheese and slivered almonds; put under broiler.

Make pancakes a party dessert.

28. Use them as a base for a shortcake: Butter them while hot, spread with fresh or frozen berries, cover with whipped cream.

29. Spread them while hot with cream cheese and heated maple syrup. Top with chopped salted nuts.

MEAT, POULTRY, FISH

30. Add a cooked-meat filling to split, unbaked canned biscuits. Bake and serve as individual meat pies for cocktail-party hors-d'oeuvre.

31. Rub inside of any poultry with ground thyme before roasting.

Serve seafood or meat salads in wedges of melon:

32. Crabmeat in honeydew, for instance, or chicken in cantaloupe.

33. Mix a good amount of crisply fried onion bits into a crust and as a topping for meat pies.

34. Marinate chicken in a mixture of lemon juice and onion slices before broiling.

35. Stud a small onion with whole cloves to use as flavoring for beef stock or stews. (Remove whole after cooking.)

36. Add green grapes to chicken salad, crabmeat salad.

37. Broil a few seedless grapes on seafood casseroles; add for the last few minutes of broiling to chicken or fish.

38. Make a sauce of black cherries for roast pork. Mix 1 can (1 pound) of pitted black cherries, 2 tablespoons brown sugar, 1 tablespoon soy sauce, and a couple of tablespoons of the drippings.

39. Serve broiled chicken with peaches or apricots added for the last few minutes of broiling.

40. Marinades are magic for turning inexpensive cuts of meat into really superb dishes. There are a number of possible combinations for this miraculous liquid, but here is one of the best:

1 cup French dressing, red wine, or wine vinegar, 2 teaspoons mixed spices (cloves, bay leaf, garlic), 2 tablespoons mixed chopped onion, parsley, chives, fresh dill or dillseeds, 1 teaspoon powdered mustard. Mix all ingredients together; soak meat in the marinade for at least 2 hours before cooking. Use excess liquid for gravy, basting, or sauce. Fish also benefits from the marinade. Soak the fish for 1 to 2 hours in 1 part vinegar or dry white wine to 2 parts oil. Lemon juice may be substituted for the vinegar or wine.

41. Do not overcook fish, for most of it takes only a few minutes provided it is at room temperature. To test doneness, use a toothpick inserted in thickest part (usually near bone). Separate meat from bone; when meat is no longer transparent, fish is done.

42. Try this for two-dish, one-operation broiling: When broiling hamburgers, small steaks, or ham on the broiler racks in the oven, put, in the drip pan underneath, a dish that will be all the better for catching the juice and drippings. Canned spaghetti or Spanish rice, as examples, with hamburger or steak; canned corn with ham. Be sure the meat is not too fat. Trim if necessary.

43. To separate excess fat from meat drippings, quickly pour into a tall cup and place immediately in cold water. The fat will rise to the top and can be skimmed off easily, leaving the substance for use in the gravy.

44. A surprise center in cocktail meatballs is a pitted ripe olive stuffed with Cheddar cheese and cooked right along with the meat.

SAUCES AND GRAVIES

Thicken gravies and sauces and add unusual flavor at the same time with:

45. A couple of slices of crumbled stale rye bread to about 2 cups gravy.

46. One cup herb-flavored bread crumbs to 2 cups gravy.

47. Don't throw away that ketchup, mustard, chili sauce, or relish bottle if there's the least bit left. Rinse them out with a small amount of vinegar and water and add to gravies, meat sauces.

48. Try leftover coffee to add richness to beef, ham, or pork gravies. About 1½ cups coffee to 3 to 4 cups gravy does the trick.

49. Slip a square of unsweetened chocolate into a brown sauce or gravy to add south-of-the-border richness.

50. Try easy-does-it mustard sauce with ham, cold meats, on sandwiches. Add 2 tablespoons powdered mustard to 1½ cups mayonnaise, 1 tablespoon sugar, 1 teaspoon vinegar or lemon juice. That's all there is to it.

51. Substitute horseradish for the mustard and you have another marvelous sauce. Perfect for boiled beef and cold cuts.

52. Instead of using water for thinning gravies and stews, try using canned consommé, bouillon, concentrated beef cubes, or homemade meat or chicken stock.

53. Make a quick sweet-and-pungent sauce for pork, tongue, or beef with 10 gingersnaps, 1 tablespoon vinegar or lemon juice, ½ cup water, 2 tablespoons brown sugar, and 1 tablespoon grated lemon rind added to 3 to 4 cups gravy.

54. Make a glaze for roast pork or ribs with ½ cup honey, ½ cup soy sauce, and 1 tablespoon powdered mustard.

55. Brush barbecued ribs, hamburgers, frankfurters with French dressing.

56. Browned flour adds more flavor and color to gravies. Make it by stirring it in a dry skillet over very low heat. Remember it has about ½ the thickening power of unbrowned flour. In addition to its other virtues, browned flour doesn't lump or thicken beyond control.

57. Thicken sauces only partially with flour. Try egg yolks for finishing the job. Use 1 egg yolk to about 2 cups basic cream sauce. A wonderfully delicate sauce for pork, ham, or chicken is made by adding 1 tablespoon tarragon vinegar and 1 egg yolk to basic cream sauce.

VEGETABLES

58. Add ground nutmeg (a couple of shakes for unexpected interest) to eggplant, spinach, squash, and also, for a surprising spiciness, to beef gravies and stews.

59. Use sugar as a seasoning. A pinch or two in vegetables gives them a fresher taste, never makes them sweet.

60. Add a pinch of ground oregano and basil to any recipe that includes tomatoes, and don't forget that pinch of sugar.

Put the baked potato in high society by:

61. Adding bits of cooked pork sausage;

62. Stuffing mealy baked ones with leftover beef ground up and mixed with browned onions and a dash of Worcestershire;

63. Adding a delectable mixture of diced celery, green pepper, and crisp bacon;

64. Switching to Swiss cheese instead of Cheddar and adding snips of scallions.

For all above suggestions, bake potatoes in usual way: oil skins, place in hot oven (400°F.), and bake until you can pierce skin easily with a fork. Remove from oven and cut into halves immediately. Scoop out potato and mash thoroughly, adding ½ to ¾ cup liquid for additional moisture (use milk for vegetables and cheese, beef stock or consomme with meats). Put mixture back into skins and broil for additional brownness and crusty tops. Try something new with new potatoes, such as:

65. Quick-fry them, after parboiling, in own jackets.

66. Broil them in the oven. First scrape; put into broiler with ample butter or margarine, shaking them frequently for overall brownness; they're done in about 15 minutes. Serve piping hot, dredged with paprika and parsley.

67. Mix them with fresh green peas in a sauce made of melted butter or margarine and crisp bits of bacon. Add lemon juice just before serving.

68. For deliciously dry boiled potatoes, drain off all water. Dry potatoes on a clean cloth and put them back into pot over low heat for a few minutes. Always remove the lid from the pot after they are done.

69. Snap up green beans with sliced water chestnuts, a few cashew nuts, almonds, bean sprouts. Mix with equal amount of fresh peas and a few of the pea pods.

70. Fry yourself a reputation with French-fried vegetables. Dip the following into egg-and-milk batter and fry quickly in deep fat: tender sprigs of parsley, cauliflower, okra, green beans, slivers of eggplant, and fresh green tomato slices. Dip individual pieces into batter (for 6 servings: 2 egg yolks, ½ cup milk, ¾ cup cake flour, ½ teaspoon salt) and drop into fat that is hot enough to brown cube of bread immediately. Fry until golden-brown and drain on paper towels. Serve immediately. To keep large quantities warm, place pieces on cookie sheet in warm oven, with space around each.

Give the hard-working onion a raise like this:

71. See what it does to ordinary summer squash when fried in golden bits and added, along with a handful of diced hard-cooked eggs. To brown onions, use half olive oil and half butter or margarine. The olive oil lends flavor and will not brown or burn as quickly as butter. This method is also good for sautéing mushrooms and green peppers.

72. Bake boiling-size onions with a glaze of honey and soy sauce. Broil them on skewers with the same sauce for company service.

73. Add a couple of tablespoons of browned minced onions to fresh spinach.

74. Parboil large, sweet onions, hollow out the middles, and stuff with corned-beef hash. Top with bread crumbs and Parmesan cheese and bake quickly until brown.

75. Add a few browned onions to macaroni and cheese, scalloped potatoes.

Be experimental in mixing vegetables as an attention-getter. Perfect partners:

76. Green peas with canned or fresh mushrooms.

77. Okra, tomatoes, green peppers, corn.

78. Baked eggplant, tomatoes, green peppers, and onions: boil eggplant for 12 minutes, dice pulp, mix with other raw vegetables. Put them all back in eggplant skin and bake in the oven for about 20 minutes. The seasonings: salt, pepper, oil, ground basil, and oregano.

79. Hominy with ripe olive slices, butter, margarine, and a little cream.

80. Whole vegetables, stuffed, make hearty, delicious main courses. In addition to the perennial pepper, here are a few other ideas:

81. Stuff tomatoes with Cheddar cheese, chips of crisp bacon, some of the tomato pulp. Top with more bacon and cheese; pop into broiler.

82. Try eggplant, boiled or baked, mixed with cooked lamb, browned onions, a tomato, dashes of ground nutmeg, and rosemary, salt, and pepper, stuffed into eggplant skin, topped with bread crumbs and grated cheese, and baked in oven.

83. Stuff flat pattypan squash with cooked hamburger, green pepper, hard-cooked egg, mixed with a little French dressing, and bake.

84. Use cornmeal as a thickener for corn pudding, using about half as much as you would of flour. You can also use fewer eggs.

85. Cook a couple of lettuce leaves (outer ones preferably) with either fresh or frozen peas. Use no, or almost no water; the lettuce furnishes the necessary moisture. Add a sprinkle of sugar and a few boiled onions if desired.

86. Never boil vegetables vigorously. Always cook them at low heat, just at boiling point. Cook them in tightly covered vessels (the tighter the cover the less water you use), with never more than the minimum amount of water (you can always add more if necessary). They are always at their best when crisp and should never be soft and mushy. It is much better to add seasonings and herbs after cooking.

87. Crisp reminders for salad: Never cut the greens. Tear them into desired size. Cutting makes them limp and bruises them. Always wash salad greens in very cold water. Shake off excess water very gently and place in a bowl that is large enough so that they won't be crushed or bruised. Place in refrigerator for about 1 hour before serving.

88. Marinate potatoes for salad in French dressing for about 1 hour before mixing with mayonnaise or other dressing.

89. Try stuffed olives with rice for a taste treat.

90. Green peas with rice, served hot or cold with a French dressing, is good.

EGGS

91. Scramble eggs in the top of a double boiler. You'll have fluffier ones. Here's the way to do it: Put 4 eggs, lightly beaten, into top part of double boiler. Add 3 tablespoons water and 2 tablespoons butter. Stir slightly. Place over boiling water and stir gently until done.

92. Add ½ cup diced Swiss cheese, ¼ cup diced scallions.

93. Add 1 cup cubed liverwurst or salami slices with 3 tablespoons minced browned onions.

94. Add 1 cup chopped parsley, ½ cup diced green pepper.

95. Add 1½ cups diced boiled potatoes, ½ cup finely chopped raw onions. The amounts given above are for each 4 eggs used.

96. Try the covered-skillet method for frying eggs. Lightly grease skillet, break eggs into it, and cook, covered, for about 5 minutes for the most beautiful and delicious fried eggs you ever tasted. Remember: use lowest possible heat.

97. Add 1 tablespoon cold water to 2-egg omelet; never use milk.

98. Flavor a cream sauce for hard-cooked eggs with curry powder. Serve over noodles mixed with browned bread crumbs flavored with salt, coarse-ground black pepper, and a dash or two of ground nutmeg.

99. Add excitement to deviled eggs with canned sardines, tuna fish, a few capers, chopped-up green olives, a slice or two of liverwurst, ham or bacon chips.

100. Use the yolks of 2 mashed, hard-cooked eggs for thickening in a delicious salad dressing. Add ½ cup oil, ¼ cup vinegar, 1 tablespoon sugar, 1 teaspoon celery seeds. Mix well. This is a semi-thick, delightful dressing.

101. Hard-cooked eggs mixed with unpeeled fresh apple chips and mayonnaise make a marvelous salad.

102. Heat deviled eggs in the broiler under a sauce of mayonnaise mixed with the juice of ½ lemon.

103. Try this change for scrambled eggs: Break 6 eggs into a bowl. Do not beat, whip, or stir. Into a cold skillet put 3½ tablespoons butter, 3 tablespoons heavy cream, and the eggs. Turn heat up to the highest temperature and stir the eggs very slowly, watching them carefully, as they cook very fast. Add salt and pepper when served.

104. Don't ever boil eggs. Always start them in cold water and bring water slowly to boiling point. When water reaches this point, lower heat. This method takes about 5 minutes longer than boiling method, but you'll rarely have a cracked shell or a misshapen egg, and never a tough, rubbery one.

105. Poached eggs are usually better than hard-cooked eggs in many recipes, because the degree of doneness can be determined visually. One method that takes a little practice, but usually works, is to put a drop or two of vinegar into the water; when the water is gently boiling, with a spoon stir a little well in the water and drop the egg into it immediately. Another method: Fill a skillet ⅔ full of water. Allow ½ teaspoon salt to 4 cups water; add vinegar. Bring water to the boiling point, then reduce heat. Break egg into saucer and gently slip into the water. As eggs cook, dip some water from the sides and pour it over the tops. When film forms over the yolks, and whites are firm, remove with a buttered skimmer or pancake turner. Eggs can also be poached in milk or stock for added flavor.

FRUITS

Use fruits unexpectedly with vegetables, meats, such as:

106. Add slivers of orange rind and the juice of the fruit to a pan of baked beans.

107. Orange juice instead of lemon juice on carrots, or mixed in with mashed sweet potatoes or squash.

108. Color a green salad with crescents of unpeeled red apple.

109. Add delightful tang to green salad with wedges of orange, grapefruit, cantaloupe, fresh pineapple.

110. For a delicious cold-weather dinner, try stuffing hollowed-out apples with pork sausage and baking slowly.

111. Use leftover frozen fruit juices instead of water in gelatin salads or desserts.

112. Hollow out large, tart apples; stuff with mincemeat topped with honey and nuts. Bake as usual.

113. Use leftover canned fruit juices for glazes for ham, pork.

114. Add thick wedges of raw apple to canned kraut; bake in oven or stew over low heat.

115. Bananas crushed through a sieve add wonderful flavor and texture to packaged custards, gelatin desserts, ice creams, and sherbets. Use 1 banana for every 3 servings.

116. Use a can of purple plums (pit them) and juice for an exotic pot-roast sauce.

117. Use brown sugar for stewing fresh fruits. Add the peel of ½ lemon, the juice of 1 whole lemon, 1 cinnamon stick. Delicious with peaches, plums, cherries, apples, similar fruits.

118. For added zip to a fruit cup, add a few drops of vanilla and a pinch of salt.

119. Cooked fresh fruits can be more delicious with half the amount of sugar if you add it after the fruit has cooked until tender or after it is done.

120. Make a really savory compote of fresh or canned fruits by adding 2 tablespoons powdered mustard and 1 cup sugar to 1 quart fruit and syrup.

121. Heat canned fruits to serve with hot cereals. Canned peaches or pineapple dusted with brown sugar and warmed in broiler are delicious.

DESSERTS AND DESSERT SAUCES

122. Try adding a dash of almond extract to peach-pie and cherry-pie fillings.

Here are some grand ice-cream sauces that turn plain vanilla into a glorious concoction!

123. White raisins, walnuts, honey, and rum flavoring.

124. Apricot preserves, lemon juice, and crushed mint leaves, well blended.

125. Packaged caramels melted in 1 cup hot strong instant coffee.

126. Whip 1 large package (8 ounces) cream cheese with 3 tablespoons milk and 1 tablespoon sugar for a dreamy topping for stewed fruits, hot fruit pies, fruitcakes.

127. Make individual upside-down cakes in custard cups.

128. Try this quick, delicious glaze for cookies, coffeecakes, or simple poundcake: 1 cup confectioners' sugar, enough water to make it spreadable, a generous handful of mixed glazed fruit.

129. Add any of these to piecrust for interesting flavor and texture: chopped nuts, ground cinnamon or nutmeg, grated lemon rind. For meat pies, add herbs such as ground thyme or dill.

130. Plain toast becomes a treat when spread with peanut butter, honey, and a crunchy topping of Grapenuts. Put it back in hot oven just long enough to brown and heat through.

131. Toast your bread and butter it before making bread pudding.

132. When using a brand-new aluminum pie pan, punch several small holes in the bottom to insure a completely browned bottom crust.

133. Always preheat the oven thoroughly before baking any pie if you want perfect results.

134. Put a pinch of salt in all desserts, whether the recipe calls for it or not.

135. For apple pie with a difference, try slicing a few dates over the apples before putting on top crust.

TRICKS, TREATS, SHORTCUTS

136. Tomatoes cut vertically instead of horizontally tend to bleed less.

137. Sprinkle lettuce for salad with lemon juice while crisping in the refrigerator.

138. Keep simple syrup on hand for making mixed drinks, flavoring iced tea or coffee. It's more economical and makes a better blend with vegetables, too. Use about equal parts sugar and water until sugar dissolves into a smooth liquid.

139. Add 1 teaspoon butter and 1 tablespoon cocoa to an 8-cup coffee brew for a delicious Dutch variation.

140. Use yogurt or buttermilk instead of oil or sour cream for salad dressing. Delicious and a delight to dieters.

141. Keep a ready-to-use shaker of sugar and cinnamon on hand at all times for cookie, coffeecake, toast toppings. Try a little instant coffee in the mixture for a change.

142. Toast cold rice cereal for quick croutons. Use with soups or tossed into green salad at the last minute.

143. Add 1 tablespoon oil, butter, or margarine to rice before boiling. Makes grains separate and glossy and rice will never stick to pot.

144. No cook should ever be caught without stock. It is the liquid resulting when meat or fish is simmered in water and is a fine seasoning for soups, sauces, gravies, aspics. Keep a closely covered jar (make it a big one) in your refrigerator to collect it. Good, vitamin-rich foods that otherwise might be wasted can be used; celery tops and parings, ends of green beans, pea pods, carrot skins, parsley stems, bits of onion. Cover these with water and simmer for about 30 minutes; strain and store, or freeze in ice-cube pans and store. You can also combine with these the juices from fresh or canned vegetables such as green beans, asparagus, peas, or any delicately flavored ones. Juices from strong-flavored vegetables, such as cabbage, Brussels sprouts, turnips, are too potent for this purpose.

145. To any basic recipe for dumplings to be served with meat or chicken, add

any of the following for added interest: ¼ cup finely chopped parsley; 2 tablespoons grated cheese; ½ teaspoon raw onion, 3 tablespoons minced parsley and green sweet pepper, mixed. To keep dumplings light and fluffy as they should be, always cook them in a covered pot and never lift the lid. A glass pie plate makes a heavy, tight cover.

146. Use drawn butter for sautéing veal or chicken, also as a sauce for asparagus, cauliflower, fresh peas. Here is a way to do it: Gently melt butter in vessel that is deeper than it is wide. Skim off foam that rises to top, then pour the melted fluid off slowly and carefully, leaving in the vessel the whitish or cloudy substance that has settled. The clear liquid is the drawn butter, and has a flavor that is delicious and altogether different from regular butter.

147. Try this for quick cookie shaping and for a lighter, crisper yield: Drop the cookie dough in teaspoon-size bits about 2 inches apart on the cookie sheet. Press down with the bottom of an ordinary drinking glass which has been covered with a cloth dampened in cold water. Do not bear down; gently does it.

148. Think of food coloring in a new light. The tiniest bit of red, for instance, added to chocolate puddings or icings makes a richer, brighter brown. The merest dash of yellow food coloring added to white sauces makes them much more attractive and looks as if egg yolks have been added.

149. Use frozen-fruit-juice ice cubes for punches and cold drinks, so that the flavor will not become diluted. Apple juice is one of the best, because of its clearness and its ability to blend with other flavors. Just pour juice into trays and freeze.

150. For the most delicious iced coffee you ever tasted, try this: freeze extra-strong coffee in ice-cube trays. Put frozen cubes in tall glasses (enough to fill), then pour warm milk over them and top with 1 tablespoon whipped cream.

Menus

100 Menus to help you plan more varied meals for your family with the recipes in this volume

*Recipes for all starred dishes found in this volume.

BREAKFASTS

Brook Trout Meunière*
Cheese Waffles*
Fresh Peaches and Cream

Orange and Banana Pieces
Crisp Breaded Tripe*
Home-Fried Potatoes
Tomato Wedges

Welsh Rabbit*
Toast
Canadian Bacon
Frozen Mixed Fruit

Strawberries and Cream
Seattle Dutch Babies*
Pork Sausages

Grapefruit and Orange Slices
Egg and Tongue with Yogurt Sauce* on Toast

Tomato Juice
Creamed Smoked Whiting*
Corn Waffles*
Honey Butter*

Melon Slices
Rainbow Trout, Rocky Mountain Style*
Hashed-Brown Potatoes
Melba Toast

Broiled Grapefruit
Golden Buck*
Crisp-Fried Sausage
Cakes
Buttered Toast
Grape Conserve

LUNCH OR SUPPER

Raspberry Applesauce
Mottram Kidney in Cream* on Biscuits
Poached Eggs
Hot Biscuits
Prune Butter

Cranberry Juice
Tuna Fritters*
Raisin Muffins
Tangerine Marmalade

Poached Mixed Dried Fruit
Venison Sausage*
Waffles*
Butter Maple Syrup

Rhubarb and Strawberries
Batter-Fried Tripe*
Chili Sauce
Corn Muffins

Turkey Salad*
Watercress Sandwiches*
Apricot-Prune Upside-Down Cake*

Tuna and Potato Tart*
California Parmesan-Walnut Salad*
Breadsticks*
Butter

Double-Boiler Tuna Soufflé*
Braised Lettuces*
Yogurt, Cucumber, and Radish Relish*
Crescent Rolls*
Orange Sherbet

Trout, English Style*
Carrots with Dill*
Raspberry Jam Scones*

Turkey Chow Mein*
Soy Sauce
Broccoli
Jellied Tomato Salad
Apple Cobbler

Ham Waffles*
Blueberry Jam
Gratin of Eggplant*
Raisin-Orange Turnovers*

Veal Brains in Mushroom Sauce*
Green Noodles
Artichoke-Heart, Mandarin-Orange, and Almond Salad
Zwieback* Butter

Frosty Watermelon Soup*
Bacon Waffles*
Maple Syrup
Guava Jelly

Jellied Veal Slices*
Anchovy Vinaigrette Sauce
Potato Salad
Sliced Tomatoes
Serbian Walnut Strips*

Duck Hash*
Baked Zucchini and Corn*
Crusty Bowknot Rolls*
Whipped Butter
Watermelon Sherbet*

Cuckoo's Eggs*
Chopped Spinach
Orange Yams*
Toasted Sesame Seed Rolls
Lemon-Lime Ice

Tripe Creole*
Batter-Fried Broad
Noodles
Stuffed Zucchini*
Marmalade Turnovers*

Stewed Tripe with
Vegetables*
Toasted Rolls Black Bread
Herb Butter
Chocolate Butterscotch
Bars*

Tuna Coleslaw with Grapes*
Open-Face Broiled
Cheddar Sandwiches
Fruit Gelatin Cookies

Split Pea Soup*
Sweetbread and Cucumber
Salad*
Crackers and Crisp Breads
Yam Spicecake*

Cream-of-Corn-and-Cress
Soup*
Crab and Grapefruit Salad
with Avocado Mayonnaise*
Pepper and Salt Sticks*

Pot-Roasted Turkey,
Jamaica Style*
Herbed Wild Rice*
Buttered Broccoli
Whole-Wheat Rolls*
Butter
Almond Deep-Dish
Apple Pie*

Cream Vichyssoise
Glacée*
Breast of Veal with
Sausage Stuffing*
Classic Ratatouille*
Sherry Tortoni*

Chicken and Watercress
Soup*
Tuna-Noodle Casserole*
Okra and Tomatoes
with Lemon*
Almond Brandy Torte*

Lamb Shanks Baked in
Fruited Wine*
Wild Rice Stuffing*
(in a casserole)
Watercress Salad*
Mocha Torte*

Roast Boneless Turkey
Roll*
Potatoes in Parsley
Sauce*
Braised Leeks, Nicoise*
Raw Vegetable Sticks
(Carrots, Cucumbers)
Strawberries de Luxe*

Jellied Herb Veal Loaf*
Potato Chips
Vegetable Salad
Bread Chive Butter
Yam Custard Pie*

Commander's Palace Trout
Alexander*
Gratin of Greens*
Orange Rye Bread*
Parsley Butter
French Chocolate Torte*

Hot Crab Salad*
Ensalada de Noche
Buena* (Christmas
Eve Salad)
Sourdough Bread*
Herb Butter
Baked Bonbons*
Black-Walnut Brittle*

Tomato Juice Cocktail
Turkey and Broccoli
Amandine*
Peas and Mushrooms
Pan Rolls* Butter Balls
Apricot Torte*

Bulgarian Cold Cucumber
Soup*
Individual Tuna Pies*
Broccoli alla Piemontese*
Blueberry Upside-Down
Cake*

Roast Pork with
Chinese Vegetables*
Yellow Rice
Butterfly Wings*
Sweet Butter
Prunes in Wine*

Marinated Whiting*
Ginger Cheese Salad
Bowl*
Hot Buttered Rye Bread
Swedish Sans Rival Torte*

Pinwheel Turkey Pie*
Avocado and Orange Salad
Assorted Crisp Breads
Swedish Varmlandstärta*

Veal Saumoné*
Rice Salad
Whole Baby Carrots
à la Grecque*
Avocado Salad*
Syrup-Poached Orange
Slices

Roast Leg of Veal*
Roasted Potatoes
Buttered Asparagus Stalks
Special Mixed Green
Salad*
Vacherin à la Suisse*
(Meringue Shell)

Chicken-Liver Turnovers*
Caesar Salad*
Cornmeal Rolls*
Sour-Cream Apple Torte*

Pressed Turkey*
Mayonnaise
Onion or Shallot Soufflé*
Romaine Hearts and
Radishes
Apple Pie and Cheese

Veal and Peppers,
Italian Style*
Zucchini and Cucumbers
in Sour Cream*
Crusty Dinner Rolls*
Almond Cookies
Orange Sherbet

Sherried Artichoke
Chicken*
Duchess Potatoes
Marinated Tomatoes
Pineapple Upside-Down
Cake*

Marinated Veal Steak*
Fettuccine
Zucchini and Tomatoes
Italian Bread
Coffee Tortoni*

Tuna en Brochette*
Stewed Tomatoes
French-Fried Onion Rings
Lima-Frosted Papaya*

Western Antipasto Salad*
Filet of Beef with
Sherry*
French-Fried Potatoes
Brownie Waffles*
Vanilla Ice Cream
Fudge Sauce

Menus

Turtle Soup*
Pilot Crackers
Prawns in Cream*
Pastry Cups
Cucumber and Onion
Salad
Pecan Pie

Sole in White Wine*
Caponata*
Italian Bread
Garlic Butter
Watermelon-Almond Sherbet*

Broiled Turkey Salad*
Zucchini in Tomato Sauce*
Parker House Rolls*
Herb Butter
Lemon Meringue Tarts

Curried Tuna*
Hot Cooked Rice
Pear Chutney*
Breadsticks
A True English Trifle*

Veal Chops Soubise*
Duchess Potatoes
Herbed Green Peas
Seeded Breadsticks
Washington Plum Dumplings*

Turtle Steak with Sour-Cream Sauce*
Home-Fried Potatoes
Succotash
Spiced Raisin Relish*
Northwest Huckleberry Buckle*

Chicken Braised with Wine*
Parsley Boiled Potatoes
Sautéed Zucchini, Italian Style*
Ripe Watermelon Pickle*
Sherry Gelatin

Sweet-and-Sour Tuna*
Chow-Mein Noodles
Avocado Salad with Yogurt Dressing*
Opera Torte*

Ho T'ao Chi Jing (Walnut Chicken)*
Fried Noodles
Radish-Garnished Chinese Cabbage Slaw
Red-Wine-Baked Pears*

Veal Cutlets, Sicilian Style*
Green Noodles
Tossed Salad
Hot Crisp Italian Bread
Biscuit Tortoni*

Veal Shoulder with Cheese Sauce*
Baked Potatoes
Braised Onion Slices*
Bibb Lettuce
French Dressing
Jaegertorte (Hunter's Torte)*

Samosas (Curried Meat Turnovers)*
Zucchini and Pepper Stew*
Sour-Cream Watercress Sauce* on Salad Greens
Fruit and Cheese

Cioppino*
Hot Garlic Bread
Old Colony Gingerbread Waffles*
Orange Hard Sauce*

Lamb Baryani*
Fluffy Turnips*
Zucchini Pickles*
Zeppole*
Honey

Fresh Tangerine and Turkey Salad*
Puerto Rican Yam and Cheese Crullers*
Guava Jelly
Walnut Crescents*

Italian Tuna Frittata*
Mayonnaise-Spread Toast
Molded Watermelon Salad*
Ginger-Mince Upside-Down Cake*

Zucchini Chicken*
Cucumber Yogurt Salad*
No-Knead Feather Rolls*
Butter
Vanilla Fresh-Fruit Cup*

Tuna Green-Bean Casserole*
Spinach-Cottage Cheese Salad*
Crisp Breads
Cherry Soup Scandinavian*

Baked Turkey and Rice*
Zucchini and Sliced Tomatoes
Breadsticks*
Cherry Upside-Down Cake*

Tuna Tetrazzini*
Cheese, Cucumber, and Grapefruit Salad*
White Corn Tortillas*
Blueberry Turnovers*

Vitella Tonnato (Veal with Tuna)*
Hot Rice Salad
Green Peas Carrot Strips
Cold Zabaglione*

Trout en Papillote*
Shoestring Potatoes
Green-Bean Soufflé*
Tossed Salad
Green Goddess Salad Dressing*
Black-Walnut Wafers
Ice Cream

Stuffed Veal Rolls*
Fried Green-Tomato Slices
Browned-Butter Wilted Lettuce*
Cherry Torte with Cream*

Hunter's Chili*
Turnip Salad*
Toasted Split Hamburger Rolls*
Plain Cake with Whipped-Cream Topping*

Turkey Curry*
Fluffy Rice
Sautéed Bananas
Cashews Chutney Raisins
Lemon Bread Pudding

Fresh Tuna Tarragon*
Herbed French-Fried Potatoes
Chilled Artichokes with
Garlic Mayonnaise*
Old Colony
Gingerbread Waffles*
Mock Devonshire Cream*

Veal Chops Paprika*
Madame Fraize's Cabbage
and Zucchini Skillet*
Refrigerator Rolls*
Herb Butter
Fresh Fruit and Cheese

Chili Whitefish*
Braised Chinese Cabbage*
Haricots Verts Maillanoise
(Green Beans,
Maillane Style)*
Chocolate Cake
Raspberry Gelatin

Sherried Turkey with
Potatoes*
Brussels Sprouts with
Almonds
Fresh-Pear-and-Orange
Salad
Walnut Shortbread*

Daube Provençale*
Boiled Onions Carrots
Macaroni Salad
Sherry Custard

Breaded Veal Cutlet
(Wiener Schnitzel)*
Braised Red-Cabbage
Dumplings
Viennese Torte*

Corned-Beef Turnovers,
Mushroom Sauce*
Green Peas
Waldorf Salad
Chocolate Soufflé

Hawaiian Veal Stew*
Patty Shells
Red-Cabbage Slaw
Yogurt Honey Cakes*
Honey Whipped Cream

Broiled King Crab Legs*
Zucchini Ziti*
Braised Celery*
Apple Crisp

Turkey with Welsh-Rabbit
Sauce* on Toast
Frozen Mixed Vegetables
Sliced Cucumbers with
French Dressing
Fresh Plums

Truite au Bleu*
Parsley Buttered Potatoes
Artichoke Fritters*
Avocado Salad
Mocha Torte*

Stuffed Veal Cutlets*
Fluffy Turnips*
Braised Endive*
Bowknot Rolls*
Garlic Butter
Chocolate Cream Pie

Tripe à la Lyonnaise*
Cauliflower Sauté with
Lemon
Pan-Browned Potatoes
Stuffed Tomato Salad
Apricot-Prune Upside-
Down Cake*

Turkey Pie with
Corn-Bread Topping*
Spinach Soufflé*
Bibb Lettuce and Radishes
Hungarian Walnut Bars*
Fresh-Fruit Slices

Venison Meatballs*
Parmesan Noodles
Stuffed Baked Eggplant*
Lemon Meringue Pie

Old-Fashioned Veal Loaf*
Creamy Mashed Potatoes
Carrots à la Sultana*
Poached Pears with Kirsch

Lamb-Stuffed Zucchini*
Fried Beans*
Tostadas*
Ambrosia Upside-Down Cake*

Turkey Paprika*
Saffron Pilau*
Cabbage in White Wine*
Italian Dinner Rolls
Sherry Tortoni*

Turkey Soup*
Shrimps Victoria*
Hot Wild Rice
Braised Celery*
Cranberry-Apple Pie

Simmered Breast of Veal*
(with Bacon, Sausage,
Carrots, Onions,
Potatoes, Cabbage)
Tomato and Cucumber Salad
Zabaglione*

Basque Barbecued Lamb*
Potatoes and Onions
(Cooked with seasoned
butter in foil)
Tomato and Lettuce Salad
Strawberry Shortcake

Barbecued Turkey Steaks*
Broccoli Soufflé*
Braised Fennel*
Pan Rolls Herbed Butter
Angel-Food Cake
Ice Cream

Venison Ragout*
Water-Chestnut and Rice
Stuffing* (Baked in
casserole)
Tomato and Cucumber Slices
Blueberry Cobbler

Braised Leg of Veal*
Tangerine Sweets*
Onions in Onions*
Cloverleaf Rolls
Sweet Butter
Cherry Torte with Cream*

Barbecued Salmon Steaks*
Finnish Stuffed Turnips*
Buttered Frenched
Green Beans
Toasted Cheese Rolls
Blueberry Pie

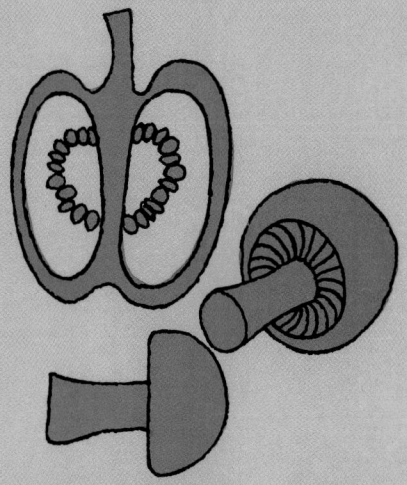

*Recipes for all starred dishes found in this volume.

GENERAL INFORMATION

The Ingredients and Measurements Used in Recipes

All recipes in this book have been tested in the Woman's Day Kitchens with standard American measuring cups (8 ounces = 16 tablespoons), measuring spoons (1 tablespoon = 3 teaspoons), and other standard kitchen equipment. All measurements are level. Liquids are measured in standard 8-ounce glass measuring cups, at eye level.

All sugar is granulated white sugar unless otherwise specified.

All flours, cake and all-purpose, are sifted before measuring unless otherwise specified. No self-rising flour is used.

All baking powder is double-acting baking powder.

All brown sugar is firmly packed when measured.

All confectioners' sugar is sifted before measuring.

All pepper is ground black pepper unless otherwise specified.

Fats and shortening are measured at room temperature, packed firmly into measuring cup and leveled with a straight knife. They are scraped out with a rubber spatula.

Salted butter or margarine, packed in ¼-pound sticks, is used unless otherwise specified. 1 stick = ½ cup = 8 tablespoons = ¼ pound.

1 tall can evaporated milk (14½ ounces) contains 1⅔ cups undiluted evaporated milk. Unsweetened condensed milk is an entirely different product, and cannot be used interchangeably with evaporated milk.

⅓ to ½ teaspoon dried herbs can be substituted for each tablespoon fresh herbs. Crumble herbs before using to release flavor.

Before starting to cook or to bake, read the recipes carefully. Assemble all ingredients and equipment. Follow recipe exactly. Do not increase or decrease recipe unless you are a skilled enough cook to recognize what adjustments must be made as to ingredients, pan sizes, and/or cooking time.

Cooking Temperatures and Times

Cooking temperatures and times are approximate for meat. They depend not only on the weight and kind of meat, but also on its shape, temperature, and its bone and fat contents. A meat thermometer was used in testing.

Cooking times for meats are as recommended by the National Live Stock and Meat Board, 36 Wabash Avenue, Chicago, Illinois 60603.

Oven Temperatures

TEMPERATURES (Degree F.)	TERM
250 to 275	VERY SLOW
300 to 325	SLOW
350 to 375	MODERATE
400 to 425	HOT
450 to 475	VERY HOT
500 to 525	EXTREMELY HOT

Important—Preheat oven for 10 to 15 minutes before placing food in it. Many a cake has been spoiled by being placed in a barely heated oven. Baking times are based on the assumption that the oven is already at the stated temperature.

Check the oven temperature control frequently, especially if baking times vary from those given in recipes. (This can be done with a portable oven thermometer.) If a control is consistently off, call your public utility. They should be able to reset the oven temperature control.

Caloric Values

The caloric values, where mentioned, for each food are based on 100 grams, about 3½ ounces edible portion, as mentioned in Composition of Foods, Agriculture Handbook No. 8, Agricultural Service of the United States Department of Agriculture, Washington, D. C., revised December 1963.

WOMAN'S DAY
Encyclopedia of Cookery

Complete Recipe Index for Volumes 1 to 12

In this cross-index of all the recipes in the twelve volumes of the Woman's Day Encyclopedia of Cookery the reader will find each recipe listed alphabetically under the name of its principal ingredient, as Chicken, Eggplant, Orange, etc. Recipes are also listed under menu categories or kind of preparation, as Appetizer, Soup, Salad, or Croquette, Meatball, Tamale, etc. Recipes with foreign names are listed by those names as well, and those recipes which have a geographical or personal description, as Danish Kringle or Kentucky Burgoo, will be found alphabetically under such descriptive names.

Immediately following each recipe is the number of the volume in which it appears (printed in bold face) and its page number (printed in light face). Those recipes which appear in Volume 10 under the entry Quantity Cooking are indicated by the symbol (QC) following the recipe.

A

Aal i Gelé (Jellied Eel), **4**-539
Aardappel-Purée met Ham en Uien (Purée of Potatoes with Ham and Onions), **4**-592

Abalone, 1-5
Chowder, **1**-5
Sauté, **1**-5
Achivades Pilafi (Clam Pilaf), **5**-818

Acorn Squash, 1-6; **11**-1759
Apple-Stuffed, **11**-1762
Baked, Supreme, **1**-7
Baked, with Whipped Potato Rosettes, **11**-1762
Grapefruit- and Tangerine-Stuffed, **11**-1762
Sausage-Stuffed, **1**-7
Slices, French-Fried, **11**-1762
Steamed, **1**-7
Adobong Manok at Baboy (Chicken and Pork), **9**-1369
Aeblekage (Apple Cake), **4**-543
Aebleskiver (Danish Doughnuts), **4**-542
Aeggestand (Cold Scrambled Eggs), **4**-538
African Style Peanut Soup, **8**-1322
Agnello alla Cacciatora (Lamb Cacciatora), **6**-954
Agourontomatosalata (Tomato and Cucumber Salad), **5**-822
Aguacates Batidos (Whipped Avocado), **11**-1709
Agurkesalat (Cucumber Salad), **4**-342
Agurkesuppe (Cucumber Soup), **4**-538
Aigo-Sau (Fish Stew), **2**-216
Aïoli, Aïoli Sauce (Garlic Mayonnaise), **1**-7; **5**-740; **10**-1614, 1621
Alabama Fruitcake, Old, **5**-759
à la King Leftovers, **7**-1050
Alaska Duck Salad, **1**-23
Alaska Pie, Mincemeat, **7**-1164

Albacore, 1-8
Broiled Fresh, **10**-1560
Divan, **1**-8
Fresh, Sauté Amandine, **1**-8
Pickled, **1**-8
Albóndigas (Meatballs), **11**-1705
Alcachofas Rellenos con Sardinas (Sardine-Stuffed Artichokes), **11**-1741
Ale, **1**-10; see also Beer
Alentejo Style Fish (Peixe a Alentejana), **9**-1455

Alewife, 1-10
Alewives Baked with Lemon, **1**-10
Algerian-Style Eggs, **5**-775
Allemande Sauce, **1**-10; **10**-1613, 1619
Allspice, **1**-11
Almásrétes (Apple Strudel), **6**-921

Almond(s), 1-11
Amandine Butter, **10**-1615, 1624
(for appetizers), **1**-89
Bacon from Heaven (Toucinho-do-Céu), **9**-1457
Bavarian Cream, **1**-15
Blanched, Blanching, **1**-13; **5**-780
Bouillon, **1**-75
Brandy Torte, **11**-1853
Bread Cookies, Brussels (Pain d'Amandes), **2**-200
Bread (Mandelbrot), **6**-992
Brittle, **1**-16
Burnt, **1**-13
Burnt-Almond Soufflé, **11**-1688
Butter Cake, **5**-783
-Butter Strips, **3**-473
Carrot Conserve, **2**-309
Celery-Almond Stuffing, **11**-1781
Cheesecakes (Queijadinhas de Amêndoas), **9**-1457
-Chicken Salad, **1**-14
Chocolate Torte (Rehruecken), **11**-1804
Coleslaw, **10**-1586
Cookies, **2**-250
Cookies, Chinese, **4**-635
Cookies, Glazed, **1**-16
Cookies (Hsing Jen Ping), **3**-404
Cream Filling, **8**-1320
Croquettes, **4**-518
Cucumber-Almond Salad, **10**-1586
Custard, Thomas Jefferson's, **1**-14
Deep-Dish Apple Pie, **12**-1933
Diamonds, **5**-709
Extract, **1**-13
-Filled Coffee Ring, **1**-15
Filling, **1**-15, 69; **8**-1308
Florentines, **8**-1272
Fondant-Dipped, **5**-708
Four Specie Dollars (Fire-Speciedalerkaker), **8**-1243
Hearts, Nonsweet, **1**-15
Ice Cream, **6**-929
Lebkuchen, Dropped, **7**-1046
Linzer Torte, **4**-535
Macaroons, **1**-15
Marzipan, **8**-1243
Mazurka (Mazurek Migdałowy), **9**-1431
Meringue Cookies, **7**-1135
Meringues, Rich, **7**-1135
and Mushroom Sauce, **7**-1152
Noodles, **1**-14
Nougat, **2**-288
-Olive Spread, **2**-279
Paste, **1**-13, 15
Pea and Cheese Salad, **8**-1315
Pfeffernüsse, **9**-1367
Popovers, **2**-238; **9**-1437
Poppy-Seed Noodles, Hungarian, **8**-1233
Praline, **9**-1480
Red Snapper Amandine, **10**-1540
Salted, **1**-14
Sauce Amandine, **1**-14
Sherry Snow Pudding, **9**-1492
Slices, **1**-74
Slivers, **5**-780
Soufflé, **1**-15
Soufflé Sandwiches, **10**-1610
Soup, **1**-14
Soup (Sopa de Almendras), **11**-1742
Soyed, **11**-1734
Spinach with, **11**-1756
Spritz Cookies, **11**-1758

Almond(s), continued
Strawberry-Almond Roll, **11**-1778
and Strawberry Cheesecake, **8**-1282
-Stuffed Kumquat Preserve, **7**-1023
Sweet-Potato Pudding, **11**-1837
Tarts and Cookies (Mandelterter), **8**-1243
Tart, Swedish (Polynees), **1**-69
Toasted, **1**-14
Torte, **1**-15; **4**-630
Torte, Swedish Sans Rival, **12**-1856
Wasps' Nests, **1**-78
Wreaths (Mandelkränze), **5**-798
Almôndegas (Meatballs), **9**-1456
Alpine Eggs, **4**-629
Alsace Salad, **9**-1469
Alsatian Carp with Sauerkraut, **5**-699
Alsatian Noodles, **1**-16
Amandine Sauce, **1**-14

Ambrosia, **1**-17; **3**-428
Cake, **7**-1044
Fresh-Pear, **8**-1331
in Frozen Orange Shells, **11**-1824
Jellied Orange Ambrosia Dessert, **8**-1270
de Luxe, **1**-17
Orange, **4**-566
Peach, **8**-1316
Texas, **1**-73
Upside-Down Cake, **12**-1882
Ameijoas a Bulhão Pato (Clams à la Bulhao Pato), **9**-1456
Ameijoas Portuguesas (Portuguese Clams), **9**-1455
Américaine Sauce, **10**-1626
American Applesauce Cake, **2**-268
American Cook Book, **1**-22
American Indian Style Pike, **9**-1401
American Onions and Tomato, **8**-1263
American Smorgasbord, Menu, **10**-1666
Amish Vanilla Pie, **9**-1355
Anadama Batter Bread, **2**-229
Anadama Bread, **8**-1225
Ananas (Pineapple) Pilau, **9**-1403
Anchoas a la Vinagreta (Anchovies Vinaigrette), **11**-1741

Anchovy(ies), **1**-80
Anchovied Mushrooms, **4**-627
Bird's Nests (Fågelbon), **11**-1786
Butter, **1**-85; **5**-694; **6**-955; **10**-1615, 1624
Canapés, **1**-80
Eggs, **6**-912
on Egg Slices, **10**-1566
Eggs Stuffed with, **4**-606
and Egg Tartlets, **11**-1811
Mayonnaise, **10**-1614, 1621
and Meat Pirozhki, **10**-1570
and Potato Casserole, **1**-80
Puffs, **8**-1306
Sauce, **11**-1738
Sauce (Salsa di Alici), **6**-959
-Stuffed Peppers, **9**-1359
Toast Butter, **11**-1829
with Toast, Fried, **11**-1826
Vinaigrette (Anchoas a la Vinagreta), **11**-1741
Andalusian Egg Platter (Oeufs sur le Plat à l'Andalouse), **6**-862
Andalusian Vinaigrette Salad (Ensalada a la Andaluza), **11**-1741
Angel Delight (QC), **10**-1525

Angel Food, Angel-Food Cake, **1**-80; **2**-262
Basic, **1**-81
Butter-Pecan, **2**-273
Cherry, **2**-273
Chocolate, **3**-410
Lemon Delight, **7**-1088
Strawberry Dessert, **11**-1778
Angelica, **1**-81
Angelica as a Garnish, **1**-81
Angel Parfait, **11**-1724
Angels on Horseback, **8**-1287

Anise, **1**-81
Aniseed Cookies, **11**-1732
Butternut Squash, **2**-255
Fruit Cup, **8**-1283
Grape and Cabbage Slaw, **10**-1586
Sesame-Anise Cookies, **10**-1647
Squash Pie, **11**-1762
Suggested Uses for, **1**-81
Anniversary Cake, **2**-268
Anniversary Punch, **9**-1502
Antebellum Spice Cake, **2**-272

Antelope, **1**-82
Antelope, Roast Saddle of, **1**-82
Antipasto, see Appetizer
Antler Cookies (Hirvensarvet), **5**-681
Antoine's Oysters Rockefeller, **1**-41
Apea Cake, **9**-1357
Apfeltorte (Apple Tart), **11**-1806
Appelschoteltje (Zwieback with Apple in the Oven), **4**-593
Appelsiinikeitto (Orange Soup), **5**-679
Äppelsoppa (Apple Soup), **11**-1787

Appetizer(s), **1**-84; see also Canapé; Cocktail; Dip; Pâté and Terrine; Pickle and Relish; Spread
Almonds, **1**-89
Anchovies Vinaigrette (Anchoas a la Vinagreta), **11**-1741
Anchovy Eggs, **6**-912
Anchovy Puffs, **8**-1306
Antipasto Combinations, **6**-952
Antipasto Plates (Antipasto Misto), **6**-952
Antipasto Variato, **1**-82
Apple, **1**-97
Apple Slices, Savory, **6**-913
Apple Snacks, **1**-97
Apple-Tomato, Hot, **11**-1832
Artichoke Hearts with Foie Gras, **5**-708
Artichoke Hearts, Marinated, **4**-643
Avocado Hors-d'Oeuvre, **6**-913
Bean and Cheese (Totopos), **7**-1138
Bean Salad, **8**-1213
Beef Tartlets, **11**-1811
Belgian Endive, **4**-618
Bird's Nest (Fågelbon), **11**-1786
Brain Salad, **8**-1211
Brandied Cheddar Cheese, **3**-355
Burritos from Taos, **11**-1732
Canapé Pie, **2**-281
Caponatina, **1**-82
Cantaloupe, Fresh, and Prosciutto, **2**-296
Cauliflower and Grape Salad (Salat iz Tsvetnoi Kapusti s Vinogradom), **10**-1566
Caviar Bowl, **7**-1146
Celery, Stuffed, **1**-89
Cheddar-Cheese Sticks, **3**-355
Cheese, **1**-78
Cheese Balls, **3**-429
Cheese Balls with Paprika, Fried, **8**-1296
Cheese Board, **1**-89
Cheese Hearts, **8**-1306
Cheese Olive Puffs, **6**-913
Cheese Pinwheels, Tiny, **8**-1306
Cheese Squares, **7**-1089
Cheese Straws, **11**-1822
Cheese Tartlets, **1**-87
Cheese Truffles (Kaastruffels), **4**-589
Chicken-Liver, **3**-391
Chicken Livers, Chopped, **6**-987
Chicken Pastries, **8**-1306
Chick-Peas, Mashed, with Sesame, **8**-1212
Chick-Peas in Olive Oil (Ceci all'Olio), **1**-82
Chili Shrimp Squares, **10**-1656
Clam Bites, **1**-89
Clam Pastries, **6**-912
Cocktail Sausages with White Wine, **8**-1276
Cocktail Snacks, Ha'Penny, **8**-1308
Cold Cuts, Cornucopias of, with Two-Cheese Molds and Mixed Fruit, **1**-89
Cold Cuts, Cubed, with Tiered Fruit Salad, **1**-89
Cottage-Stuffed Celery, **3**-355
Crabmeat Molds, **4**-568
Crabmeat-Stuffed Mushrooms, **6**-913
Cream-Cheese Miniatures, **4**-643
Cream Puffs, **8**-1306
Cream Puffs, Savory, **3**-492
Cucumber Cups, **6**-913
Cucumbers and Onions, Wilted, **6**-912
Cucumber Slices, **1**-89
Curried Chicken Tartlets, **11**-1811
Curried Shrimp Diamonds, **8**-1306
Curry Puffs, **6**-912
Custard, Steamed (Chawan-Mushi), **6**-971
Deviled Eggs, **6**-912
Deviled-Ham Pinwheels, **8**-1306
Deviled Sardines, **10**-1612
Dilled Green Beans, **4**-564
Dill Meatballs, **4**-643
Egg and Anchovy Tartlets, **11**-1811
Eggplant Caponata, Sicilian, **4**-614
Eggplant Caviar (Ikra iz Baklazhanov), **10**-1566
Eggplant Chips, **4**-614
Eggplant, Marinated (Melanzane alla Marinara), **6**-952
Eggplant Puffs, **4**-614
Eggplant with Sesame, **8**-1212
Egg Rolls, Chinese, **8**-1294
Endive Tempura, **1**-89
Fillings for Savory Appetizer Puffs, **3**-492
Fish, Pickled, **1**-49
Fish Vinaigrette (Pescado a la Vinagreta), **11**-1741
Forshmak Dragomir, **10**-1567
Frankfurter Bits, **5**-718
Frankfurter-Egg, **5**-718
Frankfurters with Cheese and Bacon, **5**-718
Frankfurters, Marinated, **5**-718
Frankfurter Sticks **5**-718
Frank-Roll Slices, **5**-718
Fresh-Grape and Lemon-Ice Cup, **5**-812
Grape Leaves, Stuffed I, **8**-1211; II, **8**-1212
Green Peppers, Pickled, **1**-82
Guadalajara Toasts (Guadalajara Tostadas), **7**-1138
Ham and Swiss, Frenched, **6**-913
Hawaiian Salad (Lomi Lomi Salmon), **1**-34
Headcheese, **6**-882
Herring and Apples in Sour Cream, **1**-87
Herring and Ham Salad (Sill och Skinksallad), **11**-1787
Herring, Pickled, **6**-903
Herring Salad, **6**-913
Herring in Sour Cream, **6**-903; **7**-1146
Herrings (Selyodka), **10**-1566
Hors-d'Oeuvre (for Parisian Luncheon), **4**-633
Kabobs, **5**-718
Karelian Pasties (Karjalanpiirat), **5**-678
Liederkranz Cheese Balls, **1**-62
Little Toasts Potosí Style (Tostaditas al Estilo de Potosí), **7**-1137
Liver-Sausage Appetizer Salad, **10**-1635
Lorenzo à la Filipini, **2**-281
Masked Liver Mold, **10**-1635
Meatballs, Cocktail, **2**-189
Meatballs, Small (Små Köttbullar), **11**-1786
Meat Crisps, Elena's Style (Carnitas al Estilo de Elena), **7**-1138
Meat Salad (Kjøttsalat), **8**-1235
Melon with Prosciutto, **4**-650
Meze, **4**-639
Mint and Parsley Salad, **8**-1213
Minted Pineapple Cup, **9**-1403
Mozzarella Cheese, Medallions of (Medaglioni di Mozzarella), **6**-952
Mushroom Beignets, **1**-89
Mushroom Caps, Broiled, **4**-644
Mushrooms, Marinated, **1**-89
Mushroom Pastries, **6**-912
Mushrooms in Sour Cream (Griby v Smetane), **10**-1567
Mushrooms, Stuffed, **4**-640; **7**-1083; **11**-1782
Olive-Avocado, **8**-1256
Olive and Bacon Rolls, **7**-1089
Olives, California Style, **1**-89
Olives in Cheese, **1**-89
Olives, Garlic, **8**-1276

Black, **8**-1257
Ripe, **1**-89
Olive Surprises, **8**-1256
Olivier Salad (Salat Olivier), **10**-1566
Oysters Bienville, Arnaud's, **4**-510
Oysters, Pickled, **1**-28
Oysters Rockefeller, Antoine's, **1**-41
Parmesan Cubes, Salty, **8**-1306
Pâtés, see Pâtés and Terrines
Peanut-Butter Ham Puffs, **8**-1324
Pecans, Salted, **8**-1335
Pepper Salad, Italian Style, **9**-1360
Pickled Turnips, **8**-1213
Pigs in Blankets, **10**-1635
Pike, Chilled, with Cocktail Sauce, **9**-1400
Pimiento Pinwheels, **8**-1306
Pineapple Fruit Cup Served in the Half Shell, **9**-1403
Piroshki, Russian, **8**-1197
Pistachio Fruit Cup, **9**-1411
Pizzas, Individual, **3**-355
Polar Bear's Eye (Isbjørnøye), **8**-1235
Potato Salad with Ham and Cherries (Kartofelnii Salat s Vechinoi i Vishniami), **10**-1566
Potatoes Mayonnaise, **1**-89
Prosciutto with Fruits, **6**-952
Quiche Lorraine, **4**-566
Raw Vegetable Tray or Bowl, **1**-87
Red Mullet Levantine (Salmonetes Levantinos), **11**-1741
Red and White Radish Salad (Salat iz Krasnoi i Beloi Rediski), **10**-1566
Relish Christmas Tree, **3**-428
Roe Salad, **8**-1211
Rollmops, **6**-903
Roquefort Pinwheels, **8**-1306
Rumaki, **1**-87
Sailboats, **10**-1589
Salmon Balls, **10**-1595
Salmon Horseradish Cones, **10**-1594
Salmon, Marinated, with Mustard Sauce (Gravad Lax med Senapssås), **11**-1786
Salmon, Salted, **10**-1594
Salmon, Smoked, with Cucumber Dip, **10**-1594
Salmon-Stuffed Eggs, **1**-87
Salmon Vinaigrette (Vinaigrette s Syomgoi), **10**-1566
Sandwiches, Mexican (Tostadas Compuestas), **7**-1137
Sardines in Tomato Sauce (Sardinas con Salsa de Tomates), **11**-1741
Sardine-Stuffed Artichokes (Alcachofas Rellenos con Sardinas), **11**-1741
Sauerkraut Balls, **10**-1632
Sausage-Ball, Spicy, **7**-1122
Sausage Slices, Hot, **3**-428
Shrimp, **10**-1656
Shrimp with Anchovy Butter, **8**-1275
Shrimp and Artichoke, **10**-1658
Shrimp and Cauliflower Salad (Maionese di Scampi e Cavolfiore), **1**-82
Shrimp, Indian Broiled, **6**-913
Shrimp, Lemon-Broiled, **7**-1052
Shrimp in Marinade, **10**-1657
Shrimp, Marinated, **10**-1656
Shrimp, Pickled, **3**-428
Shrimp, Potted, Savory, **9**-1477
Shrimp and Prosciutto, Broiled, **10**-1657
Shrimp Puffs, **8**-1306
Shrimp, Savory, **4**-642
Shrimp, Twice-Fried, **10**-1657
Smoked Whitefish Platter, **12**-1939
Snails Forestière, **10**-1667
Soyed Walnuts, **3**-428
Spinach-Cheese Strips, **8**-1306
Stuffed Eggs, **4**-606
Stuffed Eggs (Avga Gemista), **4**-639
Swiss-Cheese, Hot, **7**-1146
Sweet Fennel for Antipasto, **4**-657
Swiss Petit Puffs, **8**-1306
Teriyaki Sticks, **4**-643
Terrines, see Pâtés and Terrines
Tomato-Avocado Hors-d'Oeuvre, **6**-913
Tomato Frost, **1**-37
Tomato and Mushroom Salad, **1**-82
Tomatoes, Stuffed, **8**-1213
Tuna, **12**-1862
Tuna Fish Mound, **12**-1863
Two-Cheese Logs, **1**-78
Two-Cheese Meat Tarts, **11**-1811
Veal and Cucumber (Salat iz Teliatini s Ogurtsami), **10**-1566
White-Bean and Tuna Salad (Cannelini al Tonno), **6**-960
Won Ton, Crisp (Cha Yun Tun), **3**-403

Apple(s), 1-95
Almond Apples, Baked (Paistetut Manteliomenat), **5**-681
Appetizer, **1**-97
Baked, **1**-96
in Orange Juice, **8**-1270
Rosy Glazed, **1**-102
on Toast Rounds (Pommes Bonne Femme), **5**-746
Bavarian Slaw, **1**-100
with Beet Salad (Rödbetssallad med Äpplen), **11**-1790
Betty, **1**-77
and Blueberry Jelly, Spiced, **6**-982
Bread, **7**-1153
Bread, Autumn, **1**-100
Brown Betty, **1**-101
Butter, **1**-97
Butter, Pennsylvania Dutch, **9**-1350
-Butter Pie, **1**-79
-Buttermilk Waffles, **2**-238
Cake, Dutch, Mrs. Van's, **7**-1156
Cake, Meringue, **1**-101
Cake, Old World, **1**-102
Carrot, and Raisin Salad, **10**-1583
Charlotte (Charlotte de Pommes), **3**-348
Charoses, **6**-994
Chart, Fresh Apple Availability, **1**-92-93
Cheese-Noodle Pudding, **3**-362
Cheese-Stuffed Apple Salad, **5**-754
Chutney, West Indies, **1**-102
Cider, see Cider
Cinnamon-Apple Salad, Jellied, **10**-1587
Cobbler, **11**-1725
Coconut Betty, **9**-1490
Coconut-Crusted Apple Dessert, **3**-457
Coffeecake, **3**-463
Corn-Bread Stuffing, **4**-584
-Corn Muffins, **8**-1193
Cranberry-Apple Punch (QC), **10**-1527
Cranberry Apples, **3**-445
-Cranberry Compote, Hot, **3**-465
Cranberry-Apple Crisp, **1**-65
-Cranberry Fizz, **1**-103
-Cranberry Punch, **9**-1503
-Cranberry Shortcake, **1**-101
Cream of (Iablochnii Krem), **10**-1574
Crisp, **1**-101
Crisp (QC), **10**-1525
Cups, **5**-780
with Cuminseed, Candied, **4**-523
Curried, **1**-97
Danish Pastries, **2**-232
Dolma, Persian, **4**-571
Dumplings, **7**-1155
Dumplings, Baked, **1**-96
Flan, **5**-703
Foil-Baked, **1**-146
-Frankfurter Casserole, **1**-97
Fresh Apple Coleslaw, **10**-1586
and Fresh Tangerine Salad, **11**-1809
Fried, **2**-242; **9**-1353
Fried, with Bacon, **1**-45
Fried, Virginia, **11**-1724
Fritters, **1**-101
Fritters, Brandied, **1**-63
Fritters Regina, **5**-749
Fruit Ketchup, **6**-999
Glacé with Honey Cream Cheese, **10**-1587
Glazed, and Carrots, **2**-306
Golden-Apple Salad, **1**-77
Grape Apples, **5**-813
and Grape-Juice Ice, **6**-925
Gravy for Pork or Boiled Beef, **7**-1152
Hamburgers with Apple Rings, **1**-97
-Ham Casserole, **1**-97
-Herb Jelly, **1**-103
Honey-Glazed, **6**-910
Jelly, **1**-97; **6**-982
Jelly, Aromatic, **6**-982
Kuchen, **1**-100; **5**-799
-Lamb Curry, **1**-97
with Maple Syrup, Baked, **7**-1107
Mincemeat, Spicy, **7**-1162
Noodle-Apple Pudding, **9**-1490
-Nut Bars, **1**-103
Oatmeal Cookies, **1**-102
and Onion Dressing, **4**-574
and Onion Soup, **11**-1694
and Onions, **8**-1264
Onions, and Raisins, Sautéed, **1**-100
-and-Orange Salad, **10**-1587
and Oranges, Sliced, with Wine, **8**-1270
Pancake, **1**-100
Pancakes, German, **8**-1293
Pandowdy, **1**-101
Peanut-Butter Tea Sticks, **8**-1326
and Pears, Poached, **8**-1330
and Pecan Salad, Jellied, **8**-1334
Pie, **1**-96; **4**-626
Almond Deep-Dish, **12**-1933
with Cheese, Pam's, **1**-28
Cream, **1**-100
Caramel, **9**-1392
Deep-Dish, **1**-101
Deep-Dish Fresh, **9**-1396
Deep-Dish Pantry, **9**-1396
Dried, **1**-103
Favorite, **9**-1392
Grated-Apple, with Chicken-Fat Pastry, **9**-1393
Honey, **1**-56
Honey-Nut, **6**-910
New Hampshire, Turnover, **1**-57
and Peach, **8**-1320
and Pork, Breakfast, **8**-1224
Puddeny-Pie, **6**-949
-Raisin-Nut, **8**-1229
Rhubarb-Apple, **10**-1544
Russkii Iablochnii Pirog, **10**-1574
Upside-Down, **1**-102
and Plum Crumble, **8**-1253
Poached, **1**-101
Pomanders, Old English, **9**-1435
Pommes Meringuées, **4**-558
Pompushkes, **11**-1700
Pork Chops, and Sweet Potatoes, **9**-1443
Pork Chops, and Sweet Potatoes, Scalloped, **1**-102
Porridge (Omenapuuro), **5**-681
-Prune Dressing, **5**-808
-Prune Pudding, Steamed, **8**-1247
-Prune-Raisin Stuffing, **1**-100
Raisin, and Nut Relish, **10**-1535
-Raisin-Nut Tarts, **11**-1812
and Red Cabbage, Spicy, **1**-100
Relish, **10**-1541
Salad, Jellied Waldorf, **1**-100
Salad, Party, **1**-100
Sandwiches, **1**-102
Sausage-Apple Bake, **11**-1796
and Sausages en Brochette, **10**-1639
Sautéed, **2**-247; **11**-1796
Slice, **2**-278
Slices, Pickled, **9**-1376
Slices, Savory, **6**-913
Slump, **8**-1228
-Smothered Pork Chops, **1**-97
Snacks, **1**-97
Soup (Äppelsoppa), **11**-1787
Soup (Iablochnii Sup), **10**-1568
-Sour-Cream Sauce, **1**-96
Sour-Cream Torte, **12**-1933
and Squash Jam, **11**-1762
Stewed, **7**-1152
on a Stick, Halloween, **1**-102
Strudel, **1**-101; **11**-1780
Strudel (Almásrétes), **6**-921

Apple(s), continued
-Stuffed Acorn Squash, **11**-1762
-Stuffed Crown Roast of Pork, **9**-1442
Stuffing, Savory, **1**-97; **11**-1749
Sweet-Potato Crisp, **11**-1798
and Sweet Potatoes, Scalloped, **11**-1797
Tapioca, Baked, **1**-60, 102; **8**-1228
Tart, **5**-763
Tart (Apfeltorte), **11**-1806
Tart, French, **11**-1812
-Tomato Appetizer, Hot, **11**-1832
and Tomato Relish, Spicy, **10**-1542
-Tuna Salad, **12**-1867
Turnovers, Old-Fashioned, **8**-1247
-Walnut Griddle Cakes, **5**-826
with Wine, Baked, **1**-102
with Zwieback in the Oven (Appelschoteltje), **4**-593

Apple(s), Dried
Cake, **4**-578
and Dumplings (Schnitz un Gnepp, **1**-66, 103
and Raised Dumplings (Schnitz und Gnepp), **9**-1351
Fruit Pies (turnovers), **4**-578

Applesauce
Aplets, **1**-76
Applecake (Aeblekage), **4**-543
Apple Crème, **4**-633
Applesauce 1 (Chunky), **1**-97
Applesauce 2 (Smooth), **1**-97
Cake, American, **2**-268
Filling, **11**-1792
Frenchies, **1**-102
Jellied, **5**-789
Magic Cream (Trollkrem), **8**-1241
Peanut-Butter Apple Cake, **8**-1328
Pie, Spread Apple, **1**-75
Pork, Applesauce, and Kraut Casserole, **1**-63
Rhubarb Tangy Fresh, **10**-1544
Spongecake, **11**-1756
Swedish Applecake, **10**-1666

Apricot(s), **1**-106
and Banana Cup, **1**-107
Barbecue Sauce, **1**-147
Broiled, **1**-107
Cake
Coconut, **2**-269
Refrigerator, **1**-109
Upside-Down, **1**-108
-Cheese Salad, **1**-106
Cherry Sauce, **6**-930
Cream, **1**-108
Crescents, **1**-109
Crumb Pie, **1**-107
with Curried Pork Chops, **1**-107
Delight, **1**-108
Dessert, Jellied, **1**-109
Dessert, The Simplest, **1**-108
Frappé, **6**-926
Glaze, **1**-109; **2**-265; **5**-746,762,783; **9**-1382
-Honey Toast, **11**-1825
Ice, **6**-925
Ice Cream, Fresh Apricot Ripple, **1**-106
Ice-Cream Pie, **6**-934
-Jam Tarts, **11**-1812
with Kirsch, **1**-108
Mousse, **1**-74
Mousse, Frozen, **1**-108
Muffins, **2**-237
-Pecan Sticks, **8**-1335
Pickled, **9**-1376
-Pineapple Jam, **1**-109
-Prune Pie, **1**-108
-Prune Upside-Down Cake, **12**-1881
Rice Pudding, **1**-108
Salad, Stuffed, **1**-108
Sauce, **1**-109
Soufflé, **1**-108
Stewed, **1**-107
Strudel, **1**-108
Tarts, **7**-1089
Tarts, Cream-Cheese, **1**-106
Torte, **12**-1854

Apricot(s), Dried
Candy Roll, **8**-1328
-Cheese Sandwich Filling, **10**-1611
-Coconut Balls, **4**-578
-Date Bars, **4**-547
Filling (for Kolácky), **4**-532
-Nut Sandwiches, **10**-1611
Pineapple-Apricot Upside-Down Cake, **9**-1409
-Pineapple Jam, **6**-963
-Pineapple Pies, **9**-1396
Preserves, **9**-1481
and Prunes, Spiced, **4**-578
-Rice Custard, **9**-578
Stuffing, **4**-584
Stuffing, with Pork Chops, **4**-576
Tomato-Apricot Jam, **4**-964
Whip, Baked, **7**-1087
Arab Cheese, **8**-1213
Arab Dates, **3**-449
Arab Shish Kebab, **8**-1214
Arbutus Hermits, **4**-656
Argentina Broiled Beef (Carne Asada), **11**-1705
Argentina Meat and Vegetable Stew (Puchero), **11**-1706
Argentina Stew (Estafado I and II), **11**-1705
Arizona Pecan and Date Pie, **1**-24
Arizona Sweet Potatoes, **1**-24
Arizona's Biscuits, **11**-1732
Armenian Lamb Stew, **7**-1035
Arnaud's Ananas Flambée, **4**-513
Arnaud's Breast of Chicken en Papillote, **4**-512
Arnaud's Oysters Bienville, **4**-510
Aroostook County Potato Soup, **1**-44
Arrosto di Agnello (Roast Lamb), **6**-954
Arrosto di Vitello (Veal Roast), **12**-1889

Arrowroot, **1**-110
Blancmange, **1**-110
Flour, **5**-707
Arroz con Coco y Pasas (Rice with Coconut and Raisins), **11**-1709
Arroz con Leche (Creamed Rice), **9**-1497
Arroz Mexicano (Mexican Rice), **7**-1141
Arroz con Pollo (Rice with Chicken), **9**-1496
Ärter och Fläsk (Yellow Pea Soup), **11**-1787

Artichoke(s), **1**-110
Chicken, Sherried, **12**-1930
Fritters, **12**-1930
with Garlic Mayonnaise, Chilled, **12**-1931
German Gourmet Mixed Salad, **10**-1586
Green Heaven in a Pot, **8**-1266
Halves, **1**-112
Halves, Greek Style, **1**-112
Hearts with Foie Gras, **5**-708
Hearts au Gratin, **1**-112
Hearts, Marinated, **4**-643
Hearts Piquant, **1**-112
Hearts Salad, **1**-112
Lamb Chops with, **10**-1560
Macaroni, and Lobster Salad, **7**-1092
Omelet, **1**-112
Omelet Hollandaise, **4**-610
with Roman Pork Chops, **1**-112
Sardine-Stuffed (Alcachofas Rellenos con Sardinas), **11**-1741
and Shrimp Appetizer, **10**-1658
and Shrimp Salad, **1**-112
To Cook, Two Simple Ways, **1**-112
Artichoke Jerusalem, see Jerusalem Artichoke
Aruba Cucumber Lamb, **2**-301
Asier (Pickled Cucumbers), **4**-538
Asparagi all' Uovo, **1**-113

Asparagus, **1**-112; **12**-1900
Asparagi all' Uovo, **1**-113
Baked with Bread Crumbs and Cream (Sparzha Zapechennaya s Sukharyami i Slivkami), **10**-1572
Beef-Asparagus Moussaka, **8**-1187
and Carrots, **2**-306
Cheese-Broiled, **1**-113
French-Fried, **1**-57
Ham Rolls, **1**-113
-Ham Rolls with Macaroni and Cheese, **6**-858
with Herb Butter, **1**-115
with Lettuce Sauce, **7**-1063
and Mushrooms in Cream, **1**-113
Sauces for, **1**-114
Scalloped, **1**-114
Sesame Salad, **1**-15
Soufflé, **1**-115; **2**-324
Soup (Aspargessuppe), **4**-538
Aspargessuppe (Asparagus Soup), **4**-538

Aspic
Basic, **1**-115; **5**-787
Chaud-Froid Sauce, **10**-1620
Chicken, **1**-116
Chopped (Sky), **4**-538
Fish, **1**-116
Gelatin Mayonnaise, **7**-1116
Glaze for Sandwiches, **6**-980
Molds, To Decorate and Fill, **1**-116
Quick, **1**-116
Tomato, **1**-119; **5**-787
To Garnish with, **1**-117; **5**-780
To Glaze Food with, **1**-117
To Prepare, **5**-766
To Serve in the Mold, **1**-117
To Unmold, **1**-117

Aspic Dishes
Beef in Aspic, **5**-787
Chicken Loaves, **3**-390
Chicken Mold, Jellied, **6**-979
Cranberry-Turkey Loaf, Jellied, **3**-490
Curried Lamb Mold, **7**-1084
Eel, Jellied (Aal i Gelé), **4**-539
Desserts, see Jellied Desserts
Eggs in Aspic, **4**-603
Eggs in Aspic à la Française, **1**-117
Fish, Jellied, **6**-989
Fresh-Pear and Cucumber Aspic, **8**-1330
Galantine of Chicken, **5**-766
Galantine of Eel, **5**-766
Galantine of Pork, **5**-766
Galantine of Veal, **5**-715, 766
Glazed Cold Ham, **6**-853
Ham and Eggs in Aspic, **6**-861
Herb Veal Loaf, Jellied, **12**-1895
Lamb, Jellied (Yang Jo Kao), **3**-400
Masked Liver Mold, **10**-1635
Meat Loaf, Jellied, **6**-979
Oysters in Aspic, **10**-1665
Pâté in Aspic, **8**-1312
Pâté de Foie Gras in Aspic, **5**-708
Salads, see Salads, Jellied Salads
Salmon Mayonnaise, **12**-1928
Salmon Trout in Aspic, **10**-1665
Sandwiches en Gelée, **5**-787
Soups, see Soups, Chilled, Frosted, and Jellied
Suprêmes of Chicken Jeannette, **3**-349
Tongue Ring, Jellied, **1**-117
Tongue in White-Wine Aspic, **11**-1839
Trout in Jelly, Cold, **5**-698
Turkey Loaf, Layered, **12**-1875
Turkey, Pressed, **12**-1872
Veal in Aspic, **12**-1895
Veal, Jellied, **9**-1352
Veal Loaf, Jellied, **10**-1665
Veal Loaves, Jellied, Individual, **12**-1896
Veal Slices, Jellied, **12**-1889
Vegetables in Aspic, **1**-119
Asturian Bean Casserole (Fabada a la Asturiana), **11**-1744
Athae Chin Gyaw (Deviled Liver), **11**-1717
Aurore Sauce, **2**-173; **10**-1613, 1620
Austrian Cookery, **1**-120
Austrian Crescents, **4**-630
Austrian Ham and Noodle Dish, **8**-1233
Austrian Piquant Pork with Horseradish, **9**-1451

Aveiro Mussels (Mexilhões de Aveiro), **9**-1455
Avga Gemista (Stuffed Eggs), **4**-639
Avgolemono Sauce (Egg-Lemon Sauce), **5**-819
Avgolemono Soupa (Egg-Lemon Soup), **5**-818
Avkokt Torsk (Boiled Cod), **8**-1236

Avocado(s), 1-128
Chicken-Avocado Tostada, **12**-1930
Chicken Salad, **1**-130
-Chicken Soup, **11**-1690
-Citrus Dessert, **1**-130
and Corn Salad (Ensalada de Aguacate y Maíz), **7**-1142
Crabmeat Salad à la Ritz, **1**-130
Crabmeat-Stuffed, **1**-130
Cream, **1**-130
with Creamed Shrimps, **10**-1658
Cream, Frozen, **1**-59
Dip, **1**-130
Dressing, **10**-1588
Drink, Iced (Es Advokat), **11**-1714
Frankfurter-Avocado Dip, **5**-718
and Fresh Pineapple Salad, **9**-1408
Gelatin, Salad, **1**-130
-Grapefruit Dessert, **5**-814
Guacamole, **1**-130
Halves with Spiced Shrimps, **10**-1581
and Ham with Cauliflower Salad (Ensalada de Coliflor con Aguacate), **7**-1142
Hors-d'Oeuvre, **6**-913
Ice Cream, **1**-24
Lime Pie, **1**-130
Lobster-Avocado Sandwiches, **7**-1081
-Melon Salad, **6**-911
Olive-Avocado Appetizer, **8**-1256
Paste (Guacamole), **7**-1138
Pineapple-Avocado Spread, **9**-1403
Ring with Strawberries, **11**-1776
Romaine-Tomato Salad, **4**-566
Salad, **12**-1931
Salad (Ensalada de Aguacate), **11**-1709
Salad with Yogurt Dressing, **12**-1958
Sandwiches, **4**-635
Shrimp Boats, Puerto Rican, **1**-130
Soup, **11**-1727
Soup, Chilled, **1**-130
Soup (Sopa de Aguacate), **7**-1138
Stuffed with Veal, **12**-1896
Tomato-Avocado Hors-d'Oeuvre, **6**-913
Tomato-Avocado Salad, **10**-1586
-Tomato Cocktail, **3**-455
-Tomato Salad, **2**-300
and Tuna Salad, Molded, **5**-787
Vegetable-Avocado Salad with Paprika Dressing, **10**-1586
Whipped (Aguacates Batidos), **11**-1709
Awayuki-kan (Snow Gelatin), **6**-978

B

Baba, 1-131
Baba au Rhum (Rum Cake), **1**-131; **5**-748
Baba au Rhum, Quick, **1**-132
Babi Ketjap (Braised Pork in Soy Sauce), **11**-1714
Babka, Easter (Wielkanocna Babka), **9**-1431
Babka, Polish, **7**-1156
Babki Śmietankowe (Cream Tarts), **9**-1431
Bacalao Veracruzano (Codfish in Spicy Tomato Sauce), **7**-1140
Bacalao a la Vizcaina (Basque Salt-Cod Casserole), **11**-1743

Bacon, 1-132
Bacony Beans, **1**-132
Batter Bread, **2**-231
and Bean Casserole, **7**-1066
Bean, and Onion Chowder, **11**-1691
and Beef Succotash, **1**-133
Biscuits, **1**-134
-Buttermilk Waffles, **2**-238
-Cheese Toast, **11**-1825
Chutney and Bacon Fingers, Hot, **1**-86
-Corn Fritters, **8**-1224
Cured, **4**-523
Dip, **11**-1697
Bacon (and) Egg(s)
and Corn Cakes, **1**-134
with Noodles, **8**-1233
Pie, **4**-626
Skillet, **1**-133
with Fresh Mustard Greens, **8**-1204
Fried Apples with, **1**-45
and Green-Bean Salad, **4**-565
Island Toast with, **11**-1826
and Liver Sandwiches, **7**-1076
Muffins, **2**-237
with Mushrooms, Broiled, **8**-1200
Nutburgers, **6**-869
and Olive Rolls, **7**-1089
and Peanut Butter Sandwich, **1**-134
Peanut-Butter Spread, **8**-1324
Peanut Sandwiches, **8**-1325
and Potato Pudding (Peruna ja Pekoni Laatikko), **5**-681
Potato Salad, Hot, with, **1**-134
Relish, Sweet-and-Sour, **2**-191
Rolls, **2**-281
Sauce with Peas, **1**-134
Slaw (Spekkie Sla), **4**-592
with Succotash, **3**-484
-Topped Macaroni and Cheese, **7**-1093
and Veal Terrine, **12**-1894
Waffles, **12**-1914

Bacon, Canadian
Baked, with Port-Wine Sauce, **7**-1151
with Currant Jelly (Hamburgryg med Ribsgelé), **4**-540
-Kraut-Potato Skillet, **1**-133
and Veal Terrine, **12**-1894
Backhendl (Fried Chicken), **1**-122
Badun (curry), **4**-527
Bagels, **1**-134
Bagna Cauda, Piedmontese (Hot Bath), **10**-1627
Bahamian Tomato Canapés, **1**-86
Bahia Style Shrimps (Camarões a Bahia), **11**-1704
Baked Alaska, **1**-136
Baked Alaska, Grapefruit, **5**-814
Baked Products, To Freeze, **5**-737
Baking Powder, To Measure, **7**-1117
Baklava (Filled Pastry), **5**-823; **8**-1216
Balachong, Fresh Tomato (Pazundok Ngapi Gyaw), **11**-1716
Balinese Spiced Eggs (Telur Masak Bali), **11**-1714
Balkan Stuffed Eggplant, **4**-616
Balm, **1**-137

Bamboo Shoot(s), 1-138
Pork with (Tung Sun Ch'ao Jo), **3**-399
Salad, Chinese, **10**-1583
Sautéed, **1**-138

Banana(s), 1-138
and Apricot Cup, **1**-107
Baked, in Fresh Orange Juice, **1**-139
Baked (Maia Kalua), **9**-1435
Black-and-White Marshmallow Delight, **7**-1114
Butternut-Banana Bread, **8**-1225
and Cantaloupe Salad, **1**-142
Chiffon Pie, **9**-1397
Christmas Tarts, **11**-1812
Coffee-Banana Bavarian, **6**-980
in Cream, **5**-758
Cream Pie, **1**-139
in Currant Jelly, Baked **1**-139
Curry, **4**-527
-Filled Orange Layer Cake, **1**-142
Foster, Brennan's, **4**-513
Fried, **1**-35
Fritters, **1**-139
Fritters (Empanados de Plátanos), **11**-1708
Frosted, **7**-1160
Fruits and Roots, Sweet (Ginatan), **9**-1370
-Ham Rolls, Glazed, **6**-856
and Ham, Spiced, **6**-853
Heavenly (Maduros en Gloria), **11**-1709
with Honey, Baked, **1**-139
Ice Cream, **6**-929
-Mace Whipped Topping, **7**-1100
Meringue Pie, **9**-1392
Meringue Pudding, **1**-142
-Nut Bread, **1**-139
Nut Pie, Creamy, **5**-801
Orange, and Walnut Salad, **10**-1588
Paste with Cheese (Bananada con Queijo), **11**-1709
Peanut Salad, **8**-1323
Pie, **9**-1393
Plantain(s), **9**-1414
Baked, **9**-1414
Balls Soup, **9**-1414
Chips, **9**-1414
Curry, **4**-527
with Pork Cracklings, **9**-1414
Turnovers, Jamaican, **9**-1414
Pudding (Pudim de Bananas), **9**-1457
au Rhum, **5**-701
in Rum Custard Sauce, **2**-304
Shake, Slim, **7**-1088
-Shrimp Curry, **1**-139
Soufflé, **7**-1098
Split, **6**-934
Split Salad, **5**-755
Stoba, **2**-301
Toast, **11**-1825
Bananada con Queijo (Banana Paste with Cheese), **11**-1709
Banbury Tarts, **1**-142
Banbury Tarts, Rich, **8**-1308
Bannocks, Drop, **1**-142
Bannock, Trapper's Sweet, **1**-62
Bárány Pörkölt Árpakásával (Lamb and Barley Stew), **6**-918
Barbados Barbecue Sauce, **10**-1623
Barbecue Menus, **1**-144; **4**-644, 645

Barbecue Sauce(s), 1-146; **10**-1614, 1623
Apricot, **1**-147
Barbados, **10**-1623
Chili, **5**-725
Curry, **10**-1623
Fresh-Lemon, **7**-1053
Greek, **1**-146
Herb, **10**-1623
Honey, **10**-1623
Hot, Deep South, **10**-1623
Lemon, Savory, **1**-146
Molasses, **8**-1184
Orange, **1**-146
Pineapple-Chili, **10**-1623
Piquant, **5**-726
Red-Hot, **10**-1623
Relish, Chuck's, **10**-1543
Sherry, **10**-1624
(for Shrimps), **3**-403
Smoky, **10**-1624
Soppin' Sauce, **11**-1731
Texas Hot, **1**-146
Wine, **5**-726
Bareh Pello, **8**-1215

Barley, 1-147
Casserole, **1**-147
and Chicken Livers, **3**-391
Flour, **5**-707
and Lamb Soup, **11**-1695
Mushroom-Barley Casserole, **8**-1200
Mushroom Barley Soup, **6**-987
-Onion Soup with Beef Balls, **7**-1122
Pudding, Finnish, **1**-62
Soup (Gerstensuppe), **1**-121
Soup (Krupnik), **9**-1421
Water, **1**-147
Barmbrack, **6**-949
Barquettes, **2**-280

Barquettes, Clam, **2**-280
Barszcz Czysty (Clear Beet Soup), **9**-1420
Barszcz Zimmy (Cold Borsch with Beet Greens), **9**-1421

Basil, 1-148
Dressing, **9**-1384
and Grape Jelly, **6**-983
with Green Noodles, **8**-1233
Pesto Genovese, **1**-148
Sweet Basil Sauce, **10**-1626
Basler Lachs (Sautéed Salmon), **11**-1800
Basque Barbecue, **11**-1728
Basque Barbecued Lamb, **12**-1930
Basque Fish Soup (Sopa de Pescado a la Vasca), **11**-1743
Basque Fresh-Tuna Stew (Marmitako), **11**-1743
Basque Green Beans (Judías Verdes a la Vasca), **11**-1744
Basque Salt-Cod Casserole (Bacalao a la Vizcaina), **11**-1743
Basque Scrambled Eggs (Pipérade), **4**-608

Bass, 1-148
Baked Fish (Merluza Asado al Horno), **11**-1744
Poached Whole, **1**-149
Sea Bass, Sweet-and-Sour (Escabetseng Apahap), **9**-1368
Stuffed Baked, **1**-148
Batayaki (Butter-Cooked Meat), **6**-974

Batter(s)
Beer, **11**-1804
Beer, French, **1**-149
(for Brain Batter Cakes), **2**-217
Cake, **2**-209
Cake, One-Egg, **2**-268
Caraway Dumpling, **9**-1351
for Carolina Fruitcake, **1**-61
(for Chicken on the Wing), **3**-384
Dumpling, **3**-481; **4**-586, 587; **5**-716; **9**-1355
Dumpling, Cornmeal, **4**-586; **5**-748
Dumpling, Dessert, **4**-532, 587; **5**-808
Dumpling, Savory, **12**-1871
Fritter, Basic, **5**-748
(for Honan pork), **3**-400
Spongecake, Corn-Syrup, **9**-1486
for Tempura, **6**-972
Bavarian Cabbage (Bayerisches Kraut), **5**-796

Bavarian, Bavarian Cream, 1-150
Almond, **1**-15
Bavarois au Citron, **7**-1054
Cherry, **3**-374
Chocolate Bavarian Filling, **4**-663
Coffee-Banana, **6**-980
Lemon, **1**-150
Peach, **1**-32
Pineapple, **4**-650
Pistachio, with Strawberries, **3**-440
Strawberry, **4**-556
Strawberry-Honey, **6**-909
Vanilla, **6**-980
Bavarois au Citron, **7**-1054
Bavaroise Frutillas (Strawberry Snow), **11**-1709
Bayerisches Kraut (Bavarian Cabbage), **5**-796
Bay Leaf, **1**-150
Bay Leaves, How to Use, **1**-150

Beach Plum, 1-150
Beach Plum Jam, **1**-150

Bean(s), Fresh, 1-152
Butter Beans with Pecans, **1**-69
Cranberry-Bean Succotash, **1**-159
au Gratin, **1**-157
-and-Ham Bake, **6**-853
Salad, Cheyenne River, **1**-68
Salad, Mixed Bean, **4**-645
Sausage Casserole, **10**-1635
Succotash, Three-Bean, **1**-154
Succotash, Two-Bean, with Pork Cubes, **1**-38
Beans, Green or Wax, **1**-153
with Almonds, **3**-444
and Bacon Salad, **4**-565
Basque (Judías Verdes a la Vasca), **11**-1744
Cape Cod Style, **7**-1086
and Carrot Salad, **7**-1085
Cashew, and Mushroom Casserole, **8**-1200
and Chicken Livers, Sautéed, **7**-1075
Dilled, **4**-564
Dilly Pickles, **9**-1373
French Shallot-Beans, **10**-1650
German, Hot, **10**-1668
Hamburger, and Macaroni Casserole, **7**-1094
Hari Dal, **6**-942
with Horseradish Sauce, **6**-914
Italian, Salad, **10**-1668
Lima-Bean Casserole, Super, **7**-1066
Maillane Style (Haricots Verts Maillanoise), **12**-1903
and Mushrooms, **1**-154
and Onion Salad, **1**-157
Oriental, **10**-1668
with Pimiento and Pickle Relish, **10**-1668
Potatoes, and Onions, Skillet, **9**-1468
and Potato Salad (Insalata di Fagiolini e Patate), **6**-960
Salad, **4**-650
Salad with Potatoes, Hot (Salade Liègeoise), **2**-200
Salted, Old-Fashioned, **4**-524
Soufflé, **12**-1906
Sour, **9**-1354
in Sour-Cream Sauce, **10**-1668
Southern Style, **11**-1723
Stewed (Vrasta Fasolakia Freska), **5**-822
and Tomatoes, Glazed, **11**-1834
Tomatoes, and Squash, Savory, **11**-1832
with Tomatoes, Stewed, **1**-154
Tuna, Casserole, **12**-1864
Tuna, and Potato Salad, Genoa Style, **12**-1867
Whole, **11**-1823
and Whole Onions, **10**-1668
Beans, Lima or Fava, **1**-153
Barbecued, **8**-1184
with Cheese, **7**-1065
Chili Limas, **7**-1065
Curried, Salad, **7**-1065
with Easy White Sauce, **7**-1065
and Egg Salad, **7**-1065
Fordhook Limas and Leeks, **7**-1047
Green Lima Beans, **4**-648
Green, Salad, **7**-1065
and Lamb, Curried, **7**-1039
in Lemon Sauce, **7**-1065
Lerida (Judías Blancas a la Leridana), **11**-1744
Minted, **7**-1065
Salad, **1**-146
Succotash, **11**-1783
Succotash, Creamy, **7**-1065
Succotash, Picnic, **7**-1065

Bean(s), Dried, 1-153
Blackeye, Southern Style, **1**-159
Brown, Swedish, **10**-1666
Congo-Pea (pigeon peas) Soup, Jamaican, **6**-966
Creole Blackeye Peas, **4**-512
Hoppin', Hopping John, **1**-22; **11**-1723
Jungle Stew, **1**-79
Lamb and Fava Beans, Stewed (Vrasto Arni me Fava), **5**-819
Picnic Bean Sandwiches, **10**-1605
Pongal (mung beans), **6**-942
Rancho Salad, **10**-1583
Salads, **11**-1727
Salad, White and Red, **1**-159
Tomato-Cheese Soybeans, **1**-158
Beans, Dried, Black, **1**-153
Chiller (soup), **11**-1692
Mashed (Frijoles Negros Batidos), **11**-1708
and Rice, **1**-158
Sauce, Fruited, **10**-1554
Soup, **4**-645
Soup, Savory, **11**-1691
Stew (Feijoada), **11**-1704
Beans, Dried, Kidney or Red, **1**-153
and Beef Balls, **7**-1123
Cakes (Yokan), **6**-978
Chili con Carne (QC), **10**-1520
Hot Bean Pot, **1**-59
Italian Sausages with (Salsiccie e Fagioli), **6**-955
and Lamb Stew, **7**-1038
Macaroni. and Egg Salad, **7**-1095
and Rice, **1**-44
Salad, **1**-159
and Sauerkraut Salad, Hot, **10**-1632
Soup, Jamaican, **6**-966
Soup, Portuguese, **1**-158
Beans, Dried, Lima, **1**-153
and Bacon Casserole, **7**-1066
with Breast of Lamb, **1**-158
Casserole, French, **7**-1066
Casserole, Super, **7**-1066
and Chicken Casserole, Savory, **7**-1066
and Codfish Chowder, **7**-1065
Country-Style, **7**-1066
Creole Style, **1**-158
Flour, **5**-707
and Frankfurter Casserole, **5**-721
and Frankfurters, Barbecued, **7**-1066
and Ham Casserole, Individual, **7**-1066
Ham Soup, **6**-852
and Lamb-Bone Soup, **7**-1065
and Liver Creole, **7**-1073
-and-Pear Casserole, Baked, **1**-76
and Pork, **7**-1066
Soup with Sausage Balls, **7**-1122
Beans, Dried, Marrow or Navy, **1**-153
Bacony Beans, **1**-132
Baked, Southern Style, **1**-158
Beef, Brisket of, **6**-990
and Ham Soup with Vegetables (Garbure Basque), **5**-739
Salt Pork, Beans, and Hominy, **6**-907
Soup, Dutch, **11**-1839
Stewed, with Savory, **10**-1640
Beans, Dried, Pea or Great Northern, **1**-153
Bacon, and Onion Chowder, **11**-1691
Baked, **9**-1378
Baked (QC), **10**-1524
Baked-Bean and Peanut Sandwiches, **8**-1322
Baked, Boston, **1**-47
Baked, Michigan, **1**-48; **7**-1152
Baked, New England, **1**-159
Barbecued Baked, Quick, **8**-1184
Boiled, Chuck-Wagon, **1**-53
Boiled White Beans, **8**-1224
Breton, **1**-159
Casserole, Savory, **2**-320
Cassoulet, **2**-325
Pineapple Baked, **9**-1407
and Salt-Pork Chowder, **10**-1598
Beans, Dried, Pinto, **1**-153
Beans, Mashed Beans, and Beans Refried (Frijoles, Frijolitos, y Frijoles Refritos), **11**-1731
and Cheese Appetizers (Totopos), **7**-1138
Cowpuncher's Bean Stew, **1**-24
Crisp Fried (Frijoles Refritos), **7**-1141
Fried, **12**-1931
Fried (Frijoles Fritos), **7**-1141
Frijoles Refritos, **11**-1730
and Macaroni, Thick Soup of (Minestrone di Pasta e Fagiuoli), **6**-952
Mexican Beans (Frijoles), **7**-1141
Mexican Refried, **1**-59
Ranch-House, **1**-73
Salad, **1**-79
with Spareribs, Sooner-State, **1**-64
Stew, Western, **1**-158
Beans, Dried, White, **1**-153
Bean Paste, Fermented (Miso), **6**-970

Bean Paste Soup (Miso Shiru), **6**-971
Brandade de Thon, **12**-1864
Casserole, Asturian (Fabada a la Asturiana), **11**-1744
and Cheese Salad, **10**-1582
Chutney Baked, **1**-159
with Ham, Baked, **1**-158
Lamb and Bean Ragout, **7**-1036
Lamb Haricot, **7**-1029
Salad, **8**-1213
and Scallions, **8**-1266
Soup, Different, **1**-54
Soup, Near-East, **11**-1690
Soup, Senate, **1**-157
in Sour Cream (Tejfeles Baffözelék), **6**-919
and Tuna Salad (Cannelini al Tonno), **6**-960

Bean Sprouts, **1**-159; **7**-1022
Sautéed, **1**-159
Bear Chops, Breaded, **5**-768

Béarnaise, Béarnaise Sauce, **2**-173; **10**-1614
5-741; **6**-905; **7**-1029; **10**-1621; **11**-1766
Quick, **7**-1074; **12**-1897
Tomate, **10**-1621
True, **2**-173
Beaten Biscuits, **2**-173
Beaver, Roast Haunch of, Hotel Lexington, **5**-769

Béchamel, Béchamel Sauce, **2**-173; **10**-1613
8-1190; **10**-1618
Variations of, **2**-173

Beef, **2**-177
in Aspic, **5**-787
and Bacon Succotash, **1**-133
Bean-Pot Roast, **1**-69
Beer Marinade for, **7**-1110
Birds in Wine, **2**-183
Birmingham, **8**-1324
Boeuf à la Mode, **1**-8
Boeuf Bourguignon, **2**-253
Boiled Spanish (Cocido), **11**-1742
Bouillon, **2**-215
Bouillon or Stock (Brown Stock), **11**-1774
Braised (Stufato), **11**-1802
Braised (Sztufada), **9**-1424
Brisket of, **6**-990
Brisket of, in Horseradish Sauce, **2**-189
Brisket with Mushroom Gravy, **9**-1473
Broiled (Carne Asada), **11**-1705
Broiled (Jyuniku-Teriyaki), **6**-974
Broiled in Sauce (Jang Po), **7**-1020
Broth, **7**-1146
Brussels Sprouts and Beef Kabobs, **2**-248
Butter-Cooked Meat (Batayaki), **6**-974
Canapés, Danish, **1**-86
with Carrots and Egg Dumplings, Boiled, **4**-625
Carving, **2**-310, 311
Casserole, **2**-189
Casserole with Almonds, **6**-873
Casseroles, **2**-316
Cheese, and Noodle Casserole, Crusty, **2**-316
Chile con Carne Verde, **11**-1728
Corn and Meat All-in-One, **3**-482
Cured (Tapang Baka), **9**-1369
Curried, **2**-191
Curry, **4**-525, 527
Daube of, Béarnaise, **2**-187
Daube, Provence Style (Daube de Boeuf, Provençale), **4**-548; **12**-1947
Eye Round, Stuffed (Lechón de Mechar), **9**-1494
Filet Mignon with Mushrooms (Filety z Poledwicy), **9**-1424
Flank Steak
Chinese-Beef Casserole, **11**-1734
Deviled, **2**-183
Hodgepodge with Boiled Meat (Hutspot met Klapstuk), **4**-592
London Broil, **2**-183; **11**-1768
Orientale, Gingered, **5**-801
Pressed, **2**-183
with Rice, Fried (Bife Sauté a la Minuta con Arroz), **11**-1705
Rolled Stuffed, **2**-184
Roll-Ups, **4**-566
Stuffed, **4**-645
Teriyaki, **9**-1382
Teriyaki Barbecue, **2**-183
with Vegetables, Pot-Roasted, **9**-1473
Fruited Spiced, **4**-576
Ginger Beef, Burmese, **10**-1646
Ginger Beef Soup with Noodles (Pho), **11**-1717
Goulash, **5**-809
Hungarian, **2**-187
Hungarian (Magyar Gulyás), **6**-918
Meat and Potato, **5**-809
Oven, **2**-298
with Green Beans (Ssu Chi Tou Niu Ju), **3**-399
-and-Green-Pepper Oven Stew, **9**-1359
with Green Peppers (Niu Ju Chin Jow), **3**-403
Ground Beef, see Hamburger; Hash; Meatball; Meat Loaf
alla Italiana, **5**-775
Jerked, **1**-24
Jewish Sabbath Meal-in-One (Cholent), **6**-990
Leftover-Beef Casserole, **2**-324
Lemon Pie-Pan Steak, **6**-868
Lindström (Biff à la Lindström), **11**-1788
à la Lindstrom (Lindströmin Pihvi), **5**-680
Loaf, Loaves, see Meat Loaf
London Broil, see Flank Steak
Low-Calorie Seasonings for, **7**-1084
with Macaroni, Red-Wine, **7**-1094
Meat Cooked in Fermented Beef Juice (Rusell Fleisch in Borscht), **6**-994
Meat Pies, Individual, **9**-1387
Meat-Stuffed Cabbage (Holishkes), **6**-995
Meat and Vegetables, Main-Dish (Festive Tzimmes), **6**-990
Mounds with Noodles, **9**-1351
with Mushrooms, Chinese, **2**-189; **8**-1200
and Noodle Platter, **6**-872
and Noodles with Sour Cream and Paprika, **2**-191
-Okra Soup, **11**-1721
-and-Okra Stew, **8**-1255
and Onion Pie, **8**-1260
Oven Beef Stogonoff, **2**-183
Patties, see Hamburger; Meatball
Paupiettes, **8**-1313
Pelmeni Filling (Farsh Dlia Sibirskikh Pelmenei), **10**-1571
Picadillo, **1**-72
Pickled, Hot, **1**-52
-Pie Pastry, **8**-1261
Pie, Shepherd's, **2**-189
Pies, Spanish, **9**-1387
Plough-Roasted (Sukiyaki), **6**-974
Poitou (Boeuf du Poitou), **2**-276
Porcupines with Vegetable-Cheese Sauce, **7**-1123
Pot Roast, Pot Roasted, **9**-1472
2-184; **6**-990
with Apple Cider, **1**-77
Barbecued, **2**-186
Burgundy, **2**-186
-Chili-Sauce, **9**-1473
Coffee, with Vegetables, **9**-1473
with Dumplings (Sauerbraten mit Spätzle), **5**-793
à la Eszterhazy, **9**-1473
Fontaine, **9**-1473
Ginger, **5**-801; **9**-1473
Juniper, in Burgundy, **6**-996
Larded Herb, **7**-1041
à la Mode, **2**-186
à la Mode, Braised, **2**-220
Oven, **2**-186
Peppery, **9**-1473
with Red Wine, **10**-1598
Royal (Slottsstek), **11**-1788
Seventeenth-Century, **6**-948
Soy, **11**-1734
Special Russian Sauce for, **10**-1573
Spiced, **9**-1472
with Vegetables, **1**-55
with Vegetables, Skillet, **2**-186
West Indian, **9**-1472
Yankee, **2**-186; **8**-1224
Yankee, Company, **9**-1472
Pressed, **2**-183
Puchero, Mexican, **1**-26
Rama Bathing (Phra Ram Long Song), **11**-1715
Retail Cuts, Chart, **2**-179
Roast Beef
Barbecued, **11**-1722
and Blue-Cheese Sandwiches, **10**-1604
Bøf, **4**-536
Chili con Carne, **9**-1384
Cold, **4**-624
Filet de Boeuf à la Suisse, **11**-1802
Hash, see Hash
Rib Roast of, **3**-444
Rib Roast of, on a Spit, **1**-54; **7**-1150
Roast Beef of England, The, **4**-624
Slices, Deviled, **2**-183
on a Spit, **2**-183
Timetable for Roasting, Chart, **2**-180
Warm (for picnic), **9**-1383
Roulades with Carrots and Lima Beans, **2**-186
Round Steak
Beefsteak Stew and Dumplings, **4**-586
Birds, Different (QC), **10**-1519
Boneless Birds (Benløse Fugle), **4**-540
Deviled, **4**-558
Grillades, **4**-512
-and-Olive Casserole, **8**-1256
Oven-Barbecued (QC), **10**-1519
Panbroiled, **2**-189
Pickled, Hot, **1**-52
Rolls (sandwiches), **10**-1601
Sorrel and Spinach Steaks (Bifes com Azedas), **9**-1456
with Sour-Cream Gravy (Beefsteak na Kyselo), **4**-531
Steak and Kidney Pie, **4**-624
Stewed Meat (Hâché), **4**-590
Teriyaki, **11**-1768
Salad, French, **10**-1580
Salisbury Steak, Charcoal-Broiled, **1**-145
Salisbury Steak with Mushroom Sauce, **6**-868
Sauerbraten, **2**-186; **10**-1629
Overnight, **10**-1630
Quick, **10**-1630
with Sour-Cream Gravy, **10**-1630
with Vegetables, **10**-1630
and Sauerkraut (Kücherlkraut), **1**-121
Shin of, Red-Cooked (Hung Shao Niu Nan), **3**-399
Short Ribs
Braised, Jardinière, **2**-189
Broiled (Kalbi Kui), **7**-1022
with Vegetables, **1**-38
Soup à la Paysanne, **11**-1695
in Sour Cream, **11**-1700
with Soybean Cake (Ton Jun), **7**-1020
Steak(s)
Barbecue, Western, **1**-65
Bordelaise, **5**-741
Chateaubriand, **11**-1766
Dutch (Hollandsche Biefstuk), **1**-60
End-of-the-Month Casserole, **2**-316
Entrecôte Bercy, **11**-1767
Fire Beef (Pul Koki), **7**-1020
Fondue Bourguignonne, **5**-712; **11**-1803
Fry, **11**-1728
Grandmother's, **1**-73
(grilled over charcoal), **8**-1280
Kabobs, **12**-1957
Kabobs, Skillet, **6**-997
Korean, **1**-35

Beef, continued
Loin-Strip, **11**-1766
Meat on Skewers (San Juk), **7**-1022
Minute Steak Casserole, Wheelspoke, **1**-52
Minute Steaks, Deviled, **11**-1768
with Onion (Rozbratle z Cebula), **9**-1422
with Onions, **11**-1767
and Oysters, **1**-72
Pepper Steak, **2**-186
Pepper Steak (Steak au Poivre), **5**-740; **11**-1767
Pepper Steak with Cream, Flamed (Steak au Poivre Flambé à la Crème), **5**-741
Rib Steak, Bordelaise, **11**-1767
Rump Steak, Marinated, **11**-1767
Sauces for, **2**-193-194
Sirloin, Baked, **1**-35
Sirloin, Top, **11**-1767
Sirloin, Whole Thick, for a Large Party, **11**-1766
Skirt Steak, Deviled, **11**-1768
Skirt Steak, Marinated, **11**-1768
Smothered, **1**-27
Spencer Steak, **11**-1767
Swiss, **2**-186
Swiss Cube Steaks, **2**-184
Swiss, Spicy, **1**-11
Tartare, **2**-189; **7**-1150
Tenderloin, with Roquefort Spread, **1**-36
Teriyaki Sticks, **4**-643
Timetable for Broiling, Chart, **2**-181
Tournedos, **12**-1858
Tournedos Béarnaise, **11**-1766
Tournedos Rossini, **11**-1766
with Walnut-Anchovy Sauce, **11**-1746
Stew, **11**-1773
with Marjoram (Marjorannás Tokány), **6**-918
Old Fashioned, **2**-187
Stifado, **4**-639
Stroganoff (Bif Strogonov), **10**-1571
Stuffed Rolled (Morcon), **9**-1369
Table-Boiled (Jyuniku no Mizutaki), **6**-974
Tartlets, Appetizer, **11**-1811
Tenderloin, Filet, Fillet
with a Bouquet of Vegetables (Filet de Boeuf Bouquetière), **5**-740
Broiled Whole, **1**-144
Chateaubriand, Sauce Béarnaise, **5**-741
with Madeira Sauce and Truffles (Poledwica z Madera i Truflami), **9**-1424
Pineapple Teriyaki, **9**-1406
Roasted, **2**-183
Roast (Poledwica Pieczona), **9**-1424
Sandwiches, **10**-1601
with Sherry, **12**-1947
in Sour Cream (Poledwica w Smietanie), **9**-1424
Tartar Sandwiches (Biftecks Tartare), **11**-1802
Turkey and, **1**-72
with Vegetables (Ossenhaas à la Jardinière), **4**-590
Variety Meats, **2**-182
with Vegetables, Boiled, (Pot-au-Feu), **5**-740
and Vegetable Soup, **11**-1694
-Vegetable Soup, Stockyard Inn, **1**-36

Beef, Corned
Baked Barbecued, **3**-429
Baked in Sherry, **2**-193
Baked Spicy, **2**-193
Boiled Dinner, **1**-28
Boiled Dinner, New England Style, **8**-1224
and Cabbage, **3**-485
and Cabbage, Nebraska Style, **1**-54
and Cheese Sandwiches, **10**-1601
Hash, see Hash
and Muenster Sandwiches, **10**-1605
(To corn), **2**-193
Turnovers, Mushroom Sauce, **12**-1879

Beef, Dried
Cheese, and Celery Spread, **2**-279
Cottage Beef and Eggs, **7**-1084
Creamed, on Boiled Potatoes, **2**-193
Creamed, French-Toast Sandwiches with, **10**-1601
Eggs, Stuffed with, **4**-606
Green Noodle, Beef, and Cheese Casserole, **2**-324
with Orange Sauce, **8**-1268
in Sour-Cream Sauce, **11**-1700

Beef Heart(s)
Parsley Hearts of, **2**-191
Patties, Scotch, **6**-883
Savory Stuffed, **6**-883
Stew, **6**-883
with Vegetables, **6**-883

Beef Kidney(s)
and Beef Pie, **9**-1387
and Beef Pudding, **6**-945
and Hamburger Pie, **6**-872
and Mushroom Pie, **7**-1013
Stew, **2**-191

Beef Liver
and Bacon, Broiled, **2**-192
Bernese, Sautéed (Berner Leberli), **11**-1802
French-Fried, **7**-1073
and Limas, Creole, **7**-1073
and Noodles, Italian Style, **7**-1073
and Onions, Smothered, **7**-1073
with Onions, Venetian, **2**-192
Panfried, **2**-192
Potted, Danish Style, **2**-192
Pudding, **1**-49
and Sausage Loaf, **10**-1636
-and-Sausage Ring, Savory, **7**-1073
Sliced, with Spleen Sauce (Iscas), **9**-1456
and Vegetables, Piquant, **7**-1073

Beef Marrow, Beef Bone Marrow, **7**-1112
Balls, **2**-192
Dumplings, **7**-1113
Marrowbone Soup, **7**-1112
Poached, **2**-192
Poached (Moelle Pochée), **5**-741
Roasted, **2**-192
Sauce, **7**-1113
Toast, **7**-1112

Beef Tongue
Boiled, **2**-192; **11**-1838
Braised, **11**-1837
and Cheese Sandwiches with Cashews, **10**-1605
Columbian, **2**-193
Jellied Tongue Ring, **1**-117
Pineapple, and Cheese Spread, **9**-1403
Sandwiches, **9**-1383
with Sweet-and-Sour Sauce, **6**-990
in White-Wine Aspic, **11**-1839

Beef Tripe
Batter-Fried, **12**-1858
Breaded, Crisp, **12**-1859
Creole, **12**-1859
Fried, **1**-56
Honeycomb Tripe, Broiled, with Mustard Sauce, **8**-1224
Lyonnaise, à la Lyonnaise, **2**-193; **12**-1859
à la Mode de Caen, **12**-1858
Soup (Sopa de Mondongo), **11**-1704
Stew (Menudo), **7**-1140
with Vegetables, Stewed, **12**-1859
à la Warsaw (Flaki po Warszawsku), **9**-1424

Beer, **2**-194; see also Ale
Batter, **11**-1804
Batter, French, **1**-149
and Bread Soup (Øllebrød), **4**-539
Glaze, **7**-1151
Marinade for Beef, Game, or Shrimps, **7**-1110
Stew, Flemish (Carbonnade Flamande), **2**-197
Waffles, Brussels (Gaufres Bruxelloise), **2**-200
"Bee's Sting" Coffeecake (Bienenstich), **5**-798

Beet(s), **2**-195
Buttered, **3**-444
Cabbage-Beet Relish, **5**-726
and Cabbage Relish, **10**-1541
and Cucumber Relish, **1**-90
Fresh, in Orange Sauce, **8**-1268
Garnishes, **5**-777
Glazed, **2**-195
and Greens, **2**-195
Harvard, **1**-47
Honeyed, **6**-909
Juice, Fermented, Passover (Pesach Rusell), **6**-994
Juice, Fermented, with Horseradish, Passover (Rusell Chrain), **6**-994
Juice, Fermented, Meat Cooked in (Rusell Fleisch in Borscht), **6**-994
and Onions, Spiced, **8**-1261
Pickled, **8**-1278
Pickled (Nedlagte Rødbeter), **8**-1239
Pickled, Scandinavian, **2**-195
Pickled (Syltede Rødbeder), **4**-542
and Pineapple, Piquant, **9**-1407
Polish, **11**-1700
Red, Pickled Eggs and, **1**-66
Roses (garnish), **10**-1666
Salad with Roquefort Dressing, **4**-570
Soup, Clear (Barszcz Czysty), **9**-1420
Spiced, Buttered, **11**-1754
Spiced Pickled, **9**-1376

Beet Tops or **Greens,** **2**-195
with Cold Borsch (Barszcz Zimmy), **9**-1421
Beignet, **2**-195; for recipes see Fritter(s); Fritter(s), Dessert
Belgian Buttermilk Soup, **11**-1690
Belgian Cookery, **2**-196
Belgian Endive, see Endive
Belgian Mussels Marinière, **8**-1203
Belgian Veal Blanquette, **12**-1895
Bengalese Crab (Keksda Bengali), **6**-942
Benløse Fugle (Boneless Birds), **4**-540
Benne-Seed Cookies, **1**-68
Benne Wafers, **10**-1647
Benson (Mrs.) Receipt for Fudge, **8**-1231
Bercy Butter, **10**-1615, 1624
Bercy Sauce, **10**-1620
Berenjena con Queso (Eggplant with Cheese), **9**-1496
Berks County Potato Filling, **1**-66; **9**-1352
Bermuda Casserole, **8**-1263
Bermudas Glacés, **8**-1264
Bern, The Dish From (Bernerplatte), **11**-1803
Berner Leberli (Sautéed Liver Bernese), **11**-1802
Bernerplatte (The Dish from Bern), **11**-1803

Berry(ies), **2**-200; see also names of berries
Jam, **6**-965
Jelly, **6**-982
Beurre Blanc, **10**-1615, 1624

Beurre Manié, **2**-202, 218; **4**-595; **10**-1615
American, **2**-202
French, **2**-202
Beurres Composés (Composed Butters), see Butters

Beverage(s)
Apple-Cranberry Fizz, **1**-103
Apple-Tomato Appetizer, Hot, **11**-1832
Avocado Drink, Iced (Es Advokat), **11**-1714
Banana Slim Shake, **7**-1088
Barley Water, **1**-147
Buttermilk Shake, **1**-64

Café Frappé, Deep South, **5**-726
Café au Lait, **3**-462
Caffè Espresso, **4**-651
Chocolate, Brazilian, **3**-416
Chocolate, Frosted, **5**-752
Chocolate, Guatemalan, **3**-416
Chocolate, Mexican, **7**-1143
Chocolate, Quick, **3**-417
Christmas Eggnog, **4**-611
Cider, Mulled, **8**-1193
Cider, Mulled, Holiday, **8**-1193
Cider, Spiced, **11**-1754
Clam-Juice Cocktail, Hot, **8**-1282
Cocoa, Hot, **3**-455
Cocoa, Hot (QC), **10**-1526
Cocoa, Iced, **3**-455
Coffee, Campfire, **3**-462
Coffee, Church-Supper Method, **3**-462
Coffee, Frosted, **3**-462
Coffee, Greek, **4**-640
Coffee, Greek (Kafes), **5**-824
Coffee, Hot (instant, QC), **10**-1526
Coffee, Hot (kettle, QC), **10**-1526
Coffee, Iced, **3**-462
Coffee, Imperial, **3**-462
Coffee, Instant, for a Crowd, **3**-462
Coffee Shake, **3**-462
Coffee, Special, **4**-630
Coffee, Turkish, **3**-462
Coffee, Viennese, **4**-630
Coffee, Viennese Iced (Wiener Eiskaffee), **1**-123
Cucumber Tomato Cocktail, **11**-1832
Egg Chocolate, Spanish, **3**-416
Eggnog, **4**-611
Float(s)
  Berry, **7**-1161
  Chocolate, **7**-1161
  Dutch Delight, **7**-1161
  Mint Chocolate, Frosted, **7**-1161
  Polka-Dot Punch, **7**-1161
Flower Teas, **4**-636
Fresh-Lemon Peach Cooler, **7**-1056
Fresh-Lime Froth, **7**-1069
Frosted(s)
  Banana, **7**-1160
  Chocolate, **7**-1160
  Strawberry, **7**-1161
Ginger Buttermilk, **5**-804
Ginger-Fruit Frost, **5**-803
Ginger Tea, **5**-803
Grapefruit-Honey Nog, **1**-24
Grape Juice, Mulled, **8**-1193
Ice-Cream Sodas, **6**-932
  Coffee, **3**-462
  Strawberry, **11**-1779
Island Dream, **9**-1410
Jasmine Tea, **4**-635
Lemonade Syrup, **7**-1057
Lemonade-Tea, Iced, **7**-1057
Lime-Ginger Foam, **7**-1067
Lime Julep, **7**-1069
Milk Shakes, see Milk Shake(s)
Mocha, **3**-462
Mocha Chocolate, **7**-1167
Mocha de Luxe, **3**-462
Mocha de Luxe, Iced, **3**-462
Molasses Cider, Hot, **8**-1185
Orangeade, **8**-1273
Orange-Ginger Fizz, **5**-804
Orange-Milk Starter, **7**-1088
Peach Bowler, **8**-1321
Pomegranate Nectar, **9**-1436
Posset, Molasses, **9**-1457
Punch, **9**-1501
  Apple-Cranberry, **9**-1503
  Cider, Hot, **3**-446
  Concord (QC), **10**-1526
  Cranberry, **3**-490
  Cranberry-Apple (QC), **10**-1527
  Cranberry, Spicy, **3**-428
  Fresh-Lemon-and-Orange Party, **7**-1056
  Fresh Pineapple, **9**-1410
  Fruit, **9**-1503
  Fruit, Fresh Rhubarb, **10**-1545
  Fruit, Picnic, **7**-1057
  Fruit (QC), **10**-1527
  Golden, **9**-1503
  Lemonade-Mint, **5**-804
  Lemon-Apple, **7**-1057
  Party (QC), **10**-1527
  Patriot, **5**-804
  Raspberry Shrub, **1**-75
  Root Beer, **10**-1559
  Sarsaparilla, **10**-1613
  Soda, **10**-1669
  Soda Pop, **10**-1669
  Soda Water, **10**-1669
  Tea for a Crowd, **4**-636
  Tea, English, **4**-635
  Tea, Fennel Seed, **4**-657
  Tea, Hot (QC), **10**-1526
  Tea, Hot Spiced, **11**-1815
  Tea, Iced, **4**-636
  Tea, Lemon Iced, **11**-1816
  Tea, Minted Iced, **11**-1816
  Tomato Cocktail, **6**-999
  Tomato Cocktail, Spiced, **11**-1832
  Tomato Juice Cocktail, **3**-455
  Turkish Strawberry Sherbet Drink, **10**-1654
  Turkish Watermelon Sherbet Drink, **10**-1654
  Vegetable Cocktail, **3**-455
  Wassail Bowl, **12**-1918
  Watermelon-Lime Cooler, **12**-1920
  Yogurt Froth Ayran, **12**-1958

Beverage(s), Alcoholic
  Ale, **1**-10
  Beer, **2**-194; for recipes see Beer
  Brazilian Coconut Sherbet Drink, **10**-1654
  Café Brûlot, **3**-462
  Café Brûlot, New Orleans, **5**-702
  Cherry Bounce, **3**-372
  Claret Lemonade, **7**-1057
  Coffee Dunk, **5**-714
  Coffee, Viking (Vikingekaffe), **4**-543
  Daiquiri, **10**-1563
    Frozen, **10**-1563
    on-the-Rocks, **9**-1498
  Dandelion Wine, **4**-534
  Eggnog, **1**-52
  Eggnog, Colonial, **4**-611
  Elderberry Wine, **4**-617
  Fish-House Cooler, **1**-32
  Glögg, **11**-1796
  Grog with Honey, Hot (Krupnik), **9**-1431
  Irish Coffee, **3**-462; **6**-950
  Jamaican Gold Doubloons, **8**-1273
  Maibowle, **12**-1949
  Mint Julep, Georgia, **6**-996
  Mint Julep, Kentucky, **6**-996
  Mint Julep, Rum, **6**-996
  Mocha-Brandy Delight, **7**-1167
  Posset, Brandy or Sherry, **9**-1457
  Punch, **9**-1501
    Anniversary, **9**-1502
    Champagne, **9**-1502
    Champagne and Sauterne (QC), **10**-1527
    Fish House, Philadelphia, **9**-1502
    Milk, Hot, **9**-1502
    Pineapple, Hot (Ponche de Piña), **11**-1709
    Pineapple-Rum, **9**-1498
    Port (QC), **10**-1527
    Reception, **9**-1503
    Rum (QC), **10**-1527
    Rum, Sparkling, **10**-1563
  Sack-Posset, Old English, **4**-611
  Sake, **10**-1578
  Sherry Cobbler, **3**-454
  Shrub, **10**-1662, 1663
  Syllabub, Frothy, **4**-611
  Syllabub, Old English, **11**-1807
  Toddy, **11**-1829
  Vodka, **12**-1913
  Wassail Bowl, Old-Time, **12**-1918
  Whiskey, Whisky, **12**-1937
  Wine, Mulled, **8**-1193
Bhaji Malida Machli (Stuffed Fish with Greens), **6**-942
Biarritz (potatoes), **9**-1469
Bienenstich ("Bee's Sting" Coffeecake), **5**-798
Bif Strogonov (Beef Stroganoff), **10**-1571
Bife Sauté a la Minuta con Arroz (Fried Beef with Rice), **11**-1705
Bifes com Azedas (Sorrel and Spinach Steaks), **9**-1456
Biff à la Lindström (Beef Lindström), **11**-1788
Biftecks Tartare (Tartar Sandwiches), **11**-1802
Bigarade Sauce, **2**-202
Bigos Mysliwski (Hunter's Stew), **9**-1426
Bigos, Polish, **7**-1016
Bigos Polski (Polish Bigos), **9**-1427
Billets-Doux, **8**-1308
Biloxi Shrimp Stew, **1**-50
Birthday Cake Castle, **4**-550

Biscuit(s), **2**-225, 227, and **Scone(s),** **10**-1642
  Arizona's Biscuits, **11**-1732
  Bacon Biscuits, **1**-134
  Baking-Powder Biscuits, **2**-237
  Baking-Powder Biscuits (QC), **10**-1524
  Beaten Biscuits, **2**-173; **11**-1724
    with Ham Filling, **11**-1724
  Benne-Seed Biscuits, South Carolina, **11**-1724
  Biscuit Dough, **2**-205; **7**-1039
  Biscuit Dough for Chicken Pie, **7**-1152
  Buttermilk Biscuits, **1**-69
  Buttermilk Scones, **10**-1644
  Calico Biscuits, **11**-1732
  Cheese Biscuits, **2**-238
  Cream Biscuits, **1**-46
  Currant Scones, **2**-238
  Dropped Scones, **10**-1644
  Griddle Scones, **10**-1644
  Mammy's Sour-Milk Biscuits, **1**-22
  Mormon Biscuits with Cream Gravy, **1**-74
  Oat Scones, **10**-1643
  Pinwheel Biscuits, **4**-578
  Potato Scones, **11**-1818
  Potato Scones, Katy's Drop, **10**-1644
  Raised Biscuits, **1**-34
  Raised Biscuits, Georgia, **2**-236
  Raised Potato Biscuits, Pike's Peak, **1**-27
  Raspberry Jam Scones, **12**-1932
  Scottish Scones, **4**-634
  Sweet Potato Biscuits, **1**-61; **11**-1797
  Tea Scones, **10**-1643

Biscuit Tortoni, **2**-203; **12**-1857
  Coffee, **12**-1857
  Sherry, **12**-1858
Bishop Whipple Pudding, **1**-50
Bismarcks, **1**-63
Bisque, see Soup(s), Cream Soup(s), Bisque(s), and Purée(s)
Blabærkake (Blueberry Cake), **8**-1242

Blackberry(ies), **2**-204
  -Almond Meringue Pie, **9**-1392
  Flummery, **5**-707
  Jam, No-Cook, **6**-965
  Jam, Spiced, **6**-963
  Jelly, No-Cook, **6**-984
  -Juice Jelly, **6**-982
  Patch Salad, **2**-204
  Pie, **2**-204
  Roly-Poly, **2**-204
  Spiced Jellied, **2**-205
  Whip, **2**-205
  Wild Blackberry Cobbler, **11**-1725
Black Butter, **2**-254; **10**-1624
Black-Eyed Susans, **3**-473
Black Kettle Soup, **1**-40

Blancmange, **2**-205
  Arrowroot, **1**-110
  Chocolate, **2**-205
  Coconut, **2**-205
  Irish Moss, **6**-950
  Pineapple, **2**-205
Blanquette de Veau (Veal Stew, French Style), **2**-205

Blinde Vinken (Stuffed Fillets of Veal), **4**-590
Blini, see Pancakes(s)
Blintz, see Pancake(s)
Block Island Baked Swordfish, **1**-67
Blomkål i Rekesaus (Hot Cauliflower with Shrimps), **8**-1239
Blotch Kucha, **9**-1357

Blueberry(ies), **2**-206, and **Huckleberry(ies),** **6**-915
Blueberry(ies)
and Apple Jelly, Spiced, **6**-982
Betty, **1**-45; **2**-208
Blintzes, **6**-992
Bread Pudding, **9**-1489
Buckle, **2**-208
Cake, **2**-210
Cake (Blabærkake), **8**-1242
Cake, Breakfast, **8**-1225
Compote, Gingered Fresh, **2**-209
Cottage-Cheese Cake, **2**-210
and Cottage-Cheese Salad, **10**-1587
-Decorated Cheesecake, **3**-366
Fluff, Fresh, **2**-209
Fluff Pie, **5**-790
Flummery, **2**-209
Gingerbread, **5**-805
-Grape Mold, **5**-812
or Huckleberry Buckle, Northwest, **12**-1933
Ice Cream, **6**-929
Jam, **6**-965
and Lime Mold, **2**-208
and Lime Salad, Molded, **7**-1067
Marmalade, **7**-1111
Mousse, **8**-1191
Muffins, **2**-209; **8**-1192
-Orange Bread, **2**-210
Pancakes, **2**-209
Pandowdy, **2**-209
Parfait, **2**-209; **6**-930
and Peach Jam, Spiced, **8**-1321
-Peach Meringue, **2**-209
Peach, Meringue, **8**-1317
Pie(s), **9**-1393, 1396
Pie, Fresh, **2**-208
Pie, Lattice, **2**-208
Pies, Deep-Dish, **2**-208
Pudding, Steamed, **2**-209
Relish, **2**-210
Sauce, **2**-210; **6**-930
Sauce, Foamy, **2**-209
Sauce, Fresh, **2**-210
Shortcake, **2**-210
Soup, Norwegian, **2**-208
Spiced, **1**-23
Tarts, **2**-208
-Topped Cheesecake, **7**-1087
Torte, **7**-1156
Turnovers, **2**-208; **12**-1879
Upside-Down Cake, **1**-57; **12**-1881
Vareniki, **10**-1574
Waffles, **2**-209; **12**-1915
Huckleberry(ies)
Cobbler, **11**-1725
Cottage Pudding, **6**-915
Cream-Cheese Pie, **6**-915
Griddle Cakes, **6**-915
Shortcake, **6**-915
Sour-Cream, Pie, **9**-1355
Wild-Huckleberry Pie, **1**-77

Bluefish, **2**-211
Boneless, **2**-212
Broiled, Maître d'Hôtel, **2**-211
Cutlets, Baked, **2**-211
Potato-Stuffed, **2**-210
Bluegrass Sorghum Cake, **1**-41
Bøf (Roast Beef), **4**-536
Boeuf, see Beef
Bohemian Restaurant Cheesecake, **3**-366
Bohemian Tarts (Kolácky), **4**-532
Bok You Guy, **10**-1550
Bolivia Baked Fish (Pescado al Horno), **11**-1705
Bolivia Cheese Turnovers (Empanadas de Queso), **11**-1708

Bologna, **2**-212
Cups, Creamed Peas in, **10**-1638
Potatoes, and Onions, Fried, **10**-1638
Spread, **2**-279
Bolognese Meat Sauce, **11**-1738
Bombay Refresher, **11**-1692
Bombe, **2**-212; for recipes see Frozen Desserts

Bonbons, **2**-284; **5**-708
Baked, **12**-1918
Walnut, **12**-1917

Bonito, **2**-212
Chowder, **11**-1696
Steaks, Deviled Fresh, **2**-213
Boova Shenkel (Filled Noodles), **9**-1352
Booyaw, **1**-48
Borage, **2**-213
Bordeaux Potatoes, **9**-1470

Bordelaise Sauce, **2**-214; **10**-1613
1-144; **5**-741; **10**-1619; **11**-1766
Börek (Filled Pastry), **8**-1215
Borjú Pörkölt (Veal Paprika), **6**-918

Borsch
with Beet Greens, Cold (Barszcz Zimmy), **9**-1421
Meatless, **2**-214
Polish, **2**-195
Quick, **11**-1838
Rusell Borscht, **6**-994
Ukrainian, **2**-214; **10**-1567
Very Quick (Poproshche), **10**-1567
Boston Baked Beans, **1**-47
Boston Brown Bread, **1**-47
Boston Cream Pie, **1**-47; **8**-1229
Bouchées, **2**-280

Bouillabaisse, **2**-214
Creole, **4**-509
White-Fish, **10**-1645

Bouillon, see also Soup(s), Bouillon(s) and Consommé(s); Stock(s)
Beef, **2**-215
Bouquet Garni for, **2**-216
Chicken, **2**-215
Clam, Digby Pines, **2**-275
Fish, **2**-215
Herbed, **3**-424
Jellied, **2**-216
To Clarify, **2**-215
Tomato, **2**-216

Bouquet Garni, **10**-1615
for Bouillon, **2**-216
Herb Bouquet, **2**-218
for Soup, **2**-216
Bouquet Sauce, **5**-769
Bourride (Fish Stew), **5**-740
Boxty-on-the-Griddle, **6**-944
Boxty-on-the-Pan, **6**-944
Bozi Milosti (Celestial Crusts), **4**-532
Braendende Kaerlighed (Burning Love), **4**-540

Brains, **2**-216
Batter Cakes, **2**-217
Beef, with Scrambled Eggs, **2**-217
Calf's, Cervelle Sauce, **10**-1614, 1622
Calf's, Cutlets (Kotleciki z Mózgu), **9**-1424
Calf's, in Mushroom Sauce, **12**-1897
Lamb, Salad, **8**-1211
Mixed Fry (Fritto Misto), **7**-1040
Parboiled in Court Bouillon, **9**-1424
with Wine Sauce, **2**-217

Bran, **2**-220
Bread, **2**-220
Muffins, **2**-221
Muffins, Miniature, **4**-632
Pancakes, **2**-238
Prune Bread, **9**-1485
Brandade de Thon, **12**-1864

Brandy, Brandied, **2**-221
Almond Torte, **12**-1853
Apple Fritters, **1**-63
Cheddar Cheese, **3**-355
Hard Sauce, **5**-702; **6**-877; **9**-1493
Lobster au Brandy, **7**-1078
Mincemeat Pie, **9**-1396
Mocha-Brandy Delight, **7**-1167
Nut Cakes, **8**-1310
Orange-Brandy Toast Butter, **11**-1829
Peach Preserves, **9**-1481
Plum Pudding, **9**-1492
Posset, **9**-1457
Sauce, **9**-1492
Sweet Potatoes, **11**-1724
Toast, Fluffed, **11**-1826
Wafers, **3**-472
Bratwurst (Cooked Sausage), **2**-221; **11**-1802
Brawn, **9**-1448
Brazil Banana Paste with Cheese (Bananada com Queijo), **11**-1709
Brazil Black Bean Stew (Feijoada), **11**-1704
Brazil Farofa, **11**-1709
Brazil Fish Stew (Vatapá), **11**-1703
Brazil Shrimps, Bahia Style (Camarões a Bahia), **11**-1704
Brazilian Chocolate, **3**-416
Brazilian Coconut Sherbet Drink, **10**-1654
Brazilian Orange Cake, **8**-1272
Brazilian Stuffed Eggplant, **4**-615

Brazil Nut(s), **2**-221
Bars, Layered, **3**-471
Chips, Toasted, **2**-222
Macaroons, **7**-1096
Pie Shell, **2**-222
Pilaf, **2**-222
Stuffing, Creamy, **11**-1781

Bread
-and-Butter Pickles, Crisp, **9**-1337
Crumbs, **4**-519
Dumplings, **4**-585
Dumplings, Italian, **11**-1696
Parsley and Green-Onion Stuffed, **8**-1276
Pudding
Blueberry, **9**-1489
Cheese, **9**-1487
Old-Time Spiced, **8**-1228
Orange-Date, **9**-1490
Pineapple, **9**-1490
Plum, Refrigerator, **9**-1415
Sauce, **4**-626; **10**-1614
English, **10**-1626
Stuffed (Gefülltes Brot), **11**-1803
Stuffing, **3**-392; **6**-990; **9**-1477; **11**-1781
Bread-Crumb, **9**-1426
Chestnut, **1**-1781
Oyster, **11**-1781

Bread(s), **2**-222

Bread(s), Breadsticks
Corn Sticks, **2**-239
Herb Breadsticks, **2**-236
Shaping and Baking, **12**-1953-1954

Bread(s), Quick, **2**-225, 237 see also Biscuit(s) and Scone(s); Coffeecake(s); Doughnut(s) and Cruller(s); Muffin(s); Pancake(s); Popover(s); Waffle(s)
Bran, **2**-220
Brown, Boston, **1**-47
Corn, see Corn Bread(s)
Grits Batter Bread, **6**-907
Indian Shuck, **1**-64
Molasses Johnnycake, **8**-1225
Oatmeal, **8**-1253
Onion-Cheese, Quick, **1**-79
Onion, Southern, **8**-1265
Pinwheel Onion, **2**-239
Ripe-Olive, Visalia, **1**-26

Sally Lunn, Quick, **10**-1590
Sesame-Seed Dips, **2**-239
Soda Bread, Basic Recipe for, **6**-944
Spoon Bread(s), **11**-1724
Buttermilk, **2**-254
Cheese, **3**-361
Delaware, **1**-32
Double-Corn, **3**-485
Farina, **4**-656
Golden Cheese, **1**-65
Mushroom, **2**-247
Nebraska, **7**-1153
Virginia Batter Bread, **1**-75
Bread(s), Quick, Sweet
Allspice Orange-Nut, Quick, **1**-11
Almond (Mandelbrot), **6**-992
Apple, **7**-1153
Apple, Autumn, **1**-100
Banana-Nut, **1**-139
Blueberry-Orange, **2**-210
Butternut-Banana, **8**-1225
Carrot-Raisin, **10**-1611
Cinnamon Flop, **9**-1355
Coconut, **2**-238
Cranberry-Nut, **10**-1611
Date and Nut, **4**-547
Date-Nut Loaves, **10**-1611
Fig, **4**-658
Fruit Spice Roll, **5**-803
Maple Date-Nut, **7**-1105
Mincemeat Tea Loaf, **7**-1164
Nut, **6**-904
Orange Coconut, **10**-1611
Orange-and-Date Tea Loaf, **8**-1272
Orange Nut, **2**-238
Orange Tea, **10**-1612
Peanut-Butter Orange, **8**-1325
Pecan, Chuck Wagon, **11**-1732
Prune Pecan, **8**-1334
Saffron, **7**-1035
Saffron Tea, **10**-1577
Spiced (Pain d'Épice), **5**-804

Bread(s), Quick, Skillet
Corn Dodgers, **1**-75
Corn Oysters, **1**-28
Corn Oysters, Idaho, **1**-36
Drop Bannocks, **1**-142
Fried Bread, **1**-59
Hoecake, Old-Fashioned, **6**-904
Hush Puppies, **2**-239
Hush Puppy Batter, **5**-690
Johnnycake, **1**-67
Mexican (Tortillas), **7**-1137
Potato Cakes, **2**-278
Spiced Nut Corn, Antebellum, **1**-52
Squaw, Fried, **1**-64
Tortillas (Mexican Bread), **7**-1137
Corn (Tortillas de Maíz), **7**-1137
Flour (Tortillas de Harina), **7**-1137
Tostadas, **7**-1137

Bread(s), Yeast, **2**-222
Anadama, **8**-1225
Anadama Batter, **2**-229
Bacon Batter, **2**-231
Cheese, **2**-229
Corn Cake (Welsch Kornkuche), **9**-1354
Cracked Wheat, **1**-40
Finnish, **10**-1575
French, **2**-228
Hot Casserole, **2**-229
Indian Meal Raised, **8**-1225
Limpa, **2**-229
Oatmeal, **2**-231
Oatmeal Batter, **2**-229
Onion, **2**-229
Potato, **2**-231
Prune Bran, **9**-1485
Pumpernickel, **2**-229
Pumpernickel, Light, **7**-1153
Pumpkin, **9**-1499
Raisin, **10**-1534
Rye, Dark, **2**-228
Rye (Rågbröd), **11**-1791
Rye (Rugbrød), **4**-542; **8**-1240
Rye, Swedish, **1**-49
Sabbath or Holiday Twist (Challah), **6**-992
Sally Lunn Ring, **10**-1589
Sennebec Hill, **2**-230
Sourdough, **12**-1932
Wheat-Germ, **2**-228
White, **2**-228
Individual Loaves, **2**-228
White Batter, **2**-228
Whole-Wheat Batter Loaves, Individual, **2**-228
Whole-Wheat, Sesame, **10**-1647
Bread(s), Yeast, Sweet; see also Coffeecake(s)
Apple Kuchen, **1**-100
Apple, Plum, or Peach Kuchen, **5**-799
Baba au Rhum (Rum Cake), **5**-748
Babka, Polish, **7**-1156
Barmbrack, **6**-949
Bundkuchen, **7**-1156
Butter Braid, **2**-231
Cherry Cake, **3**-372
Christmas Bread (Julekake), **8**-1240
Christmas Coffee Ring, **3**-429
Christmas Fruitcake (Stollen), **5**-798
Christmas Tree Bread (Tannenbaum Brot), **5**-798
Coffeecake (Kaffekake), **8**-1240
Cornish Fruited Saffron, **7**-1097
Currant, **11**-1818
Easter Babka (Wielkanocna Babka), **9**-1431
Fruit Twist Coffeecake, **4**-578
Hickory-Nut Graham, **7**-1153
Kringle, Danish, **7**-1157
Kuchen Dough, **5**-799
Mohn Kuchen, **5**-799
Orange Rye, **12**-1932
Panettone (Italian Coffeecake), **3**-463
Poppy-Seed Kringle, Hungarian, **9**-1437
Sally Lunn, **2**-229
Savarin, **10**-1640
Savarin Dough (Gâteau Manon), **5**-784
Stollen, **11**-1775
Sweet Bread (Vasilopitta), **5**-823
Tea Ring, Swedish, **7**-1156
Viipuri Twists (Viipurin Rinkeli), **5**-682

Bread(s), Yeast Bun(s) and Roll(s), **2**-233-237; **12**-1952
Bagels, **1**-134
Biscuits, Georgia Raised, **2**-236
Brioche Dough, **5**-745
Brioches, Little, **2**-237
Butterhorns, **2**-233
Cloverleaf Rolls, **2**-236
Cornmeal Rolls, **12**-1956
Crescents, **2**-237
Croissants, **4**-517
Crumpets, **4**-520; **11**-1818
English Muffins, **4**-627; **8**-1193
Mixing, Kneading, and Raising, **12**-1953
No-Knead Feather Rolls, **12**-1956
Pan Rolls, **2**-237
Pan Rolls (QC), **10**-1524
Parkerhouse Rolls, **2**-233
Parker House Rolls (QC), **10**-1525
Plain Yeast Rolls, **12**-1956
Potato Rolls, **2**-233
Pumpkin Rolls, Raised, **9**-1499
Refrigerator Rolls, **12**-1956
Rolls, Frances Clark's, **9**-1354
Rolls, To Shape, **2**-237
Sally Lunn Muffins, Raised, **10**-1590
Sesame-Seed Rolls, **10**-1647
Shaping and Baking, **12**-1953-1954
Squash Rolls, **2**-233; **12**-1956
Twists and Circles, **2**-237
Whole-Wheat Rolls, **12**-1956
Bread(s), Yeast Bun(s) and Roll(s), Sweet
Apple Danish Pastries, **2**-232
Bohemian Tarts (Kolácky), **4**-532
Butterscotch Pecan Rolls, **2**-236
Cheese-Filled Rolls, **2**-236
Cinnamon Buns, Sticky, **9**-1354
Cinnamon Raisin Buns, **1**-56
Cinnamon Rolls, **2**-236
Crescents, Austrian, **4**-630
Danish Pastries, **8**-1308
Danish Pastry (Wienerbrød), **4**-543
English Bath Buns, **2**-252
Golden Glory Knots, **2**-236
Hot Cross Buns, **2**-252
Pecan Rolls, Sticky, **8**-1334
Prune Kolache, **1**-49; **7**-1157
Quick-Rising Sweet Rolls, **2**-237
Schnecken, **2**-242; **5**-799
Shrove Tuesday Buns (Semlor), **11**-1791
Swedish Saffron Buns, **2**-252
Walnut Rolls, **5**-799
Wigs, **7**-1098
Wig Buns, Christmas, **7**-1098
Bread-and-Butter Pickles, **1**-74
Breakfast Menus, **2**-241
Brennan's Bananas Foster, **4**-513
Brennan's Eggs Hussarde, **4**-512
Brennan's Hollandaise Sauce, **4**-512
Brennan's Marchand de Vin Sauce, **4**-512
Brennan's Shrimp Clemenceau, **4**-510
Breton Beans, **1**-159
Bride's Pudding, **9**-1492

Brioche(s), **2**-243
Canapés, **2**-280
Canapés, Onion, **2**-281
Dough, **5**-745
Little, **2**-237
British Guiana Main-Course Soup (Callalu), **11**-1704

Brittle, **2**-284
Almond, **1**-16
Black-Walnut, **12**-1917
Cashew, **2**-314
Peanut, **1**-75; **2**-288

Broccoli, **2**-243
Amandine, **4**-566
Bisque, Chilled, **11**-1837
Buttered, **11**-1823
-and-Cheese Custard, **2**-245
Chicken Divan, **2**-244
-and-Chicken Soup, **2**-244
Chicken or Turkey Mornay, **2**-325
and Ham Casserole, **6**-853
Italian Style, **5**-775
Marinated, Veal Salad with, **10**-1580
alla Piemontese, **12**-1904
with Pimiento Butter, **3**-445
Piquant, **2**-245
Salmon Divan, **10**-1595
Soufflé, **12**-1904
Soup, Cold, **4**-645
with Sour Cream, **2**-245
and Turkey Amandine, **12**-1872
Vinaigrette Sauce for, **2**-252
Brochette, en Brochette, **2**-245; for recipes see Skewer, Skewered
Brødboller (Bread Dumplings), **4**-542
Broodschoteltje met Sinaasappels (Bread Dish with Oranges), **4**-593

Broth, **2**-246, see also Soup(s), Bouillon(s) and Consommé(s)
Quick Mushroom Broth, **2**-246
Brown Beauty Cake, **3**-424

Brownie(s), **2**-246
Black and White, **2**-246
Chocolate (QC), **10**-1526
Brown Rice, see Rice
Brown Sauce (Sauce Espagnole), **2**-246; **7**-1039
Basic, **10**-1617
Brown Stock, **10**-1618
Brown Stock (Bouillon or Beef Stock), **11**-1774

Brown Sugar, **11**-1784
Candied Sweet Potatoes, **11**-1796
Frosting, **3**-408
Fudge Cake, **7**-1044

Brown Sugar, continued
Hard Sauce, **6**-878
Sauce, **1**-50; **7**-1151
Syrup, **10**-1629
Broyage, Swiss, **5**-781
Brunch Menus, **2**-246
Summertime, **4**-630
Viennese, **4**-629
Brunede Kartofler (Sugar-Browned Potatoes), **4**-540
Brunkålssoppa (Brown Cabbage Soup), **11**-1787
Brunswick Stew, **1**-75; **5**-770
Brunswick Stew (QC), **10**-1520
Brunswick Stew for a Crowd, **11**-1722
Brunswick Style Chicken Stew, **3**-386
Brussels Almond Bread Cookies (Pain d'Amandes), **2**-200
Brussels Beer Waffles (Gaufres Bruxelloises), **2**-200
Brussels Chef's Salad, **10**-1580
Brussels Lof (Belgian Endive), **4**-592

Brussels Sprouts, **2**-247
Baked Sweet-Sour, **2**-249
and Beef Kabobs, **2**-248
in Browned Butter, **2**-248
Brussels Chef's Salad, **10**-1580
and Chestnuts, **2**-248; **3**-440
and Cranberries with Crown Roast of Pork, **9**-1442
with Frankfurters, **5**-725
and Onions au Gratin, **11**-1838
Pork Moussaka with, **8**-1190
Purée of (Spruiten Purée), **4**-592
Bubble and Squeak, **4**-624
Bûche de Noël (Yule Log), **12**-1959
Buckeye Maple-Syrup Cake, **1**-63

Buckwheat, **2**-249
Cakes, **2**-249; **8**-1293; **9**-1354
Cakes, Maple, **5**-826
Dumplings with Cheese (Pierogi z Kaszy ze Serem), **9**-1429
Flour, **5**-707
Groats, Country-Style, **2**-249
Groats (Czarna Kasza), **9**-1428
Groats and Mushroom Filling, **9**-1429
Groats with Noodles (Kasha Varnishkas), **6**-992
Groat Stuffing, **9**-1426
Kasha, **2**-249; **11**-1838
Kasha in Chicken Soup, **5**-827
Noodles (Soba), **6**-976
Porridge (Grechnevaia Kasha), **10**-1573
Pudding, Baked, **2**-249
Budino di Ricotta (Cream-Cheese Custard), **6**-960

Buffet Menus, **2**-249
Casserole Buffet, **2**-250; **8**-1275
Chafing Dish Buffet, **2**-250
Christmas Buffet, **3**-424
Greek Taverna Buffet, **4**-639
Oriental Buffet, **2**-250
Shrimp-Curry Buffet, **4**-640
Bulgarian Appetizers, **4**-614
Bulgarian Cold Cucumber Soup, **12**-1957
Bulgur, see Cracked Wheat
Bullhead Soup, **1**-52
Bundkuchen, **7**-1156
Bun(s), **2**-252; for recipes see Bread(s), Yeast Bun(s) and Roll(s)
Buñuelos de Espinaca (Spinach Fritters), **11**-1708
Buñuelos de Viento (Wind Puffs), **9**-1497
Burgoo, Kentucky, **1**-40

Burgundy, **2**-253
Chocolate Torte, **4**-553
Juniper Pot Roast in, **6**-996
Pecanburgers, **8**-1334
Burmese Ginger Beef, **10**-1646
Burning Love (Braendende Kaerlighed), **4**-540
Burnt Sugar Frosting, **7**-1044
Burritos from Taos, **11**-1732
Butaniku-Teriyaki (Broiled Pork), **6**-974

Butter, **2**-253
Balls, **2**-253
Beurre Manié, **2**-202
Cookies, Brown-Edged, **3**-431
Cookies, Sugared, **3**-474
Creamed, **8**-1236
and Cream Sauce, **2**-193
Curls, **2**-253; **5**-780
Frosting, **3**-412
Frosting, Fluffy, **5**-751
Frosting, Fluffy Chocolate, **5**-751
Frosting, Mocha, **5**-751
Frosting, Orange, **7**-1042
Molds, **2**-253
Pats, **2**-253
Pressed, **5**-780
Sauce, **8**-1203
Sauce (dessert), **9**-1492
Sauce (dessert), Hot, **7**-1155
To Clarify, **2**-253; **5**-781
Tomato, **11**-1835

Buttercream, **12**-1854
Butterscotch Frosting, **5**-751
Cherry Frosting, **5**-751
Chocolate Frosting, **5**-751
Chocolate, Speedy, **5**-783
Coffee Frosting, **5**-751
Crème au Beurre, **9**-1366
Decorator's, Simple, **4**-549
Frosting, Basic, and Variations, **5**-751
Lemon-Orange Frosting, **2**-268
Mocha, **12**-1854
Mocha Frosting, **5**-751
Nougat, **5**-781
Orange Frosting, Cooked, **5**-751
Orange Frosting, Uncooked, **5**-751
Pineapple Frosting, **5**-751
Strawberry Frosting, **5**-751
Butterfish, Deep-Fried, with Sour-Cream Sauce, **5**-688
Butterklösse (Butter Dumplings), **4**-585

Buttermilk, **2**-254
Apple Waffles, **2**-238
Bacon Waffles, **2**-238
Beef Balls, **7**-1122
Biscuits, **1**-69
-Coconut-Cream Pie, **9**-1391
Doughnuts, **2**-237
Dressing, Cooked, **10**-1588
Dressing, Low-Calorie, **2**-254
Ginger Buttermilk, **5**-804
Horseradish Dressing, **10**-1588
Lemon Sherbet, **7**-1054
Meringue Pie, **2**-254
Orange Sherbet, **10**-1652
Pancakes, **2**-241; **8**-1292
Peach Sherbet, **8**-1320
Pudding (Karnemelk Pudding), **4**-593
Rice with (Dahi Bhath), **6**-942
Scones, **10**-1644
Shake, **1**-64
Snickerdoodles, **8**-1230
Soup, Belgian, **11**-1690
Soup, Cold (Kaernemaelkskoldskaal), **4**-539
Soup, Danish, **2**-254
Spoon Bread, **2**-254
Waffles, **2**-238

Butternut, 2-254
-Banana Bread, **8**-1225
Maple Cake, **2**-255

Butternut Squash, **2**-255; **11**-1759
Anise, **2**-255
Whole Glazed, **1**-62

Butter(s), **10**-1615
Amandine, **10**-1615, 1624
Anchovy, **5**-694; **6**-955; **10**-1615, 1624
Bercy, **10**-1615, 1624
Beurre Blanc, **10**-1615, 1624
Black, **2**-254; **10**-1624
Black-Butter Sauce for Cooked Greens, **5**-825
Brown-Butter and Caper Sauce, **10**-1663
Brown-Butter Sauce, **5**-694
Canapé Butters, **1**-85-86; **2**-279
Chervil, **5**-695
Chili-Sauce, **5**-694
Chive, **5**-695; **10**-1615, 1624
Colbert Butter Sauce, **10**-1624
for Corn-on-the-Cob, **3**-480
Curry, **2**-191
Drawn Butter Sauce, **10**-1624
Egg, **5**-679
for Fish, **5**-694-695
Garlic, **5**-695, 775; **10**-1661
Ham and Egg, **6**-866
Herb, **2**-193, 254
Herb Sweet, **3**-429
Herring, **6**-903
Honey, **6**-909; **12**-1915
Honey-Fruit, **6**-909
Horseradish, **5**-695
Lemon, **2**-254; **10**-1615, 1624
Lemon and Caper, **5**-695
Lobster, **10**-1615, 1624
Maître d'Hôtel, **2**-211, 254; **7**-1014; **10**-1615, 1624
Mustard, **8**-1205; **10**-1615, 1624
Noisette, **10**-1615, 1624
Nonsweet, **11**-1829
Onion, **5**-695
Parmesan, **1**-86
Parsley, **5**-695
Parsley Chive, **8**-1299
Pepper (capsicum), **1**-64
Pepper (nigrum), **8**-1278
Pimiento, **5**-695
Roquefort, **10**-1615, 1624
Savory, **2**-194; **5**-695
Savory (Beurres Composés), **10**-1615
Seasoned (for Sandwiches), **11**-1800
Shallot, **10**-1615, 1624
Shrimp, **10**-1615, 1626
Snail, **10**-1667
Soy Butter Sauce, **5**-695
Spreads for Hot Breads, **2**-254
Sweet, for Tea Toast, **11**-1829
Tangerine, **10**-1556
Tarragon, **10**-1615, 1626
Watercress, **1**-25
White (Beurre Blanc), **10**-1615, 1624
White Butter Sauce, Norman, **10**-1624
Butters, Fruit Jams, see Jams and Conserves

Butterscotch, **2**-255, 284
Acorns, **3**-474
Buttercream Frosting, **5**-751
Candy, **2**-288
Chocolate Bars, **12**-1918
Cream Pie, **2**-255
Filling, **2**-255
Frosting, **2**-267
-Mace Sundae Sauce, **7**-1100
-Peanut Tapioca Pudding, **9**-1487
Pecan Roll, Frozen, **8**-1335
Pecan Rolls, **2**-236
Raisin Pudding (QC), **10**-1525
Rice Pudding, **10**-1552
Sauce, **2**-225; **6**-930; **8**-1335; **10**-1615, 1628
Sauce (QC), **10**-1526
Sour-Cream Meringue Pie, **9**-1392
Tapioca Cream, **11**-1810

C

Cabbage, **2**-256; see also Salads, Coleslaw; Sauerkraut
with Bacon and Cheese Sauce, **1**-68
and Beet Relish, **10**-1541
Birds I and II, **9**-1430

Birds or stuffed Cabbage, I and II (Golabki z Kapusty), **9**-1430
with Cheese Sauce, **2**-258
in Cheese Sauce (Repollo en Salsa de Queso), **9**-1496
Chopped-Cabbage Pickle, **1**-23
Coleslaw, see Salads, Coleslaw
Corned Beef and, **3**-485
Corned Beef and, Nebraska Style, **1**-54
Curry, **4**-526
with Frankfurters, **5**-722
and Ham with Tomatoes, **6**-855
and Hamburgers, Creamed, **6**-872
Meatless Stuffed (Golabki Postne), **9**-1430
-Noodle Potpourri, **8**-1232
Pepper Cabbage, **9**-1350
Rice, and Pork, Baked, **10**-1549
Rolls, Hash-Stuffed, **6**-881
Rolls (Hvidkaalsrouladen), **4**-540
Rolls, Sour-Cream, **11**-1698
Salad, Jellied, **10**-1583
Salad with Lingonberries (Kålsallad med Lingon), **11**-1791
Salad, Two-Tone, **2**-258
Sauerkraut, see Sauerkraut
Slaws, see Salads, Coleslaw,
Soup, Brown (Brunkålssoppa), **11**-1787
Soup, Danish Browned, **11**-1690
and Spinach Salad, **11**-1756
Strudel, **6**-922
Stuffed (Couve-Lombarda Recheada), **9**-1456
Surprise Salad, **10**-1586
with Tomatoes (Paradeiskraut), **1**-122
and Tomatoes, Simmered, **7**-1087
and Tuna Pirogi, **12**-1862
in White Wine, **12**-1949
and Zucchini Skillet, Madame Fraize's, **12**-1903
Cabbage, Green and White
Almond Soup, **2**-257
-Beet Relish, **5**-726
Tomatoes, and Green Pepper, **2**-258
with Caraway (Surkål), **8**-1239
in Cream, **2**-258
with Hash-Stuffed Peppers, **9**-1359
and Lamb (Fårikål), **8**-1239
Meat-Stuffed (Holishkes), **6**-995
Pirozhki, **10**-1568
with Potatoes (Stamppot Witte Kool) **4**-592
Relish, **2**-260
Rolls, Beef-Stuffed, **6**-873
Rolls with Sauerkraut and Pork, **2**-257
Salad, Virginia City, **1**-56
Soup, French, **2**-257
Soup, Pride of Erin, **6**-945
Stuffed whole, with Béchamel Sauce, **2**-257
Wilted, **2**-258
Cabbage, Red Cabbage
Bavarian (Bayerisches Kraut), **5**-796
with Polish Sausage, **7**-1151
Rødkaal, **4**-542
Spicy Apples and, **1**-100
Sweet-and-Sour, **2**-258
Wilted, **2**-258
Cabbage, Savoy Cabbage
Braised, **6**-948
Polanaise, **2**-258

Cabbage, Chinese Cabbage, **2**-257
Braised, **12**-1902
with Egg Dressing, **2**-258
Panned, **2**-258
Cabillaud à la Flamande (Halibut, Flemish Style), **2**-197
Cactus Pear, **2**-260
Caesar Salad, **1**-27; **12**-1931
Café, Caffé, see Coffee
Cajun Crab Gumbo, **5**-830

Cake(s), **2**-262; see also Torte(n)
Almond Butter, **5**-783
Almond Mazurka (Mazurek Migdałowy), **9**-1431
Ambrosia, **7**-1044
Angel, Angel Food, **1**-80; **2**-262
Basic, **1**-81
Butter-Pecan, **2**-273
Cherry, **2**-273
Chocolate, **3**-410
Lemon Delight, **7**-1088
Peach Raspberry, **8**-1320
Anniversary, **2**-268
Antebellum Spice, **2**-272
Apea, **9**-1357
Apple Coffeecake, **3**-463
Apple Meringue, **1**-101
Apple, Old World, **1**-102
Applesauce, American, **2**-268
Apple Slice, **2**-278
Baba au Rhum, see Baba au Rhum
Babka, see Babka
Banana-Filled Orange Layer, **1**-142
Batter, One-Egg, **2**-268
Batter (for Pandowdy), **2**-209
Birthday Cake Castle, **4**-550
Blitztorte, **2**-267
Blueberry Breakfast, **8**-1225
Blueberry Buckle, **2**-208
Boston Cream Pie, **1**-47; **8**-1229
Brown Beauty, **3**-424
Brown-Sugar Fudge, **7**-1044
Broyage, Swiss, **5**-781
Burnt-Sugar, **7**-1042
Caramel, **2**-297
Caraway or Seed, **2**-298
Cardamom, Quick, **2**-299
Cheesecake, see Cheesecake(s)
Cherry, **3**-372
Chiffon Cake(s), **2**-262; **3**-393
Almond, **2**-272
Pumpkin, **9**-1500
Refrigerator, Orange, **4**-556
Chocolate Cake(s)
Chestnut Slices, **5**-783
Cheyenne, **1**-79
Cream-Filled, **2**-265
Cream Roll, **3**-410
-Filled Eight-Layer, **7**-1044
Fondant, **3**-407
Grandma's, **3**-410
Honey, **3**-410
Milk-Chocolate, **3**-407
Nutcake, **3**-410
One-Bowl, **2**-268
Peppermint, **7**-1044
Potato, **9**-1468
Rum, A Man's, **3**-408
Shadow, **7**-1044
with Sour-Cream Frosting, **11**-1701
Southern, **7**-1045
Sweet-Chocolate, **3**-407
Walnut, **7**-1044
Wisconsin, **3**-407
Citron Loaf, **3**-449
Coffeecake, see Coffeecake(s)
Coffee Spice, **7**-1045
Company Gold, **7**-1045
Crumb, **4**-654
Cupcake, see Cupcake(s)
Decorating a Cake, **4**-548
Devil's Food, **2**-267; **4**-559
with Marshmallow Frosting, **4**-559
Diva, **3**-408
Dried Apple, **4**-578
Dutch Apple, Mrs. Van's, **7**-1156
Election, **1**-28
Finnish (Vesi-Sokerikakku), **5**-681
Fresh-Blueberry, **2**-210
Fresh-Coconut, **3**-457
Frosted Marble, **2**-267
Fruitcake, see Fruitcake(s)
Fruit-Preserve Layer, **7**-1042
Funny, **9**-1356
Gâteau Manon (Savarin Dough), **5**-784
Gâteau Mousseline, **8**-1192
Gâteau Praliné, **5**-781
Génoise, **5**-781
Génoise Fine, **9**-1366
Gingerbread, see Gingerbread
Glazes for, **5**-805
Gold Butter, **2**-265
Golden Glow (QC), **10**-1525
Golden Lord Baltimore, **7**-1045
Hickory-Nut, **1**-37; **6**-904
Honey Cake(s)
Chocolate, **3**-410
Dutch, **6**-911
Lekah, **6**-993
-Orange-Almond, **6**-910
Spice, **2**-267
Ice Cream Cakes, see Frozen Desserts
Ice Cream Rolls, see Frozen Desserts
Jelly-Roll
Butterscotch Pecan Roll, Frozen, **8**-1335
Jelly Sponge Roll, **11**-1757
Strawberry Cake Roll, **11**-1779
Kentucky Jam, **2**-270
King Haakon's (Kong Haakonskake), **8**-1242
Kuchen, see Kuchen
Lady Baltimore, **1**-46
Layer, Malay (Spiku), **11**-1715
Lemon-Cheese, **11**-1725
Lemon-Orange Refrigerator, **7**-1056
Lenten (Eggless), **6**-949
Lord Baltimore, **1**-46
Maple Butternut, **2**-255
Maple-Syrup, **7**-1108
Maple-Syrup, Buckeye, **1**-63
Maraschino-Cherry, **3**-375
Midnight Lace, **3**-407
Mocha, **3**-410
Mocha-Almond, **7**-1167
Molasses Layer, **8**-1184
Molasses Spice, **2**-269
Morning-Glory, **8**-1186
Nut, Passover, **6**-995
Orange, **7**-1087
Brazilian, **8**-1272
Form, **3**-553
Gold Layer, **7**-1042
-Marmalade, **8**-1272
-Rum, **2**-269
-Rum, Italian, **8**-1272
Peach Cream, **11**-1701
Peach Slices, **7**-1155
Peanut-Butter, **8**-1328
Peanut-Butter Apple, **8**-1328
Pecan, Louisiana, **4**-513
Petits Fours, **9**-1365
Pineapple Meringue, **9**-1409
Plum Cake Cobbler, **9**-1417
Potato or Raised, **9**-1357
Potato Seedy, **6**-950
Poundcake(s), **2**-262; **9**-1479
2-270; **9**-1479
Chocolate, **2**-272; **9**-1479
Ginger, Colonial, **2**-272
Half-a-Pound, **2**-272
Holiday, **2**-272
Nut, **2**-272
Orange-and-Lemon, Canadian, **2**-272
Sour-Cream, **9**-1480
Traditional English, **2**-272
Prune Chocolate, **9**-1486
Prune, Dutch, **9**-1486
Pumpkin-Prune, **1**-40
Rainbow, **2**-264; **7**-1042
Raisin, Iranian, **10**-1535
Raisin, Rainbow Grange, **4**-656
Raisin Spice, **10**-1535
Raisin Spicecake, **4**-579
Ribbon, **8**-1229
Rich Dessert Cake (Cassata Napolitana), **6**-960
Rum, Canadian, **2**-279
Rum Chocolate, A Man's, **3**-408
Rum, Italian, **10**-1562
Scripture, **1**-38
Seedcake, **11**-1819
Shortcake, see Shortcake(s)
Silver, **7**-1042
Simnel, **4**-626
Sorghum, Bluegrass, **1**-41
Spice, Toasted, **11**-1754

Cake(s), continued
Spongecake(s), **2**-262; **11**-1756
2-273; **3**-444; **11**-1756
Applesauce, **11**-1756
Chocolate, **3**-410; **11**-1756
Corn-Syrup Batter, **9**-1486
Daffodil, **2**-273
Hot-Water, **11**-1756
Jelly Sponge Roll, **11**-1757
Sponge Sheet, Basic, **5**-783
Strawberry Circle, **1**-72
Strawberry Cream, **2**-264; **7**-1042
Strawberry Macaroon Torte, **11**-1779
Sweet-Chocolate, **3**-407
Sweet (Hojaldre), **9**-1497
Swiss Classic, **5**-781
Tea Cake, Melting, **5**-784
Telegraph (Telegrafkake), **8**-1242
Tipsy (Sopa Borracha), **9**-1497
Two-Egg, **2**-264
Upside-Down Cake(s), **12**-1881
Ambrosia, **12**-1882
Apricot, **1**-108
Apricot-Prune, **12**-1881
Blueberry, **1**-57; **12**-1881
Cherry, **3**-374; **12**-1882
Ginger-Mince, **12**-1882
Pineapple, **2**-268; **12**-1881
Pineapple-Apricot, **9**-1409
Prune, **9**-1486
Walnut (Karidopita), **4**-640
Wedding, Bride's, and Groom's, **12**-1922
Whitby Nun's, **2**-272
White Cake(s)
Delicate, **2**-264
with Double Frosting, **1**-55
Two-Minute, **2**-268
White Mountain, **11**-1819
Yam Spicecake, **12**-1951
Yellow, with Broiled Peanut Frosting, **8**-1323
Yellow Coffeecake, **3**-463
Yule Log (Bûche de Noël), **12**-1959
Zuppa Inglese, **4**-650
Calas Tout Chauds (Hot Rice Fritters), **4**-513
Caldeirada de Peixe (Potato Fish Stew), **9**-1455
Caldo de Pescado (Fish Soup), **7**-1138
Calf's Liver, see Liver; Veal
California Chef's Salad, **5**-825; **7**-1063
California Fruit Roll, **5**-758
California Omelet, **12**-1930
California Parmesan-Walnut Salad, **12**-1934
California Prune Pudding, **9**-1486
California Prunes in Claret, **9**-1485
California Succotash, **3**-482
California Turkey Bake, **12**-1875
California Walnut Sauce, **10**-1629
Callalu (A Main-Course Soup), **11**-1704
Camarões a Bahia (Shrimps, Bahia Style), **11**-1704
Cambodian Mixed Fruits (Trai Cay), **11**-1717
Canadian Cookery, **2**-274
Canadian Hamburger Pie, **6**-872
Canadian Lamb Soufflé, **7**-1040
Canadian Orange-and-Lemon Poundcake, **2**-272
Canadian Parsley Soup, **11**-1690
Canadian Rum Cake, **2**-279
Canadian Snipe, **5**-769
Canadian Spiced Gooseberries, **5**-809

Canapé(s), **1**-85; **2**-279
Brioche for, **2**-280
Butters, **1**-85; **2**-279
Spreads, **2**-279, 280; **4**-642
To Freeze, **5**-737
Canapé(s), Cold
Anchovy, **1**-80
Anchovies on Egg Slices, **10**-1566
Beef, Danish, **1**-86
Cheese, **1**-86
Cheese-Mushroom, **3**-355
Chili Shrimp Squares, **10**-1656
Copenhagen Coolers, **10**-1610
Curried-Salmon Triangles, **10**-1595
Egg-Tomato, **2**-281
Frankfurter Rounds, **1**-86
Onion Brioche, **2**-281
Onion and Parsley Finger Sandwiches, **10**-1610
Peanut-Onion, **1**-86
Pie, **2**-281
Salami-Egg, **1**-86
Sardine Rounds, **1**-86
Shrimp Canapé Paste, **1**-67
Shrimp-Caviar, **4**-632
Shrimp Spread, **10**-1658
Shrimp Toast, **11**-1828
Smithfield Ham, **6**-852
Tomato Caviar, **1**-86
Tuna and Horseradish, **12**-1862
Canapé(s), Hot
Anchovied Mushrooms, **4**-627
Bacon Rolls, **2**-281
Barquettes, **2**-280
Barquettes, Clam, **2**-280
Biscuits with Foie Gras, Hot, **5**-708
Bouchées, **2**-280
Cheese Allumettes, **2**-280
Cheese-Crab, **10**-1610
Cheese Rounds, **4**-635
Chili Cheese Fingers, **3**-395
Chutney and Bacon Fingers, Hot, **1**-86
Crab, **1**-86
Ham-and-Cheese Appetizers, **6**-852
Mushroom, **8**-1197
Savory, **1**-86
Tomato, Bahamian, **1**-86
Canard à la Bruxelloise (Duck à la Brussels), **2**-197
Canards aux Navets (Ducklings with Turnips), **5**-744
Candied Fruit, see Fruit, Candied

Candy(ies), **2**-282
Almond Diamonds, **5**-709
Apricot-Apple Drops, **2**-289
Bonbons, **2**-284; **5**-708
Brittle, **2**-284
Almond, **1**-16
Black-Walnut, **12**-1917
Cashew, **2**-314
Peanut, **1**-75; **2**-288
Peanut, Popcorn, **8**-1323
Butterscotch, **2**-288
Candied-Fruit Squares, **2**-285
Candy-Making Tests, Chart, **2**-284
Caramels, Chocolate, **2**-288
Caramels, Vanilla, **2**-285
Chocolate Creams, **5**-708
Divinity, **2**-284, 285; **4**-570
Chocolate, **2**-285
Ginger, **2**-285
Holiday, **2**-285
Seafoam, **2**-285
Fig Logs, **5**-709
Filbert Squares, **5**-709
Fondant, **2**-284; **5**-708; **9**-1365
Cooked, **5**-708
Patties, **2**-284
Uncooked, **2**-285; **5**-709
Fudge, **2**-283; **5**-764
Burnt-Sugar, **5**-764
Chocolate, **3**-472
Chocolate, Kneaded, **5**-764
Chocolate Nut (QC), **10**-1526
Chocolate, Old-Fashioned, **5**-764
Chocolate, Old-Time, **2**-285
Cocoa, **5**-764
Layered, **5**-764
Mrs. Benson's Receipt for, **8**-1231
Opera, **2**-285
Peanut-Butter Chocolate, **8**-1328
Quick, **5**-764
Vanilla, **5**-764
Glacé Nut Patties, **5**-805
Kisses, Creole, **3**-444
Maple Sugar on Snow, **1**-74
Marshmallows, **2**-288
Marshmallows, Coconut, **2**-289
Mints, Pulled, **2**-288
Mints, Thin, **7**-1166
Mint Wafers, Grandmother's, **8**-1231
Mocha Logs, **2**-285
Nougat, Almond, **2**-288
Opera Creams, **2**-285
Peanut Chews, **1**-75
Peanut Squares, **2**-285
Pecan Roll, **2**-289
Pecan-Roll Slices, **2**-289
Pennies from Heaven, **6**-910
Penuche, Panocha, Penuchi, **9**-1358
Old-Time, **2**-285
Pecan, **9**-1358
Popcorn
Balls, **2**-288; **8**-1231
Balls (QC), **10**-1526
Balls, Sugared, **9**-1437
Caramel, **9**-1437
Molasses, with Peanuts, **9**-1437
Peanut Brittle, **8**-1323
Praline(s), **4**-513
Almond, **9**-1480
Caramel, **9**-1480
Creole, **1**-44
Fresh-Coconut, **9**-1480
Pecan, **2**-285
Vanilla, **2**-285
Raisin-Peanut Clusters, **2**-289
Rum Balls, **2**-289
Seafoam, **2**-284, 285
Taffy, **11**-1808
Chocolate, **11**-1808
Molasses, **11**-1808
Molasses, Old-Fashioned, **2**-288
Peppermint, **9**-1362
Saltwater, **1**-57
Toasted-Coconut Balls, **5**-709
Toffee, **2**-28; **11**-1829
Truffles, Two-Tone, **2**-289
Cannelini al Tonno (White-Bean and Tuna Salad), **6**-960
Cannelloni, Florentine, **8**-1231
Cannelloni, Italian, **8**-1293
Cannelloni alla Parmigiana (Stuffed Pancakes, I), **6**-958

Canning, **2**-289
Chart, Acid Foods, **2**-292
Chart, Nonacid Foods, **2**-291
Cannoli, **3**-368

Cantaloupe, **2**-295; **7**-1129
and Banana Salad, **1**-142
Chiffon Pie, **9**-1397
Fresh, and Grape Cup, **2**-296
Fresh-Lime Melon Cup, **7**-1067
Fresh, and Pineapple Compote, **2**-296
Fresh, and Prosciutto Appetizers, **2**-296
Ice, **6**-925
Melon with Cointreau, Minted, **7**-1166
Melon Delight, **2**-296
Melon, Gingered, **1**-27
Melon Ice-Cream Sauce, **2**-296
Mousse, **8**-1191
and Shrimp Luncheon Salad, **2**-296
Spiced, **1**-24
Canton Beef with Green Beans, **3**-399
Canton Diced Chicken with Almonds, **3**-401
Canton Lobster Cantonese, **3**-399
Canton Pork with Bamboo Shoots, **3**-399
Canton Salted Chicken, **3**-401
Cantonese Broiled Lamb, **7**-1032
Cantonese Style Eggs (Ch'ao Tan), **3**-403
Cape Cod Style Green Beans, **7**-1086

Caper(s), **2**-296
and Brown-Butter Sauce, **10**-1663
Butter, **1**-85
Dressing, **7**-1116
and Egg Sauce, **2**-296
Eggs, Capered, **11**-1839
and Lemon Butter, **5**-695
Piquant Stuffing, **11**-1780

Sauce, **1**-63; **4**-624; **7**-1029, 1101; **10**-1614, 1620
Sauce (Kaprissås), **11**-1791
Toast Butter, **11**-1829
Tuna Open-Faced Sandwiches, **12**-1867
Capon, see Chicken
Caponata, **12**-1903
Caponatina (eggplant), **1**-82
Capsicum, **2**-296; see also Pepper(s), Capsicum

Caramel
Apple Pie, **9**-1392
Cake, **2**-297
-Cardamom Toast, **11**-1825
Chiffon Pie, **9**-1397
Custard(s), **4**-530
Crème Renversée, **3**-493
Pie, **9**-1391
Swedish, **2**-297
-Date Pies, Individual, **4**-547
Filling, Southern, **4**-663
Frosting, **1**-55; **2**-270, 297; **7**-1044
Fudge Frosting, **5**-751
Glaze, **4**-547; **5**-805
Glaze with Coffee Custard Pudding, **9**-1490
Popcorn, **9**-1437
Sauce, **10**-1615, 1628
Squares, **2**-297
Syrup, **2**-297
Topping, **1**-124
Torte, **2**-297

Caramels (candy), 2-284
Chocolate, **2**-288
Pralines, **9**-1480
Vanilla, **2**-285
Caramela, **11**-1732

Caraway, 2-298
Butter, **2**-279
Cottage or Cream Cheese, **2**-298
Dumpling Batter, **9**-1351
Pork Chops, **2**-298
Potatoes, **9**-1466
Sauerkraut with Pork Butt, **9**-1440
Seed Cake, **2**-298; **11**-1819
Soup (Kömény Leves), **6**-917
Carbonnade Flamande (Flemish Beer Stew), **2**-197

Cardamom, 2-299
Cake, Quick, **2**-299
Cookies, **3**-474
Sugar, **2**-299
Cardinal Sauce, **10**-1620
Cardoon, **2**-299
Caribbean Grapefruit, **2**-204
Caribbean Loin of Pork in Black Sauce, **9**-1442
Caribou Stew, Yukon, **2**-278
Carimañolas (Fritters), **11**-1706
Carmen Pears, **8**-1331
Carne Adobada (New Mexican Cured Pork), **11**-1728
Carne Asada (Broiled Beef), **11**-1705
Carne de Porco a Alentejana (Pork with Mussels), **9**-1456
Carneiro Transmontano (Lamb from Over the Hills), **9**-1456
Carnitas al Estilo de Elena (Meat Crisps, Elena's Style), **7**-1138
Carob Flour, **5**-707
Carolina Fruitcake, **1**-61

Carp, 2-304
Casserole, **2**-304
Fillets, Oven-Braised, **5**-699
à la Polonaise (Szczupak czy Karp po Polsku), **9**-1422
with Sauerkraut, Alsatian, **5**-699
with Sour-Cream Sauce (Kapr Peceny s Kyselou Omackou), **4**-531
Sweet-and-Sour, **5**-699

Carrot(s), 2-304
-Almond Conserve, **2**-309
Apple, and Raisin Salad, **10**-1583
and Asparagus, **2**-306
Braised (Zanahorias Natas), **2**-306
and Celery, Braised, **2**-305
with Celery Seed, **2**-306
Cheese-Glazed, **2**-306
-Coconut Salad, **2**-306
and Corn Pudding, **2**-306
Creamed, **2**-306
Curls, **2**-305
Dessert (Gajar Halwa), **6**-942
with Dill, **4**-630; **12**-1904
Dilled Crisscross, **4**-564
Garnishes, **5**-778
Ginger, **2**-306
Glazed, **4**-566
and Glazed Apples, **2**-306
and Green-Bean Salad, **7**-1085
Honey Glaze for, **6**-909
Jam, Golden, **6**-964
Lamb-Carrot Moussaka, **8**-1189
and Onions, Panned, **2**-306
and Onion Tea Sandwiches, **2**-306
-Orange Cookies, **2**-308
Oranged, **2**-306
Oven-Browned, **3**-444
Parmesan, **2**-306
and Parsley Soup, **8**-1298
and Peanut-Butter Sandwiches, **2**-306
Pickled, **2**-309
Pickles, **9**-1374
Pie, **1**-54
and Potato Soup, **9**-1462
Pudding, Steamed, **2**-308
-Raisin Bread, **10**-1611
and Raisin Salad, **2**-306
Rice, **2**-252
Salami-Carrot Salad, **10**-1589
and Sauerkraut Salad (Salat iz Morkovi i Kisloi Kapusty), **10**-1572
Scalloped, **1**-54
Slaw, **2**-306
Slieve na mBan, **6**-948
Soufflé, **2**-305
Soufflé (Porkkanakohokas), **5**-681
Sticks, Dilled, **2**-305
-Suet Pudding, Steamed, **9**-1491
à la Sultana, **12**-1958
Torte, **2**-308
-Walnut Pudding, Steamed, **2**-306
Caruso Spaghetti, **11**-1736

Casaba, 2-314; **7**-1129
Salad with Sour Cream, **2**-314

Cashew(s), Cashew Nut(s), 2-314
Brittle, **2**-314
with Buttered Noodles, **8**-1232
Coffee-Nut Macaroons, **2**-314
Curry Sandwich Spread, **10**-1611
Green Bean, and Mushroom Casserole, **8**-1200
-Rice Stuffing, **2**-314
Tuna Casserole, **12**-1866
Cassata Napolitana (Rich Dessert Cake), **6**-960
Cassava Chicken Pie, **7**-1105
Casseroles, **2**-316
Casserole Buffet, Menu, **2**-250; **8**-1275
Cassoulet, **2**-325

Catfish, 3-341
Baked Stuffed, **3**-341
Deep-Fried, **5**-699
Fried, **3**-341
Fried, Home Style, **1**-25
Soup, **1**-52
Caucasian Plum Sauce (Tkemali), **10**-1627

Cauliflower, 3-341
with Almond Butter, **3**-343
in Bread-Crumb Sauce, **7**-1097
Cheese, and Chicken Casserole, **3**-358
in Cheese Puff, **3**-343
Creamed, **3**-444
Fritters (Torrejas de Coliflor), **11**-1708
and Grape Salad (Salat iz Tsvetnoi Kapusti s Vinogradom), **10**-1566
Hot, with Shrimps (Blomkål i Rekesaus), **8**-1239
Pickles, **9**-1373
Pickles, Mixed Sweet, **9**-1376
Salad with Ham and Avocado (Ensalada de Coliflor con Aguacate), **7**-1142
Sauté with Lemon, **12**-1903
and Shrimp Salad (Maionese di Scampi e Cavolfiori), **1**-82
with Shrimps, Hot, **3**-343
Soup, **3**-341
Soup, Cream of, **1**-55
Stuffed (Fylld Blomkål), **11**-1790

Caviar, 3-343
Bowl, **7**-1146
Butter, **2**-279
Butter, Cream-Cheese, **2**-279
Butter, Toast, **11**-1829
Eggs Stuffed with, **4**-606
Red, in Cream, **1**-76
Shrimp Canapés, **4**-632
Spread, Red Caviar (Taramosalata), **4**-639
Cazuela (Sweet-Potato and Pumpkin Dessert), **9**-1497
Ceci all'Olio (Chick-Peas in Olive Oil), **1**-82

Celeriac, 2-344
Celery-Root Salad (Zeller Saláta), **6**-919
au Gratin, **3**-344
Salad, **3**-344
Céleris Braisés (Braised Celery), **5**-745

Celery, 3-344
-Almond Stuffing, **11**-1781
Braised (Céleris Braisés), **5**-745
Braised, with Peanut-Butter Sauce, **8**-1325
with Cheese and Ham, Baked, **3**-344
Chicken, and Potato Scallop, **7**-1097
Cottage-Stuffed, **3**-355
and Crabmeat Salad, **10**-1582
with Egg-Lemon Sauce (Selino Avgolemono), **5**-822
Fried, **3**-344
Fritters, **1**-73
Grape, and Pear Salad, **10**-1588
Gratin with Almonds, **1**-14
Garnishes, **5**-778
and Onions in Cream, **11**-1823
Peanut-Butter Soup, **8**-1324
-Pickle Spread, **2**-279
with Pork, Stewed Italian, **9**-1451
Salad, Oregon, **1**-65
Sauce, Creamed, **5**-694
Sauté, **3**-344
and Shrimp Salad, **10**-1662
Stuffed, **1**-89
Tomato, and Pepper Relish, **11**-1835
Celery Knob, Celery Root, see Celeriac
Celery Seed, **3**-345
Celestial Crusts (Bozi Milosti), **4**-532

Cereal, 3-345
Hot, Variations for, **3**-346
Ready-to-Eat, Serving Variations for, **3**-345
Cervelle Sauce, **10**-1614, 1622
Cha Chi (Deep-Fried Chicken), **3**-400
Chafing Dish Buffet, menu, **2**-250
Chakin Shibori (Sweet-Potato Dessert), **6**-978
Challah (Sabbath or Holiday Twist Bread), **6**-992

Champagne
Punch, **9**-1502
Sauce, **10**-1626
and Sauterne Punch (QC), **10**-1527
Champignon Schnitzel, **1**-127

Champignons Farcis (Stuffed Mushrooms, French Style), **8**-1201
Chantilly Potatoes, **3**-346; **9**-1464
Chantilly Sauce, **10**-1628
Ch'ao Fan (Fried Rice), **3**-401
Ch'ao Hsia Tan (Shrimp Omelet), **3**-403
Ch'ao Lung Hsia (Lobster Cantonese), **3**-399
Ch'ao Tan (Eggs, Cantonese Style), **3**-403
Cha Yun T'un (Crisp Won Ton), **3**-401
Charcoal Room Cheesecake, **3**-368

Chard or **Swiss Chard,** **3**-348
with Cheese Sauce, **3**-348
and Green Onions, **3**-348
Charleston She-Crab Soup, **1**-67
Charlotte de Pommes (Apple Charlotte), **3**-348
Charlotte Russe, **3**-348; **4**-556
Charlotte Russe Cake, Chocolate, **2**-269
Charlotte Russe, Southern, **11**-1725
Charoses, **6**-994
Chasseur Sauce, **10**-1619
Chateaubriand Sauce, **10**-1626; **11**-1766
Chateaubriand, Sauce Béarnaise, **5**-741
Chateaubriand Steak, **11**-1766
Cha Tom (Vietnamese Omelet), **11**-1717
Chaud-Froid, **3**-348
Sauce, **10**-1620
Chawan-Mushi (Steamed Custard), **6**-971

Chayote, **4**-349; **11**-1758
Boiled, **3**-349
au Gratin, **3**-349
Stuffed, **3**-349
Chazuke, **6**-976

Cheese, **3**-349
Balls, with Paprika, Fried, **8**-1297
-Beef Patties, **3**-358
Board (appetizer), **1**-89
Camembert (sandwich), **4**-536
Camembert, Spread, **1**-86
Canapés, **1**-86
Cornmeal Sticks (Surullitos de Maíz), **9**-1497
à la Crème, **3**-362
Crème Lorraine, **4**-608
Filling, **10**-1539
Fine Noodles for the Shepherdess (Vermicelli alla Pastora), **6**-958
and Guava Dessert, **2**-300
Hamburger Pizza Pie, **8**-1273
Lasagne with Meatballs (Lasagne con le Polpettine), **6**-958
Liederkranz Appetizer Cheese Balls, **1**-62
Macaroni and, Creamy, **3**-358
Mornay Sauce, **8**-1186; **10**-1614, 1620; **12**-1864
Muenster and Corned-Beef Sandwiches, **10**-1605
Noodles, Two-Cheese, **8**-1233
Omelet, **8**-1257
Pancakes, Rolled (Kaese Blintzes), **6**-992
Pie (Tiropitta), **5**-819
Pimiento-Cheese Bacon Spread, **2**-280
Plate, **4**-568, 643
Potatoes, **9**-1469
and Potato Patties (Llapingachos), **11**-1708
Provolone and Salami Sandwiches, **10**-1605
and Rice Balls, **3**-361
Ricotta Tart, The Gevasci's, **3**-367
Ring, Jellied, **10**-1588
Sandwich Fillings, **10**-1606
Sandwiches, Tiny, **1**-86
Soup (Sopa de Queso), **11**-1747
Spaghetti with Four Cheeses (Spaghetti ai Quattro Formaggi), **6**-958
Spinach Pie, **3**-361
-Stuffed Lettuce Salad, **7**-1063
Toast Cups, **2**-252
-Tomato Grill, **7**-1085
Town Toast, **11**-1829
Tray, **4**-650
Tray, Dessert, **3**-362
Turkey Combination Sandwiches, **12**-1877
Two-Cheese Dip, **1**-87
Two-Cheese Fusilli, **11**-1737
Two-Cheese Logs, **1**-78
Two-Cheese Meat Tarts, **11**-1811
World's Best-Known Cheeses, Chart, **3**-352
Cheese (Processed), American
Clam, and Macaroni, Casserole, **7**-1091
and Eggs, Creamy, **3**-358
Fritters, **3**-361
-Glazed Carrots, **2**-306
Golden Buck, **3**-358; **12**-1923
Ham, and Potato Casserole, **2**-317
Omelet, **3**-358
Onion Tarts, **11**-1811
Sandwiches, French-Toasted, **3**-362
Sauce, **5**-725
Sauce, Paprika, **8**-1297
Sauce, Quick, **3**-361
Parsley-Cheese Toasts, **8**-1298
-and-Shrimp Macaroni Loaf, **7**-1091
Soup with Croutons, **3**-355
Spoon Bread, **3**-361
Stratas, Individual, **3**-358
Stuffing, **11**-1780
Cheese, Blue and Roquefort
Blue-Cheese Spread, **1**-86
Chicken-Cheese Sandwiches, **10**-1602
Danish Blue, Sandwich (Roquefort Ost), **4**-536
Dressing, **3**-361; **7**-1115
and Egg Sandwiches, **10**-1605
Malaxe, **3**-355
Mayonnaise-Roquefort Dressing, Creamy, **10**-1622
and Onions, Marinated, **8**-1264
Pineapple Blue-Cheese Salad Ring, **7**-1153
and Rice Hot Salad, **10**-1555
and Roast-Beef Sandwiches, **10**-1604
Roquefort Butter, **10**-1615, 1624
Roquefort Cheese Sauce, **10**-1614, 1623
Roquefort Pinwheels, **8**-1306
Roquefort Salad, **10**-1586
Cheese, Cheddar
Almond, Pea, and Cheese Salad, **8**-1315
Appetizers, **1**-78
-and-Bacon Rice Salad, **10**-1550
Balls, **3**-429
and Bean Appetizers (Totopos), **7**-1138
and Bean Salad, **10**-1582
Beef Cheeseburgers de Luxe, **6**-869
Beef, and Noodle Casserole, Crusty, **2**-316
Biscuits, **2**-238
Brandied, **3**-355
Bread, **2**-229
and Bread Pudding, **9**-1487
and Broccoli Custard, **2**-245
Cauliflower in Cheese Puff, **3**-343
Celery with Cheese and Ham, Baked, **3**-344
Cheddar-Cheese Soup, **1**-60
Chili Cheese Fingers, **3**-395
and Chili Pancakes, Mexican, **8**-1293
Chilies Stuffed with (Chiles Rellenos con Queso), **7**-1141
Cocktail Snacks, Ha'Penny, **8**-1308
and Corned-Beef Sandwiches, **10**-1601
-Corn Fritters, **3**-361
Creole Puff, **8**-1325
Deviled-Ham Spread, **2**-279
-and-Egg Barbecue Sandwiches, **10**-1604
Egg, and Deviled-Ham Sandwiches, **10**-1605
and Egg Toast, **11**-1826
Fish-Cheese Rice, **10**-1550
Fondue, Baked, **3**-359
Fondue, Tuna and Chili, **12**-1864
Frankfurters with Macaroni and Cheese, **5**-720
Golden Buck, **12**-1923
Haggerty, **6**-949
Hamburger Potato-Cheese Pie, **9**-1463
Ham-Cheese Rice Bake, **10**-1549
Ham Rabbit Sandwiches, **10**-1604
Hearts, **8**-1306
and Hominy, **6**-907
Hominy Grits with, Baked, **1**-37
Lobster Rabbit, **7**-1081
and Macaroni, Bacon-Topped, **7**-1093
Macaroni Double-Cheese Casserole, **7**-1096
and Macaroni Soufflé, **7**-1095
Mace Cheese Puffs, **7**-1097
Meat-Cheese Rice, **10**-1550
-Mustard Sauce, **5**-694
-and-Oatmeal Snaps, **8**-1253
Olive Puffs, **6**-913
Onion-Cheese Bread, Quick, **1**-79
Onion Pie, **9**-1388
and Onion Soup, **8**-1260
Pancakes, **2**-238
Pastry, **9**-1398
Peanut-Butter Spread, **8**-1324
Peanut Macaroni and Cheese, **8**-1322
and Pea Salad in Tomato Shells, **8**-1315
Pecan-Pimiento Spread, **8**-1334
-Pickle Spread, **2**-279
Pinwheels, Tiny, **8**-1306
Popovers, **2**-238; **9**-1437
Potato-Cheese Soup, Savory, **11**-1690
Potato, and Egg Sandwiches, **10**-1605
-Potato Salad, Hot, **10**-1582
Rabbit, Wisconsin, **1**-78
and Rice, Baked, **10**-1550
Rounds, **4**-635
Salad, Oregon, **3**-361
and Sardine Salad, **10**-1612
Sauce, **7**-1049
Sauce, Easy, **3**-361
Sharp-Cheddar Dressing, **7**-1116
Soufflé, **2**-324
Soufflé, Top-Hat, **3**-359
Spoon Bread, Golden Cheese, **1**-65
Squares, **7**-1089
Sticks, **3**-355
Straws, **11**-1822
-Stuffed Squash, **11**-1762
Timbales, **11**-1824
Toast Roll-Ups, **11**-1825
Toast Squares, Puffed, **11**-1828
and Tomatoes with Macaroni, Baked, **7**-1095
and Tongue Sandwiches with Cashews, **10**-1605
Truffles (Kaastruffels), **4**-589
Tuna-Cheese Loaf, Baked, **10**-1602
Tuna-Cheese Rice Bake, **10**-1549
-Tuna Chowder, **3**-355
Tuna-Macaroni Bake, **12**-1864
Turkey Sandwiches, Baked, **12**-1877
Turkey with Welsh-Rabbit Sauce, **12**-1874
Turnovers (Empanadas de Queso), **11**-1708
Vegetable-Cheese Rice, **10**-1550
Welsh Rabbit, **1**-10; **3**-346; **12**-1923
Welsh Rabbit with Beer, **12**-1923
and Yam Crullers, Puerto Rican, **12**-1951
Zucchini with Creamy Cheese Topping, **12**-1962
Cheese, Cottage, Pot, and Farmer
-Apple-Noodle Pudding, **3**-362
Apricot-Cheese Sandwich Filling, **10**-1611
Apricot Salad, **1**-106
Blintzes, **2**-204
Blueberry Cottage-Cheese Cake, **2**-210
and Blueberry Salad, **10**-1587
Cakes, Fried (Syrniki), **10**-1572
Caraway, **2**-298
Celery, and Olive Spread, **2**-279
Cottage Beef and Eggs, **7**-1084
Crab-Cheese Dip, **7**-1083
Cucumber, and Grapefruit Salad, **12**-1958
and Cucumber Salad, **7**-1085
Dessert, **3**-362
Dressing, **10**-1588
Dumplings, Lazy (Leniwe Pierogi), **9**-1429
and Egg Tart (Vatrushki), **10**-1572
Filling, **8**-1308; **9**-1429

French Dressing, **10**-1622
Frozen Cheese and Raspberry Dessert, **10**-1536
Green-Noodle Casserole, **3**-359
Lemon-Orange Mold, **7**-1052
and Lime Salad, Jellied, **7**-1067
Macaroni, and Sour-Cream Salad, **10**-1582
Mushroom Canapé, **3**-355
and Noodle Casserole, Hungarian, **8**-1233
Noodle Pudding, **9**-1487
Orange Cups, **8**-1268
Pancakes, **3**-361
Peach Salad, **8**-1316
Pear Salad, **3**-361
Pie, **9**-1390
Pineapple Pie, **3**-362
Pompushkes, **11**-1700
Pot-Cheese Dumplings, **4**-587
Prune Soufflé, **3**-362; **9**-1485
Sag Paneer, **11**-1755
Spinach Salad, **12**-1958
Spread, **1**-86
and Strawberry Salad, Jellied, **11**-1776
Strudel, **6**-922; **11**-1780
-Stuffed Celery, **3**-355
Tarts, Tropical, **3**-367
and Tomato Salad, Jellied, **6**-980
and-Tomato Salad, Layered, **11**-1834
and Vegetable Peach Salad, **8**-1316
Cheese, Cream Cheese
with Banana Paste (Bananada com Queijo), **11**-1709
Butter Cookies, **3**-472
Caraway, **2**-298
Carrot, and Raisin Sandwiches, **10**-1605
Caviar Butter, **2**-279
Cheese-Filled Rolls, **2**-236
Cherry, and Pineapple Sandwiches, **10**-1611
Coconut-Cheese Sandwich Loaf, **10**-1611
Coeur à la Crème, **5**-788
Custard (Budino di Ricotta), **6**-960
Foldovers, **3**-434
Frosting, **5**-752
Frosting, Chocolate, **2**-267; **3**-407; **5**-752; **7**-1045
Ginger Salad Bowl, **12**-1935
Golden Fleece, **4**-608
Lemon Cookies, **3**-473
Lemon Pie, **7**-1054
Liptauer Cheese Spread, **1**-90
Loganberry-Cheese Tarts, **7**-1081
Miniatures, **4**-643
Mousse, **3**-362; **8**-1191
-and-Nut Sandwiches, Savory, **10**-1610
-Olive-Raisin Sandwiches, **8**-1257
-Olive Spread, **2**-279
Parsley Balls, **8**-1299
Pastry, **8**-1304
Pastry, Russian, **11**-1838
Peanut Sandwiches, **8**-1325
and Pear Salad, Jellied, **6**-980
and Pineapple Pie, **9**-1408
Quiche Lorraine with Cream Cheese, **10**-1527
-Roquefort Spread, **2**-279
Sage-Cheese Appetizer, **10**-1578
Sandwiches, **9**-1383
Seafoam Salad, **10**-1587
Stuffing, Syrian, **11**-1782
Topping for Ginger Bread, **3**-362; **5**-805
-Watercress Balls, **3**-424
Cheese, Gruyere and Samsø
Croquettes with Green Noodles (Croquettes au Fromage), **11**-1803
Onion Soup with Cheese, Jamaican, **6**-967
Sandwich, **4**-536
Sauce, **10**-1614, 1620
Toast Butter, **11**-1829
Cheese, Mozzarella
Eggplant, and Pimiento Long Boys, **10**-1605
French-Toasted Sandwiches, **10**-1604
Italian Mozzarella Skewers (Crostini alla Mozzarella), **6**-955
Medallions of (Medaglioni di Mozzarella), **6**-952
Pillows with Italian Ham (Cuscinetti Filanti al Prosciutto), **6**-862
Pizzas, Individual, **3**-355
Spiedino alla Romana, **3**-358
Stuffing, Italian, **11**-1782
Cheese, Parmesan and Romano
-Baked Ham and Vegetables, **3**-355
Beignets, **2**-196
Butter, **1**-86
-Crab Canapés, **10**-1610
Croutons, **4**-519; **11**-1697
Cubes, Salty, **8**-1306
Egg-Parmesan Pudding, Steamed, **4**-604
with Eggplant (Berenjena con Queso), **9**-1496
Green Noodles with Basil, **8**-1233
Fettucine Alfredo, **8**-1233
Macaroni Parmesan, **7**-1095
and Macaroni, Tossed, **7**-1095
Sauce, **3**-359; **5**-806; **6**-958; **8**-1231
Spaghetti Parmigiana, **3**-361
Spinach-Cheese Strips, **8**-1306
Waffles, **12**-1915
Cheese, Swiss
Allumettes, **2**-280
Appetizer, Hot, **7**-1146
Batter-Fried (Steak de Fromage), **11**-1803
Chicken, and Cauliflower Casserole, **3**-358
Croque Monsieur, **3**-362
Denver Sandwiches, **10**-1604
Eggs with Cream Sauce (Oeufs à la Crème), **11**-1804
Filling, **3**-492
Fondue, **3**-359; **11**-1803
Fondue, Geneva Style, **5**-712
Fondue, Neuchâtel Style, **5**-711
Glorified Cheese Strata, **2**-325
Green-Noodle, Beef, and Cheese Casserole, **2**-324
and Ham Pie (Quiche de Bourbonnaise), **6**-862
Leek Soup with, **3**-355
and Macaroni Salad, **7**-1095
Mornay Sauce, **3**-361
Onions, Swiss Style, **8**-1264
Petit Puffs, **8**-1306
Pie, **3**-359
Pie with Bacon, **3**-355
with Potatoes and Mushrooms, **8**-1201
Quiche Lorraine, **4**-566; **5**-703
Quiche Lorraine with Swiss Cheese, **10**-1529
Raclette, **5**-712
Ramekins, **10**-1535
Salad (Käsesalat), **11**-1804
Sandwich, French Style, Fried (Croque Monsieur), **6**-862
Sardine Sandwiches, **10**-1604
Sauce, Cabbage in (Repollo en Salsa de Queso), **9**-1496
Spread, Simple, **1**-86
Tartlets, **1**-87
Tartlets (Ramequins au Fromage), **11**-1804
Toast Special, **11**-1825
and Veal Steaks, **12**-1897
Walnut Sandwich, **10**-1611

Cheesecake(s), **3**-364
Blueberry-Decorated, **3**-366
Blueberry-Topped, **7**-1087
Bohemian Restaurant, **3**-366
Cannoli, **3**-368
Charcoal Room, **3**-368
Cream, with Cookie Crust, **1**-33
Dale's, **3**-368
de Luxe, **3**-368
Dream, **3**-366
Golden, **11**-1798
Grison's Steak House, **3**-367
Holiday, **3**-428
Jay's Famous Cheese Pie, **3**-368
Lemon, Frozen, **5**-791
Mad Hatter, **3**-366
Pineapple, **3**-367
Pineapple, Jellied, **9**-1409
Postre de Mamon, Elena Zelayeta's, **3**-367
Pump Room, **3**-366
Refrigerator, Jim Beard's, **3**-367
Ricotta Tart, The Gevasci's, **3**-367
Secret Harbor, **3**-368
Strawberry and Almond, **8**-1282
Strawberry-Glazed, Lindy's, **3**-367
Strawberry-Pineapple Refrigerator Cake, **3**-369
Tropical Cheese Tarts, **3**-367
Violet-Topped, **3**-369
Chef's Club Sandwich, **10**-1604

Chef's Salad
Brussels, **10**-1580
California, **5**-825; **7**-1063
Classic, **10**-1580
Orange, **10**-1580
Chello Kebab, **8**-1215
Cherkes Tavugu (Circassian Chicken), **8**-1214

Cherry(ies), **3**-369
Batter Pudding, **3**-374
Bavarian, **3**-374
Blintzes, **6**-992
Bounce, **3**-372
Buttercream Frosting, **5**-751
Cake, **3**-372
Coconut Macaroons, **7**-1096
-Coconut Pastries, **8**-1309
in Currant Jelly, **7**-1154
Deep-Fried (Cseresznye Kisütve), **6**-921
Dumplings, **3**-374
Dumplings (Knedlíky s Visnové), **4**-532
Frosting, **5**-750
Ice Cream, **1**-36
Jam, Red-Cherry, **6**-965
Jam, Sour-Cherry, **6**-965
Jam, Sour-Cherry, No-Cook, **6**-965
Jubilee, **3**-372
Jubilee, Flaming, **5**-701
Kuchen, Red-Cherry, **9**-1384
Muffins, **7**-1154
Pancakes, French (Clafoutis), **3**-372
Parfait, **3**-374
Parfait, Two-Tone, **6**-930
and Pear Halves Compote (Kompot iz Narezanykh Popolam Grush i Vishen), **10**-1573
Pickled, **1**-49
Pies, **1**-77
Bavarian, **9**-1398
Chantilly, **1**-78
Deep-Dish, **8**-1229
Deep-Dish (QC), **10**-1525
Deep-Dish, with Shortcake Crust, **3**-374
Sour-Cherry, Canned, **3**-374
Sour-Cherry, Fresh, **3**-374
Sour-Cherry, Frozen, **3**-374
Sour-Cherry (individual), **9**-1396
Sweet-Cherry, **9**-1396
Pork Chops with, **3**-372
-Port Mold, **10**-1677
Preserves, Sweet-Cherry, **9**-1481
Roly-Poly, **3**-374
Sauce I, **3**-374
Sauce II, **3**-375
Soup (Kirsebaersuppe), **4**-539
Cold, **8**-1235
Soup Scandinavian, **12**-1927
Strudel, **6**-922; **11**-1780
Tart(s), **3**-374; **5**-763; **7**-1089
Tart or Flan, **8**-1309
Tarts, Glazed, **11**-1812
Torte with Cream, **12**-1854
Torte Glacé, **4**-552
Upside-Down Cake, **3**-374; **12**-1882
Vareniki, **10**-1574
Waffles, **12**-1915

Cherry(ies), Maraschino, 3-371
-Almond Parfait Pie, 7-1108
Apricot Sauce, 6-930
Cake, 3-375
Coconut Squares, 7-1109
Cream-Cheese, and Pineapple Sandwiches, 10-1611
Creamy Strawberries Maraschino, 7-1108
-Pineapple Sauce, 5-788
-Pistachio Parfait, 3-375
Sauce, 7-1108
Watermelon-Maraschino Pickle, 12-1922
Chervil, 3-375
Butter, 5-695
Chesapeake Oyster Bisque, 2-203
Chess Pie, 9-1388

Chestnut(s), 3-375, and **Marron(s),** 7-1112
Bread Stuffing, 11-1781
Chocolate Cake (Gâteau de Marrons au Chocolat), 5-746
and Brussels Sprouts, 2-248; 3-440
-Chocolate Dessert, Italian, 3-377
-Chocolate Vanilla Tarts, 3-416
Cream, 5-783
Purée, 3-376
and Sausage Stuffing, 11-1781 for Chicken, 3-376
Stuffing for Turkey, 3-376
Sweet (Doce de Castanhas), 9-1457
and Sweet Potatoes, Scalloped, 11-1797
Chestnuts, Whole Braised, 3-376
Marron Coupe, 7-1112
Marron Purée, 7-1112
Marron Soufflé, 7-1117
Meringue with Marron Filling, 7-1112
Mont Blanc of Chestnuts (Monte Bianco di Castagne), 3-376
Cheyenne Chocolate Cake, 1-79
Chiang Lo Po (Sweet-and-Sour Radishes), 3-403

Chicken, 3-377
Alexandria (QC), 10-1521
-Almond Mousse, 1-14
-Almond Salad, 1-14
with Almonds, Diced (Hsing Jen Chi Ting), 3-401
Appetizer Pastries, 8-1306
Arroz con Pollo, 10-1550
Artichoke, Sherried, 12-1930
Aspic, 1-116
Avocado-Chicken Soup, 11-1690
-Avocado Salad, 1-130
-Avocado Tostada, 12-1930
Baked in Cream, 3-382; 8-1224
Baked (Gemisti Kotta), 5-820
Baked in Orange Sauce, 8-1268
Barbecued, 7-1089
Barbecued Broiled, 3-381
Barbecued, Texas, 4-645
Batter-Dipped Fried, 3-384
and Bean Casserole, Savory, 7-1066
Boiled (Tori no Mizutaki), 6-975
Bok You Guy, 10-1550
Booyaw, 1-49
Bordeaux, 2-213
Bouillon, 2-215
Braised, 2-219
Braised with Wine, 12-1947
Breast(s)
Boneless (Suprêmes de Volaille), 3-383
with Cream (Suprêmes de Volaille à Blanc), 3-383
Far Eastern Kebabs, 3-390
with Mushrooms, 3-384
en Papillote, Arnaud's, 4-512
Piedmont Style (Petti di Pollo alla Piemontese), 6-955
Suprêmes of, Jeanette, 3-349
Tropicale, 3-383
Broiled, Cold, 9-1378
Broiled Deviled, 3-382
Broth, Golden (Goldene Yoich), 6-987
Browned, Stew with Cornmeal Dumplings, 4-586
Brunswick Stew, 1-75
Brunswick Stew (QC), 10-1520
Brunswick Style Stew, 3-386
Cacciatora (Pollo alla Cacciatora), 6-955
Capon(s)
Cock of the North, 6-948
Roast Stuffed, Middle-East, 2-298
Twin, with Two Stuffings, 3-439
Carving, 2-313
Cassava Pie, 7-1105
Casserole, Herbed, 11-1824
Charcoal-Broiled, 1-146
Cheese, and Cauliflower Casserole, 3-358
-Cheese Sandwiches, 10-1602
Chinese Smoked, 3-386
Chinese Walnut, 3-381
and Chorizo Spaghetti, 8-1275
Circassian (Cherkes Tavugu), 8-1214
Cock-a-Leekie Soup, 6-945
Coconut (Moa Niu), 9-1435
Cooked in Burgundy Wine (Huhn im Burgunder), 5-795
Coq au Vin, 3-386
-Corn Moussaka, 8-1190
and Corn Pudding, 9-1487
Costa Brava (Pollo a la Costa Brava), 11-1746
Country Captain, 1-33; 3-382
Cracklings (Gribenes) and Fat, 6-987
with Cream (Poulet à la Crème), 5-744
Croquettes, 4-518
Curried Chicken Filling, 3-492
Curry, 4-527
Curry with Tomatoes (Murgha Kari), 6-939
Danish, 3-386
Deep-Fried, 3-384
Deep-Fried (Cha Chi), 3-400
Dinner, Menu, 8-1278
Divan, 2-244
with Dumplings, 4-586
and Eggplant, Baked Individual, 4-615
Enchiladas (Enchiladas de Gallina), 11-1706
Enchiladas (Enchiladas de Pollo), 7-1138
Fat and Gribenes (Cracklings), 6-987
with Figs, 4-576
-Filled Tortillas with Tomato Sauce, 12-1856
Filling, 8-1308
Filling in Green Corn-Husk Tamales, 11-1808
Flambée, 2-221; 5-701
Florentine, 5-704
Forcemeat, 5-715
and Frankfurters, Creamed, 5-724
and Fresh Grape Mold, 5-812
Fricassee, 3-390; 5-716
Fricassee with Cornmeal Dumplings, 5-748
Fricasseed with Meatballs, Flemish (Kiek met Ballekens), 7-1122
Fried (Backhendl), 1-122
Fried Japanese (Tatsuta-Age), 1-26
Fried, Maryland, 1-46
Fried, with Puffs and Gravy, 1-22
Fried, Topeka, 1-39
Galantine of, 5-766
How to Bone and Prepare a Chicken for a Galantine, 5-765
Gumbo, 3-386; 5-830; 8-1255
in Ham Blankets, 6-855
-Ham Mousse, 3-391
Ham and Oyster Gumbo Filé, 4-660
and Ham Three-Decker Sandwiches, 10-1611
with Hard Cider, 1-37
Hash, Baked, 3-391
Hashed in Cream, 3-390
Hash à la Ritz, 6-879
Hawaiian (QC), 10-1521
Jellied Lemon Chicken, Portuguese, 7-1052
à la King (QC), 10-1523
Korma Curry, 4-525
Lasagna, Make-Ahead, 7-1041
and Leek Casserole, 7-1047
Legs, Ham-Stuffed, 6-852
in Lemon-Caper Butter, 7-1052
Lemon-Fried, 1-29
Loaf, Loaves, 3-390; 7-1129
Loaf with Almond and Mushroom Sauce, 7-1152
and Lobster, Costa Brava, 7-1080
Low-Calorie Fried, 3-383
Low-Calorie Seasonings for, 7-1084
Luau, 1-34
-Macaroni Salad, Baked, 7-1094
Marengo, 3-381; 4-568
Marinade for Small Portions of, Uncooked, 7-1110
Minced, Sandwich Filling, 10-1611
Mold, Jellied, 6-979
Montmorency, 3-390
Mornay, 8-1186
Mornay on Broccoli, 2-325
Moussaka with Peas, 8-1190
Mousse, 8-1190
Mulligatawny, 8-1194
Mulligatawny Shorba, 11-1691
and Mushrooms, Barrister Style Hollyhock-House, 8-1200
and Mushrooms in Sour-Cream Sauce, 2-320
-Mushroom Vol-au-Vent, 12-1913
Noodle Supreme, Party, 8-1232
Normandy, 11-1736
and Okra Gumbo, 4-512
with Olive and Caper Sauce, 5-775
Olivier Salad (Salat Olivier), 10-1566
with Onions, 8-1261
à l'Orange, 3-382
Orange Salad, 8-1268
Oven-Fried, in Bread Loaf, 3-424
Oven-Fried, Crispy, 3-383
and Oyster Casserole, 2-320
and Oyster Sauté, 8-1288
Paella a la Valenciana, 8-1291
Paprika (Paprikahühner), 1-122
Paprika with Sour Cream (Csirke Paprikás), 6-919
Paprika, with Sour-Cream Sauce, 8-1296
in Paprika Sour-Cream Sauce, 11-1698
Peach Salad, 8-1316
in Peanut-Tomato Sauce, 8-1324
and Peas, Herbed, 8-1314
with Pecans, Southern, 8-1334
with Peppers, Sautéed (La Chiso Ch'ao Chi), 3-400
Picnic, 1-64
Pie, 7-1151
Pie with Corn Crust (Pastel de Maíz con Gallina), 7-1140
Pie, Old Homestead, 3-382; 9-1388
Pilaf, 3-391
Pilaf (Kotta Pilafi), 5-820
Pilau, Madras, 9-1401
and Pineapple, Hawaiian, 9-1406
-Pineapple Spread, 2-279
Pine-Nut Dressing for, 4-575
and Pork (Adobong Manok at Baboy), 9-1369
in a Pot, 3-382
Potato, and Celery Scallop, 7-1097
with Potatoes, Pot-Roasted Stuffed, 9-1477
Potpie, Boiled, 9-1352
Pot-Roasted, Jamaica Style, 9-1477
Poule au Riz, 3-387
Poulet Vallée d'Auge, 3-386
à la Providence, 3-383
and Prunes, Baked, 3-382
or Pullets, Roast à la Polonaise (Kura Lub Kurczeta po Polsku), 9-1428
Quenelles, 10-1527
Rappie Pie, 2-278
with Rice (Arroz con Pollo), 9-1496
and Rice Salad with Cashews, 2-314
with Rice, Spanish, 10-1550
with Riesling (Coq au Riesling), 5-744
Rivvel Corn Soup, 9-1350
Roast, Roasted
with Bananas, 3-381

Cold, **8**-1278
Glazed, **7**-1084
India Style, **3**-391
with Sausage-Nut Stuffing, **3**-381
Stuffed, **4**-625; **8**-1214
with Tarragon (Poulet à l'Estragon), **5**-744
Tongdak Juk, **7**-1022
Rosemary, **3**-382
Rosemary, in Cream, **10**-1560
Rosemary, with Tangerine Rice, **10**-1556
Salad, **3**-391
Chinese, **10**-1582
Nham, **11**-1717
Perfect, **10**-1582
(QC), **10**-1522
Silhouette, **7**-1086
Salted (Hsien Chi), **3**-401
Sancocho, **2**-300
Sandwich Loaf, **10**-1610
in Sauce (Pollo con Salsa), **11**-1706
Scotch Cock-a-Leekie, **7**-1047
Sesame, Spiced, **10**-1647
-Shrimp Gumbo Filé, **1**-44
on Skewers, Broiled (Sate Ajam), **11**-1714
on Skewers, Fried (Kushi-Katsu), **6**-975
Smothered in Oysters, **1**-67
Soup, **5**-716
Soup, Cool Curried, **3**-390
Soup (Moeun Sngo), **11**-1717
Soup with Sherry, **6**-967
Soup or Stew, Friar's, **11**-1721
Soup, Ujhazy, **11**-1695
Southern Fried, **11**-1723
with Cream Gravy, **3**-383
Variations in Preparing, **11**-1723
Soy, Baked, **11**-1734
Steamed (Dak Chim), **7**-1022
Steamed in Lemon Butter, **3**-387
Steamed in Lime Juice, **7**-1067
Stew, **9**-1774
Stew with Dumplings, **5**-716
Stew (Szegedi Csirke Paprikás), **6**-919
Stew (Waterzooi de Poulet), **2**-197
Stock, **11**-1775
Stuffings for, **3**-392
Supreme, Scalloped, **4**-632
-and-Sweetbread Croquettes, **1**-46
and Sweet Potatoes, Baked, **11**-1796
and Sweet-Potato Soup, **11**-1795
Sweet and Sour (Pollo en Agridulce), **9**-1496
in Sweet Wine (Pollo en Vino Dulce), **9**-1496
Tandoori, **12**-1957
Tartlets, Curried, **11**-1811
Tetrazzini, **11**-1819
Tetrazzini (QC), **10**-1522
Timetable for Roasting, Chart, **3**-378
Walnut (Ho T'ao Chi Jing), **12**-1917
and Watercress Soup, **12**-1920
on the Wing, **3**-384
Yam of Roses, **11**-1716
Zucchini, **12**-1961

Chicken Giblet(s) and **Gizzards**
Giblet Pâté, **5**-800
Giblet Sandwich Filling, **5**-800
Giblet Sauce (Sikotakia Saltsa), **5**-822
Giblet Stuffing, **3**-392
Giblets with Rice, **5**-800
Gizzards in Sauce Pietro, **3**-392

Chicken Liver(s)
Appetizers, **3**-391
-and-Bacon Sandwiches, **7**-1076
-Bacon Spread, **2**-279
and Barley, **3**-391
with Carrots and Peas, **7**-1075
Chopped, **6**-987; **7**-1075
Cutlets, **9**-1470
with Fried Noodles, **3**-391
and Green Beans, Sautéed, **7**-1075
Omelet, **7**-1075
Pâté, **4**-565; **7**-1075
Pâté, Ruby-Glazed, **6**-979
and Rice, Oriental Style, **3**-399
with Rice Soup, Italian, **7**-1075
with Sage, **10**-1578
with Sage (Fegatini di Pollo alla Salvia), **6**-955
Sauce, **7**-1076
Shrimp Spread, **2**-279
in Sour Cream, **7**-1076
Sweet-and-Pungent, **3**-391
Terrine, Quick and Easy, **8**-1312
Turnover, **12**-1879
Wine Picnic Pâté, **12**-1927

Chick-Pea(s), **3**-392
Croquettes (Falafel), **6**-992
Curry (Chinai Curry), **6**-942
Fritters (Frituras de Garbanzos), **11**-1747
Garbanzo Sauce, **11**-1737
Mashed with Sesame, **8**-1212
in Olive Oil (Ceci all'Olio), **1**-82
Salad, Italian, **3**-392
Salad, Mexican, **3**-392
and Sausage, **10**-1638
Soup with Pigs' Feet (Sopón de Garbanzos con Patas de Cerdo), **9**-1493
Soup, Spanish, **3**-392

Chicory, **3**-393
Panned, **3**-393
Chiffonade Dressing, **3**-393; **4**-573; **5**-694; **10**-1622
Chile Potato or Sweet-Corn Pie (Pastel de Papas o Choclos), **11**-1705
Chile Strawberry Snow (Bavaroise Frutillas), **11**-1709
Chile con Carne (Chili with Meat), **7**-1140
Chile con Carne Verde, **11**-1728
Chiles Rellenos con Queso (Chilies Stuffed with Cheese), **7**-1141

Chili, **3**-394
Baked Ocean Perch, **9**-1363
Barbecue Sauce, **5**-725
Beefburger Sandwiches, **10**-1601
Butter, **1**-85
con Carne (Heavy), **3**-396
con Carne (Hot), **3**-395
con Carne (Mild), **3**-395
con Carne (QC), **10**-1520
con Carne, Roast-Beef, **9**-1385
con Carne Sauce, **8**-1282
Cheese Fingers, **3**-395
Corn in Husks, **3**-482
Dip, **1**-87
-Filled Tortillas, **12**-1856
Hunter's, **12**-1909
Lamb, Pueblo, **11**-1728
Limas, **7**-1065
Mayonnaise, **7**-1116
with Meat (Chile con Carne), **7**-1140
Meatballs, **6**-870
Pie, Cowpuncher, **11**-1728
Pineapple-Chili Barbecue Sauce, **10**-1623
Popcorn, **3**-395
Pork Balls in Tomato Sauce, **9**-1449
Pumpkin Soup, **11**-1727
con Queso, **4**-643
Salsa, Mexican, **9**-1360
Sauce, **1**-64
-Sauce-Beef Pot Roast, **9**-1473
-Sauce Butter, **5**-694
Sauce, Eggs Poached in (Huevos con Salsa de Chiles), **11**-1708
Sauce, Green, **11**-1731
Sauce, Green (Salsa de Chile Verde), **7**-1142
Sauce, Homemade, **3**-396
Sauce, Quick (Salsa Rapida de Chile), **7**-1142
Sauce, Red, **11**-1731
Sauce, Red (Salsa de Chile Colorado), **7**-1142
Sauce, Southwestern, **11**-1731
Sauce, Spiked, **2**-194
Seafood in, **11**-1727
Shrimp Squares, **10**-1656
-Tomato Sauce, **8**-1273
and Tuna Fondue, **12**-1864
Whitefish, **12**-1939

Chilies, Chili Peppers
and Cheese Pancakes, Mexican, **8**-1293
Potatoes with Cold Huancayo Sauce (Papas con Salsa Huancaina Fría), **11**-1708
Stuffed with Cheese (Chiles Rellenos con Queso), **7**-1141
Chinai Curry (Chick-Pea Curry), **6**-942
Chinese Almond Cookies, **4**-635
Chinese Bamboo Shoots Salad, **10**-1583
Chinese-Beef Casserole, **11**-1734
Chinese Beef with Mushrooms, **2**-189, **8**-1200
Chinese Broiled Pork, **9**-1442
Chinese Cabbage, see Cabbage, Chinese
Chinese Chicken Salad, **10**-1582
Chinese Cookery, The Art of, **3**-396
Chinese Egg-Drop Soup (Chi Tan T'ang), **3**-401
Chinese Egg Rolls, **8**-1294
Chinese Egg Rolls (Chi Tan Chuan), **3**-401
Chinese Eggs Fu Yung, **4**-610
Chinese Fortune Cookies, **4**-635
Chinese Fried Shrimps, **10**-1660
Chinese-Pork-Fried Rice, **9**-1450
Chinese Roast Goose, **1**-81
Chinese Smoked Chicken, **3**-386
Chinese Style Pineapple and Shrimps, **9**-1406
Chinese Style Pork Spareribs, **9**-1445
Chinese Sweet-and-Sour Pork, **1**-26
Chinese Sweet-and-Sour Spareribs, **11**-1749
Chinese Vegetables, **2**-250; **3**-403
Chinese Vegetables with Roast Pork, **12**-1919
Chinese Walnut Chicken, **3**-381
Chirinabe (Fish Sukiyaki), **6**-971
Chi Tan Chuan (Chinese Egg Rolls), **3**-401
Chi Tan T'ang (Chinese Egg-Drop Soup), **3**-401
Chitterlings, see Pork

Chive(s), **3**-404
Butter, **1**-85; **2**-279; **5**-695; **10**-1615, 1624
and Cress Soup, **11**-1690
Parsley Butter, **8**-1299
Potatoes, **9**-1467
-Scrambled Eggs, **3**-404
Toast Butter, **11**-1829

Chocolate, **3**-404
Almond Torte (Rehruecken), **11**-1804
Balls, Greek, **3**-416
Black-Walnut Drops, **7**-1157
Blancmange, **2**-205
Brazilian, **3**-416
Brownies (QC), **10**-1526
Brownie Waffles, **12**-1915
Buttercream, Speedy, **5**-783
Butterscotch Bars, **12**-1918
Cake(s)
Angel Food, **3**-410
Brown-Sugar Fudge, **7**-1044
Charlotte Russe, **2**-269
Chestnut (Gâteau de Marrons au Chocolat), **5**-746
Cheyenne, **1**-79
Cream-Filled, **2**-265
Devil's Food, **4**-559
Devil's Food, with Marshmallow Frosting, **4**-559
Devil's Food Squares, **4**-559
Diva, **3**-408
-Filled Eight-Layer, **7**-1044
Fondant, **3**-407
Fudge-Cake Squares, **3**-411
Grandma's, **3**-410
Honey, **3**-410
Midnight Lace, **3**-407
Milk-Chocolate, **3**-407
Nutcake, **3**-410

Chocolate, continued
One-Bowl, **2**-268
Peppermint, **7**-1044
Potato, **9**-1468
Poundcake, **2**-272; **9**-1479
Prune, **9**-1486
Rum, A Man's, **3**-408
Shadow, **7**-1044
with Sour-Cream Frosting, **11**-1701
Southern, **7**-1045
Spongecake, **3**-410
Sweet Chocolate, **3**-407
-Walnut, **7**-1044
Wisconsin, **3**-407
Caramels, **2**-288
Chestnut Dessert, Italian, **3**-377
Chestnut Slices, **5**-783
Chestnut Vanilla Tarts, **3**-416
Cinnamon Parfait, **6**-930
-Coconut Crust, **3**-456
Confection, Viennese, **3**-416
-Covered Coffee Beans, **6**-930
Cookies, Refrigerator, **3**-474
Cream Roll, **3**-410
Creams, **5**-708
Crinkle Cups, **3**-416
Crispies, **4**-636
Cupcakes, Surprise, **3**-411
Decorating with, **4**-549
Dessert, Queen Bona's, **3**-415
Diamonds with Hazelnuts, **6**-882
Divinity, **2**-285
Doughnuts, **4**-572
Drops, **10**-1535
Filling(s), **1**-124; **11**-1812
Bavarian, **4**-663
Cream, **3**-492; **8**-1243, 1309
Float, **7**-1161
Freezer Ice Cream, **6**-929
Frosted, **5**-752; **7**-1160
Frosting, **2**-267; **7**-1044, 1157; **10**-1535; **12**-1959
Bittersweet, **3**-412
Butter, **3**-412
Butter, Fluffy, **5**-751
Buttercream, **5**-751
Choco-Peanut, **3**-412
Choco-Sour Cream, **3**-412; **5**-752
Cream-Cheese, **2**-267; **3**-407; **5**-752; **7**-1045
Creamy, **3**-412
Easy, **3**-410
Fudge, **3**-412; **4**-559; **5**-751
Fudge, Semisweet, **5**-751
Glossy, **1**-79; **3**-407
Hungarian, **5**-752
Peanut-Butter, **8**-1328
Rich, **3**-457
Rum, **3**-408
Semisweet, **3**-412
Soft, **3**-401
Fudge, **3**-472
Batter Pudding, **3**-415
Batter Pudding, Black-and-White, **3**-415
Kneaded, **5**-764
Meringues, **3**-472
Nut (QC), **10**-1526
Old-Fashioned, **5**-764
Old-Time, **2**-285
Peanut-Butter, **8**-1328
Glaze, **3**-410; **4**-594; **5**-805; **11**-1756
Glaze, Bitter, **5**-783
Glaze, Thin, **3**-411
Guatemalan, **3**-416
Ice Cream, **6**-929
Ice-Cream Roll, **6**-932
Icing, **12**-1853
Lebkuchen, **7**-1046
Macaroons, **7**-1096
Meringues, **3**-416
Mexican (Chocolate Mexicano), **7**-1143
Milk, **7**-1158
Mint Cookies, **3**-412
Mint Float, Frosted, **7**-1161
Mocha, **7**-1167
Mousse, **5**-790; **8**-1191
French, **3**-415
Low-Calorie, **3**-415
-Mint, **8**-1191
Mousse au Chocolat, **5**-746
Pastry, **8**-1304
Peppermint-Chocolate Cream, Marbled, **9**-1361
Pie(s)
Almond, **7**-1089
Angel, **3**-411
Black-Bottom, **3**-411
Black-Bottom, with Chocolate Crust, **9**-1398
Brownie, **9**-1390
Chiffon, **3**-393, 411
Coconut Syrup, **9**-1390
Fruit, **4**-578
Marble, Frozen, **9**-1398
Meringue, **9**-1392
-Pecan, **8**-1335; **9**-1390
Peppermint Chiffon, **9**-1397
Rum, Marbled, **9**-1398
Spongecake, **9**-1390
Pie Shell, **9**-1399
Pinwheel Cookies, **3**-434
Pots de Crème au Chocolat, **3**-494
Pudding, Cornstarch, **9**-1489
Pudding, Steamed, **8**-1228
Quick, **3**-417
Raspberry Cream, **3**-416
Rings, **3**-475
Sabayon, **9**-1489
Sauce, **9**-1492; **10**-1615, 1628
Bittersweet, **10**-1628
Custard, **10**-1628
Fudge, **3**-415; **6**-931
Low-Calorie, **3**-416
Mole, **5**-770
Peanut-Butter, **8**-1328
Soufflé, **3**-412; **11**-1688
Cold, **4**-557
Sour-Cream Frosting, **11**-1701
Spanish Egg, **3**-416
Spongecake, **11**-1756
Spritz Cookies, **11**-1757
Squares, **3**-433
Sticks, Spicy, **3**-412
Syrup, **3**-417; **11**-1807
Taffy, **11**-1808
-Topped Custard Pie, **9**-1391
Torte Burgundy, **4**-553
Torte, French, **12**-1853
Torte, Unbaked Warsaw, **3**-415
Chokeberry Jam, Wild, **1**-62
Cholent (Jewish Sabbath Meal-in-One), **6**-990
Chop Suey, **3**-417
Skillet, **8**-1232
Turkey, **12**-1874
Chorizo (Mexican Sausage), **7**-1140
Choron Sauce, **6**-905; **10**-1621
Choucroute Garnie, **1**-16; **10**-1632
Simple, **9**-1444
Chowder, **3**-417; for recipes see Soup(s), Chowder(s), and Thick Soup(s)
Chowchow, **8**-1231; **9**-1350
Chow Mein, **3**-417; **7**-1049
Chow Meins (leftovers), **7**-1049
Duck, **4**-584
Pork, **9**-1451
Turkey, **12**-1874
Chremslach (Matzo-Meal Fritters), **6**-994
Christmas
Bread (Julekake), **8**-1240
Eggnog, **4**-611
Eve Salad (Ensalada de Noche Buena), **7**-1142; **12**-1931
Fruitcake (Stollen), **5**-798
Fruit Salad, **10**-1588
Ham (Juleskinke), **8**-1237
Ham (Julskinka), **11**-1788
Menus, buffet, **3**-424
Menus, dinner, **3**-438, 440
Meringues, **7**-1135
Tarts, Banana, **11**-1812
Tree Bread (Tannenbaum Brot), **5**-798
Tree Cookies, **3**-428
Wig Buns, **7**-1098
Chrust Czyli Faworki (Crunch Cakes or Favors), **9**-1431
Chuck's Barbecue Sauce Relish, **10**-1543
Chuck-Wagon Boiled Beans, **1**-53
Chu Jou Pi Chi Tang (Pork and Watercress Soup), **3**-401
Churros (Mexican Crullers), **7**-1143

Chutney(s), **3**-446
Apple, West Indies, **1**-102
and Bacon Fingers, Hot, **1**-86
Baked Beans, **1**-159
Butter, **1**-85
Cream-Cheese (filling), **3**-492
Date, East Indian, **4**-579
Dressing, **7**-1116
Ginger Fresh-Peach, **8**-1321
Ham Spread, **2**-280
Mango, **3**-446
Mango, Spicy, **7**-1104
Melon, Hot, **7**-1132
Peach, **8**-1321
Pear, **12**-1878
Pineapple, **3**-446
Tomato, **3**-446
Tomato-Cumin, **10**-1556

Cider, **3**-446
Apple-Cider Raisin Pie, **1**-39
Gelatin Salad, **1**-103; **3**-446
Ham in, **6**-853
Molasses, Hot, **8**-1185
Mulled, **8**-1193
Mulled, Holiday, **8**-1193
Pie, **3**-446
Punch, Hot, **3**-446
-and-Sage Jelly, **6**-982
Sauce for Meats, **1**-103
Sauce for Pudding, **3**-446
Spiced, **11**-1754
Wassail Bowl, **12**-1918

Cinnamon, **3**-446
-Apple Salad, Jellied, **10**-1587
Buns, Sticky, **9**-1354
Cookies, Swedish (Kanelkakor), **11**-1796
Flop, **9**-1355
Frosting, **1**-56; **3**-471
Hazelnut Buns, **6**-882
-Honey Syrup, **5**-824
-Layered Quick Coffeecake, **11**-1754
Loaf, **2**-233
Mocha Frosting, **3**-410
-Nut Diamonds, **3**-432
Rolls, **2**-236
Stars, **3**-447
Sugar, **11**-1784
Syrup, **7**-1155
Toast de Luxe, **3**-447; **11**-1825
Topping, **7**-1156
Cioppino, **3**-447; **12**-1927
Fisherman's Wharf, **1**-26
Circassian Chicken (Cherkes Tavugu), **8**-1214
Cisco, Broiled, **6**-903

Citron, **3**-449
Loaf Cake, **3**-449

Citrus, **3**-449; see also names of citrus fruits
Peel, Quick Crystallized, **2**-281
Salad Plate, **3**-451
Vitamin C in varieties, Chart, **3**-451
Clabber (Sialde Mleko), **9**-1428
Clafoutis (French Cherry Pancakes), **3**-372

Clam(s), **3**-451
-Aspic Salad, **6**-979
Barquettes, **2**-280
Bisque, Chilled, **11**-1692
Bites, **1**-89
Bouillon Digby Pines, **2**-275
Brandy Sauce, **5**-700

à la Bulhao Pato (Ameijoas a Bulhão Pato), **9**-1456
Chowder, **8**-1222
Chowder, Manhattan, **3**-418
Chowder, New England, **3**-418
Coquilles, **4**-632
and Cream-Cheese Dip, **1**-87
Deviled, **3**-453
Dip, **4**-642
Eggplant Soufflé, **4**-614
Fried, or Fannie Daddies, **1**-66
Fritters with Tomato Sauce, **3**-453
on the Half Shell, Broiled, **3**-453
-Juice Cocktail, Hot, **8**-1282
Macaroni and Cheese Casserole, **7**-1091
and Oysters and Mushrooms, Fricassee of, **8**-1198
Pastries, **6**-912
Pie, **8**-1222
Pilaf (Achivades Pilafi), **5**-818
Pilaf Casserole, **10**-1554
Portuguese (Ameijoas Portuguesas), **9**-1455
Puffs, Fried, **3**-453
Razor-Clam Bisque, **1**-64
Sauce, White, **3**-453
Sauce, White, Quick, **11**-1738
Sauce, White (Salsa di Vongole), **6**-959
Scallop, **8**-1222
Soup, Italian Style, **3**-453
Soup (Sopa de Ameijos), **9**-1453
Spaghetti, **11**-1736
Steamed, **3**-452

Clarify, To Clarify
Bouillon, **2**-215
Broth to Make Consommé, **3**-467
Butter, **2**-253
Clipper Sandwich, **4**-536
Cloverleaf Rolls, **2**-236
Cloves, **3**-454
Coalfish, see Sablefish

Cobbler(s), **3**-454
Apple, **11**-1725
Huckleberry, **11**-1725
Peach, **8**-1317; **11**-1725
Peach, Old-Fashioned, **3**-454
Plum Cake Cobbler, **9**-1417
Red-Currant, **7**-1155
Strawberry, **11**-1776
Wild Blackberry, **11**-1725
Coca de Sardinas (Sardine Pie), **9**-1494
Cocido (Spanish Boiled Beef), **11**-1742
Cock-a-Leekie, Scotch, **7**-1047
Cock-a-Leekie Soup, **6**-945

Cocktail(s), **1**-85
Avocado-Tomato, **3**-455
Clam-Juice, Hot, **8**-1282
Crabmeat Rémoulade, **1**-86
Cucumber, Diced, **1**-86
Cucumber Tomato, **11**-1832
Flounder, Flaked, **5**-705
Fruit, **5**-754
Fruit, Six Suggestions, **3**-455
Grape and Avocado, Fresh, **5**-812
Lobster and Orange, **7**-1077
Mayonnaise Sauce, **10**-1626
Melon, with Guava Jelly, **5**-829
Mushroom, **8**-1197
Peach, Fresh, **1**-86
Pear, Fresh-, and Shrimp Appetizer, **8**-1330
Sardine, **10**-1612
Sauce, **7**-1077; **11**-1626
Sauce, Hot, **5**-695
Seafood, **3**-455
Seafood Cocktail Salad, **5**-786
Shrimp Rémoulade, **1**-86
Shrimp Rémoulade, Hotel Pontchartrain, **4**-510
Shrimp, Supreme, **10**-1656
Tomato, Spiced, **11**-1832
Tuna, **12**-1863
Watermelon, **1**-86
Cocktails, to drink, see Beverages

Cocoa, **3**-455
Hot, **3**-455
Hot (QC), **10**-1526
Iced, **3**-455
Kisses, **7**-1017
Marshmallow Pudding, **7**-1113
Syrup, **11**-1807
Whipped-Cream Topping, **3**-412

Coconut, **3**-455
Apple Betty, **9**-1490
Apricot-Coconut Balls, **4**-578
Blancmange, **2**-205
Bread, **2**-238
Brown-Sugared Roasted Fresh Coconut Bites, **2**-301
-Buttermilk-Cream Pie, **9**-1391
Carrot Salad, **2**-306
-Cheese Sandwich Loaf, **10**-1611
Cherry-Coconut Macaroons, **7**-1096
Cherry-Coconut Pastries, **8**-1309
Cherry Coconut Squares, **7**-1109
Chicken (Moa Niu), **9**-1435
Chocolate Crust, **3**-456
Chocolate Syrup Pie, **9**-1390
Cookies, **3**-458; **4**-634
Cookie Snowballs, **10**-1668
Cream, **9**-1370
Cream (from dried coconut), **3**-456
Cream (from fresh coconut), **3**-456
Cream, Hawaiian, **1**-35
Crust, **9**-1399
-Crusted Apple Dessert, **3**-457
Custard Pie, **4**-530; **9**-1391
Eskimos, **3**-458
Fresh-Coconut Cake, **3**-456
Fresh-Coconut Filling, **4**-662
Fresh-Coconut Ice, **6**-925
Fresh-Coconut Pralines, **9**-1480
Frosting, Boiled, **3**-457
Kisses, **7**-1017
Lemon Ambrosia Pie with Coconut Crust, **9**-1397
Macaroons, **3**-458; **7**-1096
-Marshmallow Frosting, **5**-750
Meringue Pie, **9**-1392
Milk, **1**-36; **4**-526; **9**-1370; **10**-1627
Milk (from dried coconut), **3**-456
Milk (from fresh coconut), **3**-456
Orange Bread, **10**-1611
-Orange Squares, **3**-471
-Pecan Filling, **3**-407
Poppy-Seed Bars, **9**-1438
Pot Roast, West Indian, **9**-1472
Puddin'-Pie, **3**-456
and Raisins with Rice (Arroz con Coco y Pasas), **11**-1709
Rice, Sweet Sticky, **11**-1717
Sambal, **4**-527
Sherbet Drink, Brazilian, **10**-1654
Snowballs, **3**-458
Spinach (Limu Niu), **9**-1435
Squares, **3**-431
Syrup Pie, **9**-1390
-Taro-Egg Custard (Khanom mo Kaeng), **11**-1716
Tea Rounds, **8**-1310
Toasted-Coconut Balls, **5**-709
Water, **9**-1370

Cod, Codfish, **3**-458
Baked, Piquant, **5**-688
Biarritz, **9**-1469
Boiled (Avkokt Torsk), **8**-1236
Cakes, Spooned, **1**-47
Cape Cod Turkey, **1**-47
à la Catalan, **3**-459
Creamed, and Baked Potatoes, **8**-1222
Fillet of, and Rock Lobster Sarapico, **7**-1080
Fillets with Cheese Sauce, Broiled, **5**-688
Fillets, Creole, **7**-1084
Fillets with Potatoes, Baked (Gestoofde Kabeljauw of Schelvis met Aardappelen), **4**-589
Flemish Style (Morue à la Flamande), **2**-197
Florentine, **3**-459
and Lima-Bean Chowder, **7**-1065
Lutfisk, Boiled (Kokt Lutfisk), **11**-1787
with Mushroom-and-Wine Sauce, **8**-1198
Scrod, **10**-1644
with Olive Sauce, Broiled, **5**-692
Paprika, Baked, **5**-692
Smoked, en Casserole, **5**-688
in Spicy Tomato Sauce (Bacalao Veracruzano), **7**-1140
Steaks, Deviled, **3**-459
Sunday-Morning Fish Balls, **8**-1222

Cod, Salt-Cod
Casserole, Basque (Bacalao a la Vizcaina), **11**-1743
Chowder, **2**-275
and Potato Cakes, Dropped, **3**-459
Provencal, **3**-459
Salted Dried Cod (Klipfisk), **4**-539
Coeur à la Crème, **5**-788

Coffee, **3**-460
-Banana Bavarian, **6**-980
Beans, Chocolate-Covered, **6**-930
Bombe, Italian, **2**-212
Buttercream Frosting, **5**-751
Café Brûlot, **3**-462
Café Brûlot, New Orleans, **5**-702
Café au Diable (Café Brûlot), **3**-462
Café Frappé, Deep South, **5**-726
Café au Lait, **3**-462
Caffè Espresso, **4**-651
Campfire, **3**-462
Chiffon Pie, **9**-1397
Church-Supper Method, **3**-462
Cream Filling, **12**-1959
Custard Pudding with Caramel Glaze, **9**-1490
Dunk, **5**-714
Frosted, **3**-462
Frosting, **5**-750; **7**-1045
Greek, **4**-640
Greek (Kafes), **5**-824
Hot (instant, QC), **10**-1526
Hot (kettle, QC), **10**-1526
How to Make Good Coffee, **3**-460
Ice-Cream Soda, **3**-462
Iced, **3**-462
Iced, Viennese (Wiener Eiskaffee), **1**-123
Ice with Whipped Cream, **6**-925
Imperial, **3**-462
Instant, For a Crowd, **3**-462
Irish, **3**-462; **6**-950
Mocha, **3**-462
Mocha de Luxe, **3**-462
Mocha de Luxe, Iced, **3**-462
Mousse, Kona, **1**-35
-Nut Cream Pie, **9**-1391
-Nut Macaroons, **2**-314
-Pecan Fancies, **8**-1335
Pot Roast with Vegetables, **9**-1473
Shake, **3**-462
Soufflé, Cold, **4**-565
Special, **4**-630
Spice Cake, **7**-1045
Spiced Jelly with Rum Cream, **5**-790
Sponge, **7**-1087; **11**-1837
Tortoni, **12**-1857
Turkish, **3**-462
Viennese, **4**-630
Viking (Vikingekaffe), **4**-543

Coffeecake(s), **3**-462
Coffeecake(s), Quick
Apple, **3**-463
"Bee's Sting" (Bienenstich), **5**-798
Cinnamon-Layered Quick, **11**-1754
Kaffekake, **8**-1240
Mace, **7**-1100
Peanut-Butter Marmalade, **8**-1326
Pecan, **8**-1334
Pineapple, **2**-239

Coffeecake(s), continued
Scotch, **3**-463
Yellow, **3**-463
Coffeecake(s), Yeast
Almond-Filled Coffee Ring, **1**-15
Apricot-Peanut Squares, **2**-232
Babka, Polish, **7**-1156
Cardamom Braid, Swedish, **2**-233
Christmas Coffee Ring, **3**-429
Cinnamon Loaf, **2**-232
Election Cake, **1**-28
Finnish Coffee Braids, **2**-232
Fruitcake, Raised, **2**-233
Fruit Twist, **4**-578
German Coffee Braid, **2**-231
Hungarian Poppy-Seed Kringle, **9**-1437
Italian (Panettone), **3**-463
Kringle, Danish, **7**-1157
Kugelhupf, **1**-123
Savarin, **10**-1639, 1640
Stollen, **11**-1775
Streusel, **2**-231
Tea Ring, Swedish, **7**-1156
Turban, **2**-232
Coimbra Egg Pudding (Pudim de Ovos a Moda de Coimbra), **9**-1457
Colache (Vegetable Medley), **7**-1141
Colbert Butter Sauce, **10**-1624
Colbert Sauce, **10**-1626
Colcannon, **6**-949

Cold Cuts, **3**-463; see also names of cold cuts
Cornucopias (for appetizers), **1**-89
Cubed (for appetizers), **1**-89
Head Cheese, **6**-882
Head Cheese, Pork and Veal, **6**-979
Suggestions for Serving, **3**-463
Coleslaw, see Salads, Coleslaw

Collards, **3**-464
and Salt Pork, Stewed, **3**-465
Colonial Pear Pie, **9**-1393
Colombia Avocado Salad (Ensalada de Aguacate), **11**-1709
Colombia Rice with Coconut and Raisins (Arroz con Coco y Pasas), **11**-1709
Colombia Roast Leg of Pork (Puerco Asado), **11**-1706
Columbian Tongue, **2**-193
Commander's Palace Stuffed Flounder, **4**-510
Commander's Palace Trout Alexander, **12**-1860

Compote(s), **3**-465
Apple-Cranberry, Hot, **3**-465
Fresh-Pear, **8**-1332
Fruit, Amandine, **3**-465
Fruit, Canned, **5**-758
Fruit, Chilled, **3**-465
Fruit Compote Combinations, **3**-465
Fruit, Dried, **4**-578; **6**-993
Orange and Pomegranate, **9**-1436
Peach, **8**-1316
Pear, Gingered, **8**-1332
Pear Halves and Cherry (Kompot iz Narezanykh Popolam Grush i Vishen), **10**-1573
Pear-Orange, **8**-1333
Prune-Orange (Kompot is Apelsin i Chernosliv), **10**-1573
Raisin, Rumanian, **10**-1534
Summer-Fruit, **5**-758
Tangerine, **11**-1809
Vanilla Fresh-Plum, **9**-1416

Conch, **3**-465
Chowder, **3**-466
in Marinara Sauce, **3**-466
Stewed, **3**-466
Concord Punch (QC), **10**-1526

Condiment(s), **3**-466
(for Curries), **4**-526
English Mustard, **5**-725
Figs, 5-Day Pickled, **1**-59
Ketchup
Fruit, **1**-53; **6**-999
Grape, **6**-999
Green-Tomato, **1**-41
Mushroom, **6**-999
Tomato, **6**-999
Rouille, **2**-216
Sauce, Hot, **10**-1626
Shrimp Sambal, **10**-1661
Coney Island Picnic Frankfurters, **5**-724

Confection(s), **3**-466
Aplets, **1**-76
Apples on a Stick, Halloween, **1**-102
Apricot Candy Roll, **8**-1328
Apricot-Coconut Balls, **4**-578
Arab Dates, **3**-449
Burnt Almonds, **1**-13
Buttered Honey Nuts, **6**-911
California Fruit Roll, **5**-758
Candied Cranberries, **3**-490
Chocolate Balls, Greek, **3**-416
Chocolate Crinkle Cups, **3**-416
Chocolate Meringues, **3**-416
Chocolate, Viennese, **3**-416
Cinnamon Filberts, **4**-659
Date Chews, **4**-547
Date Comfits, **8**-1335
Figs Stuffed with Almonds, **1**-16
Fondant-Dipped Almonds, **5**-708
Fondant-Stuffed Dates, **5**-708
Fruit Meringues, **7**-1135
Halva (Nut Confection), **5**-824
Hickory Nut Creams, **6**-904
Hungarian Christmas Balls, **3**-455
Marshmallows, **7**-1113
Marshmallow Sticks, Crispy, **7**-1113
Marzipan, **7**-1115
Nougat, French, **8**-1244
Nut and Honey Sweetmeats (Tayglach mit Neshomas), **6**-994
Orange Peel, Honeyed, **8**-1273
Orange Peel, Spiced, **8**-1273
Peach Leather, **1**-34
Peanut and Raisin Clusters, **8**-1323
Pecans, Sugared, **8**-1335
Popcorn Balls, **2**-288; **8**-1231
Popcorn Balls (QC), **10**-1526
Spiced Raisins, **10**-1535
Stuffed Sherried Dates, **4**-548
Turkish Dreams, **10**-1561
Turkish Paste, **5**-791
Walnut Bonbons, **12**-1917
Walnut Meringues, **7**-1135
Walnut Nougat, **8**-1244
Wasps' Nests, **1**-78

Confectioners' Sugar, **11**-1784
Frosting (or Icing), **1**-15, 50; **2**-232; **3**-410; **4**-543; **7**-1157; **8**-1309; **10**-1526
Plain, **5**-751
Glaze, **9**-1438
Vanilla, **9**-1431

Consommé, **3**-466; see also Bouillon(s); Soup(s), Bouillon(s) and Consommé(s)
Consommé, **3**-467
Julienne, **3**-467; **6**-996
Madrilene, **4**-568
Madrilene, Jellied, **3**-467; **6**-979
To Clarify Broth for, **3**-467
Watercress, Jellied, **3**-467
Conserves, see Jam(s) and Conserve(s)
Continental Club Sandwiches, **10**-1602
Cooked Foods, to Freeze, **5**-736

Cookie(s), **3**-467, and **Small Cakes**
Almond Cookies, **2**-250
Almond Cookies (Hsing Jen Ping), **3**-404
Almond Bread, Brussels (Pain d'Amandes), **2**-200
Almond Butter Cookies (Ischeler Torteletten), **1**-124
Almond-Butter Strips, **3**-473
Almond Cookies, Chinese, **4**-635
Almond Cookies, Glazed, **1**-16
Almond Cookies (Mandelterter), **8**-1243
Almond Hearts, Nonsweet, **1**-15
Almond Lebkuchen, Dropped, **7**-1046
Almond Macaroons, **1**-15
Almond Meringue Cookies, **7**-1135
Almond Meringues, Rich, **7**-1135
Almond Pfeffernüsse, **9**-1367
Almond Slices, **1**-74
Almond Spritz Cookies, **11**-1758
Almond Wreaths (Mandelkränze), **5**-798
Aniseed Cookies, **11**-1732
Antler Cookies (Hirvensarvet), **5**-681
Apple-Nut Bars, **1**-103
Apple Oatmeal Cookies, **1**-102
Apricot Crescents, **1**-109
Apricot-Date Bars, **4**-547
Apricot-Pecan Sticks, **8**-1335
Arbutus Hermits, **4**-656
Benne-Seed Cookies, **1**-68
Benne Wafers, **10**-1647
Black-Eyed Susans, **3**-473
Black-Walnut Chocolate Drops, **7**-1157
Black-Walnut Cookies, **3**-476
Black-Walnut Wafers, **12**-1917
Blotch Kucha or Sugar Leb Cake, **9**-1357
Bonbons, Baked, **12**-1918
Brandy Nut Cakes, **8**-1319
Brandy Wafers, **3**-472
Brazil-Nut Bars, Layered, **3**-471
Brazil-Nut Macaroons, **7**-1096
Brownies, **2**-246
Black and White, **2**-246
Chocolate (QC), **10**-1526
Brown-Sugar Hermits, **6**-901
Brown-Sugar Nut Mounds, **3**-474
Butter Cookies, Brown-Edged, **3**-431
Butter Cookies, Sugared, **3**-474
Butter Rings, Filled, **3**-472
Butterscotch Acorns, **3**-474
Caramel Squares, **2**-297
Cardamom Cookies, **3**-475
Carrot-Orange Cookies, **2**-308
Cheese-and-Oatmeal Snaps, **8**-1253
Cherry-Coconut Macaroons, **7**-1096
Cherry Coconut Squares, **7**-1109
Chocolate Butterscotch Bars, **12**-1918
Chocolate Crispies, **4**-636
Chocolate Cupcakes, Surprise, **3**-411
Chocolate Diamonds with Hazelnuts, **6**-882
Chocolate Drops, **10**-1535
Chocolate Fudge Meringues, **3**-472
Chocolate Lebkuchen, **7**-1046
Chocolate Macaroons, **7**-1096
Chocolate Mint Cookies, **3**-412
Chocolate Pinwheel Cookies, **3**-434
Chocolate Refrigerator Cookies, **3**-474
Chocolate Rings, **3**-475
Chocolate Spritz Cookies, **11**-1757
Chocolate Squares, **3**-433
Christmas Tree Cookies, **3**-428
Cinnamon Cookies, Swedish (Kanelkakor), **11**-1796
Cinnamon-Nut Diamonds, **3**-432
Cinnamon Stars, **3**-447
Cocoa Kisses, **7**-1017
Coconut Cookies, **3**-458; **4**-634
Coconut Cookie Snowballs, **10**-1668
Coconut Kisses, **7**-1017
Coconut Macaroons, **3**-458; **7**-1096
Coconut-Orange Squares, **3**-471
Coconut Squares, **3**-431
Coffee Molasses Cupcakes, **4**-523
Coffee-Nut Macaroons, **2**-314
Coffee-Pecan Fancies, **8**-1335
Coriander Drop Cookies, **3**-478
Cornflake-Coconut Macaroons, **1**-67
Cornflake Macaroons, **7**-1096
Cream-Cheese Butter Cookies, **3**-472
Cream-Cheese Foldovers, **3**-434
Cream Cookies, Swedish, **3**-473
Crisp Cookies (Grostoli), **6**-960
Curled Cakes (Krumkaker), **8**-1241
Currant-Orange Cupcakes, **4**-523

Dalesman Cakes, Norwegian, **9**-1471
Date Cookies, Mae's, **3**-476
Date-Nut Bars, Frosted (QC), **10**-1526
Date-Nut Kisses, **7**-1017
Date-Nut Pinwheels, **4**-547
Date Pastries, Southern, **4**-547
Date Sticks, **4**-547
Decorating Cookies, **4**-549
Devil's Food Squares, **4**-559
Dream Cookies, **3**-474; **10**-1666
Elisen Ginger Cookies (Elisen Lebkuchen), **5**-798
Farina Cakes (Maamoul), **8**-1216
Fat Rascals, **4**-525
Filbert Crescents, **4**-659
Filbert Kisses, Toasted, **3**-472
Filbert Lemon Logs, **3**-474
Filbert Spice Cookies, **4**-659
Fingers, **3**-474
Florentines, **8**-1272
Fortune Cookies, Chinese, **4**-635
Fortune Wafers, Japanese (Tsujiura), **6**-978
Four Specie Dollars (Fire-Speciedaler-Kaker), **8**-1243
Fruit Drops, Holiday, **3**-432
Fruited Molasses Bars, **3**-471
Fruit-Filled Cookies, **4**-579
Fudge-Cake Squares, **3**-411
Funnel Cakes or Plowlines, **9**-1357
Ginger Cookies, **11**-1754
Ginger Cookies, Crisp, **5**-801
Ginger Cutouts, **5**-801
Ginger Drop Cookies, **5**-801
Ginger Wafers, **5**-803
Grandmother's Jelly Cookies (Mormor's Syltkakor), **11**-1793
Hermits, **3**-471
Hermits, Old-Fashioned, **8**-1230
Hickory Crescents, **6**-904
Honey-Date Bars, **6**-911
Honey Fruit Bars, **3**-433
Honey Lebkuchen, **7**-1046
Honey Peanut-Butter Cookies, **3**-474
Hussar's Kisses (Huszárcsók), **6**-922
Jam Circles, **3**-473
Lace Cookies, **3**-472
Lebkuchen, **3**-435
Leckerli, **3**-433
Lemon-Caraway Cookies, **3**-474
Lemon-Cheese Cookies, **3**-473
Lemon-Nut Cookies, **7**-1056
Lemon Squares with Apricot Glaze, **9**-1382
Leopold Schnitten, **3**-447
Lizzies, **3**-435
Macaroons, **7**-1096
Macaroons, Danish, **7**-1096
Madeleines, **7**-1102
Maple Lace Wafers, **7**-1108
Medal Cookies (Medaljekager), **4**-543
Melt-in-the-Mouth Cookies, **3**-433
Meringues, Christmas, **7**-1135
Mincemeat Diamonds, Frosted, **3**-471
Mincemeat Hermits, **6**-901
Mincemeat Lane Cakes, **7**-1164
Mint Cookies, **3**-476; **7**-1166
Mocha Nut Butter Balls, **3**-474
Molasses Cookies, **1**-77; **8**-1185
Molasses Cookies, Old-Fashioned, **9**-1357
Molasses Crinkles, Helen's, **3**-476
Molasses Cutouts, Spicy, **3**-472
Molasses Drop Cookies, **11**-1798
Molasses Hermits, **6**-901
Moravian Cookies, **3**-431
Mother Monsen Cakes (Mor-Monsen Kaker), **8**-1243
Muscatels, Italian, **8**-1194
Muster Cookies, **4**-654
Neapolitans, **8**-1208
Newton Sugar Squares, **1**-57
Nut Butter Cookies, **2**-252
Nut-Butter Wafers, **3**-472
Nut Crescents (Nusskipferln), **1**-124
Nutmeg Date Bars, **3**-471
Nutmeg Logs, **8**-1247
Oatcakes, **4**-634
Oatmeal Chocolate-Chip Cookies, Virigina's, **3**-475
Oatmeal Cookies, Crisp, **7**-1041
Oatmeal Cookies, Filled, **8**-1253
Oatmeal Drop Cookies, **8**-1253
Oatmeal Lace Cookies, **3**-434
Oatmeal Refrigerator Cookies (QC), **10**-1526
Old-Fashioned Rocks, **3**-471
Orange Flowers, Spiced, **3**-473
Orange Shortbread, **10**-1655
Orange Wafers, **3**-472
Orange Walnut-Date Bars, **3**-431
Oregon Filbert Squares, **1**-65
Peanut-Butter Apple Tea Sticks, **8**-1326
Peanut-Butter Drop Cookies, **3**-476
Peanut Cookies, Surprise, **8**-1328
Peanut Crisps, **8**-1323
Peanut Oatmeal Cookies, **8**-1323
Pecan Bars, **3**-471
Pecan Butter Balls, **3**-432
Pecan Dainties, **8**-1335
Pecan Dainties, Southern, **8**-1335
Pecan Squares, Spicy, **8**-1335
Petits Fours, **9**-1365
Petticoat Tails, **6**-950
Pfeffernüsse, **9**-1367
Pineapple-Oatmeal Cookies, **9**-1409
Pine-Nut Cookies, **9**-1411
Poor Man's Cake (Fattigmann), **8**-1241
Poppy-Seed Coconut Bars, **9**-1438
Poppy-Seed Mace Cookies, **7**-1100
Porcupines, **1**-44
Prune Pound Cupcakes, **4**-523
Prune Refrigerator Cookies, **3**-475
Punch Rings (Punschkakor), **11**-1793
Raisin-Filled Cookies, **3**-475; **10**-1535
Raisin-Nut Pinwheels, **10**-1535
Raspberry Delights, **3**-471
Rolled Fruit Sticks, **4**-548
Rosewater Sugar Cookies, Old-Fashioned, **10**-1561
Rye Cookies, Swedish, **10**-1575
Rye-Honey Cookies, **10**-1575
Rye Rings (Rågkakor), **11**-1793
Sand Tarts, **3**-473
Sandwich Cream Cookies, **3**-434
Serina Cakes (Serinakaker), **8**-1243
Sesame-Anise Cookies, **10**-1647
Sesame-Seed Cookies, Korean, **4**-635
Shortbread(s), **10**-1655, 1656; **11**-1819
Small Frosted Cakes, **3**-428
Snickerdoodles, **1**-29
Snickerdoodles, Joanne's, **3**-476
Sour-Cream Molasses Squares, **11**-1701
Sour-Cream Raisin Nut Cookies, **11**-1701
Sour-Cream Sugar Cakes, **9**-1357
Sour-Milk Gingerbread Cupcakes, Anthelias', **8**-1230
Spiced Cookies (Speculaas), **4**-593
Spicy Chocolate Sticks, **3**-412
Spongecake Cookies (Pleskener), **8**-1243
Springerle, **1**-82
Spitzbuben, **3**-473
Spritz Cookies, **3**-435; **11**-1757
Stormy-Weather Jumbles, **3**-475
Stuffed-Date Cookies, **4**-547
Sugar Cookies, **3**-432
Sugar Crisps, **3**-472
Swirl Cookies, **3**-474
Teacakes (Polvorónes), **7**-1143
Urchins (Spitzbuben), **5**-799
Vanilla Cupcakes, **4**-523
Wafers (Goro Cakes), **8**-1243
Walnut Bars, Hungarian, **12**-1918
Walnut Crescents, **12**-1918
Walnut Shortbread, **12**-1917
Walnut Strips, Serbian, **12**-1918
Wasps' Nests, **1**-78
Wine Cookies, Italian, **3**-473
York Hermits, **9**-1357
Coon, see Raccoon
Coot, Roast, **5**-769
Copenhagen Coolers, **10**-1610
Coq au Riesling (Chicken with Riesling), **5**-744
Coq au Vin, **3**-386
Coquilles St. Jacques, **3**-478, **5**-739
Cordon Bleu, **1**-126

Coriander, **3**-478
Drop Cookies, **3**-478
with Potatoes, Baked, **8**-1282
Rice Pudding, **3**-478
Tomato Marmalade, **3**-478

Corn, **3**-478; **12**-1900; see also Hominy
Apple Corn Muffins, **8**-1193
and Avocado Salad (Ensalada de Aguacate y Maíz), **7**-1142
Bacon Corn Fritters, **8**-1224
Bacon, and Egg Pancakes, **3**-484
Bake, Creamy, **3**-482
Baked, **1**-53
Broiled, with Salt Pork, **10**-1598
Cakes, Lace-Edge, **1**-41
and Carrot Pudding, **2**-306
Cheese Fritters, **3**-361
Chicken-Corn Moussaka, **8**-1190
and Chicken Pudding, **9**-1487
Chicken Rivvel Corn Soup, **9**-1350
-Chicken Soup, Pennsylvania Dutch, **3**-481
Chili Corn in Husks, **3**-482
Chowder, **3**-419
Chowder, Iowa, **1**-38
Chowder, Kansas, **7**-1146
on-the-Cob, **8**-1278
on the Cob, Roast(ed), **7**-1152; **9**-1385
on-the-Cob, Sauces and Butters for, **3**-480
in Cream, **3**-482
and Cress Soup, Cream of, **12**-1920
Crust, Chicken Pie with (Pastel de Maíz con Gallina), **7**-1140
Dodgers, **1**-25
Dried, **9**-1354
Egg, Olive, and Raisin Casserole, **8**-1257
and Frankfurter Casserole, **5**-720
and Frankfurter Chowder, **5**-718
-Frankfurter Soup, **11**-1695
Fresh-Corn Cakes, **3**-484
Fresh-Corn Pudding, **9**-1487
Fresh-Corn Soufflé, **3**-482
Fresh-Corn Tart (Torta de Maíz Tierno), **9**-1496
Fritters, **2**-242; **3**-484
Fritters, Nebraska, **1**-54
Fritters, Parsleyed, **5**-749
Fritters, Skillet, **3**-484
Green-Corn Cakes, **1**-67
Green Corn-Husk Tamales with Chicken Filling, **11**-1808
with Green Onion, Sautéed, **3**-482
-Ham Bake, **3**-481
Hamburger-Corn Skillet Dinner, **6**-873
and Ham Fritters, **6**-856
and Meat All-in-One, **3**-482
and Meatballs, Barbecued, **3**-482; **7**-1123
Medley, Stewed, **3**-482
Muffins, Double-Corn, **2**-237
Muffins, Savory, **8**-1192
Mush, Grilled, **1**-55
and Mushrooms, Sautéed, **3**-382
Oysters, **1**-28
Oysters, Idaho, **1**-36
and Peas in Cream, **8**-1315
and Peas, Herbed, **8**-1315
and Pepper Relish, **10**-1541
Pie, **3**-484; **9**-1353
Pie, Sweet-Corn (Pastel de Papas o Choclos), **11**-1705
Pudding, **7**-1152
Quiche, **3**-482
Relish, **1**-38
Relish, Pennsylvania Dutch, **3**-484
Relish, Quick, **10**-1541
Rivvel Soup, **1**-66
Roast, **1**-145
and Sausage, Scalloped, **10**-1636
Scalloped, **1**-67

Corn, continued
Scalloped (QC), **10**-1524
and Shrimp Casserole, **3**-482
and Shrimp Pie, **1**-67
-Soufflé Pudding, Southern, **1**-22
Squaw Corn, **1**-27
Squaw Dish, **1**-61
Stewed, **11**-1723
Sticks, **2**-239; **3**-444
Sticks, Double, **3**-484
-Stuffed Pimientos, **9**-1359
-Stuffed Tomatoes, Baked, **3**-484
Stuffing Balls, **3**-445
Stuffing, Mexican, **11**-1782
Succotash, **11**-1783
Succotash, Creamy, **7**-1065
Succotash, Picnic, **7**-1065
Green Corn-Husk Tamales (Tamales de Maíz con Chile y Queso), **7**-1138
Tomato, and Celery Salad, **3**-484
Tomatoes, and Okra, **11**-1832
Tortillas (Tortillas de Maíz), **7**-1137
Waffles, **12**-1915
and Zucchini, Baked, **12**-1962

Corn Bread(s)
Anadama Batter Bread (yeast), **2**-229
Bacon, Egg, and Corn Cakes, **1**-134
Buttermilk Spoon Bread, **2**-254
Cheese-Cornmeal Croutons, **2**-301
Cheese Spoon Bread, **3**-361
Corn Bread, **3**-485
Corn Bread (QC), **10**-1524
Corn Cake (Welsch Kornkuche), **9**-1354
Corn Dodgers, **1**-25
Cornmeal Sticks (Surullitos de Maíz), **9**-1497
Corn Muffins, **3**-485
Corn Sticks, **2**-239; **3**-444
Corn Sticks, Double, **3**-484
Crackling Corn Bread, **3**-489
Crisp Golden Corn Points, **2**-304
Cush, **1**-54
Custard Corn Bread, **8**-1225
Custardy Corn Bread, **2**-239
Delaware Spoon Bread, **1**-32
Double-Corn Spoon Bread, **3**-485
Frankfurter Corn Sticks, **5**-725
Golden Cheese Spoon Bread, **1**-65
Grits Batter Bread, **6**-907
Hamburger Sandwiches, **10**-1601
Ham Corn-Bread Ring with Creamed Peas, **6**-856
Hoecake, Old-Fashioned, **6**-904
Hush Puppies, **2**-239
Hush Puppy Batter, **5**-690
Indian Shuck Bread, **1**-64
Mushroom Spoon Bread, **2**-247
Onion Bread, Southern, **8**-1265
Spiced Nut Corn Bread, Antebellum, **1**-52
Spoon Bread, **11**-1724, 1757
Spoon Bread, Nebraska, **7**-1153
Stuffing, **3**-392
Stuffing, New England, **11**-1780
Toads, Fried, **8**-1228
Virginia Batter Bread, **1**-75
Corned Beef, see Beef, Corned
Cornflake-Coconut Macaroons, **1**-67
Cornflake Macaroons, **7**-1096
Corn Flour, **5**-707
Cornish Fruited Saffron Bread, **7**-1097
Cornish Game Hen, see Rock Cornish Hen

Cornmeal, **3**-485
Batter, **11**-1728
Bread, Anadama, **8**-1225
Bread, Indian Meal Raised, **8**-1225
Chili Pie, Cowpuncher, **11**-1728
Dumpling Batter, **4**-586; **5**-748
and Frankfurter Patties, **8**-1313
Griddle Cakes, **5**-826
Hasty Pudding, **8**-1228
Indian Pudding, **8**-1228
Mush (Mamaliga), **6**-995
Polenta, **9**-1418
Polenta Casserole, **9**-1419
Polenta with Egg Sauce, **9**-1418
Polenta with Italian Sausage, **9**-1418
Polenta with Salami and Tomatoes, Baked, **9**-1419
Rolls, **12**-1956
Sauce, **12**-1886
Sticks (Surullitos de Maíz), **9**-1497
Tamale Pie, Hot, **11**-1728
Cornstarch, Cooking with, **3**-485
Costa Brava Chicken (Pollo a la Costa Brava), **11**-1746
Costa Brava Paella, **11**-1746
Costa Rica Chicken Enchiladas (Enchiladas de Gallina), **11**-1706
Costolette alla Parmigiana (Veal Chops Parmigiana), **6**-954
Côtelettes de Porc au Fromage (Pork Chops with Cheese), **11**-1802
Cottage Pie, **6**-876
Cottage Pudding, **9**-1490
Cottonseed Flour, **5**-707
Coucou Sabzi (Iranian Spinach and Parsley Pie), **8**-1215
Country Captain, **1**-33; **3**-382

Court Bouillon, **3**-486
4-595; **10**-1594; **12**-1928, 1939
Brains Parboiled in, **9**-1424
Flavored, **3**-486
for Poaching Fish, **5**-698, **9**-1421
Sauce, **5**-698
Simple, **10**-1663
Couscous, **8**-1215
Couve-Lombarda Recheada (Stuffed Cabbage), **9**-1456
Cowpuncher Chili Pie, **11**-1728
Cowpuncher's Bean Stew, **1**-24

Crab, Crabmeat, **3**-487
Avocado Crabmeat Salad à la Ritz, **1**-130
Bengalese Crab (Kekda Bengali), **6**-942
Cakes, **3**-488; **11**-1721
Cakes, Deviled, **1**-29
Canapés, **1**-86
and Celery Salad, **10**-1582
Cheese-Crab Canapés, **10**-1610
-Cheese Dip, **7**-1083
Chowder, **3**-419
Custard, **1**-33
Deviled, **3**-488
à la Dewey, **3**-346
Dressed, **4**-621
Dungeness, Louis, **1**-76
Filling, **3**-492
and Fresh Grapefruit Salad, **5**-814
and Fresh-Pear Salad, **8**-1330
Fu Yung (Hsieh Fu Yung), **3**-403
and Grapefruit Salad with Avocado Mayonnaise, **12**-1934
Gumbo, Cajun, **5**-830
Hard-Shell, Maryland Steamed, **3**-487
-Horseradish Spread, **2**-279
Imperial, **3**-488
King Crab Legs, Broiled, **12**-1928
Kona Crab (Papai), **9**-1434
Lorenzo à la Filipini, **2**-281
Louis, **3**-488
Molds, **4**-568
-Mushroom Casserole, **3**-488
with Mushrooms, **8**-1198
with Mushrooms in Shells, Baked, **8**-1198
Newburg, **3**-488
Olive Sandwiches, **8**-1257
Pilaf, **2**-321
Rémoulade, **1**-86
-Rice Soup, **11**-1696
Ring, Jellied, **7**-1080
Salad, **10**-1583
Salad, Curried, **3**-488
Salad, Hot, **12**-1928
Salad, Molded, **6**-979
and Shell Chowder, **7**-1091
Sherry Soup, **7**-1097
Shrimp-Crab Salad, Hot, **10**-1652
and Shrimps, Creamed, in Timbale Cases, **11**-1824
and Shrimps, Dixie Style, **10**-1650
Soft-Shell, Baked, Stuffed, **3**-488
Soft-Shell, Fried, **1**-45; **3**-487
Soft-Shell, Fried, Amandine, **3**-488
Soup, Charleston She-Crab, **1**-67
Soup, Martha Washington's, **1**-75
Soup, Nutmeg State, **1**-28
Stuffed, **1**-50
-Stuffed Avocados, **1**-130
-Stuffed Lobster, **7**-1080
-Stuffed Mushrooms, **1**-913

Crabapple(s), **3**-488
Spiced, **3**-488

Cracked Wheat
Bread, **1**-40
Bulgur Pilaf, **8**-1215
Couscous, **8**-1215
Kibbeh (Meat Loaf), **8**-1214
Mint and Parsley Salad, **8**-1213
Pilaf, **9**-1402
Veal with Bulgur and Dill, **12**-1895

Cracker, **3**-489
Pie, **9**-1390
Cracklings, Chicken, see Chicken
Cracklings, Pork, see Pork

Cranberry(ies), **3**-489
Apple-Cranberry Punch, **9**-1503
Apple-Cranberry Shortcake, **1**-101
-Apple Crisp, **1**-65
-Apple Punch (QC), **10**-1526
Apples, **3**-445
Candied, **3**-490
-Claret Jelly, **3**-490
-Cream Salad, **10**-1587
Dishes, Quick, **3**-490
and Fig Jam, **6**-963
-Filbert Relish, **10**-1542
Fruit Ring, **3**-424
Ham Cubes, Baked, **3**-490; **6**-853
and Horseradish Relish, **3**-490
Jelly, **6**-982
Marmalade, **7**-1111
-Mint Sauce, **3**-490; **7**-1151
Mold, **11**-1823
Mousse, **8**-1191
Muffins, **2**-237
-Nut Bread, **10**-1611
Orange, and Honey Jam, **6**-963
-Orange Jelly, **3**-490
-Orange-Raisin Pie, **9**-1393
and Orange Salad, Jellied (QC), **10**-1523
Peanut Sandwiches, **8**-1325
Pear Relish, **10**-1542
Pears, Hot (QC), **10**-1524
Pie, **9**-1393
Pudding, **7**-1155
Puddings, Steamed, **9**-1491
Punch, **3**-490
Punch, Spicy, **3**-428
and Quince Jelly, **7**-982
-Raisin Pie, **3**-490
Roly-Poly, **3**-490
Ruby Pears, **8**-1333
Salad, **4**-632
Salad, Jellied, **8**-1225
Sauce, Spicy, **6**-859
Sauce, Whole, **11**-1823
and Sweets, Scalloped, **11**-1797
Turkey Combination Sandwiches, **12**-1877
-Turkey Loaf, Jellied, **3**-490

Crappie(s), **3**-491
with Chives, Panned, **3**-491

Crayfish, **3**-491
Boiled (Raki Gotowane), **9**-1422
in Court Bouillon, **3**-491
Sauté, **1**-73
Toast Butter, **11**-1829

Cream, **3**-491
Filling, **2**-267; **8**-1192, 1229
Mayonnaise Dressing, **10**-1621

Sauce, **2**-173, 242; **10**-1620
Sauce, Rich, **3**-346
Sauce, Simple, **3**-346
To Whip, **3**-491
Whipped
Amber, **8**-1321
Amber (QC), **10**-1525
Chantilly Sauce, **10**-1628
Filling, Fluffy Cream, **8**-1309
Flavored, **6**-931
Horseradish Sauce, **5**-695
Stabilized, **4**-550; **5**-780
Sherry Ginger Cream, **9**-1493
Topping, **11**-1792; **12**-1853

Cream Desserts; see also Custard(s), Dessert
Almond Bavarian Cream, **1**-15
Apricot Cream, **1**-108
Avocado Cream, **1**-130
Chantilly Cherry Pie, **1**-78
Charlotte Russe, **3**-348; **4**-556
Cherry Bavarian, **3**-374
Chestnuts, Mont Blanc of, **3**-376
Chocolate Charlotte Russe Cake, **2**-269
Chocolate Raspberry Cream, **3**-416
Coffee-Banana Bavarian, **6**-980
Cream of Apples (Iablochnii Krem), **10**-1574
Cream Pie(s)
Apple, **1**-100
Banana, **1**-139
Butterscotch, **2**-255
Coffee-Nut, **9**-1391
Lemon, **7**-1053
Mocha-Nut, **9**-1391
Orange, **8**-1271
Pear, with Apricot Glaze, **8**-1333
Raspberry, **10**-1536
Cream Tarts (Babki Smietankowe), **9**-1431
Fresh-Lime Cream, **7**-1067
Gooseberry Fool, **5**-714
Hazelnut Cream, **6**-882
Heavenly Hash, **6**-879
Lemon Bavarian, **1**-150
Maple Cream, **1**-74
Norwegian Rum Cream, **10**-1563
Peach Bavarian Cream, **1**-32
Persimmon Pudding, Cold, **9**-1364
Pineapple Bavarian Cream, **4**-650
Pistachio Bavarian with Strawberries, **3**-440
Prune-Pineapple Dessert, **9**-1485
Rhubarb Fool, **2**-279
Russian Cream, **10**-1561
Spanish Cream, **6**-980
Strawberry Bavarian Cream, **4**-556
Strawberries à la Chantilly, **4**-568
Strawberry Cream, **1**-37
Strawberry-Honey Bavarian, **6**-909
Syllabub, Old English, **11**-1807
Vanilla Bavarian Cream, **6**-980
Cream Gravy for Southern Fried Chicken, **11**-1723

Cream Puff(s), **3**-492
Appetizer, **3**-492; **8**-1306
Petits Puffs, **8**-1308
Crème Anglaise, **10**-1615, 1628
Crème au Beurre (Buttercream), **9**-1366
Crème Brûlée, **3**-494; **4**-513
Crème Lorraine, **4**-608
Crème Louisa, **5**-790

Crème de Menthe
Peach Parfait, **8**-1320
Pear de Menthe Salad, **8**-1330
with Pineapple Ice, **9**-1410
Crème Pâtissière, **4**-494; **5**-762; **10**-1615, 1628

Crenshaw, Crenshaw Melon, **3**-495; **7**-1129
Fruit Salad Supreme, **3**-495

Creole, Creole Style
Baked Sablefish, **10**-1576
Blackeye Peas, **4**-512
Bouillabaisse, **4**-509
Cod Fillets, **7**-1084
Jambalaya, **6**-968
Kisses, **3**-444
Lamb Liver, **7**-1074
Leftovers, **7**-1049
Leg of Lamb, **7**-1029
Liver and Limas, **7**-1073
Peanut-Butter Soup, **8**-1324
Pralines, **1**-44
Puff, **8**-1325
Sauce, **5**-694; **9**-1359; **10**-1626
Sausage, **2**-242
Scallops, **10**-1642
Shrimps, **10**-1660
Stuffed Peppers, **9**-1359
Tripe, **12**-1859
Turkey in Rice Ring, **12**-1874
Vegetable Soup, **7**-1084
Whiting, **12**-1940
Creole Cookery, **4**-509
Crêpes, see Pancake(s)
Cressonière Sauce, **10**-1614, 1622

Croaker(s), **4**-517
Deep-Fried, with Tartare Sauce, **4**-517
Fillets with Herbs, Boiled, **4**-517
Croissants, **4**-517
Croque Monsieur, **3**-362
Croque Monsieur (Fried Sandwich, French Style), **6**-862

Croquette(s), **4**-517
Cheese, with Green Noodles (Croquettes au Fromage), **11**-1803
Chicken, **4**-518
Chicken-and-Sweetbread, **1**-46
Chick-Pea (Falafel), **6**-992
Cuckoo's Eggs, **12**-1874
Egg, **4**-518
Flounder and Rice, **5**-705
Ham, **6**-856
Rice, Surprise, **10**-1551
Salmon, **10**-1596
Shrimp (Garnalen Croquetten), **4**-590
Sweet-Potato, **4**-518
Tuna, **4**-518
Whitefish, **5**-692

Croquette(s), Dessert
Almond, **4**-518
Lemon-Rice, **4**-518
Crostini alla Mozzarella (Italian Mozzarella Skewers), **6**-955
Croustades, To Make, **4**-518

Croutons, **4**-519; **11**-1826
Cheese, **4**-519; **11**-1697
Cheese-Cornmeal, **2**-301
French-Bread, **4**-519
Savory, **4**-519
Cruller(s), see Doughnut(s) and Cruller(s)
Crumb Crust, **7**-1054; **9**-1399
Crumb Stuffing, Savory, **11**-1834
Crumb Topping, **9**-1357
Crumpets, **4**-520; **11**-1818
Cseresznye Kisütve (Deep-Fried Cherries), **6**-921
Csirke Paprikás (Chicken Paprika with Sour Cream), **6**-919
Cuckoo's Eggs, **12**-1874

Cucumber(s), **4**-520
-Almond Salad, **4**-522; **10**-1586
Braised, **4**-521
Braised (Svezhiye Podzharenyye Ogurtzy), **10**-1572
Cheese, and Grapefruit Salad, **12**-1958
in Cheese Sauce, **4**-522
Cooked (Oi Bokum Namul), **7**-1022
and Cottage Cheese Salad, **7**-1085
and Cress in Horseradish Dressing, **11**-1838
Cups, **6**-913
Diced, Cocktail, **1**-86
Dilled, **4**-522
Dip, Smoked Salmon with, **10**-1594
Egg-Petal Soup with, **11**-1691
and Fresh-Pear Aspic, **8**-1330
Garden Ragout, **8**-1266
Garlic Half-Sour Pickles, **6**-993
Garnishes, **5**-778; **10**-1666
and Green-Tomato Slices, Fried, **11**-1833
Hapsburg, **11**-1700
Jelly Salad, **8**-1225
Lamb, Aruba, **2**-301
Lamb, and Tomato Salad, **10**-1580
Marinated, **10**-1665
Marinated (QC), **10**-1524
-Mayonnaise Dressing, **10**-1621
with Mint, **11**-1749
Mousse, **1**-36
-Onion, and Onion(s)
Curried, **7**-1086
Olive-Oil Pickle, **9**-1374
Relish, **1**-90
Salad, **4**-521
Wilted, **6**-912
-and-Pâté Sandwiches, **5**-708
Pickled, **4**-522
Pickled (Asier), **4**-538
Pickled (Liang Pan Huang Kua), **3**-403
Pickle Relish, **10**-1542
Pineapple-Cucumber Salad, **9**-1408
Radishes, and Onions in Sour Cream, **11**-1700
Relish, Sweet, **10**-1542
Salad(s)
Agurkesalat, **4**-542
Gurkensalat, **1**-123
Mizerja I, **9**-1430
with Sour Cream (Mizerja II), **9**-1430
Sandwich Fillings, **4**-522
Sauce, **7**-1086; **11**-1700
Sauces for Fish, **4**-522
and Shrimp Sandwiches, **12**-1958
Slices, **1**-89
Soup (Agurkesuppe), **4**-538
Soup, Cold, Bulgarian, **12**-1957
with Sour Cream, **8**-1278
Sour-Cream Sauce, **5**-695
Stuffing, **11**-1781
and Sweetbread Salad, **11**-1796; **12**-1897
Tomato Cocktail, **11**-1832
Tomato Salad, **4**-566
and Tomato Soup, **4**-521
and Turnip Salad (Salat iz Repy i Ogurtzov), **10**-1572
and Veal Salad (Salat iz Teliatini s Ogurtsami), **10**-1566
Vinegared (Kyuri-Momi), **6**-978
Yogurt, and Radish Relish, **12**-1958
Yogurt Salad, **12**-1958
Yogurt, Turquoise, **8**-1213
and Zucchini in Sour Cream, **12**-1962
Cumberland Dressing, **7**-1116
Cumberland Sauce, **2**-194; **10**-1614, 1627
Cumberland Slaw, **3**-464
Cumin, **4**-522

Cupcake(s), **4**-523
Coffee-Molasses, **4**-523
Currant-Orange, **4**-523
Prune Pound, **4**-523
Sour-Milk Gingerbread, Anthelias, **8**-1230
Vanilla, **4**-523
Curaçao Banana Stoba, **2**-301
Curd, Lemon, **7**-1056

Currant(s), **4**-524
Cherries in Currant Jelly, **7**-1154
Glaze, **5**-746
-Glazed Strawberry Tarts, **9**-1384
Ice, **4**-524
Jelly, **4**-524
-Jelly and Raspberry Ice, **6**-925
Pie, **4**-524
Raspberry Jam, **6**-964
Red-Currant Cobbler, **7**-1155
Red Pudding (Rødgrød), **4**-543
Tarts, Glazed, **4**-524
Waffles, **12**-1915

Currant(s), Dried, 4-524
Bread, **11**-1818
Curry Seasoning, **10**-1555
Fat Rascals (Tea Cakes), **4**-525
Scones, **2**-238
Simnel Cake, **4**-626

Curry(ies), Curried, 4-525
Apple-Lamb, **1**-97
Apples, **1**-97
Badun, **4**-527
Banana-Shrimp, **1**-139
Barbecue Sauce, **10**-1623
Beef, **2**-191; **4**-525, 527
Butter, **1**-85; **2**-191, 297
Cabbage, **4**-526
Cashew Sandwich Spread, **10**-1611
Chicken, **4**-527
Chicken Korma, **4**-525
Chicken Soup, Cool, **3**-390
Chicken Tartlets, **11**-1811
Chicken with Tomatoes (Murgha Kari), **6**-939
Chick-Pea (Chinai Curry), **6**-942
Crab Salad, **3**-488
Currant Seasoning, **10**-1555
Curries, **7**-1049
Dressing, **3**-428
Egg, Indian, **4**-606
Eggs, **4**-626
Egg Sandwiches, **10**-1605
Fish, **4**-527
Fruit, Hot, **11**-1753
Hake, **6**-847
Ham and Fresh-Pork Loaf, **6**-856
Lamb, **4**-527
Lamb, Indian Style, **2**-299
Lamb, Indonesian (Kerie Kambing), **11**-1714
Lamb Kofta, **4**-526
Lamb and Limas, **7**-1039
Lamb Mold, **7**-1084
Lamb (Rogan Josh), **6**-939
Lentil with Rice, **7**-1059
Lima Salad, **7**-1065
Mayonnaise, **4**-573; **5**-694; **7**-1116; **10**-1622
Meat Turnovers (Samosas), **12**-1879
Mussels, **8**-1203
Mutton, Jamaican, **8**-1205
Onions, **8**-1264
Onions and Cucumber, **7**-1086
-Onion Sauce, **5**-725
Peas and Onions, **8**-1315
Pea Soup, Iced, **9**-1384
Pears, **8**-1330
Plantain or Banana, **4**-527
Popcorn, **9**-1437
Pork, **4**-527; **9**-1450
Pork Chops, Apricots with, **1**-107
Pork, Sour (Soowar ka Gosht Vindaloo), **6**-939
Potatoes, **9**-1464
Potato Soup, **9**-1462
Puffs, **6**-912
Rabbit, **12**-1930
Rice, **10**-1551
Rockfish Salad, **10**-1558
Rock Lobster, **7**-1078
Rock-Lobster Salad, **10**-1582
Salmon Loaf, **10**-1595
Salmon Sandwiches, **10**-1597
-Salmon Triangles, **10**-1595
Sauce, **2**-173; **5**-694; **6**-848; **10**-1662; **11**-1824
Sauce, French Style, **10**-1614, 1620
Sauce (Karry), **4**-539
Scallops, Broiled, **10**-1641
Schnitzel, **1**-127
Shellfish, **10**-1652
Shrimp, **4**-640; **10**-1660
Shrimp Diamonds, **8**-1306
Shrimps in Pineapples, **10**-1660
Stuffed Eggs, **4**-606
Tomato, **7**-1123
Tomato Relish, **5**-726
Tuna, **12**-1863
Tuna Sandwiches, **10**-1602
Turkey, **12**-1872
Vegetable, **4**-527
Cuscinetti Filanti al Prosciutto (Pillows with Italian Ham), **6**-862
Cush, **1**-54

Cusk, 4-530
and Potato Casserole, **4**-530
with Vegetables, Baked, **4**-530

Custard, 4-530
Corn Bread, **8**-1225
Crème Pâtissière, **5**-762
Filling, Cream, **11**-1792
Filling, Thick, **4**-543
Pastry Cream, **4**-627; **5**-746, 784
Sauce, **4**-518; **9**-1492; **10**-1666
Sauce (Crème Anglaise), **10**-1615, 1628
Sauce, Lemon, **7**-1056
Sauce, Sherry, **9**-1493
Custard Apple, **4**-530

Custard(s), Appetizer and Main-Dish
Broccoli-and-Cheese, **2**-245
Crab, **1**-33
Egg Custard Noodles (Odamaki-Mushi), **6**-976
Frankfurter Custard Tarts, **11**-1811
Golden Fleece, **4**-608
Ham, Swedish, **6**-865
Meat (Sfougato), **5**-818
Steamed (Chawan-Mushi), **6**-971

Custard(s), Dessert
Almond Cheesecakes (Queijadinhas de Amendoas), **9**-1457
Apple Crème, **4**-633
Apricot-Rice, **4**-578
Bacon from Heaven (Toucinho-do Céu), **9**-1457
Baked, **4**-530
Boiled, Tennessee, **11**-1725
Caramel, **4**-530
Caramel (Crème Renversée), **3**-493
Caramel, Swedish, **2**-297
Coconut Puddin' Pie, **3**-456
Coffee Pudding with Caramel Glaze, **9**-1490
Crème Brûlée, **3**-494; **4**-513
Custard Pie(s), **9**-1391
Caramel, **9**-1391
Chocolate-Topped, **9**-1391
Coconut, **4**-530; **9**-1391
Crisp-Crust, **9**-1391
Raisin-Pineapple, **4**-578
Yam, **12**-1951
Custard Rice Pudding, **10**-1552
Flan, Mexican, **4**-557
Floating Island, **3**-494; **5**-704
Floating Island (Isla Flotante), **9**-1497
Frangipane Pie, **5**-716
Fried Cream, **1**-69
Honey, Baked, **1**-62
Lemon, Low-Calorie Frozen, **7**-1054
Macaroon Cream, **7**-1097
Maple, **1**-56
Mrs. Parson's Receipt for Cream, **8**-1229
Pineapple Caramel (Flan de Piña), **5**-703
Pistachio, Frozen, **9**-1411
Plain Baked, **3**-493
Pots de Crème, **3**-493
Pots de Crème au Chocolat, **3**-494
Prune, Baked (Sviskekompott), **8**-1241
Pudding (Letse Plan), **9**-1370
Pumpkin Custard Pudding with Sherry Ginger Cream, **9**-1491
Pumpkin-Orange, **9**-1499
Soft, **4**-530
Soft with Fresh Plum Whip, **9**-1416
Sun and Shadow (Flan Sol y Sombra) **1**-73
Taro-Coconut-Egg (Khanom Mo Kaeng), **11**-1716
Thomas Jefferson's Almond Custard, **1**-14
Top-Stove, **3**-493
Trifle, **4**-527
Trifle, A True English, **12**-1858
Vanilla Cream Pots (Pots de Crème à la Vanille), **3**-493
Vanilla, Rich, **8**-1331
Zabaglione, **12**-1960
Zabaglione, Cold, **12**-1960
Zuppa Inglese, **4**-650

Cymling or **Pattypan Squash,** **11**-1758
Baked, **11**-1761
Cheese-Stuffed, **11**-1762
Fritters, **11**-1761
Czarna Kasza (Buckwheat Groats), **9**-1428
Czechoslovakian Cookery, **4**-531

D

Dahi Bhath (Rice with Buttermilk), **6**-942

Daiquiri, **10**-1563
Frozen, **10**-1563
on-the-Rocks, **9**-1498
Dairy Products, to Freeze, **5**-736
Daisies (garnish), **10**-1666
Dak Chim (Steamed Chicken), **7**-1022
Dale's Cheesecake, **3**-368
Dalesman Cakes, Norwegian, **9**-1471
Dampfnudeln (Raised Dumplings), **4**-587
Damson, Damson Plum, **4**-533; for recipes see Plum(s)

Dandelion, Dandelion Greens, **4**-534
Italian Style, **4**-534
with Lentils, **4**-534
Salad, **9**-1354
Salad, Raw, **4**-534
Veal with, **12**-1896
Wine, **4**-534
Danish Beef Canapés, **1**-86
Danish Blue Cheese (sandwich) (Roquefort Ost), **4**-536
Danish Browned Cabbage Soup, **11**-1690
Danish Buttermilk Soup, **2**-254
Danish Chicken, **3**-386
Danish Cookery, **4**-535
Danish Doughnuts (Aebleskiver), **4**-542
Danish Kringle, **7**-1157
Danish Liver Pâté, **7**-1074
Danish Macaroni Salad, **7**-1095
Danish Macaroons, **7**-1096
Danish Meatballs, **7**-1123
Danish Meatballs (Frikadeller), **4**-540
Danish Onions, **8**-1265
Danish Pastries, **8**-1308
Apple, **2**-232
Danish Pastry (Wienerbrød), **4**-542
Danish Pork Balls, **9**-1449
Danish Pot-Roasted Calf Hearts, **9**-1476
Danish Salad, **10**-1586
Danish Toast, **11**-1826
Danish Veal Hearts, **6**-883
Dasheen, **4**-546
Dashi (Soup Stock), **6**-970

Date(s), **4**-546
Apricot Bars, **4**-547
Arab, **3**-449
Bonbons, Baked, **12**-1918
Butterscotch-Date Tapioca Pudding, **9**-1489
Caramel-Date Pies, Individual, **4**-547
and Cheddar, **2**-243
Chews, **4**-547
Chutney, East Indian, **4**-579
Comfits, **8**-1335
Cookies, Mae's, **3**-476
Fondant-Stuffed, **5**-708
-Graham Pudding, **8**-1228
Honey-Date Bars, **6**-911
-Nut Bars, Frosted (QC), **10**-1526
and Nut Bread, **4**-547

-Nut Filling, **4**-547, 663; **8**-1253
-Nut Kisses, **7**-1017
-Nut Loaves, **10**-1611
-Nut Maple Bread, **7**-1105
Nutmeg Date Bars, **3**-471
-Nut Muffins, **4**-547
-Nut Pinwheels, **4**-547
-Nut Sandwiches, **9**-1383
Orange-Date Bread Pudding, **9**-1490
and Orange Salad, **10**-1588
-and-Orange Tea Loaf, **8**-1272
Pastries, Southern, **4**-547
Rice Pudding, **10**-1552
Sour-Cream Toast, **11**-1828
Sticks, **4**-547
Stuffed-Date Cookies, **4**-547
Stuffed Sherried, **4**-548
Waffles, **2**-1915

Daube, **4**-548
d'Agneau (Lamb Daube), **5**-741
of Beef, Béarnaise, **2**-187
of Beef, Provence Style, **4**-548
Provençale, **12**-1947
Deep South Hot Barbecue Sauce, **10**-1623
Déglacer, **10**-1615
Delmonico Potatoes, **4**-551
Delaware Spoon Bread, **1**-32
Demi-Glace Sauce, **10**-1619
Demi-Glace for Steaks, **2**-246
Denver Sandwiches, **1**-27; **10**-1604
Desserts, Frozen, see Frozen Desserts
Desserts, Jellied, see Jellied Desserts
Desserts, To Freeze, **5**-737

Deviled
Eggs, **6**-912
Eggs, Sardine-Stuffed, **9**-1378
Eggs, Smoked-Sturgeon, **11**-1782
Halibut Steaks, **5**-689; **6**-848
Ham Steak, **11**-1770
Lamb Riblets, **7**-1038
Liver (Athae Chin Gyaw), **11**-1717
Liver in Croustades, **7**-1073
Minute Steaks, **11**-1768
Ocean-Perch Fillets, **9**-1363
Rock Lobster, South African, **7**-1080
Roe, **10**-1558
Sardines, **10**-1612
Shrimps, **10**-1661
Skirt Steak, **11**-1768
Toast, **11**-1826
Deviled Ham, see Ham, Deviled

Devil's Food, Devil's-Food Cake, **2**-267
Cake, **4**-559
with Marshmallow Frosting, **4**-559
Squares, **4**-559
Devils on Horseback, **8**-1287
Devonshire Berry Tarts, **11**-1812
Devonshire Cream, Mock, **12**-1915
Devonshire Fried Eggs, **6**-865
Devonshire Pears, **11**-1701
Devonshire Sour-Cream Pears, **10**-1561

Dewberry(ies), **4**-560
Crumble, **4**-560
Flummery, **4**-560
Jelly, **4**-560
Diable, à la Diable, Sauce, **4**-559; **5**-743; **10**-1613, 1619; **11**-1768
for Grilled Chicken, **2**-246
Diamondback Terrapin, see Turtle, Tortoise, and Terrapin
Different Bean Soup, **1**-54

Dill, Dilled, **4**-563
Carrots, Crisscross, **4**-564
Dilly Green-Bean Pickles, **9**-1373
Dressing, **10**-1555
Green Beans, **4**-564
Fresh, Suggestions for Using, **4**-563
Green-Tomato Pickles (Kosher Style), **9**-1374
Meatballs, **4**-643
-Pickle Salad, **10**-1555
Pickles, **9**-1372
Fresh (Kosher Style), **9**-1373
(Kosher Style), **9**-1373
Sauce, **4**-564; **5**-694; **9**-1475; **11**-1784, 1788
Sauce for Fish, **4**-564
Sauce, Sharp (Skarpsås), **11**-1791
Sauce (Tillikastike), **5**-681
Shrimps with, **4**-564
Seed, Suggestions for Using, **4**-564
Dingle Mackerel, **6**-945
Dinner Menus, **4**-565-570
Chicken Dinner, **8**-1278
Festive Dinner, **4**-648
Roman Dinner, **4**-650
Diós Tekercs (Hungarian Walnut Roll), **6**-922
Diós Tészta (Boiled Noodles with Walnuts), **6**-920

Dips or **Dunks,** **1**-85
Avocado Dip, **1**-130
Avocado Paste (Guacamole), **7**-1138
Bacon Dip, **11**-1697
Bulgarian Appetizers (eggplant), **4**-615
Caviar Bowl, **7**-1146
Chili Dip, **1**-87
Chili con Queso, **4**-643
Clam Dip, **4**-642
Crab-Cheese Dip, **7**-1083
Cream-Cheese and Clam Dip, **1**-87
East Indian Dip, **1**-87
Frankfurter-Avocado Dip, **5**-718
Guacamole, **1**-130
Ham Dip, **6**-852
Mustard Dip for Raw Vegetables, **1**-87
Red Caviar in Cream, **1**-76
Rémoulade Dip, for Scallops or Shrimps, **1**-87
Salmon Dip, **10**-1595
Sour-Cream Ham Dip, **11**-1697
Tuna Dip, Fines Herbes, **12**-1862
Two-Cheese Dip, **1**-87
Vegetable Dip, **2**-305
Disznókaraj Magyarosan (Hungarian Pork Chops), **6**-918
Diva Cake, **3**-408

Divinity and **Seafoam,** **2**-284; **4**-570
Chocolate Divinity, **2**-285
Divinity, **2**-285
Ginger Divinity, **2**-285
Holiday Divinity, **2**-285
Seafoam, **2**-285
Dixie Style Crab and Shrimps, **10**-1650
Dobostorte (Hungarian Seven-Layer Cake), **1**-124
Doce de Castanhas (Chestnut Sweet), **9**-1457
Dock, see Sorrel
Dolmadakia me Avgolemono (Greek Stuffed Grapevine Leaves with Lemon Sauce), **4**-570
Dolmathes (Stuffed Grape Leaves), **5**-819
Domi Jun (Sea Bream Fried in Egg Batter), **7**-1020
Dominican Republic Chicken Sancocho, **2**-300

Dough(s), **4**-571
Biscuit, **7**-1039
Biscuit, for Chicken Pie, **7**-1152
Biscuit, Rich, **11**-1725
Brioche Dough, **5**-745
Kuchen, **5**-799
Noodle, Basic, **8**-1231
Pastry, Rich, **5**-747
Raised for Pirogi or Pirozhki, **10**-1570
Squares (for Boiled Potpie), **9**-1352
Strudel, **11**-1779
Suet, **4**-627
Sweet, **9**-1355
Sweet Basic, **2**-242

Doughnut(s), **4**-571, and **Cruller(s),** **4**-519
Bismarcks, **1**-63
Buttermilk Doughnuts, **2**-237
Chocolate Doughnuts, **4**-572
Crullers, **4**-519; **7**-1153
Crullers, French, **4**-519
Danish Doughnuts (Aebleskiver), **4**-542
Doughnuts, **4**-572
Doughnuts, Baked, **1**-53
Doughnuts Filled with Applesauce, **4**-572
Dumfunnies, **8**-1228
Fastnachts, **9**-1357
Fat Balls, **1**-48
Mexican Crullers (Churros), **7**-1143
Potato Doughnuts, **9**-1469
Raised Doughnuts, **4**-572
Raisin Doughnuts, Dropped, **4**-572
Sour-Cream Doughnuts, **1**-66
Sourdough Doughnuts, **1**-54
Sweet-Potato Doughnuts, **11**-1798
Yam and Cheese Crullers, Puerto Rican, **12**-1951
Down-East Sandwiches, **10**-1604
Dream Cookies, **10**-1666
Dreams (Sonhos), **9**-1457

Dressing(s), **4**-572; see also Fillings; Stuffings
Apple and Onion, **4**-574
for Goose, Three, **5**-808
Mushroom-Giblet, for Poultry, **5**-800
Oyster, for Turkey, **4**-575
Pine-Nut, for Chicken, **4**-575
Raisin-Walnut, **4**-575
Shrimp, **4**-575
Spanish-Rice, **4**-574
Drippings, Spiced (Skysovs), **4**-538
Duchesse Potatoes, **7**-1150; **11**-1470

Duck, Duckling, **4**-580
Braised, **4**-582
Braised, with Turnips, **2**-220
à la Brussels (Canard à la Bruxelloise), **2**-197
Carving, **2**-313
Cassoulet, **2**-325
Chow Mein, **4**-584
in Claret, **4**-584
Cooked like Wild Duck (Hausente als Wildente), **1**-122
Galantine
How to Bone and Prepare a Duck for a Galantine, **5**-765
Giblet Fricassee, Viennese, **4**-584
Gumbo, **5**-830
Hash, **12**-1919
Jambalaya de Canard, **1**-44
Marinated (Kaczka lub Gés Marynowana), **9**-1428
Orange Rice for, **8**-1268
Pot-Roasted Spanish Style, **9**-1477
Roast, Roasted
Bigarade, **2**-202
Boned, with Savory Rice, **4**-582
Long Island, **1**-60
à l'Orange, **4**-582
with Sage and Onion Stuffing, **4**-625
Stegt And, **4**-536
Stuffed (Gebratene Ente), **5**-795
Varnished with Coconut (Panggang Golek), **11**-1715
Rosé, **12**-1949
Salad, Alaska, **1**-23
Salmi of, **10**-1590
Spiced (Wu Hsiang Ya), **3**-401
Stuffings for, **4**-584
and Sweet-Potato Casserole, **2**-320
Timetable for Roasting, Chart, **4**-581
with Turnips (Canards aux Navets), **5**-744
Varsovia, **4**-584

Duck, Wild Duck
Mallard Stuffed with Sauerkraut, **5**-773
Roast, **1**-53; **7**-1152
Roast, with Beans, **5**-773
Dumfunnies, **8**-1228

Dumpling(s), 4-585
Batter, **3**-481; **4**-586, 587; **5**-716; **9**-1355
Batter, Savory, **12**-1871
Biscuit, Pigs' Knuckles, and Sauerkraut, **9**-1449
Bread, **4**-585
Bread (Brødboller), **4**-542
Bread, Italian, **11**-1696
Buckwheat, with Cheese (Pierogi z Kaszy ze Screm), **9**-1429
Butter Balls for Philadelphia Pepper Pot Soup, **11**-1964
Butter (Butterklösse), **4**-585
Caraway Dumpling Batter, **9**-1351
Cornmeal, **1**-61
Cornmeal Dumpling Batter, **4**-586; **5**-748
Devil Balls, **7**-1147
Egg, **4**-625
Farina, **7**-1147
Farina Balls, **4**-586
Floats, **11**-1697
Frankfurter-Potato, **4**-586
Gnocchi, **11**-1804
Gnocchi di Patate alla Piemontese, **5**-806
Gnocchi Parmesan, **5**-806
Gnocchi Romana, **5**-806
Ham, **6**-852
Italian Style (Gnocchi all'Italiana), **4**-587
Lazy (Leniwe Pierogi), **9**-1429
Liver, **4**-586; **7**-1147
Liver, Delicate, **7**-1074
Liver Dumpling Soup (Leberknödelsuppe), **5**-793
Liver Dumplings, Soup with, (Polévka s Jaternimi Knedlíky), **4**-531
Main-Course, **4**-586
Marrow (Marrow Balls), **7**-113
Marrow, in Consommé (Markklösschen), **5**-793
Matzo Balls, **7**-1147
Matzo Balls (Knaidlach), **4**-586; **6**-987
Meat Kreplach, **6**-995
Onion, Baked (Olad'i s Lukom), **10**-1573
Parsley, **8**-1298
Potato, **4**-586; **10**-1630
Potato (Kartoffelklösse), **5**-795
Potato, Swedish (Potatisbullar), **11**-1791
Pot-Cheese, **4**-587
Quenelles de Brochet, **5**-700
Raised, and Dried Apples (Schnitz und Gnepp), **9**-1351
Siberian (Sibirskie Pelmeni), **10**-1571
Small (Spätzle), **5**-794
for Soup, **4**-585
Spaetzle (German Egg Dumplings), **4**-586
for Stews, **4**-586
(for Veal Parsley Pie), **1**-78

Dumpling(s), Dessert
Apple, **7**-1155
Apple, Baked, **1**-96
Baked in Caramel Sauce, **4**-587
Batter, **4**-532; **5**-808
Cherry, **3**-374
Cherry (Knedlíky s Visnové), **4**-532
Gooseberry, **5**-808
Grandfathers (Grandpères), **4**-587
Lemon Slump, **8**-1229
Nut and Honey Sweetmeats (Tayglach mit Neshomas), **6**-994
Peach, **8**-1317
Peach and Plum, **4**-587
Plum, **9**-1417
Plum (Svestkove Knedlíky), **4**-532
Plum (Szilvás Gomboc), **6**-920
Plum, Washington, **12**-1932
Raised (Dampfnudeln), **4**-587
Vareniki, Cherry or Blueberry, **10**-1574
Dunbar's Jambalaya, **4**-510
Dunbar's Stuffed Squash, **4**-513
Dutch Apple Cake, Mrs. Van's, **7**-1156
Dutch Babies, Seattle, **12**-1932
Dutch Bean Soup, **11**-1839
Dutch Cookery, **4**-588
Dutch Delight Float, **7**-1161
Dutch Honey Cake, **6**-911
Dutch Onion Pie, **8**-1261
Dutch Prune Cake, **9**-1486
Dutch Raspberry Toast, **11**-1826
Duxelles, **4**-593; **12**-1900
Duxelles Sauce, **10**-1619

E

Early American Pear Pie, **8**-1247
East Indian Date Chutney, **4**-579
East Indian Dip, **1**-87
East Indian Marinated Lamb Chops, **7**-1034
East Indian Rose Pudding, **10**-1561
Easter Babka (Wielkanocna Babka), **9**-1431
Easter Soup (Mageritsa), **5**-818
Éclairs, **4**-594; **8**-1309
Ecuador Mashed Black Beans (Frijoles Negroes Batidos), **11**-1708
Ecuador Potato and Cheese Patties (Llapingachos), **11**-1708
Ecuador Seafood in Pickled Sauce (Escabeche de Mariscos), **11**-1704

Eel(s), 4-594
Fried, with Curry Sauce (Stegt Aal i Karry), **4**-539
Galantine of, **5**-766
Jellied (Aal i Gelé), **4**-539
Matelote of, Normandy, **4**-595
Smoked (Roget Aal), **4**-536
Stifle, **4**-595

Egg(s), 4-596
Asparagi all' Uovo, **1**-113
in Aspic à la Française, **1**-117
Bacon and Egg Skillet, **1**-133
and Bacon with Noodles, **8**-1233
and Bacon Pie, **4**-626
Baked, **1**-32; **4**-601
Algerian-Style, **5**-775
Andalusian Egg Platter (Oeufs sur le Plat à l'Andalouse), **6**-862
Celery Eggs, **4**-609
Egg-Stuffed Tomatoes, **4**-609
Ham and Egg Pie, **6**-862
with Onions and Cheese (Gebakken Eieren met Uien en Kaas), **4**-592
Parmesan, **6**-861
in Ramekins with Ham (Oeufs Cocottes au Jambon), **6**-861
in Tomatoes, **8**-1274
Barley (Tarhonya), **6**-919
Boiled, **4**-600
Butter, **1**-86; **5**-679
Cake, Viennese (Wiener Eierkuchen), **6**-865
Cantonese Style (Chao Tan), **3**-403
and Caper Sauce, **2**-296
Casserole, Hoosier, **1**-37
Caviar Spread, **2**-279
and Cheese, Creamy, **3**-358
Consommé (Pavese), **6**-952
and Cottage Beef, **7**-1084
Cottage Eggs with Rice, **2**-322
Creamed, **2**-242
with Cream Sauce (Oeufs à la Crème), **11**-1894
Creamy, **3**-429
Croquettes, **4**-518
Deviled-Egg Salad, **5**-788
Dropped in Cream, **1**-74
Dumplings, **4**-625
Flamenco (Huevos a la Flamenca), **11**-1744
Florentine, **5**-704
Fried, **4**-600
à l'Américaine, **6**-861
à la Bayonne, **6**-865
Beauvilliers, **6**-865
au Beurre Noir, **4**-607
-and-Cheese Burgers, **4**-608
Deep-Fried (Huevos Fritos), **4**-608
Devonshire, **6**-865
and Ham, Phillip's, **6**-861
Hobo, **4**-607
Jockey Club, **4**-607
Provençale, **4**-608
Ranchers' (Huevos Rancheros), **4**-607
in Toledo (Huevos en Toledo), **6**-865
Fu Yung, **6**-865
Glaze, **12**-1953
Goldenrod Sauce, **5**-694
Green Heaven in a Pot, **8**-1266
and Ham, French Style, **2**-247
and Ham Dishes, Quick, **6**-865
Ham, and Mushrooms in a Chafing Dish, Creamed, **3**-346
and Ham Roll, Parsley, **8**-1298
and Ham Smørrebrød, **6**-862
and Ham Tart, **6**-862
Hard-Cooked
Alpine, **4**-629
Anchovy, **6**-912
and Anchovy Tartlets, **11**-1811
in Aspic, **4**-603
Baked (Oeufs au Four), **11**-1804
and Blue-Cheese Sandwiches, **10**-1605
Capered, **11**-1839
-Cheese Spread, **4**-606
Creamed, Supreme, **11**-1755
Curried, **4**-626
Curry, Indian, **4**-606
Deviled, **4**-558; **6**-912
Deviled-Ham, and Cheese Sandwiches, **10**-1605
Deviled, Sardine-Stuffed, **9**-1378
Deviled, Smoked-Sturgeon, **11**-1782
English Thin Yellow Boys, **4**-603
Garnishes, **10**-1666
Goldenrod Toast, **11**-1826
au Gratin, **4**-604
and Ham Butter, **6**-866
Ham and Egg Cakes, English, **6**-862
Ham and Egg Salad, **6**-864
Ham, and Macaroni Salad, **4**-607
and Ham Piroshki (Little Russian Pies), **6**-864
and Ham Pizza (Pizza con Uovo e Prosciutto), **6**-864
and Ham, Potted, **6**-866
and Ham with Tortillas (Huevos con Tortillas y Jamon), **6**-861
Hongroise, **4**-606
and Lima-Bean Salad, **7**-1065
-Lobster Salad, Molded, **7**-1080
Macaroni, and Bean Salad, **7**-1095
-Macaroni Salad, **7**-1095
Madeira Eggs, Funchal, **4**-606
Mornay, **4**-606
and Mushroom Filling, Russian, **4**-662
and Mushrooms, Ragout of, **4**-603
and Olive Mold, **4**-606
and Onions, Baked, **4**-603
Pepper, and Cheese Sandwiches, **9**-1360
Pickled, **9**-1376
and Potato Casserole, **4**-603
and Potato Casserole (Rakott Krumpli), **6**-919
Potato-Egg Salad, Hot Creamy, **9**-1462
and Potato Pie, Indienne, **9**-1388
and Potatoes, Skillet, **4**-606
Salad, Mexican, **4**-523
Salad, Piquant, **4**-606
Salad, Savory, **4**-606
-Salad-Stuffed Tomatoes, **10**-1582
-Salad and Tongue Sandwiches, **10**-1604
Sandwiches, Curried, **10**-1605
Sauce, Creamy, **10**-1620
Sauce for Fish (Sos z Jaj do Ryby), **9**-1422
in Scallion and Mushroom Sauce, **8**-1265
and Shrimp Salad, Japanese, **10**-1580
Spiced, Balinese (Telur Masak Bali), **11**-1714
Stuffed, **4**-606
Stuffed (Avga Gemista), **4**-639
Tuna-Egg Three-Deckers, **10**-1604

and Hash (Pytt i Panne), **8**-1237
Hoppel Poppel, **9**-1463
and Lemon Sauce, **5**-694
-Lemon Sauce (Avgolemono Sauce), **5**-819
and Lemon Sauce, Greek, **10**-1627
-Lemon Soup (Avgolemono Soupa), **5**-818
Nut Spread, **2**-280
Oeufs Brouillés, **11**-1811
Omelet(s), **4**-601
Artichoke, **1**-112
Artichoke, Hollandaise, **4**-610
California, **12**-1930
Charentière, **4**-610
Cheese, **3**-358; **8**-1257
Chicken-Liver, **7**-1075
Crab Fu Yung, **3**-403
The Emperor's Omelet (Kaiserschmarrn), **1**-123
Fillings, Nonsweet, **4**-662
Fillings, Sweet, **4**-662
Frankfurter Eggs Fu Yung, **5**-720
French, **8**-1257
Fu Yung, Chinese, **4**-610
Ham, **8**-1257
Hangtown Fry, **2**-243; (Beard) I, II, and III, **8**-1287
Italian Tuna Frittata, **12**-1866
Miniature Puffy, **4**-609
Omelette à la Lyonnaise, **7**-1089
Onion, **8**-1257
Oyster, **8**-1287
Puffy, **8**-1257
Salami, **10**-1589
and Salami, **6**-991
Sandwiches, Hawaiian, **10**-1602
Shrimp (Ch'ao Hsia Tan), **3**-401
Shrimp Fu Yung, **3**-403
Shrimp Nets (La Tieng), **11**-1716
6-Egg, **4**-602
Soufflé, **2**-324
Spanish, **4**-610; **8**-1257
Spanish Omelette with Ham (Tortilla con Jamon), **6**-861
2-Egg, **4**-602
Vietnamese (Cha Tom), **11**-1717
Western, **4**-610
Zucchini, **12**-1962
and Onions, Faust, **8**-1263
and Onions (Oeufs à l'Oignon), **2**-198
-Parmesan Pudding, Steamed, **4**-604
Pickle Spread, **2**-280
Poached, **4**-600
Benedict, **4**-607
Carmen, **6**-864
Celestine, **6**-865
in Chili Sauce (Huevos con Salsa de Chiles), **11**-1708
Corned-Beef Hash with, **4**-630
in Cream, **4**-607
Florentine, Italian, **11**-1755
Florentine in Mornay Sauce, **4**-607
Golden Buck, **12**-1923
and Ham in Aspic, **6**-861
and Ham, Fried (Huevos Escalfados Fritos), **6**-862
Hussarde, Brennan's, **4**-512
Italienne, **6**-865
with Lentil Purée, **7**-1059
Mayonnaise, **4**-607
Oeufs Mollet Chasseur, **4**-607
in Purgatory (Uova in Purgatoria), **6**-955
in Red Wine (Oeufs à la Matelote), **4**-607
alla Romana, **1**-57
Zurlo, **6**-865
Pudding, Coimbra (Pudim de Ovos a Moda de Coimbra), **9**-1457
Ranch Style, **1**-59
Ranch-Style (Huevos Rancheros), **7**-1141
and Red Beets, Pickled, **1**-66
Rolls, Chinese, **8**-1294
Salami-Egg Canapés, **1**-86
-Salmon Quiche, **4**-608
Salmon-Stuffed, **1**-87
Sandwich Fillings, **10**-1606
Sauce, Creamy, **5**-694
Scotch Woodcock, **3**-346
Scrambled, **4**-600
Basque (Pipérade), **4**-608
with Brains, **2**-217
and Cheese Toast, **11**-1826
Chive-Scrambled, **3**-404
Cold (Aeggestand), **4**-538
Creamy, with Bacon, **4**-608
with Mushrooms (Houby s Vejci), **4**-532
Pipérade, **9**-1411
Raisin Scramble Toast, **11**-1828
Rialto, **8**-1200
Salami and Noodle Skillet, **10**-1638
with Smoked Salmon, **10**-1594
-and-Tomato Scramble, **11**-1833
Shirred, **4**-601
Caruso, **4**-608
with Frankfurters, **5**-720
Shreds of Gold (Foi Tong), **11**-1716
"Shushed," Mississippi, **11**-1723
Soup, Jellied, **5**-786
Soup, Portuguese, **11**-1691
Soup (Tamago Suimono), **6**-971
and Spaghetti on Ham (Spaghetti alla Carbonara), **6**-862
with Spinach Ring, Baked, **11**-1755
Swiss, **7**-1085
Tart, **11**-1811
Thousand Island, **11**-1698
Threaded (Huevos Hilados), **4**-608
Timbales with Curry Sauce, **11**-1824
and Tongue Tart, **11**-1811
and Tongue with Yogurt Sauce, **12**-1957
Watercress Spread, **2**-280
Western Long Boys, **6**-859
Eggless Muffins, **8**-1193

Eggnog, **4**-610
Chiffon Filling, **7**-1164
Christmas, **4**-611
Colonial, **4**-611
Eggnog, **1**-52; **4**-611
Old English Sack-Posset, **4**-611
Pie, Frozen, **7**-1100
Snow Pudding, **3**-445
Syllabub, Frothy, **4**-611
Tarts, **8**-1247
Egg-Petal Soup with Cucumbers, **11**-1691

Eggplant, **4**-611
Appetizer, Marinated (Melanzane alla Marinara), **6**-952
Appetizers, Bulgarian, **4**-614
Caponata, **12**-1903
Caponata, Sicilian, **4**-614
Caponatina, **1**-82
Caviar, **1**-90
Caviar (Ikra iz Baklazhanov), **10**-1566
with Cheese (Berenjena con Queso), **9**-1496
and Chicken, Baked Individual, **4**-615
Chips, **4**-614
Clam Soufflé, **4**-614
Deep-Fried, **4**-614
Fried, **4**-616
Fried, and Pimiento Long Boys, **9**-1359
Gratin of, **12**-1904
Imam Fainted, The (Turkish Imam Bayeldi), **4**-616
and Lamb Stew, **7**-1038
Lasagna, **4**-616
and Macaroni Casserole, Sicilian, **7**-1095
Moussaka, **8**-1187
Mozzarella, and Pimiento Long Boys, **10**-1605
Parmigiana, **2**-324
Parmigiana, Italian, **4**-615
Parmigiana (Melanzane alla Parmigiana), **6**-958
Puffs, **4**-614
Ratatouille, Classic, **12**-1903
Ratatouille, Provençal, **4**-616
Salad (Melitzanosalata), **5**-822
Salad, Turkish, **4**-616
-Sausage Casserole, **4**-614
Sausage-Stuffed, **10**-1638
with Sesame, **8**-1212
Stuffed Baked, **12**-1904
Stuffed, Balkan, **4**-616
Stuffed, Brazilian, **4**-615
Stuffed (Gemisti Melitzana), **5**-818
Sultan's Delight, The, **4**-614
with Yogurt, **12**-1957
-Yogurt Salad, **4**-616
Egg Rolls, Shrimp, **10**-1660
Eight Treasures Pudding (Pa Pao Fan), **3**-403
Eish el Seraya (Palace Bread), **8**-1216

Elderberry(ies), **4**-617
Fritters, **4**-617
Jelly, **4**-617
Pie, **4**-617
Wine, **4**-617
Elena Zelayeta's Postre de Mamon, **3**-367
Elisen Lebkuchen (Elisen Ginger Cookies), **5**-798
El Salvador Tropical Fruits in Liqueur (Macedoine de Frutas Exoticas), **11**-1709
Empanadas de Dulce (Sweet Turnovers), **7**-1143
Empanadas de Plátanos (Banana Fritters), **11**-1708
Empanadas de Queso (Cheese Turnovers), **11**-1708
Enchiladas de Gallina (Chicken Enchiladas), **11**-1706
Enchiladas de Pollo (Chicken Enchiladas), **7**-1138
Enchiladas (Stuffed Tortillas), **7**-1138

Endive, Belgian Endive, **4**-618
Appetizer, **4**-618
and Beet Salad, **2**-198
Braised, **12**-1902
Brussels Lof, **4**-592
Curly, with Bacon or Ham, **4**-618
Curly, Stewed in Butter, **4**-618
au Gratin, **4**-618
and Orange Salad, **8**-1268
Tempura, **1**-89
English Afternoon Tea, **4**-634
English Bath Buns, **2**-252
English Bread Sauce, **10**-1626
English Cookery, **4**-619
English Gooseberry Sauce, **10**-1627
English Ham and Egg Cakes, **6**-862
English Ham and Herb Pancakes, **8**-1293
English Herring, Grilled, **6**-903
English Mincemeat, **7**-1162
English Mint Sauce for Roast Lamb, Traditional, **7**-1165

English Muffins, **4**-627; **8**-1193
English Muffins, Nut-Spiced, **4**-627
English Mustard, **5**-725; **8**-1276
English Poundcake, Traditional, **2**-272
English Style Lobster Salad, **4**-621
English Style Roast Turkey, **4**-625
English Style Trout, **12**-1860
English Tea, **4**-635
English Thin Yellow Boys, **4**-603
English Trifle, **9**-1489
English Trifle, A True, **12**-1858
Ensalada de Aguacate (Avocado Salad), **11**-1709
Ensalada de Aguacate y Maíz (Avocado and Corn Salad), **7**-1142
Ensalada a la Andaluza (Andalusian Vinaigrette Salad), **11**-1741
Ensalada de Arroz a la Valenciana (Rice Salad Valenciana), **11**-1742
Ensalada de Coliflor con Aguacate (Cauliflower Salad with Ham and Avocado), **7**-1142
Ensalada de Naranjas (Orange, Cucumber, and Pepper Salad), **7**-1142
Ensalada de Noche Buena (Christmas Eve Salad), **7**-1142; **12**-1931

Entrecôte Bercy, **11**-1761
Erbsenpuree (Purée of Dried Peas), **5**-795
Erwtensoep (Pea Soup), **4**-589
Es Advokat (Iced Avocado Drink), **11**-1714
Escabeche de Mariscos (Seafood in Pickled Sauce), **11**-1704
Escabetseng Apahap (Sweet-and-Sour Sea Bass), **9**-1368

Escarole, **4**-651
and Lentil Soup, Italian, **4**-652
Panned, **4**-652
Espagnole, Espagnole Sauce, **4**-652; **10**-1613, 1617
Estofado, I and II (Stew), **11**-1705

F

Fabada a la Asturiana (Asturian Bean Casserole), **11**-1744
Fabulous Mixed Grill, The, **5**-827
Fågelbon (Bird's Nests), **11**-1786
Faki Soupa (Lentil Soup), **5**-818
Falafel (Chick-Pea Croquettes), **6**-992
Fannie Daddies or Fried Clams, **1**-66
Far Eastern Kebabs, **3**-390
Fårikål (Lamb and Cabbage), **8**-1239

Farina, **4**-656
Balls, **4**-586
Cakes (Maamoul), **8**-1216
Dumplings, **8**-1147
Pastries (Galotoboureko), **5**-823
Pudding, **4**-656
Spoon Bread, **4**-656
Farofa, **11**-1709
Farsh Dlia Sibirskikh Pelmenei (Pelmeni Filling), **10**-1571
Fastnachts, **9**-1357
Fat, **4**-656
Fat Balls, **1**-48
Fat Rascals (Dried Currant Tea Cakes) **4**-525
Fattigmann (Poor Man's Cake), **8**-1241
Fegatini di Pollo alla Salvia (Chicken Livers with Sage), **6**-955
Feijoada (Black Bean Stew), **11**-1704

Fennel, **4**-657
Braised, **12**-1902
Parmigiana, **4**-657
Seed Tea, **4**-657
Sweet, for Antipasto, **4**-657
Festive Tzimmes (Main-Dish Meat and Vegetables), **6**-990
Fettucine Alfredo, **8**-1233
Fiddlehead, **4**-658
Fiddleheads, Milkweed, and Other Roadside Greens, **1**-45

Fig(s) **4**-658
Bread, **4**-658
and Cranberry Jam, **6**-963
Jam, **4**-659
Logs, **5**-709
Molasses Fig Pudding, **8**-1184
Pickled, **9**-1376
Pickled, 5-Day, **1**-59
Preserves, **9**-1481
Pudding with Peanut Butter, **4**-659
Pudding, Steamed, Individual, **9**-1492
Stuffed with Almonds, **1**-16
Filbert(s), **4**-659; for recipes see Hazelnut(s) and Filbert(s)
File Kambali so Slivkami i Lukom (Fillets of Flounder with Sweet Cream and Scallions), **10**-1570
Filés com Môlho de Laranja (Fish Fillets with Orange Sauce), **9**-1455
Filés de Peixe Recheados (Stuffed Fillets of Fish), **9**-1455
Filet de Boeuf Bouquetière (Beef Fillet with a Bouquet of Vegetables), **5**-740
Filet de Boeuf à la Suisse (Roast Beef), **11**-1802
Filet Piquant (Spicy Fish Fillets), **2**-275
Filety z Poledwicy (Filet Mignon with Mushrooms), **9**-1424
Filipino Veal Pot Roast, **9**-1476

Filling(s), **4**-662; see also Stuffing(s)
Cheese, **10**-1539; **9**-1429
Chicken, **8**-1308
Chicken-Mushroom, **12**-1913
Egg and Mushroom, Russian, **4**-662
(for Florentine Cannelloni), **8**-1231
Giblet Sandwich, **5**-800
Groats and Mushroom, **9**-1429
Ham, **6**-919
Hamburger, **10**-1538
Liverwurst, **4**-662
Meat, **1**-48; **6**-995; **10**-1538
Meat, Basic, **4**-662
Mushroom, **1**-89; **9**-1429
Omelet, Nonsweet, **4**-662
Omelet, Sweet, **4**-662
Pelmeni (Farsh Dlia Sibirskikh Pelmenei), **10**-1571
Potato, **6**-992; **9**-1353
Potato, Berks County, **1**-66; **9**-1352
Sandwich, Nonsweet, **4**-662
Sandwich, Sweet, **4**-662
for Savory Appetizer Puffs, **3**-492
Shrimp, **10**-1660
(for Tea Sandwiches), **4**-636
(for Vatrushki), **10**-1572

Filling(s), Dessert; see also Buttercream
Almond, **1**-15, 69; **8**-1308
Almond Cream, **2**-209; **4**-662; **8**-1320
Apple Mincemeat, Spicy, **7**-1162
Applesauce, **11**-1792
Apricot (for Kolácky), **4**-532
(for Banbury Tarts), **1**-142
Butterscotch, **2**-255
Caramel, Southern, **4**-663
Cheese, **8**-1308
Chestnut Cream, **5**-783
Chocolate, **1**-124; **11**-1812
Chocolate Bavarian, **4**-663
Chocolate Cream, **3**-492; **8**-1243, 1309
Coconut-Pecan, **3**-407
Coffee Cream, **12**-1959
Cream, **1**-47; **2**-267; **8**-1192, 1229
Cream, Fluffy, **8**-1309
Crème Pâtissière, **3**-494; **5**-762; **10**-1628
Custard Cream, **11**-1792
Custard, Thick, **4**-543
(for Danish Kringle), **7**-1157
Date-Nut, **4**-547, 663; **8**-1253
Eggnog Chiffon, **7**-1164
(for Empanadas de Dulce), **7**-1143
Fresh Coconut, **4**-662
Fruit, **2**-238, 269; **4**-579
Green-Tomato Mincemeat, **7**-1162
(for Hungarian Walnut Roll, Diós Tekercs), **6**-922
Lemon-Cheese, **11**-1725
Lemon Curd, **7**-1056; **9**-1382
Lemon, Fancy, **11**-1792
Lemon-Orange, **1**-15; **7**-1056
Lemon, Rich, **4**-663
Mincemeat, Dressed-Up Bought, **7**-1162
Mincemeat, English, **7**-1162
Mincemeat, Make-Your-Own, **7**-1162
Mincemeat, Meatless, **7**-1162
Mincemeat, Pear, Spicy, **7**-1162
Mincemeat, Pilgrim, **7**-1162
Mint, **3**-412
Mocha Cream, **7**-1167
(for Nut and Honey Sweetmeats), **6**-994
Orange, **2**-268; **4**-663; **11**-1792
Pastry Cream, **4**-627; **5**-746, 784
Pineapple, **2**-268; **4**-663
Poppy-Seed, **6**-995; **9**-1438
Prune, **1**-50; **6**-993; **7**-1157
Prune (for Kolácky), **4**-532
Raisin, **4**-663
Raisin-Nut, **10**-1535
Strawberry Cream, **11**-1779
Vanilla Cream, **3**-407, 492; **4**-594; **8**-1309
Vanilla Cream, for Tarts, **11**-1812

Fines Herbes, **4**-663
for Meats, Poultry, and Eggs, **2**-246
Finnan Haddie, see Haddock
Finnish Barley Pudding, **1**-62
Finnish Bread, **10**-1575
Finnish Cake (Vesi-Sokerikakku), **5**-681
Finnish Coffee Braids, **2**-232
Finnish Cookery, **5**-677
Finnish Stuffed Turnips, **12**-1879
Finnish Macaroni, **7**-1095
Fireplace Road Succotash, **8**-1282
Fire-Speciedaler-Kaker (Four Specie Dollars), **8**-1243

Fish, **5**-682; see also names of fishes
Alentejo Style (Peixe a Alentejana), **9**-1455
Aspic, **1**-116
Baked in a Blanket, **1**-64
Baked in Foil (Poisson en Papillote), **11**-1800
Baked (Merluza Asado al Horno), **11**-1744
Baked (Pescado al Horno), **11**-1705
Balls (Fiskefrikadeller), **4**-539
Balls, for Whiting Chowder, **5**-694
Bouillabaisse, **2**-214
Bouillabaisse, White-Fish, **10**-1645
Bouillon **2**-215
Butters for, **5**-694-695
Cakes (Kamaboko), **6**-972
-Cheese Rice, **10**-1550
and Chips, **4**-621
Chowder, **3**-419
Chowder, Jamaican, **6**-967
Chowder, Old-Fashioned New England, **8**-1222
Chowder, Oven, **11**-1695
Cioppino, **3**-447; **12**-1927
Court Bouillon for Poaching Fish, **5**-698; **9**-1421
Court Bouillon Sauce for, **5**-698
Cucumber Sauces for, **4**-522
Curry, **4**-527
Dill Sauce for, **4**-564
Dressings, **4**-573
Fillet(s), Fillet(s) of
Florentine, **2**-321
Fried, Italian Style (Pesce Fritto), **6**-954
au Gratin, **1**-119
in Mushroom-Cheese Sauce, Baked, **8**-1198
with Orange Sauce (Filés com Môlho de Laranja), **9**-1455
Rolled, with Shrimp Sauce, **11**-1753
Spicy (Filet Piquant), **2**-275
Spinach-Stuffed, **11**-1755
Stuffed (Filés de Peixe Recheados), **9**-1455
in Foil, **1**-146
Forcemeat, **5**-715
Forcemeat (Fiskefars), **4**-539
with Fresh-Grapefruit Stuffing, Baked, **5**-814
Freshwater, Fried, **1**-37
Fried, with Puerto Rican Sauce (Mojo Isleño), **9**-1494
Gefilte, **6**-989
au Gratin (Fiskegrateng), **8**-1236
Grill, **3**-355
Grilled, with Mushrooms and Rosemary, **8**-1276
Jellied, **6**-989
Kedgeree, **4**-621
Loaf (Kalakukko), **5**-680
Low-Calorie Seasonings for, **7**-1084
and Macaroni Casserole, Company, **7**-1091
and Macaroni Salad, **7**-1092
Marinade for Small Portions of, Uncooked, **7**-1110

Marinated (I 'A Ota), **9**-1434
Mousse, Hot, **8**-1190
and Mushroom Soufflé (Hmon Nga Baung), **11**-1716
with Onions and Tomatoes (Fiskgryta), **11**-1788
Packages (Laulau I 'A), **9**-1435
Paella de la Costa Brava, **11**-1746
Pickled, **1**-49
Pickled, Cold (Ikan Goreng Atjar), **11**-1714
Pickled (Pescado en Escabeche), **9**-1494
Picnic, Menu, **8**-1276
and Potato Scallop, **2**-276
Potato Stew (Caldeirada de Peixe), **9**-1455
Pudding, **5**-715; **9**-1487
Pudding (Fiskebudding), **4**-539
Pudding (Fiskepudding), **8**-1236
Pudding, Norwegian, **1**-49
Quenelles, **5**-715
Quenelles de Brochet, **5**-700
Raw Fish Rice Ball (Nigiri Sushi), **6**-971
Raw, Pickled (Seviche), **7**-1140
Raw, Sliced (Sashimi), **6**-971
and Rice Casserole (Kala-Riisivuoka), **5**-680
Ring, Jellied, **7**-1080
Rolls, Vegetable-Stuffed, **2**-305
Salad in Clamshells, **10**-1665
Salade Russe, **10**-1587
Sandwich Fillings, **10**-1606
Sauces for, **5**-694-695
Sauces for (Swedish), **11**-1791
with Sauerkraut, German, **10**-1631
Sauté Meunière, **5**-698
Amandine, **5**-698
Fines Herbes, **5**-698
Lemon Butter, **5**-698
Seafood
Baked, Hearthside, **8**-1222
Chowder, Maine, **1**-45
Club Sandwiches, **10**-1602
Medley in Patty Shells, **3**-424
Newburg, **2**-250
in Pickled Sauce (Escabeche de Mariscos), **11**-1704
Salad, **10**-1665
Salad, Peach, **8**-1316
Stew, **8**-1222
Supreme, **10**-1645
Sicilian (Pesce alla Siciliana), **6**-954
Soup, Basque (Sopa de Pescado a la Vasca), **11**-1743
Soup (Caldo de Pescado), **7**-1138
Soup (Gentsche Waterzooi), **2**-197
Soup, Venetian (Zuppa Veneziana di Pesce), **6**-952
Steaks, **11**-1771
Steaks with Lemon Butter, **7**-1052
Stew (Aigo-Sau), **2**-216
Stew, Boatman's (Sardinhas de Caldeirada), **9**-1455
Stew (Bourride), **5**-740
Stew from Burgundy (Pauchouse Bourguignon), **4**-595
Stew (Kaeng Phed), **11**-1717
Stew (Vatapá), **11**-1703
Stock, **11**-1775
Stuffed with Greens (Bhaji Malida Machli), **6**-942
Stuffings for, **11**-1780
Sukiyaki (Chirinabe), **6**-971
Sweet-and-Sour, **6**-990
in Sweet-Sour Sauce, **11**-1734
Tartare Fish Loaf with Caper Sauce, **7**-1101
Tempura, **6**-971
To Freeze, see To Freeze Seafood, **5**-736; see also information under entry for specific fish
Truite Farcie, **5**-698
Vinaigrette (Pescado a la Vinagreta), **11**-1741
Fish Casseroles, **2**-321
Fisherman's Wharf Cioppino, **1**-26
Fish-House Cooler, **1**-32
Fish House Punch, Philadelphia, **9**-1502
Fiskebudding (Fish Pudding), **4**-539
Fiskefars (Fish Forcemeat), **4**-539
Fiskefrikadeller (Fish Balls), **4**-539
Fiskegrateng (Fish au Gratin), **8**-1236
Fiskepudding (Fish Pudding), **8**-1236
Fiskgryta (Fish with Onions and Tomatoes), **11**-1788
Flaeskesteg (Roast Pork), **4**-540
Flaki no Warszawsku (Tripe à la Warsaw), **9**-1424

Flambé, Flambéed, or **Flaming**
Ananas Flambée, Arnaud's, **4**-513
Bananas au Rhum, **5**-701
Café Brûlot, **3**-462
Café Brûlot, New Orleans, **5**-702
Cherries Jubilee, **5**-701
Chicken, **5**-701
Crêpes Carlos, **8**-1293
Crêpes Suzette, **5**-701
Kidneys (Rognons Bolo), **11**-1802
Pepper Steak with Cream (Steak au Poivre Flambé à la Crème), **5**-741
Plum Pudding, **5**-701
Rognons Flambés au Ruban Bleu, **7**-1014
Shrimps, **10**-1660
Sweet Potatoes, **11**-1796
Flan, Custard, see Custard
Flan, Tart, see Pies and Tarts
Flan de Piña (Pineapple Caramel Custard), **5**-703
Flan Sol y Sombra (Sun and Shadow Custard), **1**-73
Flannel Cakes, **5**-703; **8**-1293
Flapjacks, **5**-703
Flemish Beer Stew (Carbonnade Flamande), **2**-197
Flemish Fricasseed Chicken with Meatballs (Kiek met Ballekens), **7**-1122
Flemish Pork (Porc à la Flamande), **2**-197
Flensjes (Very Thin Pancakes), **4**-593
Float, see Beverages, Float
Floating Island, **3**-494; **5**-704
Flødebudding (Cream Pudding), **4**-543
Florentine Cannelloni, **8**-1231
Florentine Cod, **3**-459
Florentine Eggs, Italian, **11**-1755
Florentine Pork Cooked in Milk, **9**-1442
Florentine Pork Roast Arista, **10**-1560
Florentines, **8**-1272
Florida "Gaspachy" Salad, **1**-33
Florida Gingered Orange Peel, **5**-803
Florida Lime Pie, **7**-1069
Florida Meringue Orange Pudding, **7**-1135
Florida Style Baked Red Snapper, **10**-1540

Flounder, **5**-705
Cocktail, Flaked, **5**-705
Fillets, Broiled, with Puffy Cheese Sauce, **1**-57
Fillets of, with Sour Cream and Scallions (File Kambali so Slivkami i Lukom), **10**-1570
Florentine, **5**-704
Monterey, **5**-705
and Mushrooms in Cream Sauce, Poached, **5**-688
Pickled Fish (Seviche), **11**-1704
and Rice Croquettes, **5**-705
Seviche, **5**-688
and Shrimps, **5**-705
Stuffed, Commander's Palace, **4**-510
with Tartare Sauce, **5**-705

Flour, **5**-705
Peanut, **8**-1328
Potato, **9**-1471
Rice, **10**-1556
Rye, **10**-1575
To Brown, **2**-277
To Measure, **7**-1117
Flummery, see Puddings, Dessert
Foamy Sauce, **10**-1628
Foie Gras, see Liver(s); Pâté(s) and Terrine(s)
Foi Tong (Shreds of Gold), **11**-1716

Fond, **10**-1615
Blanc, **10**-1615
Brun, **10**-1615

Fondant, **2**-283, 284; **5**-708
Almond Diamonds, **5**-709
Bonbons, **5**-708
Chocolate Creams, **5**-708
Cooked, **5**-708
-Dipped Almonds, **5**-708
-Dipped Strawberries, **11**-1779
Fig Logs, **5**-709
Filbert Squares, **5**-709
Frosting, Easy (for Frosting Cakes and Petits Fours), **4**-549
Patties, **2**-284
(for Petits Four), **9**-1365
-Stuffed Dates, **5**-708
Toasted-Coconut Balls, **5**-709
Uncooked, **2**-285; **5**-709

Fondue, **5**-709
Bourguignonne, **5**-712; **11**-1803
Cheese, Baked, **3**-359
Geneva Style, **5**-712
(Melted Cheese Dish), **11**-1803
Neuchâtel Style, **5**-711
Swiss, **3**-359
Tuna and Chili, **12**-1864

Fool, **5**-714
Gooseberry, **5**-714

Forcemeat, **5**-714
Basic, **8**-1312
Chicken, **5**-715
Fish, **5**-715
Fruit, **5**-715
Potato, **5**-715
Forshmak Dragomir, **10**-1567
Fortune Cookies, Chinese, **4**-635
Fortune Wafers, Japanese (Tsujiura), **6**-978
Four Specie Dollars (Fire-Speciedaler-Kaker), **8**-1243
Frangipane Pie, **5**-716
Fragole all'Italiana (Italian Strawberries), **6**-960
Fraize (Madame) Cabbage and Zucchini Skillet, **12**-1903
Fraize (Madame) Tomatoes Provençal, **12**-1900

Frankfurter(s), **5**-717
Appetizer Kabobs, **5**-718
Apple-Frankfurter Casserole, **1**-97
-Avocado Dip, **5**-718
Baked, **5**-721
Bavarian, **5**-722
Bean Casserole, Savory, **2**-320
Bits, **5**-718
in Blankets, **5**-725
Boats, **5**-724
with Brussels Sprouts, **5**-725
Buon Gusto, **5**-721
with Cabbage, **5**-722
with Cheese, **5**-725
with Cheese and Bacon, **5**-718
-Cheese Rolls, Snappy, **5**-725
Cheese-Topped, **5**-724
and Chicken, Creamed, **5**-724
Chili, **5**-725
Coney Island Picnic, **5**-724
and Corn Casserole, **5**-720
and Corn Chowder, **5**-718
Corn-Frankfurter Soup, **11**-1695
and Cornmeal Patties, **8**-1313
Corn Sticks, **5**-725
Country-Style, **5**-721
and Creamed Corn, **5**-724
and Creamed Onions, **5**-724

Frankfurter(s), continued
in a Crispy Crust, **5**-725
-Custard Tarts, **5**-725; **11**-1811
-Egg Appetizers, **5**-718
Eggs Fu Yung, **5**-720
and Eggs, Mexican, **5**-724
Frank-Cheese Burgers, **5**-725
Frankie and Johnny, **5**-725
Frank-Roll Slices, **5**-718
with Fruit Sauce, **5**-724
Hash, **6**-879
Hawaiian, **5**-722
Hominy, and Green-Pea Casserole, **6**-907
and Hot-Potato Salad, **10**-1580
-Kraut Casserole, **5**-720
Lentil Moussaka, **8**-1187
and Lima Beans, Barbecued, **7**-1066
and Lima-Bean Casserole, **5**-721
with Macaroni and Cheese, **5**-720
Macaroni-Frankfurter Skillet, **7**-1094
Marinated Appetizer Frankfurters, **5**-718
-Mozzarella Spaghetti, **5**-720
with New Potatoes and Peas, **5**-721
and Noodles, **9**-1352
in Olive Sauce, **5**-725
Pilaf, **5**-722
Pineapple-Frankfurter Kabobs, **6**-998
-Potato Dumplings, **4**-586
and Potato Salad, Hot, **5**-722
Prune, and Onion Kabobs, **5**-721
in Pungent Sauce, **5**-722
and Puréed Lentil Soup, **5**-720
Rarebit, **5**-725
and Rice Soup, **5**-718
Rounds, **1**-86
in the Round, **5**-725
Sauces and Relishes to Serve with, **5**-725
and Sauerkraut Goulash, **5**-721
with Shirred Eggs, **5**-720
Soups with, Quick, **5**-720
in Spaghetti Sauce, **5**-725
with Spanish Rice, **5**-721
Split Franks Cooked with Relish, **5**-724
-Squash Lyonnaise, **5**-724
Stew, **5**-720
Sticks, **5**-718
Stuffed Broiled, **5**-722
-Stuffed Green Peppers, **5**-722
Stuffed with Mashed Potatoes, Onions, and Cheese, **5**-724
Succotash, **5**-725
Tetrazzini, **5**-724
and Tomatoes, Scalloped, **5**-721
and Tomato Scrambled Eggs, **5**-724
with Yellow Peas, German Style, **5**-722
Frankfurter and Sausage Casseroles, **2**-320
Frankfurter Rippchen (Pot Roast of Smoked Loin of Pork), **5**-795
Frankie and Johnny, **5**-725
Frappé(s), **5**-726; for recipes see Frozen Dessert(s)

Freezing, To Freeze, and Frozen Foods, **5**-726
Baked Products, To Freeze, **5**-737
Canapés, To Freeze, **5**-737
Cooked Foods, To Freeze, **5**-726
Dairy Products, To Freeze, **5**-736
Desserts, To Freeze, **5**-737
Fruits, To Freeze, **5**-728
Chart, **5**-730-732
Maximum Storage Times for Frozen Foods, Chart, **5**-728
Meat, To Freeze, **5**-733
Poultry, To Freeze, **5**-736
Sandwiches, To Freeze, **5**-737
Seafood, To Freeze, **5**-736
Sugar Syrup, Chart, **5**-728
Vegetables, To Freeze, **5**-732
Chart, **5**-734-735
French Apple Tart, **11**-1812
French Bean Casserole, **7**-1066
French Beef Salad, **10**-1580
French Beer Batter, **1**-149
French Bread, **2**-228
French Cabbage Soup, **2**-257
French Chocolate Mousse, **3**-415
French Chocolate Torte, **12**-1853
French Cookery, **5**-738
French Country-Style Pork Chops, **9**-1444
French Crullers, **4**-519
French Crust, Flaky, **12**-1879

French Dressing, **10**-1622
Cottage-Cheese, **10**-1622
Cream, **11**-1700
Fresh-Lime, **7**-1067
Fresh Orange, **5**-754
Garlic, **10**-1614, 1622
Lemon, **7**-1053
de Luxe, **4**-573; **10**-1622
Orange, **8**-1270
for Salad, **8**-1276
Simple, **4**-573
Special, **4**-650
Sweetened, **10**-1622
French Kirsch Parfait, **8**-1297
French Lamb Stew, **2**-216
French Nougat, **8**-1244
French Omelet, **8**-1257
French Onion Quiche, **8**-1261
French Onion Soup, **8**-1260
French Pancakes, **5**-699
French Pancakes, Basic (Crêpes), **8**-1293
French Pastry, Nonsweet (Pâte Brisée), **8**-1304
French Pastry, Sweet (Pâte Brisée Sucrée), **8**-1304
French Peas, **4**-568; **8**-1315
French Pepper Steak (Steak au Poivre), **11**-1767
French Pork Liver with Onions, **7**-1075
French Potato Salad with Onion and Parsley Dressing, **9**-1383
French Potato Soup, Quick, **11**-1690
French Rice Salad, **10**-1550
French Rolls, Pungent, **9**-1378
French Shallot-Beans, **10**-1650
French Shrimp-Mushroom Flan, **4**-633
French Stuffed Onions, **8**-1261
French Style Stuffed Mushrooms (Champignons Farcis), **8**-1201
French Tarragon Soup, **11**-1692
French Toast, **11**-1826
French Toasted Mozzarella Sandwiches, **10**-1604
French Toast Sandwiches with Creamed Dried Beef, **10**-1601
French Vanilla Ice Cream, **6**-929
French Veal Stew, **2**-216
Fresno Fruit Salad, **10**-1588
Friar's Chicken Soup or Stew, **11**-1721

Fricassee, **5**-748
Chicken, **3**-390; **5**-716
Chicken, with Cornmeal Dumplings, **5**-748
Chicken Fricasseed with Meatballs, Flemish (Kiek met Ballekens), **7**-1122
Pork, Filipino, **6**-851
Veal Breast, **5**-748
Frijoles, Frijolitos, y Frijoles Refritos (Beans, Mashed Beans, and Beans Refried), **11**-1731
Frijoles Fritos (Fried Beans), **7**-1141
Frijoles (Mexican Beans), **7**-1141
Frijoles Negros Batidos (Mashed Black Beans), **11**-1708
Frijoles Refritos (Crisp Fried Beans), **7**-1141
Frikadeller (Danish Meatballs), **4**-540
Frisk Stegt Løg (Fried Onions), **4**-538

Fritters(s), **5**-748
American-Cheese, **3**-362
Artichoke, **12**-1930
Bacon-Corn, **8**-1224
Banana (Empanados de Plátanos), **11**-1708
Batter, Basic, **5**-748
Brain Batter Cakes, **2**-217
Burritos from Taos, **11**-1732
Carimañolas, **11**-1706
Cauliflower (Torrejas de Coliflor), **11**-1708
Celery, **1**-73
Cheese Beignets, **2**-196
Cheese-Corn, **3**-361
Chick-Pea (Frituras de Garbanzos), **11**-1747
Clam Puffs, Fried, **3**-453
Clam, with Tomato Sauce, **3**-453
Corn, **2**-242; **3**-484
Corn, Nebraska, **1**-54
Corn, Skillet, **3**-484
Green Corn Cakes, **1**-67
Ham and Corn, **6**-856
Hominy Puffs, **6**-907
Meat, **5**-749
Mushroom Beignets, **1**-89
Ocean-Perch, **5**-748
Oyster-Plant, **8**-1290
Parsleyed Corn, **5**-749
Parsnip, **1**-68
Peanut, Crisp (Rempejek Katjang), **11**-1714
Potato (Kartoffel Chremsel), **6**-992
Rice Balls, **10**-1549
Rice, Hot (Calas Tout Chauds), **4**-513
Sopaipillas, **11**-1731
Spinach (Buñuelos de Espinaca), **11**-1708
Squash (Cymling), **11**-1761
Tuna, **12**-1866

Fritter(s), Dessert
Apple, **1**-101
Apple, Regina, **5**-749
Banana, **1**-139
Batter for Fruits, Thin, **5**-749
Beignets Soufflés, **11**-1804
Brandied Apple, **1**-63
Celestial Crusts (Bozi Milosti), **4**-532
Cherries, Deep-Fried (Cseresznye Kisütve), **6**-920
Country, **8**-1228
Elderberry, **4**-617
Jam, Viennese, **5**-749
Matzo-Meal (Chremslach), **6**-994
Orange, **5**-749
Plum, **5**-749
Pompushkes, **11**-1700
Rice, New Orleans, **10**-1552
Walnut-Rice, **10**-1552
Fritti Rognoni, **7**-1016
Fritto Misto (Mixed Fry), **7**-1040
Frituras de Garbanzos (Chick-Pea Fritters) **11**-1747

Frogs' Legs, **7**-1150
à la Creole, **1**-41
Poulette, **5**-749
Frosted, see Beverages, Frosted

Frosting(s), **5**-750, and **Icing(s);** see also Buttercream; Glaze(s)
Amounts Needed, Chart, **5**-750
Boiled Frosting, **5**-750
Brown-Sugar Frosting, **3**-408
Burnt-Sugar Frosting, **7**-1044
Butter Frosting, **3**-412
Butter Frosting, Fluffy, **5**-751
Butterscotch Frosting, **2**-267
Caramel Frosting, **1**-55; **2**-270, 297; **7**-1044
Caramel Fudge Frosting **5**-751
Caramel Topping, **1**-124
Chocolate Frosting, **2**-267; **7**-1044, 1157; **10**-1535; **12**-1959
Bittersweet, **3**-412
Cream-Cheese, **2**-267; **3**-407; **5**-752; **7**-1045
Creamy, **3**-412
Easy, **3**-410
Fudge, **5**-751
Glossy, **1**-79; **3**-407
Hungarian, **5**-752
Peanut-Butter, **8**-1328
Rich, **3**-457
Rum, **3**-408
Soft, **3**-407

Chocolate Icing, **12**-1853
Choco-Peanut Frosting, **3**-412
Choco-Sour-Cream Frosting, **3**-412; **5**-752
Cinnamon Frosting, **1**-56; **3**-471
Cinnamon Mocha Frosting, **3**-410
Coconut Boiled Frosting, **3**-457
Coffee Frosting, **7**-1045
Confectioners' Icing, **7**-1157
Confectioners' Sugar Frosting, **1**-15, 50; **2**-232; **3**-410; **4**-543; **7**-1157; **8**-1309; **10**-1526
Confectioners'-Sugar Frosting, Plain, **5**-751
Cream Cheese Frosting, **5**-752
Decorator's or Royal Icing (for Decorations), **4**-549
Fluffy Frosting, **1**-55
Fluffy White (Seven-Minute) Frosting, **2**-264
Fondant, **9**-1365
Fondant Frosting, Easy (for Frosting Cakes and Petits Fours), **4**-549
Frosting (for Brown Beauty Cake), **3**-424
Frosting (for Cassata Napolitana), **6**-960
Frosting (for Christmas Tree Cookies), **3**-428
Frosting (for Election Cake), **1**-29
Frosting (for Italian Muscatels), **8**-1195
Frosting (for Kolácky), **4**-532
Frosting (for Mincemeat Diamonds), **3**-471
Frosting for Pfeffernüsse, **9**-1367
Frosting for Stollen, **11**-1775
Fudge Frosting, **3**-412; **4**-559
Caramel, **5**-751
Chocolate, **5**-751
Maple-Nut, **5**-751
Raisin, **5**-751
Semisweet, **5**-751
White, **5**-751
Icing (for Stuffed-Date Cookies), **4**-547
Lemon Frosting, **7**-1046, 1056
Lemon Frosting, Fluffy, **7**-1056
Lemon-Orange Buttercream Frosting, **2**-268
Lemon Icing, **11**-1793
Lemon Icing, Simple, **12**-1853
Lime or Lemon Boiled Frosting, **5**-750
Maple Icing, **1**-63; **7**-1108
Maple-Nut Fudge Frosting, **5**-751
Maple Sugar Frosting, **2**-255
Marshmallow Frosting, **3**-375; **4**-559
Mocha Cream, **7**-1167
Mocha Frosting, Rich, **3**-410
Molasses Frosting, Fluffy, **8**-1185
Orange Frosting, **2**-238, 308
Boiled, **8**-1272
Butter, **3**-431; **7**-1042
Cream-Cheese, **3**-407; **5**-752
Thin, **7**-1046
Ornamental Frosting, **12**-1922
Peanut Frosting, Broiled, with Yellow Cake, **8**-1323
Peppermint Frosting, **7**-1044
Pink Fluffy Frosting, **2**-273
Prune Frosting, **9**-1486
Rum-Flavored Frosting, **8**-1247
Seafoam Frosting, **2**-272
Semisweet Frosting, **3**-412
Seven-Minute Frosting, **5**-750
Sour-Cream Chocolate Frosting, **11**-1701
Sour-Cream Frosting, **11**-1701
To Frost, **5**-751
Topping (for Apple Betty), **1**-77
Vanilla Frosting, **8**-1229, 1326
Wedding or Anniversary Cake Frosting, **5**-752
Whipped Cream, Stabilized (for Decorations), **4**-550
White Frosting, Fluffy, **1**-46; **3**-408; **7**-1042; **9**-1469
Yellow Jacket Frosting, **2**-273

Frozen Desserts
Ambrosia in Frozen Orange Shells, **11**-1824
Banana Split, **6**-934
Biscuit Tortoni, **2**-203; **12**-1857
Bombe
Italian Coffee, **2**-212
Raspberry, **2**-212
Butterscotch Pecan Roll, **8**-1335
Caramela, **11**-1732
Cheese and Raspberry, **10**-1536
Coconut Eskimos, **3**-458
Coconut Snowballs, **3**-458
Coffee Tortoni, **12**-1857
Crêpes, Frozen, **6**-934
Eggnog Pie, **7**-1100
Lemon Custard, Low-Calorie, **7**-1054
Frappé(s), **5**-726
Café, Deep South, **5**-726
Grape-Lime, **5**-726
Lemon, **6**-925
Strawberry, Apricot, Raspberry, or Peach, **6**-926
Tangerine, **5**-726
Gingered Lemon Pineapple, **9**-1410
Ginger-Pumpkin Pie, **9**-1500
Grated Fresh-Pear Snow, **8**-1331
Harlequin Crinkle Cups, **6**-934
Ice Cream, see Ice Cream
Ices, see Ice(s) and Sherbet(s)
Ice-Cream Bonbons, **6**-934
Ice-Cream Cake, **6**-932
Shadow Cake, **6**-932
Ladyfinger Cake, **6**-932
Chocolate Ice-Cream Roll, **6**-932
Ice-Cream Pie
Apricot, **6**-934
Coffee-Chocolate, **6**-934
Ice-Cream Snowballs, **10**-1669
Jelly-Roll Sandwiches, **6**-934
Lemon Pie, Frozen, **9**-1398
Maple Freeze, **7**-1108
Maple-Graham Cream, **7**-1107
Marble Pie, Frozen, **9**-1398
Marron Coupe, **7**-1112
Melon à la Mode, **6**-934
Parfait(s)
Angel, **11**-1724
Blueberry, **2**-209; **6**-930
Cherry, **3**-374
Cherry-Pistachio, **3**-375
Cherry, Two-Tone, **6**-930
Chocolate Coconut-Cream, **3**-457
Cinnamon Chocolate, **6**-930
French Kirsch, **8**-1297
Maple, **7**-1108
Mint, **7**-1166
Mocha, **6**-930
Peach Crème de Menthe, **8**-1320
Rainbow Sherbet, **10**-1654
Strawberry, **6**-930
Peach Cream, **8**-1320
Peach Delight, **8**-1320
Peach Marlow, **7**-1113
Peach Melba, **8**-1320
Peach Parfait Pie, **9**-1398
Peppermint-Chocolate Cream, Marbled, **9**-1361
Peppermint Freeze, **9**-1361
Pineapple, Iced, **11**-1732
Pistachio Custard, **9**-1411
Prune Whip, **9**-1485
Pumpkin Tarts, **9**-1500
Raspberry Peach Glacées, **10**-1537
Sabayon, **9**-1489
Sherbet(s), see Ice(s) and Sherbet(s)
Sherry Tortoni, **12**-1858
Spumoni, **11**-1758
Strawberries à la Mode, **6**-934
Strawberry-Almond Roll, **11**-1778
Strawberry Cake Roll, **11**-1779
Strawberry Ice Cream Tarts, **8**-1309
Strawberry-Macaroon Cream, **11**-1778
Summer Snowballs, **6**-934
Sundaes, Ice Cream, **6**-931-932
Arabian, **6**-932
Brandied Fruit, **6**-932
Brittle, **6**-931
Butterscotch-Mace Sauce for, **7**-1100
Candied Fruit, **6**-932
Caramel, Hot, **6**-931
Cereal, **6**-932
Chocolate Mint, **6**-931
Chocolate-Rum, **6**-932
Coconut, **6**-932
Cookie, **6**-932
Cranberry-Orange, **6**-932
Ginger, **6**-931
Jam or Preserves, **6**-932
Junior, **6**-932
Mango Rum, **7**-1104
Maple-Rum, **6**-931
Marshmallow, **6**-931
Mincemeat, **6**-932
Mocha, **6**-932
Molasses Chip, **6**-932
Nutmeg, **6**-931
Orange, **6**-932
Orange and Blue, **6**-931
Oriental, **6**-931
Party Pink, **6**-932
Peach, **6**-931
Pineapple, **6**-932
Pineapple-Ginger, **6**-932
Sauce, Mocha, **7**-1167
Stop-and-Go, **6**-931
Tropical, **6**-932
Zippy, **6**-932
Frugtsauce (Fruit Sauce), **4**-543

Fruit(s), **5**-752; see also names of fruits
Ambrosia, Texas, **1**-73
Berry Charlotte, **5**-758
Bowl, Mixed-Fruit, **2**-250
Brandied, **2**-221
Canned Fruit Compote, **5**-758
Canning, **2**-295
Cocktails, **5**-754
-Cocktail Salad Loaf, **5**-788
-Cocktail Whip, **7**-1088
Compote Amandine, **3**-465
Compote, Chilled, **3**-465
Compote Combinations, **3**-465
Cream Mousse, **8**-1191
Cup, Anise, **8**-1283
Cup, Pistachio, **9**-1411
Curried, Hot, **11**-1753
Dessert (Kisiel Owocowy), **9**-1431
Dessert, Party, **5**-788
Dressing, **6**-859
Dressing, Fluffy, **10**-1589
Five-Fruit Salad Plate, **5**-754
Forcemeat, **5**-715
Fresh, Compote, **2**-241
Fresh, Compote of, with Lemon Balm, **1**-138
Fresh Fruit Garnishes, **5**-777, 779-780
Fresh Fruit Platter, **4**-641
Fritter Batter for, Thin, **5**-749
Frosted Fruit for Decorations, **5**-752
Fruit Cocktails, **3**-455
Fruited Black-Bean Sauce, **10**-1554
Fruited Rice Pudding, **5**-758
Fruited Wine Gelatin, **5**-789
Ginger-Ale Fruit Mold, **5**-803
Ice, Three-Fruit, **6**-926
-Juice Ice, **6**-925
Ketchup, **1**-53; **6**-999
Kumquat, Orange, and Apple Compote, **7**-1023
Lemon-Orange-Cottage-Cheese Mold, **7**-1052
Macédoine of, **4**-568
Marinade for, **7**-1110
Meringues, **7**-1135
Milk Shake, Spiced, **7**-1160
Mincemeat, Meatless, **7**-1162
Mixed, Cambodian (Trai Cay), **11**-1717
Molded Winter Fruit Salad, **5**-755
Molasses Spiced, **8**-1184
October Salad, **10**-1587
Orange Cream, de Luxe, Frozen, **5**-791
Peach, Plum, and Apricot Medley, **5**-758
Peanut-Butter Salad, **8**-1325
Pies, Fried, **11**-1725
Pie, Swedish, **9**-1396

Fruit(s), continued
Pineapple Fruit Cup Served in the Half Shell, **9**-1403
Plate with Pistachio Cheese, **5**-755
-Preserve Layer Cake, **7**-1042
Prosciutto with, **6**-952
Punch, **9**-1503
Punch, Picnic, **7**-1057
Punch (QC), **10**-1527
Rainbow, **3**-429
and Roots, Sweet (Ginatan), **9**-1370
Rouges, **5**-758
Salad Bowl, **1**-33
Salad, Christmas, **10**-1588
Salad with Coconut Dressing, **3**-456
-Salad Dressing, **7**-1116
Salad, Fresno, **10**-1588
Salads, **11**-1727
Sauce, **10**-1615, 1628
Sauce (Frugstsauce), **4**-543
Soup, Chilled, Scandinavian, **11**-1694
Soup, Clear, **9**-1421
Soup, Jellied, **6**-979
Soups with Sour Cream, **9**-1421
Spring-Fruit Jam, **9**-1403
Squares, Fluffy, **5**-790
Stewed, Sugar Syrup for, **11**-1807
Summer-Fruit Compote, **5**-758
Sweet-Potato Dessert (Chakin Shibori), **6**-978
Tartlets, **5**-763
Tarts, Glazed, **11**-1812
Tarts (Tartes aux Fruits), **5**-746
Tarts with Pastry Cream (Tartes aux Fruits avec Crème Pâtissière), **5**-746
To Freeze, **5**-728; see also information under entry for specific fruit
Chart, **5**-730-732
-Tomato Relish, **10**-1543
Tropical, in Liqueur (Macedoine de Frutas Exoticas), **11**-1709
Vanilla Fresh-Fruit Cup, **12**-1885

Fruit(s), Candied, **2**-281; see also Glacé, Glacéed
Candied-Fruit Squares, **2**-285
Cherry-Nut Patties (Hard Sauce), **6**-878
Citrus Peel, Quick Crystallized, **2**-281
Grapefruit Peel, **2**-289
Kumquats, **7**-1023
Nesselrode Pudding, Classic, **8**-1217
Orange Peel, **2**-289
Soufflé Rothschild, **11**-1688

Fruit(s), Dried, **4**-576; see also names of dried fruits
Barmbrack, **6**-949
Beef, Fruited Spiced, **4**-576
Beef Pot Roast, Spiced, **9**-1472
Buns, **2**-238
Chocolate Fruit Pie, **4**-578
Coffeecake, Fruit Twist, **4**-578
Compote, **4**-578; **6**-993
Compote, Chilled, **3**-465
-Cream Pudding, Jellied, **9**-1489
Drops, Holiday, **3**-432
-Filled Cookies, **4**-579
Filling, **2**-238, 269; **4**-579
Honey Bars, **3**-433
Lamb Shanks Baked in Fruited Wine, **12**-1928
Plum Pudding, **9**-1418
Plum Pudding, Brandy, **9**-1492
Pudding, Scandinavian, **5**-758
Roll, California, **5**-758
Soup, Dried- and Fresh-Fruit, **4**-576
Spice Roll, **5**-803
Sticks, Rolled, **4**-548
Suet Pudding, **11**-1783
Tutti-Frutti, **4**-579
Tutti-Frutti, How to Use, **4**-579

Fruitcake(s), **5**-758
Candied Light, **5**-759
Carolina Fruitcake, **1**-61
Christmas (Stollen), **5**-798
Dark, **5**-759
Fruitcake, **2**-269; **3**-444
Golden, **5**-759
Light, **3**-429
Little White, **3**-449
Old Alabama, **5**-759
Raised, **2**-233

Fudge, **2**-283; **5**-764
Burnt-Sugar, **5**-764
Chocolate, **3**-472
Chocolate, Kneaded, **5**-764
Chocolate Nut (QC), **10**-1526
Chocolate, Old-Fashioned, **5**-764
Chocolate, Old-Time, **2**-285
Cocoa, **5**-764
Divinity, see Divinity and Seafoam
Frosting(s), see Frosting(s) and Icing(s)
Layered, **5**-764
Mrs. Benson's Receipt for, **8**-1231
Opera, **2**-285
Peanut-Butter Chocolate, **8**-1328
Quick, **5**-764
Sauce (QC), **10**-1526
Seafoam, see Divinity and Seafoam
Vanilla, **5**-764
Fukien Deep-Fried Chicken, **3**-400
Fukien Jellied Lamb, **3**-400
Fukien Red-Cooked Pork Shoulder, **3**-400
Fukien Red-Cooked Shin of Beef, **3**-399
Fukien Spiced Ducks, **3**-401
Fumet, **10**-1615
Funeral Pie, **9**-1355
Funnel Cakes, **9**-1357
Funny Cake, **9**-1356
Fusilli, see Pasta
Fyldt Svinemorbrad (Stuffed Pork Tenderloin), **4**-540
Fylld Blomkål (Stuffed Cauliflower), **11**-1790

G

Gado Gado (Vegetables with Peanut Sauce), **11**-1715
Gajar Halwa (Carrot Dessert), **6**-942

Galantine, **5**-765
of Chicken, **5**-766
of Eel, **5**-766
How to Bone and Prepare a Chicken, Duck, or Turkey for a Galantine, **5**-765
of Pork, **5**-766
Veal, **5**-715, 766
Galician Turnovers (Pastelillos Gallegos), **9**-1497
Gallina Rellena (Stuffed Turkey South-western Style), **11**-1730
Galotoboureko (Farina Pastries), **5**-823

Game, **5**-766; see also names of game animals
Beer Marinade for, **7**-1110
Booyaw, **1**-84
Canning, **2**-295
Hunter's Reward, **11**-1730
Hunters' Stew (Bigos Mysliwski), **9**-1426
Maggi's Mad Hare, **1**-29
Marinade for, Cooked, **7**-1109
Mulligan, **1**-27
Trapper's Stew, **1**-23
Wild-Fowl Salad, **5**-774
Garbure Basque (Ham and Bean Soup with Vegetables), **5**-739
Garden Sorrel, **10**-1671
Gardiners Bay Potato Salad, **8**-1278
Garides Saltsa Tomate (Shrimp with Spicy Tomato Sauce), **5**-818

Garlic, **5**-774
Bread, **2**-250
Bread, Italian, **5**-775
Butter, **1**-86; **5**-695, 775; **10**-1661
French Dressing, **10**-1614, 1622
Garlic Lover's Spaghetti, **11**-1736
-Ginger Shrimps, **10**-1661
Hamburgers on Toasted Buns, **8**-1282
Lamb Steaks, **7**-1032; **11**-1770
Olives, **8**-1276
Black, **8**-1257
Peanut-Butter Bread, **8**-1326
Pickles, Half-Sour, **6**-993
Sauce, Genoese (Pesto alla Genovese), **5**-775
Sauce, Greek, **10**-1623
Sauce, Plum, **9**-1415
Sauce (Skordalia), **5**-822
Seasoning, **5**-775
Soup, **11**-1742
Soup, Italian, **5**-775
Soup, Vera Cruz, **11**-1691
Toast Butter, **11**-1829
Toast, Italian Style, **11**-1826
-Vinegar Sauce, **5**-694
Garnalen Croquetten (Shrimp Croquettes), **4**-590

Garnish(es), **5**-776
and Accompaniments, Soup, **11**-1696-1697
Almonds, Blanched and Slivers, **5**-780
Angelica, **1**-81
Apple Cups, **5**-780
Aspic, **1**-117; **5**-780
Aspic, Chopped (Sky), **4**-538
Aspic Glaze for Sandwiches, **6**-980
Beet Roses, **10**-1666
Beets, **5**-777
Butter, Curls and Pressed, **5**-780
Carrots, **5**-778
Carrot Curls, How to Make, **2**-305
Celery, **5**-778
Cream-Cheese Watercress Balls, **3**-424
Croutons, **4**-519
Cucumber, **5**-778; **10**-1666
Serrated Slices or Twists, **10**-1666
Daisies (carrot, white turnip, cucumber), **10**-1666
Egg, Hard-Cooked, **10**-1666
Frosted Fruit for Decorations, **5**-752
Frosted Glasses, **5**-752
Grapes, Frosted, **5**-780
for Ham, **11**-1790
for Idaho Baked Potatoes, **1**-35
Lemons, **5**-779; **10**-1666
Serrated Slices or Twists, **10**-1666
Limes, **5**-779
Serrated Slices or Twists, **10**-1666
Mayonnaise, Stabilized, **5**-780
Melons, **5**-780
Nonsweet, **5**-776
(for Norwegian Reindeer Pot Roast), **10**-1541
Onions, **5**-778
Fried (Frisk Stegt Løg), **4**-538
Oranges, **5**-780; **10**-1666
Serrated Slices or Twists, **10**-1666
Slices, Spicy, **1**-11
Pickle Fans, **10**-1666
Pineapple, **5**-780
Potatoes, **5**-778
Radishes, **5**-778
Radish Flowers, **10**-1666
Scrambled Eggs, Cold (Aeggestand), **4**-538
Sliced Vegetable, **10**-1666
Spearmint Leaves, Candied, **11**-1749
Sweet, **5**-777
Tomato(es), **5**-778; **10**-1666
Truffles (cutouts), **5**-780
Turnip Roses, **10**-1666
Turnips, **5**-777
Vegetable (for Herrings), **10**-1566
for Vegetables à la Polonaise, **9**-1430
Whipped Cream, Stabilized, **5**-780
"Gaspachy" Salad, Florida, **1**-33

Gâteau, Gâteaux, **5**-780
de Marrons au Chocolat (Chestnut Chocolate Cake), **5**-746

Mousseline, **8**-1192
Praliné (Génoise), **5**-781
Gaufres Bruxelloises (Brussels Beer Waffles), **2**-200
Gazpacho (Cold Salad-Soup), **11**-1742
Gazpacho, Iced with Vegetable, Crouton, and Herb Garnish, **9**-1383
Gebackene Seezunge (Deep-Fried Sole), **5**-793
Gebakken Eieren met Uien en Kaas (Baked Eggs with Onions and Cheese), **4**-592
Gebratene Ente (Roast Stuffed Duck), **5**-795
Gebratene Kalbsleber (Baked Calf's Liver), **9**-1351
Gebratener Hummer (Fried Lobster), **5**-793
Gefilte Fish, **6**-989
Gefülltes Brot (Stuffed Bread), **11**-1803
Gelatin, Gelatine, **5**-784
Gemisti Kotta (Baked Chicken), **5**-820
Gemisti Melitzana (Stuffed Eggplant), **5**-818
Geneva Style Fondue, **5**-712
Genoa Style Tuna, Potato, and Bean Salad, **12**-1867
Génoise, **5**-781, 791
Génoise Fine, **9**-1366
Gentsche Waterzooi (Fish Soup), **2**-197
Georgia Mint Julep, **6**-996
Georgia Pork Chops, **9**-1445
Georgia Raised Biscuits, **2**-236
German Apple Pancakes, **8**-1293
German Beans, Hot, **10**-1668
German Cabbage Slaw, **3**-464
German Coffee Braid, **2**-231
German Cookery, **5**-792
German Egg Dumplings (Spaetzle), **4**-586
German Fish with Sauerkraut, **10**-1631
German Gourmet Mixed Salad, **10**-1586
German Lettuce Salad, **7**-1064
German Onion Tart, **8**-1261
German Pancakes, **8**-1293
German Pancakes with Spinach, **11**-1755
German Potato Salad, **9**-1462
German Spinach Salad, **10**-1586; **11**-1756
German Style Frankfurters and Yellow Peas, **5**-722
German Style Rabbit, **5**-769
Geröstete Kalbsleber (Calf's Liver, Sautéed), **1**-122
Gerstensuppe (Barley Soup), **1**-121
Ges po Polsku (Goose à la Polonaise), **9**-1428
Gestoofde Kabeljauw of Schelvis met Aardappelen (Baked Fillets of Haddock or Cod with Potatoes), **4**-589
Gestoofde Prei (Braised Leeks), **4**-592
Gevasci's Ricotta Tart, **3**-367
Gevulde Lamsborst (Roast Cushion Shoulder of Lamb), **4**-590

Giblet(s), **5**-801
Chicken Giblets with Rice, **5**-800
Cream or Milk Giblet Gravy for Poultry, **5**-816
Gravy, **5**-800
Mushroom-Giblet Dressing for Poultry, **5**-800
Pâté, **5**-800
Sandwich Filling, **5**-800
Sauce (Sikotakia Saltsa), **5**-822
Gigot Qui Pleure, Le (Weeping Leg of Lamb), **5**-741
Ginatan (Sweet Fruits and Roots), **9**-1370

Ginger, Gingered, **5**-800
Beef, **5**-801
Beef, Burmese, **10**-1646
Beef Pot Roast, **9**-1473
Beef Soup with Noodles (Pho), **11**-1717
Buttermilk, **5**-804
Cakes, **11**-1818
Cheese Salad Bowl, **12**-1935
Cookies, **11**-1754
Cookies, Crisp, **5**-801
Cutouts, **5**-801
Drop Cookies, **5**-801
Flank Steak Orientale, **5**-801
Fresh Gingerroot Preserve, **5**-803
Fresh-Peach Chutney, **8**-1321
-Fruit Frost, **5**-803
Garlic-Ginger Shrimps, **10**-1661
Grapefruit Peel, **5**-803
Lemon Jelly, **7**-1056
Lemon Pineapple, **9**-1410
Mayonnaise Dressing, **10**-1622
Melon, **1**-27; **5**-801
-Mince Upside-Down Cake, **12**-1882
Orange Peel, Florida, **5**-803
Peach Halves, **8**-1321
Peach Mold, **8**-1317
Pear Compote, **8**-1332
Pear Crumble, **9**-1491
Pears, **5**-801
Preserved, and Cream, **5**-803
Pudding, Quick, **11**-1839
Pumpkin Pie, **5**-801
-Pumpkin Pie, Frozen, **9**-1500
Quince Marmalade, **10**-1529
Sherry Cream, **9**-1493
Tea, **5**-803
Tomato Conserve, **5**-803
Wafers, **5**-803
Waffles, **5**-801
Waffles, Old Colony, **12**-1915
Walnut-Ginger Dressing, **11**-1700

Ginger Ale, **5**-803
Fruit Mold, **5**-803
Glaze for Baked Ham, **5**-803
Ham Simmered in, **5**-803
Lime-Ginger Foam, **7**-1067

Gingerbread, **5**-804
Blueberry, **5**-805
Busy-Day, **5**-804
Company, **2**-238
Cream Cheese Topping for, **3**-362; **5**-805
Ginger Cakes, **11**-1818
Honey, **1**-53; **5**-804
Molasses, **8**-1184
Old Colony, **5**-804; **7**-1164
Old Fashioned, **1**-45
(QC), **10**-1525
Sour-Cream, **11**-1701
Sour-Milk Cupcakes, Anthelias', **8**-1230
Gingersnap-Crumb Crust, **3**-411; **5**-791
Giouvarlakia Avgolemono (Meatballs with Egg-Lemon Sauce), **5**-819
Glace de Viande, **10**-1615

Glacé, Glacéed, **5**-805
Nut Patties, **5**-805
Oranges, **5**-805
Orange Slices, **5**-805
Pineapple Chunks, **5**-805

Glaze(s), **5**-805
Aspic, for Sandwiches, **6**-980
Beer, **7**-1151
Blueberry Relish (for ham), **2**-210
Egg (for rolls and buns), **12**-1953
Ginger-Ale, for Baked Ham, **5**-803
Ham, **6**-850; **11**-1790
for Ham, Baked, **10**-1665
Honey, **6**-909
Orange Juice, **6**-856

Glaze(s), Dessert
Apricot, **1**-109; **2**-265; **5**-746, 762, 783; **9**-1382
Bitter Chocolate, **5**-783
Caramel, **5**-805
Caramel with Coffee Custard Pudding, **9**-1490
Chocolate, **3**-410; **4**-594; **5**-805; **11**-1756
Chocolate, Thin, **3**-411
Clear, Very Thin Glaze, **5**-805
Confectioners'-Sugar, **9**-1438
Currant, **5**-746
(for Dark Fruitcake), **5**-759
(for Gâteau Mousseline), **8**-1192
(for Golden Fruitcake), **5**-759
(for Honey Lebkuchen), **7**-1046
(for Lebkuchen), **3**-435
(for Leckerli), **3**-433
Orange, **2**-233; **7**-1156
Orange-Honey, **2**-265
Orange-Lemon, **2**-265; **5**-806
Piecrust, **5**-806
Red-Jelly, **5**-762
Rum, **2**-279; **5**-806
Strawberry, **3**-367
Vanilla, **5**-806; **6**-901
Glögg, **11**-1796

Gnocchi, **5**-806
(Dumplings), **11**-1804
all'Italiana (Dumplings Italian Style), **4**-587
Parmesan, **5**-806
di Patate alla Piemontese, **5**-806
Potato, **9**-1463
Romana, **5**-806
Gohan (Rice), **6**-976
Golabki z Kapusty (Cabbage Birds or Stuffed Cabbage I and II), **9**-1430
Golabki Postne (Meatless Stuffed Cabbage), **9**-1430
Golden Buck, **3**-358; **12**-1923
Golden Fleece, **4**-608
Golden Glow Cake (QC), **10**-1525
Goldene Yoich (Golden Chicken Broth), **6**-987
Goldenrod Sauce, **5**-694
Goma-Zu (Sauce for Vegetables), **6**-976

Goose, **5**-806
Carving, **2**-313
Cassoulet, **2**-325
Dressings for, **5**-808
Liver and Greben, Chopped, **7**-1075
Livers, To cook whole, see Pâté de Foie Gras, **5**-708
Marinated (Kaczka lub Ges Marynowana), **9**-1428
à la Polonaise (Ges po Polsku), **9**-1428
Roast, Chinese, **1**-81
in Spanish Sauce, Sliced, **5**-808
Spicy, Sliced in Gravy, **5**-808
Timetable for Roasting, Chart, **5**-807
To Roast, **5**-807

Goose, Wild
Braised, **5**-769
To Prepare, **5**-807
To Roast, **5**-808
(roast), **1**-68
Roast Snow Goose, **2**-278

Gooseberry(ies), **5**-808
Dumplings, **5**-808
Fool, **5**-714
Jam, **5**-809; **6**-965
Sauce, **5**-808
Sauce, English, **10**-1627
Spiced, Canadian, **5**-809
Stewed, **5**-808
Gorditas (Fat Pancakes), **7**-1143
Goreng Bajem (Fried Spinach Leaves), **11**-1715
Goro Cakes (Wafers), **8**-1243

Goulash, **5**-809
Beef, **5**-809
Beef, Oven, **2**-298
Frankfurter and Sauerkraut, **5**-721
Hungarian, **2**-187
Hungarian (Magyar Gulyás), **6**-918
Meat and Potato, **5**-809
with Noodles, **5**-809
Pork, **5**-809
Soup (Gulyásleves), **6**-917
Szekely Sauerkraut (Székeley Gulyás), **6**-919
Veal, **5**-809
Veal (Kalbsgulasch), **1**-122

Grains, see names of grains
Grandfathers (Grandpères), **4**-587
Grandmother's Mint Wafers, **8**-1231
Grandmother's Steak, **1**-73
Grandmother Stoughton's Tomato Gravy, **9**-1354
Grandpères (Grandfathers), **4**-587
Granité, see Ice(s) and Sherbet(s)

Grape(s), **5**-810
Anise and Cabbage Slaw, **10**-1586
-and-Basil Jelly, **6**-983
and Cauliflower Salad (Salat iz Tsvetnoi Kapusti s Vinogradom), **10**-1566
and Cheese Salad, **5**-812
Concord Grape Pie, **5**-812; **7**-1157
Concord Lime Jelly, **6**-982
Conserve, **3**-466; **5**-813
Fresh Cantaloupe and Grape Cup, **2**-296
Fresh Grape(s)
and Avocado Cocktail, **5**-812
and Chicken Mold, **5**-812
and Lemon-Ice Cup, **5**-812
and Plum Salad, **5**-812
Frosted, **5**-780
Jam, Spiced, **6**-964
Jelly, **6**-982
Jelly, No-Cook, **6**-984
Jelly, Old-Fashioned, **5**-812
-Juice Jelly, **6**-983
Juice, Mulled, **8**-1193
Ketchup, **6**-999
-Lime Frappé, **5**-726
Lime-Grape Dessert, **7**-1088
Pear, and Celery Salad, **10**-1588
and Pineapple Jam, **6**-964
Sauce Véronique, **10**-1614, 1621
Tarts, Orange-Glazed, **5**-812
Thompson Seedless, in Sour Cream, **1**-27
-Turkey Salad, **5**-812
in White-Wine Gelatin, **5**-812

Grapefruit, **5**-813
Avocado-Grapefruit Dessert, **5**-814
Baked Alaska, **5**-814
Caribbean, **2**-204
and Crab Salad with Avocado Mayonnaise, **12**-1934
Cucumber, and Cheese Salad, **12**-1958
Fresh Grapefruit
and Apple Salad, Molded, **5**-814
and Crab Salad, **5**-814
Salad Dressing, **5**-814
and Salmon Salad, **5**-814
Shrimp Salad, **10**-1581
Honeyed, **5**-814
-Honey Nog, **1**-24
-Orange-Juice Jelly, **6**-984
Peel, Candied, **2**-289
Peel, Gingered, **5**-803
Persimmon, and Pomegranate Salad, **9**-1364
Rind, Pickled, **5**-814
Salad, Jellied, **5**-814
-and-Savory Jelly, **6**-983
Shrimp-Grapefruit Salad, **10**-1662
and Tangerine-Stuffed Squash, **11**-1762

Grape Leaves, Grapevine Leaves
Dolma, Turkish, **4**-570
Stuffed I, **8**-1211; II, **8**-1212
Stuffed (Dolmathes), **5**-819
Stuffed, with Lemon Sauce, Greek (Dolmadakia me Avgolemono), **4**-570
Grape-Nut Puff Pudding, **8**-1228
Gratin aux Champignons, **9**-1470
Gravad Lax med Senapssås (Marinated Salmon with Mustard Sauce), **11**-1786

Gravy(ies), **5**-815
Apple, for Pork or Boiled Beef, **7**-1152
for Beef à la Lindstrom (Lindströmin Pihvi), **5**-680
Capon Gravy, **3**-439
Cream Gravy, **1**-74
Cream or Milk Giblet, for Poultry, **5**-816
Cream, for Southern Fried Chicken, **11**-1723
Creamy Gravy, **1**-37
Creamy (for Chicken Pie), **7**-1151
Flour-Paste, **5**-816
Giblet, **5**-800
Giblet (Turkey), **11**-1823
Medium Thick, **5**-815
Onion, **8**-1265
Onion, for Panfried Steak, **2**-181
Pan Gravy, **5**-814
Pan Gravy (for Spiced Sesame Chicken), **10**-1647
Poor Man's, **9**-1354
Raisin, **1**-39
Red-Eye, for Ham, **5**-816
for Roast Fresh Ham, **3**-445
(for Slottsstek), **11**-1788
Thin, **5**-815
Tomato, Grandmother Stoughton's, **9**-1354
Turkey, **4**-625
Great Lakes Fish Boil, **7**-1147
Greben and Goose Liver, Chopped, **7**-1075
Grechnevaia Kasha (Buckwheat Porridge) **10**-1573
Grecque, à la, Basic Recipe, for Vegetables, **1**-7
Greek Barbecue Sauce, **1**-146
Greek Chocolate Balls, **3**-416
Greek Coffee, **4**-640
Greek Coffee (Kafes), **5**-824
Greek Cookery, **5**-817
Greek Egg and Lemon Sauce, **10**-1627
Greek Garlic Sauce, **10**-1623
Greek Lemon Soup, **7**-1052
Greek Potato Salad, **7**-1053
Greek Rice and Pork Pilaf, **9**-1401
Greek Rice Soup, **10**-1549
Greek Salad, **8**-1190
Greek Spinach Pie, **11**-1755
Greek Stuffed Grapevine Leaves with Lemon Sauce (Dolmadakia me Avgolemono), **4**-570
Greek Taverna Buffet, **4**-639
Green Gables Icebox Pudding, **9**-1492
Greengage, Greengage Plum, **5**-824; for recipes see Plum(s)
Green Goddess Salad Dressing, **12**-1931
Green Heaven in a Pot, **8**-1266
Green Mousseline Sauce, **10**-1622

Greens, **5**-824
Boiled (Hitashimono), **6**-976
Gratin of, **12**-1904
Mustard, Fried, **5**-825
Panned Garden, **5**-825
and Pork, Southern, **5**-825
Green Sauce, **5**-694; **10**-1652
Green Sauce, Piquant (Salsa Verde Piccante), **6**-959
Gribiche Sauce, **10**-1614, 1623
Griby v Smetane (Mushrooms in Sour Cream), **10**-1567
Griddle Cake(s), **5**-825; for recipes see Pancake(s)
Grillades, **4**-512
Grinders, Italian, **10**-1602
Grison's Steak House Cheesecake, **3**-368
Grits, Groats, **5**-827; for recipes see Buckwheat; Hominy
Groentesoep met Balletjes (Vegetable Soup with Meatballs), **4**-589
G'röste' mit Rosmarin (Home-Fried Potatoes and Rosemary), **1**-123
Grostoli (Crisp Cookies), **6**-960

Grouper, **5**-828
Baked, **5**-828

Grouse, **5**-828
Breasts of, Stuffed, **2**-278
Roast, with Orange Slices, **5**-828
Stuffed and Roasted, **5**-773
Geschnetzeltes (Minced Veal), **11**-1802

Gruel, **5**-828
Oatmeal, **5**-828
Guacamole, **1**-130
Guacamole (Avocado Paste), **7**-1138
Guadalajara Tostadas (Guadalajara Toasts), **7**-1138
Guatemala Banana Fritters (Empanadas de Plátanos), **11**-1708
Guatemalan Chocolate, **3**-416

Guava(s), **5**-828
and Cheese Dessert, **2**-300
-Cheese Pie, **5**-829
Fruit Salad, **5**-829
Jelly, **5**-829
-Pecan Pie, **5**-829
Salads, **1**-33
Sherbet, **10**-1652
Stuffed (Guayabas Rellenas), **7**-1143
Guayabas Rellenas (Stuffed Guavas), **7**-1143

Guinea Fowl, Guinea Hen, **5**-829
Breasts, Fried, **5**-830
Roast with Wild-Rice Stuffing, **5**-830
Gule Aerter (Yellow Pea Soup), **4**-538
Gulyásleves (Goulash Soup), **6**-917

Gumbo, **5**-830
Chicken, **3**-386
Chicken and Okra, **4**-512
Chicken-Shrimp Gumbo Filé, **1**-44
Crab, Cajun, **5**-830
Ham and Oyster Gumbo Filé, **4**-660
Okra Soup, **1**-22
Shrimp-Oyster, **10**-1658
Sweet-Potato, **11**-1795
Turkey, Duck, or Chicken, **5**-830
Gureevskaia Kasha (Guriev Pudding), **10**-1574
Guriev Pudding (Gureevskaia Kasha), **10**-1574
Gurkensalat (Cucumber Salad), **1**-123

H

Habitant Pea Soup, **2**-275
Hâché (Stewed Meat), **4**-590

Haddock, **6**-845
Fillets, Broiled, **6**-845
Fillets with Potatoes, Baked (Gestoofde Kabeljauw of Schelvis met Aardappelen), **4**-589
Finnan Haddie, **4**-663
Baked in Milk, **4**-663
in Cream Sauce, **5**-688
with Shrimp Sauce, **4**-663
Flaked, Newburg, **6**-846
Kippered, with Bacon, **7**-1017
Loaf, Norwegian, Baked, **5**-689
Mock Lobster Salad, **5**-689
Mornay, **5**-688
Plaki, **6**-846
-Potato Patties, **6**-846
Smoked (Røket Kolje), **8**-1236
Haggerty, **6**-949

Hake, **6**-846
Casserole, **6**-847
Curried, **6**-847
Fillets, Baked Stuffed, **5**-689
Fillets with Olives, **8**-1256
Sesame Baked, **6**-847

Halibut, **6**-848
Baked Whole, **6**-848
Country (Halibut Paysanne), **2**-276
Creamed, New England Style, **5**-689
with Creamy Mustard Sauce, **6**-848
Flemish Style (Cabillaud à la Flamande), **2**-197
Steak Hash, **5**-689
Steaks, Barbecued, **6**-848

Steaks, Deviled, **5**-689; **6**-848
Steaks, Planked, **6**-848
Steaks, Poached, with Curry Sauce, **6**-848
with Wine Sauce, **5**-689
Hallacas (Meat Pies), **11**-1706
Halva (Nut Confection), **5**-824

Ham, **6**-849
Andalusian Egg Platter (Oeufs sur le Plat à l'Andalouse), **6**-862
Apple-Ham Casserole, **1**-97
Apricot Glazed, **3**-439
Asparagus Rolls, **1**-113
-Asparagus Rolls with Macaroni and Cheese, **6**-858
and Avocado with Cauliflower Salad (Ensalada de Coliflor con Aguacate), **7**-1142
Baked Beans with, **1**-158
Baked Country Cured, North Carolina Style, **11**-1722
Baked, with Cumberland Sauce, **6**-858
Baked, with Spicy Sauce, **6**-852
Baked, Tennessee, **1**-69
Balls, **7**-1151
Balls, Candied Sweet Potatoes, and, **11**-1796
Balls and Macaroni Shells in Skillet, **7**-1093
Balls with Sour-Cream Sauce, **10**-1666
Banana-Ham Rolls, Glazed, **6**-856
and Bananas, Spiced, **6**-853
-and-Bean Bake, **6**-853
and Bean Soup with Vegetables (Garbure Basque), **5**-739
Biscuit Roll with Cheese Sauce, **6**-856
Boiled Pot, Miss Mollie's, **1**-61
Boneless, Baked (QC), **10**-1520
Bones, leftover, ways to use, **6**-860
Brine for, **11**-1788
and Broccoli Casserole, **6**-853
and Cabbage with Tomatoes, **6**-855
Carving, **2**-311-312
Celery with Cheese and Ham, Baked, **3**-344
-and-Cheese Appetizers, **6**-852
and Cheese Bites, **6**-852
Cheese, and Potato Casserole, **2**-317
-Cheese Rice Bake, **10**-1549
-Cheese Rolls, Hot, **6**-859
-Cheese-Tomato Parlay, **11**-1747
Chicken in Ham Blankets, **6**-855
Chicken Mousse, **3**-391
and Chicken Three-Decker Sandwiches, **10**-1611
Christmas (Julskinka), **11**-1788
Chunks or Cubes, leftover, 13 ways to use, **6**-859
-Chutney Spread, **2**-280
in Cider, **6**-853
in Claret, Baked, **6**-853
Cold, Glazed, **6**-853
Corn Bake, **3**-481
Corn-Bread Ring with Creamed Peas, **6**-856
and Corn Fritters, **6**-856
and Corn Potato Soup, **6**-852
Country (Jambon de Campagne), **2**-277
Cranberry Cubes, Baked, **3**-490
Cranberry-Glazed, **1**-78
Cranberry Ham Cubes, Baked, **3**-490; **6**-853
with Cream Gravy, **2**-242
à la Crème, **4**-566; **6**-858
Croquettes, **6**-856
Cuckoo's Eggs, **12**-1874
Cured, **4**-523
Curing for, **11**-1788
Custard, Swedish, **6**-865
Denver Sandwiches, **1**-27
Dip, **6**-852
Dumplings, **6**-852
and Egg(s), with Eggs
in Aspic, **6**-861
Butter, **6**-866
Cakes, English, **6**-862
Cake, Viennese (Wiener Eierkuchen), • **6**-865
Carmen, **6**-864
Devonshire Fried, **6**-865
Dishes, Quick, **6**-865
French Style, **2**-247
Fried, à l'Américaine, **6**-861
Fu Yung, **6**-865
and Macaroni Salad, **4**-607
and Mushrooms in a Chafing Dish, Creamed, **3**-346
Parmesan, **6**-861
Phillip's, **6**-861
Pie, **6**-862
Piroshki (Little Russian Pies), **6**-864
Pizza (Pizza con Uova e Prosciutto), **6**-864
Potted, **6**-866
in Ramekins (Oeufs Cocottes au Jambon), **6**-861
Roll, Parsley, **8**-1298
Salad, **6**-864
Smørrebrød, **6**-862
Tart, **6**-862
in Toledo (Huevos en Toledo), **6**-865
with Tortillas (Huevos con Tortillas y Jamon), **6**-861
Zurlo, **6**-865
Fat, leftover, ways to use, **6**-860
Filling, **3**-492; **6**-919
and Fresh-Pork Loaf, Curried, **6**-856
Fried Rice, **6**-858
with Fried Rice, **6**-865
Frizzled, with Piquant Sauce, **6**-858
Fruit Salad, **6**-858
Garnish for, **11**-1790
Glaze(s), **6**-850; **11**-1790
with Grapefruit, Baked, **5**-814
and Green-Noodle Casserole, **6**-853
Ground or Minced, leftover, 21 ways to use, **6**-860
Hash, **6**-858
Hawaiian, **6**-856
and Herring Salad (Sill och Skinksallad), **11**-1787
Honey Glaze, for, **6**-909
Jambalaya, **10**-1556
Kedgeree, **6**-858
and Kidney Ragout, **7**-1014
à la King, **1**-8
Leftover, 50 ways to use, **6**-859
and Lima-Bean Casserole, Individual, **7**-1066
-Lima Bean Soup, **6**-852
Limerick, Baked, **6**-948
Loaf, **7**-1128
Loaf, Orange-Glazed, **6**-856
Loaf in Raisin Sauce (QC), **10**-1520
Loaves, Individual, **7**-1128
and Macaroni Salad, Hot, **7**-1094
Madeira Sauce for, **3**-439
with Madeira (Skinke med Madeira), **4**-539
Main-Dish Rice Salad, **10**-1550
Mousse, **5**-716; **8**-1190
Mousse (Mousse de Jambon), **6**-865
Mousseline, **8**-1191
with Mustard Crust, **1**-39
and Noodle Casserole (Viennese Ham Fleckerl), **6**-865
and Noodle Dish, Austrian, **8**-1233
and Noodle Rabbit, **8**-1232
and Noodles, **3**-358
with Noodles (Schinkenfleckerln), **1**-122
Nuggets in Raisin Sauce, **10**-1534
Omelet, **8**-1257
Orange Rice for, **8**-1268
and Oyster Gumbo Filé, **4**-660
Pan-Barbecued, **1**-68
Parsleyed (Jambon Persillé), **5**-743
Peanut-Butter Puffs, **8**-1324
Peanut-Butter Rolls, **8**-1324
Pie with Cheese Pastry, Deep-Dish, **9**-1387
Pillows with Italian Ham (Cuscinetti Filanti al Prosciutto), **6**-962
Pineapple-Ham Loaf, **9**-1406
Pineapple-Ham Salad, **9**-1408
Pineapple, and Yam Casserole, **9**-1406
Poached Eggs and Ham, Fried (Huevos Escalfados Fritos), **6**-862
-and-Pork Balls, Baked, **6**-855
and Potatoes au Gratin, **6**-853
and Potato-Salad Sandwiches, **6**-859
Prosciutto, **9**-1483
with Fruits, **6**-952
and Shrimps, Broiled, **10**-1657
Rabbit Sandwiches, **10**-1604
Red-Eye Gravy for, **5**-816
Rice Salad Hortense, **10**-1580
and Rice-Stuffed Peppers, **10**-1549
Roast, with Beer Glaze, **7**-1151
Rollatine, **12**-1894
Salad, **1**-38; **6**-858
Salad Boats, **6**-859
Salad, Broiled, **6**-858
Salad, Molded, **6**-858
Salad Rolls, **10**-1604
Sandwich, French Style, Fried (Croque Monsieur), **6**-862
Sauces for, **6**-859
and Sauerkraut (Schinkenkraut), **1**-122
with Scalloped Potatoes, **9**-1463
Scraps, leftover, ways to use, **6**-860
Seasonings for Cooking, **11**-1790
Simmered in Ginger Ale, **5**-803
Slices, Stuffed, **6**-853
Smithfield, Baked, **1**-75; **3**-442
Smithfield, Canapés, **6**-852
Soufflé, **6**-865
Sour-Cream Dip, **11**-1697
Spaghetti and Eggs on (Spaghetti alla Carbonara), **6**-862
Spanish Omelette with (Tortilla con Jamon), **6**-861
Spread, Savory, **3**-428
Spread, Spicy, **2**-280
Steak, Deviled, **3**-429; **11**-1770
Steaks, **11**-1770
Steaks, Baked Stuffed, with Sweet Potato-Sausage Stuffing, **11**-1722
Strips, leftover, 10 ways to use, **6**-859
Stuffed, **1**-50
-Stuffed Chicken Legs, **6**-852
and Sweets, **6**-855
and Swiss-Cheese Pie (Quiche de Bourbonnaise), **6**-862
and Swiss, Frenched, **6**-913
Tamale Pie, **2**-320
Tetrazzini, **11**-1736
Timbales, **6**-865
Timetable for Roasting, Chart, **6**-850
Tomato-Ham Salad, Jellied, **10**-1583
Turnovers, **6**-852
and Veal Loaf, **6**-856
-and-Veal Pie, Cold, **9**-1387
-and-Veal Potpie, **9**-1472
and Vegetables, Cheese-Baked, **3**-355
with Vegetables, Sweet-and-Sour, **9**-1351
Waffles, **12**-1915
Western Long Boys, **6**-859

Ham, Deviled
Devil Balls, **7**-1147
Egg, and Cheese Sandwiches, **10**-1605
-Egg Spread, **2**-279
Eggs Stuffed with, **4**-606
Peanut-Butter Spread, **8**-1324
Pinwheels, **8**-1306

Ham, Fresh
Baked, Southern Style, **9**-1448
Barbecued Roast, **9**-1448
Cold, **6**-851
Christmas (Juleskinke), **8**-1237
Pork Fricassee Filipino, **6**-851
Roast, **3**-428, 445; **6**-851; **9**-1445
Roast, with Sour Cream Gravy, **7**-1150
Roast, with Savory Stuffing, **9**-1448
Spiced Pork Pot Roast, **9**-1476
Steak, **11**-1770

Ham, Fresh, continued
with Wine, Pot of (Pernil con Vino al Caldero), **9**-1496
Hamantaschen, **6**-995

Hamburger, **6**-886; see also Meatball(s); Meat Loaf
with Apple Rings, **1**-97
Bacon Nutburgers, **6**-869
Balls with Prunes, Spiced, **9**-1483
Beef-Asparagus Moussaka, **8**-1187
Beef, Carrot, and Olive Loaf, **6**-870
Beef Casserole with Almonds, **6**-873
Beef Cheeseburgers de Luxe, **6**-869
Beef Kidney and Hamburger Pie, **6**-872
Beef-Mushroom Moussaka, **8**-1187
Beef and Noodle Platter, **6**-872
Beef Patties, Barbecued, **7**-1084
Beef Patties Parmigiana, **2**-191
Beef, Potato, and Bean Casserole, **6**-873
Beef and Rice Casserole, **6**-872
Beef-and-Rice Stuffed Peppers, **9**-1358
Beef-Stuffed Cabbage Rolls, **6**-873
Beef-and-Tomato Loaf, **6**-870
Burgundy Meatballs with Raisin Sauce, **6**-869
Burgundy Pecanburgers, **8**-1334
and Cabbage, Creamed, **6**-872
Canadian Hamburger Pie, **6**-872
Cheese-Beef Patties, **3**-358
Cheeseburgers de Luxe, **6**-869
Cheese-Nut Burgers, **6**-869
with Cherry-Cheese Sauce, **6**-869
Chili Beefburger Sandwiches, **10**-1601
Chili Meatballs, **6**-870
Chopped Beef Toast, **11**-1825
Corn-Bread Sandwiches, **10**-1601
-Corn Skillet Dinner, **6**-873
Cottage Pie, **6**-876
Eggplant Moussaka, **8**-1187
Filling, **10**-1538
Garlic, on Toasted Buns, **8**-1282
Ground-Meat Stew (Zoo-Tosopy), **11**-1704
Guacamole, **6**-868
Hamburger, **6**-877
Hawaiian, **6**-868
Hot Dog and Hamburger Relish, **10**-1543
and Kidney Pie, **6**-872
Lasagne al Forno, **6**-873
-Macaroni Casserole, **6**-872
Macaroni, and Green-Bean Casserole, **7**-1094
Meat Custard (Sfougato), **5**-818
Meat Pie (Pastel de Carne), **11**-1705
Moussaka, **5**-818
Moussaka, Fried-Tomato, **8**-1187
Paprika, **6**-869
Patties, Stuffed, **6**-869
Peanut Hamburger Balls, **6**-870
Pepper-Ring Burgers, **6**-868
Pepper Steaks, **9**-1358
Picadillo, **6**-877
Pizza-Burgers, **6**-868
Pizza Pie, **8**-1273
Polish Style, **6**-868
Potato-Cheese Pie, **9**-1463
Princess, **6**-868
Rolls, **10**-1601
Salisbury Steak with Mushroom Sauce, **6**-868
Sandwiches, **11**-1770
Sandwiches, French-Fried, **6**-873
Sandwiches, Sweet-and-Sour, **10**-1601
Sauces for, **2**-191
Sauerbraten Hamburgers, **6**-869
with Sherry-Cheese Sauce, **6**-869
Sloppy Joes, **10**-1601
Steak, **2**-191
Steaks and Onions, Smothered, **6**-868
Steak Tartare, **2**-189; **7**-1150
Steak Tartare en Croûte, **11**-1770
Stew, **6**-868
Stew with Dumplings, **4**-586
Stir-Fry Ground Beef, **6**-876
Stracotto Sauce, **11**-1738
Supreme, Menu, **8**-1282
Surprise, **6**-877
Sweet and Sour, **6**-868
Tennessee, **6**-869
Texas Sombreros, **6**-872
Tomato-Meat Sauce, **2**-316
Tomato-Meat Spaghetti Sauce, **11**-1737
-Vegetable Casserole, **2**-316
Wild-West, **6**-876
-Zucchini Skillet Dinner, **6**-873
Hamburgryg med Ribs Gelé (Bacon with Currant Jelly), **4**-540
Hangtown Fry, **2**-243; (Beard), I, II, and III, **8**-1287
Hans Andersen's, **4**-536
Ha'penny Cocktail Snacks, **8**-1308
Hapsburg Cucumbers, **11**-1700

Hard Sauce, **6**-877; **10**-1615
3-445; **9**-1493; **10**-1628
Basic, **6**-877
Brandy, **5**-702; **9**-1493
Brown-Sugar, **6**-878
Fluffy, **6**-878
Lemon, **9**-1493
Orange, **12**-1915
Stars, Lighted, **9**-1493
Strawberry, **11**-1776
Variations, **6**-877-878
Haricots de Mouton (Mutton Stew), **8**-1205
Haricots Verts Maillanoise (Green Beans, Maillane Style), **12**-1903
Hari Dal (Green Beans), **6**-942
Haringsla (Herring Salad), **4**-590
Harlequin Crinkle Cups, **6**-934
Harry Hamblet's Golden-Fried Oysters, **8**-1287
Harvest Relish, **10**-1543
Hasenpfeffer, **5**-772; **6**-878

Hash, **6**-878
Chicken
Baked, **3**-391
in Cream, **3**-390
à la Ritz, **6**-879
Corned Beef, **3**-485
with Creamed Eggs, **6**-881
Lyonnaise, **2**-193; **6**-881
Maine, **6**-879
Mounds, Broiled, **6**-881
with Mustard Sauce, **6**-881
O'Brien, **6**-881
Patties, Quick, **2**-193
with Poached Eggs, **4**-630
Red Flannel, **1**-56; **2**-193
and Sauerkraut, Baked, **10**-1631
-Stuffed Cabbage Rolls, **6**-881
-Stuffed Peppers with Cabbage, **9**-1359
Stuffing, **11**-1834
and Tomatoes, Baked, **6**-879
Duck, **12**-1919
and Eggs (Pytt i Panne), **8**-1237
Frankfurter, **6**-879
Green Pepper, **6**-879
Ham, **6**-858
Lamb
Idaho, **1**-35
de Luxe, **7**-1039
Lyonnaise, **7**-1039
Meat and Vegetable, **8**-1224
with Mushrooms, **6**-879
Pork, Brown, **9**-1451
Pork, Creamy, **9**-1451
Red Flannel, **1**-56; **2**-193
Roast Beef
Barbecued, **6**-881
Casserole, **6**-881
Lyonnaise, **2**-193
and Sweet-Potato, **11**-1796
Swedish (Pytt i Panna), **11**-1790
Turkey, **6**-879
Veal, **6**-879
Hasty Pudding, **8**-1228
Haugesundsk Spedesild (Haugesund Pickled Herrings), **8**-1236
Hausente als Wildente (Duck Cooked like Wild Duck), **1**-122
Hawaiian Chicken (QC), **10**-1521
Hawaiian Coconut Cream, **1**-35
Hawaiian Frankfurters, **5**-722
Hawaiian Ham, **6**-856
Hawaiian Hamburgers, **6**-868
Hawaiian Marinated Scallops (Ophi), **9**-1434
Hawaiian Omelet Sandwiches, **10**-1602
Hawaiian Pineapple and Chicken, **9**-1406
Hawaiian Pineapple Muffins, **4**-635
Hawaiian Pork, **9**-1450
Hawaiian Shrimps, **10**-1658
Hawaiian Teriyaki Sauce, **10**-1626
Hawaiian Turkey, **12**-1872
Hawaiian Veal Stew, **12**-1896

Hazelnut(s), **6**-881, and **Filbert(s),** **4**-659
Chocolate Diamonds with Hazelnuts, **6**-882
Cinnamon Filberts, **4**-659
Cranberry-Filbert Relish, **10**-1542
Filbert Crescents, **4**-659
Filbert Kisses, Toasted, **3**-472
Filbert Lemon Logs, **3**-474
Filbert Spice Cookies, **4**-659
Filbert Squares, **5**-709
Filbert Torte, **4**-659
Hazelnut Cinnamon Buns, **6**-882
Hazelnut Cream, **6**-882
Hazelnut and Mushroom Sauce, **6**-882
Hazelnut Tarts, **6**-882
Noisette Butter, **10**-1615, 1624
Oregon Filbert Squares, **1**-65

Head Cheese, **6**-882
Pork and Veal, **6**-979

Heart(s), **6**-882
Beef
Parsley Hearts of, **2**-191
Patties, Scotch, **6**-883
Savory Stuffed, **6**-883
with Vegetables, **6**-883
Stew, **6**-883
Timetable for Cooking, Chart, **6**-883
Veal
Danish, **6**-883
with Fruit Stuffing, **6**-883
Pot-Roasted, Danish, **9**-1476
Slices, Fried, **6**-883
Hearts of Palm, see Palm
Heavenly Hash, **6**-879
Helen's Molasses Crinkles, **3**-476

Herb(s), Herbed, **6**-884; see also names of herbs
Barbecue Sauce, **10**-1623
Best-Known, Culinary Uses, Chart, **6**-886-899
Bouillon, **3**-424
Bouquet (Bouquet Garni), **2**-218
Breadsticks, **2**-236
Butter, **2**-193, 254
Butter, Sweet, **3**-429
-Buttered Rye- and White-Bread Sandwiches, **9**-1384
Chicken Casserole, **11**-1824
Chicken and Peas, **8**-1314
Corn and Peas, **8**-1315
Crust, **7**-1036
Dressing, **10**-1623
Eggs Stuffed with, **4**-606
Fines Herbes Combinations, **4**-663
Fines Herbes for Meats, Poultry, and Eggs, **2**-246
Fines Herbes Sauce, **10**-1614
Lamb Shoulder, **7**-1032
Mayonnaise, **5**-700
Mixed-Herb Mayonnaise, **5**-695; **7**-1116
Potatoes, Baked, **9**-1466
Pot Roast, Larded, **7**-1041
Ravigote Sauce, **5**-695
Sauce, **2**-173; **10**-1620
Sauce (for Veal Loaf), **7**-1128
Savory Butter, **5**-695

Seasonings (Odori Fini), **3**-345
Sour-Cream Dressing for Romaine, **10**-1556
-Stuffed Pork Birds, **9**-1444
Tomatoes, Fines Herbes, **11**-1839
-and-Tomato Soup on the Rocks, **11**-1832
Toast, **11**-1826
Tuna Dip, Fines Herbes, **12**-1862
Veal Loaf, Jellied, **12**-1895
Vinegar, **12**-1912
Wild Rice, **12**-1940
and Wine-Vinegar Sauce, **5**-694

Hermit(s), 6-901
Arbutus, **4**-656
Brown-Sugar, **6**-901
Hermits, **3**-471
Mincemeat, **6**-901
Molasses, **6**-901
Old-Fashioned, **8**-1230
York, **9**-1357
Hero Sandwiches, **10**-1604
Hero Sandwiches, Hot, **10**-1639

Herring, 6-901
and Apples in Sour Cream, **1**-87
Butter, **6**-903
Cisco, Broiled, **6**-903
English, Grilled, **6**-903
Fried (Stekt Sill Eller Strömming), **11**-1787
au Gratin, **10**-1665
and Ham Salad (Sill och Skinksallad), **11**-1787
Kippered, Broiled, **6**-903
Kipper Soufflé, **7**-1017
Pickled, **6**-903
Pickled, Haugesund (Haugesundsk Spedesild), **8**-1236
Pickled (Kryddersild), **4**-536
Rollmops, **6**-903
Salad, **6**-913
Salad (Haringsla), **4**-590
Salad, Salmagundi, **9**-1383
Salad, Salt-Herring, **10**-1665
Salad (Sillisalaatti), **5**-678
Selyodka, **10**-1566
Smoked, Fried, **6**-903
Soufflé (Soufflé ze Sledzia), **9**-1422
in Sour Cream, **6**-903; **7**-1146
Hét Vezér Tokány (Seven Chieftains' Tokany), **6**-918

Hickory, Hickory Nut, 6-903
Bread, **6**-904
Cake, **1**-37; **6**-904
Creams, **6**-904
Crescents, **6**-904
Graham Bread, **7**-1153
Himmel Torte, **7**-1045
Hingha (Shrimp and Squash Soup), **11**-1716
Hirvensarvet (Antler Cookies), **5**-681
Hitashimono (Boiled Greens), **6**-976
Hmon Nga Baung (Fish and Mushroom Soufflé), **11**-1716
Hodgepodge Relish, **5**-726
Hoecake, Old-Fashioned, **6**-904
Hog, see Pig; Pork
Hojaldre (Sweet Cake), **9**-1497
Holishkes (Meat-Stuffed Cabbage), **6**-995

Hollandaise, Hollandaise Sauce, 6-904-906; **10**-1614
1-114; **5**-695; **10**-1621
Blender, **10**-1620
Brennan's, **4**-512
Mustard, **10**-1614, 1621
Quick Blender (for Asparagus), **1**-114
Sour-Cream, **11**-1700
Variations, **6**-905-906; **10**-1614
Hollandsche Biefstuk (Dutch Steak), **1**-60
Hollyhock-House Mushrooms and Chicken, Barrister Style, **8**-1200

Hominy, 6-906
Buttery Garlic Grits, **6**-907
and Cheese, **6**-907
Frankfurter, and Green-Pea Casserole, **6**-907
Fried Salt Pork and Milk Gravy on Hominy Grits, **6**-907
au Gratin, **6**-907
Grits, **5**-827
Grits, Baked, **6**-907
Grits Batter Bread, **6**-907
Grits with Cheese, Baked, **1**-37
Grits, Fried, **6**-907
Hog and, **1**-69
Lamb Chili, Pueblo, **11**-1728
Mexican, **6**-907
and Pork, Mexican, **9**-1450
Puffs, **6**-907
Salt Pork, Beans, and Hominy, **6**-907
Honan Sweet-and-Sour Beef Bails, **3**-399
Honan Sweet-and-Sour Pork, **3**-400
Honduras Chicken in Sauce (Pollo con Salsa), **11**-1706
Honduras Eggs Poached in Chili Sauce (Huevos con Salsa de Chiles), **11**-1708
Honduras Ladyfingers in Syrup (Torrijas), **11**-1709
Honduras Hot Pineapple Punch (Ponche de Piña), **11**-1709

Honey, Honeyed, 6-908
Apple Pie, **1**-56
Barbecue Sauce, **10**-1623
Beets, **6**-909
Butter, **2**-279; **6**-909; **12**-1915
Butter, Sesame, **10**-1647
Cake, Chocolate, **3**-410
Cake, Dutch, **6**-911
Cake (Lekah), **6**-993
Cinnamon-Honey Syrup, **5**-824
Cranberry, and Orange Jam, **6**-963
-Cream Dressing, **11**-1776
-Cream Salad Dressing, **1**-79
-Cream Sauce, **6**-911
Custard, Baked, **1**-62
-Date Bars, **6**-911
Dressing, **10**-1623
Fruit Bars, **3**-433
-Fruit Butter, **6**-909
Gingerbread, **1**-53; **5**-804
-Glazed Apples, **6**-910
-Glazed Onions, **8**-1264
Glazes, **6**-909
Grapefruit, **5**-814
Lebkuchen, **7**-1046
Lemon-Honey Dressing, **7**-1053
Lemon-Honey Spread, **6**-911
-Lemon Syrup, **5**-823
Mousse, **6**-910
-Nut-Apple Pie, **6**-910
-Orange-Almond Cake, **6**-910
Orange-Honey Sherbet, **6**-980
Orange Peel, **8**-1273
-Peanut Butter Cookies, **3**-474
Peanut Sandwiches, **8**-1325
Pear Honey, **8**-1333
Pears, **6**-910
Pecan Tea Toast, **11**-1826
Pennies from Heaven, **6**-910
-Prune Pudding, **9**-1485
Rye-Honey Cookies, **10**-1575
Sage-Honey Sour-Cream Pie, **1**-55
Spice Cake, **2**-267
Syrup, **5**-823
Toast Butter, **11**-1829
Topping, **6**-911
Yogurt Cakes, **12**-1958

Honeydew, Honeydew Melon, 6-911; **7**-1129
and Orange Dessert, **6**-911
Rings with Shrimp Salad, **6**-911
Hoosier Egg Casserole, **1**-37
Hoosier Fried Tomatoes, Creamy Gravy, **1**-37
Hoppel Poppel, **9**-1463
Hoppin', Hopping John, **1**-22; **11**-1723
Hors-d'Oeuvre, **1**-85; **6**-912; for recipes see Appetizer(s)

Horseradish, 6-913
Butter, **1**-86, **2**-279; **5**-695
and Cranberry Relish, **3**-490
Cream, **9**-1383
with Fermented Beet Juice, Passover (Rusell Chrain), **6**-994
Sauce, **2**-189; **5**-726; **6**-914; **10**-1626
Sauce, Creamy, **6**-859
Sauce, Hot (Varm Peberrodssovs), **4**-542
Sauce (Pepperrotsaus), **8**-1240
Sauce Raifort, **10**-1614, 1620
Sauce (Sos Chrzanowy), **9**-1422
Sauce (Sous iz Khrena), **10**-1573
Sauce, Whipped-Cream, **5**-695; **6**-914
Sole, **10**-1670
Sour-Cream Horseradish, **2**-191
Toast Butter, **11**-1829
and Tuna Canapés, **12**-1862
Ho T'ao Chi Jing (Walnut Chicken), **12**-1917
Hot Cross Buns, **2**-252
Hotel Pontchartrain Red Snapper Court Bouillon, **4**-510
Hotel Pontchartrain Shrimp Rémoulade, **4**-510
Houby s Vejci (Mushrooms with Eggs), **4**-532
Hsieh Fu Yung (Crab Fu Yung), **3**-403
Hsien Chi (Salted Chicken), **3**-401
Hsing Jen Chi Ting (Diced Chicken with Almonds), **3**-401
Hsing Jen Ping (Almond Cookies), **3**-404

Hubbard Squash, 6-914; **11**-1759
Baked in Shells, **6**-914
Casserole, **6**-914; **11**-1762
Muffins, **6**-915
Patties, **6**-915
Pie, Company, **6**-915
Scalloped, **11**-1762
Huckleberry, **6**-915; for recipes see Blueberry and Huckleberry
Huevos Escalfados Fritos (Poached Eggs and Ham, Fried), **6**-862
Huevos a la Flamenca (Eggs Flamenco), **11**-1744
Huevos Fritos (Deep-Fried Eggs), **4**-608
Huevos Hilados (Threaded Eggs), **6**-608
Huevos Rancheros (Ranchers' Eggs), **4**-607
Huevos Rancheros (Ranch-Style Eggs), **7**-1141
Huevos con Salsa de Chiles (Eggs Poached in Chili Sauce), **11**-1708
Huevos en Toledo (Eggs in Toledo), **6**-865
Huevos con Tortillas y Jamon (Ham and Eggs with Tortillas), **6**-861
Huhn im Burgunder (Chicken Cooked in Burgundy Wine), **5**-795
Hummersaus (Lobster Sauce), **8**-1236
Hungarian Almond Poppy-Seed Noodles, **8**-1233
Hungarian Cheese Pastries, **8**-1308
Hungarian Chocolate Frosting, **5**-752
Hungarian Christmas Balls, **3**-455
Hungarian Cookery, **6**-916
Hungarian Goulash, **2**-187
Hungarian Goulash (Magyar Gulyás), **6**-918
Hungarian Noodle and Cheese Casserole, **8**-1233
Hungarian Palacsinta, **8**-1293
Hungarian Poppy-Seed Kringle, **9**-1437
Hungarian Pork Chops, **9**-1445
Hungarian Pork Chops (Disznókaraj Magyarosan), **6**-918
Hungarian Potatoes, **9**-1463
Hungarian Walnut Bars, **12**-1918
Hungarian Walnut Roll (Diós Tekercs), **6**-922
Hung Shao Chu-Tzu (Red-Cooked Pork Shoulder), **3**-400
Hung Shao Niu Nan (Red-Cooked Shin of Beef), **3**-399
Hunter's Reward, **11**-1730
Hunters' Stew (Bigos Mysliwski), **9**-1426
Hunter's Torte (Jaegertorte), **12**-1854

Hush Puppies, **2**-239
Hush Puppy Batter, **5**-690
Hussar's Kisses (Huszárcsók), **6**-922
Huszárcsók (Hussar's Kisses), **6**-922
Hutspot met Klapstuk (Hodgepodge with Boiled Meat), **4**-592
Hvidkaalsrouladen (Cabbage Rolls), **4**-540

I

Iablochnii Krem (Cream of Apples), **10**-1574
Iablochnii Sup (Apple Soup), **10**-1568
I'A Ota (Marinated Fish), **9**-1434
Ice (frozen water), **6**-923

Ice(s), **6**-924, and **Sherbet(s),** **10**-1652
Apple and Grape-Juice Ice, **6**-925
Apricot Ice, **6**-925
Café Deep South Frappé, **5**-726
Cantaloupe Ice, **6**-925
Citrus Milk Sherbet, **10**-1652
Coffee Ice with Whipped Cream, **6**-925
Currant-Jelly and Raspberry Ice, **6**-925
Five-Fruit Sherbet, **10**-1652
Fresh Coconut Ice, **6**-925
Fresh Currant Ice, **4**-524
Fresh-Lemon Sherbet, **7**-1054
Fresh Pineapple Ice, **6**-926
Fruit-Juice Ice, **6**-925
Grape-Lime Frappé, **5**-726
Guava Sherbet, **10**-1652
Lemon Buttermilk Sherbet, **7**-1054
Lemon Frappé, **6**-925
Lemon Granité, **5**-810
Lemon Ice, Instant Blender, **6**-925
Lemon-Lime Sherbet, **5**-790
Lemon Sherbet, **10**-1652
Lime Sherbet, **7**-1169; **10**-1652
Loganberry Ice, **7**-1082
Muscatel Ice, **6**-925
Orange Buttermilk Sherbet, **10**-1652
Orange-Honey Sherbet, **6**-980
Orange Ice, **6**-925; **8**-1208
Peach Buttermilk Sherbet, **8**-1320
Peach Ice, **6**-926
Peach Sherbet, **10**-1654
Peach Sherbet, Low-Calorie, **7**-1087
Persimmon Ice, **9**-1364
Pineapple Ice, **9**-1410
Pineapple Ice with Crème de Menthe, **9**-1410
Pineapple-Mint Sherbet, **7**-1166
Pineapple Sherbet, Creamy, **9**-1410
Pineapple Sherbet, Low-Calorie, **9**-1410
Plum Ice, **6**-926
Pomegranate Ice, **1**-24; **9**-1436
Rainbow Sherbet Parfait, **10**-1654
Rhubarb Ice, **6**-926
Rhubarb Ice, Tangy, **10**-1544
Roman Punch, **10**-1654
Sherbet Drink
Coconut, Brazilian, **10**-1654
Strawberry, Turkish, **10**-1654
Watermelon, Turkish, **10**-1654
Sherbet Mold, **4**-570
Strawberry, Apricot, Raspberry, or Peach Frappé, **6**-926
Strawberry Ice, **6**-926
Strawberry Ice, Italian, **11**-1779
Strawberry Sherbet, **10**-1654
Tangerine Frappé, **5**-726
Tangerine Ice in Orange Shells, **6**-926
Tangerine Sherbet, **10**-1654
Three-Fruit Ice, **6**-926
Tropical Sherbet, **11**-1701
Watermelon Almond Sherbet, **12**-1922
Watermelon Granité, **6**-926
Watermelon Ice, **5**-790
Watermelon Sherbet, **12**-1922

Ice Cream(s), **6**-926
Almond, **6**-929
Apricot Ripple, Fresh, **1**-106
Avocado, **1**-24
Avocado Cream, Frozen, **1**-59
Banana, **6**-929
Blueberry, **6**-929
Cherry, **1**-36
Chocolate, **6**-929
Chocolate Freezer, **6**-929
Fresh Strawberry, **6**-929
Ice Cream as a Dessert Sauce, **6**-934; **10**-1615
Ice 'n Cream, **6**-929
Iowa Farm, **1**-39
Lotus, **8**-1276
Mango, **7**-1104
Neapolitan, **8**-1208
Orange Velvet, **8**-1270
Peach, **6**-929
Peach Ripple, **8**-1320
Peanut-Butter, **8**-1326
Peppermint Freeze, **5**-790
Pineapple, **6**-929
Pumpkin, **9**-1500
Raspberry, **6**-929
Rum-Raisin, **6**-929
Sauces for, **6**-930
Strawberry, **6**-929; **11**-1779
Strawberry, Freezer of, **9**-1382
Tangelemon, **11**-1838
Vanilla, **6**-929
Vanilla, French, **6**-929
Ice Cream Bonbons, **6**-934
Ice-Cream Cake, see Frozen Desserts
Ice-Cream Parfait, see Frozen Desserts
Ice-Cream Pie, see Frozen Desserts
Ice-Cream Sodas, see Beverages
Ice-Cream Sundaes, see Frozen Desserts
Idaho Corn Oysters, **1**-36
Idaho Lamb Hash, **1**-35
Ikan Goreng Atjar (Cold Pickled Fish), **11**-1714
Ikra iz Baklazhanov (Eggplant Caviar), **10**-1566
Indian Broiled Shrimps, **6**-913
Indian Egg Curry, **4**-606
Indian Kitchree, **10**-1551
Indian Pilau, **4**-641
Indian Meal Raised Bread, **8**-1225

Indian Pudding, **8**-1228
Baked, **1**-47
Sour-Cream, **9**-1490
Top-Stove, **8**-1184
Indian Pumpkin Soup, **9**-1499
Indian Ravo, **10**-1561
Indian Shrimp Balls, **10**-1662
Indian Shuck Bread, **1**-64
Indian Steamed Rice and Lamb, **7**-1035
India Relish, Melon, **7**-1132
India's Cookery, **6**-935
India Style Roast Chicken, **3**-381
Indienne Sauce, **2**-194; **11**-1837
Indonesian Lamb Curry (Kerie Kambing), **11**-1714
Indonesian Skewered Pork, **7**-1052
Insalata Bandiera (Flag Salad), **6**-960
Insalata di Fagiolini e Patate (Green-Bean and Potato Salad), **6**-960
Insalata di Funghi Crudi (Italian Raw-Mushroom Salad), **8**-1197
Io Pua (Roast Pork), **9**-1434
Iowa Corn Chowder, **1**-38
Iowa Farm Ice Cream, **1**-39
Iranian Pilaf (Pello), **8**-1215
Iranian Raisin Cake, **10**-1535
Iranian Shish Kebab, **8**-1214
Iranian Spinach and Parsley Pie (Coucou Sabzi), **8**-1215
Irish Coffee, **3**-462; **6**-950
Irish Cookery, **6**-943
Irish Lamb Stew, **7**-1035
Irish Moss Blancmange, **6**-950
Irish Stew, **6**-948
Isbjørnøye (Polar Bear's Eye), **8**-1235
Iscas (Sliced Liver with Spleen Sauce), **9**-1456
Ischeler Torteletten (Almond Butter Cookies), **1**-124
Isla Flotante (Floating Island), **9**-1497
Italian Bread Dumplings, **11**-1696
Italian Cannelloni, **8**-1293
Italian Cheese Stuffing, **11**-1782
Italian Chestnut-Chocolate Dessert, **3**-377
Italian Chick-Pea Salad, **3**-392
Italian Chowder, **11**-1695
Italian Coffee Bombe, **2**-212
Italian Coffeecake (Panettone), **3**-463
Italian Cookery, **6**-950
Italian Eggplant Parmigiana, **4**-615
Italian Eggs Florentine, **11**-1755
Italian Escarole and Lentil Soup, **4**-652
Italian Garlic Bread, **5**-775
Italian Garlic Soup, **5**-775
Italian-Green-Bean Salad, **10**-1668
Italian Grinders, **10**-1602
Italian Lamb Casserole, **2**-325
Italian Marrow, see Zucchini, Vegetable Marrow
Italian Mozzarella Skewers (Crostini alla Mozzarella), **6**-955
Italian Muscatels, **8**-1194
Italian Onion Soup, **11**-1690
Italian Orange-Rum Cake, **8**-1272
Italian Parsley Sauce, **8**-1299
Italian Pork Chops with Herbs, **9**-1443
Italian Raw-Mushroom Salad (Insalata di Funghi Crudi), **8**-1197
Italian Rice and Peas, **10**-1551
Italian Rice Salad, **9**-1383
Italian Rice Salad with Veal, **10**-1550
Italian Rice Soup with Chicken Livers, **7**-1075
Italian Rum Cake, **10**-1562
Italian Salad, **10**-1587
Italian Sausage and Rice, **10**-1636
Italian Sausages with Beans (Salsicclee e Fagioli), **6**-955
Italian Scalloped Potatoes, **4**-650
Italian Sloppy Joes, **10**-1601
Italian Spaghetti and Meatballs (QC), **10**-1523
Italian Stewed Pork with Celery, **9**-1451
Italian Strawberries (Fragole all'Italiana), **6**-960
Italian Strawberry Ice, **11**-1778
Italian Style Broccoli, **5**-775
Italian Style Clam Soup, **3**-453
Italian Style Dandelion Greens, **4**-534
Italian Style Dumplings (Gnocchi all'Italiana), **4**-587
Italian Style Fried Fish Fillets (Pesce Fritto), **6**-954
Italian Style Garlic Toast, **11**-1826
Italian Style Liver and Noodles, **7**-1073
Italian Style Pepper Salad, **9**-1360
Italian Style Perch, **5**-691
Italian Style Perch (Pesce Persico), **6**-954
Italian Style Ravioli, **10**-1538
Italian Style Sautéed Zucchini, **12**-1962
Italian Style Squid, **11**-1763
Italian Style Stuffed Mushrooms, **8**-1201
Italian Style Stuffed Onions, **8**-1261
Italian Style Veal and Peppers, **12**-1896
Italian Tomato Salad, **11**-1834
Italian Tomato Sauce, **10**-1627
Italian Tuna Frittata, **12**-1866
Italian Wine Cookies, **3**-473
Italienne Sauce, **10**-1613, 1619

J

Jaegertorte (Hunter's Torte), **11**-1854

Jam(s), **6**-961, and **Conserve(s),** **3**-466; see also Marmalade; Preserve(s)
Apple Butter, **1**-97
Apple Butter, Pennsylvania Dutch, **9**-1350
Apricot-Pineapple Jam, **1**-109; **6**-963

Beach Plum Jam, **1**-150
Berry Jam, **6**-965
Blackberry Jam, No-Cook, **6**-965
Blackberry Jam, Spiced, **6**-963
Blueberry Jam, **6**-965
Cherry-Almond-Pineapple Jam, **9**-1410
Cherry-Pineapple Jam, **3**-375
Cranberry and Fig Jam, **6**-963
Cranberry, Orange, and Honey Jam, **6**-963
Damson-Plum, **9**-1415
Damson-Plum Butter, **9**-1415
Damson-Plum Conserve, **4**-534
Damson-Plum Jam, **4**-534
Fig Jam, **4**-659
Fresh Plum Jam, **9**-1417
Ginger Tomato Conserve, **5**-803
Golden Jam, **6**-964
Gooseberry Jam, **5**-809; **6**-965
Grape Conserve, **3**-466; **5**-813
Grape Jam, Spiced, **6**-964
Grape and Pineapple Jam, **6**-964
Green Tomato Jam, **11**-1836
Jam Circles, **3**-473
Jam Fritters, Viennese, **5**-749
Jam Roly-Poly, **4**-627
Jam Tarts, **4**-626; **11**-1838
Jam Toast, Rolled, **11**-1826
Lime-Orange Conserve, **7**-1069
Loganberry Jam, **6**-965; **7**-1082
Loquat Jam, **7**-1082
Mango Jam, **7**-1104
Melon Conserve, Western, **7**-1132
Peach and Blueberry Jam, Spiced, **8**-1321
Peach Jam, **6**-965
Peach Jam, No-Cook, **6**-965
Peach Jam, Spiced, **6**-964
Peach and Orange Conserve, **8**-1321
Pear and Orange Conserve, **3**-466
Pear-Pineapple Conserve, **8**-1333
Pear-Raspberry Jam, **6**-965
Pineapple-Mint Jam, **6**-964
Pineapple-Papaya Conserve, **9**-1410
Pineapple-Strawberry Jam, **6**-964
Plum Conserve, **9**-1418
Plum-Orange Jam, **6**-964
Prune Butter, **1**-76
Quince and Pear Jam, **6**-964
Raspberry Currant Jam, **6**-964
Red-Cherry Jam, **6**-965
Red-Pepper Jam, **6**-964
Red-Raspberry Jam, **6**-965
Red-Rasperry Jam, No-Cook, **6**-965
Rhubarb and Strawberry Jam, **10**-1545
Rose-Hip Jam, **10**-1560
Sour Cherry Jam, **6**-965
Sour Cherry Jam, No-Cook, **6**-965
Spring-Fruit Jam, **9**-1403
Squash and Apple Jam, **11**-1762
Strawberry Jam, No-Cook, **6**-965
Strawberry Jam, Old-Country, **6**-964
Strawberry Jam, Three-Minute, **6**-964
Tomato-Apricot Jam, **6**-964
Tomato Jam, **6**-965; **11**-1836
Watermelon Honey, Spiced, **12**-1922
Wild-Chokeberry Jam, **1**-62
Jamaica Style Pot-Roasted Chicken, **9**-1477
Jamaica Style Pot-Roasted Turkey, **12**-1871
Jamaican Congo-Pea or Kidney-Bean Soup, **6**-966
Jamaican Curried Mutton, **8**-1205
Jamaican Fish Chowder, **6**-967
Jamaican Gold Doubloons, **8**-1273
Jamaican Onion Soup with Cheese, **6**-967
Jamaican Pepperpot Soup, Myrtle Bank, **6**-966
Jamaican Plantain Turnovers, **9**-1414
Jamaican Split-Pea Soup, **6**-966

Jambalaya
de Canard, **1**-44
Creole, **6**-968
Dunbar's, **4**-510
Ham, **10**-1556
Oyster and Shrimp, **4**-510
Shrimp, **10**-1661
Shrimp and Rice, **10**-1549
Jambon de Campagne, Le, (Country Ham), **2**-277
Jambon Persillé (Parsleyed Ham), **5**-743
Jang Po (Beef Broiled in Sauce), **7**-1020
Jannson's Temptation, **10**-1664
Japanese Cookery, **6**-969
Japanese Fortune Wafers (Tsujiura), **6**-978
Japanese Shrimp and Egg Salad, **10**-1580
Jasmine Tea, **4**-635
Javanese Lamb, **11**-1753
Javanese Satay Sauce, **8**-1323
Jay's Famous Cheese Pie, **3**-368
Jeg Kan Ikke La Være (Irresistible Dessert), **8**-1241

Jellied Desserts
Angel Delight (QC), **10**-1525
Applesauce, Jellied, **5**-789
Apricot Dessert, Jellied, **1**-109
Bavarois au Citron, **7**-1054
Bean Cakes (Yokan), **6**-978
Berry Charlotte, **5**-758
Black-Bottom Pie with Chocolate Crust, **9**-1398
Blueberry Cottage-Cheese Cake, **2**-210
Blueberry Fluff Pie, **5**-790
Blueberry-Grape Mold, **5**-812
Bride's Pudding, **9**-1492
Charlotte Russe, Southern, **11**-1725
Cherry Bavarian Pie, **9**-1398
Cherry-Port Mold, **10**-1667
Chiffon Pies
Banana, **9**-1397
Cantaloupe, **9**-1397
Caramel, **9**-1397
Chocolate, **3**-393, 411
Coffee, **9**-1397
Fresh Orange, **8**-1270
Lemon, **7**-1054
Lemon-Ambrosia, with Coconut Crust, **9**-1397
Lemon, in Pastry Shell, **9**-1397
Lime, **9**-1397
Mocha, **7**-1167
Molasses, **8**-1184
Nesselrode, **9**-1397
Passion-Fruit, **8**-1300
Peanut-Butter, **8**-1328
Peanut Crunch, **9**-1397
Peppermint, **9**-1361, 1397
Peppermint Chocolate, **9**-1397
Pumpkin, **9**-1397
Pumpkin Meringue, **9**-1500
Raspberry, **6**-980
Strawberry, **6**-980
Velvety, **9**-1396
Chiffon Tarts
Orange, **8**-1272
Strawberry, **9**-1812
Chocolate Rum Pie, Marbled, **9**-1398
Coeur à la Crème, **5**-788
Coffee Sponge, **7**-1087; **11**-1837
Cranberry Mold, **11**-1823
Cream of Apples (Iablochnii Krem), **10**-1574
Crème Louisa, **5**-790
Eggnog Snow Pudding, **3**-445
Fresh Blueberry Fluff, **2**-209
Fruit-Cream Pudding, **9**-1489
Fruit Dessert, Party, **5**-788
Fruited Wine Gelatin, **5**-789
Fruit Squares, Fluffy, **5**-790
Ginger Peach Mold, **8**-1317
Grapes in White-Wine Gelatin, **5**-812
Hazelnut Cream, **6**-882
Irresistible Dessert (Jeg Kan Ikke La Være), **8**-1241
Jellied Fresh Plums, with Golden Fresh-Lemon Sauce, **9**-1416
Lemon Fluff Dessert (QC), **10**-1525
Lime-Grape Dessert, **7**-1088
Litchi Gelatin Dessert, **7**-1072
Litchi and Peach, Jellied, **7**-1072
Macaroon Cream, **7**-1096
Mandarin Oranges, Jellied, **8**-1270
Maple Gelatin, **7**-1107
Maraschino-Almond Pie, **7**-1108
Minted Fresh-Lime Mold with Watermelon Balls, **7**-1067
Mocha Molds, Low-Calorie, **7**-1167
Mousses, see Mousse(s), Dessert
Nesselrode Pie, **8**-1218
Nesselrode Pudding, Jellied, **8**-1218
Norwegian Rum Cream, **10**-1563
Orange Ambrosia, Jellied, **8**-1270
Orange Delight, **8**-1270
Orange Fluff Pudding, **8**-1270
Orange Pie with Whipped Cream, **8**-1272
Peach Melba, Jellied, **5**-790
Pineapple-Ginger-Ale Jelly with Peaches, **5**-803
Plum Snow Pudding, **9**-1417
Prune Molds, Individual, **5**-789
Prune Whip, **9**-1485
Rhubarb, Jellied, **10**-1544
Rice à l'Impératrice, **10**-1552
Russian Cream, **10**-1561
Sherry Almond Snow Pudding, **9**-1492
Sherry Jelly, **1**-60; **5**-789
Sherry Parfait, **5**-790
Snow Gelatin (Awayuki-kan), **6**-978
Snow Pudding with Nesselrode Sauce, **8**-1218
Spanish Cream, **6**-980
Spiced Jellied Blackberries, **2**-205
Spiced Jelly with Rum Cream, **5**-790
Strawberry Angel-Food Dessert, **11**-1778
Strawberry Charlotte Dessert, **5**-788
Strawberry Fluff, **7**-1087
Strawberry Snow (Bavaroise Frutillas), **11**-1709
Sweet Rice and Pineapple Dessert, **9**-1409
Two-Tone Jelly (Nishiki-kan), **6**-978
Jellied Salads, see Salad(s), Jellied
Jellied Soups, see Soup(s), Chilled, Frosted, and Jellied

Jelly(ies), **6**-981
Apple, **1**-97; **6**-982
Apple, Aromatic, **6**-982
Apple and Blueberry, Spiced, **6**-982
Apple-Herb, **1**-103
Berry, **6**-982
Blackberry-Juice, **6**-982
Blackberry, No-Cook, **6**-984
Black Raspberry, **6**-982
Cider-and-Sage, **6**-982
Concord Lime, **6**-982
Cranberry, **6**-982
Cranberry-Claret, **3**-490
Cranberry-Orange, **3**-490
Dewberry, **4**-560
Elderberry, **4**-617
Fresh Currant, **4**-524
Ginger Lemon, **7**-1056
Grape, **6**-982
Grape-and-Basil, **6**-983
Grape-Juice, **6**-983
Grape, No-Cook, **6**-984
Grape, Old-Fashioned, **5**-812
Grapefruit-and-Savory, **6**-983
Guava, **5**-829
Lemon-Honey Spread, **6**-911
Mint, **6**-982; **7**-1166
Mulberry, **8**-1193
Orange, **6**-983
Orange-Grapefruit-Juice, **6**-984
Plum, **6**-984
Prickly Pear, **9**-1483
Quince, **6**-984
Quince and Cranberry, **6**-982
Quince, without Pectin, **10**-1529
Red Raspberry, **6**-984
Red Raspberry, No-Cook, **6**-984
Rhubarb and Strawberry, **10**-1545
Rose-Geranium, **5**-791
Strawberry, No-Cook, **6**-984
Wild-Plum, **1**-40
Jelly Cookies, Grandmother's (Mormor's Syltkakor), **11**-1793
Jelly Sauce, **1**-40

Jelly-Roll Sandwiches, **6**-934
Jerusalem Artichokes with Tomatoes, **6**-985
Jewish Cookery, **6**-985
Jewish Sabbath Meal-in-One (Cholent), **6**-990
Jim Beard's Refrigerator Cheesecake, **3**-367
Joanne's Snickerdoodles, **3**-476
Jockey Club Eggs, **4**-607
Johnnycake(s), **1**-67; **8**-1293
Johnnycake, Molasses, **8**-1225
Judías Blancas a la Leridana (Lima Beans Lerida), **11**-1744
Judías Verdes a la Vasca (Basque Green Beans), **11**-1744
Juju Gakuan (Salad), **6**-976
Julekake (Christmas Bread), **8**-1240

Julep, **6**-996
Lime, **7**-1069
Mint, Georgia, **6**-996
Mint, Kentucky, **6**-996
Rum Mint, **6**-996
Juleskinke (Christmas Ham), **8**-1237
Julskinka (Christmas Ham), **11**-1788
July Day Salad, **1**-14
Jungle Stew, **1**-79
Junidanya Sauce, **6**-975

Juniper Berry, **6**-996
Juniper Pot Roast in Burgundy, **6**-996
Sauce, **6**-996
Jyuniku no Mizutaki (Table-Boiled Beef), **6**-974
Jyuniku-Teriyaki (Broiled Beef), **6**-974

K

Kaastruffels (Cheese Truffles), **4**-589

Kabob(s), Kebab(s), **6**-997; see also Skewer(s), Skewered
Appetizer, **5**-718
Brussels Sprouts and Beef, **2**-248
Far Eastern (chicken), **3**-390
Frankfurter, Prune and Onion, **5**-721
Lamb Shish-Kabob, **6**-997
Pork, Malayan, **8**-1324
Pork, Spicy, **6**-997
Pineapple-Frankfurter, **6**-998
Shish Kebab, **10**-1654
Arab, **8**-1214
Iranian, **8**-1214
Turkish, **8**-1214
Shrimp, **6**-998; **10**-1660
Skillet, **6**-997
Steak, **12**-1957
Kaczka lub Ges Marynowana (Marinated Duck or Goose), **9**-1428
Kadayif (Shredded-Wheat Dessert), **8**-1216
Kaeng Phed (Fish Stew), **11**-1717
Kaernemaelkskoldskaal (Cold Buttermilk Soup), **4**-539
Kaese Blintzes (Rolled Cheese Pancakes), **6**-992
Kafes (Greek Coffee), **5**-824
Kaffekake (Coffeecake), **8**-1240
Kaiserschmarrn (The Emperor's Omelet), **1**-123
Kakejiru (Sauce), **6**-972
Kalakukko (Fish Loaf), **5**-680
Kala-Riisivuoka (Fish and Rice Casserole), **5**-680
Kalbi Kui (Broiled Short Ribs), **7**-1022
Kalbsbraten (Veal Roast), **5**-794
Kalbsgulasch (Veal Goulash), **1**-122

Kale, **6**-998
Bacon, and Oatmeal, **6**-999
Colcannon, **6**-949
Country Style, **6**-999
with Pork, **1**-48
with Potatoes and Sausage (Stamppot van Boerenkool met Worst), **4**-592
Kålsallad med Lingon (Cabbage Salad with Lingonberries), **11**-1791
Kalvkotlett à la Oscar (Veal Cutlet à la Oscar), **11**-1788
Kamaboko (Fish Cakes), **6**-972
Kanari Milch (Canary's Milk), **1**-123
Kanelkakor (Swedish Cinnamon Cookies), **11**-1796
Kansas Corn Chowder, **7**-1146
Kapr Peceny s Kyselou Omackou (Carp with Sour-Cream Sauce), **4**-531
Kaprissås (Caper Sauce), **11**-1791
Kapusniak (Cabbage Soup), **9**-1420
Karelian Hot Pot (Karjalanpaisti), **8**-1205
Karelian Pasties (Karjalanpiiraat), **5**-678
Karidopita (Walnut Cake), **4**-640
Karjalanpaisti (Karelian Hot Pot), **8**-1205
Karjalanpiiraat (Karelian Pasties), **5**-678
Karnemelk Pudding (Buttermilk Pudding), **4**-593
Karry (Curry Sauce), **4**-539
Kartofelnii Salat s Vechinoi i Vishniami (Potato Salad with Ham and Cherries), **10**-1566
Kartofel's Anchousami (Scalloped Potatoes with Anchovies), **10**-1572
Kartoffel Chremsel (Potato Fritters), **6**-992
Kartoffelklösse (Potato Dumplings), **5**-795
Kartoffel Latkes (Potato Pancakes), **6**-991
Kartoffelsalat (Potato Salad), **5**-796
Käsesalat (Cheese Salad), **11**-1804
Kasha, **2**-249; **11**-1838
Kasha in Chicken Soup, **5**-827
Kasha Varnishkas (Buckwheat Groats with Noodles), **6**-992
Katy's Drop Potato Scones, **10**-1644
Kedgeree, **4**-621
Keema Matar (Chopped Meat with Peas), **6**-939
Keja Chae (Salad with Mustard), **7**-1023
Kekda Bengali (Bengalese Crab), **6**-942
Kentucky Burgoo, **1**-40
Kentucky Jam Cake, **2**-270
Kentucky Lamb Roast, **1**-40
Kentucky Mint Julep, **6**-996
Kerie Kambing (Indonesian Lamb Curry), **11**-1714
Kesäkeitto (Summer Vegetable Soup), **5**-679

Ketchup, **6**-999
Fruit, **1**-53; **6**-999
Grape, **6**-999
Green-Tomato, **1**-41
Mushroom, **6**-999
Tomato, **6**-999
Tomato, and Tomato Cocktail, **6**-999
Key Lime Pie, **7**-1069
Key Lime Pie with Peaches, **8**-1320
Khanom mo Kaeng (Taro-Coconut-Egg Custard), **11**-1716
Khvorost (Twigs), **10**-1573
Kibbeh (Meat Loaf), **8**-1214
Kibbeh bi Laban (Meatballs in Yogurt), **8**-1214
Kibbeh bi Sanieh (Stuffed Meat Loaf), **8**-1214

Kid, **6**-999
Roast, **6**-999
Stuffed Roast, **8**-1214

Kidney(s), **7**-1013
Beef
Beef and Kidney Pie, **9**-1387
Beef and Kidney Pudding, **6**-945
Beef Kidney Stew, **2**-191
Hamburger and Kidney Pie, **6**-872
Kidney Stew, **7**-1014
Mushroom and Kidney Pie, **7**-1013
Steak and Kidney Pie, **4**-624
Lamb
with Eggs, Guetaria, **7**-1014
Fritti Rognoni, **7**-1016
Lancaster Hot Pot, **7**-1033
Riñones a la Pamplona, **7**-1014
Rognons d'Agneau à la Lully, **7**-1014
Stew, Brunch, **7**-1040
Pork, Braised, **7**-1016
Veal
with Anchovies, **7**-1014
Bonne Femme, **7**-1014
Brochettes de Rognons Panés et Grillés, **7**-1014
Casserole Jerez, **7**-1014
in Cream, Mottram, **12**-1897
Flambéed (Rognons Bolo), **11**-1802
and Ham Ragout, **7**-1014
Nyre Sauté, Gammeltoft, **7**-1014
Pot-Roasted, au Citron, **9**-1476
Roast, **12**-1897
Rognoncini di Vitello Trifolato, **7**-1016
Rognons Flambés au Ruban Bleu, **7**-1014
Soup (Nier Soep), **4**-589
Turbigo, **7**-1014
in Vermouth, **12**-1897
Kiek met Ballekens (Flemish Fricasseed Chicken with Meatballs), **7**-1122

Kielbasa, Kolbasi, or Kolbassy, **7**-1016
Homemade, **10**-1636
Kilich Shish (Turkish Swordfish on Skewers), **8**-1215
Kimchi (Korean Pickle), **7**-1023
Kim Kui (Toasted Seaweed), **7**-1022

Kingfish, **7**-1016
Steaks au Gratin, Baked, **7**-1016
King Haakon's Cake (Kong Haakonskake), **8**-1242
Kingston Potato Soup, **6**-967

Kipper(s), Kippered, **7**-1016
Haddock with Bacon, **7**-1017
Salmon with Rice, **7**-1017
Soufflé, **7**-1017
Kirsebærsuppe (Cherry Soup), **4**-539
Kirsebærsuppe (Cherry Soup, Cold), **8**-1235
Kisiel Owocowy (Fruit Dessert), **9**-1431

Kiss(es), **7**-1017
Cocoa, **7**-1017
Coconut, **7**-1017
Date-Nut, **7**-1017
Kissel, **10**-1573
Kiveve (Creamed Squash), **11**-1708
Kjøttkaker (Meatballs), **8**-1237
Kjøttsalat (Meat Salad), **8**-1235
Klejner (Fried Twists), **8**-1241
Klipfisk (Salted Dried Cod), **4**-539

Knackwurst, **7**-1017
in Ale, **1**-10
Knaidlach (Matzo Balls), **4**-586; **6**-987
Knedlíky s Visnové (Cherry Dumplings), **4**-532
Knishes, Potato, **6**-991
Koenigsberger Klops, **1**-62

Kohlrabi, **7**-1018
with Cheese, Spiced, **7**-1018
Kokt Lamm med Dillsås (Boiled Lamb with Dill), **11**-1788
Kokt Lutfisk (Boiled Lutfisk), **11**-1787
Kokt Ørrett (Boiled Trout), **8**-1236
Kolache, Prune, **7**-1157
Kolácky (Bohemian Tarts), **4**-532
Kolokythia Krokettes (Zucchini Pancakes), **5**-822
Kömèny Leves (Caraway Soup), **6**-917
Kompot iz Apelsin i Chernosliv (Prune-Orange Compote), **10**-1573
Kompot iz Narezanykh Popolam Grush i Vishen (Pear Halves and Cherry Compote), **10**-1573
Kona Coffee Mousse, **1**-35
Kona Crab (Papai), **9**-1434
Kong Haakonskake (King Haakon's Cake), **8**-1242
Königsberger Meatballs, **6**-870
Kopfsalat mit Erbsen (Romaine Lettuce with Peas), **1**-123
Korean Cookery, **7**-1019
Korean Pickle (Kimchi), **7**-1023

Korean Sesame-Seed Cookies, **4**-635
Korean Steak, **1**-35
Kori Kuk (Oxtail Soup), **7**-1020
Kosher Style Dill Green-Tomato Pickles, **9**-1374
Kosher Style Dill Pickles, **9**-1373
Kosher Style Fresh Dill Pickles, **9**-1373
Kotleciki z Mózgu (Brain Cutlets), **9**-1424
Kotlety z Grzybów (Mushroom Patties), **9**-1429
Kotta Pilafi (Chicken Pilaf), **5**-820
Köttbullar (Swedish Meatballs), **2**-191
Kreplach (Meat Dumplings), **6**-995
Krumkaker (Curled Cakes), **8**-1241
Krupnik (Barley Soup), **9**-1421
Krupnik (Hot Grog with Honey), **9**-1431
Kryddersild (Pickled Herring), **4**-536
Ktenia me Ryzi (Scallops with Rice), **5**-818

Kuchen
Apple, Plum, or Peach, **5**-799
Dough, **5**-799
Mohn, **5**-799
Peach, **8**-1320
Red-Cherry, **9**-1384
Kuchenteig (Tart Pastry), **11**-1804
Kücherlkraut (Beef and Sauerkraut), **1**-121
Kugelhupf (Coffeecake), **1**-123
Kul Jun (Oysters Fried in Egg Batter), **7**-1020
Kumu Niu Pu'uwai (Hearts of Palm), **9**-1435

Kumquat(s), **7**-1023
Candied, **7**-1023
-Ginger Relish, **7**-1023
Orange, and Apple Compote, **7**-1023
Preserves, Almond-Stuffed, **7**-1023
Kura Lub Kurczeta po Polsku (Roast Chicken or Pullets à la Polonaise), **9**-1428
Kushi-Katsu (Fried Chicken on Skewers), **6**-975
Kyuri-Momi (Vinegared Cucumbers), **6**-978

L

Lace Cookies, **3**-472
Lace Praline, **2**-304
La Chiso Ch'ao Chi (Chicken Sautéed with Peppers), **3**-400
Lady Baltimore Cake, **1**-46

Ladyfinger(s)
Crust, **6**-980
Dessert, Mela's, **11**-1747
in Syrup (Torrijas), **11**-1709
Lake Michigan Trout, Butter-Stuffed, **7**-1147
Lake Superior Whitefish, Baked, with Savory Dressing and Lobster Sauce, **7**-1150
Lake Superior Whitefish, Planked, **7**-1147

Lamb, **7**-1024
Apple-Lamb Curry, **1**-97
Balls with Tomato Curry, **7**-1123
Barbecued in Foil, **7**-1032
Barbecued, on Riced Potato, **7**-1039
Bareh Pello, **8**-1215
and Barley Soup, **11**-1695
and Barley Stew (Bárány Pörkölt Árpakásával), **6**-918
Baryani, **12**-1957
and Bean Ragout, **7**-1036
Boiled, with Dill and Dill Sauce, Swedish, **4**-564
-Bone and Lima-Bean Soup, **7**-1065
Breast, Breast of
Baked Stuffed, **7**-1034
Baked Sweet-Sour, **7**-1034
with Beans, **1**-158
Pot-Roasted, with Dill Sauce, **9**-1475
Pot-Roasted Rosé, **9**-1475
Pot Roast with Raisin Sauce, **9**-1476
Rosé, **7**-1034
with Vegetables, Braised, **7**-1034
Broiled Cantonese, **7**-1032
and Cabbage (Fårikål), **8**-1239
Cacciatora (Agnello alla Cacciatora), **6**-954
-Carrot Moussaka, **8**-1189
Carving, **2**-312
Casserole, Italian, **2**-325
Casserole, Savory, **2**-320
Chafing-Dish (Yang Jo Kuo), **3**-400
Chili, Pueblo, **11**-1728
Chop(s)
with Apples and Potatoes, **7**-1034
with Artichokes, **10**-1560
Baked, **4**-568
Baked (Psita Paidakia), **5**-819
Barbecued, **7**-1033
Lancashire Hot Pot, **7**-1033
and Macaroni Skillet, **7**-1094
Marinated, East Indian, **7**-1034
Napa Valley, **1**-26
and Shallots in Casserole, **10**-1650
Stuffed, **7**-1033
Chutney, **7**-1039
Creamed, in Puff Shells, **7**-1039
Crown Roast of, **7**-1029
Cubes, Spiced Browned, **10**-1555
Cucumber, Aruba, **2**-301
Cucumber, and Tomato Salad, **10**-1580
Curry(ied), **4**-527
Indian Style, **2**-299
Indonesian (Kerie Kambing), **11**-1714
Jamaican, **8**-1205
Mold, **7**-1084
Rogan Josh, **6**-939
Daube (Daube d'Agneau), **5**-741
with Dill, Boiled (Kokt Lamm med Dillsås), **11**-1788
Easter Soup (Mageritsa), **5**-818
and Eggplant Stew, **7**-1038
and Fava Beans, Stewed (Vrasto Arni me Fava), **5**-819
Garlic Steaks, **11**-1770
Green Peppers, Stuffed, **8**-1216
Haricot, **7**-1029
Hash
Idaho, **1**-35
de Luxe, **7**-1039
Lyonnaise, **7**-1039
Hearts, **7**-1026
Irish Stew, **6**-948
Javanese, **11**-1753
Jellied (Yang Jo Kao), **3**-400
Kofta Curry, **4**-526
Lancashire Hot Pot, **4**-624
and Leek Skillet, **7**-1047
Leg(s), Leg of
Barbecue(d), Basque, **11**-1728; **12**-1930
Boiled, with Caper Sauce, **4**-624; **7**-1029
Boned, Broiled, **1**-146
Creole, **7**-1029
from Over the Hills (Carneiro Transmontano), **9**-1436
Roast, with Herb Mustard Glaze, **7**-1029
Roast, with Hot Curried Fruit, **11**-1753
Roast, Polish, **7**-1029
Roast, Rare, **7**-1029
Roast (Rôti d'Agneau), **2**-278
Roast with Sour-Cream Sauce, **11**-1698
Shashlik, **10**-1571
Weeping (Le Gigot Qui Pleure), **5**-741
and Limas, Curried, **7**-1039
Loaf, Pressed, **7**-1128
Loin of
Béarnaise, **7**-1029
Cold Roast, Garnished, **7**-1029
Low-Calorie Seasonings for, **7**-1084
Meatballs in Yogurt (Kibbeh bi Laban), **8**-1214
Meat Loaf (Kibbeh), **8**-1214
Meat Loaf, Stuffed (Kibbeh bi Sanieh), **8**-1214
Meat Roll (Rullepølse), **4**-536
Navarin, **7**-1032
-Neck Slices with Vegetables, **7**-1035
Nigerian Groundnut Stew, **8**-1324
and Onion Casserole, **2**-320
Patties, Baked, **8**-1313
Patties with Cranberry Mint Sauce, **7**-1151
Pie with Herb Crust, **7**-1036
Pie with Poppy-Seed Crust, **9**-1387
Pie, Shepherd's, **9**-1387
Pilaf, Savory Turkish, **7**-1038
and Potato Salad, Minted, **10**-1580
Ragout in Carrot-Potato Ring, **10**-1533
and Red-Bean Stew, **7**-1038
and Red Noodles, **7**-1039
Retail Cuts of, Chart, **7**-1026
Rib Roast (Rack) of, with Chutney Glaze, **7**-1029
Riblets, Deviled, **7**-1038
Roast, Roasted
Arrosto di Agnello, **6**-954
Cushion Shoulder of (Gevulde Lamsborst), **4**-590
Kentucky, **1**-40
with Mint Sauce and New Peas, **4**-624
Roll with Brown Sauce, **7**-1038
Salmagundi Salad, **7**-1039
Scotch Broth, **7**-1038
Serendipity, **9**-1406
Shanks
Baked in Fruited Wine, **12**-1928
Barbecued, **7**-1035
Braised, **2**-220; **7**-1034
Milanaise, **7**-1034
and Rice, Steamed, Indian, **7**-1035
Rice-Stuffed, **7**-1035
with Sour-Cream Sauce (Lammekjøtt i Sursaus), **8**-1239
Shish-Kabob (Kebab), **6**-997
Arab, **8**-1214
Iranian, **8**-1214
Turkish, **8**-1214
Shoulder
Herbed, **7**-1032
Spicy Roast, **7**-1032
on Skewers, **1**-53
Soufflé, Canadian, **7**-1040
in Sour Cream, Braised, **7**-1035
with Spinach (Palak Gosht), **6**-939
Steak(s)
Garlic, **7**-1032
in Marinade, **7**-1032
Orange, Baked, **7**-1032
Stew, **11**-1773
Armenian, **7**-1035
Brown, **11**-1773
French, **2**-216
Fruited, **9**-1485
Irish, **7**-1035
with Manestra (Vrasto Arni me Manestra), **5**-819
Mexican, **7**-1038
with Okra and Cuminseed, **4**-522
Puss Pass, **8**-1239
Spiced Meat (Masak Nadi), **11**-1715
Stuffed Grapvine Leaves with Lemon Sauce, Greek (Dolmadakia me Avgolemono), **4**-570
-Stuffed Green Peppers, **7**-1039
-Stuffed Zucchini, **12**-1961
Sweetbreads, **7**-1026
Timetable for Braising, Chart, **7**-1026
Timetable for Broiling, Chart, **7**-1026
Timetable for Roasting, Chart, **7**-1025
and Vegetable Casserole, **2**-320
-Vegetable Moussaka, **8**-1189
and Vegetable Soup, **7**-1038
in White Wine, **7**-1035

Lamb Brains, **7**-1026
Salad, **8**-1211
Lamb Casseroles, **2**-320

Lamb Kidney(s), **7**-1026
with Eggs, Guetaria, **7**-1014
Fritti Rognoni, **7**-1016
Lancashire Hot Pot, **7**-1033
Riñones a la Pamplona, **7**-1014

Lamb Kidney(s), continued
Rognons d'Agneau à la Lully, **7**-1014
Stew, Brunch, **7**-1040

Lamb Liver(s), **7**-1026
Balls and Noodles, **7**-1074
Creole, **7**-1074
Pot Roast with Noodles, **7**-1074
with Rice, **7**-1040
Savory Baked, **7**-1074

Lamb Tongue(s), **7**-1026
Potted, **7**-1040; **11**-1838
Lamb's-Quarters (Quelites), **11**-1731
Lammekjøtt i Sursaus (Lamb Shanks with Sour-Cream Sauce), **8**-1239
Lancashire Hot Pot, **4**-624; **7**-1033
Lancaster Squares, **8**-1310
Lapin Sauté à l'Estragon, **5**-772

Lard, **7**-1040
Pastry, **7**-1041
Larding, **2**-218; **7**-1041

Lasagna, **2**-316
Chicken, Make-Ahead, **7**-1041
Eggplant, **4**-616
Lasagne al Forno, **6**-873
with Marinara Sauce, Hearty, **7**-1041
with Meatballs (Lasagne con le Polpettine), **6**-958
Las Vegas Stuffed Tomatoes, **11**-1730
La Tieng (Shrimp Nets), **11**-1716
Laulau I'A (Fish Packages), **9**-1435
Laulau Pua (Pork and Salmon Packages), **9**-1435
Layer Cake, **7**-1042; for recipes see Cake(s)
Leavening, **7**-1045
Lebanese Pineapple, **9**-1408
Leberknödelsuppe (Liver Dumpling Soup), **5**-793

Lebkuchen, **3**-435
Almond, Dropped, **7**-1046
Chocolate, **7**-1046
Elisen, **5**-798
Honey, **7**-1046
Lechón de Mechar (Stuffed Eye Round), **9**-1494
Leckerli, **3**-433

Leek(s), **7**-1046
Braised (Gestoofde Prei), **4**-592
Braised, Niçoise, **12**-1902
and Chicken Casserole, **7**-1047
Cock-a-Leekie, Scotch, **7**-1047
Cock-a-Leekie Soup, **6**-945
and Fordhook Limas, **7**-1047
and Green-Pea Purée, **7**-1047
and Lamb Skillet, **7**-1047
Salad, **1**-57
Sausage-Leek Pie, **9**-1387
Soup, **7**-1047
Soup with Cheese, **3**-355
Lefser (Griddle Cakes), **8**-1241
Leipsiger Allerlei (Vegetable Medley), **5**-796
Lekah (Honey Cake), **6**-993

Lemon, **7**-1050
Ambrosia Pie with Coconut Crust, **9**-1397
Angel Cake Lemon Delight, **7**-1088
-Apple Punch, **7**-1057
Barbecue Sauce, Savory, **1**-146
Bavarian, **1**-150
Bavarois au Citron, **7**-1054
-Broiled Shrimps, **7**-1052
Butter, **2**-254, 279; **10**-1615, 1624
Buttermilk Sherbet, **7**-1054
Cake Pudding, **9**-1490
and Caper Butter, **5**-695
Cheesecake, Frozen, **5**-791
Cheese Pie, **7**-1054
Chicken, Portuguese, Jellied, **7**-1052
Chiffon Pie, **7**-1054
Chiffon Pie in Pastry Shell, **9**-1397
Cream Pie, **7**-1053
Cream Rice Pudding, **9**-1491
Cream Sauce, **11**-1757
Curd, **7**-1056
-Curd Filling, **9**-1382
Custard, Low-Calorie Frozen, **7**-1054
Custard Sauce, **7**-1056
and Egg Sauce, Greek, **10**-1627
Filling, Fancy, **11**-1792
Filling, Lemon-Orange, **1**-15
Filling, Rich, **4**-663
Fluff Dessert (QC), **10**-1525
Frappé, **6**-925
French Dressing, **7**-1053
Fresh Lemon(s)
Barbecue Sauce, **7**-1053
Browned-Butter Sauce, **7**-1053
Dessert Sauce, **7**-1056
Golden Sauce, **9**-1417
-and-Orange Party Punch, **7**-1056
Peach Cooler, **7**-1056
Sherbet, **7**-1054
Frosting, **7**-1046, 1056
Frosting, Boiled, **5**-750
Frosting, Fluffy, **7**-1056
Garnishes, **5**-779; **10**-1666
Gelatin Salad, Spiced Prunes in, **11**-1754
Ginger Jelly, **7**-1056
Gingered Lemon Pineapple, **9**-1410
Granité, **5**-810
Hard Sauce, **6**-878; **9**-1493
-Honey Dressing, **7**-1053
-Honey Spread, **6**-911
-Honey Syrup, **5**-823
Ice, Instant Blender, **6**-925
Lemonade-Mint Punch, **5**-804
-Lime Sherbet, **5**-790
Iced Tea, **11**-1816
Icing, **11**-1793
Icing, Simple, **12**-1853
Lemon-Cheese Cake, **11**-1725
Lemon-Cheese Filling, **11**-1725
Lemon-Cheese Tarts, **11**-1725
Lotus Ice Cream, **8**-1276
Marmalade, **7**-1057
Meringue Pie, **7**-1053
Meringue Pie, Old-Fashioned, **9**-1392
Mousse, **8**-1191
-Nut Cookies, **7**-1056
-Orange Filling, **7**-1056
-Orange Refrigerator Cake, **7**-1056
and Orange Salad, **7**-1052
Pie, Frozen, **9**-1398
Pudding, Steamed, **7**-1054
Sauce, **2**-210; **5**-790, 804; **9**-1493; **10**-1628
Sauce, Clear, **7**-1054
Sauce (QC), **10**-1525
Sherbet, **10**-1652
Sliced-Lemon Pie, **7**-1053
Slump, **8**-1229
Soufflé, **7**-1054
Soup, Greek, **7**-1052
Sponge Pie, **7**-1053; **9**-1390
Squares with Apricot Glaze, **9**-1382
Strip Pie, **9**-1355
Sweet-Potato Pudding, **11**-1724
Tarts, **8**-1309
Toast, **11**-1826
Toast Butter, **11**-1829
Topping, **7**-1088
Velvet Pudding, **1**-52
Wedges, Pickled, **7**-1057

Lemonade, **7**-1057
Claret, **7**-1057
Syrup, **7**-1057
-Tea, Iced, **7**-1057
Lemon Balm, Compote of Fresh Fruits with, **1**-138
Leniwe Pierogi (Lazy Dumplings), **9**-1429
Lenten Cake (Eggless), **6**-949

Lentil(s), **7**-1058
Curry with Rice, **7**-1059
with Dandelion Greens, **4**-534
and Escarole Soup, Italian, **4**-652
Frankfurter and Puréed Lentil Soup, **5**-720
Indian Kitchree, **10**-1551
Moussaka, **8**-1187
and Potato Casserole, **7**-1059
Purée with Poached Eggs, **7**-1059
Salad, **7**-1059
Sauce, **7**-1059
with Sausage, **7**-1059
Soup, **1**-39
Chilled, Syrian Style, **11**-1692
Cream-of-, **7**-1059
Faki Soupa, **5**-818
and Spinach, Thick, **7**-1059
Thick, **7**-1059
Spicy, with Tomato Sauce, **7**-1059
Leopold Schnitten (cookies), **3**-447
Lerida Lima Beans (Judías Blancas a la Leridana), **11**-1744
Letse Plan (Custard Pudding), **9**-1370

Lettuce, **7**-1061
Braised, **12**-1902
Browned-Butter, Wilted, **12**-1934
Cheese-Stuffed, Salad, **7**-1063
Garden, with Bacon Dressing, **7**-1061
Green Onions, and Peas, **7**-1061
German, Salad, **7**-1064
and Green Peas, **7**-1063
Green Salad, **4**-650
Norwegian Fashion (Salat), **8**-1240
Romaine, **10**-1559
with Peas (Kopfsalat with Erbsen), **1**-123
Salad, **4**-633
Salad, **4**-646
Sauce with Asparagus, **7**-1063
Soup, Cream-of-, **7**-1061
and Tomato Avocadaise, **11**-1837
Wilted, **1**-38; **7**-1063; **9**-1354
Leverpostej (Liver Pâté), **4**-536
Liaison, **10**-1615
Liang Pan Huang Kua (Pickled Cucumbers), **3**-403
Liberal Pancakes, **1**-39
Liffey Trout with Mushroom Sauce, **6**-945
Liha ja Perunamureke (Sliced Beef and Potato Loaf), **5**-680
Lihakohokas (Meat Soufflé), **5**-680
Lima Bean(s), **7**-1064; for recipes see Bean(s), Lima; Bean(s), Dried
Lima Style Soup (Sopa a la Limeña), **11**-1703

Lime, **7**-1067
Avocado Pie, **1**-130
and Blueberry Salad, Molded, **7**-1067
and Cheese Salad, Jellied, **7**-1067
Chicken Soup, **11**-1717
Chiffon Pie, **9**-1397
Concord Lime Jelly, **6**-982
Dressing, **3**-451
Fresh Lime(s)
Cream, **7**-1067
French Dressing, **7**-1067
Froth, **7**-1069
Melon Cup, **7**-1067
Minted Mold with Watermelon Balls, **7**-1067
-Frosted Papaya, **12**-1933
Frosting, Boiled, **5**-750
Garnishes, **5**-779; **10**-1666
-Ginger Foam, **7**-1067
-Grape Dessert, **7**-1088
Julep, **7**-1069
Key Lime Pie, **7**-1069
Key Lime Pie with Peaches, **8**-1320
-Orange Conserve, **7**-1069
-Pear Salad, **8**-1330
Pie, Florida, **8**-1069
Relish, **10**-1542
Sherbet, **7**-1069; **10**-1652
Tarts, **7**-1069
Watermelon-Lime Cooler, **12**-1920

Limpa Bread, **2**-229
Limu Niu (Coconut Spinach), **9**-1435
Lindströmin Pihvi (Beef à la Lindstrom), **5**-680
Lindy's Strawberry-Glazed Cheesecake, **3**-367
Lingonberries with Cabbage Salad (Kålsallad med Lingon), **11**-1791
Linguado Recheado (Ana of Povoa's Stuffed Sole), **9**-1455
Linzer Torte, **4**-635

Liqueur, **7**-1069
Soufflé, **11**-1688
Liquids, To Measure, **7**-1117
Lisbon Turkey Stuffing (Recheio a Moda de Lisboa Para Peru), **9**-1457

Litchi or **Lichee Nut,** **7**-1071
Gelatin Dessert, **7**-1072
and Peach Dessert, Jellied, **7**-1072
Salad, **7**-1072
Litsong Baboy (Barbecued Suckling Pig), **9**-1369

Liver, **7**-1072
Beef
and Bacon, Broiled, **2**-192
French-Fried, **7**-1073
and Limas, Creole, **7**-1073
Liver Dumpling Soup (Leberknödelsuppe), **5**-793
and Noodles, Italian Style, **7**-1073
and Onions, Smothered, **7**-1073
with Onions, Venetian, **2**-192
Panfried, **2**-192
Potted, Danish Style, **2**-192
Pudding, **1**-49
and Sausage Loaf, **10**-1636
-and-Sausage Ring, Savory, **7**-1073
Sautéed, Bernese (Berner Leberli), **11**-1802
and Vegetables, Piquant, **7**-1073
and Brown-Rice Ring, **7**-1073
Calf's Liver (Veal)
Baked, **9**-1351
Deviled (Athae Chin Gyaw), **11**-1717
Dumplings, Delicate, **7**-1074
Loaf, **7**-1128
Pirozhki, **10**-1568
Sautéed (Geröstete Kalbsleber), **1**-122
Steak Béarnaise, **7**-1073; **12**-1897
Swiss, **7**-1073
Chicken
-and-Bacon Sandwiches, **7**-1076
with Carrots and Peas, **7**-1075
Chopped, **6**-987; **7**-1075
Cutlets, **9**-1470
and Green Beans, Sautéed, **7**-1075
Omelet, **7**-1075
Pâté, **7**-1075
Pâté, Ruby-Glazed, **6**-979
with Rice Soup, Italian, **7**-1075
with Sage, **10**-1578
with Sage (Fegatini di Pollo alla Salvia), **6**-955
Sauce, **7**-1076
in Sour Cream, **7**-1076
Terrine, Quick and Easy, **8**-1312
in Curry-Tomato Sauce, Braised, **7**-1072
Deviled in Croustades, **7**-1073
Dumplings, **4**-586; **7**-1147
Goose
and Greben, Chopped, **7**-1075
To Cook whole, see Pâté de Foie Gras, **5**-708
Lamb
Balls and Noodles, **7**-1074
Creole, **7**-1074
Pot Roast with Noodles, **7**-1074
with Rice, **7**-1040
Savory Baked, **7**-1074
and Mushrooms, **7**-1072; **8**-1198
Pâté (Leverpostej), **4**-536
Pork
with Barbecue Sauce, **7**-1074
in Mustard Sour-Cream Sauce, **11**-1698
with Onions, French, **7**-1075
Pâté, Danish, **7**-1074
Pot-Roasted, with Barbecue Sauce, **9**-1476
Pudding, Old-Fashioned, **9**-1448
Sauce, **9**-1369
and Vegetable Pie, Savory, **7**-1075
and Vegetables, **7**-1074
Pudding (Maksalaatikko), **5**-680
Sausage, see Liverwurst
Sliced, with Spleen Sauce (Iscas), **9**-1456
Steaks, **11**-1771

Liverwurst or **Liver Sausage,** **7**-1076
Appetizer Salad, **10**-1635
with Creole Sauce, **7**-1076
Filling, **4**-662
Masked Liver Mold, **10**-1635
Mushroom Liver Pâté, **7**-1076; **8**-1197
Patties, **7**-1076
Potato, and Egg Salad, **7**-1076
Sandwiches, **7**-1076
Spread, **2**-280
Lizzies, **3**-435
Llapingachos (Potato and Cheese Patties), **11**-1708

Lobster, **7**-1076
-Avocado Sandwiches, **7**-1081
Bisque, **7**-1077
Bordelaise, **2**-213
au Brandy, **7**-1078
Broiled, **1**-146
Butter, **10**-1615, 1624
Cantonese (Ch'ao Lung Hsia), **3**-399
Casserole à la Costa, **7**-1080
Chowder, **3**-419
Chowder, Fish, Jamaican, **6**-967
Crab-Stuffed, **7**-1080
Egg-Lobster Salad, Molded, **7**-1080
Fried (Gebratener Hummer), **5**-793
Liguanea, **7**-1081
Lobsterburgers, **10**-1602
Macaroni, and Artichoke Salad, **7**-1092
Macaroni, and Orange Salad, **7**-1092
Marinade for, Uncooked, **7**-1110
-Muffin Sandwiches, **11**-1722
and Mushrooms Parmesan, **8**-1198
Newburg, **7**-1078; **8**-1218
-Noodle Casserole, **2**-321
and Orange Cocktail, **7**-1077
Pie (Quiche de Langouste), **5**-740
Pilaf, **2**-321
Quiche, **10**-1529
Rabbit, **7**-1081
Ring, Jellied, **7**-1080
Salad, **10**-1583
Salad, English Style, **4**-621
Salad Tropicale, **10**-1581
Sauce, **5**-695; **7**-1150
Sauce (Hummersaus), **8**-1236
and Shell Chowder, **7**-1091
Soufflé, **7**-1078
Spread, **2**-280
Stew, **7**-1078
Stew, Wiscasset, **1**-45

Lobster, Rock-Lobster Tails
in Almond Sauce, **7**-1078
Boiled, **9**-1384
and Chicken, Costa Brava, **7**-1080
Chowder, **7**-1078
Curried, **7**-1078
Deviled, South African, **7**-1080
and Fillet of Cod Sarapico, **7**-1080
French-Fried Butterfly, **7**-1078
Salad, Curried, **10**-1582
Steamed, **7**-1078
Stuffed, **7**-1081

Loganberry(ies), **7**-1081
-Cheese Tarts, **7**-1081
Ice, **7**-1082
Jam, **6**-965; **7**-1082
Pie, **7**-1081
Loggers' Flapjacks, **5**-703
Løksaus (Onion Sauce), **8**-1240

Lokshen Kugel (Noodle Pudding), **6**-993
Lomi Lomi Salmon (Hawaiian Salad), **1**-34
London Broil, see Beef, Flank Steak

Loquat(s), **7**-1082
Jam, **7**-1082
Spiced, **7**-1082
Lord Baltimore Cake, **1**-46
Lord Baltimore Cake, Golden, **7**-1045
Lorenzo à la Filipini, **2**-281
Lorraine Salad, **9**-1469
Losós do Sosów Goracych i Zimnych (Poached Salmon), **9**-1422
Lotus Ice Cream, **8**-1276
Louis Dressing, **10**-1614, 1622
Louisiana Pancakes, **11**-1797
Louisiana Pecan Cake, **4**-513

Low Calorie, **7**-1082
Angel Cake Lemon Delight, **7**-1088
Apricot Whip, Baked, **7**-1087
Banana Slim Shake, **7**-1088
Beef Patties, Barbecued, **7**-1084
Blueberry-Topped Cheesecake, **7**-1087
Buttermilk Dressing (salad), **2**-254
Canapé, Cheese Mushroom, **3**-355
Cheese-Tomato Grill, **7**-1085
Chicken, Fried, **3**-383
Chicken, Glazed Roast, **7**-1084
Chocolate Mousse, **3**-415
Chocolate Sauce, **3**-416
Cod Fillets, Creole, **7**-1084
Coffee Sponge, **7**-1087
Cottage Beef and Eggs, **7**-1084
Cottage Cheese and Cucumber Salad, **7**-1085
Crab-Cheese Dip, **7**-1083
Cucumber Sauce, **7**-1086
Curried Lamb Mold, **7**-1084
Eggs, Swiss, **7**-1085
Fruit-Cocktail Whip, **7**-1088
Green-Bean and Carrot Salad, **7**-1085
Green Beans, Cape Cod Style, **7**-1086
Green Peppers, Sautéed, **7**-1086
Lemon Custard, Frozen, **7**-1054
Lemon Topping, **7**-1088
Lime-Grape Dessert, **7**-1088
Mocha Molds, **7**-1167
Mushrooms, Stuffed, **7**-1083
Onions and Cucumber, Curried, **7**-1086
Orange Cake, **7**-1087
Orange-Milk Starter, **7**-1088
Peach Sherbet, **7**-1087
Pineapple Sherbet, **9**-1410
Radishes, Braised, **7**-1087
Radish Salad, Panama, **7**-1086
Salad Dressing, Cooked, **7**-1086
Salad Dressing, Piquant, **7**-1086
Salad, Patio, **7**-1085
Salad, Silhouette, **7**-1086
Seasonings for Fish, Meat, and Poultry, **7**-1084
Seasonings for Vegetables, **7**-1086
Shrimps and Vegetables, Skewered, **7**-1084
Slick Chick Soup, **7**-1083
Strawberry Fluff, **7**-1087
Tomatoes and Cabbage, Simmered, **7**-1087
Tomato Salad Dressing, **7**-1086
Tuna Salad, Jellied, **7**-1085
Tuna, Scalloped, **7**-1084
Vegetable Soup, Creole, **7**-1084
Luau, Chicken, **1**-34

Luncheon Menus
Buffet Luncheon, **7**-1089
Intimate Luncheon, **4**-632
Parisian Luncheon, **4**-633
Salad Luncheon, **7**-1189
Spring Luncheon, **4**-632
Lusitanian Oysters (Ostras Lusitanas), **9**-1456
Lutfisk, see Cod, Codfish

M

Maamoul (Farina Cakes), **8**-1216

Macaroni, **7**-1090
Bean, and Egg Salad, **7**-1095
and Beans, Thick Soup of (Minestrone di Pasta e Fagiuoli), **6**-952
with Beef, Red-Wine, **7**-1094
and Cheese, Bacon-Topped, **7**-1093
and Cheese, Creamy, **3**-358
and Cheese with Frankfurters, **5**-720
and Cheese with Ham-Asparagus Rolls, **6**-858
and Cheese, Peanut, **8**-1322
and Cheese Salad, **7**-1095
and Cheese Soufflé, **7**-1095
Cheese, and Sour-Cream Salad, **10**-1582
and Cheese, Tossed, **7**-1095
Chicken-Macaroni Salad, Baked, **7**-1094
Clam, and Cheese Casserole, **7**-1091
Crab and Shell Chowder, **7**-1091
Double-Cheese Casserole, **7**-1096
Egg-Macaroni Salad, **7**-1095
and Eggplant Casserole, Sicilian, **7**-1095
Finnish, **7**-1095
and Fish Casserole, Company, **7**-1091
and Fish Salad, **7**-1092
-Frankfurter Skillet, **7**-1094
Hamburger, and Green-Bean Casserole, **7**-1094
Hamburger-Macaroni Casserole, **6**-872
and Ham Salad, Hot, **7**-1094
and Lamb-Chop Skillet, **7**-1094
Lobster, and Artichoke Salad, **7**-1092
Lobster, and Orange Salad, **7**-1092
Lobster and Shell Chowder, **7**-1091
-Meat Timbale, **7**-1094
Parmesan, **7**-1095
with Pork Balls, **7**-1094
Salad (QC), **10**-1523
Salad, Danish, **7**-1095
Shell, and Peas (Piselli e Pasta), **6**-959
Shells and Ham Balls in Skillet, **7**-1093
Shrimp-and-Cheese Loaf, **7**-1091
Shrimp, and Orange Salad, **7**-1092
Shrimp Salad, **10**-1662
Shrimp and Shell Chowder, **7**-1091
Sour-Cream Casserole, **7**-1095
Stuffing, **11**-1834
with Tomatoes and Cheese, Baked, **7**-1095
Tuna-Macaroni Bake, **12**-1864
Tuna Mushroom, **12**-1864
Tuna, and Orange Salad, **7**-1092

Macaroon(s), **7**-1096
Almond, **1**-15
Angel Pudding, **7**-1096
Brazil-Nut, **7**-1096
Cherry-Coconut, **7**-1096
Chocolate, **7**-1096
Coconut, **3**-458; **7**-1096
Coffee-Nut, **2**-314
Cornflake, **7**-1096
Cornflake-Coconut, **1**-67
Cream, **7**-1097
Cream, Strawberry-Macaroon, **11**-1778
Danish, **7**-1096
Macaroons, **7**-1096

Mace, **7**-1097
Banana-Mace Whipped Topping, **7**-1100
Butterscotch-Mace Sundae Sauce, **7**-1100
Cheese Puffs, **7**-1097
Coffeecakes, **7**-1100
Poppy-Seed Cookies, **7**-1100
Macédoine of Fruit, **4**-568
Macedoine de Frutas Exoticas (Tropical Fruits in Liqueur), **11**-1709
Macédoine of Vegetables, **7**-1100

Mackerel, **7**-1100
Baked, **7**-1101
Baked, with Mushroom Stuffing, Savory, **5**-689
Baked Stuffed, **7**-1101
Broiled, with Mustard Sauce, **5**-689; **7**-1101
Dingle, **6**-945
Pickled, with Cucumber Slices, **7**-1101
Pie, **7**-1101
Salt Mackerel, Baked in Cream, **7**-1101
Sautéed Meunière, **7**-1101
Tartare Fish Loaf with Caper Sauce, **7**-1101
Madame Fraize's Cabbage and Zucchini Skillet, **12**-1903
Madame Fraize's Tomatoes Provençal, **12**-1900
Madeira Sauce, **9**-1424; **11**-1766
Madeira Sauce for Ham, **3**-439
Madeira Sauce (Sauce Madère), **5**-740; **6**-865
Madeleines, **7**-1102
Madère Sauce, **10**-1613, 1619
Mad Hatter Cheesecake, **3**-366
Madras Chicken Pilau, **9**-1401
Madrilene, **7**-1102; for recipes see Soup(s), Bouillon(s) and Consommé(s) and Soup(s), Chilled, Frozen, or Jellied
Maduros en Gloria (Heavenly Bananas), **11**-1709
Mae's Date Cookies, **3**-476
Mageritsa (Easter Soup), **5**-818
Magic Cream (Trollkrem), **8**-1241
Magyar Gulyás (Hungarian Goulash), **6**-918
Maia Kalua (Baked Banana), **9**-1435
Maiale Affogato (Stewed Pork with Celery), **6**-954
Maibowle, **12**-1949
Maids of Honour, **4**-626
Raspberry, **8**-1309
Maillane Style Green Beans (Haricots Verts Maillanoise), **12**-1903
Maine Corned-Beef Hash, **6**-879
Maine Seafood Chowder, **1**-45
Maionese di Scampi e Cavolfiori (Shrimp and Cauliflower Salad), **1**-82
Maître d'Hôtel Butter, **2**-211, 254; **7**-1014; **10**-1615, 1624
Majorannás Tokány (Beef Stew with Marjoram), **6**-918
Makos Tészta (Boiled Noodles with Poppy Seeds), **6**-920
Makovy Kolác (Poppy-Seed Layer Torte), **4**-532
Maksalaatikko (Liver Pudding), **5**-680
Malaxe (Cheese Spread), **3**-355
Malay Layer Cake (Spiku), **11**-1715
Malayan Pork Kabobs, **8**-1324
Mallung (vegetables for curry dinner), **4**-527
Maltaise Sauce, **6**-906; **10**-1614, 1621
Mamaliga (Cornmeal Mush), **6**-995
Mandarin Orange(s), see Orange(s)
Mandelbrot (Almond Bread), **6**-992
Mandelkränze (Almond Wreaths), **5**-798
Mandelterter (Almond Tarts and Cookies), **8**-1243

Mango(es), **7**-1102
Chutney, **3**-446
Chutney, Spicy, **7**-1104
Ice Cream, **7**-1104
Jam, **7**-1104
Pie, **7**-1103
Rum Sundae, **7**-1104
Stewed, **7**-1103
Tarts, **7**-1103
Manhattan Clam Chowder, **3**-418

Manicotto, Manicotti, **7**-1104
à la Béchamel, **7**-1104
Meat-Filled, **7**-1104
with Meat Sauce, Baked, **7**-1104
Stuffed Pancakes, II, **6**-958
Manila Meat Loaf, **7**-1128

Manioc, **7**-1104
Farofa, **11**-1709
Manitaria Toursi (Pickled Mushrooms), **4**-639

Maple, **7**-1105
Buckwheat Cakes, **5**-826
Butternut Cake, **2**-255
Candied-Sweet Potatoes, **11**-1796
Cottage Pudding, **7**-1107
Cream, **1**-74
Custard, **1**-56
Date-Nut Bread, **7**-1105
Freeze, **7**-1108
Gelatin, **7**-1107
Graham Cream, Frozen, **7**-1107
Icing, **1**-63; **7**-1108
Lace Wafers, **7**-1108
-Nut Fudge Frosting, **5**-751
Parfait, **7**-1108
Pineapple Sauce, **7**-1107
Sea Foam Frosting, **5**-750
Sugar, **11**-1784
Sugar Frosting, **2**-255
Sugar on Snow, **1**-74
Sugaring-Off Pie, **7**-1108
Syrup with Baked Apple, **7**-1107
-Syrup Cake, **7**-1108
-Syrup Cake, Buckeye, **1**-63
Syrup, Hot Spiced, **11**-1807
Maracay Pumpkin Soup (Sopa de Calabaza Maracay), **11**-1704
Marängsuisse (Cream Meringue Torte), **11**-1792
Maraschino, **7**-1108; for recipes, see Cherry(ies), Maraschino
Marchand de Vin Sauce, Brennan's, **4**-512
Margarine, **7**-1109

Marinade(s), **7**-1109
Beer, for Beef, Game, or Shrimps, **7**-1110
(for Canton beef), **3**-399
(for Canton pork), **3**-399
Cooked, for Meats and Game, **7**-1109
(for Duck), **1**-122
for Fruits, **7**-1110
(for Fukien chicken), **3**-400
Oil, **5**-769
for Pheasant, **9**-1367
Uncooked, for Meats, **7**-1110
Uncooked, for Shrimps or Lobster, **7**-1110
Uncooked, for Small Portions of Chicken, Meat, Fish, or Seafood, **7**-1110
for Vegetables, **7**-1110
Vinegar, for Meat, **9**-1422
Marinara Sauce, **7**-1041; **11**-1737
Mariner's Sauce (Salsa alla Marinara), **6**-959

Marjoram, **7**-1110
Veal Chops, **7**-1110
Markklösschen (Marrow Dumplings in Consommé), **5**-793

Marmalade, **7**-1111
Blueberry, **7**-1111
Coriander Tomato, **3**-478
Cranberry, **7**-1111
Green Tomato, **11**-1836
Lemon, **7**-1057
Orange-Ginger, **3**-429
Orange-Marmalade Cake, **8**-1272
Peach, **7**-1111
Peanut-Butter Marmalade Coffeecake, **8**-1326
Pudding, **9**-1492
Quince, **7**-1111
Quince Ginger, **10**-1529
Seville-Orange, **6**-1111
Toast, Spiced, **11**-1828
Tropical, **6**-980

Turnovers, **12**-1880
Valencia-Orange, **7**-1111
Marmitako (Basque Fresh-Tuna Stew), **11**-1743
Marron, **7**-1112; for recipes see Chestnut(s) and Marron(s)

Marrow, Beef, **7**-1112
Balls (Dumplings), **2**-192; **7**-1113
Beef Bone, Poached, **2**-192
Beef Bone, Roasted, **2**-192
Dumplings in Consommé (Markklösschen), **5**-793
Poached (Moelle Pochée), **5**-741
Sauce, **7**-1113
Soup, Marrowbone, **7**-1112
Toast, **4**-627; **7**-1112
Marrow, Vegetable, **7**-1113; **11**-1759; for recipes see Zucchini

Marshmallow(s), **2**-284; **7**-1113
Black-and-White Delight, **7**-1114
Cocoa Pudding, **7**-1113
Coconut, **2**-289
Dessert, Fluffy, **7**-1113
Frosting, **3**-375; **4**-559; **5**-750
Marshmallow, **2**-288; **7**-1113
Peach Delight, **8**-1320
Peach Marlow, **7**-1113
Pineapple Rice Pudding, **10**-1554
Sticks, Crispy, **7**-1113
Sweet-Potato Balls, **11**-1797
Martha Washington's Crab Soup, **1**-75
Maryland Diamondback Terrapin Stew, **11**-1819
Maryland Fried Chicken, **1**-46
Maryland Muskrat, **5**-769
Maryland Steamed Hard-Shell Crabs, **3**-487
Marzipan, **7**-1114, 1115; **8**-1243
Masa, To Make, **3**-480
Masak Nadi (Spiced Meat Stew), **11**-1715
Matelote of Eels, Normandy, **4**-595
Matsutaki Dobin (Steamed Mushrooms), **6**-976

Matzo(s)
Balls, **7**-1147
Balls (Knaidlach), **4**-586; **6**-987
Fried (Matzo Brie), **6**-994
-Meal Fritters (Chremslach), **6**-994
-Meal Pudding (Matzo Kugel), **6**-994
Matzo Brie (Fried Matzos), **6**-994
Matzo Kugel (Matzo-Meal Pudding), **6**-994

Mayonnaise, **4**-573; **7**-1115; **10**-1614
Aïoli, Aïoli Sauce (Garlic Mayonnaise), **1**-7; **5**-740; **10**-1614, 1621
Anchovy, **10**-1614, 1621
Basic Recipe, **7**-1115; **10**-1621
Blender, **7**-1116
Blue-Cheese Dressing, **7**-1115
Caper Dressing, **7**-1116
Chantilly, **4**-573
Chili, **7**-1116
Chutney Dressing, **7**-1116
Cocktail Sauce, **10**-1626
with Cooked Base, **7**-1116
Cream Dressing, **10**-1621
Cucumber-Mayonnaise Dressing, **10**-1621
Cumberland Dressing, **7**-1116
Curry, **4**-573; **5**-694; **7**-1116; **10**-1622
for Fish, **5**-695
Fruit-Salad Dressing, **7**-1116
Garlic (Aïoli Sauce), **1**-7; **5**-740; **10**-1614, 1621
Gelatin, **7**-1116
Ginger Dressing, **10**-1622
Green Goddess Salad Dressing, **12**-1931
Green Sauce, **10**-1652
Herbed, **5**-700
Louis Dressing, **10**-1614, 1622
Mixed Herb, **5**-695; **7**-1116
Mustard, **5**-695; **8**-1205; **10**-1614, 1622
Mustard Cream, **10**-1614, 1622
Paprika Dressing, **10**-1622
Piquant Sauce, **5**-695
-Roquefort Dressing, Creamy, **10**-1622
Rosemary, **5**-695
Rouge, **10**-1614, 1622
Russian Dressing, **4**-573; **7**-1116; **10**-1614, 1622
Sauce Verte, **10**-1614, 1622
Sharp-Cheddar Dressing, **7**-1116
Stabilized, **5**-780
Tartare Sauce, **4**-517, 574; **5**-695; **7**-1116; **10**-1614, 1622
Tartare Sauce, Hot, **5**-695
Thousand Island Dressing, **4**-574; **5**-695; **7**-1116; **10**-1614, 1622
Tomato, **5**-695
Mazarin Torte (Mazarintårta), **11**-1793
Mazarintårta (Mazarin Torte), **11**-1793
Mazurek Migdałowy (Almond Mazurka), **9**-1431

Measures
Equivalent Amounts, various foods, chart, **7**-1117
Equivalent Measures, chart, **7**-1117

Meat(s), **7**-1119; see also names of meats
and Anchovy Pirozhki, **10**-1570
Blind Rabbit, **1**-53
Brunswick Stew for a Crowd, **11**-1722
Burgoo, Kentucky, **1**-40
Canning, **2**-295
Casserole, Slavic, **11**-1698
Cassoulet, **2**-325
-Cheese Rice, **10**-1550
with Chili (Chile con Carne), **7**-1140
Chili con Carne (QC), **10**-1520
Chili con Carne Sauce, **8**-1282
Chopped, with Peas (Keema Matar), **6**-939
Chow Meins, **7**-1049
Curried Turnovers (Samosas), **12**-1879
Curries, **7**-1049
Dressings, **4**-573
Dumplings (Kreplach), **6**-995
Filled Manicotti, **7**-1104
Filling, **1**-48; **6**-995; **10**-1538
Filling, Basic, **4**-662
Fondue Bourguignonne, **5**-712; **11**-1803
Fritters, **5**-749
Hash and Eggs (Pytt i Panne), **8**-1237
Hunters' Stew (Bigos Mysliwski), **9**-1426
Karelian Hot Pot (Karjalanpaisti), **8**-1205
Leftovers, à la King, **7**-1050
Leftovers, Barbecue-Style, **7**-1050
Leftovers, Creole-Style, **7**-1049
Luncheon Meat, Potato-Topped, **9**-1463
Macaroni-Meat Timbale, **7**-1094
Marinade for, Cooked, **7**-1109
Marinade for Small Portions of, Uncooked, **7**-1110
Marinade for, Uncooked, **7**-1110
Mixed Grill, **11**-1803
Mixed Grill, The Fabulous, **5**-827
Noodle Casseroles, **7**-1049
Noodle Dish, The Poor Parson's, **8**-1233
Paella de la Costa Brava, **11**-1746
Pancake Roll Ups, **7**-1049
Pancakes, **2**-247
Pastries, **11**-1696
Pâté, King's Point, **8**-1278
Pemmican, **9**-1349
Pichelsteiner Casserole (Pichelsteiner Fleisch), **1**-121
Pie, Baked, **9**-1351
Pie (Pastel de Carne), **11**-1705
Pies (Hallacas), **11**-1706
Pies, Mexican, **7**-1049
Pies, Special Pastry for, **8**-1304
Pinwheels, **7**-1049
Puchero, **9**-1486
Ragout of Variety Meats, **12**-1885
Rhubarb Sauce for, **11**-1753
Rice Casseroles, **7**-1049
-and-Rice Stuffing, Turkish, **11**-1782
Rolls with Pine Nuts, **9**-1410
Salad (Kjøttsalat), **8**-1235
Sandwich Fillings, **10**-1606
Sauce, Bolognese, **11**-1738
Sauce for Spaghetti, **2**-193
Sauces for (Swedish), **11**-1791
Shepherd's Pies, **7**-1049
Shish Kebab, **1**-146
Soufflé (Lihakohokas), **5**-680
Spaghetti Sauce (QC), **10**-1523
Stew, Spiced (Masak Nadi), **11**-1715
Stuffed Bread (Gefülltes Brot), **11**-1803
Stuffed Vegetables, **7**-1050
Stuffings for, **11**-1781
Szekely Sauerkraut Goulash (Székely Gulyás), **6**-919
To Corn, **3**-485
To Freeze, **5**-733; see also information under entry for specific meat
Tokany, Seven Chieftains' (Hét Vezér Tokány), **6**-918
Two-Cheese Meat Tarts, **11**-1811
and Vegetable Hash, **8**-1224
and Vegetable Salad, **10**-1580
and Vegetable Stew (Puchero), **11**-1706

Meatball(s), **7**-1122
Albóndigas, **11**-1705
Almôndegas, **9**-1456
with Almond-Mushroom Noodles, **6**-870
Barley-Onion Soup with Beef Balls, **7**-1122
Beef Balls, Spicy, in Milk Gravy, **7**-1122
Beef Balls Stroganoff, **2**-250
Beef Balls, Sweet-and-Sour (T'ang Ts'u Niu Ju Wan), **3**-399
Beef and Kidney-Bean Balls, **7**-1123
Beef and Pork, Sweet-and-Sour, **7**-1126
Burgundy, with Raisin Sauce, **6**-869
Buttermilk Beef Balls, **7**-1122
Chili, **6**-870
Chili Pork Balls in Tomato Sauce, **9**-1449
Cocktail, **2**-189
and Corn, Barbecued, **3**-482; **7**-1123
in Curried Tomato Sauce, **6**-870
Danish, **7**-1123
Danish (Frikadeller), **4**-540
Dill, **4**-643
with Egg-Lemon Sauce (Giouvarlakia Avgolemono), **5**-819
with Fricasseed Chicken, Flemish (Kiek met Ballekens), **7**-1122
Ham Balls, **7**-1151
Ham Balls and Macaroni Shells in Skillet, **7**-1093
Hamburger Balls with Prunes, Spiced, **9**-1483
Ham-and-Pork Balls, Baked, **6**-855
and Italian Spaghetti (QC), **10**-1523
Kjøttkaker, **8**-1237
Koenigsberger Klops, **1**-62
Königsberger, **6**-870
Lamb Balls with Tomato Curry, **7**-1123
with Lasagna (Lasagne con le Polpettine), **6**-958
Lima-Bean Soup with Sausage Balls, **7**-1122
Liver Balls and Noodles, **7**-1074
Meatball Shepherd's Pie, **6**-872
Mexican, **8**-1273
-Noodle Skillet, **8**-1232
Peanut Hamburger Balls, **6**-870
Polish Style, **7**-1123
Porcupines with Vegetable-Cheese Sauce, **7**-1123
Pork Balls, Danish, **9**-1449
Pork Balls with Noodles, **9**-1450
Sausage-Ball Appetizers, Spicy, **7**-1122
Sausage-Beef Patties, Smothered, **10**-1638
Small (Små Köttbullar), **11**-1786
Soup, **1**-24
Soup Meatballs (Soepballetjes), **4**-589
Soup (Sopa de Albóndigas), **1**-59
with Spaghetti, **11**-1736
with Spaghetti (Spaghetti con le Polpettine), **6**-955
Swedish, **7**-1123; **10**-1665
Swedish (Köttbullar), **2**-191
Swedish (QC), **10**-1520

Meatballs, continued
Sweet-and-Sour, **2**-250; **3**-424; **7**-1123
Umani, **6**-974
Veal, **7**-1122
Venison, **12**-1909
(for White Soup), **7**-1122
in Yogurt (Kibbeh bi Laban), **8**-1214
Meatless Casseroles, **2**-322

Meat Loaf, Loaves, **7**-1126
Basic, **2**-190; **7**-1126
Basic, Variations on, **7**-1126
Beef, Carrot, and Olives, **6**-870
Beef, Farmer Style, **6**-870
Beef, Individual, **2**-191
Beef-and-Onion, Layered, **7**-1128
Beef and Pork, with Vegetables, Broiled, **9**-1449
Beef and Potato, Sliced (Liha ja Perunamureke), **5**-680
Beef-and-Tomato, **6**-870
Beef, with Wine, **2**-190
Chicken, **7**-1129
Chicken, with Almond and Mushroom Sauce, **7**-1152
Ham, **7**-1128
Ham and Fresh-Pork, Curried, **6**-856
Ham, Individual, **7**-1128
Ham, Orange-Glazed, **6**-856
Ham, in Raisin Sauce (QC), **10**-1520
Ham and Veal, **6**-856
Individual, **2**-191
Jellied, **6**-979
Kibbeh, **8**-1214
Lamb, Pressed, **7**-1128
Liver, **7**-1128
Manila, **7**-1128
Olive, **9**-1382
Orange-Glazed, **6**-870
Pineapple-Ham, **9**-1406
Spanish, **8**-1256
Stuffed (Kibbeh bi Sanieh), **8**-1214
Veal, **7**-1126
Veal, Old-Fashioned, **12**-1896
Veal (Pain de Veau), **2**-278
Veal, Sour-Cream, **11**-1698
Tomato Beef, **11**-1810
-Vegetable Casserole, **2**-316
Medaglioni di Mozzarella (Medallions of Mozzarella Cheese), **6**-952
Medaljekager (Medal Cookies), **4**-543
Melanzane alla Marinara (Marinated Eggplant Appetizer), **6**-952
Melanzane alla Parmigiana (Eggplant Parmigiana), **6**-958
Melba Toast, **2**-280; **11**-1826
Melitzanosalata (Eggplant Salad), **5**-822

Melon(s), **7**-1129; see also names of melons
Avocado Salad, **6**-911
Chutney, Hot, **7**-1132
Circles of, **4**-630
Cocktail with Guava Jelly, **5**-829
Conserve, Western, **7**-1132
Delight, **2**-296
Garnishes, **5**-780
Gingered, **1**-27; **5**-801
Ice-Cream Sauce, **2**-296
India Relish, **7**-1132
à la Mode, **6**-934
Patio Salad, **7**-1085
with Prosciutto, **4**-650
Simplicity, **7**-1132
Melting Tea Cake, **5**-784
Melt-in-the-Mouth Cookies, **3**-433

Menu(s), **7**-1132; see also 100 Menus in each volume
Barbecue, **1**-144
Holiday Barbecue, **4**-645
Small Barbecue, **4**-644
Southern Barbecue, **4**-645
Breakfast, **2**-241
Brunch, **2**-246
Summertime Brunch, **4**-630
Viennese Brunch, **4**-629
Buffet, **2**-249
Casserole Buffet, **2**-250; **8**-1275
Chafing Dish Buffet, **2**-250
Greek Taverna Buffet, **4**-639
Oriental Buffet, **2**-250
Shrimp-Curry Buffet, **4**-640
Christmas dinner, **3**-438; **3**-440
Christmas Hospitality (buffets), **3**-424
Dinner
Chicken Dinner, **8**-1278
Dinner for 8, 6, 4, **4**-565-570
Festive Dinner, **4**-648
Roman Dinner, **4**-650
Tongue Dinners, **11**-1837-1839
Luncheon
Buffet Luncheon, **7**-1089
Intimate Luncheon, **4**-632
Parisian Luncheon, **4**-633
Salad Luncheon, **7**-1089
Spring Luncheon, **4**-632
Picnic
Beach Picnic, **9**-1378
Camping Picnic, **9**-1384
Cookout Picnic, **9**-1384
Fish Picnic, **8**-1276
Hamburgers Supreme, **8**-1282
Holiday Picnic, **9**-1382
Roadside Picnic, **9**-1378
Sandwich and Salad Picnic, **9**-1382
Simply Elegant Picnic, A, **9**-1383
Steak Party, **8**-1280
Rice Casseroles, **10**-1554-1556
Smorgasbord, American, **10**-1666
Tea
for a Crowd, **4**-635
English Afternoon Tea, **4**-634
Oriental Tea, **4**-635
Thanksgiving, **11**-1822
Menudo (Tripe Stew), **7**-1140

Meringue(s), **7**-1134
Almond Cookies, **7**-1135
Almond, Rich, **7**-1135
Apple Meringue Cake, **1**-101
Black-Walnut, **1**-63
Blueberry-Peach, **2**-209
Cake Pudding, **9**-1490
Chocolate, **3**-416
Chocolate Fudge, **3**-472
Christmas, **7**-1135
Floating Island, **5**-704
Floating Island (Isla Flotante), **9**-1497
Fruit, **7**-1135
Lebanese Pineapple, **9**-1408
with Marron Filling, **7**-1112
Meringue, **2**-254; **7**-1053, 1164; **10**-1544; **11**-1754
Meringue (for Maräng Suisse), **11**-1792
Meringue Pie(s)
Banana, **9**-1392
Blackberry-Almond, **9**-1392
Chocolate, **9**-1392
Chocolate Angel, **3**-411
Coconut, **9**-1392
Lemon, Old-Fashioned, **9**-1392
Mincemeat Alaska, **7**-1164
Peach, **9**-1398
Rhubarb, **9**-1392
Sour-Cream Butterscotch, **9**-1392
Vanilla, **9**-1391
Meringues Glacées, **6**-934
Molasses-Peach, **8**-1184
Orange Pudding, Florida, **7**-1135
with Orange Sauce, **7**-1135
Peach-Blueberry, **8**-1317
Pie Shell, **7**-1135
Pie Topping, Never-Fail, **7**-1134
Pineapple Cake, **9**-1409
Pommes Meringuées, **4**-558
Pumpkin Chiffon, **9**-1500
Raspberry Peach Glacées, **10**-1537
Rhubarb, Baked, **10**-1544
Salzburger Nockerln (Dessert Puffs), **1**-123
Shell, **9**-1500
Shells, Individual, **7**-1134
Shell (Vacherin à la Suisse), **12**-1884
Strawberry Pavlova, **8**-1313
Strawberry Schaumtorte, **7**-1156
Topping for Pies or Puddings, Quick, **7**-1134
Torte, Cream (Marängsuisse), **11**-1792
Walnut, **7**-1135
Merluza Asado al Horno (Baked Fish), **11**-1744
Mexican Beans (Frijoles), **7**-1141
Mexican Bread (Tortillas), **7**-1137
Mexican Cheese and Chili Pancakes, **8**-1293
Mexican Chick-Pea Salad, **3**-392
Mexican Chili Salsa, **9**-1360
Mexican Chocolate (Chocolate Mexicano), **7**-1143
Mexican Cookery, **7**-1136
Mexican Corn Stuffing, **11**-1782
Mexican Crullers (Churros), **7**-1143
Mexican Egg Salad, **4**-523
Mexican Flan, **4**-557
Mexican Frankfurters and Eggs, **5**-724
Mexican Hominy, **6**-907
Mexican Lamb Stew, **7**-1038
Mexican Meatballs, **8**-1273
Mexican Panned Potatoes, **9**-1465
Mexican Pies, **7**-1049
Mexican Pork and Hominy, **9**-1450
Mexican Pork Pot Roast, **9**-1475
Mexican Potato Chips, **8**-1283
Mexican Puchero, **1**-26
Mexican Rice, **10**-1551
Mexican Refried Beans, **1**-59
Mexican Rice (Arroz Mexicano), **7**-1141
Mexican Salad, **12**-1931
Mexican Sandwiches (Tostadas Compuestas), **7**-1137
Mexican Sausage (Chorizo), **7**-1140
Mexican Style Perch, **9**-1363
Mexican Veal, **12**-1896
Mexicanos Onions and Noodles, **8**-1261
Mexilhões de Aveiro (Aveiro Mussels), **9**-1455
Meze (Appetizers), **4**-639
Michigan Baked Beans, **1**-48; **7**-1152
Michigan Shortcake, **1**-48
Middle-East Roast Stuffed Capon, **2**-298
Midnight Lace Cake, **3**-407
Midwestern Cookery, **7**-1144
Mi Krob (Fried Noodles), **11**-1715
Milan Style Rice (Risotto alla Milanese), **6**-958

Milk, **7**-1158
Buttermilk, **7**-1158, 1159
Chocolate Milk, **7**-1158
Condensed, **7**-1158, 1159
Dried, **7**-1159
Evaporated, **7**-1158, 1159
Orange-Milk Starter, **7**-1088
Punch, Hot, **9**-1502
Skim, **7**-1158
Sour Milk, **11**-1701
Toast, **11**-1828
Whey, **12**-1936

Milk Shake, **7**-1160
Banana Frosted, **7**-1160
Banana Slim Shake, **7**-1088
Berry Float, **7**-1161
Chocolate Float, **7**-1161
Chocolate Frosted, **7**-1160
Dutch Delight Float, **7**-1161
Fruit Shake, Spiced, **7**-1160
Mint Chocolate Float, Frosted, **7**-1161
Mocha Cream Shake, **7**-1160
Peach-Rum Shake, **8**-1321
Polka-Dot Punch Float, **7**-1161
Prune Shake, **7**-1160
Strawberry Frosted, **7**-1161
Vanilla Shake, **7**-1160

Millet, **7**-1161
Pilaf, **7**-1161
Porridge, **7**-1161
Milt, see Roe

Mincemeat, **7**-1161
Alaska Pie, **7**-1164
Apple, Spicy, **7**-1162
Delight, **7**-1164
Diamonds, Frosted, **3**-471
Dressed-Up Bought, **7**-1162
English, **7**-1162
Ginger-Mince Upside-Down Cake, **12**-1882
Green-Tomato, **7**-1162
Hermits, **6**-901
Lane Cakes, **7**-1164
Make-Your-Own, **7**-1162
Meatless, **7**-1162
Mince Pie, Brandied, **9**-1396
Mince Tarts, **11**-1824
Pear, Spicy, **7**-1162
Pie with Cheese Crust, **9**-1396
Pilgrim, **7**-1162
Plum, **9**-1417
Pumpkin-Mince Pie, **9**-1500
Roly-Poly, **4**-627
with Sweet Potatoes, **11**-1797
Tea Loaf, **7**-1164
Venison, **1**-76

Minestrone, **7**-1164; **11**-1691
alla Genovese, **7**-1165
Milanese, **6**-952
Milanese alla Savini, **7**-1164
di Pasta e Fagiuoli (Thick Soup of Macaroni and Beans), **6**-952
alla Romana, **7**-1165

Mint, Minted, **7**-1165
Chocolate Float, Frosted, **7**-1161
Chocolate-Mint Mousse, **8**-1191
Cookies, **3**-476; **7**-1166
Cranberry Sauce, **7**-1151
Cucumbers with, **11**-1749
Filling, **3**-412
Fresh-Lime Mold with Watermelon Balls, **7**-1067
Fresh-Mint Dressing, **11**-1700
Green Peas, **11**-1749
Iced Tea, **11**-1816
Jelly, **6**-982; **7**-1166
Julep, Georgia, **6**-996
Julep, Kentucky, **6**-996
Julep, Rum, **6**-996
Lamb and Potato Salad, **10**-1580
Limas, **7**-1065
Melon with Cointreau, **7**-1166
Onions, **7**-1166
Parfait, **7**-1166
and Parsley Salad, **8**-1213
Peppermint, **9**-1361
Chiffon Pie, **9**-1361, 1397
-Chocolate Cream, Marbled, **9**-1361
Chocolate Peppermint Cake, **7**-1044
Freeze, **5**-790; **9**-1361
Frosting, **5**-750; **7**-1044
Taffy, **9**-1362
Pineapple Cup, **9**-1403
Pineapple-Mint Sherbet, **7**-1166
Pineapple Topping, **6**-931
Relish, **10**-1543
Sauce, **4**-624; **10**-1627
Sauce for Roast Lamb, Traditional English, **7**-1165
Spearmint Leaves, Candied, **11**-1749
Stuffing, **11**-1781
Vinegar, Green, **7**-1166

Mints (Candy)
Pulled, **2**-288
Thin, **7**-1166
Wafers, Grandmother's, **8**-1231
Mirepoix, **7**-1166; **10**-1615
Miso (Fermented Bean Paste), **6**-970
Miso Shiru (Bean Paste Soup), **6**-971
Miss Mollie's Boiled Pot, **1**-61
Mississippi "Shushed" Eggs, **11**-1723
Mizerja I (Cucumber Salad), **9**-1430
Mizerja II (Cucumber Salad with Sour Cream), **9**-1430
Moa Niu (Coconut Chicken), **9**-1435

Mocha, **7**-1166
-Almond Cake, **7**-1167
(beverage), **3**-462
de Luxe, **3**-462
de Luxe, Iced, **3**-462
Buttercream, **12**-1854
Buttercream Frosting, **5**-751
Butter Frosting, **5**-751
-Brandy Delight, **7**-1167
Cake, **3**-410
Chiffon Pie, **7**-1167
Chocolate, **7**-1167
Cinnamon, Frosting, **3**-410
Cream, **7**-1167
Cream Shake, **7**-1160
Frosting, Rich, **3**-410
Hard Sauce, **6**-878
Logs, **2**-285
Molds, Low-Calorie, **7**-1167
Mousse, **7**-1167
Nut Butterballs, **3**-474
-Nut Cream Pie, **9**-1391
Parfait, **6**-930
Soufflé (Soufflé Moka), **5**-746
Southwestern, **11**-1732
Sundae Sauce, **7**-1167
Torte, **12**-1854
Mochomas (Minced Pork), **7**-1140
Moelle Pochée (Poached Marrow), **5**-741
Moeun Sngo (Chicken Soup), **11**-1717
Mohn Kuchen, **5**-799
Mojo Isleño (Fried Fish with Puerto Rican Sauce), **9**-1494

Molasses, **8**-1181
Barbecue Sauce, **8**-1184
Bars, Fruited, **3**-471
Chiffon Pie, **8**-1184
Cider, Hot, **8**-1185
Cookies, **1**-77; **8**-1185
Cookies, Drop, **11**-1798
Cookies, Old-Fashioned, **9**-1357
Crinkles, Helen's, **3**-476
Cutouts, Spicy, **3**-472
Fig Pudding, **8**-1184
Frosting, Fluffy, **8**-1185
Gingerbread, **8**-1184
Hermits, **6**-901
Hermits, Old-Fashioned, **8**-1230
-Honey-Butter Sauce, **8**-1184
Johnnycake, **8**-1225
Layer Cake, **8**-1184
-Oat Waffles, **8**-1184
-Peach Meringues, **8**-1184
Popcorn with Peanuts, **9**-1437
Posset, **9**-1457
Pudding, Baked, **9**-1490
Pudding, Steamed, **9**-1355
Sour-Cream Squares, **11**-1701
Spice Cake, **2**-269
Spiced Fruit, **8**-1184
Taffy, **11**-1808
Taffy Sundae Sauce, **8**-1185
Mole Sauce, **5**-770
Monaco Style Onions (Oignons à la Monégasque), **5**-745
Monsodium Glutamate (MSG), **8**-1185
Mont d'Or, **9**-1470
Monte Bianco di Castagne (Mont Blanc of Chestnuts), **3**-376
Monte Cristo Sandwiches, **10**-1602
Moose Stew, Yukon, **2**-278
Moravian Cookies, **3**-431
Morcon (Stuffed Rolled Beef), **9**-1369
Mormon Biscuits with Cream Gravy, **1**-74
Mormon Vegetable Stew, **1**-73
Mor-Monsen Kaker (Mother Monsen Cakes), **8**-1243
Mormor's Syltkakor (Grandmother's Jelly Cookies), **11**-1793

Mornay, Mornay Sauce, **7**-1186; **10**-1614
2-173; **3**-361; **8**-1186; **9**-1400; **10**-1620; **12**-1864
Morning-Glory Cake, **8**-1186
Morue à la Flamande (Codfish, Flemish Style), **2**-197
Mother Monsen Cakes (Mor-Monsen Kaker), **8**-1243
Mottram Kidneys in Cream, **12**-1897

Moussaka, **5**-818
Beef-Asparagus, **8**-1187
Beef-Mushroom, **8**-1187
Chicken-Corn, **8**-1190
Chicken, with Peas, **8**-1190
Eggplant, **8**-1187
Fried-Tomato, **8**-1187
Lamb-Carrot, **8**-1189
Lamb-Vegetable, **8**-1189
Lentil, **8**-1187
Pork, with Brussels Sprouts, **8**-1190

Mousse(s), **8**-1190
Chicken, **8**-1190
Chicken-Almond, **1**-14
Chicken-Ham, **3**-391
Cucumber, **1**-36
Fish, Hot, **8**-1190
Ham, **5**-716; **8**-1190
Ham (Mousse de Jambon), **6**-865
Salmon, Cold, **10**-1597
Salmon, Hot, **5**-691

Mousse(s), Dessert
Apricot, **1**-74
Apricot, Frozen, **1**-108
Blueberry, **8**-1191
Cantaloupe, **8**-1191
Chocolate, **5**-790; **8**-1191
Chocolate, French, **3**-415
Chocolate, Low-Calorie, **3**-415
Chocolate-Mint, **8**-1191
Chocolate (Mousse au Chocolat), **5**-746
Coffee Mousse, Kona, **1**-35
Cranberry, **8**-1191
Cream-Cheese, **3**-362; **8**-1191
Fruit Cream, **8**-1191
Honey, **6**-910
Lemon, **8**-1191
Mocha, **7**-1167
Pineapple, Heavenly, **9**-1409
Strawberry, **11**-1778
Tutti-Frutti, **4**-632

Mousseline, Mousseline Sauce, **8**-1191; **10**-1614
6-906; **8**-1192; **10**-1621
Green, **10**-1622
Mrs. Benson's Receipt for Fudge, **8**-1231
Mrs. Parson's Receipt for Cream, **8**-1229
MSG (Monosodium Glutamate), **8**-1185

Muffin(s), **2**-227; **8**-1192
Apple-Corn, **8**-1193
Apricot, **2**-237
Bacon, **2**-237
Blueberry, **2**-209; **8**-1192
Bran, **2**-221
Bran, Miniature, **4**-632
Cherry, **7**-1154
Corn, **3**-485
Corn, Savory, **8**-1192
Cornmeal or Graham, Hot, **4**-630
Cranberry, **2**-237
Date-Nut, **4**-457
Double-Corn, **2**-237
Eggless, **8**-1193
English, **4**-627; **8**-1193
Fruit Buns, **2**-238
Hazelnut Cinnamon Buns, **6**-882
Peanut-Butter, **8**-1326
Pineapple, Hawaiian, **4**-635
Potato-Flour, à la Marshall Field's, **1**-37
Raised, **8**-1193
Raisin Bran, **2**-237

Muffin(s), continued
Rice, **8**-1192
Rich, **2**-237
Sally Lunn, Raised, **10**-1590
Soy-Wheat, **11**-1734
Squash, **6**-915
Sweet-Potato, **8**-1192

Mulberry(ies), **8**-1193
Jelly, **8**-1193

Mullet, **8**-1194
Baked, **8**-1194
Broiled, **8**-1194
Fish-Fry Mullet and Hush Puppies, **5**-690
Levantine (Salmonetes Levantinos), **11**-1741
Mulligatawny, **8**-1194
Mulligatawny Shorba, **11**-1691
Murgha Kari (Chicken Curry with Tomatoes), **6**-939
Muscatels, Italian, **8**-1194
Mush, Grilled Corn, **1**-55

Mushroom(s), **8**-1195
and Almond Sauce, **7**-1152
with Bacon, Broiled, **8**-1200
Baked, **1**-77
-Barley Casserole, **8**-1200
Barley Soup, **6**-987
with Beef, Chinese, **8**-1200
Beef-Mushroom Moussaka, **8**-1187
Beignets, **1**-89
Broth, Quick, **2**-246
Butter, **2**-279
Canapés, **8**-1197
Caps, Broiled, **4**-644
Cheese-Mushroom Canapé, **3**-355
-Cheese Sauce, **2**-324
and Chicken, Barrister Style, Hollyhock-House, **8**-1200
Cocktail, **8**-1197
Consommé, **11**-1822
Consommé, Swiss, **8**-1198
and Corn, Sautéed, **3**-382
Crab Casserole, **3**-488
with Crab in Shells, Baked, **8**-1198
with Crabmeat, **8**-1198
Crabmeat-Stuffed, **6**-913
in Cream, Baked, **8**-1200
Cream Sauce, **12**-1866
Deviled, Casino, **4**-558
Duxelles, **4**-593; **12**-1900
Duxelles Sauce, **10**-1619; **12**-1900
and Egg Filling, Russian, **4**-662
with Eggs (Houby s Vejci), **4**-532
and Eggs, Ragout of, **4**-603
Eggs Rialto, **8**-1200
Eggs Stuffed with **4**-606
Filling, **1**-89; **9**-1429
and Fish Soufflé (Hmon Mga Baung), **11**-1716
in Foil, **1**-144
Fried (Paistetut Sienet), **5**-681
Gratin aux Champignons, **9**-1470
Green Bean, and Cashew Casserole, **8**-1200
Ham and Eggs in a Chafing Dish, Creamed, **3**-346
Hash, with, **6**-879
Ketchup, **6**-999
and Kidney Pie, **7**-1013
and Liver, **7**-1072; **8**-1198
Liver Pâté, **7**-1076; **8**-1197
and Lobster Parmesan, **8**-1198
Marinated, **1**-89
Morel, **8**-1185
Newburg, **8**-1201
-Olive Sauce, **11**-1737
and Onions with Peas, **8**-1315
and Onions, Russian, **8**-1263
with Oregano, Savory, **8**-1274
and Oyster Pie, **8**-1288
and Oysters, Crusted, **8**-1198
and Oysters, Fricassee of, **8**-1198
and Oysters and Clams, Fricassee of, **8**-1198
Pastries, **6**-912
Patties (Kotlety z Grzybów), **9**-1429
Peas, and Pimiento, **11**-1823
Pickled, **8**-1197
Pickled Cooked, **1**-90
Pickled (Manitaria Toursi), **4**-639
-Pimiento Peas, **8**-1315
Piroshki, Russian, **8**-1197
Polish Style, **8**-1201
with Pork Chops, Neapolitan, **8**-1200
with Pork, Oriental, **8**-1200
Potato Pie, **8**-1201
and Potatoes with Cheese, **8**-1201
and Potatoes (Potatis och Svamp), **11**-1790
Raw, Salad, Italian (Insalata di Funghi Crudi), **8**-1197
à la Russe, **11**-1838
Sandwiches, **8**-1200
Sauce, **2**-193; **8**-1282; **12**-1874
Sauce, Creamy, for Pasta, **8**-1247
Sauce, Sherry, **5**-695
Sautéed, **8**-1201
Shrimp-Mushroom Flan, French, **4**-633
Soup, Cream-of-, **8**-1198
in Sour Cream (Griby v Smetane), **10**-1567
Sour-Cream Sauce, **9**-1430
and Spinach, Creamed, **8**-1202
Steamed (Matsutaki Dobin), **6**-976
Stewed in Wine, **8**-1201
Stuffed, **4**-640; **7**-1083; **11**-1782
Stuffed, French Style (Champignons Farcis), **8**-1201
Stuffed, Italian Style, **8**-1201
-Stuffed Pork Chops, **8**-1200
Stuffed with Purée of Green Peas, **8**-1201
Sweet-Cream Sauce, **9**-1430
and Tomatoes, Scalloped, **8**-1201
and Tomato Salad, **1**-82
Tuna Macaroni, **12**-1864
with Veal, **8**-1273
and Wild-Rice Stuffing, **11**-1781

Muskellunge or **Musky,** **8**-1202
Baked in Spanish Sauce, **9**-1401
with Crabmeat and Lobster Dressing, **8**-1202
Muskrat, Maryland, **5**-769
Musky, **8**-1202
Muslinger i Seng (Mussels in Bed), **4**-536

Mussel(s), **8**-1203
Aveiro (Mexilhões de Aveiro), **9**-1455
in Bed (Muslinger i Seng), **4**-536
Curried, **8**-1203
Marinière, **8**-1203
Marinière, Belgian, **8**-1203
with Pork (Carne de Porco à Alentejana), **9**-1456
Salad, **8**-1203
Stuffed, **8**-1203

Mustard, **8**-1204
Butter, **2**-279; **8**-1205; **10**-1615, 1624
Cream Mayonnaise, **10**-1614, 1622
Cream Sauce, **8**-1205
Dip for Raw Vegetables, **1**-87
Dressing, **10**-1566, 1601, 1623
English, **5**-725; **8**-1276
Hollandaise, **10**-1614, 1621
Mayonnaise, **5**-695; **8**-1205; **10**-1614, 1622
Pickle, **9**-1374
Sauce, **2**-173; **4**-622; **5**-726; **6**-881; **8**-1224, 1280; **9**-1350
Creamy, **11**-1700
Hot, **6**-859
Sauce Moutarde, **5**-743
Senapssås, **11**-1786
Sennepssaus, **8**-1240
Sennepssovs, **4**-542
Sweet-and-Sour, **7**-1128
Sweet-Sour, **10**-1627
with Whipped Cream, **8**-1205
Spread, **8**-1205
Toast Butter, **11**-1829

Mustard Greens, **8**-1204
Fresh, with Bacon, **8**-1204
Fried, **5**-825
with Irish Potatoes, **11**-1723
Spiced, **8**-1204
Mustard Seed, **8**-1204
Muster Cookies, **4**-654

Mutton, **8**-1205
Chops, Broiled, **8**-1205
Curried, Jamaican, **8**-1205
Leg of, Boiled, with Caper Sauce, **1**-79
Steak, **8**-1205
Stew (Haricots de Mouton), **8**-1205
Tart, **1**-79
Myrtle Bank Jamaican Pepperpot Soup, **6**-966

N

Nalesniki (Rolled Pancakes), **9**-1429
Napa Valley Lamb Chops, **1**-26

Napoleon, **8**-1206
Easy, **8**-1206
Nasi Goreng (Fried Rice), **11**-1714
Nasturtium Seeds, Pickled, **8**-1208
Natur Schnitzel, **1**-126
Neapolitan Ice Cream, **8**-1208
Neapolitan Pork Chops with Mushrooms, **8**-1200
Neapolitan Pork Chops and Spaghetti, **8**-1208
Neapolitan Rigatoni, **8**-1274
Neapolitans, **8**-1208
Near Eastern Cookery, **8**-1209
Near-East White-Bean Soup, **11**-1690
Nebraska Corn Fritter, **1**-54
Nebraska Spoon Bread, **7**-1153
Nectarine, **8**-1216
Nedlagte Rødbeter (Pickled Beets), **8**-1239
Nepalese Potato Salad, **4**-522
Nerkówka Lub Mostek Nadziewane po Polsku (Stuffed Breast or Shoulder of Veal à la Polonaise), **9**-1425

Nesselrode, à la Nesselrode, **8**-1216
Chiffon Pie, **9**-1397
Pie, **8**-1218
Pudding, Classic, **8**-1217
Pudding, Jellied, **8**-1217
Sauce, **8**-1218
Neuchâtel Style Fondue, **5**-711

Newburg
Lobster, **7**-1078
Salmon, **10**-1596
Scallops, **10**-1641
Shellfish, **10**-1652
New England Baked Beans, **1**-159
New England Clam Chowder, **3**-418
New England Cook Book, **8**-1221
New England Corn-Bread Stuffing, **11**-1780
New England Fish Chowder, Old-Fashioned, **8**-1222
New England Griddle Cakes, **8**-1292
New England Style Creamed Halibut, **5**-689
New Hampshire Turnover Apple Pie, **1**-57
New Mexican Cured Pork (Carne Adobada), **11**-1728
New Orleans Café Brûlot, **5**-702
New Orleans Rice Fritters, **10**-1552
Newton Sugar Squares, **1**-57
Nham (Salad), **11**-1717
Nibbles or Tidbits, **1**-85
Nicaragua Heavenly Bananas (Maduros en Gloria), **11**-1709
Nicaragua Stuffed Turkey (Pavo a la Nicaragüense), **11**-1706
Nicaragua Tripe Soup (Sopa de Mondongo), **11**-1704
Nier Soep (Kidney Soup), **4**-589
Nigerian Groundnut Stew, **8**-1324

Nigiri Sushi (Raw Fish Rice Ball), **6**-971
Noisette Butter, **10**-1615, 1624
Nishiki-kan (Two-Tone Jelly), **6**-978
Niu Ju Chin Jow (Beef with Green Peppers), **3**-403

Noodle(s), 8-1231
Almond, **1**-14
Almond Poppy-Seed, Hungarian, **8**-1233
Alsatian, **1**-16
-Apple Pudding, **9**-1490
with Beef Mounds, **9**-1351
Beef and Noodles with Sour Cream and Paprika, **2**-191
and Beef Platter, **6**-872
Boiled, with Poppy Seeds (Makos Tészta), **6**-920
Boiled, with Walnuts (Diós Tézta), **6**-920
Buckwheat (Soba), **6**-976
with Buckwheat Groats (Kasha Varnishkas), **6**-992
Buffet, Three-Tone, **8**-1233
Buttered, with Cashew Nuts, **8**-1233
Cabbage-Noodle Potpourri, **8**-1232
Cannelloni, **8**-1231
Cannelloni, Florentine, **8**-1231
Casseroles, **7**-1049
and Cheese Casserole, Hungarian, **8**-1233
Chop-Suey Skillet, **8**-1232
Cottage-Cheese Pudding, **9**-1487
Cottage Green-Noodle Casserole, **3**-359
Crisp-Fried, **2**-247
Crusty Beef, Cheese, and Noodle Casserole, **2**-316
Dish, The Poor Parson's, **8**-1233
Dough, Basic, **8**-1231
Egg Custard Noodles (Odamaki-Mushi), **6**-976
with Eggs and Bacon, **8**-1233
Fettucine Alfredo, **8**-1233
Filled (Boova Shenkel), **9**-1352
Fine Noodles for the Sherpherdess (Vermicelli alla Pastora), **6**-958
and Frankfurters, **9**-1352
Fried, with Chicken Livers, **3**-391
with Fried Foods (Tempura Soba), **6**-972
Fried (Mi Krob), **11**-1715
Fried Stewed (Pansit Gisado), **9**-1369
with Ginger Beef Soup (Pho), **11**-1717
Green, with Basil, **8**-1233
Green, with Cheese Croquettes (Croquettes au Fromage), **11**-1803
Green-Noodle, Beef, and Cheese Casserole, **2**-324
and Ham, **3**-358
and Ham Casserole (Viennese Ham Fleckerl), **6**-865
and Ham Dish, Austrian, **8**-1233
Ham and Green-Noodle Casserole, **6**-853
and Ham Rabbit, **8**-1232
with Ham (Schinkenfleckerln), **1**-122
Lasagna, **8**-1231
and Liver Balls, **7**-1074
and Liver, Italian Style, **7**-1073
Lobster Casserole, **2**-321
Meatball-Noodle Skillet, **8**-1232
Meatballs with Almond-Mushroom Noodles, **6**-870
and Onions, Mexicanos, **8**-1261
Polonaise, **8**-1233
and Pork-Chop Skillet, **8**-1233
Prune-Noodle Pudding, **8**-1233
Pudding (Lokshen Kugel), **6**-993
Red Noodles and Lamb, **7**-1039
with Rice, **8**-1215
Rumanian, **8**-1232
Shrimp Skillet, **8**-1232
Spanish Casserole, **10**-1638
Supreme, Party, **8**-1232
Tagliatelli, **8**-1231
and Tongue Rabbit, **8**-1232
Tuna-Noodle Casserole, **12**-1863
Tuna Tetrazzini, **12**-1866
Two-Cheese, **8**-1233
Won Ton, **3**-403
Won Ton, Crisp (stuffed and fried), **3**-401
Noppe Jiru (Vegetable Stew), **6**-976
Norfolk Shad without Bones, **1**-75
Nori-Chazuke (Rice with Seaweed), **6**-976
Normande Sauce, **10**-1613, 1620
Norman White Butter Sauce, **10**-1624
Normandy Chicken, **11**-1736
Normandy Style Sweetbreads, **11**-1796
North Carolina Style Baked Country Cured Ham, **11**-1722
Northwest Blueberry or Huckleberry Buckle, **12**-1933
Norwegian Blueberry Soup, **2**-208
Norwegian Cookery, **8**-1234
Norwegian Dalesman Cakes, **9**-1471
Norwegian Fashion Lettuce (Salat), **8**-1240
Norwegian Fish Pudding, **1**-49
Norwegian Haddock Loaf, Baked, **5**-689
Norwegian Reindeer Pot Roast with Mushrooms, Tomatoes, Grapes, and Pineapple, **10**-1541
Norwegian Rum Cream, **10**-1563

Nougat, 2-284; **8**-1244
Almond, **2**-288
Buttercream, **5**-781
French, **8**-1244
Walnut, **8**-1244
Nóźki Wieprzowe z Grochiem (Pickled or Fresh Pigs' Knuckles with Split Peas), **9**-1426
Nusskipferln (Nut Crescents), **1**-124

Nut(s), 8-1244; see also names of nuts
Aplets, **1**-76
Apple-Nut Bars, **1**-103
Brandy Nut Cakes, **8**-1310
Butter, **11**-1829
Butter Cookies, **2**-252
Buttered Honey, **6**-911
Cake, Passover, **6**-995
Candied, **2**-281
Charoses, **6**-994
Cheese-Nut Burgers, **6**-869
Cheese-and-Nut Sandwiches, Savory, **10**-1610
Chess Pie, **9**-1388
Chocolate Nut Fudge (QC), **10**-1526
Confection (Halva), **5**-824
Cranberry-Nut Bread, **10**-1611
Date-Nut Bars, Frosted (QC), **10**-1526
Date-Nut Fillings, **4**-547, 663; **8**-1253
Date-Nut Loaves, **10**-1611
Date-Nut Muffins, **4**-547
Mocha Nut Butterballs, **3**-474
Nut Crescents (Nusskipferln), **1**-124
Orange Nut Bread, **2**-238
Pastries (Pura), **5**-824
Patties, Glacé, **5**-805
Poundcake, **2**-272
Raisin, and Apple Relish, **10**-1535
Raisin-Nut Filling, **10**-1535
Raisin-Nut Pie, **9**-1390
Shortbread, **10**-1655
Sour-Cream Raisin Nut Cookies, **11**-1701
Strudel, **6**-922
Stuffing, **3**-392
Waffles, **12**-1915
Nuta (Seafood Salad), **6**-972
Nut Butter, **8**-1246

Nutmeg, 8-1246
Logs, **8**-1247
Nutmeg State Crab Soup, **1**-28
Nyre Sauté, Gammeltoft, **7**-1014

O

Oat(s), Oatmeal, 8-1252
Apple, Cookies, **1**-102
Batter Bread, **2**-229
Bread, **2**-231; **8**-1253
Cheese-and-Oatmeal Snaps, **8**-1253
Cookies, Chocolate-Chip, Virginia's, **3**-476
Cookies, Crisp, **7**-1041
Cookies, Drop, **8**-1253
Cookies, Filled, **8**-1253
Cookies, Refrigerator (QC), **10**-1526
Drop Bannocks, **1**-142
Griddle Cakes, **5**-826
Gruel, **5**-828
Kale, Bacon, and Oatmeal, **6**-999
Lace Cookies, **3**-434
Molasses-Oat Waffles, **8**-1184
Oatcakes, **4**-634
Oatcakes, Hot, **11**-1818
Peanut Cookies, **8**-1323
Pineapple-Oatmeal Cookies, **9**-1409
Porridge, Old-Fashioned, **9**-1452
Scones, **10**-1643
Oat Flour, **5**-707
O'Brien Potatoes, **9**-1467
October Salad, **10**-1587
Odamaki-Mushi (Egg Custard Noodles), **6**-976
Odori Fini (Herb Seasonings), **3**-345
Oeufs Brouillés, **11**-1811
Oeufs Cocottes au Jambon (Eggs in Ramekins with Ham), **6**-861
Oeufs à la Crème (Eggs with Cream Sauce), **11**-1804
Oeufs au Four (Baked Eggs), **11**-1804
Oeufs à la Matelote (Poached Eggs in Red Wine), **4**-607
Oeufs Mollet Chasseur, **4**-607
Oeufs à l'Oignon (Eggs and Onions), **2**-198
Oeufs sur le Plat à l'Andalouse (Andalusian Egg Platter), **6**-862
Oi Bokum Mamul (Cooked Cucumbers), **7**-1022
Oignons à la Monégasque, (Onions, Monaco Style), **5**-745

Okra, 8-1254
Baked, **8**-1255
Beef-Okra Soup, **11**-1721
-and-Beef Stew, **8**-1255
and Chicken Gumbo, **4**-512; **8**-1255
Fried, **11**-1723
Lamb Stew with Okra and Cuminseed, **4**-522
Pickles, **9**-1373
Soup, **1**-22
Stew, **8**-1255
Tomatoes, and Corn, **11**-1832
and Tomatoes with Lemon, **12**-1903
Olad'i s Lukom (Baked Onion Dumplings), **10**-1573
Old Colony Gingerbread Waffles, **12**-1915

Olive(s), 8-1255
-Avocado Appetizer, **8**-1256
and Bacon Rolls, **7**-1089
Black, Garlic, **8**-1257
Butter, **2**-279; **11**-1829
California Style, **1**-89
in Cheese, **1**-89
Cheese Olive Puffs, **6**-913
Corn, Egg, and Raisin Casserole, **8**-1257
Crabmeat Sandwiches, **8**-1257
Dressing, **4**-573; **11**-1700
Eggs Stuffed with, **4**-606
Garlic, **8**-1276
Garlic Ripe, **1**-89
with Hake Fillets, **8**-1256
Meat Loaf, **9**-1382
Mushroom-Olive Sauce, **11**-1737
Oil, **8**-1257
Parsley-Olive Sauce, **11**-1738
Ripe-Olive Bread, Visalia, **1**-26
Salmon-Olive Sandwiches, **10**-1597
-and-Steak Casserole, **8**-1256
Stuffing, **11**-1782
Surprises, **8**-1256
Two-Cheese Fusilli, **11**-1737
Øllebrød (Beer and Bread Soup), **4**-539
Omelet, **8**-1257; for recipes see Egg(s), Omelet(s)
Omenapuuro (Apple Porridge), **5**-681
Onigari Yaki (Broiled Shrimps), **6**-972

Onion(s), **8**-1259
and Apples, **8**-1264
Apples, and Raisins, Sautéed, **1**-100
and Apple Soup, **11**-1694
Bacon, and Bean Chowder, **11**-1691
Baked, **1**-36
Bake with Mushroom-Cheese Sauce, **2**-322
Bake, Spanish, **8**-1264
Barley-Onion Soup with Beef Balls, **7**-1122
-and-Beef Loaf, Layered, **7**-1128
and Beef Pie, **8**-1260
and Beets, Spiced, **8**-1261
Bermuda Casserole, **8**-1263
Bermudas Glacés, **8**-1264
and Blue Cheese, Marinated, **8**-1264
Bread, **2**-229
Bread, Southern, **8**-1265
Brioche Canapés, **2**-281
and Brussels Sprouts au Gratin, **11**-1838
Butter, **1**-86; **5**-695
and Celery in Cream, **11**-1823
-Cheese Bread, Quick, **1**-79
Cheese Pie, **9**-1388
and Cheese Soup, **8**-1260
Cheese Tarts, **11**-1811
with Chicken, **8**-1261
Constantine, **8**-1264
Creamed, **8**-1264
Cream Sauce, **1**-41
and Cucumber, Curried, **7**-1086
Cucumber-Onion Olive-Oil Pickle, **9**-1374
Curried, **8**-1264
Danish, **8**-1265
Dumplings, Baked (Olad'i s Lukom), **10**-1573
and Eggs, Faust, **8**-1263
Eggs in Scallion and Mushroom Sauce, **8**-1265
with Fish and Tomatoes (Fiskgryta), **11**-1788
French-Fried, **8**-1264
Fried (Frisk Stegt Løg), **4**-538
Garden Ragout, **8**-1266
Garnishes, **5**-778
Glazed, **8**-1264
Glazed, Amandine, **8**-1264
Gourmet Relish, **8**-1265
Gravy, **8**-1265
Gravy for Panfried Steak, **2**-181
Green Heaven in a Pot, **8**-1266
Green Onion and Parsley Stuffed Bread, **8**-1276
Green-Onion Sauce, **8**-1282
Honey Glaze for, **6**-909
Honey-Glazed, **8**-1264
and Lamb Casserole, **2**-320
and Liver, Smothered, **7**-1073
Ménagère, **3**-361
Minted, **7**-1166
Monaco Style (Oignons à la Monégasque), **5**-745
and Mushrooms, Russian, **8**-1263
and Noodles, Mexicanos, **8**-1261
Omelet, **8**-1257
in Onions, **12**-1906
and Orange Salad, **8**-1264, 1268
Oven-Browned, **3**-444
and Parsley Finger Sandwiches, **10**-1610
Peanut Creamed, **8**-1264
and Peas, Curried, **8**-1315
Pickles, **9**-1373
Pie, Dutch, **8**-1261
Pie Niçoise, **9**-1388
Pork Chops with, **8**-1261
with Pork Liver, French, **7**-1075
-and-Potato Cake, **9**-1468
Potato, and Cheese Pie, **9**-1463
Potatoes, and Beans, Skillet, **9**-1468
and Potatoes, Charlene, **8**-1263
Pudding, Baked, **9**-1487
Quiche, French, **8**-1261
Rhubarb-Onion Relish, **10**-1542
Rings, Marinated, **5**-726
Rings, French-Fried, **1**-77
Rolls, Pinwheel, **2**-239
and Sage Stuffing, **11**-1781
Sauce, Creamed, **5**-694
Sauce (Løksaus), **8**-1240
Scallions and Beans, **8**-1266
Slices, Braised, **12**-1903
Smothered, **2**-243
Soubise Sauce, **10**-1614, 1620
Soufflé, **12**-1904
Soup with Cheese, Jamaican, **6**-967
Soup with Cheese (Soupe à l'Oignon au Gratin), **5**-739
Soup, French, **8**-1260
Soup, Italian, **11**-1690
Soup, South American, **8**-1260
and Spinach Salad, **1**-73
and Squash, Skillet, **11**-1761
Stuffed, French, **8**-1261
Stuffed, Italian Style, **8**-1261
Sweet, with Oregano, **1**-145
Swiss Style, **8**-1264
Tart, German, **8**-1261
Toast, Texas-Style, **11**-1828
To Brown, **2**-192
and Tomato, American, **8**-1263
Turk's Onion Delight, **8**-1264
-Vinegar Sauce, **5**-694
White, and Yams with Roast Pork, **9**-1443
Whole, and Green Beans, **10**-1668
Yogurt, **12**-1957
Opakapaka Koala (Grilled Red Snapper), **9**-1434
Open Sandwiches, see Canapés; Sandwiches
Opera Torte, **12**-1856
Ophi (Hawaiian Marinated Scallops), **9**-1434

Opossum, **8**-1266
Roast, **5**-769
Roast, with Yams, **1**-25

Orange(s), **8**-1266
Ambrosia, **3**-428; **4**-566
Ambrosia Dessert, Jellied, **8**-1270
Ambrosia in Frozen Orange Shells, **11**-1824
Apple-and-Orange Salad, **10**-1587
and Apples, Sliced, with Wine, **8**-1270
-Baked Pork Chops, **9**-1444
Banana, and Walnut Salad, **10**-1588
Barbecue Sauce, **1**-146
and Belgian-Endive Salad, **8**-1268
-Brandy Toast Butter, **11**-1829
Bread Dish with (Broodschoteltje met Sinaasappels), **4**-593
Buttercream Frosting, Cooked, **5**-751
Buttercream Frosting, Uncooked, **5**-751
Butter Frosting, **3**-431; **7**-1042
Buttermilk Sherbet, **10**-1652
Cake, **7**-1087
Cake, Brazilian, **8**-1272
Chef's Salad, **10**-1580
Chicken Salad, **8**-1268
Chiffon Refrigerator Cake, **4**-556
Chiffon Tarts, **8**-1272
Coconut Bread, **10**-1611
Cottage-Cheese Cups, **8**-1268
and Cranberry Salad, Jellied (QC), **10**-1523
Cream Cheese Frosting, **5**-752
Cream Dressing, **8**-1268
Cream, de Luxe, Frozen, **5**-791
Cream Pie, **8**-1271
Cream Pudding, **9**-1491
Cucumber, and Pepper Salad (Ensalada de Naranjas), **7**-1142
-and-Date Tea Loaf, **8**-1272
and Date Salad, **10**-1588
Delight, **8**-1270
Filling, **2**-268; **4**-663; **11**-1792
Fluff Pudding, **8**-1270
Form Cake, **4**-553
French Dressing, **8**-1270
Fresh Orange Chiffon Pie, **8**-1270
Fresh Orange French Dressing, **5**-754
Fritters, **5**-749
Frosting, **2**-237, 308
Frosting, Boiled, **8**-1272
Frosting, Thin, **7**-1046
Garnishes, **5**-780; **10**-1666
-Ginger Fizz, **5**-804
Glacées, **5**-805
Glaze, **2**-233; **7**-1156
Glazed, **8**-1270
-Glazed Meat Loaves, **6**-870
Gold Layer Cake, **7**-1042
-Grapefruit-Juice Jelly, **6**-983
à la Grecque, **4**-557
Hard Sauce, **6**-878; **12**-1915
and Honeydew Dessert, **6**-911
-Honey Glaze, **2**-265
-Honey Sherbet, **6**-980
Ice, **6**-925; **8**-1208
Jelly, **6**-983
Juice, Apples Baked in, **8**-1270
Juice Glaze, **6**-856
Layer Cake, Banana-Filled, **1**-142
-Lemon Glaze, **2**-265; **5**-806
Lemon-Orange Filling, **7**-1056
and Lemon Salad, **7**-1052
-and-Lemon, Sauce, **3**-445
Lime, Conserve, **7**-1069
and Lobster Cocktail, **7**-1077
Macaroni, and Lobster Salad, **7**-1092
Macaroni, and Shrimp Salad, **7**-1092
Macaroni, and Tuna Salad, **7**-1092
Mandarin Oranges, Jellied, **8**-1270
Mandarin Squash, **11**-1759
-Marmalade Cake, **8**-1272
Marmalade, Tropical, **6**-980
Meringue Pudding, Florida, **7**-1135
-Milk Starter, **7**-1088
Nut Bread, **2**-238
and Onion Salad, **8**-1264, 1268
-Pastry Tart Shells, **8**-1272
and Peach Conserve, **8**-1321
Peanut-Butter, Bread, **8**-1325
Pear-Orange Compote, **8**-1333
Peel, Candied, **2**-289
Peel, Florida Gingered, **5**-803
Peel, Honeyed, **8**-1273
Peel, Spiced, **8**-1273
Pie with Whipped Cream, **8**-1272
Pineapple-Orange Salad, **9**-1408
-Pineapple Salad, **5**-788
Plum-Orange Jam, **6**-964
-Plum Twists, **8**-1309
and Pomegranate Compote, **9**-1436
Pork Chop Skillet, **9**-1444
Prune-Orange Compote (Kompot iz Apelsin i Chernosliv), **10**-1573
Raisin-Orange Turnovers, **12**-1879
in Red Wine, **8**-1270
Rice for Duck or Ham, **8**-1268
-Rum Cake, **2**-269
-Rum Cake, Italian, **8**-1272
-Rum Topping, **8**-1272
Rye Bread, **12**-1932
Sauce, **7**-1135; **9**-1486; **10**-1628
Chicken Baked in, **8**-1268
Dried Beef with, **8**-1268
Fresh Beets in, **8**-1268
Seville-Orange Marmalade, **7**-1111
Shortbread, **10**-1655
Slices, Glacées, **5**-805
Slices, Spicy, **1**-11
Soufflé, **8**-1270; **11**-1688
Soup (Appelsiinikeitto), **5**-679
Spiced, **11**-1754
-Stuffed Veal, **8**-1268
Sunset Soup, **11**-1694
Sweet Potatoes, **11**-1797
Syrup, **10**-1629; **11**-1807
Tartlets, **8**-1271
Tea Bread, **10**-1612
Toast Butter, **11**-1829
Valencia-Orange Marmalade, **7**-1111
Velvet Ice Cream, **8**-1270
Wafers, **3**-472
and Watercress Salad, **8**-1268
Yams, **12**-1951
Orangeade, **8**-1273

Oregano, **8**-1273
Mushrooms with, Savory, **8**-1274
Oregon Celery Salad, **1**-65
Oregon Cheese Salad, **3**-361
Oriental Buffet, **2**-250
Oriental Coffee (Coffee Imperial), **3**-462
Oriental Green Beans, **10**-1668
Oriental Pineapple and Tuna, **9**-1406
Oriental Pork with Mushrooms, **8**-1200
Oriental Style Chicken Livers and Rice, **3**-391
Oriental Tea, **4**-635
Oshitashi (Spanish with Sesame), **6**-976
Ossenhaas à la Jardinière (Filet of Beef with Vegetables), **4**-590
Ossobuco, **8**-1274
Ostras Lusitanas (Lusitanian Oysters), **9**-1456
Oswego Tea, **2**-200
Oxford Sauce, **8**-1283

Oxtail(s), **8**-1283
à la Bourgeoisie, **2**-192
Ragout, Sour (Savanyu Ököfarok), **6**-918
Soup, **2**-192
Soup I (Clear), **4**-620
Soup (Kori Kuk), **7**-1020
Soup II (Thick), **4**-621
and Vegetable Soup, **8**-1283

Oyster(s), **8**-1284
Angels on Horseback, **8**-1287
in Aspic, **10**-1665
Beefsteak and, **1**-72
Bienville, Arnaud's, **4**-510
Bisque, **8**-1290
Bisque, Chesapeake, **2**-203
Bread Stuffing, **11**-1781
en Brochette, **8**-1286
Casino, **8**-1287
and Chicken Casserole, **2**-320
and Chicken Sauté, **8**-1288
Chicken Smothered in, **1**-67
and Clams and Mushrooms, Fricassee of, **8**-1198
Club Sandwich, **8**-1287
Devils on Horseback, **8**-1287
Dressing for Turkey, **4**-575
Escalloped, **11**-1823
Fricassee, **1**-45
Fried in Egg Batter (Kul Jun), **7**-1020
Golden-Fried, Harry Hamblet's, **8**-1287
and Ham Gumbo Filé, **4**-660
Hangtown Fry, **2**-243
Hangtown Fry I, II, and III (Beard), **8**-1287
Loaf, **8**-1287
Lusitanian (Ostras Lusitanas), **9**-1456
and Mushroom Pie, **8**-1288
and Mushrooms, Crusted, **8**-1198
and Mushrooms, Fricassee of, **8**-1198
Omelet, **8**-1287
Pancakes, **8**-1287
Pan Roast, **8**-1286
Patties, Creamed, **8**-1286
Pepper Pan Roast, **12**-1928
Pickled, **1**-28
Pie, **8**-1286
-Potato Pie, **9**-1351
Poulette, **8**-1290
Rockefeller, Antoine's, **1**-41
Salad, **8**-1290
Sauce, **5**-695
Sauté, **8**-1290
Scallop, **8**-1222
Scalloped, **8**-1287
in Shells, Baked, **8**-1222
and Shrimp Jambalaya, **4**-510
Shrimp-Oyster Gumbo, **10**-1658
and Shrimp Pie, **8**-1222
Steamed, **1**-60
Stew I and II, **8**-1286
Turkey and, Creamed, **1**-47

Oyster Plant or **Salsify,** **8**-1290
Fritters, **8**-1290
Ozark Pudding, **1**-25

P

Pachadi (Yogurt Salad), **6**-939

Paella, **8**-1291
de la Costa Brava, **11**-1746
a la Valenciana, **8**-1291
Pain d'Amandes (Brussels Almond Bread Cookies), **2**-200
Pain d'Épice (Spiced Bread), **5**-804
Pain de Veau (Veal Loaf), **2**-278
Paistetut Manteliomenat (Baked Almond Apples), **5**-681
Paistetut Sienet (Fried Mushrooms), **5**-681
Paksiw Na Litson (Sour Pork Stew), **9**-1369
Palace Bread (Eish el Seraya), **8**-1216
Palacsinta, Hungarian, **8**-1293
Palak Gosht (Lamb with Spinach), **6**-939

Palm (Cabbage Palm), Hearts of, **2**-260
with Butter Sauce, **2**-260
in Cream, **1**-32
Kumu Niu Pu'uwai, **9**-1435
Salad, **2**-260
Pam's Apple Pie with Cheese, **1**-28
Panama Fritters (Carimañolas), **11**-1706
Panama Radish Salad, **7**-1086
Panama Whipped Avocado (Aguacates Batidos), **11**-1709

Pancake(s), **8**-1292; see also Waffle(s)
Apple Pancakes, **1**-100
Apple Pancakes, German, **8**-1293
Bacon, Egg, and Corn Cakes, **1**-134
Bacon, Egg, and Corn Pancakes, **3**-484
Blini, **2**-205
Quick, **2**-206
Raised, **2**-206
Russian, **8**-1293
Blintz(es), **2**-206; **4**-516; **8**-1294
Blueberry, **6**-992
Cheese, **2**-206
Cheese Pancakes, Rolled (Kaese Blintzes), **6**-992
Cherry, **6**-992
Blueberry Pancakes, **2**-209
Boxty-on-the-Griddle, **6**-944
Boxty-on-the-Pan, **6**-944
Bran Pancakes, **2**-238
Buckwheat Cakes, **2**-249; **8**-1293; **9**-1354
Buttermilk Pancakes, **2**-241; **8**-1292
Cannelloni, Italian, **8**-1293
Cheese Pancakes, **2**-238
Cheese and Chili Pancakes, Mexican, **8**-1293
Chinese Egg Rolls, **8**-1294
Chinese Egg Rolls (Chi Tan Chuan), **3**-401
Corn Cakes, Lace-Edge, **1**-41
Cottage (Cheese) Pancakes, **3**-361
Crêpe(s), **4**-514
Basic French, **8**-1293
Casserole, **4**-516
Gâteau, **4**-516
as a Main Dish, **4**-516
Fat Pancakes (Gorditas), **7**-1143
Flannel Cakes, **5**-703; **8**-1293
French Pancakes, **5**-699
Basic (Crêpes), **8**-1293
Fresh-Corn Cakes, **3**-484
German Pancakes, **8**-1293
with Spinach, **11**-1755
Griddle Cakes, **2**-227
Apple-Walnut, **5**-826
Cornmeal, **5**-826
Huckleberry **6**-915
Lefser, **8**-1241
New England, **8**-1292
Oatmeal, **5**-826
Rhode Island, **5**-825
Sour-Milk, **9**-1354
Ham and Herb Pancakes, English, **8**-1293
Oatcake, Old-Fashioned, **6**-904
Johnnycakes, **8**-1293
Lefser, **8**-1241
Liberal Pancakes, **1**-39
Logger's Flapjacks, **5**-703
Louisiana Pancakes, **11**-1797
Maple Buckwheat Cakes, **5**-826
Matzo Brie (Fried Matzos), **6**-994
Meat Pancakes, **2**-247
Oatcakes, Hot, **11**-1818
Oyster Pancakes, **8**-1287
Palacsinta, Hungarian, **8**-1293
Pancake(s), **2**-238
with Bacon (Spekpannekoeken), **4**-593
Layered with Minced Ham (Sonkás Palacsinta), **6**-919
Roll Ups, **7**-1049
Stuffed, I (Cannelloni alla Parmigiana), **6**-958
Stuffed, II (Manicotti), **6**-958
Stuffed, with Cheese Sauce, **3**-359
Peanut-Butter Pancakes, **8**-1326
Plättar, **11**-1792
Potato Pancakes, **9**-1468
Potato Pancakes (Kartoffel Latkes), **6**-991
Rice Pancakes, **10**-1551
Rolled Pancakes (Nalesniki), **9**-1429
Sour-Cream Pancakes, **8**-1292
Sourdough Pancakes, **1**-23; **8**-1292
Squash Pancakes, **1**-63
Syrniki (Fried Cheese Cakes), **10**-1572
Tiny Pancakes (Plättar or Pannekaker), **8**-1240
Very Thin Pancakes (Flensjes), **4**-593
Yeast Pancakes, **8**-1292
Zucchini Pancakes (Kolokythia Krokettes), **5**-822

Pancake(s), Dessert
Blintzes, **4**-516
Blueberry Blintzes, **6**-992
Cheese Pancakes, Rolled (Kaese Blintzes), **6**-992
Cherry Blintzes, **6**-992
Clafoutis (French), **3**-372
Crêpes Carlos, **8**-1293
Crêpes Suzette, **4**-516; **5**-701
Dessert Crêpes, **4**-516
Frozen Crêpes, **6**-934
German Pancakes, **8**-1293
Seattle Dutch Babies, **12**-1932
Pandowdy, Apple, **1**-101
Pandowdy, Blueberry, **2**-209
Panettone (Italian Coffeecake), **3**-463
Panggang Golek (Roast Duck Varnished with Coconut), **11**-1715
Pannhaas or Scrapple, **1**-66
Pansit Gisado (Fried Stewed Noodles), **9**-1369
Pa Pao Fan (Eight Treasures Puddings), **3**-403
Papa Empanada al Horno (Potato Soufflé), **9**-1497
Papai (Kona Crab), **9**-1434
Papas con Salsa Huancaina Fría (Potatoes with Cold Huancayo Sauce), **11**-1708
Papaw or Pawpaw, **8**-1296

Papaya, **8**-1296
Lime-Frosted, **12**-1933
Pineapple-Papaya Conserve, **9**-1410

Paprika, **8**-1296
Butter, **2**-279
Cheese Sauce, **8**-1297
Chicken (Paprikahühner), **1**-122
Chicken with Sour-Cream Sauce, **8**-1296
Hamburgers, **6**-869
Mayonnaise Dressing, **10**-1622
Schnitzel, **1**-127
Toast Butter, **11**-1829
Turkey, **12**-1872
Veal Paprikash, **8**-1296
Paprikahühner (Paprika Chicken), **1**-122
Paradeiskraut (Cabbage with Tomatoes), **1**-122

Paraguay Creamed Squash (Kiveve), **11**-1708
Paraguay Ground-Meat Stew (Zoo-Tosopy), **11**-1704
Paraguay Meatballs (Albóndigas), **11**-1705
Parfait, see Frozen Desserts, Parfait
Pariser Schnitzel, **1**-126
Parisian Luncheon, **4**-633
Parisienne Sauce, **10**-1613
Parkerhouse Rolls, **2**-233
Parker House Rolls (QC), **10**-1525
Parmesanschlegel (Leg of Veal with Cheese), **1**-121

Parsley, Parsleyed, **8**-1297
Butter, **1**-86; **5**-695
and Carrot Soup, **8**-1298
Cheese Balls, **8**-1299
-Cheese Toasts, **8**-1298
Chive Butter, **8**-1299
Corn Fritters, **5**-749
Dumplings, **8**-1298
Egg and Ham Roll, **8**-1298
Fried, **8**-1298
and Green-Onion Stuffed Bread, **8**-1276
Green Sauce, **5**-694
Ham (Jambon Persillé), **5**-745
and Mint Salad, **8**-1213
-Olive Sauce, **11**-1738
and Onion Finger Sandwiches, **10**-1610
Parmesan Parsley Sauce, **11**-1738
Pinwheels, **12**-1875
Potato Balls, **9**-1463
Salad, **8**-1298
Salsa Verde, **8**-1299
Sauce, **8**-1299
Sauce, Italian, **8**-1299
Soup, Canadian, **11**-1690
and Spinach Pie, Iranian (Coucou Sabzi), **8**-1215

Parsnip(s) **8**-1299
Cakes, **8**-1224
Fritters, **1**-68
Glazed, **8**-1224
Stew, **8**-1299
Parson (Mrs.) Receipt for Cream, **8**-1229

Partridge(s), **8**-1299
with Cabbage and Juniper Berries, **8**-1300
in Marinade, **8**-1300
Party Pudding, **1**-68
Party Punch (QC), **10**-1527

Passion Fruit, **8**-1300
Chiffon Pie, **8**-1300
Passover Fermented Beet Juice (Pesach Rusell), **6**-994
Passover Nut Cake, **6**-995

Pasta, **8**-1300
Cannelloni alla Parmigiana (Stuffed Pan-Cakes I), **6**-958
Egg Barley (Tarhonya), **6**-919
Fusilli, Two-Cheese, **11**-1737
Lasagna, **7**-1041; for recipes see Lasagna
Macaroni, **7**-1090; for recipes see Macaroni
Manicotti, **7**-1104; for recipes see Manicotto, Manicotti
Mushroom Sauce for, Creamy, **8**-1247
Noodles, **8**-1231; for recipes see Noodle(s)
Pasta Fazula (Thick Soup of Macaroni and Beans), **6**-952
Ravioli, **10**-1538; for recipes see Ravioli
Rigatoni, Neapolitan, **8**-1274
with Sausage Sauce, **10**-1636
Spaghetti, **11**-1735; for recipes see Spaghetti
Vermicelli, **12**-1910
Zucchini Ziti, **12**-1962
Pastel de Carne (Meat Pie), **11**-1705
Pastel de Maíz con Gallina (Chicken Pie with Corn Crust), **7**-1140
Pastel de Papas o Choclos (Potato or Sweet-Corn Pie), **11**-1705
Pastelillos Gallegos (Galician Turnovers), **9**-1497

Pastries, Appetizer and **Main-Course;** see also Pie(s) and Tart(s); Turnover(s)
Anchovy Puffs, **8**-1306
Cabbage and Tuna Pirog, **12**-1802
Cheese Hearts, **8**-1306
Cheese Pinwheels, Tiny, **8**-1306
Chicken Appetizers, **8**-1306
Chicken-Mushroom Vol-au-Vent, **12**-1913
Cream Puffs, Appetizer, **8**-1306
Curried Shrimp Diamonds, **8**-1306
Curry Puffs, **6**-912
Deviled-Ham Pinwheels, **8**-1306
Filled Pastry (Börek), **8**-1215
Karelian Pasties (Karjalanpiiraat), **5**-678
Meat Pastries, **11**-1696
Meat Pies (Hallacas), **11**-1706
Parmesan Cubes, Salty, **8**-1306
Parsley Pinwheels, **12**-1875
Pâté en Croûte, **8**-1312
Pimiento Pinwheels, **8**-1306
Pissaladière, **5**-745
Profiterole, **9**-1483
Roquefort Pinwheels, **8**-1306
Shrimp Puffs, **8**-1306
Spinach-Cheese Strips, **8**-1306
Swiss Petit Puffs, **8**-1306
Tuna Pastries, **12**-1866
Zeppole, **12**-1960

Pastries, Dessert; see also Pie(s) and Tart(s), Dessert; Turnover(s), Dessert
Apple Strudel, **11**-1780
Baklava (Filled Pastry), **5**-823; **8**-1216
Cheese Pastries, Hungarian, **8**-1308
Cheese Strudel, **11**-1780
Cherry-Coconut Pastries, **8**-1309
Cherry Strudel, **11**-1780
Coconut Tea Rounds, **8**-1310
Cream Puffs, **3**-492; **8**-1308
Petits Puffs, **8**-1308
Crunch Cakes or Favors (Chrust Czyli Faworki), **9**-1431
Danish Pastries, **8**-1308
Dreams (Sonhos), **9**-1457
Éclairs, **4**-594; **8**-1309
Farina Pastries (Galotoboureko), **5**-823
Fresh Raspberry Pastries, **10**-1536
Fried Cakes (Rosquillas), **11**-1747
Fried Twists (Klejner), **8**-1241
Hamantaschen, **6**-995
Hungarian Walnut Roll (Diós Tekercs), **6**-922
Lancaster Squares, **8**-1310
Mela's Ladyfinger Dessert, **11**-1747
Mohn (Poppy-Seed) Strudel, **11**-1780
Napoleons, **8**-1206
Napoleons, Easy, **8**-1206
Nut Pastries (Pura), **5**-824
Orange-Plum Twists, **8**-1309
Plum-Orange Twists, **9**-1417
Profiterole, **9**-1483
Prune Piroshkis, **6**-993
Raspberry Maids of Honour, **8**-1309
Sour-Cream Twists, **8**-1309
Strudel Filled with Preserves, **11**-1780
Twigs (Khvorost), **10**-1573
Wind Puffs (Buñuelos de Viento), **9**-1497
Yogurt Honey Cakes, **12**-1958

Pastry, **8**-1302
Beef-Pie, **8**-1261
Biscuit Dough, Rich, **11**-1725
Boiling-Water, **8**-1303
Cheese, **9**-1398
Cheese, Russian, **11**-1838
Chicken-Fat, **9**-1399
Chocolate, **8**-1304
Chocolate Pie Shell, **9**-1399
Coconut Crust, **9**-1399
Cookie-Dough Crust, **1**-33
Cream, **4**-627; **5**-746, 784
Cream-Cheese, **8**-1304
Cream (Crème Pâtissière), **5**-762
French Crust, Flaky, **12**-1879
French, Nonsweet (Pâte Brisée), **8**-1304
French, Sweet (Pâte Brisée Sucrée), **8**-1304
for Individual Deep-Dish Pies, **9**-1399
Lattice Pies, **8**-1303
for Meat Pie, **9**-1399
for Meat Pies, Special, **8**-1304
Oil, **8**-1303
for 1-crust shell, baked and unbaked, **8**-1304
Pâte à Choux, **11**-1804
Patty Shells, **8**-1313
Phyllo, Homemade, **5**-823
Pie Shells, Baked and Unbaked, **8**-1303
Pie Top, Unbaked (for meat pies or deep-dish pies), **8**-1303
Potato Pastry Shells, **6**-912
Puff Paste, **2**-280; **8**-1304
Puff Shells, **7**-1039
for Samosas, **12**-1879
Special (for turkey pie) (QC), **10**-1523
Standard, **9**-1399; **11**-1814
Standard, Ingredients for, Chart, **8**-1303
Strudel Dough, **11**-1779
Sweet, **11**-1814
Sweet Dough, **9**-1355
Tart (Kuchenteig), **11**-1804
Tart Shells, **11**-1814
Tart Shells, Baked, **8**-1303
Tart, Sweet (Pâte Sucrée), **5**-762
Two-Crust Pies, **8**-1302

Pâte (French pastry); see also Pastry
Brisée (Nonsweet French Pastry), **8**-1304
Brisée Sucrée (Sweet French Pastry), **8**-1304
à Choux, **11**-1804
Sucrée (Sweet Tart Pastry), **5**-762

Pâté(s), **8**-1310, and **Terrine(s),** **11**-1819
Chicken Liver Pâté, **4**-565; **7**-1075
Chicken-Liver Pâté, Ruby-Glazed, **6**-979
Chicken-Liver Terrine, Quick and Easy, **8**-1312
Foie Gras, Artichoke Hearts with, **5**-708
Foie Gras, Hot Biscuits with, **5**-708
Forcemeat, Basic, **8**-1312
Giblet Pâté, **5**-800
King's Point Pâté, **8**-1278
Liver Pâté, Danish, **7**-1074
Liver Pâté (Leverpostej), **4**-536
Liver, Tomato, and Cream-Cheese Loaf, **5**-787
Mushroom Liver Pâté, **7**-1076; **8**-1197
Pâté-and-Cucumber Sandwiches, **5**-708
Pâté(s)
in Aspic, **8**-1312
Butter, **1**-86
en Croûte, **8**-1312
de Foie Gras, **5**-708
de Foie Gras in Aspic, **5**-708
Lise, **3**-439
Pâtés and Terrines, Keeping, **8**-1313
Pork Pâté, **1**-90
Pork Pâté, Basic, **8**-1313
Pork and Veal Pâté with Ham (Terrine de Porc, Veau, et Jambon), **5**-715
Shrimp Paste, **2**-242
Terrine, Country-Style, **8**-1312
Turkey Pâté, **12**-1872
Veal and Bacon Terrine, **12**-1894
Wine Picnic Pâté, **12**-1927
Patriot Punch, **5**-804
Patty, **8**-1313
Pattypan Squash, see Cymling(s)
Patty Shells, **8**-1313
Pauchouse Bourguignon (Fish Stew from Burgundy), **4**-595
Pavese (Egg Consommé), **6**-952
Pavlova, Strawberry, **8**-1313
Pavo a la Nicaragüense (Stuffed Turkey), **11**-1706
Pazundok Ngapi Gyaw (Fresh Tomato Balachong), **11**-1716

Pea(s), **8**-1314
Almond and Cheese Salad, **8**-1315
and Cheese Salad in Tomato Shells, **8**-1315
and Chicken, Herbed, **8**-1314

Chicken Moussaka with, **8**-1190
Chopped Meat with (Keema Matar), **6**-939
and Corn in Cream, **8**-1315
and Corn, Herbed, **8**-1315
Creamed, in Bologna Cups, **10**-1638
French, **4**-568; **8**-1315
Green, and Lettuce, **7**-1063
Green, Minted, **11**-1749
Green, and New Potatoes with Cream, **1**-28
Green-Pea Pudding, **9**-1487
Leek and Green-Pea Purée, **7**-1047
Mushroom-Pimiento, **8**-1315
with Mushrooms and Onions, **8**-1315
Mushrooms, and Pimiento, **11**-1823
Mushrooms Stuffed with Purée of Green Peas, **8**-1201
and New Potatoes in Cream, **9**-1466
and Onions, Curried, **8**-1315
and Potatoes, Creamed (QC), **10**-1524
and Rice, Italian, **10**-1551
and Rice (Risi e Bisi), **4**-570
with Romaine Lettuce (Kopfsalat mit Erbsen), **1**-123
Salmon Wiggle, **10**-1596
Savory, **8**-1315
and Shell Macaroni (Piselli e Pasta), **6**-959
Soup, Iced Curried, **9**-1384
Soup Variations, **11**-1696
Tuna Peas and Rice, **8**-1315
with Tuna (Tonno con Piselli), **12**-1864

Pea(s), Dried
Frankfurters with Yellow Peas, German Style, **5**-722
Hoppin John, **11**-1723
Pureé of (Erbsenpuree), **5**-795
Sausage and Split-Pea Casserole, **2**-320
Soup, Basic Recipe, **11**-1696
Soup (Erwtensoep), **4**-589
Soup, Habitant, **2**-275
Soup, Jamaican Split-Pea, **6**-966
Split-Pea Purée, **8**-1314
Split-Pea Soup, **12**-1927
Yellow Pea Soup (Ärter och Fläsk), **11**-1787
Yellow Pea Soup (Gule Aerter), **4**-538
Yellow Pea Soup with Smoked Pork, **8**-1314

Peach(es), 8-1315
Ambrosia, **8**-1316
Angel Peach Raspberry Cake, **8**-1320
and Apple Pie, **8**-1320
Bavarian Cream, **1**-32
Betty, **8**-1317
and Blueberry Jam, Spiced, **8**-1321
Blueberry Meringue, **2**-209; **8**-1317
Bowler, **8**-1321
Buttermilk Sherbet, **8**-1320
Chili, **8**-1321
Chutney, **8**-1321
Cobbler, **8**-1317; **11**-1725
Cobbler, Old-Fashioned, **3**-454
Compote, **8**-1316
Cream, **8**-1320
Cream Cake, **11**-1701
Cream Tarts, **11**-1812
Crème de Menthe Parfait, **8**-1320
Crisp, **8**-1317
Crumble, **8**-1317
Crumb Pudding, **8**-1317
Delight, **8**-1320
Dessert, Quick, **8**-1321
Dumplings, **8**-1317
Frappé, **6**-926
Fresh-Lemon Peach Cooler, **7**-1056
Fresh Peach(es)
Cocktail, **1**-86
Pie, Lattice-Crust, **8**-1320
Tart, **5**-763
Ginger Fresh-Peach Chutney, **8**-1321
Ginger Mold, **8**-1317
Halves, Gingered, **8**-1321
Ice, **6**-926
Ice Cream, **6**-929
Ice Cream, Ripple, **8**-1320
Jam, **6**-965
Jam, No-Cook, **6**-965
Jam, Spiced, **6**-964
with Key Lime Pie, **8**-1320
Kuchen, **5**-799; **8**-1320
Leather, **1**-34
and Litchi Dessert, Jellied, **7**-1072
Marlow, **7**-1113
Marmalade, **7**-1111
Melba, **8**-1320
Melba, Jellied, **5**-790
Meringue Pie, **9**-1398
Molasses-Peach Meringues, **8**-1184
and Orange Conserve, **8**-1321
Orange-Ginger-Ale Mold, **5**-803
Parfait Pie, **9**-1398
Pickled, **1**-34; **8**-1321
Pickled, Spicy, **9**-1376
Pie, Cream Almond, **1**-65
Pineapple-Ginger-Ale Jelly with Peaches, **5**-803
Plum, and Apricot Medley, **5**-758
and Plum Dumplings, **4**-587
-Plum Milk Shake, **8**-1321
Preserves, Brandied, **9**-1481
Pudding Toast, **11**-1828
Pudding, Upside-Down, **9**-1491
Relish, **10**-1542
à la Russe, **8**-1316
Salads, Four, **8**-1316
Sherbet, **10**-1654
Sherbet, Low-Calorie, **7**-1087
Shortcake, **8**-1320
Slices, **7**-1155
Slump, **1**-67
Soufflé, **8**-1317
Sour-Cream Pie, **7**-1157
Sundae Sauce, **8**-1320
Tapioca, **8**-1317
-Tomato Relish, **10**-1542

Peanut(s), 8-1322
and Baked-Bean Sandwiches, **8**-1322
Banana, Salad, **8**-1323
Brittle, **1**-75; **2**-288
Brittle, Popcorn, **8**-1323
Chews, **1**-75
Cookies, Surprise, **8**-1328
Creamed Onions, **8**-1264
Crisps, **8**-1323
Crunch Chiffon Pie, **9**-1397
Fritters, Crisp (Rempejek Katjang), **11**-1714
Frosting, Broiled, with Yellow Cake, **8**-1323
Macaroni and Cheese, **8**-1322
with Molasses Popcorn, **9**-1437
Oatmeal Cookies, **8**-1323
Potato Cakes, **8**-1323
and Raisin Clusters, **8**-1323
Raisin-Peanut Clusters, **2**-289
Satay Sauce, Javanese, **8**-1323
Satay Sauce, Singapore, **10**-1627
Sauce, **11**-1709
Soup, African Style, **8**-1322
Squares, **2**-285
Stuffing, **8**-1323
Sweet Potatoes, **11**-1797
-Tomato Sauce, Chicken in, **8**-1324

Peanut Butter, 8-1323
Apple Cake, **8**-1328
Apple Tea Sticks, **8**-1326
Apricot Candy Roll, **8**-1328
and Bacon Sandwich, **1**-134
Cake, **8**-1328
Celery Soup, **8**-1324
Chiffon Pie, **8**-1328
Chocolate Frosting, **8**-1328
Chocolate Fudge, **8**-1328
Chocolate Sauce, **8**-1328
Cookies, Surprise Peanut, **8**-1328
Drop Cookies, **3**-476
Fruit Salad, **8**-1325
Garlic Bread, **8**-1326
Hamburger Balls, **6**-870
Ham Puffs, **8**-1324
Ham Rolls, **8**-1324
Honey Cookies, **3**-474
Ice Cream, **8**-1326
Marmalade Coffeecake, **8**-1326
Muffins, **8**-1326
Nigerian Groundnut Stew, **8**-1324
-Onion Canapés, **1**-86
Orange Bread, **8**-1325
Pancakes, **8**-1326
Peanut Loaf, **8**-1325
Pineapple-Peanut Spread, **9**-1403
Pineapple Salad Dressing, **8**-1325
Potato Salad, **8**-1325
and Prune Sandwiches, **9**-1485
Quick Tricks with, **8**-1324
Salad Dressing, Old Colonial, **8**-1325
Sandwiches, **8**-1325
Sandwich Fillings, **10**-1606
Sauce, **8**-1325
Sauce with Braised Celery, **8**-1325
Sour-Cream Sauce, **8**-1325
Spreads, Three, **8**-1324
Stuffed Tomatoes, **8**-1325
Sweet-Potato Casserole, **8**-1325
Topping, **8**-1328
Vegetables with Peanut Sauce (Gado Gado), **11**-1715
Pear, Prickly or Cactus, see Prickly Pear

Pear(s), 8-1329
and Apples, Poached, **8**-1330
Baked (Poires Cuites), **2**-200
and Blue-Cheese Salad, **5**-788
Carmen, **8**-1331
-Cheese Salad, **8**-1330
Chutney, **12**-1878
Compote, Gingered, **8**-1332
Condé, **10**-1552
Cottage Pear Salad, **3**-361
Cranberry, Hot (QC), **10**-1524
Cranberry Relish, **10**-1542
and Cream-Cheese Salad, Jellied, **6**-980
Cream Pie with Apricot Glaze, **8**-1333
in Crème de Cacao, **8**-1333
Curried, **8**-1330
Dessert, **8**-1331
Devonshire, **11**-1701
Fresh Pear(s)
Ambrosia, **8**-1331
Cactus Salad, **8**-1330
Cheese, and Anchovy Salad, **8**-1330
with Chocolate, **8**-1331
Compote, **8**-1332
and Crabmeat Salad, **8**-1330
Crumble, **8**-1333
Crumb Pudding, **8**-1331
and Cucumber Aspic, **8**-1330
Grated, Snow, **8**-1331
Hélène, **8**-1332
as Meat Accompaniment, **8**-1330
Pie, **2**-278
Relish, **8**-1333
Sauce, **8**-1331
and Shrimp Appetizer, **8**-1330
Snacks, **8**-1330
Garnished, **4**-629
Ginger Crumble, **9**-1491
Gingered, **5**-801
Grape, and Celery Salad, **10**-1588
Halves and Cherry Compote (Kompot iz Narezanykh Popolam Grush i Vishen), **10**-1573
Hélène, **3**-415
Honey, **8**-1333
Honeyed, **6**-910
Lima-Bean-and-Pear Casserole, Baked, **1**-76
Lime-Pear Salad, **8**-1330
de Luxe, **8**-1332
de Menthe Salad, **8**-1330
Mincemeat, Spicy, **7**-1162
-Orange Compote, **8**-1333
and Orange Conserve, **3**-466
in Orange Sauce, **5**-758

Pear(s), continued
Pie, Colonial, **9**-1393
Pie, Early American, **8**-1247
-Pineapple Conserve, **8**-1333
Poached in Fresh Grape Juice, **8**-1331
Poires à l'Impératrice, **10**-1554
Preserves, **9**-1482
Pudding, Bird's-Nest, **7**-1098
and Quince Jam, **6**-964
-Raspberry Jam, **6**-965
in Red Wine, **4**-557
Red-Wine-Baked, **12**-1933
Relish, **10**-1542
Ruby, **8**-1333
Seafoam Salad, **10**-1587
Sour-Cream Devonshire, **10**-1561
Stewed (Stoofperen), **4**-593
Stuffed, with Apricot Glaze (Poires Glacées), **5**-746
Tart with Cream, **8**-1333
Varieties of Fresh Pears, Chart, **8**-1329
Whole, with Raisin-Nut Filling, Baked, **8**-1331
Winter-Pear Halves, Baked, **8**-1331

Pecan(s), **8**-1333
and Apple Salad, Jellied, **8**-1334
Apricot-Pecan Sticks, **8**-1335
Bars, **3**-471
Bread, Chuck Wagon, **11**-1732
Butter Balls, **3**-432
Butter Beans with, **1**-69
Butterscotch, Roll, Frozen, **8**-1335
Cake, Louisiana, **4**-513
Caramel Pralines, **9**-1480
with Chicken, Southern, **8**-1334
Chocolate-Pecan Pie, **8**-1335; **9**-1390
Coconut, Filling, **3**-407
Coffeecake, **8**-1334
Coffee-Pecan Fancies, **8**-1335
Cracker Pie, **9**-1390
Dainties, **8**-1335
Dainties, Southern, **8**-1335
Date Comfits, **8**-1335
and Date Pie, Arizona, **1**-24
Guava-Pecan Pie, **5**-829
Honey Tea Toast, **11**-1826
Kisses, Creole, **3**-444
Lemon-Nut Cookies, **7**-1056
Mincemeat Delight, **7**-1164
Pastries, **4**-646
Pecanburgers, Burgundy, **8**-1334
Penuche, **9**-1358
Pie, **1**-34
Pie, Southern, **8**-1335; **9**-1390
-Pimiento Cheese Spread, **8**-1334
Porcupines, **1**-44
Praline Confections, **9**-1480
Pralines, **2**-285
Praline Toast, **11**-1828
Praline Topping, Broiled, **9**-1480
Prune Bread, **8**-1334
Pumpkin Nut Waffles, **9**-1499
-Rice Loaf, **8**-1334
Roll, **2**-289
-Roll Slices, **2**-289
Rolls, Sticky, **8**-1334
Salted, **8**-1335
Squares, Spicy, **8**-1335
Stuffing, **8**-1334; **10**-1558
Sugared, **8**-1335
Sweet-Potato Pie, **11**-1798
Tarts, **4**-513
-Tuna-Cheese Sandwiches, **8**-1334
Two-Cheese Logs, **1**-78
Vinegar Pie, "Piebox" Special, **11**-1732
Pechennaia Ryba v Slivkakh s Shafranom (Porgies Baked in Saffron Cream), **10**-1570
Peixe à Alentejana (Fish Alentejo Style), **9**-1455
Pello (Iranian Pilaf), **8**-1215
Pennies from Heaven, **6**-910
Pennsylvania Dutch Apple Butter, **9**-1350
Pennsylvania Dutch Chowchow, **1**-90
Pennsylvania Dutch Cookery, **9**-1349
Pennsylvania Dutch Corn-Chicken Soup, **3**-481
Pennsylvania Dutch Corn Relish, **3**-484

Penuche, Panocha, or **Penuchi,** **9**-1358
Old-Time, **2**-285
Pecan, **9**-1358
Peperoni con Patate (Peppers and Potatoes), **6**-959

Pepper(s), capsicum, **9**-1358
Butter, **1**-64
and Corn Relish, **10**-1541
Hash, **6**-879
Pipérade, **9**-1411
and Potatoes (Peperoni con Patate), **6**-959
Roasted-Pepper Sauce, **11**-1738
Pepper(s), Green
Anchovy-Stuffed, **9**-1359
Baked Stuffed, **5**-715
-and-Beef Oven Stew, **9**-1359
Beef-and-Rice Stuffed, **9**-1358
Butter, **2**-279
and Cabbage Slaw (QC), **10**-1524
Creole Stuffed, **9**-1359
Frankfurter-Stuffed, **5**-722
and Green Tomatoes, Stewed, **11**-1832
Grilled, **9**-1360
Hamburger Pepper Steaks, **9**-1358
Ham- and Rice-Stuffed, **10**-1549
Hash-Stuffed, with Cabbage, **9**-1359
Lamb Chili, Pueblo, **11**-1728
Lamb-Stuffed, **7**-1039
Pepper Cabbage, **9**-1350
Pickled, **1**-82
Relish, **9**-1360
Salad, Italian Style, **9**-1360
Salad (Zöld Paprika Saláta), **6**-919
Salmon-Stuffed, **10**-1596
Sauerkraut-Sausage-Stuffed, **10**-1638
Sautéed, **7**-1086
Strips, **2**-301
Strips, Marinated, **10**-1554
Strips, Sautéed, **9**-1359
Stuffed, **8**-1216
Stuffed with Grated Carrots (Pertzy Farshirovannye Tiortoi Morkov'yu), **10**-1573
Tomato, and Celery Relish, **11**-1835
and Tomatoes, **9**-1360
and Veal, Italian Style, **12**-1896
and Veal Long Boys, **9**-1359
and Zucchini Stew, **12**-1962
Pepper(s), Red
Jam, **6**-964
Stuffed with Rice and Cheese, **9**-1359

Pepper, nigrum, **9**-1360
Butter, **8**-1278
Steak, French (Steak au Poivre), **11**-1767
Peppermint, **9**-1361; for recipes see Mint, Minted
Pepper Pot Soup, **1**-65
Pepper Pot Soup with Dumplings, **9**-1350
Pepperpot Soup, Myrtle Bank, Jamaican, **6**-966
Pepper Pot Soup, Philadelphia, **11**-1694
Pepperrotsaus (Horseradish Sauce), **8**-1240

Perch, **9**-1362
Baked in Tomato Sauce, **5**-690
Casserole, **5**-691
Italian Style, **5**-691
Italian Style (Pesce Persico), **6**-954
Mexican Style, **9**-1363
Ocean-Perch, Chili Baked, **9**-1363
Ocean-Perch Fillets, Deviled, **9**-1363
Ocean-Perch Fritters, **5**-748
Périgueux Sauce, **10**-1613, 1619
Pernil con Vino al Caldero (Pot of Fresh Ham with Wine), **9**-1496
Persian Apple Dolma, **4**-571

Persimmon(s), **9**-1363
Graham-Cracker Dessert, **1**-38
Grapefruit, and Pomegranate Salad, **9**-1364
Ice, **9**-1364
à la Mode, **9**-1364
Pudding, **1**-25
Pudding, Baked, **9**-1364
Pudding, Cold, **9**-1364
Pulp, **9**-1364
Pertzy Farshirovannye Tiortoi Morkov'yu (Green Peppers Stuffed with Grated Carrots), **10**-1573
Peru Cauliflower Fritters (Torrejas de Coliflor), **11**-1708
Peru Lima Style Soup (Sopa a la Limeña), **11**-1703
Peru Pickled Fish (Seviche), **11**-1704
Peru Potatoes with Cold Huancayo Sauce (Papas con Salsa Huancaina Fría), **11**-1708
Peruna ja Pekoni Laatikko (Potato and Bacon Pudding), **5**-681
Pesach Rusell (Passover Fermented Beet Juice), **6**-994
Pescado en Escabeche (Pickled Fish), **9**-1494
Pescado al Horno (Baked Fish), **11**-1705
Pescado a la Vinagreta (Fish Vinaigrette), **11**-1741
Pesce alla Siciliana (Sicilian Fish), **6**-954
Pesce Fritto (Fried Fish Fillets, Italian Style), **6**-954
Pesce Persico (Perch, Italian Style), **6**-954
Pesto Genovese (sauce), **1**-148
Pesto alla Genovese (Genovese Garlic Sauce), **5**-755
Petite Marmite I and II, **9**-1364
Petits Fours, **9**-1365
Petticoat Tails, **6**-950
Petti di Pollo alla Piemontese (Chicken Breast, Piedmont Style), **6**-955
Petto di Vitello (Veal Breast), **6**-954

Pfeffernüsse, **9**-1367
Almond, **9**-1367
Pflaumensuppe (Prune Soup), **9**-1350

Pheasant, **9**-1367
in Casserole with Sausage, **5**-773
with Sauerkraut, Braised, **9**-1367
Sautéed, **9**-1368
Stuffed Roast, **4**-625; **9**-1367
Stuffed (wet dressing) and Roasted, **5**-773
Philadelphia Fish House Punch, **9**-1502
Philadelphia Pepper Pot Soup, **11**-1694
Philadelphia Vegetable Relish, **9**-1350
Philippine Cookery, **9**-1368
Pho (Ginger Beef Soup with Noodles), **11**-1717
Phra Ram Long Song (Rama Bathing), **11**-1715
Phyllo or Filo, **5**-822
Phyllo, Homemade, **5**-823
Picadillo, **6**-877
Piccalilli, **9**-1372
Piccata à la Kerzenstuberl, **1**-127
Pichelsteiner Fleisch (Pichelsteiner Casserole), **1**-121
Pichola, **1**-24
Pickerel, Marinated, **9**-1401

Pickle(s), **9**-1372, and **Relish(es),** **10**-1541; see also Chutney; Ketchup
Apple Relish, **10**-1541
Apple Slices, Pickled, **9**-1376
Apple and Tomato Relish, Spicy, **10**-1542
Apricots, Pickled, **9**-1376
Apricots and Prunes, Spiced, **4**-578
Barbecue Sauce Relish, Chuck's, **10**-1543
Beet and Cabbage Relish, **10**-1541
Beet and Cucumber Relish, **1**-90
Beets, Pickled, **8**-1278
Beets, Pickled (Nedlagte Rødbeter), **8**-1239
Beets, Pickled (Syltede Rødbeder), **4**-542
Beets, Pickled, Scandinavian, **2**-195
Beets, Spiced Pickled, **9**-1376
Blueberry Relish, **2**-210
Bread-and-Butter Pickles, **1**-74

Bread-and-Butter Pickles, Crisp, **9**-1373
Cabbage Relish, **2**-260
Cabbage-Beet Relish, **5**-726
Carrot Pickles, **9**-1374
Carrots, Pickled, **2**-309
Carrot Sticks, Dilled, **2**-305
Cauliflower Pickles, **9**-1373
Chili Sauce, **1**-64
Chopped-Cabbage Pickle, **1**-23
Chowchow, **8**-1231; **9**-1350
Chowchow, Pennsylvania Dutch, **1**-90
Corn and Pepper Relish, **10**-1541
Corn Relish, **1**-39
Corn Relish, Pennsylvania Dutch, **3**-484
Corn Relish, Quick, **10**-1541
Cranberry-Filbert Relish, **10**-1542
Cranberry and Horseradish Relish, **3**-490
Cranberry Pear Relish, **10**-1542
Crystal Mixed Pickles, **9**-1376
Crystal Tomato Pickles, **9**-1373
Cucumber-Onion Relish, **1**-90
Cucumber Pickle Relish, **10**-1542
Cucumber Relish, Sweet, **10**-1542
Cucumbers, Pickled, **4**-522
Cucumbers, Pickled (Asier), **4**-538
Cucumbers, Pickled (Liang Pan Huang Kua), **3**-403
Curried Tomato Relish, **5**-726
Dilled Crisscross Carrots, **4**-564
Dilled Green Beans, **4**-564
Dill Green-Tomato Pickles (Kosher Style), **9**-1374
Dill Pickles, **9**-1372
Dill Pickles, Fresh (Kosher Style), **9**-1373
Dill Pickles (Kosher Style), **9**-1373
Eggs, Pickled, **9**-1376
Eggs and Red Beets, Pickled, **1**-66
Figs, 5-Day Pickled, **1**-59
Figs, Pickled, **9**-1376
Fresh-Pear Relish, **8**-1333
Fresh Tomato Balachong (Pazundok Ngapi Gyaw), **11**-1716
Fruit-Tomato Relish, **10**-1543
Garlic Half-Sour Pickles, **6**-993
Gooseberries, Spiced, Canadian, **5**-809
Gourmet Relish, **8**-1265
Grapefruit Rind, Pickled, **5**-814
Green-Bean Pickles, Dilly, **9**-1373
Green Peppers, Pickled, **1**-82
Green-Tomato Mustard Pickle, **9**-1350
Green-Tomato Pickle, **9**-1373
Green-Tomato Relish, **10**-1542
Green Tomatoes, Pickled, **6**-993
Harvest Relish, **10**-1543
Hodgepodge Relish, **5**-726
Hot Dog and Hamburger Relish, **10**-1543
Korean Pickle (Kimchi), **7**-1023
Kumquat-Ginger Relish, **7**-1023
Lemon Wedges, Pickled, **7**-1057
Lime Relish, **10**-1542
Mallung (for curry), **4**-527
Marinated Onion Rings, **5**-726
Melon India Relish, **7**-1132
Mint Relish, **10**-1543
Mixed Sweet Pickles, **9**-1376
Molasses Spiced Fruit, **8**-1184
Mushrooms, Pickled, **8**-1197
Mushrooms, Pickled Cooked, **1**-90
Mushrooms, Pickled (Manitaria Toursi), **4**-639
Mustard Pickle, **9**-1374
Nasturtium Seeds, Pickled, **8**-1208
Okra Pickles, **9**-1373
Olive-Oil Cucumber-Onion Pickle, **9**-1374
Onion Pickles, **9**-1373
Onions and Beets, Spiced, **8**-1261
Peach Chili, **8**-1321
Peaches, Pickled, **1**-34
Peaches, Spicy Pickled, **9**-1376
Peach Relish, **10**-1542
Peach-Tomato Relish, **10**-1542
Pear Relish, **10**-1542
Pepper Cabbage, **9**-1350
Pepper Hash, **6**-879
Pepper Relish, **9**-1360
Piccalilli, **9**-1372
Pickle Butter, **1**-86
Pickle Fans, **10**-1666
Pickle-Preserve Syrup, **5**-814
Pickle Stuffing, **11**-1781
Pickling Spice, **9**-1377
Pickling Syrup, **9**-1374
Pineapple and Beets, Piquant, **9**-1407
Pineapple Relish, Spiced, **9**-1408
Prune Plums, Pickled Idaho, **1**-36
Prunes in Sherry, **4**-578
Pumpkin, Pickled, **6**-993
Raisin, Apple, and Nut Relish, **10**-1535
Raisin Relish, Spiced, **12**-1912
Raw-Vegetable Relish, **1**-34
Red-Hot Sauce Relish, **10**-1543
Refrigerator Summer Relish, **1**-90
Rhubarb-Onion Relish, **10**-1542
Ripe Watermelon Pickle, **12**-1920
Spicy Jellied Raisins, **10**-1535
Tomato Appetizer, **1**-89
Tomato, Pepper, and Celery Relish, **11**-1835
Tomato Relish, Spiced, **10**-1543
Tomato Relish, Sweet Spicy, **11**-1835
To Serve with Frankfurters, **5**-726
Turnips, Pickled, **8**-1213
Vegetable Relish, **8**-1315
Vegetable Relish, Philadelphia, **9**-1350
Watermelon-Maraschino Pickle, **12**-1922
Watermelon Pickle, **9**-1374
Yogurt, Cucumber, and Radish Relish, **12**-1958
Zucchini Pickles, **9**-1374; **12**-1962

Pickling, To Pickle, **9**-1376
Pickling Spice, **9**-1377
Pickling Syrup, **9**-1374

Picnic, **9**-1377
A Simply Elegant Picnic, Menu, **9**-1383
Beach Picnic, Menu, **9**-1378
Camping Picnic, Menu, **9**-1384
Chicken, **1**-64
Cookout Picnic, Menu, **9**-1384
Dinner, Sand-Pail, **1**-73
Fish Picnic, Menu, **8**-1276
Holiday Picnic, Menu, **9**-1382
Roadside Picnic, Menu, **9**-1378
Sandwich and Salad Picnic, Menu, **9**-1382

Pie(s), **9**-1385, and **Tart(s),** **11**-1811, **Appetizer** and **Main-Dish**
Bacon and Egg Pie, **4**-626
Beef and Kidney Pie, **9**-1387
Beef and Onion Pie, **8**-1260
Beef Pies, Spanish, **9**-1387
Beef Tartlets, Appetizer, **11**-1811
Carrot Pie, **1**-54
Cassava Chicken Pie, **7**-1105
Cheese and Egg Tart (Vatrushki), **10**-1572
Cheese Pie with Bacon, **3**-355
Cheese Pie (Tiropitta), **5**-819
Cheese Spinach Pie, **3**-361
Cheese Tartlets, **1**-87
Cheese Tartlets (Ramequins au Fromage), **11**-1804
Chicken Pie, **7**-1151
Chicken Pie with Corn Crust (Pastel de Maíz con Gallina), **7**-1140
Chicken Pie, Old Homestead, **3**-382; **9**-1388
Clam Pastries, **6**-912
Clam Pie, **8**-1222
Corn Pie, **3**-484
Corn Quiche, **3**-482
Curried Chicken Tartlets, **11**-1811
Egg and Anchovy Tartlets, **11**-1811
Egg and Potato Pie, Indienne, **9**-1388
Egg-Salmon Quiche, **4**-608
Egg Tart, **11**-1811
Frankfurter-Custard Tarts, **5**-725; **11**-1811
Ham and Egg Pie, **6**-862
Ham and Egg Piroshki (Little Russian Pies), **6**-864
Ham and Egg Tart, **6**-862
Ham Pie with Cheese Pastry, Deep-Dish, **9**-1387
Ham and Swiss-Cheese Pie (Quiche de Bourbonnaise), **6**-862
Hamburger and Kidney Pie, **6**-872
Hamburger Pie, Canadian, **6**-872
Lamb Pie with Herb Crust, **7**-1036
Lamb Pie with Poppy-Seed Crust, **9**-1387
Lamb Shepherd's Pie, **9**-1387
Liver and Vegetable Pie, Savory, **7**-1075
Lobster Pie (Quiche de Langouste), **5**-740
Lobster Quiche, **10**-1529
Mackerel Pie, **7**-1101
Meat Pie, Baked, **9**-1351
Meat Pie (Pastel de Carne), **11**-1705
Meat Pies, Individual, **9**-1387
Mexican Pies, **7**-1049
Mushroom and Kidney Pie, **7**-1013
Mushroom and Oyster Pie, **8**-1288
Mushoom Pastries, **6**-912
Mushroom Potato Pie, **8**-1201
Onion Cheese Pie, **9**-1388
Onion Cheese Tarts, **11**-1811
Onion Pie, Dutch, **8**-1261
Onion Pie Niçoise, **9**-1388
Onion Quiche, French, **8**-1261
Onion Tart, German, **8**-1261
Oyster Pie, **8**-1286
Oyster-Potato Pie, **9**-1351
Oyster and Shrimp Pie, **8**-1222
Pork and Apple Pie, Breakfast, **8**-1224
Pork Pie (Tourtière), **2**-277
Potato, Cheese, and Onion Pie, **9**-1463
Potato or Sweet-Corn Pie (Pastel de Papas o Choclos), **11**-1705
Quiche Lorraine, **4**-566; **5**-703
Quiche Lorraine with Cream Cheese, **10**-1527
Quiche Lorraine with Swiss Cheese, **10**-1529
Ramekins, **10**-1535
Salmon Pie (Pirok), **1**-23
Sardine Pie (Coca de Sardinas), **9**-1494
Sausage-Leek Pie, **9**-1387
Shepherd's Pies, **7**-1049
Shrimp-Mushroom Flan, French, **4**-633
Shrimp Potpie, **10**-1661
Spinach and Parsley Pie, Iranian (Coucou Sabzi), **8**-1215
Spinach Pie, Greek, **11**-1755
Steak and Kidney Pie, **4**-624
Swiss-Cheese Pie, **3**-359
Tamale Pie, **1**-59
To Freeze Pies, **9**-1385
Tomato Pie, Red and Green, **9**-1388
Tongue and Egg Tart, **11**-1811
Tuna Pies, Individual, **12**-1866
Tuna and Potato Tart, **12**-1864
Tuna Tarts, Hot, **11**-1811
Tuna-Vegetable Pie with Cheese Pastry, **9**-1388
Turkey Pie, **9**-1388
Turkey Pie, Breadstick Topping, **12**-1872
Turkey Pie with Corn-Bread Topping, **12**-1875
Turkey Pie with Pastry Crust (QC), **10**-1523
Turkey Pie, Pinwheel, **12**-1875
Two-Cheese Meat Tarts, **11**-1811
Veal-and-Ham Pie, Cold, **9**-1387
Veal Parsley Pie with Dumplings, **1**-78

Pie(s), **9**-1385, and **Tart(s),** **11**-1811, **Dessert**
Almond Tarts (Mandelterter), **8**-1243
Almond Tarts, Swedish (Polynees), **1**-69
Anise Squash Pie, **11**-1762
Apple-Butter Pie, **1**-79
Apple-Cider Raisin Pie, **1**-39
Apple Flan, **5**-703
Apple Pie, **1**-96; **4**-626
Almond Deep-Dish, **12**-1933
Caramel, **9**-1392
with Cheese, Pam's, **1**-28
Cream, **1**-100
Deep-Dish, **1**-101
Deep-Dish Fresh-Apple, **9**-1396

Pie(s) and **Tart(s), Dessert,** continued
Deep-Dish Pantry, **9**-1396
Dried-Apple, **1**-103
Favorite, **9**-1392
Grated-Apple, with Chicken-Fat Pastry, **9**-1393
Honey, **1**-56
New Hampshire Turnover, **1**-57
Puddeny-Pie, **6**-949
Raisin-Nut, **8**-1229
Russkii Iablochnii Pirog, **10**-1574
Spread Apple, **1**-75
Upside-Down, **1**-102
Apple Tart, **5**-763
Apfeltorte, **11**-1806
French, **11**-1812
-Raisin-Nut, **11**-1812
Apricot Cream-Cheese Tarts, **1**-106
Apricot-Jam Tarts, **11**-1812
Apricot Pie(s)
Crumb, **1**-107
-Pineapple, **9**-1396
-Prune, **1**-108
Avocado Lime Pie, **1**-130
Banana Christmas Tarts, **11**-1812
Banana Pie, **9**-1393
Chiffon, **9**-1397
Cream, **1**-139
Meringue, **9**-1392
Nut, Creamy, **5**-801
Berry Tarts, Devonshire, **11**-1812
Blackberry-Almond Meringue Pie, **9**-1392
Blackberry Pie, **2**-204
Black-Bottom Pie, **3**-411
with Chocolate Crust, **9**-1398
Blueberry Pie, **9**-1393; **9**-1396
Deep-Dish, **2**-208
Fluff, **5**-790
Fresh Blueberry, **2**-208
Lattice, **2**-208
Blueberry Tarts, **2**-208
Brandied Mince Pie, **9**-1396
Brazil-Nut Pie Shell, **2**-222
Buttermilk-Coconut-Cream Pie, **9**-1391
Buttermilk Meringue Pie, **2**-254
Butterscotch Cream Pie, **2**-255
Cantaloupe Chiffon Pie, **9**-1397
Caramel Chiffon Pie, **9**-1397
Caramel Custard Pie, **9**-1391
Caramel-Date Pies, Individual, **4**-547
Cheese Pie, Jay's Famous, **3**-368
Cheese Tarts, Tropical, **3**-367
Cherry Flan, **8**-1309
Cherry Pie, **1**-77
Bavarian, **9**-1398
Chantilly, **1**-78
Deep-Dish, **8**-1229
Deep-Dish (QC), **10**-1525
Deep-Dish, with Shortcake Crust, **3**-374
Sour-Cherry, **9**-1396
Sour-Cherry, Canned, **3**-374
Sour-Cherry, Fresh, **3**-374
Sour-Cherry, Frozen, **3**-374
Sweet-Cherry, **9**-1393
Cherry Tart(s), **3**-374; **5**-763; **8**-1309
and Apricot, **7**-1089
Glazed, **11**-1812
Chess Pie, **9**-1388
Chestnut-Chocolate Vanilla Tarts, **3**-416
Chocolate Pie(s)
Almond, **7**-1089
Angel, **3**-411
Brownie, **9**-1390
Chiffon, **3**-393, 411
Coconut Syrup, **9**-1390
Fruit, **4**-578
Meringue, **9**-1392
-Pecan, **8**-1335; **9**-1390
Spongecake, **9**-1390
Cider Pie, **3**-446
Coconut Pie(s)
Custard, **4**-530; **9**-1391
Meringue, **9**-1392
Puddin'-Pie, **3**-456
Syrup, **9**-1390
Coffee Chiffon Pie, **9**-1397
Coffee-Nut Cream Pie, **9**-1391
Concord Grape Pie, **5**-812; **7**-1157
Cottage-Cheese Pie, **9**-1390
Cracker Pie, **9**-1390
Cranberry Pie, **9**-1393
Cranberry-Raisin Pie, **3**-490
Cream Tarts (Babki Śmietankowe), **9**-1431
Custard Pie, **9**-1391
Chocolate-Topped, **9**-1391
Crisp-Crust, **9**-1391
Damson-Plum Pie, **4**-533
Eggnog Pie, Frozen, **7**-1100
Eggnog Tarts, **8**-1247
Elderberry Pie, **4**-617
Frangipane Pie, **5**-716
Fresh Currant Pie, **4**-524
Fresh Currant Tarts, Glazed, **4**-524
Fresh Peach Tart, **5**-763
Frozen Marble Pie, **9**-1398
Fruit Pies, Fried, **11**-1725
Fruit Pie, Swedish, **9**-1396
Fruit Tartlets, **5**-763
Fruit Tarts, Glazed, **11**-1812
Fruit Tarts (Tartes aux Fruits), **5**-746
Fruit Tarts with Pastry Cream (Tartes aux Fruits avec Crème Pâtissière), **5**-746
Funeral Pie, **9**-1355
Grape Tarts, Orange-Glazed, **5**-812
Guava-Cheese Pie, **5**-829
Guava-Pecan Pie, **5**-829
Hazelnut Tarts, **6**-882
Honey-Nut-Apple Pie, **6**-910
Huckleberry Cream-Cheese Pie, **6**-915
Jam Tarts, **4**-626; **11**-1838
Key Lime Pie, **7**-1069
Key Lime Pie with Peaches, **8**-1320
Lemon-Cheese Tarts, **11**-1725
Lemon Pie(s)
Ambrosia, with Coconut Crust, **9**-1397
Cheese, **7**-1054
Chiffon, **7**-1054
Chiffon, in Pastry Shell, **9**-1397
Cream, **7**-1053
Frozen, **9**-1398
Meringue, **7**-1053
Meringue, Old-Fashioned, **9**-1392
Sliced-Lemon, **7**-1053
Sponge, **7**-1053; **9**-1390
Strip, **9**-1355
Lemon Tarts, **8**-1309
Lime Chiffon Pie, **9**-1397
Lime Pie, Florida, **7**-1069
Lime Tarts, **7**-1069
Loganberry-Cheese Tarts, **7**-1081
Loganberry Pie, **7**-1081
Maids of Honour, **4**-626
Mango Pie, **7**-1103
Mango Tarts, **7**-1103
Maraschino-Almond Parfait Pie, **7**-1108
Marbled Chocolate Rum Pie, **9**-1398
Meringue Pie Topping, Never-Fail, **7**-1134
Meringue Topping for Pies, Quick, **7**-1134
Mincemeat Alaska Pie, **7**-1164
Mincemeat Pie with Cheese Crust, **9**-1396
Mince Tarts, **11**-1823
Mocha Chiffon Pie, **7**-1167
Mocha-Nut Cream Pie, **9**-1391
Molasses Chiffon Pie, **8**-1184
Nesselrode Chiffon Pie, **9**-1397
Nesselrode Pie, **8**-1218
Orange Pie
-Cranberry-Raisin, **9**-1393
Cream, **8**-1271
Fresh Orange Chiffon, **8**-1270
with Whipped Cream, **8**-1272
Orange Chiffon Tarts, **8**-1272
Orange Tartlets, **8**-1271
Passion-Fruit Chiffon Pie, **8**-1300
Peach Cream Tarts, **11**-1812
Peach Pie(s)
and Apples, **8**-1320
Cream Almond, **1**-65
Fresh-Peach, Lattice-Crust, **8**-1318
Meringue, **9**-1398
Parfait, **9**-1398
Peanut-Butter Chiffon Pie, **8**-1328
Peanut Crunch Chiffon Pie, **9**-1397
Pear Pie(s)
Colonial, **9**-1393
Cream, with Apricot Glaze, **8**-1333
Early American, **8**-1247
Fresh Pear, **2**-278
Pear Tart with Cream, **8**-1333
Pecan Pastries, **4**-646
Pecan Pie, **1**-34
and Date, Arizona, **1**-24
Southern, **8**-1335; **9**-1390
Pecan Tarts, **4**-513
Peppermint Chiffon Pie, **9**-1361, 1397
Peppermint Chocolate Chiffon Pie, **9**-1397
Piecrust Glazes, **5**-806
Pineapple Pie(s)
-Cheese, **3**-362
and Cream-Cheese, **9**-1408
Fresh-Pineapple, **8**-1247
-Rhubarb, **9**-1393
Two-Crust, **9**-1409
Plum Pie, Deep-Dish, **9**-1417
Pork and Apple Pie, Breakfast, **8**-1224
Prune-Whip Pie, **9**-1486
Pumpkin Pie(s)
Chiffon, **9**-1397
Chiffon Meringue, **9**-1500
Ginger, **5**-801
Ginger-, Frozen, **9**-1500
-Mince, **9**-1500
One-Bowl, **9**-1391
Tawny, **9**-1499
Topped with Ginger Rosettes, **11**-1823
Pumpkin Tarts, Frozen, **9**-1500
Raisin-Nut Pie, **9**-1390
Raisin Pie, **10**-1534
Raisin-Pineapple Custard Pie, **4**-578
Raspberry Chiffon Pie, **6**-980
Raspberry Cream Pie, **10**-1536
Rhubarb Pie, **1**-69
-Apple, **10**-1544
Lattice, **9**-1393
Meringue, **9**-1392
and Strawberry, **10**-1544
Ricotta Tart, The Gevasci's, **3**-367
Sage-Honey Sour-Cream Pie, **1**-55
Shoofly Pie, **1**-66; **9**-1390
Shoofly Pie, Spicy, **9**-1356
Sour-Cream Pie(s)
Butterscotch Meringue, **9**-1392
Huckleberry, **9**-1355
Peach, **7**-1157
-Raisin, **9**-1391
Squash Pie, **8**-1229
Squash Pie, Company, **6**-915
Strawberry Pie(s)
Chiffon, **6**-980
Glacé, **11**-1778
Snowbank, **11**-1778
Strawberry Tart, **5**-763
Chess, **1**-72
Chiffon, **11**-1812
Currant-Glazed, **9**-1384
Lattice, **11**-1778
Sugaring-Off Pie, **7**-1108
Sweet-Potato Pecan Pie, **11**-1798
Sweet Potato Pie, **9**-1391
Tart Shells, Orange-Pastry, **8**-1272
Vanilla Meringue Pie, **9**-1391
Vanilla Pie, Amish, **9**-1355
Velvety Chiffon Pies, **9**-1396
Vinegar Pie, "Piebox" Special, **11**-1732
Wild-Huckleberry Pie, **1**-77
Yam Custard Pie, **12**-1951
Piebox Special Vinegar Pie, **11**-1732

Piecrust
Almond-Crumb, for Chocolate Chiffon Pie, **3**-411
Beef-Pie Pastry, **8**-1261
Boiling-Water Pastry, **8**-1303
Cheese Pastry, **9**-1398
Chicken-Fat Pastry, **9**-1399
Chocolate-Coconut Crust, **3**-456
Chocolate Pastry, **8**-1304
Chocolate Pie Shell, **9**-1399

Coconut Crust, **9**-1399
Cookie Crust, **3**-367
Cookie-Dough Crust, **3**-369, 428
Cream-Cheese Pastry, **8**-1304
Crumb Crust, **3**-366; **7**-1054, 1167; **9**-1399
French Crust, Flaky, **12**-1879
Gingersnap-Crumb Crust, **3**-411; **5**-791
Glazes, **5**-806
Graham-Cracker Tart Shells, **8**-1310
Herb Crust, **7**-1036
Ladyfinger Crust, **6**-980
Lard Pastry, **7**-1041
Lattice Pies, **8**-1303
Meat Pie Pastry, **9**-1399
Meat Pies, Special Pastry for, **8**-1304
Meringue
Pie Shell, **7**-1135
Shell, **9**-1500
Shells, Individual, **7**-1134
Nonsweet French Pastry (Pâte Brisée), **8**-1304
Oil Pastry, **8**-1303
for 1-crust shell, baked and unbaked, **8**-1304
Orange-Pastry Tart Shells, **8**-1272
Pastry, **7**-1075
Pastry for Individual Deep-Dish Pies, **9**-1399
Pastry Crust (for Meat Loaf), **7**-1128
Pie Shells, Baked and Unbaked, **8**-1303
Pie Top, Unbaked (for meat pies or deep-dish pies), **8**-1303
Special Pastry (QC), **10**-1523
Standard Pastry, **9**-1399; **11**-1814
Standard Pastry, Ingredients for, Chart, **8**-1303
Sweet French Pastry (Pâte Brisée Sucrée), **8**-1304
Sweet, Pastry, **11**-1814
Tart Shells, **11**-1814
Tart Shells, Baked, **8**-1303
Two-Crust Pies, **8**-1302
Vanilla-Wafer Crust, **9**-1361
Pieczeń Cieleca z Sardelami (Veal Roast with Anchovies), **9**-1425
Piedmontese Bagna Cauda (Hot Bath), **10**-1627
Piedmont Stuffing, **11**-1782
Piedmont Style Chicken Breast (Petti di Pollo alla Piemontese), **6**-955
Pieds de Porc St. Menehould (Grilled Pigs' Feet), **5**-743
Pierogi z Kaszy ze Serem (Buckwheat Dumplings with Cheese), **9**-1429

Pig, **9**-1399; see also Bacon; Ham; Pork; Sausage
Pigs' Feet
with Chick-Pea Soup (Sopón de Garbanzos con Patas de Cerdo), **9**-1493
Grilled (Pieds de Porc St. Menehould), **5**-743
Pickled, **9**-1351, 1376
Pickled, Spicy, **9**-1448
and Sauerkraut, **9**-1448
Souse, Pickled, **9**-1351
Pigs' Knuckles
Breaded, **9**-1449
Pickled or Fresh, with Split Peas (Nózki Wieprzowe z Grochiem), **9**-1426
Sauerkraut, and Biscuit Dumplings, **9**-1449
and Sauerkraut with Caraway Dumplings, **9**-1351
Sauerkraut, and Potato Dumplings (Schweinekniestücke mit Sauerkraut und Kartoffelklösse), **5**-795
Suckling Pig
Barbecued (Litsong Baboy), **9**-1369
Roast Stuffed, **9**-1399
Roast Stuffed (Prosie Pieczone Nadziewane), **9**-1425
To Carve, **9**-1400
Pigs in Blankets, **10**-1635

Pike, **5**-699; **9**-1400
American Indian Style, **9**-1401
Appetizer with Cocktail Sauce, Chilled, **9**-1400
Baked in Almond Sauce, **9**-1401
Baked in Cream (Tejfeles Sült Ponty), **6**-919
Baked Stuffed (Täytetty Uunihauki), **5**-680
Braised Stuffed, **5**-700
Creamed Broiled, **9**-1400
with Egg Sauce, **9**-1401
Fillets, Baked Mornay, **9**-1400
Fillets, Lemon-Broiled, **9**-1400
with Herbed Mayonnaise, Cold, **5**-700
Loaf, **5**-700
Poached, **5**-700
à la Polonaise (Szczupak czy Karp po Polsku), **9**-1422
Quenelles, **10**-1527
Roasted, Izaak Walton's Recipe from The Compleat Angler, **5**-700
with White-Wine Sauce (Snoek in Witte Wijn Saus), **4**-590

Pilaf, **9**-1401
Bareh Pello, **8**-1215
Brazil-Nut, **2**-222
Bulgur, **8**-1215
Chicken, **3**-391
Chicken (Kotta Pilafi), **5**-820
Chicken Pilau, Madras, **9**-1401
Clam (Achivades Pilafi), **5**-818
Clam Pilaf Casserole, **10**-1554
Crabmeat, **2**-321
Cracked-Wheat, **9**-1402
Frankfurter, **5**-722
Iranian (Pello), **8**-1214
Lamb, Savory Turkish, **7**-1038
Lobster, **2**-321
Millet, **7**-1161
Parsleyed (Pilaffi), **4**-639
Pilafi, **5**-822
Pilau, Indian, **4**-641
Pilau, Saffron, **12**-1878
Pineapple (Ananas), **9**-1403
Plain, **9**-1401
Rice, **1**-146
with Almonds, **1**-14
and Peas, **2**-299
and Pork, Greek, **9**-1401
Vegetable, **9**-1402
Pilaffi, Pilafi, Pilau, see Pilaf
Pilgrim Mincemeat, **7**-1162

Pimiento(s), Pimiento Pepper, **9**-1359
Butter, **2**-279; **5**-695
Corn-Stuffed, **9**-1359
and Fried Eggplant Long Boys, **9**-1359
Peas, and Mushrooms, **11**-1823
Pinwheels, **8**-1306
Rice, **10**-1554
Two-Cheese Fusilli, **11**-1737

Pineapple(s), **9**-1402
Ananas Flambée, Arnaud's, **4**-513
(Ananas) Pilau, **9**-1403
Apricot Jam, **1**-109
Apricot-Pineapple Jam, **6**-963
Apricot-Pineapple Pies, **9**-1396
-Apricot Upside-Down Cake, **9**-1409
-Avocado Spread, **9**-1403
Baked Beans, **9**-1407
Bavarian Cream, **4**-650
and Beets, Piquant, **9**-1407
Blancmange, **2**-205
Blue-Cheese Salad Ring, **7**-1153
Bread Pudding, **9**-1490
Broiled, **1**-146
Buttercream Frosting, **5**-751
Cantaloupe and Pineapple Compote, Fresh, **2**-296
Caramel Custard (Flan de Piña), **5**-703
Cheesecake, **3**-367
Cheesecake, Jellied, **9**-1409
Cheese Mold, **5**-788
-Cheese Pie, **3**-362
Cherry-Almond-Pineapple Jam, **9**-1410
and Chicken, Hawaiian, **9**-1406
-Chili Barbecue Sauce, **10**-1623
Chunks Glacées, **5**-805
Chutney, **3**-446
Coffeecake, **2**-239
and Cream-Cheese Pie, **9**-1408
Crumb Pudding, **8**-1326
-Cucumber Salad, **9**-1408
Cup, Minted, **9**-1403
Curried Shrimps in, **10**-1660
Dressing, Fluffy, **3**-495
Filling, **2**-268; **4**-663
Finger Toast, **11**-1828
Fresh Pineapple(s)
and Avocado Salad, **9**-1408
Ice, **6**-926
Pie, **8**-1247
Punch, **9**-1410
Fruit Cup Served in the Half Shell, **9**-1403
Garnishes, **5**-780
-Ginger-Ale Jelly with Peaches, **5**-803
Gingered Fresh, **2**-301
Gingered Pineapple, Lemon, **9**-1410
and Grape Jam, **6**-964
-Ham Loaf, **9**-1406
-Ham Salad, **9**-1408
Ice, **9**-1410
with Crème de Menthe, **9**-1410
Ice Cream, **6**-929
Iced, **11**-1732
Island Dream (beverage), **9**-1410
Island Toast with Bacon, **11**-1826
Lebanese, **9**-1408
Maple Pineapple Sauce, **7**-1105
Marshmallow Rice Pudding, **10**-1554
Meringue Cake, **9**-1409
-Mint Jam, **6**-964
-Mint Sherbet, **7**-1166
Mint Topping, **6**-931
Mousse, Heavenly, **9**-1409
Muffins, Hawaiian, **4**-635
-Nut Pudding, **9**-1408
-Oatmeal Cookies, **9**-1409
-Orange Salad, **9**-1408
-Papaya Conserve, **9**-1410
Peanut-Butter, Salad Dressing, **8**-1325
-Peanut Spread, **9**-1403
Pear-Pineapple Conserve, **8**-1333
Pie, Two-Crust, **9**-1409
and Pork Casserole, **9**-1406
Pork, Sweet-and-Sour, **9**-1406
Prune-Pineapple Dessert, **9**-1485
Punch, Hot (Ponche de Piña), **11**-1709
Relish, Spiced, **9**-1408
-Rhubarb Pie, **9**-1393
Rice, **9**-1407
Rice Pudding, **10**-1554
-Rum Punch, **9**-1498
Salad, Two-Tone, **9**-1408
Sherbet, Creamy, **9**-1410
Sherbet, Low-Calorie, **9**-1410
and Shrimps, Chinese Style, **9**-1406
Slaw, **9**-1408
Slices, Broiled, **9**-1407
Spareribs, **9**-1406
Sticks, **4**-645
-Strawberry Jam, **6**-964
-Strawberry Salad, **5**-758; **7**-1089
and Sweet Rice Dessert, **9**-1409
Teriyaki, **9**-1406
Tongue, and Cheese Spread, **9**-1403
and Tuna, Oriental, **9**-1406
Tuna, and Rice Salad, **9**-1408
Upside-Down Cake, **2**-268; **12**-1881
Waldorf Salad, **10**-1588
Yam, and Ham Casserole, **9**-1406
Pine-Bark Stew, **1**-61

Pine Nut(s), **9**-1410
Cookies, **9**-1411
Dressing for Chicken, **4**-575
Pinwheels, **7**-1049
Pipérade, **9**-1411

Pipérade (Basque Scrambled Eggs), **4**-608
Piquant Butter, **2**-279
Piquant, Piquante Sauce, **5**-695; **10**-1613, 1619
Pirog, Cabbage and Tuna, **12**-1862
Pirogi, Raised Dough for, **10**-1570
Pirok (Salmon Pie), **1**-23

Piroshki
Cabbage, **10**-1568
Liver, **10**-1568
Meat and Anchovy, **10**-1570
Prune, **6**-993
Raised Dough for, **10**-1570
Russian, **8**-1197
Piselli e Pasta (Peas and Shell Macaroni), **6**-959
Pissaladière (French pizza), **5**-745

Pistachio, **9**-1411
Bavarian with Strawberries, **3**-440
Custard, Frozen, **9**-1411
Fruit Cup, **9**-1411

Pizza, **9**-1411
-Burgers, **6**-868
Hamburger Pizza Pie, **8**-1273
Ham and Egg (Pizza con Uova e Prosciutto), **6**-864
Individual, **3**-355; **8**-1274
Little, **9**-1412
Picnic, **9**-1412
Pissaladière, **5**-245
Rolls, Hot, **9**-1412
Tuna, **12**-1864
con Uova e Prosciutto (Ham and Egg Pizza), **6**-864
Western Style, **10**-1604
Plaki, Haddock, **6**-846
Plantain, **9**-1414; for recipes see Banana(s)
Plättar (Pancakes), **11**-1792
Plättar or Pannekaker (Tiny Pancakes), **8**-1240
Pleskener (Spongecake Cookies), **8**-1243
Plough-Roasted (Sukiyaki), **6**-974
Plowlines, **9**-1357

Plum(s), **9**-1414
and Apple Crumble, **8**-1253
Damson Plum(s)
Butter, **9**-1415
Conserve, **4**-534
Jam, **4**-534
-Orange Twists, **9**-1417
Pie, **4**-533
Preserves, **9**-1418
Stewed, **4**-533
Dumplings (Svestkove Knedlíky), **4**-532
Dumplings (Szilvás Gombóc), **6**-920
Dumplings, Washington, **12**-1932
Fresh Plum(s)
Dumplings, **9**-1417
Jam, **9**-1417
Jellied, with Golden Fresh-Lemon Sauce, **9**-1416
Refrigerator Bread Pudding, **9**-1415
Salad, Jellied, **9**-1417
Sauce, **9**-1415
Stewed, **9**-1415
Vanilla Compote, **9**-1416
Whip, **9**-1416
Fritters, **5**-749
Greengage Plum
Fresh Greengage Plum Betty, **5**-824
Ice, **6**-926
Jelly, **6**-984
Kuchen, **5**-799
-Orange Jam, **6**-964
Orange-Plum Twists, **8**-1309
and Peach Dumplings, **4**-587
Peach-Plum Milk Shake, **8**-1321
Prune-Plum(s), fresh
Cake Cobbler, **9**-1417
Conserve, **9**-1418
Garlic Sauce, **9**-1415
and Grape Salad, **9**-1415
Mincemeat, **9**-1417
with Mock Devonshire Cream, **9**-1417
Pickled Idaho, **1**-36
Pie, Deep-Dish, **9**-1417
Pudding, **9**-1415
Shortcake, Individual, **9**-1417
Preserves, **9**-1482
Sauce, Caucasian (Tkemali), **10**-1627
Snow Pudding, **9**-1417
Soup, Cold, **11**-1697
Wild-Plum Jelly, **1**-40

Plum Pudding, **9**-1418
Brandy, **9**-1492
Flaming, **5**-701
Light, with Hard Sauce, **3**-444
with Rum Sauce, **3**-440
Poi, **9**-1418
Poires Cuites (Baked Pears), **2**-200
Poires Glacées (Stuffed Pears with Apricot Glaze), **5**-746
Poires à l'Impératrice, **10**-1554
Poisson en Papillote (Fish Baked in Foil), **11**-1800
Polar Bear's Eye (Isbjørnøye), **8**-1235
Poledwica z Madera i Truflami (Tenderloin with Madeira Sauce and Truffles), **9**-1424
Poledwica Pieczona (Roast Beef Tenderloin), **9**-1424
Poledwica w Śmietanie (Beef Fillet in Sour Cream), **9**-1424
Poledwica Wieprzowa Duszona na Winie (Pork Pot Roast in Wine), **9**-1426

Polenta, **9**-1418
Casserole, **9**-1419
with Egg Sauce, **9**-1418
with Italian Sausage, **9**-1418
with Salami and Tomatoes, Baked, **9**-1419
Polévka s Jaternimi Knedlíky (Soup with Liver Dumplings), **4**-531
Polish Babka, **7**-1156
Polish Beets, **11**-1700
Polish Bigos, **7**-1016
Polish Bigos (Bigos Polski), **9**-1427
Polish Borsch, **2**-195
Polish Cookery, **9**-1419
Polish Roast Leg of Lamb, **7**-1029
Polish Sausage with Red Cabbage, **7**-1151
Polish Style Hamburgers, **6**-868
Polish Style Meatballs, **7**-1123
Polish Style Mushrooms, **8**-1201

Pollack or **Pollock,** **9**-1431
Chowder, Uncle Ed's, **5**-691
Pollo en Agridulce (Sweet and Sour Chicken), **9**-1496
Pollo alla Cacciatora (Chicken Cacciatora), **6**-955
Pollo a la Costa Brava (Costa Brava Chicken), **11**-1746
Pollo con Salsa (Chicken in Sauce), **11**-1706
Pollo en Vino Dulce (Chicken in Sweet Wine), **9**-1496
Polonaise Noodles, **8**-1233
Polonaise Sauce, **2**-194; **10**-1624; **11**-1837
(for asparagus), **1**-114
Polvorónes (Teacakes), **7**-1143
Polynees (Swedish Almond Tarts), **1**-69
Polynesian Cookery, **9**-1432
Pomander Balls, How to Make, **9**-1435
Pomander, Old English Apple, **9**-1435

Pomegranate(s), **9**-1435
Ice, **1**-24; **9**-1436
Nectar, **9**-1436
and Orange Compote, **9**-1436
Persimmon, and Grapefruit Salad, **9**-1364
Pommes Anna, **9**-1466
Pommes Bonne Femme (Apples Baked on Toast Rounds), **5**-746
Pommes Fondante, **9**-1463
Pommes Frites (Fried Potatoes), **5**-744
Pommes Meringuées, **4**-558
Pommes Mousseline, **8**-1191
Pommes de Terre en Salade (Hot Potato Salad), **5**-745
Pommese de Terre Sautées (Sautéed Potatoes), **5**-744

Pompano, **9**-1436
Broiled, **1**-32
en Papillote, **1**-41
en Papillote, Simple, **9**-1436
Pompushkes, **11**-1700
Ponche de Piña (Hot Pineapple Punch), **11**-1709
Pongal, **6**-942
Ponzu (Dipping Sauce), **6**-975
Poor Man's Cake (Fattigmann), **8**-1241
Poor Man's Gravy, **9**-1354
Poor Parson's Noodle Dish, The, **8**-1232

Popcorn, **3**-480; **9**-1436
Balls, **2**-288; **8**-1231
Balls (QC), **10**-1526
Balls, Sugared, **9**-1437
Caramel, **9**-1437
with Cheese, **3**-484
Chili, **3**-395
Curried, **9**-1437
Molasses, with Peanuts, **9**-1437
Peanut Brittle, **8**-1323

Popovers, **2**-227; **9**-1437
Almond, **2**-238; **9**-1437
Cheese, **2**-238; **9**-1437
Popovers, **2**-238, 242
Whole-Wheat, **2**-238; **9**-1437

Poppy Seed(s), **9**-1437
Boiled Noodles with (Makos Tészta), **6**-920
Butter, **2**-279
Coconut Bars, **9**-1438
Filling, **6**-995; **9**-1438
Kringle, Hungarian, **9**-1437
Layer Torte (Makovy Kolác), **4**-532
Mace Cookies, **7**-1100
Mohn Kuchen, **5**-799
Mohn Strudel, **11**-1780
Strudel, **6**-922
Torte, **9**-1437
Two-Cheese Fusilli, **11**-1737
Porc, see Pork
Porcupines, **1**-44
Porcupines with Vegetable-Cheese Sauce, **7**-1123

Porgy(ies), **9**-1438
Baked in Saffron Cream (Pechennaia Ryba v Slivkakh s Shafranom), **10**-1570
en Papillote, **5**-691
Sautéed, **9**-1438
with Sherry-Almond Sauce, Panfried, **5**-691
with Tomatoes, Baked, **9**-1438

Pork, **9**-1438; see also Bacon; Ham; Pig; Sausage
Bigos, Polish (Bigos Polski), **9**-1427
Carving, **2**-311-312
Pigs' Feet, see Pig
Pigs' Knuckles, see Pig
Retail Cuts, Where They Come From, Chart, **9**-1439
Suckling Pig, see Pig
Pork Casseroles, **2**-317

Pork, Cured, **9**-1440
and Apple Pie, Breakfast, **8**-1224
Booyaw, **1**-48
Butt, Brown Glazed, **9**-1452
Chops, Smoked (Uha Pua), **9**-1434
and Greens, Southern, **5**-825
Loin of, Smoked, with Burgundy-Cherry Sauce, **9**-1452
New Mexican (Carne Adobada), **11**-1728
Picnic Shoulder with Currant-Mustard Sauce, Simmered Smoked, **9**-1452

and Potato Scallop, **9**-1452
Pot Roast of Smoked Loin of (Frankfurter Rippchen), **5**-795
Salt Pork, **10**-1598
and Bean Chowder, **10**-1598
Beans, and Hominy, **6**-907
Broiled Corn with, **10**-1598
Fried, and Milk Gravy on Hominy Grits, **6**-907
and Potato Chowder, **9**-1462
and Potatoes, Baked, **9**-1452
Soup with Dumplings, Old-Time, **1**-56
Sausage, see Sausage
Smoked Butt Boiled Dinner, **9**-1452
Smoked Butt (Selchfleish), **1**-122
Smoked, with Yellow Pea Soup, **8**-1314
Stew, Sheepherder's, **1**-55
Vegetable Side Dish for Cocido (Verduras), **11**-1743

Pork, Fresh, **9**-1438
Applesauce, Pork, and Kraut Casserole, **1**-63
Balls with Macaroni, **7**-1094
with Bamboo Shoots (Tung Sun Ch'ao Jo), **3**-399
and Beef Meatballs, Sweet-and-Sour, **7**-1126
Brawn, **9**-1448
Broiled (Butaniku-Teriyaki), **6**-974
Butt
Boston, with Vegetables, Pot-Roasted, **9**-1476
with Caraway Sauerkraut, **9**-1440
with Cranberries, Braised, **9**-1440
with Celery, Stewed, Italian, **9**-1451
with Celery, Stewed (Maiale Affogato), **6**-954
and Chicken (Adobong Manok at Baboy), **9**-1369
Chitterlings, Boiled, **3**-404
Chitterlings, Deep-Fried, **3**-404
Chop(s)
Apple-Smothered, **1**-97
with Apricot Stuffing, **4**-576
à l'Auvergne, **2**-317
Barbecued, **9**-1443
Boneless, Baked, **9**-1444
Breaded, Apple Rings, **9**-1443
Caraway, **2**-298
with Cheese (Côtelettes de Porc au Fromage), **11**-1802
Choucroute Garnie, Simple, **9**-1444
Curried, Apricots with, **1**-107
and Curried-Coleslaw Sandwiches, **10**-1602
French Country-Style, **9**-1444
Georgia, **9**-1445
and Grits, **5**-827
with Herbs, Italian, **9**-1443
Herb-Stuffed Birds, **9**-1444
Hungarian, **9**-1445
Hungarian (Disznókaraj Magyarosan), **6**-918
with Mushrooms, Neapolitan, **8**-1200
Mushroom-Stuffed, **8**-1200
and Noodle Skillet, **8**-1233
with Onions, **8**-1261
Orange-Baked, **9**-1444
Party, **7**-1151
with Prunes, **9**-1444
with Prune or Sour-Cherry Sauce (Svinye Kotlety s Sousom iz Chernosliv ili Kislykh Vishen), **10**-1571
Roman, Artichokes with, **1**-112
Scalloped Apples, and Sweet Potatoes, **1**-102
with Scalloped Potatoes, **9**-1463
Skillet, Orange, **9**-1444
Smothered, **9**-1443
and Spaghetti, Neapolitan, **8**-1208
Sweet Potatoes, and Apples, **9**-1443
and Sweet-Potato Skillet, **11**-1796
Tamale Pie, **9**-1444
Chop-Suey Skillet, **8**-1232
Chow Mein, **9**-1451
Cracklings and Lard, **9**-1449
Cracklings with Plantain, **9**-1414
Crown Roast, Crown Roast of
Apple-Stuffed, **9**-1442
Florida Style, **1**-32
with Sprouts and Cranberries, **9**-1442
Curried Ham and Fresh-Pork Loaf, **6**-856
Curry, **4**-527; **9**-1450
Curry, Sour (Soowar ka Gosht Vindaloo), **6**-939
Fillet in Sour Cream, **7**-1111
Fillets, Stuffed, **6**-945
Flemish (Porc à la Flamande), **2**-197
Fresh Ham, see Ham, Fresh
Fricassee Filipino, **6**-851
-Fried Rice, Chinese, **9**-1450
Galantine of, **5**-766
Goulash, **5**-809
Goulash with Noodles, **5**-809
Ground Pork, see Meatballs; Meat Loaf, Meat Loaves
Hash, see Hash
Hawaiian, **9**-1450
Hock Stew (Ragoût de Pattes), **2**-277
Hocks with Vegetables, **9**-1449
Hog and Hominy, **1**-69
Hog Jowl, Turnip Greens with, **1**-69
and Hominy, Mexican, **9**-1450
with Horseradish, Piquant, Austrian, **9**-1451
Kabobs, Malayan, **8**-1324
Kabobs, Spicy, **6**-997
Kale with, **1**-48
Leftover-Pork Casserole, **9**-1451
Leftover Pork in Olive Sauce, **9**-1451
Leg of, Roast (Puerco Asado), **11**-1706
and Lima Beans, **7**-1066
Loin of, Loin Roast
Barbecued, Foil-Baked Potatoes, **9**-1442
in Black Sauce, Caribbean, **9**-1442
Braised, **2**-220
Broiled, Chinese, **9**-1442
with Browned Vegetables, **9**-1442
Cooked in Milk, Florentine, **9**-1442
Io Pua, **9**-1434
with Oranges, **9**-1443
Roast, **1**-57, 146
with Sauerkraut and Apples, **9**-1442
au Vin Blanc, **9**-1442
with Yams and White Onions, **9**-1443
Meat Crisps, Elena's Style (Carnitas al Estilo de Elena), **7**-1138
Minced (Mochomas), **7**-1140
Moussaka with Brussels Sprouts, **8**-1190
with Mushrooms, Oriental, **8**-1200
with Mussels (Carne de Porco à Alentejana), **9**-1456
and Noodles, Baked, **9**-1450
Noodles, Rumanian, **8**-1232
Pâté, **1**-90
Pâté, Basic, **8**-1313
Pâté Lise, **3**-439
with Peas, **1**-34
-and-Pepper Casserole with Fruited Black-Bean Sauce, **10**-1554
Pichola, **1**-24
Picnic Pot Roast with Vegetables, **9**-1476
Picnic Shoulder Stuffed with Sauerkraut, **9**-1442
Pie (Tourtière), **2**-277
and Pineapple Casserole, **9**-1406
Pineapple Sweet-and-Sour, **9**-1406
Piquant, with Horseradish (Veprové s Krenem), **4**-532
Pot Roast, Mexican, **9**-1475
Pot Roast, Spiced, **9**-1476
Ribs, Barbecued, **1**-77
Ribs, Rolled (Varkensschijf), **4**-590
Rice, and Cabbage, Baked, **10**-1549
and Rice Casserole, **10**-1549
and Rice Pilaf, Greek, **9**-1401
Roast
Arista, Florentine, **10**-1560
with Chinese Vegetables, **12**-1919
Flaeskesteg, **4**-540
with Sage Onions, **9**-1442
Trastevere, **4**-650
Roll for Cocido (Relleno), **11**-1743
and Salmon Packages (Laulau Pua), **9**-1435
Scrapple, **10**-1644
2-242; **9**-1351
Homemade, **10**-1644
or Pannhaas, **1**-66
South Carolina, **1**-68
Shoulder, Red-Cooked (Hung Shao Chu-Tzu), **3**-400
Shoulder Steak Teriyaki, **11**-1770
Skewered, Indonesian, **7**-1052
in Soy Sauce, Braised (Babi Ketjap), **11**-1714
Spareribs
Apple-Stuffed, **11**-1749
Baked, **1**-61
Barbecued, **1**-25; **4**-644; **8**-1184, 1283
Barbecued, Spicy, **11**-1749
Beans with, Sooner-State, **1**-64
Chinese Style, **9**-1445
Pineapple, **9**-1406
and Sauerkraut, **7**-1151
Soya, **9**-1445
Spiced, **11**-1748
Stuffed, **11**-1781
Sweet-and-Sour, Chinese, **11**-1749
Steaks, Bouillon, **9**-1442
Steaks, Tomato, **9**-1442
Stew (Sianlihakastike), **5**-681
Stew, Sour (Pasiw Na Litson), **9**-1369
Stroganoff Style, **9**-1451
Sweet and Pungent, **9**-1450
Sweet-and-Sour, Chinese, **1**-26
Sweet-and-Sour (T'ang Ts'u Chu Jo), **3**-400
-Tail Stew, **9**-1449
Tenderloin(s)
Baked, **9**-1445
Pot Roast in Wine (Poledwica Wieprzowa Duszona na Winie), **9**-1426
Savory, **9**-1445
Stuffed, **9**-1445
Stuffed (Fyldt Svinemorbrad), **4**-540
Tomato, **9**-1445
Timetable for Braising, Chart, **9**-1439
Timetable for Roasting, Chart, **9**-1439
and Veal Head Cheese, **6**-979
and Veal Ragout, **2**-317; **10**-1533
-Vegetable Bake, **9**-1451
-Vegetable Skillet, **9**-1451
and Watercress Soup (Chu Jou Pi Chi T'ang), **3**-401

Pork Kidneys
Braised, **7**-1016

Pork Liver
Balls and Noodles, **7**-1074
with Barbecue Sauce, **7**-1074
in Mustard Sour-Cream Sauce, **11**-1698
with Onions, French, **7**-1075
Pâté, Danish, **7**-1074
Pot-Roasted, with Barbecue Sauce, **9**-1476
Pudding, Old-Fashioned, **9**-1448
Sauce, **9**-1369
Savory Baked, **7**-1074
and Vegetable Pie, Savory, **7**-1075
and Vegetables, **7**-1074
Porkkanakohokas (Carrot Soufflé), **5**-681

Port, **9**-1452
Cherry-Port Mold, **10**-1667
Port-Wine Sauce, **7**-1151
Prunes in Port, **9**-1485
Prunes in Wine, **12**-1949
Punch (QC), **10**-1527
Porto, au Porto Sauce, **10**-1613, 1619
Portuguese Bean Soup, **1**-158
Portuguese Clams (Ameijoas Portuguesas), **9**-1455

Portuguese Cookery, **9**-1453
Portuguese Egg Soup, **11**-1691
Portuguese Lemon Chicken, Jellied, **7**-1052
Portuguese Stewed Squid, **11**-1763

Posset, **9**-1457
Brandy or Sherry, **9**-1457
Molasses, **9**-1457
Postre de Mamon, Elena Zelayeta's, **3**-367
Potage au Cresson (Watercress Soup), **5**-739
Potage Parmentier (Potato Soup), **5**-739
Potatisbullar (Swedish Potato Dumplings), **11**-1791
Potatis och Svamp (Potatoes and Mushrooms), **11**-1790

Potato(es), **9**-1457; see also Sweet Potato(es)
and Anchovy Casserole, **1**-80
Anna, **4**-566
Bacon-Kraut-Potato Skillet, **1**-133
and Bacon Pudding (Peruna ja Pekoni Laatikko), **5**-681
Baked, with Coriander, **8**-1282
Baked and Creamed Codfish, **8**-1222
Balls, Parsleyed, **9**-1463
and Beef Loaf, Sliced (Liha ja Perunamureke), **5**-680
Biarritz, **9**-1469
Boiled (Salzkartoffeln), **5**-795
Bordeaux, **9**-1470
Boulangère, **7**-1111
Boules, **9**-1470
Boxty-on-the-Griddle, **6**-944
Boxty-on-the-Pan, **6**-944
Bread, **2**-231
Bretonne, **9**-1471
Cakes, **2**-278
Cakes alla Calabrese, **9**-1468
Caraway, **9**-1466
and Carrot Soup, **9**-1462
Chantilly, **3**-346; **9**-1464
Chasseur, **9**-1471
Cheese, **9**-1469
-Cheese Hamburger Pie, **9**-1463
Cheese, and Onion Pie, **9**-1463
and Cheese Patties (Llapingachos), **11**-1708
-Cheese Soup, Savory, **11**-1690
Chicken, and Celery Scallop, **7**-1097
Chips, Mexican, **8**-1283
Chive, **9**-1467
Chocolate, Cake, **9**-1468
Chuck-Wagon, **4**-645
Colcannon, **6**-949
with Cold Huancayo Sauce (Papas con Salsa Huancaina Fría), **11**-1708
Collops, **6**-949
Creamed, Double-Boiler, **9**-1465
Creamed, Swedish (Skånsk Potatis), **11**-1790
Country-Fried, **9**-1468
à la Crème, **9**-1470
Curried, **9**-1464
Cutlets, **9**-1470
and Dab, **5**-712
Delmonico, **4**-551
Deviled Stuffed, **4**-558
Dishes with Frozen French Fries, **9**-1468
Doughnuts, **9**-1469
Dressing, **10**-1588
Duchesse, **7**-1150; **9**-1470
Duchesse, with Yellow Turnip, **11**-1823
Dumplings, **4**-587; **10**-1630
Dumplings (Kartoffelklösse), **5**-795
Dumplings, Swedish (Potatisbullar), **11**-1791
and Egg Casserole, **4**-603
and Egg Casserole (Rakott Krumpli), **6**-919
Egg, and Cheese Sandwiches, **10**-1605
and Egg Pie, Indienne, **9**-1388
and Eggs, Skillet, **4**-606
Eggs Zurlo, **6**-865
Filling, **6**-992; **9**-1353
Filling, Berks County, **1**-66; **9**-1352
Fish Stew (Caldeirada de Peixe), **9**-1455
in Foil, **4**-566
Foil-Baked, Barbecued Pork, **9**-1442
Forcemeat, **5**-715
Frankfurter-Potato Dumplings, **4**-586
Fried (Pommes Frites), **5**-744
Fried (Stegte Kartofler), **4**-540
Frites Provençales, **9**-1471
Fritters (Kartoffel Chremsel), **6**-992
Frosting, **7**-1126
Galette, **9**-1470
Garnishes, **5**-778
Gnocchi, **9**-1463
Golden, **9**-1465
au Gratin, **9**-1467
Gratin aux Champignons, **9**-1470
Green Peas and New Potatoes with Cream, **1**-28
Griddle Cakes (Lefser), **8**-1241
Haggerty, **6**-949
Ham, Cheese, and Potato Casserole, **2**-317
Ham and Corn Potato Soup, **6**-852
and Ham au Gratin, **6**-853
Ham with Vegetables, Sweet-and-Sour, **9**-1351
Hashed in Cream, **6**-879
Hashed or Home-Fried, with Rosemary, **10**-1561
Herbed, Baked, **9**-1466
Home-Fried, with Rosemary (Geröstete mit Rosmarin), **1**-123
Home-Fried (Rösti), **11**-1804
Hoppel Poppel, **9**-1463
Hungarian, **9**-1463
Idaho Baked-Potato Garnitures, Suggestions for, **1**-35
Irish, with Mustard Greens, **11**-1723
Jannson's Temptation, **10**-1664
Jeanette, **9**-1470
Knishes, **6**-991
and Lentil Casserole, **7**-1059
Lyonnaise, **7**-1089; **9**-1467
Mashed, with Sage Onions, **9**-1464
Mayonnaise, **1**-89
Mont d'Or, **9**-1470
Mounds, Amandine, **9**-1466
Mushroom Pie, **8**-1201
and Mushroom (Potatis och Svamp), **11**-1790
and Mushrooms with Cheese, **8**-1201
in Mustard Sauce, **9**-1466
New Potatoes, Crisp, **9**-1467
New Potatoes and Peas in Cream, **9**-1466
Nutmeg Cheese, **8**-1246
O'Brien, **9**-1467
-and-Onion Cake, **9**-1468
Onions, and Beans, Skillet, **9**-1468
and Onions, Charlene, **8**-1263
Oven-Browned, **3**-444
Oyster-Potato Pie, **9**-1351
Pancakes, **9**-1468
Pancakes (Kartoffel Latkes), **6**-991
Panned, Mexican, **9**-1465
à la Parisienne, **9**-1470
in Parsley Sauce, **12**-1930
Pastry Shells, **6**-912
Patties, **8**-1313
Peanut Cakes, **8**-1323
and Peas, Creamed (QC), **10**-1524
and Peppers (Peperoni con Patate), **6**-959
Pie (Pastel de Papas o Choclos), **11**-1705
Pommes Anna, **9**-1466
Pommes Fondante, **9**-1463
Pommes Mousseline, **8**-1191
and Pork Scallop, **9**-1452
with Pot-Roasted Stuffed Chicken, **9**-1477
Princess, **9**-1468
Puff, **9**-1466
Purée of, with Ham and Onions (Aardappel-Purée met Ham en Uien), **4**-592
or Raised Cake, **9**-1357
Raw Fried, **1**-38
Rector, Baked, **9**-1466
Rissole, **9**-1467
Rolls, **2**-233
Rosettes, **3**-439
Rösti, Swiss, **9**-1467
Salad(s), see Salad(s), Potato Salad(s)
Salmon-and-Potato Bake, **10**-1596
and Salt Pork, Baked, **9**-1452
and Salt-Pork Chowder, **9**-1462
Saucisses, **9**-1471
Sausage-Potato Pot, **10**-1636
Sautéed (Pommes de Terre Sautées), **5**-744
Savarin, **9**-1470
Savory Stuffed, **9**-1466
Scalloped, **9**-1467
Scalloped, with Anchovies (Kartofel' s Anchousami), **10**-1572
Scalloped, with Ham, **9**-1463
Scalloped, Italian, **4**-650
Scalloped, with Pork Chops, **9**-1463
Scalloped (QC), **10**-1524
Scones, **11**-1818
Scones, Katy's Drop, **10**-1644
Seedy Cake, **6**-950
Soufflé, **9**-1467
Soufflé (Papa Empanada al Horno), **9**-1497
Souffléed, **9**-1468
Soup Amphitryon, **9**-1469
Soup, Aroostook County, **1**-44
Soup with Bacon and Browned Bread Cubes, **9**-1350
Soup, Curried, **9**-1462
Soup, Kingston, **6**-967
Soup Parmentier, **9**-1469
Soup (Potage Parmentier), **5**-739
Soup, Quick French, **11**-1690
Sour-Cream, **9**-1464
Sour-Cream, and Mushroom Chowder, **11**-1697
Sour-Cream Patties, **9**-1467
in Spaghetti Sauce, Baked, **9**-1466
-Spinach Casserole, **9**-1467
-and-Spinach Pie, **11**-1755
Spuds, Baked, **4**-645
Stewed, **9**-1352
Stuffed Baked, **4**-568; **9**-1466
Stuffing, **3**-392
Sugar-Browned (Brunede Kartofler), **4**-540
Sunday-Morning Fish Balls, **8**-1222
-Topped Luncheon Meat, **9**-1463
-Tuna Casserole, **9**-1462
and Tuna Tart, **12**-1864
with Turkey, Sherried, **12**-1874
Turkey Soup, Parmentier, **11**-1695
and Turnips, **9**-1352
Vichy, **9**-1471
Waffles, **9**-1462
White Dome, **12**-1896
White and Sweet, Oven-Browned, **3**-445
Potato-Flour Muffins à la Marshall Field's, **1**-37
Pot-au-Feu (Boiled Beef with Vegetables), **5**-740
Potosí Style Little Toasts (Tostaditas al Estilo de Potosí), **7**-1137
Potpourri, Rose, How to Make, **9**-1472

Pots de Crème, **3**-493
au Chocolat, **3**-494
à la Vanille (Vanilla Cream Pots), **3**-493
Poule au Riz, **3**-387
Pouletià la Crème (Cricken with Cream), **5**-744
Poulet à l'Estragon (Roast Chicken with Tarragon), **5**-744
Poulet Vallée d'Auge, **3**-386
Poulette Sauce, **10**-1620

Poultry, **9**-1477; see also names of poultry
Canning, **2**-295
Chow Meins, **7**-1049
Cream or Milk Giblet Gravy for, **5**-816
Curries, **7**-1049
Dressings, **4**-573
Giblet Gravy, **5**-800
Leftovers à la King, **7**-1050
Leftovers, Barbecue-Style, **7**-1049

Leftovers, Creole-Style, **7**-1049
Mushroom-Giblet Dressing for, **5**-800
Noodle Casseroles, **7**-1049
Pancake Roll Ups, **7**-1049
Pies, Mexican, **7**-1049
Pinwheels, **7**-1049
Rice Casseroles, **7**-1049
Sandwich Fillings, **10**-1606
Shepherd's Pies, **7**-1049
Stuffed Vegetables, **7**-1050
Stuffings for, **11**-1781
To Freeze, **5**-736; see also information under entry for specific poultry
Poultry Casseroles, **2**-320

Poundcake(s), **2**-262; **9**-1479
Antebellum Spice Cake, **2**-272
Chocolate, **2**-272; **9**-1479
English, Traditional, **2**-272
Ginger, Colonial, **2**-272
Half-a-Poundcake, **2**-272
Holiday, **2**-272
Nut, **2**-272
Orange-and-Lemon, Canadian, **2**-272
Poundcake, **2**-270; **9**-1479
Sour-Cream, **9**-1480
Whitby Nun's Cake, **2**-272

Praline(s), **9**-1480
Almond, **9**-1480
Almond Brittle, **1**-16
Caramel, **9**-1480
Confections, **9**-1480
Creole, **1**-44
Fresh-Coconut, **9**-1480
Fresh-Gingerroot, **5**-803
Frosting, **5**-750
Lace, **2**-304
Pecan, **2**-285
Pralines, **4**-513
Toast, **11**-1828
Topping, Broiled, **9**-1480
Vanilla, **2**-285
Prawn, see Shrimp(s)

Preserve(s), **9**-1481
Almond-Stuffed Kumquat Preserves, **7**-1023
Beets, Spiced, Pickled, **9**-1576
Blueberries, Spiced, **1**-23
Brandied Peach Preserves, **9**-1481
Cantaloupe, Spiced, **1**-24
Carrot-Almond Conserve, **2**-309
Cherries in Currant Jelly, **7**-1154
Cherries, Pickled, **1**-49
Crabapples, Spiced, **3**-488
Damson-Plum Preserves, **9**-1418
Dried-Apricot Preserves, **9**-1481
Eggs, Pickled, **9**-1376
Fig Preserves, **9**-1481
Figs, Pickled, **9**-1376
Kumquat-Ginger Relish, **7**-1023
Loquats, Spiced, **7**-1082
Peaches, Pickled, **8**-1321
Peaches, Pickled, Spicy, **9**-1376
Pear Preserves, **9**-1482
Plum Preserves, **9**-1482
Pumpkin Preserves, **9**-1500
Pumpkin Chips, Preserved, **8**-1230
Quince Preserves, **9**-1482
Ripe-Watermelon Preserves, **9**-1482
Strawberry Preserves, **9**-1482
Sweet-Cherry Preserves, **9**-1481
Tomato Butter, **11**-1835
Yellow-Tomato Preserves, **11**-1835
Pretzel, **9**-1482

Prickly Pear, **9**-1483
Jelly, **9**-1483
Pride of Erin Soup, **6**-945
Prosciutto, see Ham
Prosie Pieczone Nadziewane (Roast Stuffed Suckling Pig), **9**-1425

Prune(s), dried prune-plums, **9**-1483
Apple-Prune Pudding, Steamed, **8**-1247
-Apple-Raisin Stuffing, **4**-584
-Apricot Pie, **1**-108
Apricot-Prune Upside-Down Cake, **12**-1881
and Apricots, Spiced, **4**-578
Black-and-White Marshmallow Delight, **7**-1114
Bran Bread, **9**-1485
Butter, **1**-76
Cake, Dutch, **9**-1486
-Cheese Soufflé, **9**-1485
and Chicken, Baked, **3**-382
Chocolate Cake, **9**-1486
in Claret, California, **9**-1485
Cottage (cheese) Soufflé, **3**-362
Cottage Pudding with Orange Sauce, **9**-1485
Crumble Pudding, **9**-1485
Custard, Baked (Sviskekompott), **8**-1241
Filling, **1**-50; **6**-993; **7**-1157
Filling (for kolácky), **4**-532
Frankfurter, and Onion Kabobs, **5**-721
Frosting, **9**-1486
Fruited Lamb Stew, **9**-1485
Fruited Veal Stew, **9**-1483
with Hamburger Balls, Spiced, **9**-1483
Honey-Prune Pudding, **9**-1485
Kolache, **1**-49; **7**-1157
Molds, Individual, **5**-789
-Noodle Pudding, **8**-1233
-Nut Sandwiches, **9**-1485
-Orange Compote (Kompot iz Apelsin i Chernosliv), **10**-1573
and Peanut-Butter Sandwiches, **9**-1485
Pecan Bread, **8**-1334
-Pineapple Dessert, **9**-1485
Piroshki, **6**-993
with Pork Chops, **9**-1444
in Port, **9**-1485
Pudding, California, **9**-1486
Pumpkin-Prune Cake, **1**-40
Refrigerator Cookies, **3**-475
Shake, **7**-1160
in Sherry, **4**-578
Soup (Pflaumensuppe), **9**-1350
Spiced, in Lemon Gelatin Salad, **11**-1754
Torte, Seven-Layered, **4**-553
Upside-Down Cake, **9**-1486
Whip, **9**-1485
Whip, Frozen, **9**-1485
-Whip Pie, **9**-1486
in Wine, **12**-1949
Prune-Plum, see Plum
Psita Paidakia (Baked Lamb Chops), **5**-819
Puchero, **9**-1486
Puchero (Meat and Vegetable Stew), **11**-1706

Pudding(s) Appetizer and **Main-Dish,** **9**-1486
Almond Sweet-Potato, **11**-1837
Barley, Finnish, **1**-62
Beef-and-Kidney, **6**-945
Bread and Cheese, **9**-1487
Carrot and Corn, **2**-306
Cheese Stratas, Individual, **3**-358
Chicken and Corn, **9**-1487
Corn, **7**-1152
Corn-Soufflé, Southern, **1**-22
Egg-Parmesan, Steamed, **4**-604
Fish, **5**-715; **9**-1487
Fish (Fiskebudding), **4**-539
Fish (Fiskepudding), **8**-1236
Fish, Norwegian, **1**-49
Fresh-Corn, **9**-1487
Green-Pea, **9**-1487
Ham Timbales, **6**-865
Hasty, **8**-1228
Liver, **1**-49
Liver (Maksalaatikko), **5**-680
Noodle Cottage-Cheese, **9**-1487
Noodle (Lokshen Kugel), **6**-993
Onion, Baked, **9**-1487
Pork-Liver, Old-Fashioned, **9**-1448
Potato and Bacon (Peruna ja Pekoni Laatikko), **5**-681
Sweet-Potato Pone, **1**-33
Turkey, **12**-1875
Yorkshire, **3**-444; **9**-1487; **12**-1958
Yorkshire I and II, **4**-624

Pudding(s), Dessert, **9**-1486
Apple Betty, **1**-77
Apple Brown Betty, **1**-101
Apple Charlotte (Charlotte de Pommes), **3**-348
Apple Crisp (QC), **10**-1525
Apple Porridge (Omenapuuro), **5**-681
Apple-Prune, Steamed, **8**-1247
Apple Puddeny-Pie, **6**-949
Apple Slump, **8**-1228
Apple Tapioca, Baked, **1**-60, 102; **8**-1228
Apricot Rice, **1**-108
Arrowroot Blancmange, **1**-110
Banana Meringue, **1**-142
Banana (Pudim de Bananas), **9**-1457
Bird's-Nest, **7**-1098
Bishop Whipple, **1**-50
Blackberry Flummery, **5**-707
Blackberry Roly-Poly, **2**-204
Black-and-White Fudge Batter, **3**-415
Blancmange, **2**-205
Blueberry Betty, **1**-45; **2**-208
Blueberry Flummery, **2**-209
Blueberry or Huckleberry Buckle, Northwest, **12**-1933
Blueberry Pandowdy, **2**-209
Blueberry, Steamed, **2**-209
Brandy Plum, **9**-1492
Bread Dish with Oranges (Broodschoteltje met Sinaasappels), **4**-593
Bread Pudding(s)
Blueberry, **9**-1489
Old-Time Spiced, **8**-1228
Orange-Date, **9**-1490
Pineapple, **9**-1490
Plum, Refrigerator, **9**-1415
Raspberry-Jam, **1**-23
Bride's, **9**-1492
Buckwheat, Baked, **2**-249
Buttermilk (Karnemelk Pudding), **4**-593
Butterscotch-Peanut Tapioca, **9**-1487
Butterscotch Raisin (QC), **10**-1525
Butterscotch Tapioca Cream, **11**-1810
Carrot Dessert (Gajar Halwa), **6**-942
Carrot, Steamed, **2**-308
Carrot-Suet, Steamed, **9**-1491
Carrot-Walnut, Steamed, **2**-306
Cheese-Apple-Noodle, **3**-362
Cherry Batter, **3**-374
Cherry Roly-Poly, **3**-374
Chestnut Sweet (Doce de Castanhas) **9**-1457
Chocolate Blancmange, **2**-205
Chocolate Cornstarch, **9**-1489
Chocolate Sabayon, **9**-1489
Chocolate, Steamed, **8**-1228
Cocoa Marshmallow, **7**-1113
Coconut Apple Betty, **9**-1490
Coconut Blancmange, **2**-205
Coffee Custard, with Caramel Glaze, **9**-1490
Cottage, **9**-1490
Cranberry, **7**-1155
Cranberry Roly-Poly, **3**-490
Cranberry, Steamed, **9**-1491
Cream (Flødebudding), **4**-543
Date-Graham, **8**-1228
Dewberry Crumble, **4**-560
Dewberry Flummery, **4**-560
East Indian Rose, **10**-1561
Egg, Coimbra (Pudim de Ovos a Moda de Coimbra), **9**-1457
Eight Treasures (Pa Pao Fan), **3**-403
English Trifle, **9**-1489
English Trifle, A True, **12**-1858
Farina, **4**-656
Fig with Peanut Butter, **4**-659
Fig, Steamed, Individual, **9**-1492
Fresh-Pear Crumb, **8**-1331
Fresh-Pear Crumble, **8**-1333
Fresh Prune-Plum, **9**-1415
Fruit-Cream, Jellied, **9**-1489
Fruit Dessert (Kisiel Owocowy), **9**-1431

Pudding(s), Dessert, continued
Fruited Rice, **5**-758
Fruit, Scandinavian, **5**-758
Fudge Batter, **3**-415
Ginger Pear Crumble, **9**-1491
Ginger, Quick, **11**-1839
Grape-Nuts Puff, **8**-1228
Green Gables Icebox, **9**-1492
Guriev (Gureevskaia Kasha), **10**-1574
Honey-Prune, **9**-1485
Huckleberry Cottage, **6**-915
Indian, **8**-1228
Indian, Baked, **1**-47
Indian Ravo, **10**-1561
Indian, Top-Stove, **8**-1184
Irish Moss Blancmange, **6**-950
Kissel, **10**-1573
Lemon Cake, **9**-1490
Lemon, Steamed, **7**-1054
Lemon Sweet-Potato, **11**-1724
Lemon Velvet, **1**-52
Macaroon Angel, **7**-1096
Maple Cottage, **7**-1107
Marmalade, **9**-1492
Matzo-Meal (Matzo Kugel), **6**-994
Meringue Cake, **9**-1490
Meringue Orange, Florida, **7**-1135
Meringue Topping for, Quick, **7**-1134
Michigan Shortcake, **1**-48
Molasses, Baked, **9**-1490
Molasses Fig, **8**-1184
Molasses, Steamed, **9**-1354
Nesselrode, Classic, **8**-1217
Nesselrode, Jellied, **8**-1218
Noodle-Apple, **9**-1490
Noodle (Lokshen Kugel), **6**-993
Orange Cream, **9**-1491
Ozark, **1**-25
Party, **1**-68
Peach Betty, **8**-1317
Peach Cobbler, **8**-1317
Peach Cobbler, Old-Fashioned, **3**-454
Peach Crisp, **8**-1317
Peach Crumb, **8**-1317
Peach Crumble, **8**-1317
Peach Dessert, Quick, **8**-1321
Peach Tapioca, **8**-1317
Persimmon, **1**-25
Persimmon, Baked, **9**-1364
Persimmon, Cold, **9**-1364
Pineapple Blancmange, **2**-205
Pineapple Crumb, **8**-1326
Pineapple-Nut, **9**-1408
Plum, **9**-1418
Plum and Apple Crumble, **8**-1253
Plum, Brandy, **9**-1492
Plum, Flaming, **5**-701
Plum, Light, with Hard Sauce, **3**-444
Plum, with Rum Sauce, **3**-440
Plum Snow, **9**-1417
Prune, California, **9**-1486
Prune Cottage, with Orange Sauce, **9**-1485
Prune Crumble, **9**-1485
Prune-Noodle, **8**-1233
Pumpkin Custard, with Sherry Ginger Cream, **9**-1491
Raspberry, **10**-1536
Red-Currant Cobbler, **7**-1155
Red Pudding (Rødgrød), **4**-543
Rhubarb, **1**-28; **9**-1355
Rhubarb Betty, **10**-1544
Rhubarb Flummery, **10**-1544
Rhubarb (Rabarbragrøt), **8**-1241
Rice, **10**-1552
Apricot, **1**-108
Butterscotch, **10**-1552
Coriander, **3**-478
Creamed (Arroz con Leche), **9**-1497
Custard, **10**-1552
Date, **10**-1552
Every-Day, **9**-1491
Fruited, **5**-758
à l'Impératrice, **10**-1552
Lemon Cream, **9**-1491
Marshmallow Pineapple, **10**-1554
Old-Time, **10**-1552
Pears Condé, **10**-1552
Pineapple, **10**-1554
Poires à l'Impératrice, **10**-1554
Rich, **10**-1552
Rijstpudding, **4**-593
Strawberry, **11**-1778
Sweet Scrambled, **10**-1552
Sabayon, **9**-1489
with Fresh Strawberries or Peaches, **9**-1489
Frozen, **9**-1489
Sauces for, **9**-1492
Sherry Almond Snow, **9**-1492
Sour-Cream Indian Pudding, **9**-1490
Spotted Dog, **4**-627
Squash, Spiced, **7**-1098
Strawberry Betty, **11**-1776
Strawberry Cobbler, **11**-1776
Strawberry, Steamed, **9**-1492
Suet, **4**-627; **11**-1783
Sweet-Potato, **1**-22
Sweet-Potato Apple Crisp, **11**-1798
Sweet-Potato, Spicy, **9**-1491; **11**-1798
Tapioca, Apple, Baked, **1**-60, 102
Tapioca Cream, **11**-1810
Telephone, **1**-41
Upside-Down, **9**-1491
Vanilla Cornstarch, **9**-1489
Zwieback with Apple in the Oven (Appelschoteltje), **4**-593
Pudim de Bananas (Banana Pudding), **9**-1457
Pudim de Ovos a Moda de Coimbra (Coimbra Egg Pudding), **9**-1457
Pueblo Lamb Chili, **11**-1728
Puerco Asado (Roast Leg of Pork), **11**-1706
Puerto Rican Avocado Shrimp Boats, **1**-130
Puerto Rican Cookery, **9**-1493
Puerto Rican Sauce with Fried Fish (Mojo Isleño), **9**-1494
Puerto Rican Turkey Sausage, **12**-1871
Puerto Rican Yam and Cheese Crullers, **12**-1951
Puff Paste, **8**-1304
Puff Shells, **7**-1039
Pul Koki (Fire Beef), **7**-1020
Pummelo, **10**-1648
Pumpernickel, **2**-229
Pumpernickel Bread, Light, **7**-1153

Pumpkin(s), **9**-1498
Baked, **8**-1224
Bread, **9**-1499
Chiffon Cake, **9**-1500
Chiffon Meringue, **9**-1500
Chiffon Pie, **9**-1397
Chili Pumpkin Soup, **11**-1727
Custard Pudding with Sherry Ginger Cream, **9**-1491
Ginger Pie, Frozen, **9**-1500
Ice Cream, **9**-1500
-Mince Pie, **9**-1500
Nut Waffles, **9**-1499
-Orange Custards, **9**-1499
Pickled, **6**-993
Pie, Ginger, **5**-801
Pie, One-Bowl, **9**-1391
Pie, Tawny, **9**-1499
Pie Topped with Ginger Rosettes, **11**-1823
Preserved Pumpkin Chips, **8**-1230
Preserves, **9**-1500
-Prune Cake, **1**-40
Rolls, Raised, **9**-1499
Soufflé, **9**-1499
Soup, **6**-967
Soup, Indian, **9**-1499
Soup Maracay (Sopa de Calabaza Maracay), **11**-1704
and Sweet-Potato Dessert (Cazuela), **9**-1497
Tarts, Frozen, **9**-1500
Pump Room Cheesecake, **3**-366
Punch, **9**-1501; for recipes see Beverage(s); Beverage(s), Alcoholic
Punschkakor (Punch Rings), **11**-1793
Pura (Nut Pastries), **5**-824
Puss Pass (Lamb Stew), **8**-1239
Puszta Schnitzel, **1**-127
Pytt i Panna (Swedish Hash), **11**-1790
Pytt i Panne (Hash and Eggs), **8**-1237

Q

Quail(s), **10**-1517
Braised, **1**-25
Broiled, **5**-774
Broiled, on Toast, **10**-1518
Panbroiled, **10**-1518
Roast, **10**-1518
Steamed, **5**-774
on Toast, **1**-36
Yugoslav Style, **10**-1518

Quantity Cooking, **10**-1518
[Note: Quantity Cooking recipes are identified in the index by the symbol (QC) following the recipe name.]
Queen Bona's Dessert, **3**-415
Queijadinhas de Amêndoas (Almond Cheesecakes), **9**-1457
Quelites (Lamb's-Quarters), **11**-1730

Quenelles, **10**-1527
de Brochet, **5**-700
Chicken, **10**-1527
(Fish), **5**-715
Pike, **10**-1527

Quiche, **10**-1527
de Bourbonnaise (Ham and Swiss-Cheese Pie), **6**-862
Corn, **3**-482
Egg-Salmon, **4**-608
de Langouste (Lobster Pie), **5**-470
Lobster, **10**-1529
Lorraine, **4**-566; **5**-703
Lorraine with Cream Cheese, **10**-1527
Lorraine with Swiss Cheese, **10**-1529
Onion, French, **8**-1261

Quince(s), **10**-1529
Baked, **10**-1529
and Cranberry Jelly, **6**-980
Ginger Marmalade, **10**-1529
Jelly, **6**-984
Jelly without Pectin, **10**-1529
Marmalade, **7**-1111
and Pear Jam, **6**-964
Preserves, **9**-1482

R

Rabarbragrøt (Rhubarb Pudding), **8**-1241

Rabbit(s), **10**-1530, and **Hare,** **6**-878
Curried Rabbit, **12**-1930
Hare, Roast (Zajac Pieczony), **9**-1427
Hasenpfeffer, **5**-772; **6**-878
Jugged Rabbit, **10**-1531
Lapin Sauté à l'Estragon, **5**-772
Maggi's Mad Hare, **1**-29
Rabbit, Braised, **1**-62
Rabbit, German Style, **5**-769
Rabbit and Onions, Smothered, **1**-52
Rabbit Stew, **5**-772; **10**-1531
Wild Rabbits, **10**-1530
Raclette, **5**-712

Raccoon or **Coon,** **10**-1531
Coon, Roast, **5**-769
Roast, with Sweet-Potato Stuffing, **10**-1531

Radish(es), **10**-1531
Braised, **7**-1087
Cucumbers, and Onions in Sour Cream, **11**-1700
Flowers, **10**-1666
Garnishes, **5**-778
Salad, **10**-1533

Salad, Panama, **7**-1086
Salad, Red and White (Salat iz Krasnoi i Beloi Rediski), **10**-1566
Sweet-and-Sour (Chiang Lo Po), **3**-403
Yogurt, and Cucumber Relish, **12**-1958
Rågbröd (Rye Bread), **11**-1791
Råkakor (Rye Rings), **11**-1793
Ragoût de Pattes (Pork Hock Stew), **2**-277
Raifort Sauce, **10**-1614, 1620
Rainbow Cake, **7**-1042
Rainbow Grange Raisin Cake, **4**-656
Rainbow Sherbet Parfait, **10**-1654

Raisin(s), 10-1534
-Apple-Nut Pie, **8**-1229
Apple, and Nut Relish, **10**-1535
-Apple-Nut Tarts, **11**-1812
Bread, **10**-1534
Butterscotch Raisin Pudding (QC), **10**-1525
Cake, Iranian, **10**-1535
Carrot-Raisin Bread, **10**-1611
-Cheese-Olive Sandwiches, **8**-1257
Compote, Rumanian, **10**-1534
Corn, Egg, and Olive Casserole, **8**-1257
Cream-Cheese, and Carrot Sandwiches, **10**-1605
-Filled Cookies, **3**-475; **10**-1535
Filling, **4**-663
Fudge Frosting, **5**-751
Funeral Pie, **9**-1355
Gravy, **1**-39
-Nut Filling, **10**-1535
-Nut Pie, **9**-1390
-Nut Pinwheels, **10**-1535
-Nut Sandwiches, **10**-1534
-Orange-Cranberry Pie, **9**-1393
-Orange Turnovers, **12**-1879
-Peanut Clusters, **2**-289
and Peanut Clusters, **8**-1323
Pie, **10**-1534
-Pineapple Custard Pie, **4**-578
Relish, Spiced, **12**-1912
-Rice Stuffing, **11**-1781
Rum-Raisin Ice Cream, **6**-929
Sauce, **7**-1150
Scramble Toast, **11**-1828
-Sour-Cream Pie, **9**-1391
Sour-Cream Raisin Nut Cookies, **11**-1701
Spice Cake, **4**-579; **10**-1535
Spiced, **10**-1535
Spicy Jellied, **10**-1535
Stewed, **8**-1216
Waffles, **12**-1915
-Walnut Dressing, **4**-575
Raki Gotowane (Boiled Crayfish), **9**-1422
Rakott Krumpli (Potato and Egg Casserole), **6**-919
Rama Bathing (Phra Ram Long Song), **11**-1715
Ramekins, **10**-1535
Ramequins au Fromage (Cheese Tartlets), **11**-1804
Rancho Salad, **10**-1583
Rancho Salad Dressing, **10**-1584
Rappie Pie, **2**-278
Rarebit, see Welsh Rabbit

Raspberry(ies), 10-1536
Angel Peach Cake, **8**-1320
Berry Float, **7**-1161
Black-Raspberry Jelly, **6**-982
Bombe, **2**-212
and Cheese Dessert, Frozen, **10**-1536
Chiffon Pie, **6**-980
Chocolate Cream, **3**-416
Cream Pie, **10**-1536
Currant Jam, **6**-964
and Currant-Jelly Ice, **6**-925
Frappé, **6**-926
Fresh Raspberry Pastries, **10**-1536
Ice Cream, **6**-929
Jam Scones, **12**-1932
Maids of Honour, **8**-1309
Meringue with Marron Filling, **7**-1112
Peach Glacées, **10**-1537
Pear-Raspberry Jam, **6**-965
Pudding, **10**-1536
Red Raspberry(ies)
Jam, **6**-965
Jam, No-Cook, **6**-965
Jelly, **6**-984
Jelly, No-Cook, **6**-984
-Rhubarb Compote, **2**-247
Sauce, **6**-931; **10**-1538
Shrub, **1**-75
Soup, **9**-1421
Toast, Dutch, **11**-1826
Rassolnik s Yachmenem (Soup with Pickles), **10**-1568

Ratatouille, 10-1538
Classic, **12**-1903
Provençal, **4**-616
Ravigote, Ravigote Sauce, **10**-1538, 1620
3-573; **5**-695

Ravioli, 10-1538
Fillings
Cheese, **10**-1539
Hamburger, **10**-1538
Meat, **10**-1538
Italian Style, **10**-1538
Reception Punch, **9**-1503
Recheio a Moda de Lisboa Para Peru (Lisbon Turkey Stuffing), **9**-1457
Redfish, see Rosefish
Red Flannel Hash, **1**-56; **2**-193
Red and Green Sauce, **2**-194
Red-Hot Sauce, **10**-1623
Red-Hot Sauce Relish, **10**-1543

Red Snapper, 10-1540
Amandine, **10**-1540
Baked, Florida Style, **10**-1540
Court Bouillon, Hotel Pontchartrain, **4**-510
Fried, with Tamarind Sauce, **11**-1809
Grilled (Opakapaka Koala), **9**-1434
Gulf-Baked, **1**-22
Pine-Bark Stew, **1**-61
Steaks with Shrimps, **10**-1540
Reduce, **10**-1615
Refrigerator Oatmeal Cookies (QC), **10**-1526
Rehruecken (Chocolate Almond Torte), **11**-1804

Reindeer, 10-1541
Pot Roast, Norwegian, with Mushrooms, Tomatoes, Grapes, and Pineapple, **10**-1541
Saddle of (Reinsdyrsteik), **8**-1239
Reinsdyrsteik (Saddle of Reindeer), **8**-1239
Rejer i Traengsel (Rush Hour Shrimp), **4**-536
Rekesaus (Shrimp Sauce), **8**-1236
Relish(es), **10**-1541; for recipes see Pickle(s) and Relish(es)
Relleno (Pork Roll for Cocido), **11**-1743
Relyenong Hipon (Stuffed Shrimps), **9**-1369
Rémolade, see Rémoulade

Rémoulade, Rémoulade Sauce, 10-1543, 1614
4-573; **9**-1382; **10**-1622
Dip for Scallops or Shrimps, **1**-87
Rempejek Katjang (Crisp Peanut Fritters), **11**-1714
Rennet, **10**-1543
Repollo en Salsa de Queso (Cabbage in Cheese Sauce), **9**-1496
Rhein Lachs vom Grill (Broiled Salmon), **5**-793
Rhode Island Griddle Cakes, **5**-825

Rhubarb, 10-1543
-Apple Pie, **10**-1544
Applesauce, Tangy Fresh, **10**-1544
Baked Rosy, **10**-1544
Flummery, **10**-1544
Fool, **2**-279
Fresh Rhubarb Betty, **10**-1544
Fresh Rhubarb Fruit Punch, **10**-1545
Golden Jam, **6**-964
Ice, **6**-926
Ice, Tangy, **10**-1544
Jellied, **10**-1544
Meringue, Baked, **10**-1544
Meringue Pie, **9**-1392
-Onion Relish, **10**-1542
Pie, **1**-69
Pie, Lattice, **9**-1393
Pineapple-Rhubarb Pie, **9**-1393
Pudding, **1**-28; **9**-1355
Pudding (Rabarbragrøt), **8**-1241
Raspberry Compote, **2**-247
Sauce for Meats, **11**-1753
and Strawberry Jam, **10**-1545
and Strawberry Jelly, **10**-1545
and Strawberry Pie, **10**-1544
Ribbon Cake, **8**-1229

Rice, 10-1545
Arroz con Pollo, **10**-1550
Bake, Ham-Cheese, **10**-1549
Ball, Raw Fish (Nigiri Sushi), **6**-971
Balls, **10**-1549
Bareh Pello, **8**-1215
and Beef Casserole, **6**-872
Brazil-Nut Pilaf, **2**-222
with Buttermilk (Dahi Bhath), **6**-942
Carrot Rice, **2**-252
Cashew Stuffing, **2**-314
Casseroles, **7**-1049
Casserole, Wheelspoke, **1**-52
Chazuke, **6**-976
Cheese-and-Bacon Salad, **10**-1550
and Cheese, Baked, **10**-1550
and Cheese Balls, **3**-361
and Cheese, Peppers Stuffed with, **9**-1359
with Chicken (Arroz con Pollo), **9**-1496
with Chicken, Spanish, **10**-1550
and Chicken Livers, Oriental Style, **3**-391
Chicken Pilaf, **3**-391
Chicken Pilaf (Kotta Pilafi), **5**-820
Chicken Pilau, Madras, **9**-1401
and Chicken Salad with Cashews, **2**-314
(Chinese), **3**-401
Clam Pilaf (Achivades Pilafi), **5**-818
Clam Pilaf Casserole, **10**-1554
with Coconut and Raisins (Arroz con Coco y Pasas), **11**-1709
Company, Casserole, **11**-1734
Coriander Pudding, **3**-478
Cottage Eggs with, **2**-322
Crabmeat Pilaf, **2**-321
Creole-Style Leftovers, **7**-1049
Croquettes, Surprise, **10**-1551
Curried, **10**-1551
Fish-Cheese, **10**-1550
Frankfurter Pilaf, **5**-722
Fried, **10**-1551
Fried (Ch'ao Fan), **3**-401
Fried, with Ham, **6**-865
Fried (Nasi Goreng), **11**-1714
Fritters, Hot (Calas Tout Chauds), **4**-513
Fritters, New Orleans, **10**-1552
Gohan, **6**-976
Green, **1**-39; **4**-565
Ham Fried, **6**-858
and Ham-Stuffed Peppers, **10**-1549
Hopping John, **1**-22
Indian Kitchree, **10**-1551
Jambalaya de Canard, **1**-44
Jambalaya, Creole, **6**-968
Lamb Baryani, **12**-1957
Lamb Pilaf, Savory Turkish, **7**-1038
and Lamb, Steamed, Indian, **7**-1035
with Lentil Curry, **7**-1059
Lobster Pilaf, **2**-321
Main-Dish Salad, **10**-1550
Meat-Cheese, **10**-1550
-and-Meat Stuffing, Turkish, **11**-1782
Mexican, **10**-1551
Mexican (Arroz Mexicano), **7**-1141
Milan Style (Risotto alla Milanese), **6**-958
Muffins, **8**-1192
with Noodles, **8**-1215
Orange, for Duck or Ham, **8**-1268
Paella de la Costa Brava, **11**-1746
Paella a la Valenciana, **8**-1291

Rice, continued
Pancakes, **10**-1551
Parsleyed Pilaf (Pilaffi), **4**-639
Peanut Loaf, **8**-1325
and Peas, Italian, **10**-1551
and Peas Pilaf, **2**-299
and Peas (Risi e Bisi), **4**-570
Pecan-Rice Loaf, **8**-1334
Pilaf, **1**-146
Pilaf with Almonds, **1**-14
Pilaf, Iranian (Pello), **8**-1215
Pilaf (Pilafi), **5**-822
Pilaf, Plain, **9**-1401
Pilau, Indian, **4**-641
Pimiento Rice, **10**-1554
Pineapple, **9**-1407
Pineapple (Ananas) Pilau, **9**-1403
Pineapple, and Tuna Salad, **9**-1408
Pongal, **6**-942
Pork, and Cabbage, Baked, **10**-1549
and Pork Casserole, **10**-1549
Pork-Fried, Chinese, **9**-1450
and Pork Pilaf, Greek, **9**-1401
Pudding, **10**-1552
Apricot, **1**-108
Butterscotch, **10**-1552
Coriander, **3**-478
Creamed (Arroz con Leche), **9**-1497
Custard, **10**-1552
Date, **10**-1552
Every-Day, **9**-1491
Fruited, **5**-758
à l'Impératrice, **10**-1552
Lemon Cream, **9**-1491
Marshmallow Pineapple, **10**-1554
Old-Time, **10**-1552
Pears Condé, **10**-1552
Pineapple, **10**-1554
Poires à l'Impératrice, **10**-1554
Rich, **10**-1552
Rijstpudding, **4**-593
Strawberry, **11**-1778
Sweet Scrambled Rice, **10**-1552
Purée of, **10**-1549
Raisin-Rice Stuffing, **11**-1781
Red, **1**-68
Red Beans and Rice, **1**-44
Ring, Tuna Mornay in, **12**-1864
Ring, Turkey Creole in, **12**-1874
Saffron, **10**-1577
Saffron Pilau, **12**-1878
Salad(s), see Salad(s), Rice Salad(s)
and Sausage, Italian, **10**-1636
with Seaweed (Nori-Chazuke), **6**-976
and Shrimp Jambalaya, **10**-1549
Shrimp Stew, Biloxi, **1**-50
and Smoked Whitefish, **12**-1939
Soup with Chicken Livers, Italian, **7**-1075
Soup, Greek, **10**-1549
Spanish, with Frankfurters, **5**-721
Spanish-Rice Dressing, **4**-574
Spinach Curry Casserole, Layered, **10**-1555
and Spinach (Spanakoryzo), **5**-822
Steamed, **2**-300
-Stuffed Lamb Shanks, **7**-1035
Stuffing, **3**-392; **11**-1781, 1834
Sushi, **6**-971
Sweet, and Pineapple Dessert, **9**-1409
Sweet Sticky, **11**-1717
Toasted, **1**-73
and Tuna, **12**-1863
Tuna-Cheese Bake, **10**-1549
and Tuna Peas, **8**-1315
and Turkey, Baked, **10**-1549; **12**-1874
Vegetable-Cheese, **10**-1550
Vegetable Pilaf, **9**-1402
Viennese, **10**-1551
Waffles, **10**-1552; **12**-1915
Walnut-Rice Fritters, **10**-1532
and Water-Chestnut Stuffing, **12**-1919
Waxy Rice Flour, **5**-707
Yellow, **10**-1551
Rice Casseroles, **10**-1554-1556

Rice, Brown
Ginger, **2**-301
and Liver Ring, **7**-1073
and Mushrooms, Sautéed, **10**-1551
Rice, Wild, see Wild Rice
Rijstpudding (Rice Pudding), **4**-593
Riñones a la Pamplona, **7**-1014
Risi e Bisi (Rice and Peas), **4**-570
Risotto alla Milanese (Rice, Milan Style), **6**-958
Rivvel Soup, **1**-66
Robert Sauce, **10**-1619

Rock Cornish Hen(s), **10**-1558
with Apples, **1**-57
Glazed Roasted Stuffed, **10**-1558
with Rice, Baked, **4**-648
with Sauerkraut, **1**-52

Rockfish, **10**-1558
Muddle, **1**-61
en Papillote, **10**-1558
Salad, Curried, **10**-1558
Rock Lobster, Rock Lobster Tails, see Lobster
Rödbetssallad med Äpplen (Beet Salad with Apples), **11**-1790
Rødgrød (Red Pudding), **4**-543
Rødkaal (Red Cabbage), **4**-542

Roe, **10**-1558; see also Caviar; Shad Roe
in Casserole, **10**-1559
Deviled, **10**-1558
Salad, **8**-1211
Rogan Josh (Lamb Curry), **6**-939
Roget Aal (Smoked Eel), **4**-536
Roget Laks (Smoked Salmon), **4**-536
Rognoncini di Vitello Trifolato, **7**-1016
Rognons d'Agneau à la Lully, **7**-1014
Rognons Bolo (Flambéed Kidneys), **11**-1802
Rognons Flambés au Ruban Bleu, **7**-1014
Røket Kolje (Smoked Haddock), **8**-1236
Rollmops, **6**-903
Rolls, see Bread(s), Yeast Buns and Rolls

Roly-Poly
Blackberry, **2**-204
Cherry, **3**-374
Cranberry, **3**-490
Jam, **4**-627
Mincemeat, **4**-627
Romaine Lettuce, see Lettuce
Roman Dinner, **4**-650
Roman Punch, **10**-1654
Root Beer, **10**-1559
Roquefort Ost (Danish Blue Cheese Sandwich), **4**-536

Rosefish, **10**-1559
Baked in Paprika Sauce, **10**-1559
Marinara, **10**-1559
Sesame-Baked, **10**-1559
Rose-Geranium Jelly, **5**-791

Rose Hip, **10**-1560
Jam, **10**-1560

Rosemary, **10**-1560
Chicken in Cream, **10**-1560
Chicken with Tangerine Rice, **10**-1556
Mayonnaise, **5**-695
Veal, **10**-1560
-Wine Seasoning, **10**-1556
Rose Potpourri, How to Make, **9**-1472
Roses, Candied, **2**-281
Rosettes, **10**-1561

Rosewater, **10**-1561
East Indian Rose Pudding, **10**-1561
Sugar Cookies, Old-Fashioned, **10**-1561
Rosquillas (Fried Cakes), **11**-1747
Rösti (Home-Fried Potatoes), **11**-1804
Rôti d'Agneau (Roast Leg of Lamb), **2**-278
Rouille (condiment), **2**-216
Roux, **10**-1562, 1615
Rozbratle z Cebula (Beef Steaks with Onion), **9**-1422
Rue, **10**-1562
Rugbrød (Rye Bread), **4**-542; **8**-1240
Rullepølse (Meat Roll), **4**-536

Rum, **10**-1562
Balls, **2**-289
Cake (Baba au Rhum), **5**-748
Cake, Canadian, **2**-279
Cake, Italian, **10**-1562
Chocolate Cake, A Man's, **3**-408
Chocolate Frosting, **3**-408
-Cinnamon Toast Sticks, **11**-1828
Cream, Norwegian, **10**-1563
Daiquiri, **10**-1563
Frozen, **10**-1563
Frosting, Rum-Flavored, **8**-1247
Glaze, **2**-279; **5**-806
Jamaican Gold Doubloons, **8**-1273
Mango Rum Sundae, **7**-1104
Mint Julep, **6**-996
Orange-Rum Topping, **8**-1272
Pears de Luxe, **8**-1332
Pineapple Punch, Hot (Ponche de Piña), **11**-1709
Pineapple-Rum Punch, **9**-1498
Punch (QC), **10**-1527
Punch, Sparkling, **10**-1563
-Raisin Ice Cream, **6**-929
Sauce, **3**-440
Syrup, **1**-132; **10**-1640
Syrup (Sirop de Rhum), **5**-748
Rumaki, **1**-87
Rumanian Noodles, **8**-1232
Rumanian Raisin Compote, **10**-1534
Rumanian Sauerkraut Soup, **10**-1631
Rusell Borscht, **6**-994
Rusell Chrain (Passover Horseradish with Fermented Beet Juice), **6**-994
Rusell Fleisch in Borscht (Meat Cooked in Fermented Beet Juice), **6**-994
Russian Blini, **8**-1293
Russian Cheese Pastry, **11**-1838
Russian Cookery, **10**-1563
Russian Cream, **10**-1561
Russian Dressing, **4**-573; **7**-1116; **10**-1614, 1622
Russian Egg and Mushroom Filling, **4**-662
Russian Onions and Mushrooms, **8**-1263
Russian Piroshki, **8**-1197
Russian Sturgeon Champagne Soup, **10**-1568
Russkii Iablochnii Pirog (Apple Pie), **10**-1574
Rutabaga, **10**-1574; for recipes see Turnip(s)

Rye, **10**-1575
Bread, Dark, **2**-228
Bread, Orange, **12**-1932
Bread (Rågbröd), **11**-1791
Bread (Rugbrød), **4**-542; **8**-1240
Bread, Swedish, **1**-49
Cookies, Swedish, **10**-1575
-Honey Cookies, **10**-1575
Rings (Rågkakor), **11**-1793

S

Sabayon, Sabayon Sauce, **9**-1489; **10**-1576, 1615, 1629
Chocolate, **9**-1489
with Fresh Strawberries or Peaches, **9**-1489
Frozen, **9**-1489
Sabbath Bread (Challah), **6**-992

Sablefish, **10**-1576
Baked, Creole, **10**-1576
Saccharin, **10**-1576
Sack-Posset, Old English, **4**-611
Saewu Jun (Shrimps Fried in Egg Batter), **7**-1020
Safflower or Bastard Saffron, **10**-1577

Saffron, **10**-1577
Bread, **7**-1053

Bread, Cornish Fruited, **7**-1097
Buns, Swedish, **2**-252
Pilau, **12**-1878
Rice, **10**-1577
Tea Bread, **10**-1577
Veal, **10**-1577

Sage, 10-1577
-Cheese Appetizer, **10**-1578
and Cider Jelly, **6**-982
and Onion Stuffing, **11**-1781
Stuffing, **10**-1578
Sago, **10**-1578
Sag Paneer, **11**-1755
Sailboats, **10**-1589

Salad(s), 10-1578
Albacore, Pickled, **1**-8
Almond, Pea, and Cheese, **8**-1315
Antipasto, Western, **12**-1935
Apple, Carrot, and Raisin, **10**-1583
Artichoke, **12**-1931
Artichoke Hearts, **1**-112
Artichokes with Garlic Mayonnaise, Chilled, **12**-1931
Avocado and Corn (Ensalada de Aguacate y Maíz), **7**-1142
Avocado (Ensalada de Aguacate), **11**-1709
Avocado-Tomato, **2**-300
Bacon and Green-Bean, **4**-565
Bamboo Shoots, Chinese, **10**-1583
Bean, **1**-79; **8**-1213; **11**-1727
Bean, Cheyenne River, **1**-68
Bean, Mixed, **4**-645
Bean, White and Red, **1**-159
Beet with Apples (Rödbetssallad med Äpplen), **11**-1790
Beet, with Roquefort Dressing, **4**-570
Cabbage with Lingonberries (Kålsallad med Lingon), **11**-1791
Caesar, **1**-27; **12**-1931
Carrot and Raisin, **2**-306
Carrot and Sauerkraut (Salat iz Morkovi i Kisloi Kapusty), **10**-1572
Cauliflower and Grape (Salat iz Tsvetnoi Kapusti s Vinogradom), **10**-1566
Cauliflower, with Ham and Avocado, **7**-1142
Celeriac, **3**-344
Celery, Oregon, **1**-65
Celery-Root (Zeller Saláta), **6**-919
Cheese, Cucumber, and Grapefruit, **12**-1958
Chick-Pea, Italian, **3**-392
Chick-Pea, Mexican, **3**-392
Corn, Tomato, and Celery, **3**-484
Cottage Cheese and Cucumber, **7**-1085
Country Salad Bowl, **2**-213
Cucumber (Agurkesalat), **4**-542
Cucumber-Almond, **4**-522; **10**-1586
Cucumber Cups, **6**-913
Cucumber (Gurkensalat), **1**-123
Cucumber (Mizerja I), **9**-1430
Cucumber-Onion, **4**-521
Cucumber-Onion, with Sour-Cream Dressing, **4**-521
Cucumber with Sour Cream (Mizerja II), **9**-1430
Cucumber Yogurt, **12**-1958
Cucumbers and Cress in Horseradish Dressing, **11**-1838
Cucumbers, Dilled, **4**-522
Cucumbers, Marinated (QC), **10**-1524
Dandelion, **9**-1354
Dandelion, Raw, **4**-534
Danish, **10**-1586
Dill-Pickle, **10**-1555
Eggplant (Melitzanosalata), **5**-822
Eggplant, Turkish, **4**-616
Eggplant-Yogurt, **4**-616
Endive and Beet (Salade aux Endives et Betteraves), **2**-198
Finger Salad with Dunking Sauce, **9**-1382
Flag (Insalata Bandiera), **6**-960
Florida "Gaspachy," **1**-33
Garden Lettuce with Bacon Dressing, **7**-1061
German Gourmet Mixed, **10**-1586
Ginger Cheese Salad Bowl, **12**-1935
Greek, **8**-1190
Green, **4**-650
Green-Bean, **4**-650
Green-Bean and Carrot, **7**-1085
Green-Bean with Potatoes, Hot (Salade Liègeoise), **2**-200
Green-Lima-Bean, **7**-1065
Green, Mixed, **5**-825
Green-Pepper (Zöld Paprika Saláta), **6**-919
Green, Special Mixed, **12**-1934
Greens à la Polonaise (Sałatka po Polsku), **9**-1430
Hawaiian (Lomi Lomi Salmon), **1**-34
Hearts of Palm, **2**-260
Herring (Sillisalaatti), **5**-678
Italian, **10**-1587
Italian-Green-Bean, **10**-1668
Juju Gakuan, **6**-976
Leek, **1**-57
Lentil, **7**-1059
Lettuce, **4**-646
Lettuce, Cheese-Stuffed, **7**-1063
Lettuce, German, **7**-1064
Lettuce, Norwegian Fashion (Salat), **8**-1240
Lettuce and Tomato Avocadaise, **11**-1837
Lettuce, Wilted, **9**-1354
Lettuce, Browned-Butter-Wilted, **12**-1934
Lima-Bean, **1**-146
Lima-Bean and Egg, **7**-1065
Lima, Curried, **7**-1065
Macaroni, Danish, **7**-1095
Macaroni (QC), **10**-1523
Macédoine of Vegetables, **7**-1100
Mexican Salad, **12**-1931
Mint and Parsley, **8**-1213
with Mustard (Keja Chae), **7**-1023
Onion and Orange, **8**-1264
Orange and Belgian-Endive, **8**-1268
Orange, Cucumber, and Pepper (Ensalada de Naranjas), **7**-1142
Orange and Onion, **8**-1268
Orange and Watercress, **8**-1268
Parmesan-Walnut, California, **12**-1934
Parsley, **8**-1298
Parsley Cheese Balls, **8**-1299
Pea and Cheese, in Tomato Shells, **8**-1315
Pepper, Italian Style, **9**-1360
Pineapple-Cucumber, **9**-1408
Radish, **10**-1533
Radish, Panama, **7**-1086
Radish, Red and White (Salat iz Krasnoi i Beloi Rediski), **10**-1566
Rancho, **10**-1583
Raw-Mushroom, Italian (Insalata di Funghi Crudi), **8**-1197
Roe, **8**-1211
Romaine, **4**-633
Romaine-Avocado-Tomato, **4**-566
Roquefort, **10**-1586
Salata, **4**-639; **5**-822
and Sandwich Picnic, Menu, **9**-1382
Sauerkraut (Sauerkrautsalat), **5**-796
Sesame Asparagus, **1**-115
Shrimp and Cauliflower (Maionese di Scampi e Cavolfiore), **1**-82
Sour-Cream Spinach, **11**-1700
Spinach and Cabbage, **11**-1756
Spinach Cottage-Cheese, **12**-1958
Spinach, German, **10**-1586; **11**-1756
Spinach and Onion, **1**-73
Summer (Sommersalat), **8**-1240
Tomato-Avocado, **10**-1586
Tomato-Avocado Hors-d'Oeuvre, **6**-913
Tomato, Bacon, and Egg, **10**-1586
Tomato-and-Cottage-Cheese, Layered, **11**-1834
Tomato-Cucumber, **4**-566
Tomato and Cucumber (Agourontomato-salata), **5**-822
Tomato, Italian, **11**-1834
Tomato and Mushroom, **1**-82
Tomato (Salade de Tomates), **5**-745
Tomatoes, Fines Herbes, **11**-1839
Tomatoes, Marinated, **10**-1586
Tomatoes Stuffed with Dilled Cucumbers, **4**-522
Tomatoes Vinaigrette, **8**-1278
Tossed, **10**-1583
Tossed Green, **8**-1276
Tossed, Variations, **10**-1583
Turnip, **12**-1879
Turnip and Cucumber (Salat iz Repy i Ogurtzov), **10**-1572
Vegetable-Avocado, with Paprika Dressing, **10**-1586
Vegetable, Cooked, **10**-1665
Vegetable, with Deviled Ham, **10**-1587
Vegetable, Marinated, **10**-1667
Vegetable, Mixed, **10**-1587
Vegetable-Rice, **10**-1587
Vegetables Vinaigrette, **4**-632
Vinaigrette, Andalusian (Ensalada a la Andaluza), **11**-1741
Watercress, **12**-1920
Watercress Salad Bowl, **2**-301
Watercress-Tomato, **4**-641
Wax Bean and Onion, **1**-157
Yogurt (Pachadi), **6**-939

Salad(s), Coleslaw
Almond Coleslaw, **10**-1586
Anise Grape and Cabbage Slaw, **10**-1586
Apple Bavarian Slaw, **1**-100
Apple Horseradish Slaw, **2**-260
Buttermilk Herb Slaw, **2**-260
Cabbage and Green-Pepper Slaw (QC), **10**-1524
Cabbage Slaws, **2**-258, 260
Carrot Slaw, **2**-306
Celery and Cabbage Slaw, **3**-464
Coleslaw, **3**-464; **4**-645
Country-Style Coleslaw, **2**-258
Creamy Slaw with Carrots, **2**-260
Cumberland Slaw, **3**-464
Curried-Coleslaw and Pork Sandwiches, **10**-1602
Curried Pear Slaw, **2**-260
Dill Mustard Slaw, **2**-260
Everyday Slaw, **2**-260
Fresh-Apple Coleslaw, **10**-1586
German Cabbage Slaw, **3**-464
Heavenly Slaw, **2**-260
Hot Bacon Slaw, **2**-260
Hot Slaw, **3**-464
Pineapple Slaw, **9**-1408
Red Cabbage Slaw, **2**-260
Soy Ginger Slaw, **2**-260
Surprise Salad, **10**-1586
Tuna Coleslaw with Grapes, **12**-1867
Two-Tone Cabbage Salad, **2**-258
Virginia City Salad, **1**-56

Salad(s), Fruit
Apple Glacé with Honey Cream Cheese, **10**-1587
Apple-and-Orange, **10**-1587
Apple, Party, **1**-100
Apricot-Cheese, **1**-106
Apricot, Stuffed, **1**-108
Avocado-Citrus Dessert, **1**-130
Avocado-Melon, **6**-911
Avocado, with Yogurt Dressing, **12**-1958
Banana and Cantaloupe, **1**-142
Banana Peanut, **8**-1323
Banana Split Salad, **5**-755
Blackberry Patch, **2**-204
Carrot-Coconut, **2**-306
Casaba, with Sour Cream, **2**-314
Cheese, Oregon, **3**-361
Cheese-Stuffed Apple, **5**-754
Christmas, **10**-1588
Christmas Eve (Ensalada de Noche Buena), **7**-1142; **12**-1931
Cinnamon-Apple, Jellied, **10**-1587
Citrus Salad Plate, **3**-451

Salad(s), Fruit, continued
Cottage-Cheese and Blueberry, **10**-1587
Cranberry-Cream, **10**-1587
Cranberry and Orange, Jellied (QC), **10**-1523
Crenshaw Fruit Salad Supreme, **3**-495
Five-Fruit Salad Plate, **5**-754
Fresh Grape and Plum, **5**-812
Fresh-Pear Cactus, **8**-1330
Fresh-Pear, Cheese, and Anchovy, **8**-1330
Fresh Pineapple and Avocado, **9**-1408
Fresh Tangerine and Apple, **11**-1809
Fresno, **10**-1588
Fruit, with Coconut Dressing, **3**-456
Fruit Plate with Pistachio Cheese, **5**-755
Fruit Salad Bowl, **1**-33
Grape and Cheese, **5**-812
Grape, Pear, and Celery, **10**-1588
Guava, **1**-33; **5**-829
Golden-Apple, **1**-77
Lemon and Orange, **7**-1052
October, **10**-1587
Orange, Banana, and Walnut, **10**-1588
Orange and Date, **10**-1588
Patio, **7**-1085
Peach, Four, **8**-1316
Peanut-Butter, **8**-1325
Pear-Cheese, **8**-1330
Persimmon, Grapefruit, and Pomegranate, **9**-1364
Pineapple-Orange, **9**-1408
Pineapple-Strawberry, **5**-758; **7**-1089
Pineapple, Two-Tone, **9**-1408
Prune-Plum and Grape, **9**-1415
Seafoam, **10**-1587
Southwestern, **11**-1727
Virginia City, **1**-56
Waldorf, **1**-60; **10**-1588
Waldorf, Pineapple, **10**-1588

Salad(s), Jellied
Avocado, **1**-130
Avocado Ring with Strawberries, **11**-1776
Cabbage, **10**-1583
Cheese Ring, **10**-1588
Cheese and Strawberry, **11**-1776
Cider, **1**-103; **3**-446
Cinnamon-Apple, **10**-1587
Clam-Aspic, **6**-979
Cottage-Cheese and Tomato, Jellied, **6**-980
Cottage Pear, **3**-361
Crabmeat, **10**-1583
Crabmeat, Molded, **6**-979
Crabmeat Ring, Jellied, **7**-1080
Cranberry, **4**-632
Cranberry-Cream, **10**-1587
Cranberry Fruit Ring, **3**-424
Cranberry, Jellied, **8**-1225
Cranberry and Orange (QC), **10**-1523
Cucumber, **8**-1225
Deviled-Egg, **5**-788
Egg-Lobster, Molded, **7**-1080
Egg and Olive Mold, **4**-606
Fish Ring, Jellied, **7**-1080
Fresh Blueberry and Lime Mold, **2**-208
Fresh Grape and Chicken Mold, **5**-812
Fresh-Grapefruit and Apple, Molded, **5**-814
Fresh-Pear and Cucumber Aspic, **8**-1330
Fresh-Plum, Jellied, **9**-1417
Fruit-Cocktail Loaf, **5**-788
Ginger-Ale Fruit Mold, **5**-803
Ginger Peach Mold, **8**-1317
Grapefruit, Jellied, **5**-814
Ham, Molded, **6**-858
July Day Salad, **1**-14
Lemon-Orange-Cottage-Cheese Mold, **7**-1052
Lemon, Spiced Prunes in, **11**-1754
Lime and Blueberry, Molded, **7**-1067
Lime and Cheese, Jellied, **7**-1067
Lime-Pear, **8**-1330
Litchi, **7**-1072
Liver, Tomato, and Cream-Cheese Loaf, **5**-787
Lobster, **10**-1583
Lobster Ring, Jellied, **7**-1080
October, **10**-1587
Orange Cottage-Cheese Cups, **8**-1268
Orange-Ginger-Ale Mold, **5**-803
Orange-Pineapple, **5**-788
Pâté de Foie Gras in Aspic, **5**-708
Pear and Blue-Cheese, **5**-788
Pear and Cream-Cheese, Jellied, **6**-980
Pear de Menthe, **8**-1330
Pecan and Apple, Jellied, **8**-1334
Pineapple Blue-Cheese Ring, **7**-1153
Pineapple Cheese Mold, **5**-788
Pineapple, Two-Tone, **9**-1408
Potato, Jellied, **5**-787
Salmon Loaf, Curried, **10**-1595
Salmon Salad Ring, Molded, with Cucumbers in Sour Cream, **5**-786
Seafoam, **10**-1587
Seafood Cocktail, **5**-786
Shrimp Mold, Savory, **6**-979
Shrimp Ring, Jellied, **7**-1080
Silhouette, **7**-1086
Spinach Mold with Ham, **5**-787
Tomato-Ham, **10**-1583
Tomato-Juice Squares (QC), **10**-1523
Tomato, Masked, **7**-1115
Tuna and Avocado, Molded, **5**-787
Tuna, Jellied, **7**-1085
Tuna and Salmon Mold, **10**-1583
Tuna-Vegetable Mold, **12**-1866
Vegetable, **5**-787
Vegetable Ring, Jellied, **6**-980
Vegetable Salad, Jellied, **3**-424
Waldorf, Jellied, **1**-100
Watermelon, Molded, **12**-1920
Western Perfection, **2**-258
Winter Fruit, Molded, **5**-755

Salad(s), Main-Dish Salads
Albacore, Pickled, **1**-8
Almond-Chicken, **1**-14
Apple-Tuna, **12**-1867
Artichoke and Shrimp, **1**-112
Avocado Crabmeat, à la Ritz, **1**-130
Avocado Halves with Spiced Shrimps, **10**-1581
Avocado Shrimp Boats, Puerto Rican, **1**-130
Bean and Cheese, **10**-1582
Beef, French, **10**-1580
Brain, **8**-1211
Cantaloupe and Shrimp Luncheon Salad, Fresh, **2**-296
Celery and Crabmeat, **10**-1582
Cheese-and-Bacon Rice, **10**-1550
Cheese (Käsesalat), **11**-1804
Cheese-Potato, Hot, **10**-1582
Chef's, Brussels, **10**-1580
Chef's, California, **5**-825; **7**-1063
Chef's, Classic, **10**-1580
Chef's, Orange, **10**-1580
Chicken, **3**-391
Chicken-Avocado, **1**-130
Chicken, Chinese, **10**-1582
Chicken-Macaroni, Baked, **7**-1094
Chicken, Perfect, **10**-1582
Chicken (QC), **10**-1522
Chicken and Rice, with Cashews, **2**-314
Crab, Curried, **3**-488
Crab, Dressed, **4**-621
Crab and Grapefruit, with Avocado Mayonnaise, **12**-1934
Crab, Hot, **12**-1928
Crab Louis, **3**-488
Crabmeat, **10**-1583
Duck, Alaska, **1**-23
Dungeness Crab Louis, **1**-76
Egg, Ham, and Macaroni, **4**-607
Egg-Macaroni, **7**-1095
Egg, Mexican, **4**-523
Egg, Piquant, **4**-606
Egg-Salad-Stuffed Tomatoes, **10**-1582
Egg, Savory, **4**-606
Fish, in Clamshells, **10**-1665
Fish and Macaroni, **7**-1092
Frankfurter and Potato, Hot, **5**-722
Frankfurters and Hot-Potato, **10**-1580
Fresh-Grapefruit and Crab, **5**-814
Fresh-Grapefruit and Salmon, **5**-814
Fresh-Grapefruit Shrimp, **10**-1581
Fresh-Pear and Crabmeat, **8**-1330
Grape-Turkey, **5**-812
Green-Bean, with Potatoes, Hot (Salade Liègeoise), **2**-200
Green-Bean and Potato (Insalata di Fagiolini e Patate), **6**-960
Ham, **1**-38; **6**-858
Ham, Broiled, **6**-858
Ham and Egg, **6**-864
Ham Fruit Salad, **6**-858
Ham and Macaroni, Hot, **7**-1094
Herring, **6**-913
Herring and Ham (Sill och Skinksallad), **11**-1787
Herring (Haringsla), **4**-590
Herring, Salmagundi, **9**-1383
Honeydew Rings with Shrimp Salad, **6**-911
Kidney-Bean, **1**-159
Lamb, Cucumber, and Tomato, **10**-1580
Lamb and Potato, Minted, **10**-1580
Liver-Sausage Appetizer, **10**-1635
Liverwurst, Potato, and Egg, **7**-1076
Lobster, **10**-1583
Lobster, English Style, **4**-621
Lobster, Tropicale, **10**-1581
Macaroni, Bean, and Egg, **7**-1095
Macaroni and Cheese, **7**-1095
Macaroni, Cheese, and Sour-Cream, **10**-1582
Macaroni, Lobster, and Artichoke, **7**-1092
Macaroni, Lobster, and Orange, **7**-1092
Macaroni, Shrimp, and Orange, **7**-1092
Macaroni, Tuna, and Orange, **7**-1092
Meat (Kjøttsalat), **8**-1235
Meat and Vegetable, **10**-1580
Mock Lobster, **5**-689
Mussel, **8**-1203
Nham, **11**-1717
Olivier (Salat Olivier), **10**-1566
Orange Chicken, **8**-1268
Oyster, **8**-1290
Peanut-Butter Potato, **8**-1325
Pineapple-Ham, **9**-1408
Pineapple, Tuna, and Rice, **9**-1408
Potato, with Ham and Cherries (Kartofelnii Salat s Vechinoi i Vishniami), **10**-1566
Rockfish, Curried, **10**-1558
Rock-Lobster, Curried, **10**-1582
Salade Niçoise, **9**-1384; **10**-1582
Salade Parisienne, **10**-1580
Salade Russe, **10**-1587
Salami-Carrot, **10**-1589
Salmagundi, **7**-1039
Salmagundi, with Salami and Liverwurst, **10**-1580
Salmon, **10**-1582
Salmon Louis, **10**-1597
Salmon-Potato, **10**-1597
Salt-Herring, **10**-1665
Sardine and Cheese, **10**-1612
Sauerkraut and Bean, Hot, **10**-1632
Seafood, **10**-1665
Seafood (Nuta), **6**-972
Shellfish Plate, **10**-1652
Shrimp, **6**-911; **10**-1580
Shrimp and Celery, **10**-1662
Shrimp-Crab, Hot, **10**-1652
Shrimp and Egg, Japanese, **10**-1580
Shrimp, Exotic, **10**-1662
Shrimp-Grapefruit, **10**-1662
Shrimp Macaroni, **10**-1662
Smoked-Sturgeon Deviled Eggs, **11**-1782
Supper Salad, **5**-775
Sweetbread and Cucumber, **11**-1796; **12**-1897
Tomato-Ham, Jellied, **10**-1583
Tuna-Fish, **10**-1582
Tuna, Marinated, **12**-1867
Tuna Plate (Thon en Salade), **11**-1802

Tuna, Potato, and Bean, Genoa Style, **12**-1867
Tuna-Potato, Hot, **12**-1867
Tuna Radiccio, **12**-1867
Tuna and Salmon Mold, **10**-1583
Tuna, Salubrious, **12**-1867
Tuna, with Sour-Cream Horseradish Sauce, **6**-914
Turkey, **12**-1875
Turkey, Broiled, **12**-1876
Turkey and Fresh Tangerine, **12**-1876
Veal, **12**-1897
Veal and Cucumber (Salat iz Teliatini s Ogurtsami), **10**-1566
Veal, with Marinated Broccoli, **10**-1580
West Coast, **12**-1867
White-Bean and Tuna (Cannelini al Tonno), **6**-960
Wild-Fowl, **5**-774
Yam of Roses, **11**-1716

Salad(s), Potato
Alsace, **9**-1469
Cheese-Potato, Hot, **10**-1582
Cold (QC), **10**-1523
with Eggs, **9**-1462
Frankfurter and Potato, Hot, **5**-722
Frankfurters and Hot-Potato, **10**-1580
French, with Onion and Parsley Dressing, **9**-1383
Gardiners Bay, **8**-1278
German, **9**-1462
Greek, **7**-1053
Green-Bean and Potato (Insalata di Fagiolini e Patate), **6**-960
Green-Bean, with Potatoes, Hot (Salade Liègeoise), **2**-200
with Ham and Cherries (Kartofelnii Salat s Vechinoi i Vishniami), **10**-1566
Hot, **9**-1462
Hot, with Bacon, **1**-134
Hot-and-Cold, **10**-1586
Hot Mashed, **9**-1462
Hot (Pommes de Terre en Salade), **5**-745
Italian, **10**-1587
Jellied, **5**-787
Kartoffelsalat, **5**-796
Lorraine, **9**-1469
Lamb and Potato, Minted, **10**-1580
Liverwurst, and Egg, **7**-1076
Nepalese, **4**-522
Peanut-Butter, **8**-1325
Potato-Egg, Hot Creamy, **9**-1462
Salmon-Potato, **10**-1597
with Sour Cream, **9**-1462
Texas, **9**-1462
Tuna, and Bean, Genoa Style, **12**-1867
Tuna-Potato, Hot, **12**-1867

Salad(s), Rice
Blue-Cheese and Rice, Hot, **10**-1555
French, **10**-1550
Hortense, **10**-1580
Italian, **9**-1383
Pineapple, Tuna, and Rice, **9**-1408
and Seafood, **10**-1550
Valenciana (Ensalada de Arroz a la Valenciana), **11**-1742
with Veal, Italian, **10**-1550
Vegetable-Rice, **10**-1587

Salad Dressings, **4**-572; see also Mayonnaise
Aïoli, **1**-7
Avocado, **10**-1588
Basil, **9**-1384
Blue-Cheese, **3**-361
Buttermilk, Cooked, **10**-1588
Buttermilk Horseradish, **10**-1588
Buttermilk, Low-Calorie, **2**-254
Chiffonade, **3**-393; **4**-573; **5**-694; **10**-1622
Cooked, **4**-574; **7**-1086
Cottage-Cheese, **10**-1588
Cream, **9**-1364
Curry, **3**-428
Dill, **10**-1555
Double-Boiler, **8**-1225
French, **8**-1276; **10**-1622
Cottage-Cheese, **10**-1622
Cream, **11**-1700
Fresh-Lime, **7**-1067
Fresh-Orange, **5**-754
Garlic, **10**-1614, 1622
Lemon, **7**-1053
de Luxe, **4**-573; **10**-1622
Orange, **8**-1230
Simple, **4**-573
Special, **4**-650
Sweetened, **10**-1622
Fresh Grapefruit, **5**-814
Fresh-Mint, **11**-1700
Fruit, **6**-859
Fruit, Fluffy, **10**-1589
Green Goddess, **12**-1931
Herb, **10**-1623
Herbed Sour-Cream, for Romaine, **10**-1556
for Herring Salad (Sillisalaatti), **5**-678
Honey, **10**-1623
Honey-Cream, **1**-79; **11**-1776
Lemon-Honey, **7**-1053
Lime, **3**-451
Louis, **10**-1614, 1622
Mayonnaise, **7**-1115; for recipes, see Mayonnaise
Mustard, **10**-1601, 1623
Old Colonial, **8**-1325
Olive, **4**-573; **11**-1700
Orange Cream, **8**-1268
Peanut-Butter Pineapple, **8**-1325
Pineapple, Fluffy, **3**-495
Piquant, **7**-1086
Piquant Sauce, **5**-695
Potato, **10**-1588
Rancho, **10**-1583
Ravigote Sauce, **4**-573
Rémoulade Sauce, **4**-573; **9**-1382
Russian, **4**-573; **10**-1614, 1622
Sauce Louis, **3**-488
Sherry, **10**-1589
Snow, **1**-56
Sour-Cream, **10**-1588; **11**-1700
Sour-Cream, Cooked, **10**-1588
Sour-Cream, for Cucumber-Onion Salad, **4**-521
Sour-Cream, Plain (Sous iz Smetany), **10**-1572
Soy Sauce, **10**-1626
Spanish, **4**-573
Tartare Sauce, **4**-574; **5**-695
Thousand Island, **1**-60; **4**-574; **5**-695; **7**-1116; **10**-1614, 1622
Tomato, **7**-1086; **10**-1623
Vinaigrette, **4**-573; **5**-695, 745
Walnut-Ginger, **11**-1700
Wisconsin, for Shredded Cabbage, **3**-464
Yogurt, **12**-1958
Salade, Salat, Salata, Sałatka, see Salad(s)

Salami, **10**-1589
-Carrot Salad, **10**-1589
-Egg Canapés, **1**-86
Egg, and Noodle Skillet, **10**-1638
and Eggs, **6**-991
Omelet, **10**-1589
and Provolone Sandwiches, **10**-1605
Sailboats, **10**-1589
Skillet, **10**-1589
Sweet-and-Sour, **10**-1589
and Tomatoes, with Baked Polenta, **9**-1419

Sally Lunn, **2**-229; **10**-1589
Muffins, Raised, **10**-1590
Quick, **10**-1590
Ring, **10**-1589

Salmagundi, **10**-1590
Herring Salad, **9**-1383
Salad, **7**-1039
Salad with Salami and Liverwurst, **10**-1580
Salmi, Salmis, of Duckling, **10**-1590

Salmon, **10**-1590
Baked, **1**-76
Baked, with Caper Butter, **4**-622
Balls, **10**-1595
Broiled with Herbs, **5**-691
Broiled (Rhein Lachs vom Grill), **5**-793
Casserole, **2**-325
Casseroles, Individual, **7**-1097
Columbia River, Barbecued, **1**-65
Croquettes, **10**-1596
with Cucumber Sauce, **10**-1597
Curried-Salmon Sandwiches, **10**-1597
Curried-Salmon Triangles, **10**-1595
Cutlets, Deep-Fried, **10**-1594
Dip, **10**-1595
Divan, **10**-1595
Egg-Salmon Quiche, **4**-608
and Fresh-Grapefruit Salad, **5**-814
Kippered, with Rice, **7**-1017
Lime Salmon-Salad Spread, **7**-1067
Loaf, **10**-1595
Loaf, Curried, **10**-1595
Lomi Lomi (Hawaiian Salad), **1**-34
Louis, **10**-1597
Marinated, with Mustard Sauce (Gravad Lax med Senapssås), **11**-1786
Mayonnaise, **12**-1928
Mounds with Curry Mushroom Sauce, **10**-1596
Mousse, Cold, **10**-1597
Mousse, Hot, **5**-691
Newburg, **10**-1596
-Olive Sandwiches, **10**-1597
Patties, **10**-1596
Pie (Pirok), **1**-23
Poached (Losós do Sosów Goracych i Zimnych), **9**-1422
and Pork Packages (Laulau Pua), **9**-1435
-and-Potato Bake, **10**-1596
-Potato Salad, **10**-1597
Salad, **10**-1582
Salad Ring, Molded, with Cucumbers in Sour Cream, **5**-786
Salted, **10**-1594
Sautéed (Basler Lachs), **11**-1800
and Shrimp Casserole, **10**-1596
Smoked (Roget Laks), **4**-536
Soufflé, **10**-1596
with Souffléed Caper Sauce, **10**-1595
Soup, Cream of, **10**-1595
-Spaghetti Casserole, **10**-1596
Spread, **2**-280
Steaks, Barbecued, **12**-1928
Steaks with Caviar Sauce (Syomga s Sousom iz Ikri), **10**-1570
-Stuffed Peppers, **10**-1596
and Tomato Bisque, **10**-1595
and Tomato Soup, **10**-1595
and Tuna Mold, **10**-1582
with Veal (Veau Saumoné), **12**-1889
Wiggle, **10**-1596

Salmon, Smoked
with Cucumber Dip, **10**-1594
Horseradish Cones, **10**-1594
Scrambled Eggs with, **10**-1594
Vinaigrette (Vinaigrette s Syomgoi), **10**-1566
Salmonetes Levantinos (Red Mullet Levantine), **11**-1741
Salmon Trout in Aspic, **10**-1665
Salmon Trout Poached, with Tomato-Mustard Hollandaise Sauce, **4**-621
Salsa, **7**-1141
Salsa di Alici (Anchovy Sauce), **6**-959
Salsa de Chile Colorado (Red Chili Sauce), **7**-1142
Salsa de Chile Verde (Green Chili Sauce), **7**-1142
Salsa Cruda (Spiced Tomato Sauce), **7**-1142
Salsa alla Marinara (Mariner's Sauce), **6**-959
Salsa Parmigiana (Basic Tomato Sauce), **6**-959
Salsa Rapida de Chile (Quick Chili Sauce), **7**-1142
Salsa Verde, **1**-115; **8**-1299

Salmon, Smoked, continued
Salsa Verde Piccante (Piquant Green Sauce), **6**-959
Salsa di Vongole (White Clam Sauce), **6**-959
Salsiccie e Fagioli (Italian Sausages with Beans), **6**-955
Salsify, **8**-1290; **10**-1597; for recipes see Oyster Plant

Salt, 10-1597
Sticks, **11**-1828
To Measure, **7**-1117
Salt Pork, **10**-1598; for recipes see Pork, Cured
Saltsa Tomate (Tomato Sauce), **5**-818
Saltwater Taffy, **1**-57
Salzburger Nockerln (Dessert Puffs), **1**-123
Salzkartoffeln (Boiled Potatoes), **5**-795
Sambal, Coconut, **4**-527
Samosas (Curried Meat Turnovers), **12**-1879
Sam Saek Namul (Tricolored Vegetables), **7**-1022
San Juk (Meat on Skewers), **7**-1022

Sand Dab(s), 10-1598
Meunière, **10**-1598
Sand-Pail Picnic Dinner, **1**-73
Sand Tarts, **3**-473

Sandwich(es), 10-1598
Almond Soufflé, **10**-1610
Apple, **1**-102
Applesauce Frenchies, **1**-102
Apricot-Nut, **10**-1611
Aspic Glaze for, **6**-980
Avocado, **4**-635
Baked-Bean and Peanut, **8**-1322
Barbecue Bonanza, **10**-1605
Beef Tenderloin, **10**-1601
Blue-Cheese and Egg, **10**-1605
Breads, **10**-1599
Broadway Special, **10**-1605
Carrot and Onion Tea Sandwiches, **2**-306
Carrot and Peanut Butter, **2**-306
Cheese, Denver, **10**-1604
Cheese-and-Egg Barbecue, **10**-1604
Cheese, French-Toasted, **3**-362
Cheese-and-Nut, Savory, **10**-1610
Cheese-Olive-Raisin, **8**-1257
Cheese, Tiny, **1**-86
Chicken-Cheese, **10**-1602
Chicken and Ham, Three-Decker, **10**-1611
Chicken Loaf, **10**-1610
Chili Beefburger, **10**-1601
Club, Chef's, **10**-1604
Club, Continental, **10**-1602
Coconut-Cheese Loaf, **10**-1611
Cold Cuts Pyramid, **10**-1605
Copenhagen Coolers, **10**-1610
Corned-Beef and Cheese, **10**-1601
Corned-Beef and Muenster, **10**-1605
Country Club Luncheon, **10**-1605
Crabmeat Olive, **8**-1257
Cream-Cheese, Carrot, and Raisin, **10**-1605
Cream-Cheese, Cherry, and Pineapple, **10**-1611
Croque Monsieur, **3**-362
Cucumber Fillings, **4**-522
Curried Egg, **10**-1605
Curry Surprise, **10**-1605
Date-Nut Bread Slices, **4**-636
Denver, **1**-27
Down-East, **10**-1604
Egg-and-Cheese Burgers, **4**-608
Egg, Deviled-Ham, and Cheese, **10**-1605
Egg, Pepper, and Cheese, **9**-1360
Eggplant, Mozzarella, and Pimiento Long Boys, **9**-1359
Eggplant, Fried, and Pimiento Long Boys, **10**-1605
Egg-Salad and Tongue, **10**-1604
Frenched Ham and Swiss, **6**-913
French-Toast, with Cream Dried Beef, **10**-1601
Fried, French Style (Croque Monsieur), **6**-862
Fried Toast with Anchovies, **11**-1826
Garnishes, **10**-1599; **11**-1800
en Gelée, **5**-787
Giblet Filling, **5**-800
Grinders, Italian, **10**-1602
Guadalajara Toasts (Guadalajara Tostadas)), **7**-1138
Hamburger, **11**-1770
Hamburger Corn-Bread, **10**-1601
Hamburger, French-Fried, **6**-873
Hamburger Rolls, **10**-1601
Hamburger, Sweet-and-Sour, **10**-1601
Ham and Cheese Bites, **6**-852
Ham-Cheese Rolls, Hot, **6**-859
Ham and Potato-Salad, **6**-859
Ham Rabbit, **10**-1604
Ham Salad Boats, **6**-859
Ham Salad Rolls, **10**-1604
Hawaiian Omelet, **10**-1602
Herb-Buttered Rye- and White-Bread, **9**-1384
Hero, **10**-1604
Hero, Hot, **10**-1639
Little Toasts, Potosí Style (Tostaditas al Estilo de Potosí), **7**-1137
Liver-and-Bacon, **7**-1076
Liverwurst, **7**-1076
Lobster-Avocado, **7**-1081
Lobsterburgers, **10**-1602
Lobster-Muffin, **11**-1722
Mexican (Tostadas Compuestas), **7**-1137
Monte Cristo, **10**-1602
Mozzarella, French-Toasted, **10**-1604
Mushroom, **8**-1200
Onion and Parsley Finger, **10**-1610
Oyster Club, **8**-1287
Pâté-and-Cucumber, **5**-708
Peanut-Butter, **8**-1325
Peanut Butter and Bacon, **1**-134
Peanut-Butter and Prune, **9**-1485
Pecan-Tuna-Cheese, **8**-1334
Picnic Bean, **10**-1605
Pillows with Italian Ham (Cuscinetti Filanti al Prosciutto), **6**-862
Pizza, Western Style, **10**-1604
Pork and Curried Coleslaw, **10**-1602
Potato, Egg, and Cheese, **10**-1605
Provolone and Salami, **10**-1605
Prune-Nut, **9**-1485
Pungent French Rolls, **9**-1378
Raisin-Nut, **10**-1534
Roast-Beef and Blue-Cheese, **10**-1604
Roman Holiday, **10**-1605
and Salad Picnic, Menu, **9**-1382
Salmon, Curried, **10**-1597
Salmon-Olive, **10**-1597
for Sandwich and Salad Picnic, **9**-1383
Sardine, **10**-1612
Sardine Swiss-Cheese, **10**-1604
Sauerkraut, **10**-1632
Seafood Club, **10**-1602
Seafood Delight, **10**-1605
Shapes, **10**-1599
Shrimpburgers, **10**-1602
Shrimp and Cucumber, **12**-1958
Shrimp Spread, **10**-1658
Skyscraper, **10**-1605
Sloppy Joes, **10**-1601
Sloppy Joes, Italian, **10**-1601
Snitter, **4**-538
Sour-Cream Date Toast, **11**-1828
Spreading, **10**-1599
Steak Rolls, **10**-1601
Steak Tartare en Croûte, **11**-1770
Sunday Night Supper, **10**-1605
Tartar (Biftecks Tartare), **11**-1802
Tea Sandwiches, **4**-636
To Freeze, **5**-737; **10**-1599
Tongue and Cheese, with Cashews, **10**-1605
Toppings, **11**-1800
Tuna-Cheese Loaf, Baked, **10**-1602
Tuna, Curried, **10**-1602
Tuna-Egg Three-Deckers, **10**-1604
Turkey-Cheddar, Baked, **12**-1877
Turkey Combination, **12**-1877
Turkey, Hot, with Mushroom Sauce, **10**-1602
Turkey Loaf, **10**-1610
Veal and Pepper Long Boys, **9**-1359
Walnut Swiss-Cheese, **10**-1611
Watercress, **12**-1920
West Coast Extravaganza, **10**-1605
Western Long Boys, **6**-859
Western Sunday-Night, **10**-1604

Sandwich(es), Open, Open-Face(d), 10-1599; see also Canapé(s)
Bacon-Cheese Toast, **11**-1825
Banana Toast, **11**-1825
Callie-Toast, **11**-1825
Cheese Toast Special, **11**-1825
Chopped Beef Toast, **11**-1825
Creole Puff, **8**-1325
Danish, **4**-536
Danish Toast, **11**-1826
Deviled Toast, **11**-1826
Egg and Cheese Toast, **11**-1826
Ham and Egg Smørrebrød, **6**-862
Honey Pecan Tea Toast, **11**-1826
Mace Cheese Puffs, **7**-1097
Praline Toast, **11**-1828
in the Scandinavian Manner, **10**-1607-1610
Swiss, **11**-1800
Toast Luncheonettes, **11**-1829
Town Toast, **11**-1829
Tuna Caper, **12**-1867
Tuna Treat, **12**-1863
Turkey with Cheese Sauce, **12**-1876

Sandwich Filling(s), 10-1599; see also Spread(s)
Apricot-Cheese, **10**-1611
Cheese, **10**-1606
Curry Cashew, **10**-1611
Eggs, **10**-1606
Fish, **10**-1606
Meat, **10**-1606
Minced-Chicken, **10**-1611
Nonsweet, **4**-662
Peanut Butter plus, **10**-1606
Poultry, **10**-1606
Seasoned Butters, **11**-1800
Shellfish, **10**-1606
Sweet, **4**-662
Sans Rival Torte, Swedish, **12**-1856
Sardellenschnitzel (Veal Cutlets with Anchovies), **10**-1642
Sardinas con Salsa de Tomates (Sardines in Tomato Sauce), **11**-1741

Sardine(s), 10-1612
-Beet Spread, **2**-280
Broiled, on Toast, **10**-1612
Butter, **1**-86; **2**-279
and Cheese Salad, **10**-1612
Cocktail, **10**-1612
Deviled, **10**-1612
Pie (Coca de Sardinas), **9**-1494
Rounds, **1**-86
Sandwiches, **10**-1612
with Spinach and Cheese, **10**-1612
-Stuffed Artichokes (Alcachofas Rellenos con Sardinas), **11**-1741
-Stuffed Deviled Eggs, **9**-1378
Swiss-Cheese Sandwiches, **10**-1604
in Tomato Sauce (Sardinas con Salsa de Tomates), **11**-1741
Sardinhas de Caldeirada (Boatman's Stew), **9**-1455
Sarson Bhara Kekda (Shrimps with Mustard), **6**-942
Sashimi (Sliced Raw Fish), **6**-971
Satay Sauce, Javanese, **8**-1323
Sate Ajam (Broiled Chicken on Skewers), **11**-1714

Sauce(s), 10-1613; see also Butters; Gravy(ies); Mayonnaise; Salad Dressings; Sauce(s), Dessert; Stock(s)
Aïoli (Garlic Mayonnaise), **1**-7; **5**-740; **10**-1614, 1621
Allemande, **1**-10; **10**-1613, 1619
Almond and Mushroom, **7**-1152
Amandine, **1**-14
Américaine, **10**-1626
Anchovy, **11**-1738
Anchovy (Salsa di Alici), **6**-959
Apple-Sour-Cream, **1**-96
for Asparagus, **1**-114
Aurore, **2**-173; **10**-1613, 1620
Avocado Paste (Guacamole), **7**-1138
Bacon, with Peas, **1**-134
Bagna Cauda, Piedmontese, **10**-1627
Barbecue, see Barbecue Sauces
Basting, for Venison, **12**-1909
Béarnaise, **2**-173; **5**-741; **6**-905; **7**-1029; **10**-1614, 1621; **11**-1766
Quick, **7**-1074; **12**-1897
Tomate, **10**-1621
True, **2**-173
Béchamel, **2**-173; **8**-1190; **10**-1613, 1618
Variations of, **2**-173
for Beef and Potato Loaf, Sliced (Liha ja Perunamureke), **5**-680
Bercy, **10**-1620
Beurre Manié, **2**-202
Bigarade, **2**-202
Black-Butter, for Cooked Greens, **5**-825
Bordelaise, **1**-144; **2**-214; **5**-741; **10**-1613, 1619; **11**-1766
Bouquet, **5**-769
Brandy Clam, **5**-700
Bread, **4**-626; **10**-1614
English, **10**-1626
Brown, **2**-246; **7**-1039
Brown-Butter, **5**-694
Brown Butter and Caper, **10**-1663
Browned-Butter Fresh-Lemon, **7**-1053
Brown-Sugar, **7**-1151
Butter, **8**-1203
Butters (Beurres Composés), see Butters
Caper, **1**-63; **4**-624; **7**-1029, 1101; **10**-1614, 1620
Caper (Kaprissås), **11**-1791
Cardinal, **10**-1620
Cervelle, **10**-1614, 1622
Champagne, **10**-1626
Chasseur, **10**-1619
Chateaubriand, **10**-1626; **11**-1766
Chaud-Froid, **10**-1620
Cheese
American or Cheddar, **5**-725; **7**-1049; **10**-1620
Easy, **3**-361
Gruyère, **10**-1620
-Mustard, **5**-694
Parmesan, **3**-359; **5**-806; **6**-956; **8**-1231
Quick, **3**-361
Chicken-Liver, **7**-1076
Chili
con Carne, **8**-1282
Green, **11**-1731
Green (Salsa de Chile Verde), **7**-1142
Homemade, **3**-396
Quick (Salsa Rapida de Chile), **7**-1142
Red, **11**-1731
Red (Salsa de Chile Colorado), **7**-1142
Salsa, Mexican, **9**-1360
Southwestern, **11**-1731
-Tomato, **8**-1273
Choron, **6**-905; **10**-1621
Cider, for Meats, **1**-103
Clam, White, **3**-453
Clam, White (Salsa di Vongole), **6**-959
Cocktail, **7**-1077; **10**-1626
Cocktail, Hot, **5**-695
Cocktail for Turkey, **12**-1872
Colbert, **10**-1626
Colbert Butter, **10**-1624
Condiment, Hot, **10**-1626
Condiment (for Shantung lamb), **3**-400
for Corn-on-the-Cob, **3**-480
Cornmeal, **12**-1886
Court Bouillon, **5**-698
(for Crab Fu Yung), **3**-403
Cranberry-Mint, **3**-490; **7**-1151
Cream, **2**-173, 242; **10**-1640
Cream, Rich, **3**-346
Cream, Simple, **3**-346
Creamed Celery, **5**-694
Creamed Onion, **5**-694
Creamy Egg, **10**-1620
Creole, **5**-694; **9**-1359; **10**-1626
Cressonière, **10**-1614, 1622
Cucumber, **7**-1086; **11**-1700
Cumberland, **2**-194; **10**-1614, 1627
Curry, **2**-173; **5**-694; **6**-848; **10**-1662; **11**-1824
French Style, **10**-1614, 1620
Karry, **4**-539
-Onion, **5**-725
Demi-Glace, **10**-1619
Demi-Glace for Steaks, **2**-246
Devonshire Cream, Mock, **12**-1915
Diable, à la Diable, **4**-559; **5**-743; **10**-1613, 1619; **11**-1768
for Grilled Chicken, **2**-246
Dill, **4**-564; **5**-694; **9**-1475; **11**-1784, 1788
for Fish, **4**-564
Sharp (Skarpsås), **11**-1791
Tillikastike, **5**-681
Dipping (Ponzu), **6**-975
Drawn Butter, **10**-1624
Duxelles, **10**-1619
Egg
and Caper, **2**-296
Creamy, **5**-694
for Fish (Sos z Jaj do Ryby), **9**-1422
and Lemon, **5**-694
-Lemon (Avgolemono Sauce), **5**-818
and Lemon, Greek, **10**-1627
Espagnole, **4**-652; **10**-1613, 1617
Fines Herbes, **10**-1614
for Meats, Poultry, and Eggs, **2**-246
for Fish, **5**-694, 695
Fruited Black-Bean, **10**-1554
Garbanzo, **11**-1737
Garlic
Genoese (Pesto alla Genovese), **5**-775
Greek, **10**-1623
Skordalia, **5**-822
-Vinegar, **5**-694
Giblet (Sikotakia Saltsa), **5**-822
Glossary of Terms, **10**-1615
Goldenrod, **5**-694
Gooseberry, **5**-808
English, **10**-1627
à la Grecque, **1**-7; **12**-1902
Green (for Fish), **5**-694
Green (for Salad), **10**-1652
Green, Piquant (Salsa Verde Piccante), **6**-959
Gribiche, **10**-1614, 1623
for Ham, **6**-859
for Hamburger Steak, **2**-191
Hawaiian Teriyaki, **10**-1626
Hazelnut and Mushroom, **6**-882
Herb, **2**-173; **10**-1620
Herb (for Veal Loaf), **7**-1128
Herb and Wine-Vinegar, **5**-694
Hollandaise, **1**-114; **5**-695; **6**-904-906; **10**-1614, 1621
Blender, **10**-1620
Blender, Quick, **1**-114
Brennan's, **4**-512
Mustard, **10**-1614, 1621
(for Honan beef balls), **3**-399
Horseradish, **2**-189; **5**-726; **6**-914; **10**-1627
Hot (Varm Peberrodssovs), **4**-542
Pepperrotsaus, **8**-1240
Sos Chrzanowy, **9**-1422
Sous iz Khrena, **10**-1573
Whipped-Cream, **5**-695; **6**-914
Indienne, **2**-194; **11**-1837
Italienne, **10**-1613, 1619
Jelly, **1**-40
Junidanya (for Japanese beef), **6**-975
Juniper-Berry, **6**-996
Kakejiru (for Tempura), **6**-972
Lentil, **7**-1059
Liver, **9**-1369
Lobster, **5**-695; **7**-1150
Lobster (Hummersaus), 8-1236
Madeira, **9**-1424; **11**-1766
for Ham, **3**-439
Madère, **5**-740; **6**-865; **10**-1613, 1619
Maltaise, **6**-906; **10**-1614, 1621
Marchand de Vin, Brennan's, **4**-512
Marinara, **7**-1041; **11**-1737
Mariner's (Salsa alla Marinara), **6**-959
Marrow, **7**-1113
Mayonnaise, **7**-1115; **10**-1614; for recipes see Mayonnaise
Meat, Bolognese, **11**-1738
Meat, for Spaghetti, **2**-193
Meat for Spaghetti (QC), **10**-1523
Mint, **4**-624; **10**-1627
Mint, Traditional English, for Roast Lamb, **7**-1165
Mirepoix, **7**-1166
Molasses-Honey-Butter, **8**-1184
Mole, **5**-770
Mornay, **2**-173; **3**-361; **8**-1186; **9**-1400; **10**-1614, 1620; **12**-1864
Mousseline, **6**-906; **8**-1191, 1192; **10**-1614, 1621
Mushroom, **8**-1282; **12**-1874
-Cheese, **2**-324
Cream, **12**-1866
Creamy, for Pasta, **8**-1247
-Olive, **11**-1737
Sherry, **5**-695
Sour-Cream, **9**-1430
Sweet-Cream, **9**-1430
Mustard, **2**-173; **4**-623; **5**-726; **6**-881; **8**-1224, 1280; **9**-1350
Cream, **8**-1205
Creamy, **11**-1700
Dressing, **10**-1566, 1601
Sauce Moutarde, **5**-743
Senapssås, **11**-1786
Sennepssaus, **8**-1240
Sennepssovs, **4**-542
Sweet-and-Sour, **7**-1128
Sweet-Sour, **10**-1627
with Whipped Cream, **8**-1205
Normande, **10**-1613, 1620
Onion Cream, **1**-41
Onion (Løksaus), **8**-1240
Onion-Vinegar, **5**-694
Oxford (Cumberland), **8**-1283
Oyster, **5**-695
Paprika Cheese, **8**-1297
Parisienne, **10**-1613
Parmesan, **6**-958
Parmesan-Parsley, **11**-1738
Parsley, **8**-1299
Parsley, Italian, **8**-1299
Parsley-Olive, **11**-1738
Peanut, **11**-1709
Peanut-Butter, **8**-1325
with Braised Celery, **8**-1325
Sour-Cream, **8**-1325
Périgueux, **10**-1613, 1619
Pesto Genovese, **1**-148
Piquante, **10**-1613, 1619
Plum, Caucasian (Tkemali), **10**-1627
Plum Garlic, **9**-1415
Polonaise, **1**-114; **2**-194; **10**-1624; **11**-1837
Porto, au Porto, **10**-1613, 1619
Port-Wine, **7**-1151
Poulette, **10**-1620
Raifort, **10**-1614, 1620
Raisin, **7**-1150
Ravigote, **4**-573; **5**-695; **10**-1538, 1620
Rémoulade, **4**-573; **9**-1382; **10**-1543, 1614, 1622
Rhubarb, for Meats, **11**-1753
Roasted-Pepper, **11**-1738
Robert, **10**-1619
Roquefort, **10**-1614, 1623
Roux (brown, blond, white), **10**-1562; 1615

Sauce(s), continued
Russian, Special, for American Pot Roast (Spetsialni Russki Sous Dlia Zharenoi Goviadini), **10**-1573
Salsa (for Eggs, Ranch-Style), **7**-1141
Salsa Verde, **1**-115; **8**-1299
Satay, Javanese, **8**-1323
Satay, Singapore, **10**-1627
to Serve with Frankfurters, **5**-725-726
Shallot or Green-Onion, **8**-1282
Sharp, **10**-1665
Sherry Shrimp, **5**-700
Shrimp, **5**-695; **11**-1753
Shrimp Cocktail Sauce with Mustard, **1**-86
Shrimp (Rekesaus), **8**-1236
Soubise, **10**-1614, 1620
Soup, **10**-1614
Sour Cream, **10**-1666
Sour-Cream Cucumber, **5**-695
Sour-Cream Watercress, **12**-1920
Soy Butter, **5**-695
Spaghetti, **10**-1614; **11**-1737
Spanish, **4**-610
for Steak, **2**-193-194
Stracotto, **11**-1738
Suprême, **10**-1613, 1620
Sweet Basil, **10**-1626
Sweet-and-Sour, **3**-400; **10**-1627
Sweet-Sour (for fish), **11**-1734
Tamarind (Fried Fish with Tamarind Sauce), **11**-1809
Tartare, **4**-517, 575; **10**-1614, 1622
Tartare, Hot, **5**-695
for Tempura, **6**-972
Tomato, **5**-806; **9**-1450; **10**-1539; **11**-1834
Basic (Salsa Parmigiana), **6**-959
Italian, **10**-1627
-Meat, **2**-316
-Meat Spaghetti, **11**-1737
Purée, **11**-1738
Saltsa Tomate, **5**-818
Spaghetti, **11**-1737
Spiced (Salsa Cruda), **7**-1142
for Tongue, Three, **2**-194
Trevisano, **11**-1738
Tuna, White, **11**-1738
for Vegetables (Goma-Zu), **6**-976
Velouté, **2**-173; **10**-1613, 1618
Véronique, **10**-1614, 1621
Verte, **10**-1614, 1622
Vinaigrette, **5**-745; **10**-1614; **12**-1910
for Asparagus or Broccoli, **2**-252
Basic, **10**-1622
Vinegar-Soy, **7**-1023
Whipped-Cream Horseradish, **5**-695; **6**-914
White, **11**-1722; **12**-1939
Medium, **3**-362
Thick, **10**-1660
White Butter, Norman, **10**-1624
White Clam, Quick, **11**-1738
Whole Cranberry, **11**-1823
Wine, **7**-1152
Wine-Shallot, **11**-1767
Wine (for Veal Roast), **4**-531
Worcestershire, **12**-1949

Sauce(s), Dessert, 10-1615
Apricot, **1**-109
Blueberry, **2**-210
Blueberry, Foamy, **2**-209
Blueberry, Fresh, **2**-210
Brandy, **9**-1492
Brandy Hard Sauce, **5**-702
Brown Sugar, **1**-50
Butter, **9**-1492
Butter, Hot, **7**-1155
Butterscotch, **2**-255; **8**-1335; **10**-1615, 1628
Butterscotch-Mace Sundae, **7**-1100
Butterscotch (QC), **10**-1526
California Walnut, **10**-1629
Caramel, **10**-1615, 1628
Chantilly, **10**-1628
Cherry, I, **3**-374
Cherry, II, **3**-375
Cherry-Pineapple, **5**-788
Chocolate, **9**-1492; **10**-1615, 1628
Bittersweet, **10**-1628
Custard, **10**-1628
Low-Calorie, **3**-416
Cider, for Pudding, **3**-446
Cinnamon-Honey Syrup, **5**-824
Coconut Cream, Hawaiian, **1**-35
Crème Pâtissière, **10**-1615, 1628
Custard, **4**-518; **9**-1492; **10**-1666
Custard (Crème Anglaise), **10**-1615, 1628
(for Eight Treasures Pudding), **3**-404
Foamy, **9**-1492; **10**-1628
Fresh-Lemon, **7**-1056
Fresh-Lemon, Golden, **9**-1417
Fresh-Pear, **8**-1331
Fresh Plum, **9**-1415
Fruit, **10**-1615, 1628
Fruit (Frugtsauce), **4**-543
Fudge, **3**-415
Fudge (QC), **10**-1526
Hard Sauce, **3**-445; **6**-877; **9**-1493, **10**-1615, 1628
Basic, **6**-877
Brandy, **9**-1493
Brown-Sugar, **6**-878
Fluffy, **6**-878
Lemon, **9**-1493
in lemon shells, **3**-445
Orange, **12**-1915
Spicy, **6**-878
Stars, Lighted, **9**-1493
Strawberry, **11**-1776
Variations, **6**-877-878
Honey-Cream, **6**-911
Honey Syrup, **5**-823
Ice Cream, **6**-934; **10**-1615
for Ice Cream, **6**-930-931
Kanari Milch (Canary's Milk), **1**-123
Lemon, **2**-210; **5**-790, 804; **9**-1493; **10**-1628
Clear, **7**-1054
Cream, **11**-1757
Custard, **7**-1056
-Honey Syrup, **5**-823
(QC), **10**-1525
Maple Pineapple, **7**-1107
Maraschino, **7**-1108
Melon Ice-Cream, **2**-296
Mocha Sundae, **7**-1167
Nesselrode, **8**-1218
Orange, **7**-1135; **9**-1486; **10**-1628
Orange-and-Lemon, **3**-445
Peach Sundae, **8**-1320
Peanut-Butter Chocolate, **8**-1328
Pear Honey, **8**-1333
Raspberry, **10**-1538
Rum, **3**-440
Rum Syrup, **1**-132
Rum Syrup (Sirop de Rhum), **5**-748
Sabayon, **10**-1576, 1615, 1629
Sesame Honey Butter, **10**-1647
Sherry Custard, **9**-1493
Sherry Ginger Cream, **9**-1493
Strawberry Velvet, **11**-1776
Suzette, **5**-701
Taffy Sundae, **8**-1185
Vanilla, **9**-1493; **10**-1629; **11**-1839
Wine Custard (Weinschaum), **10**-1628

Sauerbraten, 10-1629
Overnight, **10**-1630
Quick, **10**-1630
Sauerbraten, **2**-186
with Sour-Cream Gravy, **10**-1630
mit Spätzle (Pot Roast with Dumplings), **5**-793
with Vegetables, **10**-1630

Sauerkraut, 10-1630
and Apples, Pork Loin with, **9**-1442
Bacon-Kraut-Potato Skillet, **1**-133
Balls, **10**-1632
and Bean Salad, Hot, **10**-1632
Beef and (Kücherlkraut), **1**-121
Bern, The Dish from (Bernerplatte), **11**-1803
with Braised Pheasant, **9**-1367
Browned, **2**-258
Cabbage Soup (Kapusniak), **9**-1420
Caraway, with Pork Butt, **9**-1440
Carp with, Alsatian, **5**-699
and Carrot Salad (Salat iz Morkovi i Kisloi Kapusty), **10**-1572
Casserole, Savory, **10**-1632
Choucroute Garnie, **1**-16; **10**-1632
Choucroute Garnie, Simple, **9**-1444
and Corned-Beef Hash, Baked, **10**-1631
Cornish Game Hens with, **1**-52
Dressing, **5**-808
Fish with, German, **10**-1631
and Frankfurter Goulash, **5**-721
Frankfurter-Kraut Casserole, **5**-720
Goulash, Szekely (Székely Gulyás), **6**-919
and Ham (Schinkenkraut), **1**-122
Picnic Shoulder Stuffed with, **9**-1442
and Pigs' Feet, **9**-1448
Pigs' Knuckles, and Biscuit Dumplings, **9**-1449
Pork, Applesauce, and Kraut Casserole, **1**-63
Salad (Sauerkrautsalat), **5**-796
Sandwich, **10**-1632
-Sausage-Stuffed Peppers, **10**-1638
Soup, Rumanian, **10**-1631
Soup, Soldiers' (Soldatskie Shchi), **10**-1568
and Spareribs, **7**-1151
Stuffing, **11**-1781
Transylvanian Casserole, **10**-1632
Viennese, **10**-1632

Sausage(s), 10-1632
in Ale, **10**-1635
-Apple Bake, **11**-1796
and Apples en Brochette, **10**-1639
Bake, Slavic, **10**-1636
-Ball Appetizers, Spicy, **7**-1122
Balls with Lima-Bean Soup, **7**-1122
Bean Casserole, **10**-1635
-Beef Patties, Smothered, **10**-1638
Bockwurst, **2**-212
Bologna, **2**-212; for recipes see Bologna
Bratwurst, **2**-221; **11**-1802
Casserole, Quick, **10**-1638
and Chestnut Stuffing, **11**-1781
and Chestnut Stuffing for Chicken, **3**-376
and Chick-Peas, **10**-1638
Chorizo and Chicken Spaghetti, **8**-1275
Chorizo (Mexican Sausage), **7**-1140
Cocktail, with White Wine, **8**-1276
Cooked (Bratwurst), **11**-1802
and Corn, Scalloped, **10**-1636
Creole, **2**-242
Eggplant-Sausage Casserole, **4**-614
Hero Sandwiches, Hot, **10**-1639
Italian, with Beans (Salsiccie e Fagioli), **6**-955
Italian, with Polenta, **9**-1418
Italian, with Veal Loaf, **12**-1896
Kielbasa, Kolbasi, or Kolbassy, **7**-1016; for recipes see Kielbasa
Knackwurst in Ale, **1**-10
-Leek Pie, **9**-1387
with Lentils, **7**-1059
and Liver Loaf, **10**-1636
and Liver Ring, Savory, **7**-1073
Liver Sausage, see Liverwurst
Loaf, **10**-1635
Loaf, Hot, **10**-1636
Luncheon Meat à la King, **10**-1638
Mettwurst, **7**-1135
Mexican (Chorizo), **7**-1140
-Nut Stuffing, **3**-381
Pepperone, **9**-1362
Peppy Pork, **2**-297
Pigs in Blankets, **10**-1635
Polish, with Red Cabbage, **7**-1151
-Potato Pot, **10**-1636
Pork, Old-Fashioned, **10**-1635

Ragout, **10**-1635
and Rice, Italian, **10**-1636
Salami, **10**-1589; for recipes see Salami
Sauce with Pasta, **10**-1636
-Sauerkraut-Stuffed Peppers, **10**-1638
Seasoning, **10**-1639
Slices, Hot, **3**-428
Sloppy Joes, Italian, **10**-1601
Spanish Casserole, **10**-1638
and Split-Pea Casserole, **2**-320
-Stuffed Acorn Squash, **1**-7
-Stuffed Eggplant, **10**-1638
Sweet-Potato Cakes, **9**-1352
Sweet-Potato, and Fruit Bake, **10**-1636
Turkey, Puerto Rican, **12**-1871
Turkey-Sausage Squares, **12**-1875
Venison, **12**-1909

Sauterne, 10-1639
and Champagne Punch (QC), **10**-1527
Savanyu Ökörfarok (Sour Oxtail Ragout), **6**-918
Savarin, **10**-1639, 1640
Savarin Dough (Gâteau Manon), **5**-784

Savory, 10-1640
Butter, **5**-695
and Grapefruit Jelly, **6**-983
Summer, **10**-1640
Winter, **10**-1640

Scallion(s), 10-1640
and Beans, **8**-1266
Garden Ragout, **8**-1266
and Mushroom Sauce, Eggs in, **8**-1265

Scallop(s), 10-1641
Bisque, **2**-275
Boniface, **10**-1642
en Brochette, **10**-1642
Broiled Curried, **10**-1641
Coquilles St. Jacques, **3**-478; **5**-739
Cream Soup, **11**-1695
Creole, **10**-1642
Marinated, Hawaiian (Ophi), **9**-1434
Meunière, **10**-1641
Minced, in Wine-Cheese Sauce, **10**-1642
Mornay, **8**-1186
Newburg, **10**-1641
Rémoulade Dip for, **1**-87
with Rice (Ktenia me Ryzi), **5**-818
Sautéed, with Lemon Butter, **10**-1642
Sauté Provençale, **10**-1641
Scalloped, **1**-45
Seafood Salad (Nuta), **6**-972
Stew, **10**-1641
in Vermouth, **10**-1662
Scaloppine di Vitello (Veal Scaloppine), **6**-954
Scampi ai Ferri (Garlic Broiled Shrimps), **6**-954
Scandinavian Cherry Soup, **12**-1927
Scandinavian Fruit Pudding, **5**-758
Scandinavian Fruit Soup, Chilled, **11**-1694
Scandinavian Pickled Beets, **2**-195
Schav (Sorrel Soup), **6**-987
Schinkenfleckerln (Noodles with Ham), **1**-122
Schinkenkraut (Ham and Sauerkraut), **1**-122
Schlee (vegetables), **1**-76
Schnecken (sweet rolls), **2**-242; **5**-799
Schnitz und Gnepp (Dried Apples and Dumplings), **1**-66, 103
Schnitz und Gnepp (Dried Apples and Raised Dumplings), **9**-1351
Schnitzel, see Veal, Schnitzel
Schweinekniestücke mit Sauerkraut und Kartoffelklösse (Pigs' Knuckles, Sauerkraut, and Potato Dumplings), **5**-795
Scone(s), **10**-1642; for recipes see Biscuit(s) and Scone(s)
Scotch Broth, **1**-147; **4**-621; **7**-1038
Scotch Cock-a-Leekie, **7**-1047
Scotch Coffeecake, **3**-463
Scotch Heart Patties, **6**-883
Scotch Woodcock, **3**-346
Scottish Scones, **4**-634

Scrapple, 10-1644
2-242; **9**-1351
Homemade, **10**-1644
or Pannhaas, **1**-66
South Carolina, **1**-68
Scripture Cake, **1**-38
Scrod, **10**-1644; for recipes see Cod, Codfish
Sculpin, **10**-1644
Sea Bream Fried in Egg Batter (Domi Jun), **7**-1020
Seafoam (candy), **2**-284, 285
Seafoam Frosting, **2**-272; **5**-750
Seafoam Salad, **10**-1587
Seafood, see Fish; Shellfish

Seasoning, 10-1645; see also Bouquet Garni
Currant Curry, **10**-1555
Garlic, **5**-775
Herb (Odori Fini), **3**-345
Low-Calorie, for Fish, Meat, and Poultry, **7**-1086
Low-Calorie, for Vegetables, **7**-1086
Poultry Seasoning, **9**-1479
Rosemary-Wine, **10**-1556
Spice Mixture, **2**-298
Seattle Dutch Babies, **12**-1932

Seaweed, 10-1645
Seaweed with Rice (Nori-Chazuke), **6**-976
Seaweed, Toasted (Kim Kui), **7**-1022
Secret Harbor Cheesecake, **3**-368
Seedcake, **11**-1819
Selchfleisch (Smoked Butt), **1**-122
Selino Avgolemono (Celery with Egg-Lemon Sauce), **5**-822
Selyodka (Herrings), **10**-1566
Semlor (Shrove Tuesday Buns), **11**-1791
Semolina, **10**-1646
Senapssas (Mustard Sauce), **11**-1786
Sennebec Hill Bread, **2**-230
Sennepssaus (Mustard Sauce), **8**-1240
Sennepssovs (Mustard Sauce), **4**-542
Serbian Walnut Strips, **12**-1918
Serina Cakes (Serinakaker), **8**-1243
Serinakaker (Serina Cakes), **8**-1243

Sesame, Sesame Seed(s), 10-1646
-Anise Cookies, **10**-1647
Asparagus Salad, **1**-115
Baked Hake, **6**-847
Benne-Seed Biscuits, South Carolina, **11**-1724
Benne Wafers, **10**-1647
Chicken, Spiced, **10**-1647
Cookies, Korean, **4**-635
Dips (rolls), **2**-239
Ground Toasted, **7**-1020
Honey Butter, **10**-1647
Rolls, **10**-1647
Shrimps, Southern, **10**-1647
Toast, **11**-1828
To Toast, **4**-635
Whole-Wheat Bread, **10**-1647
Seven Chieftains Tokany (Hét Vezér Tokány), **6**-918
Seviche (Pickled Raw Fish), **5**-688; **7**-1140; **11**-1704
Sfougato (Meat Custard), **5**-818

Shad, 10-1647
Baked, **10**-1648
with Herb-Bread Stuffing, **10**-1648
with Mushroom Stuffing, **10**-1648
with Oyster Stuffing, **1**-29
without Bones, Norfolk, **1**-75
Broiled
Connecticut River, **1**-28
Golden, **10**-1648
Fillets, Sautéed, **10**-1648
Planked, **10**-1648
Shaddock, **10**-1648

Shad Roe
with Bacon, **2**-247
Broiled, **5**-692
Broiled, with Bacon, **10**-1648
Smothered, **10**-1648

Shallot(s), 10-1648
Bercy Butter, **10**-1615, 1624
Butter, **10**-1615, 1624
and Lamb Chops in Casserole, **10**-1650
Sauce, **8**-1282
Soufflé, **12**-1904
and Tomatoes, **10**-1650
-Veal Chops, **10**-1649
Wine-Shallot Sauce, **11**-1767
Shantung Chafing-Dish Lamb, **3**-400
Shashlik, **10**-1571
Sheepherder's Stew, **1**-55
Sheepshead, Sheephead, **10**-1650

Shellfish, 10-1650; see also names of shellfish
Bouillabaisse, White-Fish, **10**-1645
Cioppino, **3**-447; **12**-1927
Cioppino, Fisherman's Wharf, **1**-26
Curried, **10**-1652
Marinade, Uncooked, for Small Portions of, **7**-1110
Musical Comedy of (Zarzuela de Mariscos), **11**-1743
Newburg, **10**-1652
Paella de la Costa Brava, **11**-1746
Paella a la Valenciana, **8**-1291
Peach Seafood Salad, **8**-1316
Potato Fish Stew (Caldeirada de Peixe), **9**-1455
Rice and Seafood Salad, **10**-1550
Salad Plate, **10**-1652
Sandwich Fillings, **10**-1606
Seafood
Baked, Hearthside, **8**-1222
Bisque, **4**-648
in Chili, **11**-1727
Chowder, Maine, **1**-45
Club Sandwiches, **10**-1602
Cocktail, **3**-445
Cocktail Salad, **5**-786
Medley in Patty Shells, **3**-424
Newburg, **2**-250
in Pickled Sauce (Escabeche de Mariscos), **11**-1704
Stew, **8**-1222
Supreme, **10**-1645
-Vegetable Chowder, **11**-1696
Soufflé, **10**-1652
To Freeze, see To Freeze Seafood, **5**-736; see also information under entry for specific shellfish
-Vegetable Chowder, **10**-1650

Shepherd's Pies, 7-1049
Beef, **1**-189
Lamb, **9**-1387
Poultry, **7**-1049
Soybean, **11**-1734
Sherbet(s), **10**-1652; for recipes see Ice(s) and Sherbet(s)

Sherry, Sherried, 10-1654
Artichoke Chicken, **12**-1930
Barbecue Sauce, **10**-1624
Cobbler, **3**-454
Crab Soup, **7**-1097
Custard Sauce, **9**-1493
Dressing, **10**-1589
Filet of Beef with, **12**-1947
Ginger Cream, **9**-1493
Hard Sauce, **6**-877
Jelly, **1**-60; **5**-789
Parfait, **5**-790
Posset, **9**-1457
Smoked Sturgeon in Ramekins, **11**-1782
Stuffed Dates, **4**-548
Sweet Potatoes, **11**-1724
Tortoni, **12**-1858
Turkey with Potatoes, **12**-1874

Shish Kebab, see Kabob, Kebab; Skewer, Skewered
Shoofly Pie, **1**-66; **9**-1390
Shoofly Pie, Spicy, **9**-1356

Shortbread(s), 10-1654
Nut, **10**-1655
Orange, **10**-1655
Shortbread, **10**-1655; **11**-1819
Walnut, **12**-1917

Shortcake(s), 10-1655
Apple-Cranberry, **1**-101
Blueberry, **2**-210
Huckleberry, **6**-915
Peach, **8**-1320
Plum, Individual, **9**-1417
Strawberry, **10**-1655; **11**-1779
Shortening, **10**-1655
To Measure, **7**-1117

Shredded Wheat
Dessert (Kadayif), **8**-1216
Turkish Dreams, **10**-1561
Shreds of Gold (Foi Tong), **11**-1716

Shrimp(s), 10-1655
with Anchovy Butter, **8**-1775
Appetizer, **10**-1656
and Artichoke Appetizer, **10**-1658
and Artichoke Salad, **1**-112
Avocado Shrimp Boats, Puerto Rican, **1**-130
Bahia Style (Camarões a Bahia), **11**-1704
Balls, Indian, **10**-1662
Banana, Curry, **1**-139
Beer Marinade for, **7**-1110
Bisque, **3**-442; **10**-1658
Bisque, Quick, **10**-1658
Bisque (Sopa de Camarões), **9**-1453
Boiled with Dill, **10**-1665
Broiled, Indian, **6**-913
Broiled (Onigari Yaki), **6**-972
Butter, **1**-86; **2**-279; **10**-1615, 1626
Butterfly (Wu Dep Har), **3**-403
Cacciattore, **10**-1661
Cakes, **10**-1658
Canapé Paste, **1**-67
Canapé or Sandwich Spread, **10**-1658
and Cantaloupe Luncheon Salad, **2**-296
Casserole, **2**-325; **10**-1658
Cauliflower with, Hot, **3**-343
with Cauliflower, Hot (Blomkål i Rekesaus), **8**-1239
and Cauliflower Salad (Maionese di Scampi e Cavolfiori), **1**-82
-Caviar Canapés, **4**-632
and Celery Salad, **10**-1662
-and-Cheese Macaroni Loaf, **7**-1091
Chicken-Liver Spread, **2**-279
Chicken-Shrimp Gumbo Filé, **1**-44
Chili Shrimp Squares, **10**-1656
Chowder, **10**-1658
Clemenceau, Brennan's, **4**-510
Cocktail Sauce with Mustard, **1**-86
Cocktail Supreme, **10**-1656
Company, Casserole, **11**-1734
Cooked in Beer, **2**-195; **10**-1661
and Corn Casserole, **3**-482
and Corn Pie, **1**-67
and Crab, Dixie Style, **10**-1650
-Crab Salad, Hot, **10**-1652
and Crabs, Creamed, in Timbale Cases, **11**-1824
Cracker-Fried (Tempura Sembei), **6**-972
Creamed, with Avocado, **10**-1658
Creole, **10**-1660
Creole Jambalaya, **6**-968
Creole-Style Leftovers, **7**-1049
Croquettes (Garnalen Croquetten), **4**-590
and Cucumber Sandwiches, **12**-1958
Curried, in Pineapples, **10**-1660
Curried Shrimp Diamonds, **8**-1306
Curry, **4**-640; **10**-1660
Deviled, **10**-1661
with Dill, **4**-564
with Dill and Mushrooms, **10**-1662
Dressing, **4**-575
Egg Rolls, **10**-1660
and Egg Salad, Japanese, **10**-1580
Filling, **10**-1660
Fish Stew (Vatapá), **11**-1703
Flambé, **10**-1660
and Flounder, **5**-705
Fresh-Grapefruit, Salad, **10**-1581
and Fresh-Pear Appetizer, **8**-1330
Fresh Tomato Balachong (Pazundok Ngapi Gyaw), **11**-1716
Fried, Chinese, **10**-1661
Fried in Egg Batter (Saewu Jun), **7**-1020
Fu Yung, **3**-403
Garlic Broiled (Scampi ai Ferri), **6**-954
Garlic-Ginger, **5**-775; **10**-1661
-Grapefruit Salad, **10**-1662
Hawaiian, **10**-1658
Jambalaya, **10**-1661
de Jonghe, **11**-1722
Jumbo, Grilled, Venetian Style, **10**-1661
Kabobs, **6**-998; **10**-1660
à la King, **1**-8
Lemon-Broiled, **7**-1052
Macaroni, and Orange Salad, **7**-1092
Macaroni Salad, **10**-1662
in Marinade, **10**-1657
Marinade for, Uncooked, **7**-1110
Marinated, **10**-1656
Mixed Cooked Foods (Yose-Nabe), **6**-975
Mold, Savory, **6**-979
-Mushroom Flan, French, **4**-633
with Mustard (Sarson Bhara Kekda), **6**-942
Nets (La Tieng), **11**-1716
Newburg, **8**-1218
Noodle Skillet, **8**-1232
Omelet (Ch'ao Hsia Tan), **3**-403
in the Oven, **10**-1660
-Oyster Gumbo, **10**-1658
and Oyster Jambalaya, **4**-510
and Oyster Pie, **8**-1222
Paste, **2**-242; **10**-1657
Pickled, **3**-428
Pilau St. Augustine, **1**-32
and Pineapple, Chinese Style, **9**-1406
Potted, **4**-622
Potted, Savory, **9**-1477
Potpie, **10**-1661
Prawns in Cream, **12**-1927
and Prosciutto, Broiled, **10**-1657
Puffs, **8**-1306
Rémoulade, **1**-86
Rémoulade Dip for, **1**-87
Rémoulade, Hotel Pontchartrain, **4**-510
and Rice Jambalaya, **10**-1549
Ring, Jellied, **7**-1080
Rush Hour (Rejer i Traengsel), **4**-536
Salad, **6**-911; **10**-1580
Salad, Exotic, **10**-1662
and Salmon Casserole, **10**-1596
Sambal, **10**-1661
Sauce, **5**-695; **11**-1753
Sauce (Rekesaus), **8**-1236
Sauté, **5**-775
Sauté, Quick, **10**-1660
Savory, **4**-642
Seafood Salad, **10**-1665
Sesame, Southern, **10**-1646
and Shell Chowder, **7**-1091
Shrimpburgers, **10**-1602
Soup, English Style, **10**-1658
Spiced, Avocado Halves with, **10**-1581
with Spicy Tomato Sauce (Garides Saltsa Tomate), **5**-818
and Squash Soup (Hingha), **11**-1716
Stew, **2**-300; **10**-1658
Stew, Biloxi, **1**-50
Stuffed (Relyenong Hipon), **9**-1369
Sweet-and-Sour, **10**-1660
Teriyaki, **10**-1661
Toast, **11**-1828
Toast Butter, **11**-1829
Tomato-Shrimp Bisque, Sherried, **11**-1832
Twice-Fried, for Appetizers, **10**-1657
and Vegetables, Skewered, **7**-1084
Victoria, **12**-1927
with Wild Rice, **12**-1940
Shrove Tuesday Buns (Semlor), **11**-1791
Shrub, **10**-1662
Siadle Mleko (Clabber), **9**-1428
Sianlihakastike (Pork Stew), **5**-681
Siberian Dumplings (Sibirskie Pelmeni), **10**-1571
Sicilian Eggplant Caponata, **4**-614
Sicilian Fish (Pesce alla Siciliana), **6**-954
Sicilian Macaroni and Eggplant Casserole, **7**-1095
Sicilian Spaghetti, **11**-1737
Sicilian Style Veal Cutlets, **12**-1893
Sikotakia Saltsa (Giblet Sauce), **5**-822
Sill och Skinksallad (Herring and Ham Salad), **11**-1787
Sillisalaatti (Herring Salad), **5**-678
Silver Cake, **7**-1042
Simnel Cake, **4**-626
Singapore Satay Sauce, **10**-1627
Sirop de Rhum (Rum Syrup), **5**-748
Skånsk Potatis (Swedish Creamed Potatoes), **11**-1790
Skarpsås (Sharp Dill Sauce), **11**-1791

Skate, 10-1663
with Brown Butter and Caper Sauce, **10**-1663

Skewer, Skewered, 10-1633; see also Kabob(s), Kebab(s)
Apples and Sausages en Brochette, **10**-1639
Beef on a Spit, Rib Roast of, **7**-1150
Beef on a Spit, Roast, **2**-183
Brochettes de Rognons Panés et Grillés, **7**-1014
Broiled Beef (Jyuniku-Teriyaki), **6**-974
Broiled Pork (Butaniku-Teriyaki), **6**-974
Chicken Livers with Sage, **10**-1578
Chicken on Skewers, Broiled (Sate Ajam), **11**-1714
Chicken on Skewers, Fried (Kushi-Katsu), **6**-975
Cocktail Sausages with White Wine, **8**-1276
Corn and Meatballs, Barbecued, **7**-1123
Fire Beef (Pul Koki), **7**-1020
Garlic-Ginger Shrimps, **10**-1661
Meat on Skewers (San Juk), **7**-1022
Mozzarella Skewers, Italian (Crostini alla Mozzarella), **6**-955
Oysters en Brochette, **8**-1286
Pineapple Teriyaki, **9**-1406
Pork, Indonesian, **7**-1052
Pork Shoulder Steak Teriyaki, **11**-1770
Scallops en Brochette, **10**-1642
Shashlik, **10**-1571
Shish Kebab, **1**-146; **10**-1654
Shrimps Teriyaki, **10**-1661
Shrimps and Vegetables, **7**-1084
Spiedino alla Romana, **3**-358
Suggestions for Skewered Dishes, **1**-146
Swordfish, Skewered, **4**-565
Swordfish on Skewers, Turkish (Kilich Shish), **8**-1215
Teriyaki (beef round steak), **11**-1768
Teriyaki Sticks, **4**-643
Tuna en Brochette, **12**-1802
Skil, see Sablefish
Skinke med Madeira (Ham with Madeira), **4**-539
Skordalia (Garlic Sauce), **5**-822
Sky (Chopped Aspic), **4**-538
Skysovs (Spiced Drippings), **4**-538
Slavic Casserole, **11**-1698
Slavic Sausage Bake, **10**-1636
Slieve na mBan Carrots, **6**-948
Sloe, **10**-1663
Sloppy Joes, **10**-1601
Sloppy Joes, Italian, **10**-1601
Slottsstek (Royal Pot Roast), **11**-1788
Små Köttbullar (Small Meatballs), **11**-1786

Smelt(s), 10-1664
with Caper Sauce, **10**-1664
Fillets, Fried (Stekt Sill Eller Strömming), **11**-1787
with Lobster or Crabmeat Stuffing, **7**-1147
Panfried, **1**-78
Sautéed, **7**-1147
Smoked Salmon, see Salmon, Smoked
Salmon

Smorgasbord, 10-1664
American, Menu, **10**-1666
Garnishes, **10**-1666
Smørrebrød (Danish open-faced sandwiches), **4**-536; for recipes see Sandwich(es), Open, Open-Face(d)

Snail(s), 10-1667
Butter, **10**-1667
Forestière, **10**-1667
Snap Bean, **10**-1667; for recipes see Bean(s), Fresh; Bean(s), Green or Wax
Snapper, Red, see Red Snapper
Snickerdoodles, **1**-29
Snickerdoodles, Buttermilk, **8**-1230
Snickerdoodles, Joanne's, **3**-476
Snipe, Canadian, **5**-769
Snitter, **4**-536
Snoek in Witte Wijn Saus (Pike with White-Wine Sauce), **4**-590
Snow Dressing, **1**-56
Snow Pudding with Nesselrode Sauce, **8**-1218
Soba (Buckwheat Noodles), **6**-976
Soda Bread, Basic Recipe for, **6**-944
Sodas, Ice-Cream, **6**-932
Soepballetjes (Soup Meatballs), **4**-589
Soft Roe, see Roe
Soldatskie Shchi (Soldiers' Sauerkraut Soup), **10**-1568
Soldiers' Sauerkraut Soup (Soldatskie Shchi), **10**-1568

Sole, 10-1670
Bonne Femme, **10**-1670
Deep-Fried (Gebackene Seezunge), **5**-793
Fillet(s) of
en Casserole, **10**-1670
in Court Bouillon, **3**-486
Supreme, **5**-692
Véronique, **5**-812
Grilled, with Mustard Sauce, **4**-622
Horseradish, **10**-1670
Meunière, **10**-1670
Stuffed, Ana of Povoa's (Linguado Recheado), **9**-1455
in Vermouth, **10**-1670
in White Wine, **12**-1947
Sommersalat (Summer Salad), **8**-1240
Sonhos (Dreams), **9**-1457
Sonkás Palacsinta (Pancakes Layered with Minced Ham), **6**-919
Sooner-State Beans with Spareribs, **1**-64
Soowar ka Gosht Vindaloo (Sour Pork Curry), **6**-939
Sopa de Aguacate (Avocado Soup), **7**-1138
Sopa de Ajos (Garlic Soup), **11**-1742
Sopa de Albóndigas (Meatball Soup), **1**-59
Sopa de Almendras (Almond Soup), **11**-1742
Sopa de Ameijoas (Clam Soup), **9**-1453
Sopa Borracha (Tipsy Cake), **9**-1497
Sopa de Calabaza Maracay (Pumpkin Soup Maracay), **11**-1704
Sopa de Camarões (Shrimp Bisque), **9**-1453
Sopa a la Limeña (Soup, Lima Style), **11**-1703
Sopa de Mondongo (Tripe Soup), **11**-1704
Sopa de Pescado a la Vasca (Basque Fish Soup), **11**-1743
Sopa de Queso (Cheese Soup), **11**-1747
Sopapillas, **11**-1731
Soppin' Sauce, **11**-1731
Sopón de Garbanzos con Patas de Cerdo (Chick-Pea Soup with Pigs' Feet), **9**-1493

Sorghum, 10-1670
Sorghum Cake, Bluegrass, **1**-41

Sorrel or **Dock, 10**-1671
Garden Sorrel, **10**-1671
Purée, **10**-1671
Soup, **10**-1671
Soup, Cream of, **10**-1671
Soup with Rice, **10**-1671
Soup (Schav), **6**-987
Soup (Sóska Leves), **6**-917
Soup with Vermicelli, **10**-1671
and Spinach Steaks (Bifes con Azedas), **9**-1456
Sos Chrzanowy (Horseradish Sauce), **9**-1422
Sos z Jaj do Ryby (Egg Sauce for Fish), **9**-1422
Sóska Leves (Sorrel Soup), **6**-917
Soubise Sauce, **10**-1614, 1620

Soufflé(s), 11-1685
Asparagus, **1**-115; **2**-324
Broccoli, **12**-1904
Carrot, **2**-305
Carrot (Porkkanakohokas), **5**-681
Cassoulettes, **11**-1688
Cheese, **2**-324
Cheese, Top-Hat, **3**-359
Corn-Soufflé Pudding, Southern, **1**-22
Eggplant Clam, **4**-614
Fish and Mushroom (Hmoh Nga Baung), **11**-1716
Fresh-Corn, **3**-482
Green-Bean, **12**-1906
Ham, **6**-865
Herring (Soufflé ze Śledzia), **9**-1422
Kipper, **7**-1017
Lamb, Canadian, **7**-1040
Laurette, **11**-1688
Lobster, **7**-1078
Macaroni and Cheese, **7**-1095
Meat (Lihakohokas), **5**-680
Omelet, **2**-324
Onion or Shallot, **12**-1904
Potato, **9**-1467
Potato (Papa Empanada al Horno), **9**-1497
Salmon, **10**-1596
Savory, Basic, **11**-1685
Shellfish, **10**-1652
Spinach, **4**-604; **12**-1906
Tomato, **11**-1688
Tuna, Double-Boiler, **12**-1866

Soufflé(s), Dessert, 11-1688
Almond, **1**-15
Apricot, **1**-108
Banana, **7**-1098
Burnt Almond, **11**-1688
Chocolate, **3**-412; **11**-1688
Cottage-Prune, **3**-362
Lemon, **7**-1054
Liqueur, **11**-1688
Marron, **7**-1112
Mocha (Soufflé Moka), **5**-746
Orange, **8**-1270; **11**-1688
Peach, **8**-1317
Prune-Cheese, **9**-1485
Pumpkin, **9**-1499
Rothschild, **11**-1688
Sweet-Potato, **11**-1796
Vanilla, **11**-1688
Soufflé(s), Dessert, Cold
Chocolate, **4**-557
Coffee, **4**-565
Strawberry, **4**-632

Soup(s), 11-1690
Almond (Sopa de Almendras), **11**-1742
Avocado (Sopa de Aguacate), **7**-1138
Barley (Gerstensuppe), **1**-121
Barley-Onion with Beef Balls, **7**-1122
Bean Paste (Miso Shiru), **6**-971
Borsch, Meatless, **2**-214
Borsch, Polish, **2**-195
Borsch, Quick, **11**-1838
Borsch, Ukrainian, **2**-214
Borsch, Very Quick (Borsch Poproshche), **10**-567
Bouquet Garni for, **2**-216
Bullhead or Catfish, **1**-52
Cabbage, Brown (Brunkålssoppa), **11**-1787
Cabbage, Danish Browned, **11**-1690
Caraway (Kömény Leves), **6**-917
Cheese (Sopa de Queso), **11**-1747
Cherry (Kirsebaersuppe), **4**-539
Chicken Broth, Golden (Goldene Yoich), **6**-987
Chicken, with Sherry, **6**-967
Chicken and Watercress, **12**-1920
Dumplings for, **4**-585
Easter (Mageritsa), **5**-818
Egg-Drop, Chinese (Chi Tan T'ang), **3**-401
Egg-Lemon (Avgolemono Soupa), **5**-818
Egg-Petal, with Cucumbers, **11**-1691
Egg, Portuguese, **11**-1691
Egg (Tamago Suimono), **6**-971
Fish (Gentsche Waterzooi), **2**-197
with Frankfurters, Quick, **5**-720
Fruit, Dried- and Fresh-, **4**-576
Garlic, Italian, **5**-775
Garlic (Sopa de Ajos), **11**-1742
Garlic, Vera Cruz, **11**-1691
Garnishes and Accompaniments, **11**-1696-1697
(garnish) Won Ton, Crisp (Cha Yun T'un), **3**-401
Ginger Beef with Noodles (Pho), **11**-1717
Leek with Cheese, **3**-355
Lemon, Greek, **7**-1052
Liver Dumpling (Leberknödelsuppe), **5**-793
with Liver Dumplings (Polévka s Jaternimi Knedlíky), **4**-531
Marrow Dumplings in Consommé (Markklösschen), **5**-793
Meatball, **1**-24
Meatball (Sopa de Albóndigas), **1**-59
Mushroom Broth, Quick, **2**-246
Onion, with Cheese, Jamaican, **6**-967
Onion with Cheese (Soupe à l'Oignon au Gratin), **5**-739
Onion, French, **8**-1260
Onion, Italian, **11**-1690
Onion, South American, **8**-1260
Oxtail, **2**-192
Oxtail (Kori Kuk), **7**-1020
Plantain Balls, **9**-1414
Pork and Watercress (Chu Jou Pi Chi T'ang), **3**-401
Rice with Chicken Livers, Italian, **7**-1075
Rice, Greek, **10**-1549
Rusell Borscht, **6**-994
Russian Sturgeon Champagne, **10**-1568
Shrimp, English Style, **10**-1658
Slick Chick, **7**-1083
Sorrel, **10**-1671
with Rice, **10**-1671
with Vermicelli, **10**-1671
Spinach (Spinatsuppe), **8**-1235
Stock (Dashi), **6**-970
Toasts for, **11**-1697
Tomato, Pale-Pink, **11**-1690
Turkey, **12**-1872
Turtle, **12**-1880
Vegetable, with Meatballs (Groentesoep met Balletjes), **4**-589
Watercress, **6**-945
White, with Meatballs, **7**-1122

Soup(s), Bouillon(s) and **Consommé(s);** see also Stock(s)
Avocado, **11**-1727
Beef Bouillon, **2**-215
Beef Broth, **7**-1146
Beet, Clear (Barszcz Czysty), **9**-1420
Chicken Bouillon, **2**-215
Clam Bouillon Digby Pines, **2**-275
Clear Soup (Suimono), **6**-970
Consommé, **3**-466, 467
Consommé Julienne, **3**-467, **6**-996
Consommé Madrilène, **4**-568
Consummé Madrilène, Hot, **7**-1102
Consommé Madrilène, Jellied, **7**-1102

Soup(s), Bouillon(s), Consommé(s), continued
Egg Consommé (Pavese), **6**-952
Fish Bouillon, **2**-215
Herbed Bouillon, **3**-424
Jellied Bouillon, **2**-216
Juice-into-Soup, **11**-1691
Mushroom Consommé, **11**-1822
Mushroom Consommé, Swiss, **8**-1198
Oxtail I (Clear), **4**-620
Tomato Bouillon, **2**-216
Tomato Bouillon, Spicy, **11**-1832

Soup(s), Chilled, Frozen, or **Jellied**
Apple (Äppelsoppa), **11**-1787
Apple and Onion, **11**-1694
Avocado, Chilled, **1**-130
Black-Bean Chiller, **11**-1692
Blueberry, Norwegian, **2**-208
Bombay Refresher, **11**-1692
Bouillon, Jellied, **2**-216
Broccoli Bisque, Chilled, **11**-1837
Broccoli, Cold, **4**-645
Buttermilk, Cold (Kaernemaelkskoldskaal), **4**-539
Buttermilk, Danish, **2**-254
Cherry, Cold (Kirsebærsuppe), **8**-1235
Cherry, Scandinavian, **12**-1927
Chicken, Cool Curried, **3**-390
Clam Bisque, Chilled, **11**-1692
Consommé Madrilène, Jellied, **3**-467; **6**-979; **7**-1102
Crème Mongole, **11**-1692
Cucumber (Agurkesuppe), **4**-538
Cucumber, Bulgarian, **12**-1957
Cucumber and Tomato, **4**-521
Curried Pea, Iced, **9**-1384
Egg Soup, Jellied, **5**-786
Fruit, Clear, **9**-1421
Fruit, Jellied, **6**-979
Fruit, Scandinavian, Chilled, **11**-1694
Fruit, with Sour Cream, **9**-1421
Gazpacho, Iced with Vegetable, Crouton, and Herb Garnish, **9**-1383
Gazpacho (Salad-Soup, Cold), **11**-1742
Jellied Soup, **1**-117
Lentil, Chilled, Syrian Style, **11**-1692
Orange (Appelsiinikeitto), **5**-679
Plum, Cold, **11**-1698
Raspberry, **9**-1421
on the Rocks, **4**-632
Seafood Bisque, Chilled, **2**-203
Sherry Tomato Bouillon, **5**-786
Sorrel (Schav), **6**-987
Sorrel (Sóska Leyes), **6**-917
Sour-Cream Tomato, Chilled, **11**-1697
Sunset, **11**-1694
Tarragon, French, **11**-1692
Tomato, Chilled Creamy, **11**-1832
Tomato Frost, **1**-37
Tomato-and-Herb, on the Rocks, **11**-1832
Tomato Quickie, **11**-1694
Turquoise Yogurt, **8**-1213
Vichyssoise Glacée, The Original Cream, **12**-1910
Watercress Consommé, Jellied, **3**-467
Watermelon, Frosty, **12**-1920
Wild Strawberry, **9**-1421

Soup(s), Chowder(s) and **Thick Soup(s)**
Abalone Chowder, **1**-5
Bacon, Bean, and Onion Chowder, **11**-1691
Barley (Krupnik), **9**-1421
Bean, Dutch, **11**-1839
Bean, Portuguese, **1**-158
Bean, Senate, **1**-157
Beef-Okra, **11**-1721
Beef, à la Paysanne, **11**-1695
Beef and Vegetable, **11**-1694
Beef-Vegetable, Stockyard Inn, **1**-36
Beer and Bread (Øllebrød), **4**-539
Bonito Chowder, **11**-1696
Borsch with Beet Greens, Cold (Barszcz Zimmy), **9**-1421
Bouillabaisse, **2**-214
Bouillabaisse, Creole, **4**-509
Bouillabaisse, White-Fish, **10**-1645
Cabbage, French, **2**-257
Cabbage (Kapusniak), **9**-1420
Callalu (Main-Course Soup), **11**-1704
Cheddar-Tuna Chowder, **3**-355
Chicken, **5**-716
Chicken (Moeun Sngo), **11**-1717
Chicken Rivvel Corn, **9**-1350
Chicken Soup or Stew, Friar's, **11**-1721
Chicken and Sweet-Potato, **11**-1795
Chicken, Ujhazy, **11**-1695
Chick-Pea, with Pigs' Feet (Sopón de Garbanzos con Patas de Cerdo), **9**-1493
Chick-Pea, Spanish, **3**-392
Cioppino, **3**-447
Cioppino, Fisherman's Wharf, **1**-26
Clam Chowder, **8**-1222
Clam Chowder, Manhattan, **3**-418
Clam Chowder, New England, **3**-418
Clam, Italian Style, **3**-453
Clam (Sopa de Ameijos), **9**-1453
Cock-a-Leekie, **6**-945
Cock-a-Leekie, Scotch, **7**-1047
Codfish and Lima-Bean Chowder, **7**-1065
Conch Chowder, **3**-466
Corn-Chicken Soup, Pennsylvania Dutch, **3**-481
Corn Chowder, **3**-419
Corn Chowder, Iowa, **1**-38
Corn Chowder, Kansas, **7**-1146
Corn-Frankfurter, **11**-1695
Crabmeat Chowder, **3**-419
Crabmeat-Rice, **11**-1696
Crab and Shell Chowder, **7**-1091
Escarole and Lentil, Italian, **4**-652
Fish, Basque (Sopa de Pescado a la Vasca), **11**-1743
Fish (Caldo de Pescado), **7**-1138
Fish Chowder, **3**-419
Fish Chowder, Jamaican, **6**-967
Fish Chowder, Old-Fashioned New England, **8**-1222
Fish Chowder, Oven, **11**-1695
Fish Stew (Bourride), **5**-740
Fish Stew from Burgundy (Pauchouse Bourguignon), **4**-595
Fish, Venetian (Zuppa Veneziana di Pesce), **6**-952
Frankfurter and Corn Chowder, **5**-718
Frankfurter and Rice, **5**-718
Goulash (Gulyásleves), **6**-917
Ham and Bean with Vegetables (Garbure Basque), **5**-739
Ham and Corn Potato, **6**-852
Ham Lima-Bean, **6**-852
Italian Chowder, **11**-1695
Lamb and Barley, **11**-1695
Lamb and Vegetable, **7**-1038
Lamb-Bone and Lima-Bean, **7**-1065
Leek, **7**-1047
Lentil (Faki Soupa), **5**-818
Lentil and Spinach, Thick, **7**-1059
Lentil, Thick, **7**-1059
Lima-Bean with Sausage Balls, **7**-1122
Lima Style (Sopa a la Limeña), **11**-1703
Lobster Chowder, **3**-419
Lobster and Shell Chowder, **7**-1091
Macaroni and Beans, Thick Soup of (Minestrone di Paste e Fagiuoli), **6**-952
Marrowbone, **7**-1112
Minestrone, **11**-1691
Minestrone alla Genovese, **7**-1165
Minestrone Milanese, **6**-952
Minestrone Milanese alla Savini, **7**-1164
Minestrone alla Romana, **7**-1165
Mulligatawny, **8**-1194
Mulligatawny Shorba, **11**-1691
Okra, **1**-22
Oxtail Soup II (Thick), **4**-621
Oxtail and Vegetable, **8**-1283
Pea (Erwtensoep), **4**-589
Pea, Habitant, **2**-275
Peanut, African Style, **8**-1322
Pepper Pot, **1**-65
Pepper Pot, with Dumplings, **9**-1350
Pepperpot, Myrtle Bank, Jamaican, **6**-966
Pepper Pot, Philadelphia, **11**-1694
Petite Marmite I and II, **9**-1364
with Pickles (Rassolnik s Yachmenem), **10**-1568
Pot-au-Feu (Boiled Beef with Vegetables), **5**-740
Potato, Aroostook County, **1**-44
Potato, with Bacon and Browned Bread Cubes, **9**-1350
Potato and Carrot, **9**-1462
Potato-Cheese, Savory, **11**-1690
Prune (Pflaumensuppe), **9**-1350
Rivvel, **1**-66
Rock-Lobster Chowder, **7**-1078
Salmon and Tomato, **10**-1595
Salt Cod Chowder, **2**-275
Salt-Pork and Bean Chowder, **10**-1598
Salt-Pork and Potato Chowder, **9**-1462
Salt-Pork, with Dumplings, Old-Time, **1**-56
Sauerkraut, Rumanian, **10**-1631
Sauerkraut, Soldiers' (Soldatskie Shchi), **10**-1568
Scotch Broth, **1**-147; **4**-621; **7**-1038
Seafood Chowder, Maine, **1**-45
Seafood Stew, **8**-1222
Seafood-Vegetable Chowder, **11**-1696
Shellfish-Vegetable Chowder, **10**-1650
Shrimp Chowder, **10**-1658
Shrimp-Oyster Gumbo, **10**-1658
Shrimp and Shell Chowder, **7**-1091
Shrimp and Squash (Hingha), **11**-1716
Sour-Cream, Potato, and Mushroom Chowder, **11**-1697
Spring Vegetable, **4**-621
Squirrel, **5**-774
Sweet-Potato Gumbo, **11**-1795
Tripe (Sopa de Mondongo), **11**-1704
Tuna Chowder, **12**-1863
Turkey, Parmentier, **11**-1695
Ukrainian Borsch, **10**-1567
Uncle Ed's Chowder, **5**-691
Veal-Vegetable, **11**-1694
Vegetable, Creole, **7**-1084
Vegetable, Summer (Kesäkeitto), **5**-679
White-Bean, Near-East, **11**-1690
Whiting Chowder with Fish Balls, **5**-694
Yellow Pea (Ärter och Fläsk), **11**-1787
Yellow Pea (Gule Aerter), **4**-538
Yellow Pea, with Smoked Pork, **8**-1314

Soup(s), Cream Soup(s) and **Purée(s)**
Almond, **1**-14
Almond Bouillon, **1**-75
Apple (Iablochnii Sup), **10**-1568
Asparagus (Aspargessuppe), **4**-538
Avocado-Chicken, **11**-1690
Bean, Different, **1**-54
Black-Bean, **4**-645
Black-Bean, Savory, **11**-1691
Black Kettle, **1**-40
Bourbon Black Bean, **4**-565
Broccoli-and-Chicken, **2**-244
Buttermilk, Belgian, **11**-1690
Cabbage Almond, **2**-257
Carrot and Parsley, **8**-1298
Cauliflower, **3**-341
Cauliflower, Cream of, **1**-55
Cheddar-Cheese, **1**-60
Cheese with Croutons, **3**-355
Chili Pumpkin, **11**-1727
Chive and Cress, **11**-1690
Congo-Pea or Kidney-Bean, Jamaican, **6**-966
Corn and Cress, Cream of, **12**-1920
Crab, Martha Washington's, **1**-75
Crab, Nutmeg State, **1**-28
Curried Potato, **9**-1462
Frankfurter and Puréed Lentil, **5**-720
Fresh-Tomato, Cream-of, **11**-1832
Kidney (Nier Soep), **4**-589
Leek and Green-Pea Purée, **7**-1047
Lentil, **1**-39
Lentil, Cream of, **7**-1059
Lettuce, Cream of, **7**-1061

Lobster Bisque, **7**-1077
Mock Lobster, **4**-568
Mushroom Barley, **6**-987
Mushroom, Cream-of-, **8**-1198
Onion and Cheese, **8**-1260
Oyster Bisque, **8**-1290
Oyster Bisque, Chesapeake, **2**-203
Parsley, Canadian, **11**-1690
Pea Soup, Basic Recipe, **11**-1696
Variations, **11**-1696
Peanut-Butter Celery, **8**-1324
Peanut-Butter Creole, **8**-1324
Potato, Amphitryon, **9**-1469
Potato, Kingston, **6**-967
Potato, Parmentier, **9**-1469
Potato (Potage Parmentier), **5**-739
Potato, Quick French, **11**-1690
Pride of Erin, **6**-945
Pumpkin, **6**-967
Pumpkin, Indian, **9**-1499
Pumpkin Maracay (Sopa de Calabaza Maracay), **11**-1704
Razor-Clam Bisque, **1**-64
Rice, Purée of, **10**-1549
Salmon, Cream of, **10**-1595
Salmon and Tomato Bisque, **10**-1595
Scallop Bisque, **2**-275
Scallop Cream, **11**-1695
Seafood Bisque, **4**-648
She-Crab, Charleston, **1**-67
Sherried Tomato-Shrimp Bisque, **11**-1832
Sherry Crab, **7**-1097
Shrimp Bisque, **3**-442; **10**-1658
Shrimp Bisque, Quick, **10**-1658
Shrimp Bisque (Sopa de Camarões), **9**-1453
Shrimp Stew, **10**-1658
Sorrel, Cream of, **10**-1671
Split Pea, **12**-1927
Split-Pea, Jamaican, **6**-966
Sweet-Potato, Cream-of, **11**-1796
Tapioca Tuna, **11**-1810
Watercress (Potage au Cresson), **5**-739

Sour Cream, **3**-491; **11**-1697
Apple Torte, **12**-1933
Beef in, **11**-1700
Butterscotch Meringue Pie, **9**-1392
Cabbage Rolls, **11**-1698
Chicken Livers in, **7**-1076
Chocolate Frosting, **11**-1701
Choco-Sour-Cream Frosting, **5**-752
Cranberry-Cream Salad, **10**-1587
with Cucumbers, **8**-1278
Cucumbers, Radishes, and Onions in, **11**-1700
Cucumber Sauce, **5**-695
Date Toast, **11**-1828
Devonshire Pears, **10**-1561
Doughnuts, **1**-66
Dressing, **4**-521; **10**-1588
Dressing, Cooked, **10**-1588
Dressing, Plain (Sous iz Smetany), **10**-1572
Dressing for Romaine, Herbed, **10**-1556
Frosting, **11**-1701
with Fruit Soups, **9**-1421
Gingerbread, **11**-1701
Ham Dip, **11**-1697
Hapsburg Cucumbers, **11**-1700
Hollandaise, **11**-1700
-Horseradish (sauce), **2**-191
Horseradish Cream, **9**-1383
Huckleberry Pie, **9**-1355
Indian Pudding, **9**-1490
Lamb in, Braised, **7**-1035
Macaroni Casserole, **7**-1095
Macaroni, and Cheese Salad, **10**-1582
Molasses Squares, **11**-1701
Mushroom Sauce, **9**-1430
Pancakes, **8**-1292
Paprika, Sauce, Chicken in, **11**-1698
Peach Pie, **7**-1157
Peanut-Butter Sauce, **8**-1325
Pork Fillet in, **7**-1111
Potatoes, **9**-1464
Potato, and Mushroom Chowder, **11**-1697
Potato Patties, **9**-1467
Poundcake, **9**-1480
Raisin Nut Cookies, **11**-1701
-Raisin Pie, **9**-1391
Salad Dressings, **11**-1700
Sauce, **10**-1666
Sauce, Dried Beef in, **11**-1700
Smetana, Smitane, **10**-1664
Spinach Salad, **11**-1700
Sugar Cakes, **9**-1357
Tacos (Tacos de Jocoqui), **7**-1138
Tomato Soup, Chilled, **11**-1697
Tropical Sherbet, **11**-1701
Twists, **8**-1309
Veal Loaf, **11**-1698
Watercress Sauce, **12**-1920
Zucchini with Creamy Cheese Topping, **12**-1962

Sourdough
Bread, **12**-1932
Doughnuts, **1**-54
Pancakes, **1**-23; **8**-1292
Starter, **8**-1292; **12**-1932
Sous iz Khrena (Horseradish Sauce), **10**-1573
Sous iz Smetany (Plain Sour-Cream Dressing), **10**-1572
Souse or Pigs' Feet, Pickled, **9**-1351
South African Deviled Rock Lobster, **7**-1080
South American Cookery, **11**-1702
South American Onion Soup, **8**-1260
South Carolina Benne-Seed Biscuits, **11**-1724
South Carolina Scrapple, **1**-68
Southeast Asian Cookery, **11**-1710
Southern Caramel Filling, **4**-663
Southern Charlotte Russe, **11**-1725
Southern Chicken with Pecans, **8**-1334
Southern Chocolate Cake, **7**-1045
Southern Cookery, **11**-1718
Southern Corn-Soufflé Pudding, **1**-22
Southern Date Pastries, **4**-547
Southern Fried Chicken, **11**-1723
Southern Onion Bread, **8**-1265
Southern Pecan Dainties, **8**-1335
Southern Pecan Pie, **8**-1335; **9**-1390
Southern Pork and Greens, **5**-825
Southern Sesame Shrimps, **10**-1646
Southern Style Green Beans, **11**-1723
Southwestern Chili Sauce, **11**-1731
Southwestern Cookery, **11**-1726
Southwestern Fried Trout (Trucha Frita), **11**-1727
Southwestern Mocha, **11**-1732
Southwestern Style Stuffed Turkey (Gallina Rellena), **11**-1730

Soy, Soyed
Almonds, **11**-1734
Butter Sauce, **5**-695
Chicken, Baked, **11**-1734
-Sauce Dressing, **10**-1626
Pot Roast, **11**-1734
Vinegar-Soy Sauce, **7**-1023
-Wheat Muffins, **11**-1734

Soybean(s), **11**-1733
Flour, **5**-707
Shepherd's Pie, **11**-1734
Stew, **11**-1734
Tomato-Cheese Soybeans, **1**-158
Spaetzle (German Egg Dumplings), **4**-586

Spaghetti, **11**-1735
Amatriciana, **11**-1736
alla Carbonara (Spaghetti and Eggs on Ham), **6**-862
Caruso, **11**-1736
Chicken and Chorizo, **8**-1275
Chicken Normandy, **11**-1736
Clam, **11**-1736
and Eggs on Ham (Spaghetti alla Carbonara), **6**-862
with Four Cheeses (ai Quattro Formaggi), **6**-958
Frankfurter-Mozzarella, **5**-720
with Garbanzo Sauce, **1**-159
Garlic Lover's, **11**-1736
Ham Tetrazzini, **11**-1736
Home-Fried, **11**-1737
Lentil Sauce (for), **7**-1060
with Meatballs, **11**-1736
and Meatballs, Italian (QC), **10**-1523
with Meatballs (con le Polpettine), **6**-955
Meat Sauce for, **2**-193
Meat Sauce (QC), **10**-1523
Parmigiana, **3**-361
con le Polpettine (with Meatballs), **6**-955
and Pork Chops, Neapolitan, **8**-1208
Quattro Formaggi (with Four Cheeses), **6**-958
Salmon-Spaghetti Casserole, **10**-1596
Sauces for, **11**-1737
Sicilian, **11**-1737
with Tuna Sauce, **11**-1736
Turkey Tetrazzini, **11**-1736
with Zucchini Sauce, **11**-1737
Spanakoryzo (Spinach and Rice), **5**-822
Spanish Beef-Pies, **9**-1387
Spanish Boiled Beef (Cocido), **11**-1742
Spanish Casserole, **10**-1638
Spanish Chicken with Rice, **10**-1550
Spanish Chick-Pea Soup, **3**-392
Spanish Cookery, **11**-1740
Spanish Cream, **6**-980
Spanish Egg Chocolate, **3**-416
Spanish Meat Loaf, **8**-1256
Spanish Omelet, **4**-610; **8**-1257
Spanish Omelette with Ham (Tortilla con Jamon), **6**-861
Spanish Onion Bake, **8**-1264
Spanish-Rice Dressing, **4**-574
Spanish Rice with Frankfurters, **5**-721
Spanish Salad Dressing, **4**-573
Spanish Sauce, **4**-610
Spanish Style Pot-Roasted Duckling, **9**-1477
Spareribs, **11**-1747; for recipes see Pork, Fresh, Spareribs
Sparzha Zapechennaya s Sukharyami i Slivkami (Asparagus Baked with Bread Crumbs and Cream), **10**-1572
Spätzle (Small Dumplings), **5**-794
Spearmint, **11**-1749; for recipes see Mint, Minted
Speculaas (Spiced Cookies), **4**-593
Spekkie Sla (Bacon Slaw), **4**-592
Spekpannekoeken (Pancakes with Bacon), **4**-593
Spetsialni Russki Sous Dlia Zharenoi Goviadini (Special Russian Sauce for American Pot Roast), **10**-1573

Spice, **11**-1749; see also names of spices
Cake, Coffee, **7**-1045
Cake, Toasted, **11**-1754
Chart, **11**-1750-1751
-Crumb Topping, **12**-1933
Mixture, **2**-298
Mixture, for Pâtés, **8**-1312
Pumpkin Pie Spice, **9**-1501
Waffles, **12**-1915
Spiedino alla Romana, **3**-358
Spiku (Malay Layer Cake), **11**-1715

Spinach, **11**-1754
with Almonds, **11**-1756
and Cabbage Salad, **11**-1756
Cheese Pie, **3**-361
and Cheese, Sardines with, **10**-1612
-Cheese Strips, **8**-1306
Chicken Florentine, **5**-704
Coconut (Limu Niu), **9**-1435
Cottage-Cheese Salad, **12**-1958
Creamed, **11**-1756
Curry Casserole, Layered, **10**-1555
Eggs Florentine, **5**-704
Eggs Florentine, Italian, **11**-1755
Flounder Florentine, **5**-704
Fritters (Buñuelos de Espinaca), **11**-1708
with German Pancakes, **11**-1755
with Lamb (Palak Gosht), **6**-939
Layer, **10**-1555

Spinach, continued
Leaves, Fried (Goreng Bajem), **11**-1715
and Lentil Soup, Thick, **7**-1059
Mixed Cooked Foods (Yose-Nabe), **6**-975
and Mushrooms, Creamed, **8**-1202
and Onion Salad, **1**-73
and Parsley Pie, Iranian (Coucou Sabzi), **8**-1215
Pie, Greek, **11**-1755
-and-Potato Pie, **11**-1755
Potato-Spinach Casserole, **9**-1467
Raw, Wilted, **11**-1756
and Rice (Spanakoryzo), **5**-822
Ring with Eggs, Baked, **11**-1755
Sag Paneer, **11**-1755
Salad, German, **10**-1586; **11**-1756
Salad Mold with Ham, **5**-787
with Sesame (Oshitashi), **6**-976
and Sorrel Steaks (Bifes com Azedas), **9**-1456
Soufflé, **4**-604; **12**-1906
Soup (Spinatsuppe), **8**-1235
Sour-Cream, Salad, **11**-1700
Spinazie, **4**-592
Steamed (Spinaci Stufati), **6**-959
-Stuffed Fish Fillets, **11**-1755
Tuna Florentine, **12**-1863
Wilted, **1**-38
Spinaci Stufati (Steamed Spinach), **6**-959
Spinatsuppe (Spinach Soup), **8**-1235
Spinazie (Spinach), **4**-592
Spitzbuben, **3**-473
Spitzbuben (Urchins), **5**-799

Spongecake(s), **2**-262; **11**-1756
Applesauce, **11**-1756
Chocolate, **3**-410; **11**-1756
Cookies (Pleskener), **8**-1243
Daffodil, **2**-273
Hot-Water, **11**-1756
Jelly Sponge Roll, **11**-1757
Spongecake, **2**-273; **3**-444
Sponge Sheet, Basic (jelly roll), **5**-783
Spoon Bread, **11**-1757; for recipes see Bread(s), Quick Bread(s); Corn Bread(s)
Spotted Dog, **4**-627
Sprat, **11**-1757

Spread(s), **1**-85
Butter, for Hot Breads, **2**-254
Canapé, **2**-279; **4**-642
for Cheese Canapés, **1**-86
Curry Cashew, **10**-1611
Egg-Cheese, **4**-606
Eggplant Caviar, **1**-90
Ham and Egg Butter, **6**-866
Ham and Eggs, Potted, **6**-866
Ham, Savory, **3**-428
Lime Salmon-Salad, **7**-1067
Liptauer Cheese, **1**-90
Liver Pâté, Danish, **7**-1074
Malaxe, **3**-355
Mustard, **8**-1205
Peanut-Butter, Three, **8**-1324
Pecan Pimiento-Cheese, **8**-1334
Pineapple-Avocado, **9**-1403
Pineapple-Peanut, **9**-1403
Pineapple, Tongue, and Cheese, **9**-1403
Pork Pâté, **1**-90
Potted Shrimps, **4**-622
Red Caviar in Cream, **1**-76
Red Caviar (Taramosalata), **4**-639
Sage-Cheese Appetizer, **10**-1578
Shrimp, for Canapé or Sandwich, **10**-1658
Shrimp Paste, **10**-1657
Shrimps, Potted, Savory, **9**-1477
Tuna Sandwich, Savory, **12**-1867
Walnut, **1**-90
Walnut Tuna, **12**-1867
Springerle, **1**-82

Spritz Cookies, **11**-1757
Almond, **11**-1758
Chocolate, **11**-1757
Cookies, **3**-435; **11**-1757
Spruiten Purée (Purée of Brussels Sprouts), **4**-592
Spumoni, **11**-1758

Squab, **11**-1758; see also Rock Cornish Hen
Roast Stuffed, **11**-1758

Squash, **11**-1758
Acorn, **1**-6; **11**-1759; for recipes see Acorn Squash
Anise, Pie, **11**-1762
and Apple Jam, **11**-1762
Buttercup, **11**-1759
Butternut, **2**-255; **11**-1759; for recipes see Butternut Squash
Caserta, **11**-1758
Chayote, **3**-349; **11**-1758; for recipes see Chayote(s)
Cocozelle, **11**-1758
Creamed (Kiveve), **11**-1708
Cymling or Pattypan, **12**-1758; for recipes see Cymling
Frankfurter-Squash Lyonnaise, **5**-724
Hubbard, **6**-914; **11**-1759; for recipes see Hubbard Squash
Mandarin, **11**-1759
and Onions, Skillet, **11**-1761
Pancakes, **1**-63
Patties, **8**-1313
Pie, **8**-1229
Pudding, Spiced, **7**-1098
Pumpkin, see Pumpkin
Rolls, **2**-233; **12**-1956
and Shrimp Soup (Hingha), **11**-1716
Stuffed, Dunbar's, **4**-513
Summer, Baked, **11**-1761
Summer-Squash Casserole, **1**-63; **7**-1152
Tomatoes, and Beans, Savory, **11**-1832
Warren Turban, **11**-1759
Yellow Crookneck, **11**-1758
Yellow Straightneck, **11**-1758
Zucchini, **11**-1758; **12**-1960; for recipes see Zucchini
Squaw Bread, Fried, **1**-64
Squaw Bread Syrup, **1**-64

Squid(s), **11**-1762
Italian Style, **11**-1763
Stewed in the Portuguese Manner, **11**-1763
Stuffed, Sautéed, **11**-1763

Squirrel(s), **11**-1763
Brunswick Stew, **5**-770
Fricasseed, **11**-1763
Soup, **5**-774
Ssu Chi Tou Niu Ju (Beef with Green Beans), **3**-399
Stamppot van Boerenkool met Worst (Kale with Potatoes and Sausage), **4**-592
Stamppot Witte Kool (White Cabbage with Potatoes), **4**-592
Steak, **11**-1763; for recipes see also names of meats and fishes
Steak de Fromage (Batter-Fried Cheese), **11**-1803
Steak Party, Menu, **8**-1280
Stegt Aal i Karry (Fried Eel with Curry Sauce), **4**-539
Stegt And (Roast Duck), **4**-536
Stegte Kartofler (Fried Potatoes), **4**-540
Stegte Tomater (Fried Tomatoes), **4**-540
Stekt Sill Eller Strömming (Fried Herring or Smelt Fillets), **11**-1787
Stews, see name of chief ingredient
Stifado (Beef Stew), **4**-639

Stock(s), **11**-1774
Brown, **10**-1618
Brown (Bouillon or Beef Stock), **11**-1774
Chicken, **11**-1775
Fish, **11**-1775
Soup Stock (Dashi), **6**-970
To Clarify, **10**-1615
Vegetable, **11**-1775
White, **10**-1618
White or Veal, **11**-1774
Stockyard Inn Beef-Vegetable Soup, **1**-36
Stollen, **11**-1775
Stollen (Christmas Fruitcake), **5**-798
Stoofperen (Stewed Pears), **4**-593
Stormy Weather Jumbles, **3**-475
Stracotto Sauce, **11**-1738

Strawberry(ies), **11**-1776
and Almond Cheesecake, **8**-1282
-Almond Roll, **11**-1778
Angel-Food Dessert, **11**-1778
with Avocado Ring, **11**-1776
Bavarian Cream, **4**-556
Berry Tarts, Devonshire, **11**-1812
Betty, **11**-1776
Buttercream Frosting, **5**-751
Cake Roll, **11**-1779
à la Chantilly, **4**-568
Charlotte Dessert, **5**-788
and Cheese Salad, Jellied, **11**-1776
Cheese Tarts, **1**-72
Chiffon Pie, **6**-980
Chiffon Tarts, **11**-1812
Circle Cake, **1**-72
Cobbler, **11**-1776
Cream, **1**-37
Cream Cake, **2**-264; **7**-1042
Cream Filling, **11**-1779
Dream Cake, **2**-272
Fluff, **7**-1087
Fondant-Dipped, **11**-1779
Frappé, **6**-926
Fresh, **4**-636
Fresh, Ice Cream, **6**-929
Frosted, **7**-1161
Fruits Rouges, **5**-758
Glacé Pie, **11**-1778
Glaze, **3**-367
Hard Sauce, **11**-1776
-Honey Bavarian, **6**-909
Ice, **6**-926
Ice, Italian, **11**-1779
Ice Cream, **6**-929; **11**-1779
Ice Cream, Freezer of, **9**-1382
Ice-Cream Soda, **11**-1779
Ice Cream Tarts, **8**-1309
Italian (Fragole all'Italiana), **6**-960
Jam, No-Cook, **6**-965
Jam, Old-Country, **6**-964
Jam, Three-Minute, **6**-964
Jelly, No-Cook, **6**-984
Lattice, Tarts, **11**-1778
de Luxe, **12**-1933
-Macaroon Cream, **11**-1778
-Macaroon Torte, **11**-1779
Maraschino, Creamy, **7**-1108
Meringues Glacées, **6**-934
à la Mode, **6**-934
Mousse, **11**-1778
with Orange Juice, **2**-243
Pavlova, **8**-1313
Pie, Snowbank, **11**-1778
Pineapple-Strawberry Jam, **6**-964
Pineapple-Strawberry Salad, **7**-1089
Preserves, **9**-1482
Pudding, Steamed, **9**-1492
and Rhubarb Jam, **10**-1545
and Rhubarb Jelly, **10**-1545
and Rhubarb Pie, **10**-1544
Rice Pudding, **11**-1778
Romanoff, **4**-558
Sauce, Velvet, **11**-1776
Schaumtorte, **7**-1156
Sherbet, **10**-1654
Sherbet Drink, Turkish, **10**-1654
Shortcake, **10**-1655; **11**-1779
Snow (Bavaroise Frutillas), **11**-1709
Soufflé, Cold, **4**-632
Tart, **5**-763
Tarts, Currant-Glazed, **9**-1384
Whip, **11**-1778
Wild Strawberry Soup, **9**-1421
Streusel Coffeecake, **2**-231
Streusel Topping, **5**-799
String Hoppers (noodles for curry), **4**-527

Strudel, 11-1779
Apple, **1**-101; **11**-1780
Apple (Almásrétes), **6**-921
Apricot, **1**-108
Cabbage, **6**-922
Cheese, **6**-922; **11**-1780
Cherry, **6**-922; **11**-1780
Dough, **11**-1779
Filled with Preserves, **11**-1780
Mohn (Poppy-Seed), **11**-1780
Nut, **6**-922
Poppy-Seed, **6**-922
Stufato (Braised Beef), **11**-1802

Stuffing(s), 11-1780; see also Filling(s)
Apple Corn-Bread, **4**-584
Apple-Prune-Raisin, **1**-100
Apple, Savory, **1**-97; **11**-1749
Apricot, **4**-584
Brazil-Nut, Creamy, **11**-1781
Bread, **6**-990; **9**-1477; **11**-1781
Bread, Chestnut, **11**-1781
Bread-Crumb, **9**-1426
Bread, Oyster, **11**-1781
Cashew-Rice, **2**-314
Celery-Almond, **11**-1781
Cheese, **11**-1780
Cheese, Italian, **11**-1782
Chestnut and Sausage, **11**-1781
Chestnut, for Turkey, **3**-376
for Chicken, **3**-392
Chicken Forcemeat, **5**-715
for Chicken, Roast Stuffed, **4**-625
Corn-Bread, New England, **11**-1780
Corn, Mexican, **11**-1782
Corn Stuffing Balls, **3**-445
Corned-Beef Hash, **11**-1834
Crumb, Savory, **11**-1834
Cucumber, **11**-1781
for Duck, **4**-584
for Eye Round (Lechón de Mechar), **9**-1496
Fruit Forcemeat, **5**-715
Giblet-Butternut, Savory, **1**-74
Groat, **9**-1426
(for Ham), **1**-50
Macaroni, **11**-1834
Meat-and-Rice, Turkish, **11**-1782
Mint, **11**-1781
Mushroom and Wild Rice, **11**-1781
Numbers 1 and 2 (for Twin Capons), **3**-439
Olive, **11**-1782
Peanut, **8**-1323
Pecan, **8**-1334; **10**-1558
Pickle, **11**-1781
Piedmont, **11**-1782
Piquant, **11**-1780
Potato Forcemeat, **5**-715
Prune-Apple-Raisin, **4**-584
Raisin-Rice, **11**-1781
Rice, **11**-1781, 1834
for Roast Turkey, English Style, **4**-625
Sage, **10**-1578
Sage and Onion, **11**-1781
Sauerkraut, **11**-1781
Sausage and Chestnut, for Chicken, **3**-376
Sausage-Nut, **3**-381
Sweet-Potato Savory, **11**-1798
Syrian, **11**-1782
Turkey, Lisbon (Recheio a Moda de Lisboa Para Peru), **9**-1457
Veal-and-Vegetable, **11**-1781
Vegetable, **11**-1780, 1834
Water-Chestnut and Rice, **12**-1919
(for Wild Goose), **1**-68
Wild Rice, **1**-62; **12**-1940

Sturgeon, 11-1782
Champagne Soup, Russian, **10**-1568
Sherry Smoked Sturgeon in Ramekins, **11**-1782
Smoked-Sturgeon Deviled Eggs, **11**-1782

Succotash, 11-1783
with Bacon, **3**-484
Bacon and Beef, **1**-133
California, **3**-482
Cranberry-Bean, **1**-159
Creamy, **7**-1065
Fireplace Road, **8**-1282
Frankfurter, **5**-725
Picnic, **7**-1065
Three-Bean, **1**-154
Two-Bean, with Pork Cubes, **1**-38
Sucker, **11**-1783
Suckling Pig, see Pig

Suet, 11-1783
Carrot-Suet Pudding, Steamed, **9**-1491
Dough, **4**-627
Pudding(s), **4**-627; **11**-1783

Sugar, 11-1783
Brown, **11**-1784; for recipes see Brown Sugar
Burnt-Sugar Frosting, **7**-1044
Cardamom, **2**-299
Confectioners', **11**-1784; for recipes see Confectioners' Sugar
Cookies, **3**-432
Cookies, Rosewater, Old-Fashioned, **10**-1561
Crisps, **3**-472
Granulated, **11**-1784
Invert, **6**-942
Leb Cake, **9**-1357
Maple, **11**-1784; for recipes see Maple
Rock Candy, **9**-1784
Sour-Cream Cakes, **9**-1357
Superfine or powdered, **11**-1784
Syrup for Freezing, Chart, **5**-728
Syrup, Thin, **8**-1193
To Measure, **7**-1117
Vanilla, **1**-124; **2**-200; **6**-904; **12**-1885
Sugaring-Off Pie, **7**-1108
Suimono (Clear Soup), **6**-970
Sukiyaki, Fish (Chirinabe), **6**-971
Sukiyaki (Plough-Roasted), **6**-974
Sultan's Delight, The, **4**-614
Summer Salad (Sommersalat), **8**-1240
Sundaes, **6**-931; **11**-1784; for recipes see Frozen Desserts
Sunday-Night Western Sandwiches, **10**-1604

Sunfish, 11-1784
Panfried, with Dill Sauce, **11**-1784
Suprême Sauce, **10**-1613, 1620
Suprêmes de Volaille (Boneless Chicken Breasts), **3**-383
Suprêmes de Volaille à Blanc (Chicken Breasts with Cream), **3**-383
Surprise Salad, **10**-1586
Surkål (Cabbage with Caraway), **8**-1239
Surullitos de Maíz (Cornmeal Sticks), **9**-1497
Sushi Rice, **6**-971
Suzette Sauce, **5**-701
Svestkove Knedlíky (Plum Dumplings), **4**-532
Svezhiye Podharenyye Ogurtzy (Braised Cucumbers), **10**-1572
Svinye Kotlety s Sousom iz Chernosliv ili Kislykh Vishen (Breaded Pork Chops with Prune or Sour-Cherry Sauce), **10**-1571
Sviskekompott (Baked Prune Custard), **8**-1241
Swedish Almond Tarts (Polynees), **1**-69
Swedish Applecake, **10**-1666
Swedish Boiled Lamb with Dill and Dill Sauce, **4**-564
Swedish Brown Beans, **10**-1666
Swedish Caramel Custard, **2**-297
Swedish Cardamom Braid, **2**-233
Swedish Cinnamon Cookies (Kanelkakor), **11**-1790
Swedish Cookery, **11**-1785
Swedish Cream Cookies, **3**-473
Swedish Fruit Pie, **9**-1396
Swedish Ham Custard, **6**-865
Swedish Hash (Pytt i Panna), **11**-1790
Swedish Meatballs, **7**-1123; **10**-1665
Swedish Meatballs (QC), **10**-1520
Swedish Meatballs (Köttbullar), **2**-191
Swedish Potato Dumplings (Potatisbullar), **11**-1791
Swedish Rye Bread, **1**-49
Swedish Rye Cookies, **10**-1575
Swedish Saffron Buns, **2**-252
Swedish Sans Rival Torte, **12**-1856
Swedish Tea Ring, **7**-1156
Swedish Varmlandstårta, **12**-1854

Sweetbread(s), 11-1794
Chicken-and-Sweetbread Croquettes, **1**-46
Creamed, **11**-1794
and Cucumber Salad, **11**-1794; **12**-1897
Mixed Fry (Fritto Misto), **7**-1040
Normandy Style, **11**-1794
Sweeteners, Nonnutritive, **11**-1784

Sweet Potato(es), 11-1795, and **Yam(s), 12**-1950
with Allspice, **1**-11
Almond Porcupines, **11**-1797
Almond, Pudding, **11**-1837
Apple Crisp, **11**-1798
Apples, and Pork Chops, Scalloped, **1**-102
and Apples, Scalloped, **11**-1797
Arizona, **1**-24
Biscuits, **1**-61; **11**-1797
Brandied, **11**-1724
Brazil-Nut Porcupines, **11**-1797
Brown-Sugar Candied, **11**-1796
Candied, **1**-50
Candied, and Ham Balls, **11**-1796
Candied Yams, **3**-444
Candied Yams, Amandine, **4**-512
and Chestnuts, Scalloped, **11**-1797
and Chicken, Baked, **11**-1796
and Chicken Soup, **11**-1795
and Cranberries, Scalloped, **11**-1797
Creamed, **11**-1797
Croquettes, **4**-518
Dessert (Chakin Shibori), **6**-978
Doughnuts, **11**-1798
and Duck Casserole, **2**-320
Flambéed, **11**-1796
Fritters (Carimañolas), **11**-1706
Fruits and Roots, Sweet (Ginatan), **9**-1370
Golden Cheesecake, **11**-1798
Guava Yams with Baked Ham, **5**-829
Gumbo, **11**-1795
Ham and Sweets, **6**-855
Home-Fried, **11**-1797
Lemon, Pudding, **11**-1724
Maple-Candied, **11**-1796
Marshmallow Balls, **11**-1797
with Mincemeat, **11**-1797
Molasses Drop Cookies, **11**-1798
Muffins, **8**-1192
New Indian Style, **11**-1730
Orange, **11**-1797
Orange Yams, **12**-1951
Pancakes, Louisiana, **11**-1797
Peanut, **11**-1797
Peanut-Butter Casserole, **8**-1325
Pecan Pie, **11**-1798
Pie, **9**-1391
Pineapple, Yam, and Ham Casserole, **9**-1406
Poi, **1**-35
Pone, **1**-33
and Pork-Chop Skillet, **11**-1796
Pork Chops, and Apples, **9**-1443
Pudding, **1**-22
Pudding, Spicy, **9**-1491; **11**-1798
Puff, **2**-322
and Pumpkin Dessert (Cazuela), **9**-1497
à la Rector, **11**-1797
and Roast-Beef Hash, **11**-1796
Sausage-Apple Bake, **11**-1796
Sausage Cakes, **9**-1352

Sweet Potato(es), Yam(s), continued
Sausage, and Fruit Bake, **10**-1636
Sherried, **11**-1724
Soufflé, **11**-1796
Soup, Cream of, **11**-1796
Stuffing, Savory, **11**-1798
Tangerine Sweets, **12**-1906
with Tomatoes, **11**-1797
Tournedos, **11**-1796
and Turkey Casserole, **11**-1796
with Veal in Sour-Cream Sauce, **11**-1796
Waffles, **11**-1798
Yams, Almond Candied, **11**-1823
Yam and Cheese Crullers, Puerto Rican, **12**-1951
Yam Custard Pie, **12**-1951
Yam Spicecake, **12**-1951
Yams and White Onions with Roast Pork, **9**-1443
and Yellow Turnips, Mashed, **11**-1797
Sweetsop, **11**-1798

Sweet-and-Sour, Sweet-Sour, Sweet-and-Pungent
Bacon Relish, **2**-191
Beef Balls (T'ang Ts'u Niu Ju Wan), **3**-399
Beef and Pork Meatballs, **7**-1126
Carp, **5**-699
Chicken Livers, **3**-391
Chicken (Pollo en Agridulce), **9**-1496
Fish, **6**-990
Hamburgers, **6**-868
Hamburger Sandwiches, **10**-1601
Ham with Vegetables, **9**-1351
Lamb, Baked Breast of, **7**-1034
Meatballs, **2**-250; **3**-424; **7**-1123
Mustard Sauce, **7**-1128; **10**-1627
Pineapple Pork, **9**-1406
Pork, **9**-1450
Pork (T'ang Ts'u Chu Jo), **3**-400
Radishes (Chiang Lo Po), **3**-403
Salami, **10**-1589
Sauce, **10**-1627
Sauce, Fish in, **11**-1734
Shrimps, **10**-1660
Sea Bass (Escabetseng Apahap), **9**-1368
Spareribs, Chinese, **11**-1749
Tuna, **12**-1863
Tuna Fish, Panned, **5**-692
Swiss Chard, see Chard
Swiss Classic (Swiss Broyage), **5**-783
Swiss Cookery, **11**-1799
Swiss Cube Steaks, **2**-184
Swiss Eggs, **7**-1085
Swiss Fondue, **3**-359
Swiss Liver, **7**-1073
Swiss Mushroom Consommé, **8**-1198
Swiss Open-Face Sandwiches, **11**-1800
Swiss Petit Puffs, **8**-1306
Swiss Rösti Potatoes, **9**-1467
Swiss Steak, **2**-186
Swiss Style Onions, **8**-1264

Swordfish, 11-1806
Amandine, **11**-1806
Baked, Block Island, **1**-67
Deep-Fried, **11**-1806
Mayonnaise, **11**-1806
Skewered, **4**-565
on Skewers, Turkish (Kilich Shish), **8**-1215
with Tomato Sauce, **11**-1806

Syllabub, 11-1807
Frothy, **4**-611
Old English, **11**-1807
Syllabub, **1**-68
Syltede Rødbeder (Pickled Beets), **4**-542
Syomga s Sousom iz Ikri (Salmon Steaks with Caviar Sauce), **10**-1570
Syrian Stuffing, **11**-1782
Syrian Style Lentil Soup, Chilled, **11**-1692
Syrniki (Fried Cheese Cakes), **10**-1572

Syrup(s) or **Sirup(s), 11**-1807
Brown-Sugar, **10**-1629
Caramel, **2**-297
Chocolate, **3**-417; **11**-1807
Cinnamon, **7**-1155
Cinnamon-Honey, **5**-824
Cocoa, **11**-1807
for Halva, **5**-824
Honey, **5**-823
Lemonade, **7**-1057
Lemon-Honey, **5**-823
Maple, **10**-1615
for Nut and Honey Sweetmeats, **6**-994
Orange, **10**-1629; **11**-1807
(for Peach Dumplings), **8**-1317
Pickle-Preserve, **5**-815
Pickling, **9**-1374
Rum, **1**-132; **10**-1640
Rum (Sirop de Rhum), **5**-748
Sauces, **10**-1615
Spiced, Hot, **11**-1807
Squaw Bread Syrup, **1**-64
Sugar, for freezing, chart, **5**-728
Sugar, for Stewed Fruits, **11**-1807
Sugar, Thin, **8**-1193
Szczupak czy Karp po Polsku (Pike or Carp à la Polonaise), **9**-1422
Szechwan Chicken Sautéed with Peppers, **3**-400
Szegedi Csirke Paprikás (Chicken Stew), **6**-919
Székely Gulyás (Szekely Sauerkraut Goulash), **6**-919
Szilvás Gombóc (Plum Dumplings), **6**-920
Sztufada (Braised Beef), **9**-1424

T

Tacos
Fried Filled Tortillas, **7**-1138
Sour-Cream (Tacos de Jocoqui), **7**-1138
Taos, **11**-1731

Taffy, 2-284; **11**-1808
Chocolate, **11**-1808
Molasses, **11**-1808
Molasses, Old-Fashioned, **2**-288
Peppermint, **9**-1362
Saltwater, **1**-57
Sundae Sauce, **8**-1185
Tamago Suimono (Egg Soup), **6**-971

Tamale(s), 7-1138; **11**-1808
Green Corn-Husk (Tamales de Maíz con Chile y Queso), **7**-1138
Green Corn-Husk, with Chicken Filling (Tamales de Maíz con Pollo), **11**-1808
Ham Tamale Pie, **2**-320
Pie, **1**-59
Pie, Hot, **11**-1728
Pork Tamale Pie, **9**-1444

Tamarind, 11-1809
Sauce, Fried Fish with, **11**-1809
Tangelemon Ice Cream, **11**-1838
Tangelo, **11**-1809

Tangerine(s), 11-1809
Butter, **10**-1556
Compote, **11**-1809
Frappé, **5**-726
Fresh, and Apple Salad, **11**-1809
Fresh, and Turkey Salad, **12**-1876
Ice Cream, Tangelemon, **11**-1838
Ice in Orange Shells, **6**-926
Sherbet, **10**-1654
Sweets, **12**-1906
T'ang Ts'u Chu Jo (Sweet-and-Sour Pork), **3**-400
T'ang Ts'u Niu Ju Wan (Sweet-and-Sour Beef Balls), **3**-399
Tannenbaum Brot (Christmas Tree Bread), **5**-798
Taos Tacos, **11**-1731
Tapang Baka (Cured Beef), **9**-1369

Tapioca, 11-1810
Apple, Baked, **1**-60, 102; **8**-1228
Butterscotch, Cream, **11**-1810
Butterscotch-Peanut, Pudding, **9**-1487
Cream Pudding, **11**-1810
Peach, **8**-1317
Tomato Beef Loaf, **11**-1810
Tuna Soup, **11**-1810
Taramosalata (Red Caviar Spread), **4**-639
Tarhonya (Egg Barley), **6**-919

Taro, 11-1810
-Coconut-Egg Custard (Khanom Mo Kaeng), **11**-1716

Tarragon, 11-1810
Butter, **1**-86; **10**-1615, 1626
Fish Loaf with Caper Sauce, **7**-1101
Fresh Tuna, **12**-1862
Soup, French, **11**-1692
Tart(s), **11**-1811; for recipes see Pie(s) and Tart(s)

Tartare Sauce, 4-517, 574; **5**-695; **7**-1116; **10**-1614, 1622
Hot, **5**-695
Tartare Steak, **7**-1150
Tartar Sandwiches (Biftecks Tartare), **11**-1802
Tartes aux Fruits avec Crème Pâtissière (Fruit Tarts with Pastry Cream), **5**-746
Tatsuta-age, **1**-26
Tayglach mit Neshomas (Nut and Honey Sweetmeats), **6**-994
Täytetty Uunihauki (Baked Stuffed Pike), **5**-680

Tea, 11-1814
Black Teas, **11**-1814
for a Crowd, **4**-636
for a Crowd, Menu, **4**-635
English, **4**-635
English Afternoon, Menu, **4**-634
Fennel Seed Tea, **4**-657
Flower Teas, **4**-636
Ginger, **5**-803
Green Teas, **11**-1815
Hot (QC), **10**-1526
Iced, **4**-636
Jasmine, **4**-635
Lemonade-Tea, Iced, **7**-1057
Lemon Iced, **11**-1816
Minted Iced, **11**-1816
Oolong Teas, **11**-1815
Oriental, Menu, **4**-635
Spiced, Hot, **11**-1815
Tejfeles Baffözelék (Dried Beans in Sour Cream), **6**-919
Tejfeles Sült Ponty (Pike Baked in Cream), **6**-919
Telecí Maso s Vinnou Omackou (Veal Roast with Wine Sauce), **4**-531
Telegrafkake (Telegraph Cake), **8**-1242
Telegraph Cake (Telegrafkake), **8**-1242
Telephone Pudding, **1**-41
Teliachia Grudinka s Sousom iz Tsvetnoi Kapusty, Krevetok, i Limona (Breast of Veal with Cauliflower, Shrimps, and Lemon Sauce), **10**-1571
Telur Masak Bali (Balinese Spiced Eggs), **11**-1714

Tempura
Domburi (Tempura over Rice), **6**-972
Sembei (Cracker-Fried Shrimps), **6**-972
Soba (Fried Foods with Noodles), **6**-972
Tempura, **6**-971
Tendon (Tempura over Rice), **6**-972
Tennessee Baked Ham, **1**-69
Tennessee Boiled Custard, **11**-1725
Tennessee Hamburgers, **6**-869
Teriyaki, see Skewer, Skewered

Terrapin, **11**-1819; for recipes see Turtle, Tortoise, and Terrapin
Terrine(s), **11**-1819; for recipes see Pâté(s) and Terrine(s)
Texas Ambrosia, **1**-73
Texas Barbecued Chicken, **4**-645
Texas Hot Sauce, **1**-146
Texas Potato Salad, **9**-1462
Texas Sombreros, **6**-872
Texas-Style Onion Toast, **11**-1828
Thanksgiving Menu, **11**-1822
Thomas Jefferson's Almond Custard, **1**-14
Thon en Salade (Tuna Salad Plate), **11**-1802
Thousand Island Dressing, **1**-60; **4**-574; **5**-695; **7**-1116; **10**-1614, 1622
Thousand Island Eggs, **11**-1698
Thousand Leaves Torte (Tusenbladstårta), **11**-1972
Thyme, **11**-1824
Tillikastike (Dill Sauce), **5**-681

Timbale(s), 11-1824
Cases, **11**-1824
Cases, Creamed Crabs and Shrimps in, **11**-1824
Cheese, **11**-1824
Egg, with Curry Sauce, **11**-1824
Ham, **6**-865
Macaroni-Meat, **7**-1094
Tiropitta (Cheese Pie), **5**-819
Tkemali (Caucasian Plum Sauce), **10**-1627
Toads, Fried, **8**-1228

Toast(s), 11-1825
with Anchovies, Fried, **11**-1826
Apricot-Honey, **11**-1825
Boxes, **11**-1828
Brandy, Fluffed, **11**-1826
Butters, Nonsweet, **11**-1829
Butters, Sweet, for Tea Toast, **11**-1829
Caramel-Cardamom, **11**-1825
Celery-Seasoned, **11**-1697
Cheese Bread, Toasted, **1**-145
Cheese Roll-Ups, **11**-1825
Cheese Toast Cups, **2**-252
Cinnamon, de Luxe, **3**-447; **11**-1825
Croustades, **4**-518
Croutons, **4**-519
French, **11**-1826
Garlic, Italian Style, **11**-1826
Goldenrod, **11**-1826
Herbed, **11**-1826
Island Toast with Bacon, **11**-1826
Jam, Rolled, **11**-1826
Lemon, **11**-1826
Luncheonettes, **11**-1829
Marmalade, Spiced, **11**-1828
Marrow, **4**-627; **7**-1112
Melba Toast, **2**-280; **11**-1826
Milk, **11**-1828
Onion, Texas-Style, **11**-1828
Parsley-Cheese, **8**-1298
Peach Pudding, **11**-1828
Peanut-Butter Garlic Bread, **8**-1326
Pineapple Finger, **11**-1828
Pulled, **11**-1828
Raspberry, Dutch, **11**-1826
Rum-Cinnamon Sticks, **11**-1828
Rounds and Sticks, Toasted, **11**-1829
Salt Sticks, **11**-1828
Sesame, **11**-1828
for Soup, **11**-1697
Sour-Cream Date, **11**-1828
Squares, Puffed, **11**-1828
Toast Cups, **3**-346; **11**-1828
Tomato-Soup, **11**-1829
Town, **11**-1829
Twist, **11**-1697
Waffle, with Cinnamon-Nut Topping, **11**-1829
Zwieback, **12**-1962
Toddy, **11**-1829
Toffee, **2**-288; **11**-1829
Tokany, Seven Chieftains' (Hét Vezér Tokány), **6**-918

Tomato(es), 11-1829
Appetizer, **1**-89
and Apple Relish, Spicy, **10**-1542
Apple-Tomato Appetizer, Hot, **11**-1832
-Apricot Jam, **6**-964
Aspic, **1**-119; **5**-787
Avocado Cocktail, **3**-455
-Avocado Hors-d'oeuvre, **6**-913
Balachong, Fresh Tomato (Pazundok Ngapi Gyaw), **11**-1716
Beans and Squash, Savory, **11**-1832
Beef Loaf, **11**-1810
Broiled, **4**-630
Broiled, Seasonings for, **11**-1830
Butter, **2**-279; **11**-1835
Cabbage with (Paradeiskraut), **1**-122
and Cabbage, Simmered, **7**-1087
Canapés, Bahamian, **1**-86
Candied, Baked, **1**-22
Caviar, **1**-86
Cheese-Tomato Grill, **7**-1085
and Cheese, with Macaroni, Baked, **7**-1095
Chutney, **3**-446
Cocktail, Spiced, **11**-1832
Cocktail and Tomato Ketchup, **6**-999
Coriander Marmalade, **3**-478
Corn, and Okra, **11**-1832
Crystal, Pickles, **9**-1373
Cucumber, Cocktail, **11**-1832
-Cumin Chutney, **10**-1556
Curry, **7**-1123
Dressing, **10**-1623
-and-Egg Scramble, **11**-1833
Eggs Baked in, **8**-1274
Fines Herbes, **11**-1839
with Fish and Onions (Fiskgryta), **11**-1788
and Frankfurters, Scalloped, **5**-721
Fried, Country Style, **11**-1700
Fried, with Creamy Gravy, **11**-1833
Fried, Moussaka, **8**-1187
Fried (Stegte Tomater), **4**-540
Frost, **1**-37
Fruit-Tomato Relish, **10**-1543
Garnishes, **5**-778; **10**-1666
Gazpacho, Iced, with Vegetable, Crouton, and Herb Garnish, **9**-1383
Ginger Conserve, **5**-803
Glazed, and Green Beans, **11**-1834
Gravy, Grandmother Stoughton's, **9**-1354
Halves, Broiled, **4**-565
-Ham-Cheese Parlay, **11**-1747
with Herbs, **11**-1834
Hoosier Fried, Creamy Gravy, **1**-37
Hot Spiced Whole, **1**-55
Jam, **6**-965; **11**-1836
Juice Cocktail, **3**-455
-Juice Squares, Jellied (QC), **10**-1523
Ketchup, **6**-999
Marinated, **10**-1586
Mayonnaise, **5**-695
and Mushrooms, Scalloped, **8**-1201
and Okra with Lemon, **12**-1903
and Onions, American, **8**-1263
Peach-Tomato Relish, **10**-1542
Pepper, and Celery Relish, **11**-1835
and Peppers, **9**-1360
Pie, Red and Green, **9**-1388
with Porgies, Baked, **9**-1438
Pork Steaks, **9**-1442
Provençal, Madame Fraize's, **12**-1900
Purée, **11**-1834
Quickie, **11**-1694
Red-Hot Sauce Relish, **10**-1543
Relish, Curried, **5**-726
Relish, Spiced, **10**-1543
Relish, Sweet Spicy, **11**-1835
Salad
-Avocado, **10**-1586
Bacon, and Egg, **10**-1586
-and-Cottage-Cheese, Layered, **11**-1834
-Cucumber, **4**-566
and Cucumber (Agourontomatosalata), **5**-822
Dressing, **7**-1086
-Ham, Jellied, **10**-1583
Italian, **11**-1834
Lamb, and Cucumber, **10**-1580
and Lettuce Avocadaise, **11**-1837
Masked, **7**-1115
and Mushroom, **1**-82
-Romaine-Avocado, **4**-566
Salade de Tomates, **5**-745
Vinaigrette, **8**-1278
-Watercress, **4**-641
and Salami, with Baked Polenta, **9**-1419
Sauce, **5**-806; **9**-1450; **10**-1539; **11**-1834
Basic (Salsa Parmigiana), **6**-959
Chili-Tomato, **8**-1273
Italian, **10**-1627
Mariner's (Salsa alla Marinara), **6**-959
-Meat, **2**-316
-Meat Spaghetti, **11**-1737
Purée Sauce, **11**-1738
Saltsa Tomate, **5**-818
Spaghetti, **11**-1737
Spiced (Salsa Cruda), **7**-1142
Scalloped, **11**-1834
and Shallots, **10**-1650
Slices, Hot, **7**-1153
Soup
Bouillon, **2**-216
Bouillon, Sherry Tomato, **5**-786
Bouillon, Spicy, **11**-1832
Chilled Creamy, **11**-1832
Cream of Fresh-Tomato, **11**-1832
-and-Herb, on the Rocks, **11**-1832
Juice-into-Soup, **11**-1691
Pale Pink, **11**-1690
on the Rocks, **4**-632
and Salmon Bisque, **10**-1595
and Salmon Soup, **10**-1595
-Shrimp Bisque, Sherried, **11**-1832
Sour-Cream, Chilled, **11**-1697
Sunset, **11**-1694
-Soup Toast, **11**-1829
Stewed, with Green Beans, **1**-154
Stuffed, **8**-1213
Baked, **11**-1834
Cold, **11**-1834
Corn-Stuffed, Baked, **3**-484
with Dilled Cucumbers, **4**-522
Egg-Salad-Stuffed, **10**-1582
Egg-Stuffed, **4**-609
Las Vegas, **11**-1730
Peanut-Butter Stuffed, **8**-1325
Shells, Pea and Cheese Salad in, **8**-1315
Stuffings for, **11**-1834
with Sweet Potatoes, **11**-1797
Tomato(es), Cherry (for breakfast), **2**-243
Tomato(es), Green
and Cucumber Slices, Fried, **11**-1833
Fried (Tomato Dish), **1**-46
Jam, **11**-1836
Ketchup, **1**-41
Marmalade, **11**-1836
Mincemeat, **7**-1162
and Peppers, Stewed, **11**-1832
Pickle, Pickled, **6**-993; **9**-1373
Dill, Kosher Style, **9**-1374
Mustard, **9**-1350
Pie, Red and Green, **9**-1388
Relish, **10**-1542
Tomato(es), Yellow
Preserves, **11**-1835
Tongdak Juk (Roasted Chicken), **7**-1022

Tongue(s), 11-1836
Beef
Boiled, **2**-192; **11**-1838
Braised, **11**-1837
and Cheese Sandwiches with Cashews, **10**-1605
Columbian, **2**-193
Jellied Tongue Ring, **1**-117
Pineapple, and Cheese Spread, **9**-1403
Sandwiches, **9**-1383
with Sweet-and-Sour Sauce, **6**-990
in White-Wine Aspic, **11**-1839

Tongue(s), continued
Callie-Toast, **11**-1825
Dinners, Menus, **11**-1837-1839
and Egg-Salad Sandwiches, **10**-1604
and Egg Tart, **11**-1811
and Egg in Yogurt Sauce, **12**-1957
Lamb, Potted, **7**-1040; **11**-1838
and Noodle Rabbit, **8**-1232
with Raisin Sauce, **7**-1150
Ring, Jellied, **1**-117
Three Sauces for, **2**-194
Tunge (sandwich), **4**-536
Ton Jun (Beef with Soybean Cake), **7**-1020
Tonno con Piselli (Tuna with Peas), **12**-1864
Topeka Fried Chicken, **1**-39

Topping(s), Dessert, **12**-1853
(for Almond Meringue Cookies), **7**-1135
(for Almond Torte), **4**-630
Amber Whipped Cream, **8**-1321
Amber Whipped Cream (QC), **10**-1525
Banana-Mace Whipped, **7**-1100
Cinnamon, **7**-1156
Cinnamon and Sugar, for Kuchen, **5**-799
Cream-Cheese, for Gingerbread, **3**-362; **5**-805
Crumb, **2**-208; **9**-1357
Honey, **6**-911
for Ice Cream Sundaes, **6**-931-932
(for Italian Rum Cake), **10**-1562
Lemon, **7**-1088
Whipped (low-calorie), **7**-1167
for Mace Coffeecakes, **7**-1100
Meringue, **7**-1164
Meringue, for Pies and Puddings, Quick, **7**-1134
Meringue Pie Topping, Never-Fail, **7**-1134
Orange-Rum, **8**-1272
Peanut-Butter, **8**-1328
Praline, Almond, **9**-1480
Praline, Broiled, **9**-1480
(for Scotch Coffeecake), **3**-463
Spice-Crumb, **12**-1933
Strawberry Whip, **11**-1778
Streusel, **5**-799
Whipped-Cream, **3**-412; **11**-1792; **12**-1853
Whipped Cream, Amber, **8**-1321
Whipped Cream, Amber (QC), **10**-1525
Tori no Mizutaki (Boiled Chicken), **6**-975
Torrejas de Coliflor (Cauliflower Fritters), **11**-1708
Torrijas (Ladyfingers in Syrup), **11**-1709
Torta de Maíz Tierno (Fresh Corn Tart), **9**-1496

Torte(n), **12**-1853; see also Cake(s)
Almond, **1**-15; **4**-630
Almond Brandy, **12**-1853
Apple Cake (Aeblekage), **4**-543
Apricot, **12**-1854
Apricot-Coconut Cake, **2**-269
Apricot Delight, **1**-108
Apricot Refrigerator Cake, **1**-109
Blitz, **2**-267
Blueberry, **7**-1156
Blueberry Cake (Blabærkake), **8**-1242
Caramel, **2**-297
Carrot, **2**-308
Cherry, with Cream, **12**-1854
Cherry, Glacé, **4**-552
Chocolate Almond (Rehruecken), **11**-1804
Chocolate, Burgundy, **4**-553
Chocolate, French, **12**-1853
Chocolate, Unbaked, Warsaw, **3**-415
Cream Meringue (Marängsuisse), **11**-1792
Filbert, **4**-659
Himmel, **7**-1045
Hunter's (Jaegertorte), **12**-1854
Linzer, **4**-635
Mazarin (Mazarintårta), **11**-1793
Mincemeat Delight, **7**-1164
Mocha, **12**-1854
Opera, **12**-1856
Poppy-Seed, **9**-1437
Poppy-Seed Layer (Makavy Kolác), **4**-532
Prune, Seven-Layered, **4**-553
Sans Rival, Swedish, **12**-1856
Seven-Layer Cake, Hungarian (Dobostorte), **1**-124
Sour-Cream Apple, **12**-1933
Strawberry Dream Cake, **2**-272
Strawberry-Macaroon, **11**-1779
Strawberry Schaumtorte, **7**-1156
Swedish Applecake, **10**-1666
Thousand Leaves (Tusenbladstårta), **11**-1792
Garnishing for, **11**-1793
Varmlandstårta, Swedish, **12**-1854
Viennese, **12**-1853

Tortilla(s), **12**-1856
Chicken-Filled with Tomato Sauce, **12**-1856
Chili-Filled, **12**-1856
Corn (Tortillas de Maíz), **7**-1137
Corn, White, **12**-1856
Flour (Tortillas de Harina), **7**-1137
Fried Filled (Tacos), **7**-1138
de Harina de Trigo (Wheat Tortillas), **12**-1856
con Jamon (Spanish Omelette with Ham), **6**-861
Mexican Bread, **7**-1137
Stuffed (Enchiladas), **7**-1138
Wheat (Tortilla de Harina de Trigo), **12**-1856

Tortoni, **12**-1857
Biscuit, **2**-203; **12**-1857
Coffee, **12**-1857
Sherry, **12**-1858

Tostada(s), **7**-1137; **12**-1857
Chicken-Avocado, **12**-1930
Compuestas (Mexican Sandwiches), **7**-1137
Indio, **11**-1731
Tostaditas al Estilo de Potosí (Little Toasts, Potosí Style), **7**-1137
Totopos (Bean and Cheese Appetizers), **7**-1138
Toucinho-do-Céu (Bacon from Heaven), **9**-1457
Tournedos Béarnaise, **11**-1766
Tournedos Rossini, **11**-1766
Tourtière (Pork Pie), **2**-277
Trai Cay (Cambodian Mixed Fruits), **11**-1717
Transylvanian Casserole, **10**-1632
Trapper's Sweet Bannock, **1**-62
Trevisano Sauce, **11**-1738

Trifle, **4**-627
English, **9**-1489
English, A True, **12**-1858
Trinidad Stew Shrimp, **2**-300

Tripe, **12**-1858
Batter-Fried, **12**-1858
Breaded, Crisp, **12**-1859
Creole, **12**-1859
Fried, **1**-56
Honeycomb, Broiled, with Mustard Sauce, **8**-1224
Lyonnaise, à la Lyonnaise, **2**-193; **12**-1859
à la Mode de Caen, **12**-1858
Soup (Sopa de Mondongo), **11**-1704
Stew (Menudo), **7**-1140
with Vegetables, Stewed, **12**-1859
à la Warsaw (Flaki po Warszawsku), **9**-1424
Trollkrem (Magic Cream), **8**-1241

Trout, **12**-1859
Alexander, Commander's Palace, **12**-1860
with Almonds and Cream, **1**-14
Baked, **1**-54
Boiled (Kokt Ørrett), **8**-1236
Broiled, with Watercress Butter, **1**-25
Brook, Fried, **2**-242
Brook, Meunière, **12**-1860
Campfire, **1**-27
in a Chemise, **5**-699
Cold, with Dill Sauce, **5**-698
Cold, in Jelly, **5**-698
English Style, **12**-1860
Fish Boil, Great Lakes, **7**-1147
Foiled, **5**-698
Fried, Southwestern (Trucha Frita), **11**-1727
Lake Michigan Butter-Stuffed, **7**-1147
Liffey, with Mushroom Sauce, **6**-945
Panfried, with Anchovy Fillets, **5**-692
en Papillote, **12**-1859
Rainbow, Rocky Mountain Style, **12**-1860
Truite au Bleu, **5**-698; **12**-1860
Truite Farcie, **5**-698
Trucha Frita (Southwestern Fried Trout), **11**-1727
Truffles, Two-Tone (candy), **2**-289
Truite au Bleu, **5**-698; **12**-1860
Truite Farcie, **5**-698
Trumpet Cake, **8**-1186
Tsujiura (Japanese Fortune Wafers), **6**-978

Tuna, Tuna Fish, **12**-1862
Appetizer, **12**-1862
Apple-Tuna Salad, **12**-1867
and Avocado Salad, Molded, **5**-787
Brandade de Thon, **12**-1864
en Brochette, **12**-1862
and Cabbage Pirog, **12**-1862
Caper Open-Faced Sandwiches, **12**-1867
in Caper Sauce, **2**-296
-Cashew Casserole, **2**-314; **12**-1866
Casserole, Festive, **2**-322
Cheddar-Tuna Chowder, **3**-355
-Cheese Loaf, Baked, **10**-1602
-Cheese Rice Bake, **10**-1549
and Chili Fondue, **12**-1864
Chowder, **12**-1863
Cocktail, **12**-1863
Coleslaw with Grapes, **12**-1867
Cornish Pies, **12**-1866
Croquettes, **4**-518
Curried, **12**-1863
Dip, Fines Herbes, **12**-1862
-Egg Three-Deckers, **10**-1604
Florentine, **12**-1863
Fresh-Tuna Stew, Basque (Marmitako), **11**-1743
Fresh Tuna Tarragon, **12**-1862
Frittata, Italian, **12**-1866
Fritters, **12**-1866
Green-Bean Casserole, **12**-1864
and Horseradish Canapés, **12**-1862
à la King (QC), **10**-1523
-Macaroni Bake, **12**-1864
Macaroni, and Orange Salad, **7**-1092
Marinated, **12**-1867
Marka, **12**-1863
Mornay in Rice Ring, **12**-1864
Mound, **12**-1863
Mushroom Macaroni, **12**-1864
-Noodle Casserole, **12**-1863
Pastries, **12**-1866
Peas and Rice, **8**-1315
with Peas (Tonno con Piselli), **12**-1864
-Pecan-Cheese Sandwiches, **8**-1334
Pies, Individual, **12**-1866
and Pineapple, Oriental, **9**-1406
Pineapple, and Rice Salad, **9**-1408
Pizza, **12**-1864
Potato, and Bean Salad, Genoa Style, **12**-1867
-Potato Salad, Hot, **12**-1867
and Potato Tart, **12**-1864
Potato-Tuna Casserole, **9**-1463
Radiccio, **12**-1867
and Rice, **12**-1863
Salad, **10**-1582
Jellied, **7**-1085
Plate (Thon en Salade), **11**-1802
Salade Niçoise, **9**-1384
Salubrious, **12**-1867
with Sour-Cream Horseradish Sauce, **6**-914

and Salmon Mold, **10**-1583
Sandwiches, Curried, **10**-1602
Sandwich Spread, Savory, **12**-1867
Sauce with Spaghetti, **11**-1736
Sauce, White, **11**-1738
Scalloped, **7**-1084
Seafood Club Sandwiches, **10**-1602
Soufflé, Double-Boiler, **12**-1866
Spread, **2**-280
Sweet-and-Sour, **12**-1863
Sweet and Sour, Panned, **5**-692
Tapioca Soup, **11**-1810
Tarts, Hot, **11**-1811
Tetrazzini, **12**-1866
Treat, **12**-1863
with Veal (Vitello Tonnato), **12**-1889
-Vegetable Mold, **12**-1866
-Vegetable Pie with Cheese Pastry, **9**-1388
Véronique, **12**-1866
Walnut Spread, **12**-1867
West Coast Salad, **12**-1867
and White-Bean Salad (Cannelini al Tonno), **6**-960
Tunge (tongue sandwich), **4**-536
Tung Sun Ch'ao Jo (Pork with Bamboo Shoots), **3**-399
Turbigo Kidney, **7**-1014
Turbot, **12**-1867

Turkey, **12**-1868
Bake, California, **12**-1875
Barbecued, **1**-72
and Beef Tenderloin, **1**-72
Bread Stuffing, Basic, Chart, **12**-1869
and Broccoli Amandine, **12**-1872
Broiled, **12**-1871
Carving, **2**-313
-Cheddar Sandwiches, Baked, **12**-1877
Chop Suey, **12**-1874
Chow Mein, **12**-1874
and Cocktail Sauce, **12**-1872
Cranberry Loaf, Jellied, **3**-490
Creole in Rice Ring, **12**-1874
Cuckoo's Eggs, **12**-1874
Curry, **12**-1872
and Fresh Tangerine Salad, **12**-1876
Galantine, How to Bone and Prepare a Turkey for a Galantine, **5**-765
Giblet Gravy, **11**-1823
Grape-Turkey Salad, **5**-812
Gravy, **4**-625
Gumbo, **5**-830
Hash, **6**-879
Hawaiian, **12**-1872
à la King (QC), **10**-1523
Loaf, Layered, **12**-1875
Mornay on Broccoli, **2**-325
Open Sandwiches with Cheese Sauce, **12**-1876
and Oysters, Creamed, **1**-47
Oyster Dressing for, **4**-575
Panfried, **12**-1871
Paprika, **12**-1872
Pâté, **12**-1872
Pie, **9**-1388
Pie, Breadstick Topping, **12**-1872
Pie with Corn-Bread Topping, **12**-1875
Pie with Pastry Crust (QC), **10**-1523
Pie, Pinwheel, **12**-1875
with Potatoes, Sherried, **12**-1874
Pot-Roasted, Jamaica Style, **12**-1871
Pressed, **12**-1872
Pudding, **12**-1875
Ragout, **12**-1872
and Rice, Baked, **10**-1549; **12**-1874
Roast, **3**-442; **11**-1822
Roast, English Style, **4**-625
Roast, with Savory Giblet-Butternut Stuffing, **1**-74
Roll, Barbecued, **12**-1871
Roll, Roast Boneless, **12**-1871
Salad, **12**-1875
Salad, Broiled, **12**-1876
Sandwich Loaf, **10**-1610
Sandwiches, Combination, **12**-1877
Sandwiches, Hot, with Mushroom sauce, **10**-1602
Sandwiches, Sliced, **9**-1383
Sausage, Puerto Rican, **12**-1871
-Sausage Squares, **12**-1875
Soup, **12**-1872
Soup, Parmentier, **11**-1695
Spit-Roasted, **12**-1871
Squares with Mushroom Sauce, Savory, **12**-1874
Steaks, **11**-1771
Steaks, Barbecued, **12**-1871
Stuffed (Pavo a la Nicaragüense), **11**-1706
Stuffed Southwestern Style (Gallina Rellena), **11**-1730
Stuffing, Lisbon (Recheio a Moda de Lisboa Para Peru), **9**-1457
and Sweet-Potato Casserole, **11**-1796
Tetrazzini, **11**-1736
Timetable for Roasting, Chart, **11**-1823; **12**-1868
Vegetable, and Dumpling Dinner, Boiled, **12**-1871
with Welsh-Rabbit Sauce, **12**-1874

Turkey, Wild
in Mole Sauce, **5**-770
Turkish Coffee, **3**-462
Turkish Dreams, **10**-1561
Turkish Eggplant Salad, **4**-616
Turkish Grapevine Leaves Dolma, **4**-570
Turkish Imam Bayeldi (The Iman Fainted), **4**-615
Turkish Lamb Pilaf, Savory, **7**-1038
Turkish Meat-and-Rice Stuffing, **11**-1782
Turkish Paste, **5**-791
Turkish Shish Kebab, **8**-1214
Turkish Strawberry Sherbet Drink, **10**-1654
Turkish Swordfish on Skewers (Kilich Shish), **8**-1215
Turkish Watermelon Sherbet Drink, **10**-1654
Turk's Onion Delight, **8**-1264
Turmeric, **12**-1878

Turnip(s), **12**-1878
with Braised Duck, **2**-220
and Cucumber Salad (Salat iz Repy i Ogurtzov), **10**-1572
Fluffy, **12**-1878
Garnishes, **5**-777
Hashed, **1**-56
with Mushrooms, **3**-440
Pickled, **8**-1213
and Potatoes, **9**-1352
Rutabaga, **10**-1574
au Gratin, **10**-1575
Mashed, with Onion, **10**-1575
Ring, **1**-49
with Salt Pork, **10**-1575
Salad, **12**-1879
in Sour Cream, **12**-1878
Stuffed, Finnish, **12**-1879
White, Roses (garnish), **10**-1666
Yellow, with Duchesse Potatoes, **11**-1823
Yellow, and Sweet Potatoes, Mashed, **11**-1797

Turnip Greens
with Hog Jowl, **1**-69
with Raw Vegetable Relish, **1**-34

Turnover(s), **12**-1879
Cabbage Pirozhki, **10**-1568
Cheese (Empanadas de Queso), **11**-1708
Chicken-Liver, **12**-1879
Corned-Beef, Mushroom Sauce, **12**-1879
Curried Meat (Samosas), **12**-1879
Curry Puffs, **6**-912
Fried Pies, **4**-578
Galician (Pastelillos Gallegos), **9**-1497
Ham, **6**-852
Liver Pirozhki, **10**-1568
Meat and Anchovy Pirozhki, **10**-1570
Pasties, **1**-48
Pirogi and Pirozhki, Raised Dough for, **10**-1570
Tuna Cornish Pies, **12**-1866

Turnover(s), Dessert, **12**-1879
Apple, Old-Fashioned, **8**-1247
Banbury Tarts, **1**-142
Banbury Tarts, Rich, **8**-1308
Billets-Doux, **8**-1308
Blueberry, **2**-208; **12**-1879
Marmalade, **12**-1880
Plantain, Jamaican, **9**-1414
Raisin-Orange, **12**-1879
Sweet (Empanadas de Dulce), **7**-1143
Turquoise Yogurt, **8**-1213

Turtle, Tortoise, and **Terrapin,** **12**-1880
Diamondback Terrapin, **1**-46
Diamondback Terrapin Stew, Maryland, **11**-1819
Turtle Soup, **12**-1880
Turtle Steak with Sour-Cream Sauce, **12**-1880
Tusenbladstårta (Thousand Leaves Torte), **11**-1792
Tutti-Frutti, **4**-579
Tutti-Frutti Mousse, **4**-632
Twigs (Khvorost), **10**-1573

U

Uha Pua (Smoked Pork Chops), **9**-1434
Ujhazy Chicken Soup, **11**-1695
Ukrainian Borsch, **2**-214; **10**-1567
Ukrainskii Borsch (Ukrainian Borsch), **10**-1567
Umani (Meatballs), **6**-974
Uncle Ed's Chowder, **5**-691
Uova in Purgatorio (Eggs in Purgatory), **6**-955
Upside-Down Cake, **12**-1881; for recipes see Cake(s)
Urchins (Spitzbuben), **5**-799
Uruguay Meat Pie (Pastel de Carne), **11**-1705
Uruguay Spinach Fritters (Buñuelos de Espinaca), **11**-1708

V

Vacherin à la Suisse (Meringue Shell), **12**-1884
Vaffler (Waffles), **8**-1241
Valenciana Rice Salad (Ensalada de Arroz a la Valenciana), **11**-1742

Vanilla, **12**-1844
Bavarian Cream, **6**-980
Caramels, **2**-285
Confectioners' Sugar, **9**-1431
Cornstarch Pudding, **9**-1489
Cream Filling, **3**-407, 492; **4**-594; **8**-1309; **11**-1812
Cream Pots (Pots de Crème à la Vanille), **3**-493
Custard, Rich, **8**-1331
Fresh-Fruit Cup, **12**-1885
Fresh-Plum Compote, **9**-1416
Frosting, **8**-1229, 1326
Fudge, **5**-764
Glaze, **5**-806; **6**-901
Ice Cream, **6**-929
Ice Cream, French, **6**-929
Meringue Pie, **9**-1391
Milk Shake, **7**-1160

Vanilla, continued
Pie, Amish, **9**-1355
Pralines, **2**-285
Sauce, **9**-1493; **10**-1629; **11**-1839
Soufflé, **11**-1688
Sugar, **1**-124; **2**-200; **6**-904; **12**-1885
Suggested Uses for, **12**-1885
-Wafer Crust, **9**-1361
Vareniki, Cherry or Blueberry, **10**-1574
Variety Meat, **12**-1885; for recipes see names of variety meats
Varkensschijf (Rolled Pork Rib), **4**-590
Varm Peberrodssovs (Hot Horseradish Sauce), **4**-542
Vasilopitta (Sweet Bread), **5**-823
Vatapá (Fish Stew), **11**-1703
Vatrushki (Cheese and Egg Tart), **10**-1572

Veal, **12**-1886
in Aspic, **12**-1895
Avocados Stuffed with, **12**-1896
Birds, **2**-203
Blanquette, Belgian, **12**-1895
Breast, Breast of
with Cauliflower, Shrimps, and Lemon Sauce (Teliachia Grudinka s Sousom iz Tsvetnoi Kapusty, Krevetok, i Limona), **10**-1571
Fricassee, **5**-748
with Mayonnaise Mask, **7**-1115
in Mushroom Sauce, **12**-1895
Orange-Stuffed, **8**-1268
Petto di Vitello, **6**-954
Raisin-Rice Stuffed, **4**-576
with Sausage Stuffing, **12**-1894
Simmered, **12**-1894
Stuffed, **6**-990
and Vegetables, Barbecued, **12**-1895
with Bulgur and Dill, **12**-1895
Carving, **2**-312, 313
and Cheese Steaks, **12**-1897
Chop(s)
Lucullus, **3**-358
Marjoram, **7**-1110
Paprika, **12**-1892
Parmigiana (Costolette alla Parmigiana), **6**-954
Shallot-Veal, **10**-1649
Soubise, **12**-1892
Supreme, **11**-1698
and Cucumber Salad (Salat iz Teliatini s Ogurtsami), **10**-1566
Cutlet(s)
with Anchovies (Sardellenschnitzel), **10**-1642
Breaded (Wiener Schnitzel), **12**-1893
à la Oscar (Kalvkotlett à la Oscar), **11**-1788
Sicilian Style, **12**-1893
Stuffed, **12**-1957
Stuffed, Rolls, **12**-1894
with Sweet Potatoes in Sour-Cream Sauce, **11**-1796
with Dandelion Greens, **12**-1896
Galantine of, **5**-715, 766
with Garlic Sauce, **12**-1896
Goulash, **5**-809
Goulash (Kalbsgulasch), **1**-122
-and-Ham Pie, Cold, **9**-1387
-and-Ham Potpie, **9**-1472
Hash, **6**-879
Herb Loaf, Jellied, **12**-1895
Hot Pot, **6**-945
Jellied, **9**-1352
Leg, Leg of
Braised, **12**-1889
with Cheese (Parmesan Schlegel), **1**-121
Roast, **12**-1889
with Salmon (Veau Saumoné), **12**-1889
with Salmon, Veau Saumoné, with Tarragon, **12**-1889
Loaf, **7**-1128
Loaf with Italian Sausages, **12**-1896
Loaf, Jellied, **10**-1665
Loaf, Old-Fashioned, **12**-1896
Loaf (Pain de Veau), **2**-278
Loaves, Jellied, Individual, **12**-1896
Low-Calorie Seasonings for, **7**-1084
Marengo, **2**-324
Meatballs, **7**-1122
Mexican, **12**-1896
Minced (Geschnetzeltes), **11**-1802
with Mushrooms, **8**-1273
Paprika (Borjú Pörkölt), **6**-918
Paprikash, **8**-1296
Parmigiana, **3**-358
Parsley Pie with Dumplings, **1**-78
and Pepper Long Boys, **9**-1359
and Peppers, Italian Style, **12**-1896
and Pork Head Cheese, **6**-979
and Pork Ragout, **2**-317; **10**-1533
Pot Roast, Filipino, **9**-1476
Pot Roast with Raisin Sauce, **9**-1476
Pot Roast, Spicy, **9**-1476
Retail Cuts of, Chart, **12**-1887
with Rice Salad, Italian, **10**-1550
Roast with Anchovies (Pieczeń Cieleca z Sardelami), **9**-1425
Roast (Arrosto di Vitello), **12**-1889
Roast (Kalbsbraten), **5**-794
Roast with Wine Sauce (Telecí Maso s Vinnou Omackou), **4**-531
Rosemary, **10**-1560
Saffron, **10**-1577
Salad, **12**-1897
Salad with Marinated Broccoli, **10**-1580
Scallops, Escalopes, Scaloppine, **12**-1894
and Bacon Terrine, **12**-1894
with Dill, **4**-651
Fillets of, Stuffed (Blinde Vinken), **4**-590
with Lemon, **12**-1894
Marsala, **12**-1894
Milanese, **7**-1052
Plain, **4**-651
Rollatine with Ham, **12**-1894
Scaloppine di Vitello, **6**-954
with Vermouth and Tarragon, **4**-651
with White Wine and Tarragon, **4**-651
Schnitzel
Champignon, **1**-127
Cordon Bleu, **1**-126
Curry, **1**-127
Florentine, **1**-128
à la Holstein, **1**-126
Natur, **1**-126
Paprika, **1**-127
Pariser, **1**-126
Piccata, **1**-126
Piccata à la Kerzenstuberl, **1**-127
Puszta, **1**-127
Wiener, **1**-126
Shanks, Ossobuco, **8**-1274
Shoulder with Cheese Sauce, **12**-1890
Shoulder of, with Ravioli Stuffing, **12**-1890
Slices, Jellied, **12**-1889
Soup, Black Kettle, **1**-40
Sour-Cream Loaf, **11**-1698
Steak, Marinated, **11**-1770; **12**-1892
Stew, **12**-1896
with Almonds in Sour Cream, **1**-14
Creamy, with Mushrooms, **11**-1774
French, **2**-216
French Style (Blanquette de Veau), **2**-205
Fruited, **9**-1483
Hawaiian, **12**-1896
Stock (White Stock), **11**-1774
Stuffed Birds (Zrazy Cielece Zawijane), **9**-1425
Stuffed Breast or Shoulder of, à la Polonaise (Nerkówka Lub Mostek Nadziewane po Polsku), **9**-1425
Timetable for Braising, Chart, **12**-1887
Timetable for Roasting, Chart, **12**-1886
with Tuna (Vitello Tonnato), **12**-1889
-Vegetable Soup, **11**-1694
-and-Vegetable Stuffing, **11**-1781
White Dome, **12**-1896
White Soup with Meatballs, **7**-1122

Veal, Calf's Brains
Cutlets (Kotleciki z Mózgu), **9**-1424
in Mushroom Sauce, **12**-1897

Veal, Calf's Liver
Baked, **9**-1351
Deviled (Athae Chin Gyau), **11**-1717
Dumplings, Delicate, **7**-1074
Loaf, **7**-1128
Pirozhki, **10**-1568
Sautéed (Geröstete Kalbsleber), **1**-122
Swiss, **7**-1073
Steak Béarnaise, **7**-1073; **12**-1897

Veal Heart(s)
Danish, **6**-883
with Fruit Stuffing, **6**-883
Pot Roasted, Danish, **9**-1476
Slices, Fried, **6**-883
Stew, **6**-883

Veal Kidney(s)
with Anchovies, **7**-1014
Bonne Femme, **7**-1014
Brochettes de Rognons Panés et Grillés, **7**-1014
Casserole Jerez, **7**-1014
au Citron, Pot Roasted, **9**-1476
in Cream, Mottram, **12**-1897
Flambéed (Rognons Bolo), **11**-1802
Fritti Rognoni, **7**-1016
and Ham Ragout, **7**-1014
and Mushroom Pie, **7**-1013
Nyre Sauté, Gammeltoft, **7**-1014
Roast, **12**-1897
Rognoncini di Vitello Trifolato, **7**-1016
Rognons Flambés au Ruban Bleu, **7**-1014
Turbigo, **7**-1014
in Vermouth, **12**-1897

Veal Sweetbread(s)
Chicken-and-Sweetbread Croquettes, **1**-46
Creamed, **11**-1794
and Cucumber Salad, **11**-1794; **12**-1897
Normandy Style, **11**-1794
Veau Saumoné (Veal with Salmon), **12**-1889
with Tarragon, **12**-1889

Vegetable(s), **12**-1897; see also names of vegetables
in Aspic, **1**-119
-Avocado Salad with Paprika Dressing, **10**-1586
Balls, **2**-219
Beef Pot Roast with, **1**-55
Beef Stew, **11**-1773
Boiled Pot, Miss Mollie's, **1**-61
Braised, **12**-1902
with Breast of Lamb, Braised, **7**-1034
Brunswick Stew, **1**-75
Brunswick Stew for a Crowd, **11**-1722
Brunswick Stew (QC), **10**-1520
Burgoo, Kentucky, **1**-40
Canning, **2**-295
-Cheese Rice, **10**-1550
Chinese, **2**-250; **3**-403
Chinese, with Roast Pork, **12**-1919
Chowchow, **9**-1350
Spanish Boiled Beef (Cocido), **11**-1742
Cocktail, **3**-455
with Coffee Pot Roast, **9**-1473
Cooked-Vegetable Salad, **10**-1665
Curry, **4**-527
Cutlets, **4**-994
Dip, **2**-305
Finger Salad with Dunking Sauce, **9**-1382
Flag Salad (Insalata Bandiera), **6**-960
with Flank Steak, Pot-Roasted, **9**-1473
with Fresh Pork Picnic Pot Roast, **9**-1476
Garnish, **10**-1566
Garnishes, Decorative, **5**-777
Garnish, Sliced, **10**-1666
à la Grecque, **12**-1900

à la Grecque, Basic Recipe, **1**-7
Green Onions, Peas, and Lettuce, **7**-1061
Green Vegetable Dressing, **5**-808
Hamburger Casserole, **2**-316
Hunter's Reward, **11**-1730
and Lamb Casserole, **2**-320
with Lamb-Neck Slices, **7**-1035
Lamb Stew, **11**-1773
Lamb-Vegetable Moussaka, **8**-1189
and Liver Pie, Savory, **7**-1075
and Liver, Piquant, **7**-1073
Low-Calorie Seasonings for, **7**-1086
Macédoine of, **7**-1100
Marinade for, **7**-1110
and Meat Hash, **8**-1224
Meat-Loaf Casserole, **2**-316
and Meat, Main-Dish (Festive Tzimmes), **6**-990
and Meat Salad, **10**-1580
Medley (Colache), **7**-1141
Medley (Leipziger Allerlei), **5**-796
Mixed Fry (Fritto Misto), **7**-1040
Mustard Dip for, **1**-87
with Peanut Sauce (Gado Gado), **11**-1715
Pickle, Korean (Kimchi), **7**-1023
Pilaf, **9**-1402
Platter, **7**-1089
à la Polonaise, Garnish for, **9**-1430
with Pork Hocks, **9**-1449
and Pork Liver, **7**-1074
Pork-Vegetable Bake, **9**-1451
Pot Roast, **6**-990
with Pot-Roasted Fresh Boston Butt, **9**-1476
Puchero, **9**-1486
Ratatouille, **10**-1538
Ratatouille, Classic, **12**-1903
Ratatouille Provençale, **4**-616
Raw (for appetizers), **1**-87
Raw Vegetable Relish, **1**-34
Relish, **8**-1315
Relish, Philadelphia, **9**-1350
-Rice Salad, **10**-1587
Ring, Jellied, **6**-980
Salad, **5**-787
Salad with Deviled Ham, **10**-1587
Salad, Jellied, **3**-424
Salad, Marinated, **10**-1667
Salad, Mixed, **10**-1587
Salade Parisienne, **10**-1580
Sauce for (Goma-Zu), **6**-976
Schlee, **1**-76
Seafood-Vegetable Chowder, **11**-1696
Shellfish-Vegetable Chowder, **10**-1650
Shepherd's Pies, **7**-1049
Short Ribs with, **1**-38
and Shrimps, Skewered, **7**-1084
Side Dish for Cocido (Verduras), **11**-1743
Skillet Pot Roast with, **2**-186
Soup(s)
and Beef, **11**-1694
Beef-Vegetable, Stockyard Inn, **1**-36
Black Kettle, **1**-40
Creole, **7**-1084
and Lamb, **7**-1038
with Meatballs (Groentesoep met Balletjes), **4**-589
and Oxtail, **8**-1283
Pepper Pot, with Dumplings, **9**-1350
Spring Vegetable, **4**-621
Summer (Kesäkeitto), **5**-679
Veal-Vegetable, **11**-1694
Soybean Shepherd's Pie, **11**-1734
Stew(s)
Estofado I and II, **11**-1705
Jungle, **1**-79
and Meat (Puchero), **11**-1706
Mormon, **1**-73
Noppe Jiru, **6**-976
Soybean, **11**-1734
Stock, **11**-1775
Stuffed, **7**-1050
-Stuffed Fish Rolls, **2**-305
Stuffing, **11**-1780, 1834
Stuffings for, **11**-1782
To Freeze, **5**-732; see also information under entry for specific vegetable Chart, **5**-734, 735
Tricolored (Sam Saek Namul), **7**-1022
with Tripe, Stewed, **12**-1859
Tuna-Vegetable Mold, **12**-1866
Tuna-Vegetable Pie with Cheese Pastry, **9**-1388
Turkey, and Dumpling Dinner, Boiled, **12**-1871
and Veal Breast, Barbecued, **12**-1895
-and-Veal Stuffing, **11**-1781
Vinaigrette, **4**-632
Vegetable Marrow, see Zucchini, Vegetable Marrow
Velouté, Velouté Sauce, **2**-173; **10**-1613, 1618
Venetian Beef Liver with Onions, **2**-192
Venetian Fish Soup (Zuppa Veneziana di Pesce), **6**-952
Venetian Style Grilled Jumbo Shrimps, **10**-1661
Venezuela Fried Beef with Rice (Bife Sauté a la Minuta con Arroz), **11**-1705
Venezuela Meat Pies (Hallacas), **11**-1706
Venezuela Pumpkin Soup Maracay (Sopa de Calabaza Maracay), **11**-1704

Venison, 12-1908
Basting Sauce for, **12**-1909
in Chafing Dish, **4**-512
Chops Parmesan, **12**-1909
Deer Stew, Western, **5**-769
Flanks with Rosemary, **12**-1909
Hunter's Chili, **12**-1909
Jerked, **1**-24
Marinated, **1**-23
Meatballs, **5**-773; **12**-1909
Meat-on-a-Stick, **12**-1908
Mincemeat, **1**-76
Pit-Cooked, **12**-1908
Pot Roast, **12**-1908
Ragout, **12**-1908
Roast, **7**-1152
Roast, Spicy Barbecued, **12**-1908
Roll, Brine-cured, **12**-1909
Saddle of (Reinsdyrsteik), **8**-1239
Saddle or Haunch, Roast, **5**-772
Sausage, **12**-1909
Steaks or Chops, **12**-1908
Steaks or Cutlets, Broiled, **5**-773
Stroganoff, **12**-1908
Vepřové s Krenem (Piquant Pork with Horseradish), **4**-532
Vera Cruz Garlic Soup, **11**-1691
Verbena, Lemon, **12**-1909
Verduras (Vegetable Side Dish for Cocido), **11**-1743
Vermicelli alla Pastora (Fine Noodles for the Shepherdess), **6**-958
Véronique Sauce, **10**-1614, 1621
Vesi-Sokerikakku (Finnish Cake), **5**-681
Vet's Breakfast, **4**-536
Vichyssoise Glacée, The Original Cream, **12**-1910
Viennese Brunch, Menu, **4**-629
Viennese Chocolate Confection, **3**-416
Viennese Coffee, **4**-630
Viennese Egg Cake (Wiener Eierkuchen), **6**-865
Viennese Giblet Fricassee, **4**-584
Viennese Ham Fleckerl (Ham and Noodle Casserole), **6**-865
Viennese Jam Fritters, **5**-749
Viennese Rice, **10**-1551
Viennese Sauerkraut, **10**-1632
Viennese Torte, **12**-1853
Vietnamese Omelet (Cha Tom), **11**-1717
Viipurin Rinkeli (Viipuri Twists), **5**-682
Viipuri Twists (Viipurin Rinkeli), **5**-682
Vikingekaffe (Viking Coffee), **4**-543

Vinaigrette, Vinaigrette Dressing, Vinaigrette Sauce, 10-1614; **12**-1910
4-573; **5**-695, 745
for Asparagus or Broccoli, **2**-252
Basic, **10**-1622
Vinaigrette s Syomgoi (Salmon Vinaigrette), **10**-1566

Vinegar, 12-1910
Herb, **12**-1912
Marinade for Meat, **9**-1422
Mint, Green, **7**-1166
Pie, "Piebox" Special, **11**-1732
-Soy Sauce, **7**-1023
Violets, Candied, **2**-281
Virginia Batter Bread, **1**-75
Virginia City Salad, **1**-56
Virginia Fried Apples, **11**-1724
Virginia's Oatmeal Chocolate-Chip Cookies, **3**-475
Vitamin, **12**-1912
Vitello Tonnato (Veal with Tuna), **12**-1889
Vodka Grog with Honey, Hot (Krupnik) **9**-1431
Vol-au-Vent, Chicken-Mushroom, **12**-1913
Vrasta Fasolakia Freska (Stewed Green Beans), **5**-822
Vrasto Arni me Fava (Stewed Lamb and Fava Beans), **5**-819
Vrasto Arni me Manestra (Lamb Stew with Manestra), **5**-819

W

Waffle(s), 2-227, 228; **12**-1914
Apple-Buttermilk, **2**-238
Bacon, **12**-1914
Bacon-Buttermilk, **2**-238
Basic, **12**-1914
Beer, Brussels (Gaufres Bruxelloises) **2**-200
Blueberry, **2**-209
Blueberry, Currant, Raisin, Nut, or Date, **12**-1915
Brownie, **12**-1915
Buttermilk, **2**-238
Cheese, **12**-1915
Cherry, **12**-1915
Corn, **12**-1915
Ginger, **5**-801
Gingerbread, Old Colony, **12**-1915
Ham, **12**-1915
Molasses-Oat, **8**-1184
Potato, **9**-1462
Pumpkin Nut, **9**-1499
Rice, **10**-1552; **12**-1915
Rosettes, **10**-1561
Spice, **12**-1915
Sweet Potato, **11**-1798
Vaffler, **8**-1241

Waldorf Salad, 1-60; **10**-1588
Jellied, **1**-100
Pineapple, **10**-1588
Walleyed Pike, **1**-78

Walnut(s), 12-1915
Apricot-Nut Sandwiches, **10**-1611
Baklava (Filled Pastry), **8**-1216
Bars, Hungarian, **12**-1918
Boiled Noodles with (Diós Tészta), **6**-920
Bonbons, **12**-1917
Bonbons, Baked, **12**-1918
Cake (Karidopita), **4**-640
Carrot Pudding, Steamed, **2**-306
Chicken (Ho T'ao Chi Jing), **12**-1917
Circassian Chicken (Cherkes Tavugu), **8**-1214
Colored, **7**-1044
Crescents, **12**-1918
Date-Nut Kisses, **7**-1017
-Ginger Dressing, **11**-1700
Kadayif (Shredded-Wheat Dessert), **8**-1216

Walnut(s), continued
Meringues, **7**-1135
Nougat, **8**-1244
Orange Walnut-Date Bars, **3**-431
Parmesan-Walnut Salad, California, **12**-1934
Raisin-Walnut Dressing, **4**-575
-Rice Fritters, **10**-1552
Rolls, **5**-799
Roll, Hungarian (Diós Tekercs), **6**-922
Sauce, California, **10**-1629
Shortbread, **12**-1917
Soyed, **3**-428
Spread, **1**-90
Strips, Serbian, **12**-1918
Swiss-Cheese Sandwich, **10**-1611
Tuna Spread, **12**-1867
Zucchini with, **12**-1904

Walnut(s), Black Walnut(s)
Brittle, **12**-1917
Chocolate Drops, **7**-1157
Cookies, **3**-476
Meringue, **1**-63
Wafers, **12**-1917
Warsaw Chocolate Torte, Unbaked, **3**-415
Washington Plum Dumplings, **12**-1932
Wasps' Nests (cookies), **1**-78
Wassail Bowl, **12**-1918
Wassail Bowl, Old-Time, **12**-1918

Water Chestnut(s), **12**-1919
and Rice Stuffing, **12**-1919

Watercress, **12**-1919
Butter, **1**-25, 86
and Chicken Soup, **12**-1920
Chive and Cress Soup, **11**-1690
Consommé, Jellied, **3**-467
and Corn Soup, Cream of, **12**-1920
Cressonière Sauce, **10**-1614, 1622
and Orange Salad, **8**-1268
Salad, **12**-1920
Salad Bowl, **2**-301
Sandwich, **12**-1920
Soup, **6**-945
Soup (Potage au Cresson), **5**-739
Sour-Cream Sauce, **12**-1920
-Tomato Salad, **4**-641

Watermelon, **7**-1129; **12**-1920
Almond Sherbet, **12**-1922
Balls with Minted Fresh-Lime Mold, **7**-1067
Cocktail, **1**-86
Granité, **6**-926
Honey, Spiced, **12**-1922
Ice, **5**-790
-Lime Cooler, **12**-1920
-Maraschino Pickle, **12**-1922
Pickle, **9**-1374
Ripe-Watermelon Pickle, **12**-1920
Ripe-Watermelon Preserves, **9**-1482
Salad, Molded, **12**-1920
Sherbet, **12**-1922
Sherbet Drink, Turkish, **10**-1654
Soup, Frosty, **12**-1920
Waterzooi de Poulet (Chicken Stew), **2**-197

Wedding Cake, **12**-1922
Bride's Cake, **12**-1922
Groom's Cake, **12**-1922
Weights and Measures, Charts, **12**-1923
Weinschaum (Wine Custard Sauce), **10**-1628
Welsch Kornkuche (Corn Cake), **9**-1354

Welsh Rabbit (or **Rarebit),** **12**-1923
1-10; **3**-346; **12**-1923
with Beer, **12**-1923
West Coast Salad, **12**-1867
Western Antipasto Salad Bowl, **12**-1935
Western Bean Stew, **1**-158
Western Cookery, **12**-1924
Western Deer Stew, **5**-769
Western Long Boys, **6**-859
Western Melon Conserve, **7**-1132
Western Omelet, **4**-610
Western Perfection Salad, **2**-258
Western Sandwiches, Sunday-Night, **10**-1604
Western Steak Barbecue, **1**-65
Western Style Pizza, **10**-1604
West Indian Pot Roast, **9**-1472
West Indies Apple Chutney, **1**-102
Whale, **12**-1935

Wheat, **12**-1935
Hickory-Nut Graham Bread, **7**-1153
Semolina, **10**-1646
Soy-Wheat Muffins, **11**-1734
Tortillas, **12**-1856
Wheat-Germ Bread, **2**-228
Whole-Wheat Popovers, **9**-1437
Whole-Wheat Rolls, **12**-1956
Wheat, Cracked, see Cracked Wheat
Wheat, Shredded, see Shredded Wheat
Wheelspoke Casserole, **1**-52
Whipped Cream, see Cream
Whiskey or Whisky, **12**-1937
Whitby Nun's Cake, **2**-272

Whitebait, **12**-1937
Panfried, **12**-1937
White Cake with Double Frosting, **1**-55
White Dome, **12**-1896

Whitefish, **5**-699; **12**-1938
Baked, with Bread Stuffing, **12**-1939
Baked Stuffed, **5**-699
Chili, **12**-1939
Cold, **5**-699; **12**-1939
Croquettes, **5**-692
Fish Boil, Great Lakes, **7**-1147
Lake Superior, Baked, with Savory Dressing and Lobster Sauce, **7**-1150
Lake Superior Planked, **7**-1147
with Piquant Sauce, **5**-692
Smoked, Platter, **12**-1939
Smoked, and Rice, **12**-1939
Stew, Piquant, **1**-48

White Sauce, **12**-1939
10-1618; **11**-1722
Medium, **3**-362
Thick, **10**-1660
White Stock, **10**-1618
White Stock (Veal Stock), **11**-1774

Whiting, **12**-1940
Chowder with Fish Balls, **5**-694
Creole, **12**-1940
Marinated, **12**-1940
Marinated, Broiled, **5**-694
Smoked, Creamed, **12**-1940
Wielkanocna Babka (Easter Babka), **9**-1431
Wienerbrød (Danish Pastry), **4**-543
Wiener Eierkuchen (Viennese Egg Cake), **6**-865
Wiener Eiskaffee (Viennese Iced Coffee), **1**-123
Wiener Schnitzel, **1**-126
Wiener Schnitzel (Breaded Veal Cutlet), **12**-1893
Wig Buns, Christmas, **7**-1098
Wigs, **7**-1098

Wild Rice, **12**-1940
Casserole, **1**-49; **7**-1153
Herbed, **12**-1940
and Mushroom Stuffing, **11**-1781
with Shrimps, **12**-1940
Stuffing, **1**-62; **12**-1940
Wind Puffs (Buñuelos de Viento), **9**-1497

Wine, **12**-1941
Barbecue Sauce, **5**-726
Beef, Braised (Stufato), **11**-1802
Burgundy, **2**-253; for recipes see Burgundy
Cabbage in White Wine, **12**-1949
California Prunes in Claret, **9**-1485
Champagne, see Champagne
Cheese Dish, Melted (Fondue), **11**-1803
Chicken Braised with Wine, **12**-1947
Claret Lemonade, **7**-1057
Cocktail Sausage with White Wine, **8**-1276
Cookies, Italian, **3**-473
Cooking with, **12**-1947
Custard Sauce (Weinschaum), **10**-1628
Dandelion, **4**-534
Duckling Rosé, **12**-1949
Ducklings in Claret, **4**-584
Eggs in Red Wine, Poached, **4**-607
Elderberry, **4**-617
with Food, **12**-1943
with Fresh Ham, Pot of (Pernil con Vino al Caldero), **9**-1496
Ham Baked in Claret, **6**-853
Lamb, Breast of, Rosé, **7**-1034
Lamb, Pot-Roasted Breast of, Rosé, **9**-1475
Lamb in White Wine, **7**-1035
Mulled, **8**-1193
Muscat, Muscatel, **8**-1194
Muscatel Ice, **6**-925
Mushrooms Stewed in Wine, **8**-1201
Oranges and Apples, Sliced, with Wine, **8**-1270
Oranges in Red Wine, **8**-1270
Peach Cream, **8**-1320
Pears, Red-Wine-Baked, **12**-1933
Picnic Pâté, **12**-1927
Port, **9**-1452; for recipes see Port
Red-Wine Beef with Macaroni, **7**-1094
Sack-Posset, Old English, **4**-611
Sake, **10**-1578
Sauce, **7**-1152
Sauterne, **10**-1639; for recipes see Sauterne
Serving, **12**-1943
-Shallot Sauce, **11**-1767
Sherry, **10**-1654; for recipes see Sherry
Sole in White Wine, **12**-1947
Storage, **12**-1943
Syllabub, **1**-68
Tipsy Cake (Sopa Borracha), **9**-1497
Tongue in White-Wine Aspic, **11**-1839
Types, **12**-1942
Vermouth, **12**-1910
Wassail Bowl, Old-Time, **12**-1918
Wineglasses, **12**-1944
Wintergreen, **12**-1949
Wiscasset Lobster Stew, **1**-45
Wisconsin Cheese Rabbit, **1**-78
Wisconsin Chocolate Cake, **3**-407
Wisconsin Dressing for Shredded Cabbage, **3**-464
Won Ton Noodles, **3**-403
Won Ton Noodles, Crisp, **3**-401
Woodchuck in Cream, **5**-770

Woodcock, **12**-1949
Baked, **12**-1949
Broiled, **5**-774
Steamed, **5**-774

Woodruff, Sweet, **12**-1949
Maibowle, **12**-1949
Wormwood, **12**-1949
Wu Dep Har (Butterfly Shrimps), **3**-403
Wu Hsiang Ya (Spiced Duck), **3**-401

Y

Yam, **12**-1950; for recipes see Sweet Potato(es) and Yam(s)
Yam of Roses, **11**-1716
Yang Jo Kao (Jellied Lamb), **3**-400
Yang Jo Kuo (Chafing-Dish Lamb), **3**-400
Yankee Pot Roast, **2**-186; **8**-1224
Yankee Pot Roast, Company, **9**-1472

Yeast, 12-1951
Breads, see Bread(s), Yeast
Buns and Rolls, see Bread(s), Yeast Buns and Rolls
Pancakes, **8**-1292
Using Yeast, **12**-1952
Yellow Crookneck or Straightneck Squash, see Squash
Yellow Rice, **10**-1551

Yogurt, 12-1957
Arab Cheese, **8**-1213
Carrots à la Sultana, **12**-1958
Chicken Tandoori, **12**-1957
Cucumber, and Radish Relish, **12**-1958
Cucumber, Salad, **12**-1958
Dressing, **12**-1958
Eggplant with, **12**-1957
Eggplant-Yogurt Salad, **4**-616
Froth Ayran, **12**-1958
Homemade, **12**-1957
Honey Cakes, **12**-1958
Lamb Baryani, **12**-1957
Meatballs in Yogurt (Kibbeh bi Laban), **8**-1214
Onions, **12**-1957
Salad (Pachadi), **6**-939
Sauce, Egg and Tongue with, **12**-1957
Turquoise, **8**-1213
Yokan (Bean Cakes), **6**-978
York Hermits, **9**-1357

Yorkshire Pudding, 12-1958
3-444; **9**-1487; **12**-1958
I and II, **4**-624
Yose-Nabe (Mixed Cooked Foods), **6**-975
Yugoslav Style Quails, **10**-1518
Yukon Moose or Caribou Stew, **2**-278
Yule Log (Bûche de Noël), **12**-1959

Z

Zabaglione, 12-1960
Cold, **12**-1960
Zajac Pieczony (Roast Hare), **9**-1427
Zanahorias Natas (Braised Carrots), **2**-306
Zarzuela de Mariscos (Musical Comedy of Shellfish), **11**-1743
Zeppole, **12**-1960
Zoo-Tosopy (Ground-Meat Stew), **11**-1704

Zucchini, 11-1758; **12**-1960
Baked, **11**-1762
al Burro (Squash with Butter), **6**-959
and Cabbage Skillet, Madame Fraize's, **12**-1903
Chicken, **12**-1961
and Corn, Baked, **12**-1962
with Creamy Cheesé Topping, **12**-1962
and Cucumbers in Sour Cream, **12**-1962
Fried Squash (Zucchini Fritti), **6**-959
Hamburger-Zucchini Skillet Dinner, **6**-873
Lamb-Stuffed, **12**-1961
Omelet, **12**-1962
Pancakes (Kolokythia Krokettes), **5**-822
and Pepper Stew, **12**-1962
Pickles, **9**-1374; **12**-1962
Sauce with Spaghetti, **11**-1737
Sautéed, Italian Style, **12**-1962
Squash with Butter (Zucchini al Burro), **6**-959
Stuffed, **12**-1904
in Tomato Sauce, **12**-1903
Vegetable Marrow(s), **7**-1113; **11**-1759
Cooked, **7**-1113
Stuffed, **7**-1113
with Walnuts, **12**-1904
Ziti, **12**-1962
Zeller Saláta (Celery-Root Salad), **6**-919
Zest, **10**-1615
Zöld Paprika Saláta (Green-Pepper Salad), **6**-919
Zrazy Cielece Zawijane (Stuffed Veal Birds), **9**-1425
Zuppa Inglese, **4**-650
Zuppa Veneziana di Pesce (Venetian Fish Soup), **6**-952
Zwieback, **12**-1962

ACKNOWLEDGEMENTS

The editors and publisher of *Woman's Day* wish to thank the authors, publishers, and copyright owners listed below for their permission to reprint special material.

Six recipes in **Austrian Cookery, Volume 1,** from *The Viennese Cookbook* by Irma Rhode, copyright 1951 by Hill and Wang, Inc., and reprinted by permission of Hill and Wang.

Eight recipes in **Belgian Cookery, Volume 2,** from *A Belgian Cookbook* by Juliette Elkon, copyright © 1958 by Farrar, Straus & Giroux, Inc., and reprinted by permission of Farrar, Straus and Cudahy, Inc.

Seven recipes in the **Bread** entry, **Volume 2,** from *The Pepperidge Farm Cookbook* by Margaret Rudkin, copyright © 1963 by Margaret Rudkin, and reprinted by permission of Atheneum Publishers; registered trade mark ® Pepperidge Farm, Inc.

The Art of Chinese Cookery in **Volume 3,** from *The Art of Chinese Cooking* by Mimi Ouei, copyright © 1960 by Mimi Ouei, and published by Random House, Inc.

The Twelve Days Before Christmas in **Volume 3,** originally published in *Woman's Day,* December, 1962, and incorporated in *A Sense of Seasons* by Jean Hersey, copyright © 1964 by Jean Hersey; used by permission of Dodd, Mead & Co., Inc.

Six recipes in **Czechoslovakian Cookery, Volume 4,** from the *Bohemian-American Cook Book* by Marie Rosicky, and reprinted by permission of Automatic Printing Co.

Dutch Cookery in **Volume 4,** from *The Art of Dutch Cooking* by C. Countess van Limburg Stirum, copyright © 1961 by C. Countess van Limburg Stirum, and reprinted by permission of Doubleday & Company, Inc.

Thirteen recipes in the **Game** entry, **Volume 5,** from *The Wild Game Wild Fowl Cook Book* by Martin Rywell, copyright © 1952 by Martin Rywell, and published by Pioneer Press, Harriman, Tennessee.

Irish Cookery in **Volume 6,** from *Feasting Galore* by Maura Laverty, copyright 1952, 1955, © 1957, 1961 by Maura Laverty, and reprinted by permission of Holt, Rinehart and Winston, Inc.

Norwegian Cookery in **Volume 8** and **Swedish Cookery** in **Volume 11,** from *The Art of Scandinavian Cooking,* copyright © 1965 by Nika Standen Hazelton and published by The Macmillan Company, New York, and Collier-Macmillan Canada, Ltd., Toronto, Ontario.

Puerto Rican Cookery in **Volume 9,** from *The Art of Caribbean Cookery* by Carmen Aboy Valldejuli, copyright © 1957, 1963 by Carmen Aboy Valldejuli, and published by Doubleday & Company, Inc.

Russian Cookery in **Volume 10,** from *The Best of Russian Cookery* by Alexandra Kropotkin, copyright © 1964 by Alexandra Kropotkin and published by Charles Scribner's Sons.

DILL